Christopher

from Madeleine & Richard

1993

Robin Bush lives in Taunton, and his credentials to be author of this Guide could hardly be bettered. He worked as an archivist and historian in Somerset from his arrival in the county in 1967 until his retirement as Deputy County Archivist in 1993 while compiling this Guide. He is the author of numerous books and monographs on the county's heritage, including the highly-successful *Somerset, A Portrait in Colour*, for which Julian Comrie took the photographs. He has given some 500 weekly broadcasts on local radio on the history, archaeology and folklore of Somerset, and is a member of *Time Team*, Channel 4's archaeological action programme. He has lectured widely throughout southern England and the United States. He is a former Chairman of Somerset Archaeological and Natural History Society, current Chairman of the Taunton Deane Archaeological and Research Committee and serves as President of Taunton Operatic Society.

Somerset, The Complete Guide is the second collaboration between Robin Bush and the photographer Julian Comrie. Julian Comrie is a professional photographer living and working in Somerset. He is a Fellow of the Royal Photographic Society and an Associate of the British Institute of Professional Photography. The nearly 400 photographs in this Guide represent only a small part of his extensive photographic library illustrating Somerset, both in black and white and in colour.

Following page
Burrow Mump and floods at Burrowbridge

ROBIN BUSH

SOMERSET

The Complete Guide

Photographs by Julian Comrie

THE DOVECOTE PRESS

*To Hilary, my wife, who has suffered both this
book and myself throughout its protracted
preparation.*

*An angel in the church porch,
Buckland St Mary*

First published in 1994 by
The Dovecote Press Ltd,
Stanbridge, Wimborne, Dorset BH21 4JD

ISBN 1 874336 27 X (Casebound)
ISBN 1 874336 26 1 (Paperback)

Text © Robin Bush 1994
Photographs © Julian Comrie 1994

Designed by Humphrey Stone
Photoset in Palatino by
The Typesetting Bureau Ltd, Wimborne
Origination by Chroma Graphics
Printed by Kim Hup Lee Printing Co Pte,
Singapore

A CIP catalogue record is available
for this book from the British Library

Contents

The main MAP *and six pages of colour plates
fall between pages 144/145*

Using this Guide

The introductory 'Land of Summer' supplies summary descriptions of each of the main areas of the county and lists all the most interesting places in it. Special sections on mansions and houses, churches, etc., detail all the finest in those categories and serve as an index to them, while other sections supply accounts of general topics such as Arthur and Alfred or the Monmouth Rebellion.

In the alphabetical Gazetteer I have included every village in the modern county which has its own parish church, and obviously every town. Major places open to the public have their own entries or are cross-referenced as necessary. The county map at the centre of the colour section in the middle of the book marks the location of virtually every entry in the Gazetteer and thus forms a further index. The letter bracketed after the title of each entry identifies the relevant square in which it can be found on the map. Outline plans of the centres of larger towns locate features of interest, car parks, etc. A glossary explains possibly unfamiliar words.

The Lists at the end of the book give opening times and other information, including a rough price guide to admission charges (indicated in the Gazetteer by 'fee'). For driving or cycling around the county the Ordnance Survey's Landranger (1¼in. to 1 mile) maps are recommended and these indicate tourist attractions and viewpoints. Somerset falls within sheets 180, 181, 182, 192 and 193. For walking, try the larger scale 1:25,000 (the old 2½ in.).

My decisions regarding star ratings will inevitably cause disagreement and I am bound to suffer for them in the years to come. I am certainly going to be the *only* person to agree with all of them. The gradings reflect quantity as well as quality, and also accessibility, but basically I have reserved ★★★★ for venues worth making a special journey to see.

I would welcome details of any omissions or errors, which should be addressed to me c/o my publishers: Dovecote Press Ltd, Stanbridge, Wimborne, Dorset BH21 4JD.

ROBIN BUSH

The Land of Summer

A verie large and wealthy region ... The soile verie rich, yeelding for the most part thereof passing great plentie, both of pasture and corne, and yet not without stonie hilles; exceeding populous, and full of inhabitants, furnished also with commodious havens and ports sufficiently.

WILLIAM CAMDEN *Britannia* 1586

Camden went on, however, to emphasize that in winter the county was 'so wet and weely, so miry and moorish', that travel was extremely difficult or, as an 18th century proverb put it, the place was 'bad for the rider but good for the abider'. Happily transport has improved since Elizabethan times. The swathe cut through the county by the M5, initially resented, has proved a great boon, syphoning heavy lorries and holiday through-traffic off the country roads and enabling residents to leave Somerset (and return) with great rapidity.

Before Roman times the area seems to have been split between three late Iron-Age peoples: the Dobunni in the north, the Durotriges in the south and the Dumnonii in the west. The Romans arrived in the 1st century, principally to exploit the lead mines on the Mendips, building the Foss Way through the area and establishing their principal settlement at Ilchester, which they called Lindinis. The West Saxons followed in the 7th century and the county was first recorded by name in the Anglo-Saxon Chronicle in 845, when 'all the men of Somerset' (*Sumorsetae Ealle* – still the motto of the County Council) with those of Dorset defeated a Viking army at the mouth of the River Parret. The name suggests an early tribe centred on Somerton who in summer drove their beasts on to the Levels to pasture, withdrawing to the higher ground as the winter floodwaters advanced. Somerset, even since it lost its northern area to create the hybrid county of Avon in 1974, is still a region of incredible variety. There are no fewer than five separate ranges of hills (the Brendons, Quantocks, Blackdowns, Poldens and Mendips), the broad wetland expanse of the Levels, the remote wilderness of Exmoor and the lushness of the southern and eastern borders. The varied geology has also provided a range of building stones: golden Ham stone, blue lias, red sandstone, cob and finally brick. It has always been a rich farming area but there were mines producing lead, coal and iron from Roman times and it was, from the 14th to the 18th centuries, a heavily-industrialised clothmaking region. Time has healed Somerset's industrial scars and it is today a place of great beauty, attracting visitors and a new generation of settlers, of whom this author is one.

TAUNTON AND THE BLACKDOWNS

Towns: Milverton, Taunton, Wellington.
Villages: ★★★ Bradford-on-Tone, Corfe, Hatch Beauchamp.
Archaeology: ★★★ Norton hillfort, Castle Neroche (Staple Fitzpaine).
Churches: ★★★ Bradford-on-Tone, Creech St Michael, Pitminster, Taunton St Mary Magdalene, Taunton Mary Street Chapel, Trull.
Houses: ★★★ Hatch Court (Hatch Beauchamp), Poundisford Park (Pitminster).
Walking: ★★★ Otterford, Staple Fitzpaine (Neroche Nature Trail), Wellington Monument.
Gardens: ★★★★ Hestercombe.
Museums: ★★★★ Somerset County Museum (Taunton Castle).
Other: ★★★ Bridgwater and Taunton Canal, Widcombe Bird Gardens (Churchstanton).

BELOW *South porch, St Mary Magdalene church, Taunton*
RIGHT *West Buckland from the south*

Centred on the county town, the rich arable Vale of Taunton has been intensively cultivated from before Roman times. Indeed, its natives used to boast that their land was so fertile that it needed no manuring. The hillfort at Norton Fitzwarren, dating back over 3,000 years, has nature and archaeological trails and was occupied until the Romans left. Taunton itself was by 904 the market centre of one of the largest manors in England, Taunton Deane, including up to twenty villages in its area, ruled by the bishops of Winchester until the early 19th century. The inner area under the direct control of the bishops was known as the 'infaring', while the more distant estates (whose lords held their lands under the bishop but managed them themselves) were termed the 'outfaring'. Taunton today is a major (and growing) shopping and entertainment centre and, with the exception of some Medieval, Tudor and Stuart buildings in the centre, is largely 19th and 20th century in date. The Castle houses the extensive County Museum, there are attractive parks and gardens, and the sporting magnetism of the Somerset County Cricket ground recalls the heady days of Botham, Richards and Garner. To the west, Wellington is a small friendly town which gave the Iron Duke of Wellington his title and was once a centre of the textile trade. A little to the north, Milverton is a happy sleepy little place: a former royal borough with the Georgian intimacy of North Street, one of my favourite thoroughfares. There is a host of delightful villages, of which Pitminster has the Tudor grandeur of Poundisford Park, built by lawyer William Hill from 1546, and Hatch Beauchamp has Hatch Court, created in 1755 for John Collins, complete with its own park still stocked with deer.

The long leafy ridge of the Blackdown Hills, its name meaning literally 'black hill', forms the border with Devon and provides a succession of wonderful viewpoints to the north: the finest from the top of the Wellington Monument. The high ground is ideal for walkers, particularly in the grounds of the former Otterhead House and along the forest trail which includes the long-abandoned Norman earthworks of Castle Neroche.

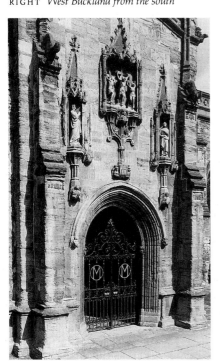

ABOVE *Robin Hood's Butts, the Blackdowns*   BELOW *Landscape between Bruton and Milton Clevedon*

FROME AND SELWOOD

Towns: Bruton, Frome, Wincanton.
Villages: ★★★★ Lullington, Mells,
★★★ Batcombe, Beckington, Castle Cary,
Great Elm, Nunney.
Archaeology: ★★★★ Farleigh Castle,
★★★ Nunney Castle.
Churches: ★★★★ Lullington, Mells.
★★★ Beckington, Berkley, Bruton,
Evercreech, Rook Lane Chapel (Frome),
Great Elm, Witham Friary.
Walking: ★★★ Orchardleigh Park.
Gardens: ★★★ Hadspen House
(Pitcombe).
Other: ★★★ George Inn (Norton St
Philip), Rode Bird Gardens, East Somerset
Railway (West Cranmore).

East Somerset was formerly dominated by the royal forest of Selwood, 'the sallow wood', which the British called *coit mawr*, 'the great wood'. It stretched eastwards into Dorset and Wiltshire and St Aldhelm's bishopric, centred on Sherborne in Dorset, was described c.709 as Selwoodshire. The forest was progressively felled and was finally disafforested by Charles I in 1630, although an area known as Woodlands, south-east from Frome, continued to be a notorious haunt of criminals and outlaws until cleared in the 18th century.

The region is focused on Frome, a substantial stone-built town which often seems to have more in common with Wiltshire than Somerset. The link is the medieval reliance on clothmaking which also typifies the villages lining the west bank of the River Frome: particularly Norton St Philip (don't miss the

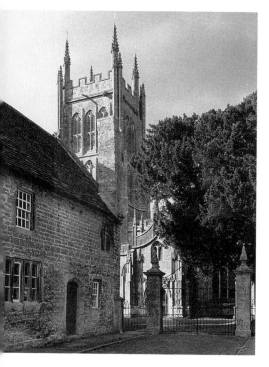

George Inn), Beckington and Rode: a reliance which persisted in Frome well into the 19th century – longer than elsewhere in Somerset. Frome itself retains many picturesque narrow streets and fine buildings, although its commercial heart and sense of activity have been somewhat diluted with the removal of its market to Standerwick in 1990. The villages hereabouts are some of the most charming in the county and the casual visitor might never perceive that they were once literally hives of industry: places like Mells, Beckington and Nunney. Lullington is largely the 19th century picture-postcard creation of the Duckworths of nearby Orchardleigh, whose park provides an idyllic stroll to visit its island church. Lullington church is the best example of scaled-down Norman architecture and detailed carving in Somerset, while the plain severity of the same period can be appreciated at Witham Friary. The flavour of the medieval can also be captured in the ruined castles at Farleigh Hungerford and Nunney.

In the south of the region, Bruton is deliciously unspoilt, with elegant medieval church, hospital and school, and Wincanton is still surprisingly busy since its bypassing, with views out over the leafy surrounding landscape from all its main streets. Castle Cary has a wonderful 18th century feel to its streets, matching the atmosphere conjured up for readers of Parson Woodforde's famous diary. Very different clienteles are catered for by Rode Tropical Bird Gardens, the East Somerset Railway at West Cranmore and the gardens at Hadspen House.

THE MENDIPS

Towns: Axbridge, Cheddar, Shepton Mallet, Wells.
Villages: ★★★ Pilton, Rodney Stoke.
Churches: ★★★★ Croscombe, Downside Abbey, Wells Cathedral, ★★★ Babington, Pilton, Rodney Stoke, Shepton Mallet, Wells St Cuthbert.
Houses: ★★★★ Bishop's Palace (Wells).
Walking: ★★★★ Cheddar Gorge, Mendips (hills generally), ★★★ Ebbor Gorge.
Gardens: ★★★ Milton Lodge (Wells).
Other: ★★★★ Cheddar Caves, Wookey Hole Cave. ★★★ Ston Easton Park.

ABOVE *Mells church*
RIGHT *Compton Bishop from Crook Peak, the Mendips*
OPPOSITE TOP *The Mendips near Priddy*
OPPOSITE BOTTOM *Cheddar Gorge*

Forming the northern boundary of the present county, this striking range of hills takes its name from a Celtic word for hill, *mynydd* (also present in the name of Minehead), to which may have been added the Saxon *hop*, meaning 'valley'. The views out across the Levels to Brent Knoll are spectacular and there is fine walking along the crest and up the dramatic clefts of Cheddar and Ebbor gorges. Excavations above Westbury-sub-Mendip have revealed worked flints which may date back over half a million years and supply the earliest evidence of man in Britain. Caves at Wookey and Cheddar have provided further remains of the presence of prehistoric man, while high up near Priddy are three Neolithic wood henge monuments and two groups of Bronze Age barrows. Lead and silver were probably mined here from 250 BC and it was almost certainly these resources which brought the Romans to Mendip by 49 AD. A Roman town was established at Charterhouse, with fort,

11

garrison and amphitheatre, linked to the Foss Way by a road along the spine of the hill. The area was a royal hunting forest by Saxon times and the kings of the West Saxons (later of England) had a 'palace' at Cheddar from the 9th to the 13th century.

The hills were divided into four mining Liberties, owned by the bishops of Bath and Wells and the lords of Charterhouse, Chewton and Harptree. Minery courts were held twice a year and customs evolved to regulate mining activity. One such custom required miners at their own cost to recover the body of any of their fellows who died, 'although hee bee threescore fathom under the earth', and give him Christian burial. Another stated that any miner found stealing lead or lead ore should be shut up in his hut with all his tools and that the hut should be then set on fire: a practice later known as 'burning the hill'. Pollution was a perennial problem and lead poisoning, once thought to be caused by breathing smoke from the smelting, killed people, livestock and trees. Mining decreased as surface seams were worked out, ending c.1800, although the smelting of spoil heaps continued until 1908. Calamine to make zinc was mined at Shipham and coal was produced at the east end of the hills. Today limestone quarrying for road building is the principal industry on Mendip.

Wells, 'the smallest city in England', is a captivating and unspoilt medieval town at the foot of the hills. The superb Gothic cathedral is justly celebrated for the gallery of sculpture on its west front, its delicate chapter house and the oldest clock dial in the world. The Cathedral Green has two gateways, including Penniless Porch, the 14th century Vicars Close, one of the oldest planned medieval streets in Europe, and the delightful Wells Museum. The moated and fortified Bishop's Palace is merely the finest of a number of early buildings concentrated in the vicinities of the Market Place and St Cuthbert's church. The best of Axbridge also surrounds its former market-place: church, town hall and King John's Hunting Lodge. Shepton Mallet still possesses many of the buildings associated with its former clothmaking, its church with a superlative wagon roof and the oldest prison in the country still on its original site. Of village churches, the finest are the magnificent Downside Abbey, Croscombe with its feast of Jacobean woodwork, Babington's Georgian delights and setting, and the profusion of Rodney Stoke's feudal memorials.

THE SOMERSET LEVELS

Towns: Bridgwater, Burnham-on-Sea, Glastonbury, Langport, Somerton, Street.
Villages: ★★★ Butleigh, Cannington, Muchelney, North Curry, Shapwick.
Archaeology: ★★★★ Glastonbury Abbey, Muchelney Abbey.
Churches: ★★★ Brent Knoll, Burnham-on-Sea, Cannington, Curry Rivel, Glastonbury St John, Meare, Muchelney, North Curry, Somerton, Swell, Westonzoyland.
Houses: ★★★★ Priest House (Muchelney), ★★★ Midelney Manor (Drayton).
Walking: ★★★★ Brean Down, Brent Knoll, Glastonbury Tor, ★★★ Burrow Mump (Burrowbridge), Compton Dundon.
Museums: ★★★★ Somerset Rural Life Museum (Glastonbury), ★★★ Tribunal (Glastonbury); Shoe Museum (Street).
Other: ★★★★ Bridgwater Carnival and St Matthew's Fair, George and Pilgrim (Glastonbury), Sedgemoor Battlefield (Westonzoyland), ★★★ Bridgwater and Taunton Canal, Burnham beach, Meare Fish House, Peat Moors Visitor Centre (Meare), Willows and Wetlands Centre (Stoke St Gregory).

A fascinating region, probably the most important wetland area in England, which stretches inland from Bridgwater Bay and the estuary of the River Parret. It is often paradoxically called 'the Moors', a term elsewhere reserved for high barren land. Those of the natives who live there probably represent the old Somerset more faithfully than any other part of the county. In the 17th century that old gossip, John Aubrey, described the Levels people as 'large, faire, good-natur'd, without designe, not given to quarrelinge; but rather to propagate their race'. The lowest-lying land, formerly regularly inundated by the sea, was progressively embanked and drained from the 12th century. The work was at first mainly carried out by the church: the bishops of Bath and Wells and the abbots of Glastonbury, Muchelney and Athelney, who owned most of the manors in the vicinity. After the Reformation the pace of drainage activity slowed, although the great inland lake, Meare Pool, gradually disappeared during the 17th and early 18th centuries.

The present landscape of regular ditches (known locally as 'rhines', pronounced 'reens'), all feeding into the rivers Brue and Parret and two great artificial channels (King's Sedgemoor Drain and the Huntspill River), is largely the creation of the last 200 years. Periodic winter flooding still occurs but is now generally controlled by a succession of clyses (sluice gates) and pumping stations. Concern over the continued lowering of the water table and its effect on the wealth of wetland plant life in the grazing meadows has led to the creation of a number of SSIs (Sites of Special Scientific Interest). There are National Nature Reserves over the mud flats and salt marsh of Bridgwater Bay, designed to protect the large flocks of wading birds and wildfowl, and at Shapwick Heath, to conserve the raised peat moor. Much of the peat has already been extracted to serve the demands of the gardeners of England, although one fortunate spin-off has been the discovery of a network of prehistoric timber trackways, dating back to c.4000 BC: the oldest in Europe. All these aspects of the Levels can be explored at visitors' centres near Westhay and at Meare Green in Stoke St Gregory: the latter being also concerned with basket-making, a Levels craft pursued since prehistoric times.

It was the very remoteness of the Levels which brought Alfred the Great to seek refuge at Athelney (near Lyng) in 878 and whence he sallied off to defeat the Danes, baptising their king, Guthrum, at Aller, before leading him onward

OPPOSITE PAGE *Glastonbury Tor*
RIGHT *Sedgemoor from Walton Hill*

ABOVE *Aller church at sunset*
OPPOSITE TOP *The River Tone in flood near Curload*
OPPOSITE BELOW *The junction of the rivers Parrett and Tone, Burrowbridge*

to Wedmore. The vicinity of Langport was in 1645 the site of a major Civil War victory for a Roundhead army led by Sir Thomas Fairfax and Oliver Cromwell, followed by the bitter siege of Bridgwater and its surrender. And it was from Bridgwater that forty years later the Duke of Monmouth led his rebel army out to defeat at the Battle of Sedgemoor, near Westonzoyland: the last major battle on English soil.

The best overview of the Levels is obtained, for those with the necessary energy, by scaling three natural hills of varying heights: Brent Knoll (456 ft), surmounted by an Iron-Age hillfort, Glastonbury Tor (158 ft), topped with the tower of St Michael's church, and Burrow Mump, capped by an unfinished 18th century church, also dedicated to St Michael, at Burrowbridge. The low ridge of the Polden Hills and the outlook from Walton Hill above Street also give splendid prospects. There are no spectacularly beautiful villages but plenty of attractive ones. Muchelney (with its ruined abbey), Meare, Wedmore and Shapwick probably best convey the atmosphere of the lowland area while, on the higher ground, North Curry, Butleigh, High Ham and Cannington have always appealed to me. Lympsham is an intriguing village, wholly transformed by an eccentric family of 19th century rectors. Midelney Manor, on the moors beside the River Isle, is still home to the family that built it over four centuries ago.

Of Levels towns, Glastonbury is a place of myth as much as history, its massive abbey, now ruined, once dominated the region and it has a splendid Rural Life Museum housed in a medieval barn. Indeed, the area's finest churches are those built by the monks: churches such as Glastonbury St John, Meare and Westonzoyland. Street is a place of recent growth whose fortunes were founded on shoeleather and now boasts a shoe museum and factory village. Langport began as a Saxon fort with its causewayed Bow Street, while Bridgwater is a former medieval port with a modern shopping centre and conserved dock area: renowned for its annual carnival and fair. Somerton has an enchanting centre and served as the early focus of the developing county. On the coast, Burnham-on-Sea is a seaside resort whose fortunes were founded on the arrival of the railway and which still preserves much of its Victorian charm.

THE QUANTOCKS

Towns: Watchet.
Villages: ★★★★ East Quantoxhead. ★★★ Aisholt, Bicknoller, Crowcombe, Nether Stowey, Spaxton, Stogursey, West Bagborough.
Archaeology: ★★★ Quantocks (hills generally), Stogursey Castle.
Churches: ★★★★ Crowcombe, Goathurst, Stogursey, ★★★ Bicknoller, Cothelstone, East Quantoxhead, Kingston St Mary, Spaxton, St Decuman's (Watchet).
Houses: ★★★★ Barford Park (Enmore), ★★★ Fyne Court (Broomfield), Coleridge's Cottage (Nether Stowey), Orchard Wyndham (Williton).
Walking: ★★★★ Holford, Quantocks (hills generally), ★★★ Fyne Court (Broomfield), Kilve, Over Stowey (Forestry Trail).
Other: ★★★★ West Somerset Railway.

North-west from Wills Neck, the Quantocks

This twelve-mile range of hills extends from just north of Taunton, running northwest to the sea at East and West Quantoxhead and recorded in the 7th century as 'Cantucuudu' – 'the wood of Cantuc': a British word meaning 'rim' or 'circle'. The hills were intensively used by early man and there are nearly a hundred burial mounds, many linear ditches and enclosures, the most significant being Trendle Ring (Bicknoller) and the oval Iron-Age hillfort of Dowsborough (Dodington). For walkers and riders it is ideal, with the best views to the north across the Bristol Channel to the Welsh coast and west towards the Brendons. Drive up on to the uplands by all means (there are plenty of places to park) but then leave the car and strike out away from the road. The higher ground has wonderful open expanses of heather and gorse, punctuated with tree-filled combes cut by silvery streams down which the walker can descend to enjoy the liquid charms of the Plough at Holford, the Hood Arms at Kilve, the Carew Arms at Crowcombe, the Traveller's Rest at Enmore or the Blue Ball at Triscombe. Among those inspired by the natural beauty of the hills were William and Dorothy Wordsworth at Alfoxton (Holford) and Samuel Taylor Coleridge, whose lodgings can be visited at Nether Stowey. In contrast to hillwalking, there is a charming stroll along the coast between East Quantoxhead and Kilve. Alternative transport is provided by the West Somerset Railway, the longest privately-owned line in the country, which runs steam trains north-west from Bishops Lydeard through this enchanting countryside.

Only the two villages of Aisholt and Broomfield are sited high up on the hills, as is Fyne Court (Broomfield): the outbuildings of the former home of the Crosse family and now the headquarters of the Somerset Wildlife Trust. West Bagborough and Cothelstone are further down the slope but still have panoramic views over the lowlands. Much of the area was long held by a small number of families: the Luttrells at East Quantoxhead, the Acland-Hoods and their predecessors at West Quantoxhead and Stogursey, the Wyndhams at Orchard Wyndham, Carews and the Trollope-Bellews at Crowcombe. Other villages given their present complexion by their owners

include Goathurst by the Halswells and Kemys-Tyntes, Enmore by the earls of Egmont and Over Stowey by Lord Taunton. There are castle sites at Stogursey and Nether Stowey, and possibly at Over Stowey. Also at Stogursey is one of the finest Norman churches in the county, there are two superb Perpendicular church towers at Kingston St Mary and Bishops Lydeard, and three of my other favourite churches are those at Crowcombe, Goathurst and St Decuman's (Watchet). Major houses open to the public include the delightful early 18th century Barford Park and Orchard Wyndham, both surrounded by appealing parkland.

Watchet is a small coastal town of considerable importance in Saxon times. Its harbour, now closed to commercial traffic, has a small-scale charm which is continued through its narrow streets and its engaging little museum. Nether Stowey is a former borough now centred on its Jubilee clock tower rather than its covered market cross.

EXMOOR AND THE BRENDONS
DULVERTON
DUNSTER
MINEHEAD

Towns: Dulverton, Dunster, Minehead, Porlock, Wiveliscombe.

Villages: ★★★★ Porlock Weir, Selworthy, Winsford, ★★★ Allerford, Bossington, Brompton Regis, Luccombe, Monksilver, Old Cleeve, Selworthy, Stogumber.

Archaeology: ★★★★ Cleeve Abbey, Exmoor (generally).

Churches: ★★★ Dunster, Nettlecombe, Oare, Old Cleeve, Selworthy, Stawley.

Houses: ★★★★ Dunster Castle, Nettlecombe, Combe Sydenham.

Walking: ★★★★ Culbone, Exmoor (generally), Porlock Weir.
★★★ Cutcombe, Exford, Simonsbath, Tarr Steps (Hawkridge), Timberscombe, Withypool.

Other: ★★★★ Clatworthy Reservoir, West Somerset Railway, ★★★ Wimbleball Reservoir (Brompton Regis), Blue Anchor beach (Old Cleeve), Tropiquaria (Stogumber).

TOP *Lydeard Hill, the Quantocks*
RIGHT *The Brendon Hills near Raddington*

Exmoor is Somerset's last wilderness, although the once royal forest has contracted over the centuries. It can be explored by car but the true joy of its high wide open spaces can only really be appreciated on foot or on horseback. Whatever one feels about field sports, this has also been hunting country since the beginning of recorded time: home of the red deer as well as the Exmoor pony. The moorland has almost as much to offer the archaeologist, with a legion of burial mounds, the occasional enclosure or fort, and isolated standing stones. Most of Exmoor's secluded villages, each with at least one welcoming inn, nestle in picturesque valleys cut by rivers such as the Exe, Quarme and Barle. Oare church, where R. D. Blackmore set the wedding of his heroine in *Lorna Doone*, draws thousands of his readers each year. The northern coastal areas are beautifully wooded, particularly from Selworthy west to the county border, and throughout their length runs the Somerset and North Devon Coast Path with extensive views, especially around Porlock Bay. Much of the most captivating countryside focused around Selworthy formed the Holnicote estate, given to the National Trust by Sir Richard Acland in 1944.

Porlock itself is a rewarding small coastal town, although outclassed by the

ABOVE *The Quantocks from Brendon Hill*
OPPOSITE TOP *Dunkery Beacon*
OPPOSITE BELOW *The Horner Valley, Exmoor*

loveliness of nearby Porlock Weir. Minehead is a no-nonsense seaside resort with gardens, shops and entertainments, but it also has an unspoilt region around St Michael's church on North Hill. Almost beyond praise is Dunster, with its romantically situated castle and gardens above the Lawns, where Maharajahs once rode their polo ponies. The feudal little town that stretches below it down the main street to the Yarn Market and the Luttrell Arms is a jewel, spoilt only by somewhat garish shops and the crowds which it attracts in high season. To the south Dulverton is the capital of the moor: narrow streets running up the slope from the bridged Barle, small-scale shops and inns of character. Wiveliscombe, formerly known for its bishop's mansion and its clothmaking, was dominated from 1806 by brewing. The best churches are at Old Cleeve and Selworthy, and I am particularly fond of Stawley, but the Victorians rebuilt many more churches in this region than elsewhere in the county.

The Brendon Hills extend east from Exmoor, mostly within the Exmoor National Park, and have largely been enclosed for farming. Iron was probably smelted at Syndercombe near Clatworthy from the earliest times, but only systematically exploited on Brendon from 1839: the workings linked to Watchet by the West Somerset Mineral Railway. There are two major Elizabethan houses; Nettlecombe Court is home to a multitude of field study courses, while educational events also feature in the extensive programme at Combe Sydenham Hall, former home of Sir Francis Drake's second wife. Gaulden Manor is a family-sized 17th century house with elegant plasterwork and fine gardens, while Cleeve Abbey is the most completely preserved monastery in the county. Somerset's most picturesque reservoirs at Wimbleball and Clatworthy furnish a range of water sports and walks around their perimeters.

THE SOUTHERN BORDERS

Towns: Chard, Crewkerne, Ilminster, Yeovil.

Villages: ★★★★ Barrington, Compton Pauncefoot, Dowlish Wake, Hinton St George, North Cadbury, ★★★ East Coker, Ilchester, Kingsdon, Long Sutton, Martock, Montacute, Pendomer, Shepton Beauchamp, Stocklinch.

Archaeology: ★★★★ Cadbury Castle (South Cadbury).

Churches: ★★★★ Brympton D'Evercy, Hinton St George, ★★★ Crewkerne, Curry Mallet, Dowlish Wake, East Coker, Ilminster, Isle Abbots, Martock, Milborne Port, Montacute, North Cadbury, Pendomer, Stocklinch Ottersey, Stoke-sub-Hamdon, Sutton Bingham, Yeovil St John.

Houses: ★★★★ Barrington Court, Brympton D'Evercy, Lytes Cary (Charlton Mackrell), Montacute, ★★★ Dillington House (Ilminster), Treasurer's House (Martock).

Walking: ★★★ Ham Hill, Montacute.

Museums: ★★★★ Fleet Air Arm (Yeovilton), ★★★ Chard, Haynes Motor Museum.

Gardens: ★★★ Clapton Court (Crewkerne), East Lambrook, Tintinhull House.

Other: ★★★ Hornsbury Mill (Chard), Cricket St Thomas Wild Life Park.

South Somerset is distinguished by undulating green countryside with sunken lanes and nucleated villages. It is typified by the warm golden Ham stone from which its great houses are constructed: Barrington Court, built by the Cliftons in the 16th century, with gardens laid out by Gertrude Jekyll; Hinton House, former home of the earls Poulett; Brympton D'Evercy, with its 17th century south front and harmonious grouping with church, chantry house and small clock tower; Montacute House, created c.1590-1600 by Sir Edward Phelips, Speaker of the House of Commons, and blessed with the longest long gallery in England, crammed with Tudor and Stuart portraits from the National Portrait Gallery. Dillington House, built by the Spekes and occupied by a Prime Minister, Lord North, is now used as an adult education college with its own little theatre. On a smaller scale, Lytes Cary was put up in the local lias stone in the 16th and 17th centuries by the Lyte family, while the Treasurer's House at Martock, dating from the 13th century, is probably the oldest occupied domestic building in the county. Most of these houses have excellent gardens: to which should be added those at Clapton Court and Tintinhull House, together with the Margery Fish garden at East Lambrook.

The major source of building stone, Ham Hill, its crest encircled by the largest Iron-Age hillfort in Europe, is now a country park with panoramic views over the area. A second excellent vantage point is the nearby Montacute Hill, crowned by a Phelips folly tower, but the most intriguing summit is that occupied by Cadbury Castle. Claimed for over four centuries (without justification) to be King Arthur's Camelot, Cadbury was the principal Somerset fortress of the Durotriges, built c.500 BC and refortified in the 5th and 11th centuries. The Roman Foss Way runs diagonally through the region, serving Ilchester. This settlement, now little more than a village, was as 'Lindinis' the principal Roman town in the county, and indeed served as the county town until its gaol closed in 1843. Chard, Crewkerne and Ilminster were all market towns which have preserved their attractive centres, Chard in particular having a large number of excellent 16th and 17th century houses. Yeovil is an excellent shopping centre, known for its glovemaking and Westlands helicopters, but has destroyed much of its heritage since the last war.

Ham stone also characterises many of the villages, of which the best are

RIGHT *A lane to Pendomer in early summer*
OPPOSITE TOP *Milborne Wick*
OPPOSITE BOTTOM *Kingstone from the Ilminster road*

Montacute, Barrington, Compton Pauncefoot, Dowlish Wake, Hinton St George and North Cadbury, although I also have a very soft spot for Kingsdon, East Coker, Martock and Pendomer. The problem is that this region has a greater number of attractive villages than any other part of Somerset. The same is true of its churches. There are fine large churches at Ilminster, Martock, Crewkerne and Yeovil, and the choicest smaller ones will be found at Brympton D'Evercy, Hinton St George, Isle Abbotts, Sutton Bingham (superb wall paintings) and Stoke-sub-Hamdon. Among other attractions are the Fleet Air Arm Museum, with a wide range of historic aircraft, Haynes Motor Museum and the extensive wild-life park at Cricket St Thomas.

Gazetteer

AISHOLT (D) The parish lies in a romantic cleft high on the Quantocks, its site determined by the course of the Cannington Brook, its name defining its original surroundings: 'the ash copse'. If arriving by car, leave it in the car park above the church and stroll down through the delightfully unspoilt village: no pub, not even a shop. In 1800 Coleridge would have liked to have taken a cottage here but the place was too isolated to suit his wife, and on his last visit to Somerset in 1807 he walked up from Nether Stowey to take a glass of port with the rector, John Brice. A later literary visitor was Sir Henry Newbolt (1862-1938) who spent his holidays at the former schoolhouse here and hoped that 'no one will ever spread the fame of Aisholt'. The simple immaculately-kept church of All Saints clings precariously to the hillside. It dates mainly from the early 14th century, a period which corresponds with the earliest recorded vicar in 1313 and features an unusual chancel arch of red sandstone, an unrestored west tower and an ancient iron-bound oak register chest.

To the north-east of the village stretches the small Hawkridge Reservoir, built 1960-62 to supply Bridgwater. To the south-east, near Merridge, is the Quantocks' only underground cave, Holwell Cavern (not open to the public): once famous for its stalactites but wrecked in the 19th century by souvenir hunters.

★★★ *Village, setting.*

ALFORD (F) A small lias-stone village set in flat lush countryside to the west of Castle Cary, named for 'Ealdgyth's ford' ('Aldedeford', 1086), evidently a crossing of the River Brue here. In 1086 the manor was held by Ansgar under the count of Mortain, to whom were due eight 'blooms' of iron from his villeins, although there is no later evidence of iron-working here. By 1236 it had passed to the Raleghs of Nettlecombe, and in 1455 to the FitzJames family of Redlynch and Bruton. It was bought by Elizabeth I's solicitor, William Rosewell (died 1566), whose descendant, Sir Henry Rosewell, sold the manor to Simon Court in 1634. Most of the houses stand on the Somerton to Castle Cary road (B 3153), while to the south, beyond the

OPPOSITE *Glastonbury Abbey (see page 104)*   ABOVE *Aisholt from the Slades*

railway line lies Alford Well Farm. This marks the site of a mineral spring, discovered in 1670 by the rector, the Rev Thomas Earl, after flocks of pigeons were observed to drink there. The well was patronised c.1690 by Celia Fiennes, who portrayed the Alford natives as 'a clounish rude people', and its waters, sent (surprisingly) to Bath, were described as having 'a nauseous bitter taste' but were 'highly recommended in gouty cases and bilious colics' and, by others, for scurvy, jaundice and 'obstructions'. This mini-spa had ceased to be popular by the late 18th century. North of the village beside the Brue is the charming unrestored Perpendicular church of All Saints, its west tower crowned with a little pyramid roof. There is a good set of early benchends, including carvings of a pelican vulning herself to feed her young and a dragon encircling a disembodied head, an ornate pulpit of 1625 and a rood screen which lacks its loft. From the church stretch the grounds of the substantial pile, Alford House, built by John Thring (died 1834), descended from a Wiltshire family. In 1877 his grandson, Theodore Thring (1816-91), employed F.C. Penrose to remodel the house 'in an insensitive neo-Elizabethan' (Pevsner). Theodore's talented brothers included Henry, 1st (and only) Baron Thring (1818-1907), the Rev Edward Thring (1821-87), headmaster of Uppingham, and

Preb Godfrey Thring (1823-1903), a celebrated hymn writer, rector here and builder of Hornblotton church.

★★ *Church and setting.*

ALFOXTON PARK (D), *see* **HOLFORD**

ALLER (E) The village, whose name means simply 'alder tree', possibly a local landmark when the first settler arrived, lies on the edge of the Levels to the north-west of Langport. It is mainly strung out along a single street which runs below the ridge of Aller Hill. The original settlement was probably on the former Aller 'island' on the moors to the west of the village where church and former manor-house, Aller Court Farm, stand. Its isolated character suggests that there may have been a semi-monastic site here in 878 when, following the Treaty of Wedmore, King Alfred baptised Guthrum, king of the Danes, at Aller. The drainage of the Levels west of the village began in the 13th century with the construction of a great wall around Aller Moor and the digging of Pathelake, a rhine (ditch) between Aller and Othery.

The parish church of St Andrew dates from the 12th and 13th centuries, although its tower and porch were added in the 14th. The older of its two fonts is 12th century and cannot be that at which Guthrum was baptised, as is sometimes claimed. Two effigies can probably be

Toll House at Aller

identified with early lords of the manor: Sir John of Aller (died c.1272), who legend credits with slaying a local dragon hereabouts, and Sir John of Clevedon (died c.1373). The parish council bought the lordship of the manor in 1910 solely to acquire the manor pound as a site for the village telephone box. The wealthy living attracted a succession of national figures as rector in the 15th and 16th centuries, including the secretary of Henry VI, the chaplain of Edward IV and Henry VII, the future archbishop of York and the personal physician of Henry VII and Henry VIII: although it is unlikely that any of them ever lived or ministered here.

The fine former rectory, west of Beer Road, dates from c.1500 and has a turret with two garderobes (i.e. loos), although much altered in the 19th century. In 1586 the living was bought by Emmanuel College, Cambridge, and for three centuries all the rectors were former fellows of that college. To one of them, Ralph Cudworth in 1618, it was 'a barren place' where 'the air is very bad, especially in spring, so that I have been often in danger of death by reason of agues, etc., which makes me desirous to remove'. The blessings of modern civilization have since improved matters.

Oath Hill to the south was the site of a medieval hermitage which housed two hermits by 1328. It had become a disused chapel by 1559 although nonconformist members of the resident Broadmead family were buried there as late as 1828.

★★ *Village and church.*

ALLERFORD (C), *see* **SELWORTHY**

AMMERDOWN (B), *see* **KILMERSDON**

ANGERSLEIGH (H) At the foot of the Blackdown Hills lies what is claimed at 403 acres to be the smallest parish in the diocese, centred on a small village originally known simply as Leigh ('glade') and later as Knightsleigh. The manor was bought from Henry of Leigh by John Anger shortly before 1279 and thus became known as 'Anger's leigh' (soft 'g'). Thereafter it passed successively to the families of Rydon, Cheddar, their heirs the Capels, Proctors and the Proctor Gales. The original manor-house was probably the medieval Leigh Farm but a 19th century squarson, the Rev Henry Tippets Tucker, built the substantial Leigh Court c.1830. The church of St Michael, at the end of a short lane, has a 14th century tower: the rest mostly 15th century with a Norman tub font. The benchends and panelling look Tudor but are 20th century by an amateur carver, Arthur Edgell Eastwood (died 1949) of Leigh Court. A small tablet commemorates the lord of Taunton Deane manor, the eccentric misogynist Thomas Southwood (died 1830) of nearby Lowton House, who left his vast estate to his parish apprentice, Robert Mattock. Mattock's pack of Lowton harriers, sold off in 1876, christened the nearby inn on top of the Blackdowns, the Harriers (formerly the Merry Harriers).

★ *Setting.*

ANSFORD (F) A former village immediately north of Castle Cary and with which town it is now almost continuously built up, its name ('Almundesford', 1086) meaning 'Ealhmund's ford'. After the Conquest the manor was granted to Walter de Douai and subsequently was always held with Castle Cary. Housing development at Churchfields in the 1970s revealed tools and pottery of the Neolithic, early Bronze and Romano-British periods. Ansford's significance lay in its position on the main road from Bristol and Bath, south to the resorts of Sidmouth and Weymouth, and was reflected in the early 19th century by the presence of no fewer than five inns on Ansford Hill. The church of St Andrew lies amid a sea of modern red-brick, signed off to the south from the A 371 down Tuckers Lane. It is a small and friendly building with a Perpendicular west tower, but much of the rest dates from the restoration and enlargement by C.E. Giles in 1861. There is a Jacobean pulpit and a fine early wooden

chest with linen-fold carving. The living was held from 1719 until 1836 by members of the Woodforde family and here, nearby at the Old Parsonage, was born the Rev James Woodforde in 1740. His diary, after that of Samuel Pepys, is one of the most famous in the English language and includes the period (1764-73) when James lived here as curate. He chronicled the everyday and the unusual: his own eating, drinking and card-playing, as well as the murder of Mrs Tucker by her husband with a hammer in 1775. The church is full of Woodforde memorials, including the one that James inscribed to the memory of his parents.

ASH (J) This parish was created in 1895 from the north-eastern quarter of Martock and presumably named from a once-prominent ash tree. The village itself was formed from two manors, Ash Boulogne and Pykesash, named from their medieval owners, the Boulogne and Pyke families. The parish also includes the hamlets of Witcombe and Milton Falconbridge, the latter held by the Fauconbergs by 1243 but forming part of the Duchy of Cornwall for the last four centuries. Court Cottage, at the southern end of the latter village beside the manor pound, can be identified with the manorial chapel built in 1287 by Sir Peter de Fauconberg and probably converted into a house in the 16th century.

★ *Setting.*

ASHBRITTLE (H) Bordering Devon to the west of Wellington and the River Tone, the parish takes its name from ash trees with the additional name of Bretel (de St Clair), the Norman lord in 1086, and the St Clair family owned the manor until the 14th century. The place has a highland landscape of scattered farmhouses whose buildings date mainly from the 16th and 17th centuries. The sturdy-looking village is centred on a green and on the church of St John the Baptist. Its north aisle, tower and chancel were rebuilt and the nave restored in 1874. In the chancel are monuments to members of the Quicke family, lords of the manor and rectors here in the 19th century, one of whom, the Rev Charles Penrose Quicke, paid for the brutal reconstruction.

★ *Landscape.*

ASHCOTT (E) A small village built of blue lias stone at the east end of the Polden Hills, originally founded around 'the cottage by the ash tree' which named it. The manor was held under that of Walton by Glastonbury Abbey from Saxon times and

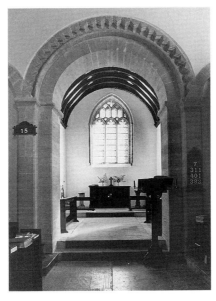

its church was one of the seven directly held by that house. The church of All Saints has a west tower built by Abbot John Selwood (1456-93), which bears his monogram. The remainder was largely rebuilt in 1832 and again altered in 1889, the Norman tub font being preserved from the old church. An informative 18th century monument near the south porch commemorates four generations of the Miles family. The chapel of St Martin, its site long forgotten, stood in the nearby hamlet of Pedwell in the early 14th century. The Duke of Monmouth camped with his rebel army at Pedwell Plain on his return to Bridgwater before the Battle of Sedgemoor and two Ashcott men were later presented for carrying provisions to his forces. The parish has two well-known public houses: the Piper's Inn on the A39, dating from the 17th century with an 18th century facade, where Wordsworth breakfasted on his last visit to Somerset in 1841, and in the village the Ashcott Inn, of similar vintage. During the Commonwealth in 1656 at the lost Black Boy Inn, local royalists daringly sang 'Let us drink, let us sing, here's a health to our King, and 'twill never be well till we have one again'.

★★ *Village, inns and setting.*

ASHILL (J) Triumphantly bypassed in 1992, this village bids fair to regain a peace it has not known for centuries. Its name is self-explanatory, the Domesday Book mentioning its extensive woodland. The manor descended from the de Vaux family to the Moultons, Sir Thomas Moulton securing in 1317 the grant of a Wednesday market and two three-day fairs here. A September fair was still being held in 1768. Thereafter the estate passed in turn through the Stretche and Beauchamp families to the Spekes. The parkland that once surrounded the Speke mansion of Jordans (demolished in the 1960s) is now cut by the new road south-

east to Ilminster, although the Spekes still live nearby at Rowlands, a delicious 16th century house of very human scale. Just off the centre of Ashill village the church of the Virgin Mary has Norman doorways to the north and south and a fine Norman chancel arch, with dogtooth decoration, flanked by smaller twin arches, now blocked, which once led to side chapels. In the north wall of the nave lie two early effigies. In the larger is that of a woman in a wimple, identified as Lady Maud de Moulton (died 1293): in the smaller that of a knight claimed to represent Sir John Stretche (died 1390). Intriguing shields carved around the base of the nave roof bear semi-heraldic coats of arms which probably once represented those of families connected with the manor or the area until amateurishly repainted. The tower screen, in memory of the village schoolmistress, is surmounted by a glazed

panel charmingly inscribed with a modern Virgin and child (1987) by parishioner Chester Read. The advowson was given to the bishop by Richard de Vaux in the early 13th century and Ashill has named a prebend in Wells Cathedral ever since.

★★ *Church and village.*

ASHINGTON (J) This 'place east of the town' ('Essentone', 1086) probably takes its name from its position to the east of Ilchester. It lies in flat countryside: north of Yeovil, beside the river Yeo. The idyllic village with its white fencing comprises only the church, manor-house, farm and a few cottages. The manor was held after the Conquest by Vital under Roger de Courcelles, later passing to the FitzWilliam, Furneaux and St Barbe families. The St Barbes seem to have lived mainly at Ashington until 1605 when they acquired Broadlands, Hants (more recently home to the Mountbattens), although the last of the line, Sir John St Barbe, Bart., chose to be buried at Ashington beside his first wife in 1723. There is an ornate monument to him in the chancel of the little Early English church of St Vincent, describing him as 'posses'd of those amiable Qualities which Birth, Education, Travel, Greatness of Spirit and Goodness of Heart produce'. He was created a baronet at the age of eight and served briefly as MP for Ilchester in 1681. The church is distinguished by its large western bellcot (as at Brympton and Chilthorne Domer) and delightful, if uncomfortable, shell-top box-pews, reader's desk and pulpit (dated 1637), evidently by the same craftsman as those at Mudford. The manor-house, visible from the north side of the churchyard, dates from the 15th century, although the eastern half of the building was demolished in the 19th century.

★★ *Village and scenery.*

Ashington church and Manor Farm

ASH PRIORS (D) Named after a long-vanished ash tree, the parish lies to the west of Bishops Lydeard, of which it once formed a part. Held in Saxon times by the bishop of Wells, the manor was seized by William the Conqueror and granted to Roger Arundel by 1086. Roger's son gave it to Taunton Priory, from which the second part of its name is derived. In more recent times Ash was dominated by the Periams and Lethbridges of Sandhill Park.

To the south of the village still stretches Ash Common where the 16th century bellfounder, Roger Semson, probably cast his bells. From the same century (the two-storey porch bears the date 1529) survives the house called the Priory although, contrary to later tradition, there was never a monastery here. The Lethbridges added a south aisle to the church and the village school, both in 1833. The church of the Holy Trinity, formerly a chapelry to Bishops Lydeard, was largely rebuilt in 1874 and includes several Lethbridge monuments.
★ *Village.*

ASHWICK (F) A parish of confusing narrow lanes which wind through the hills and vales of the lush Mendip countryside north of Shepton Mallet. This 'dairy-farm by the ash-trees', given in 1061 by Edward the Confessor to 'his abbot', Wulfwold, was soon after transferred by the abbot to Bath Priory (later Abbey), which retained it until the dissolution. Latterly the manor was held by the Hippisleys of Ston Easton. Yellow ochre was quarried here and this was also the site of some of the earliest coal-mining on Mendip, which led to the development of neighbouring hamlets such as Nettlebridge, Neighbourne and Benter, the last colliery, Moorewood, closing in 1933.

It is a dispersed community, formerly centred on the church of St James, a chapelry of Kilmersdon until 1826, which gained its own cemetery only in 1413. The Perpendicular west tower survives from the medieval building, but the rest was rebuilt in 1825 and wholly remodelled 1876-81 by Messrs Browne and Gill of Bath. It forms an attractive picture with the tree-girt Ashwick Court of c.1700, set well back from the road but in view from the churchyard. Nearby and to the north-east, until demolished in 1955-6, stood Ashwick Grove, described in 1791 as 'newly built' but on an older site: long the home (c.1820-1937) of a junior branch of the family of Strachey baronets of Sutton Court. This was the birthplace and home of

The "Priory", Ash Priors

John Billingsley (1747-1811), author in 1794 of a celebrated account of Somerset agriculture and one of the founders of the Bath and West Society. At Ashwick was baptized in 1815 William Braine, a Royal Marine who sailed on Sir John Franklin's ill-fated Arctic expedition, died in 1846 and was buried on Beechey Island. In 1984 his body, marvellously preserved in the permafrost, was exhumed and it was shown that he died of lead poisoning from the tinned food on which the expedition subsisted.

Oakhill is a substantial village strung out along a single street in the south-west of Ashwick parish. It grew up around the extensive Oakhill brewery, founded in 1767, whose buildings still give an industrial feel to the place and of which Billingsley was an original partner. Subsequently it passed to the Jillard family and in 1882 to the Spencers, becoming a limited company in 1889 when dinner for 25 was served in a 500-barrel vat to celebrate the occasion. The brewery never recovered from a disastrous fire in 1925, although production of malt here continued until 1987. Between 1904 and 1921 a narrow-gauge railway took supplies of Oakhill 'Invalid Stout' to Binegar station for distribution. The rather dour church of All Saints, architect J.L. Pearson, was built here in 1861 and became a parish church in 1866. It had been preceded by Methodist (1825) and Congregational (1873) chapels.

ATHELNEY (E), *see* **LYNG**

AXBRIDGE (A) A small but delightful former town at the foot of the Mendips, its name suggesting that it was founded to control a crossing of the River Axe. The town now centres on the Square, the former market-place, which is surrounded by a happy mix of buildings dating from the 15th to 19th centuries. With the parish church as a focal point in one corner at the head of a flight of stone steps, the whole effect is almost continental: an atmosphere enhanced by the table umbrellas outside the excellent Oak House Hotel. In origin the place was evidently carved out of the Saxon royal estate of Cheddar by the 10th century with a mint and walled fortification of some 550 yards in circuit, now thought to have lain south of the Square. In 1086 it had 32 burgesses, a number which remained constant throughout eight centuries. Axbridge ceased to be a royal borough when King John granted the manor to Hugh, archdeacon of Wells, in 1204, from whom it passed before 1209 to his relation, Thomas of Wells, then to Maurice de Gaunt, and finally c.1227 to the bishops of Bath and Wells. There had probably been a market here from the beginning but a fair was added in 1229, another in 1279 and two more in 1557. The borough, which sent MPs to parliament 1295-1344, seems to have been governed by the two stewards or masters of the guild of the Blessed Virgin Mary until the mayoralty was established in 1557. A common council was set up under a charter of 1599 and the borough

extended to include West Street in 1623, continuing thus until the place lost its corporation in 1883. The old guildhall was replaced on the south-east side of the Square by the **Town Hall** of 1833, now used mainly for social functions. The town has been headed by a mayor again since 1974 and the Axbridge Town Trust today retains a superb collection of borough records.

On the west side of the Square rises a fine three-storey merchant's house known as **King John's Hunting Lodge**. Dating from the late 15th century, it served as the King's Head Inn by 1645 until the mid 18th century but has no known connection with King John. Rescued by Miss K. Ripley for the National Trust, the building now houses an excellent local museum (fee: lists). Exhibits cover the geology, history and archaeology not only of Axbridge but also of Cheddar and the surrounding district, with special displays on Axbridge Union Workhouse (1837-1930) and World War II. Above the arched Church Wells (mentioned in 1290 as 'the great spring') rises the substantial Perpendicular **Church of St John the Baptist**, granted to Archdeacon Hugh in 1205 and to the bishops of Bath and Wells in 1214. Wonderfully lofty, despite the lack of a clerestory, it had altars dedicated to the Virgin Mary, Holy Trinity and St George until the Reformation. Below the tower is a superb fan vault of c.1400 and the nave has a most unusual plaster ceiling of 1636 with pendants, most attractively painted blue. There are several memorials to the Prowse

family, leaders of the town in the 18th century, who formerly hailed from Compton Bishop. Thomas Prowse (died 1767) was an amateur architect and MP for the county (as was his father), rejecting the office of Speaker of the Commons in 1761 because of ill-health. His mother Abigail, daughter of Bishop George Hooper, took seven years to work the altar frontal of 1720 displayed in front of a tomb bearing the kneeling effigy of Anne Prowse (died 1668). In the north transept is a brass depicting merchant Roger Harper and his wife, who died within a month of each other in 1493. A cupboard by the south door still houses loaves distributed to 'poor housekeepers' attending Saturday services. In 1583 the Wells schoolmaster was fined 2s (10p) for performing a play in the church here with his pupils and the cathedral

choristers. In 1789 Hannah More described the vicar as being drunk six times a week and often unable to preach because of black eyes sustained in fighting.

On the A 371 bypass, which opened in 1967 and follows the former course of the Cheddar Valley railway, are the **Cheddar Valley Vineyards** (lists) where wines can be tasted and bought, and light meals are served.

★★★ *Town, museum,* ★★ *Church.*

BABCARY (E) This quiet lias-built village east of Somerton, 'Babba's (settlement) on the river Cary', runs south from the inviting Red Lion Inn. Its parish seems to have been intensively farmed at the time of the Norman Conquest when there were two estates based on Babcary itself, two at Foddington ('hill for grazing'), now a small hamlet to the east, and a fifth at Stert, the last being held in 1086 by the two porters of Montacute Castle. The main manor was held by the Erlegh family from the 13th century and later by their descendants, the St Mawrs and Stawells, and was sold in 1828 to the Messiters of Barwick House. The Perpendicular church of Holy Cross, in the centre of the village, has a later north aisle of 1876, a pulpit dated 1632 and some fine old table tombs in the churchyard. The curacy here was held from 1764 by the young diarist, Parson James Woodforde. There was also a free chapel at Foddington until it was closed in 1548.

BABINGTON (B) A depopulated parish north-west from Frome, 'the settlement of Babba's people', which features one of the most harmonious Georgian groups of buildings in the county. The manor was held by Azelin under the bishop of Coutances in 1086 but by the 13th century had passed to the Botreaux family, who were granted a short-lived three-day fair

here in 1285. The estate was bought from Sir William Botreaux in 1371 by William Cheddre, from whom it descended through a succession of different families until inherited by the wife of Henry Mompesson (died 1715) and, probably soon after his marriage in 1692, Mompesson built the fine seven-bay facade of the present Babington House.

Mompesson's niece, Elizabeth Long (died 1765), erected the delightful church of St Margaret in front of the house 1748-50. It has a cupola-topped west tower, a pastel blue-domed apse, its original panelling and pews, and a slender fluted font which is more like a tall vase. Mrs Long's son-in-law, Maj Norton Knatchbull (died 1782), left a daughter who married her cousin, Capt Charles Knatchbull (died 1826), and the last added substantial rooms at the side of the house in 1790. The staircase includes four 15th century stained-glass saints: possibly from the former church. The beech-lined (private) drive up to the house is open to those visiting the church, the key to which can be obtained by calling at the side door of the house. The last remnants of the medieval village (25 tax-payers in 1327) were probably demolished by Mompesson.

★★★ *Church and its setting with Babington House.*

BADGWORTH (A)

The approach from the A 38 to 'Baecga's homestead', south-west from Axbridge, is by the delightfully-sited Biddisham and Badgworth cricket field, although there is no real village near the church. Before 1066 the place was held by two thegns, whose holdings may represent the later manors of Nether Badgworth and Over or West Badgworth, although united in 1086 under Walter de Douai. The main manor was held by the Mordaunt baronets from the 18th century. Also within the parish was the small manor of Tarnock (formerly 'Ternuc', possibly Celtic for 'winding stream'), today a scatter of houses lining the A 38. The parish church's dedication is uniquely to St Congar (whose name is also linked with Congresbury), a 6th century Welsh missionary, who may possibly have founded the first church on the site. The present building is mainly 14th century in date and can possibly be attributed to John de Hamtone or Hanton, lord of Nether Badgworth manor and patron in 1309, whose arched tomb with a Norman-French inscription lies on the north side of the sanctuary. There is a medieval tomb slab in the centre of the chancel, the piscina can be dated c.1320-50

Church and farmhouse, Badgeworth

and is reset, the chancel having been rebuilt in 1864. There is a fine Jacobean pulpit but it rests on a 15th century stone one, carved with the defaced figures of the Latin doctors: Saints Ambrose, Augustine, Jerome and Gregory. The exterior of the church was badly damaged in the great storm of 1703. Badgworth Court, south-east of the village, is a substantial early Georgian five-bay mansion to which a nine-bay wing was added in 1820. Further south, to the west of Quarrylands Lane, accumulations of late Iron Age and Romano-British pottery have been found.

★ *Church and scenery.*

BALTONSBOROUGH (E)

A village south-east from Glastonbury whose name means 'Bealdhun's hill or barrow'. It is a little like the curate's egg, good in parts, but modern development has been less well handled than in neighbouring Butleigh, and many of those who live here commute to Street and Glastonbury. The estate here was granted in 744 to Glastonbury Abbey by Lulla, who described herself as 'handmaid of Christ', and the manor was retained by the abbey until its dissolution. The link with Glastonbury resulted in the place's greatest distinction as the probable birthplace of St Dunstan c.909. It is known that he was born 'near Glastonbury' and, as the church here is the only one in the diocese dedicated to the saint, this seems the most likely location. He was the son of Heorstan, later reeve of the Glastonbury estates, and nephew of Aethelhelm, first bishop of Wells. Dunstan went on to become, abbot of Glastonbury, archbishop of Canterbury and the most influential cleric of his day. Local traditions that identify his precise place of birth in Ham

Lane are fanciful. The former most prominent feature of the parish was its oak woodland which even in the early 16th century occupied 800 acres with oak trees, divided into Northwood and Southwood. The church of St Dunstan lies at the end of an attractive short lane which is graced with the Old Vicarage and Glebe House. The living was a chapelry to Butleigh, served by chaplains and curates, until its own benefice was created in 1895. The church is uniformly 15th century, including the font, stone pulpit and benches. The 19th century 'large scrolly ironwork' supporting the tower weathervane particularly attracted Pevsner. The sedilia in the chancel has coats of arms identified with the wealthy Walton family who lived here in the 16th and 17th centuries. The Jacobean hinged extension seat to one pew is unlikely to have been a 'penance seat', as often stated, but was probably an additional sitting for the family that owned that particular bench and had outgrown it. The south door still has its original knocker, although this is rather late to have been a sanctuary knocker. A delicious epitaph commemorates the amatory prowess of William Martin (died 1639):

'Would you know whom this tombe covers,
Tis the nonpareil of lovers.
It's a sweet William, sweeter far
Than the flowers that so stil'd are.'

Gatehouse is a fine E-shaped house built by Ralph Walton c.1550, extended in the 17th century and named after the Gatehouse family of linen weavers, occupiers 1699-1839.

★ *Church and vicinity.*

BARFORD PARK (D), *see* ENMORE

The church and River Brue at Baltonsborough

BARLYNCH PRIORY (C), *see* BROMPTON REGIS

BARRINGTON (J) Lining both sides of a single winding street, this beautiful village lies to the north-east of Ilminster and is an enchanting essay in Ham stone, its name meaning 'the settlement of Barra's people'. Of its many attractive houses, the Priory (which has no ecclesiastical links and was only so-called from c.1880) dates from the late 14th century, the Knapp and Vinces from a century later. The Royal Oak, a favourite port of call, was loyally named the Victoria when licensed in 1839 but rechristened in 1854. Part of the eastern end of the village is known as Little Puckington from an estate given in 1301 to endow a chantry in the nearby parish of Puckington. Barrington formed part of the manor of South Petherton after the Norman Conquest, both the property of the Crown, but by 1225 the estate had passed to Philip Daubeney from Brittany and

remained in his family, with only short interruptions, until the death of Henry Daubeney, earl of Bridgewater, in 1548. The Barrington estate was bought by a London merchant, William Clifton in 1552.

An old medieval manor-house lay at the end of a lane leading north-east from the eastern end of the village. This was replaced by a splendid mansion, **Barrington Court**, formerly attributed to Henry Daubeney c.1514, but now thought to have been put up by Clifton (died 1564) in the years following his purchase and completed by his son, Sir John. It is largely two-storeyed with a third floor in the gables and dormers (and a fourth above the porch) and is ornamented with elegant twisted finials and gables. The house, although not the manor, was bought by William Strode (died 1666) and his son, another William, added a fine brick stable block in 1674. The latter entertained the Duke of Monmouth here in 1680 on his progress through the West Country. The

Court suffered severely during the 19th century, when it was held by the Hanning, Lee and Peters families: stripped of its internal timberwork and part converted to a cider cellar. It was purchased by Miss Woodward of Clevedon for the National Trust in 1905, and in 1920 was leased to the Lyle family (of Tate and Lyle sugar fame). The Lyles proved to be the Court's salvation. The Strode stable block was converted to living quarters, a new farm and tenants' houses were put up, connected by avenues, and formal gardens, designed by Gertrude Jekyll, were laid out to the west of the house. Inside the Court Col Abraham Lyle installed his personal collection of antique panelling, screens and other fittings. The Court is now occupied by Stuart Interiors, a firm who use it as a showcase for their antique and reproduction furniture. The delightful grounds (fee:lists), laid out in three walled 'rooms', are open, courtesy of the National Trust, plants are sold and there is a shop and restaurant.

The church of St Mary stands at the eastern end of the village, set above the street. It was formerly a daughter chapel to South Petherton and served by curates until 1968, although it gained its own cemetery as early as 1241 because of 'the risk and inconvenience' of carrying bodies to the mother church for burial. Its octagonal central tower, transepts and chancel were put up in the 13th century, the nave in the 15th and the south aisle in 1861 at the time of an over-thorough general restoration. A 13th century piscina in the south transept features a dog and monkey supporting its canopy.

★★★★ *Village, Barrington Court and gardens,* ★★ *church.*

BELOW *Barrington Court*

Geology and Building Materials

The varied landscape of the county reflects the diversity of the geology which underlies it and the differing textures of stones from which its older buildings are constructed. In the west the high lands of Exmoor, Brendon and Quantock are formed from the oldest rocks in Somerset, the Devonian sandstone, slate (formerly quarried around Treborough) and shale, while the Mendips and Brean Down are composed of grey Carboniferous (coal-bearing) Limestone. The southern edge of the Mendips is fringed with the underlying Old Red Sandstone, a pink Dolomitic Conglomerate containing limestone pebbles (which also occurs to the north of the ridge). From Cheddar in the west to Frome in the east, controversial large-scale quarrying for aggregate to build roads continues, although coalmining there, like leadmining before it, has now finished.

A small outcrop of lias on the coast north of the Quantocks extends west to Watchet, where alabaster was formerly taken from the cliffs, and oil-bearing shale occurs at Kilve, oil that fortunately it has never proved economic to extract (40 gallons per ton), also providing a rich harvest of fossil ammonites. Lias also composes the Polden ridge across the Levels and a wide area to the east and south of Taunton, extending as far as Castle Cary. Outcrops of lias are also responsible for the striking survival of the isolated hills of Brent Knoll and Glastonbury Tor. Notable quarries in the vicinity of Keinton Mandeville produced this flaky blue grey stone, used generally for domestic and church building but also for paving. Some of the lias will take a polish and was used as a local substitute for marble. Beyond the lias, the south and the east of the county is rimmed by a wide belt of Oolitic limestone of the Middle Jurassic period, which at Doulting provided most of the

TOP *Stonework at Litton on the Mendips* ABOVE *Thatch and Ham-stone, Merriott* BELOW *Almshouses at Donyatt*

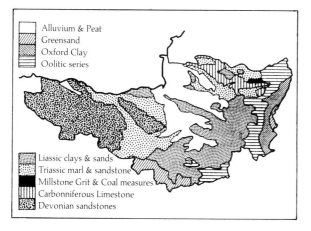

Alluvium & Peat
Greensand
Oxford Clay
Oolitic series

Liassic clays & sands
Triassic marl & sandstone
Millstone Grit & Coal measures
Carbonniferous Limestone
Devonian sandstones

raw material for Wells Cathedral and Glastonbury Abbey. Ham Hill was quarried from Roman times for the golden stone from which whole villages were built to the west of Yeovil and which was used for window and door frames and decorative details further afield in the county. Bounding the east of the county from Beckington to Henstridge is a strip of Oxford Clay.

The Blackdown Hills comprise Upper Greensand, rich in fossils, and Gault Clay with flints, together with small outcrops of chalk near Chard. The soils are poor and the small farms concentrate largely on dairying. The flint here, or more properly chert, distinguishes churches and houses to the west of Chard, with former major quarries at Whitestaunton and Combe St Nicholas. Cob was occasionally used as a cheaper alternative to building stone.

The fertile valley of the Tone and the lower land both east and west of the Quantocks lie on a clay foundation of Keuper Marl, formerly providing the raw material for brick and tile making, particularly around Taunton, Wellington and Bridgwater. There is an isolated reference to bricks carried from Taunton to Rimpton in 1498, but extensive use of brick in the county dates only from the early 17th century and for major houses only from the building of Ven House (Milborne Port) from 1696. The Levels are formed from peat beds overlaid with alluvium, the former exploited for horticultural use and the latter once used around Bridgwater to make Bath bricks: a scouring product. Along the coast there is a belt of marine clay, which acts as a barrier to fresh water drainage and has caused much of the flooding in the peat moors over the centuries.

ABOVE *Ham Hill quarry workings*
BELOW *Coastal shale at Kilve*
BOTTOM *13th century stone tombs, Curry Rivel church*

LEFT *Needle Folly, Barwick.* ABOVE *The Guildhall, Stoford (Barwick)*

BARTON ST DAVID (E) A no-nonsense working village, a mixture of old and new building, north-east from Somerton, its name identifying 'a demesne (or corn) farm', the 'demesne' being the land reserved to the lord of the manor, with the addition of the church's dedication. There were two manors here in Saxon times and in 1086, each with its own mill. In the early 13th century a cleric, Robert de Meysi, gave the church to Wells Cathedral which was used to found a prebend there. The church of St David stands at the south-western end of the village with a Perpendicular tower: the only one in Somerset which is octagonal from the ground. It has a Norman zigzag north doorway and most of the rest is of c.1300, apart from the south transept, rebuilt in 1894. The interior is relatively austere with few monuments. In the chancel, however, flanked by small flags, is a plaque to the memory of Henry Adams, born here in 1583, set up in 1926 by a descendant. Henry was ancestor of two American presidents, John Adams and John Quincy Adams, 'whose exalted services to their country evoke a testimony of respect for their ancestral home'.

BARWICK (J) A small village (*berewic* – 'corn farm') immediately south of Yeovil which has been somewhat swamped by modern suburban development. With Chilton Cantelo it formed the tiny hundred of Barwick. The manor seems originally to have been held under Yeovil but by 1160 had been acquired by William de Cantilupe, whose family named Chilton Cantelo. From him it was eventually inherited by George de Cantilupe (died 1272), who had here a

'well-built' manor-house, dovecot and 40 acre park. The manor was bought by John Newman of Yeovil in 1758 and it was probably Newman who built the present Barwick House north-east from the old village (remodelled in the 19th century and described as 'recently erected' in 1861). Four celebrated rubble follies define the boundaries of the park and can readily be seen from the surrounding roads. Some of these appear in the background of Newman family portraits of c.1770 and comprise to the west a 75 ft cone surmounted by a ball and standing on an arched support, to the south a slender needle, tilted at the top, to the north the cylindrical Fish Tower, 50 ft tall on a square plinth, topped by a Ham stone drum which formerly had a fish weathervane (the tithe map of 1837 shows two such towers side by side), and to the east Jack the Treacle Eater. This last takes the form of a tower mounted on an arch, allegedly named after a spritely messenger, trained on treacle, who used to carry letters to London for the Messiters, bankers from Wincanton, who inherited Barwick from the Newmans. There is also an elaborate grotto in the grounds of the house: the property formerly used as a reformatory but, at the time of writing (1994), empty for several years. The small church of St Mary Magdalene, west of an attractive group of cottages, was a chapelry of Yeovil. It is basically 15th century: the cost of the ornate north aisle evidently contributed to in 1489 by Syon Abbey, holders of Yeovil rectory. It has a 13th century transeptal tower and a Norman font, although the chancel was rebuilt in 1885. The surprise is the delightful

bench ends, dated 1533 and illustrating rural scenes.

The largest settlement in the parish is the attractive hamlet of **Stoford**, named for a 'stone ford' over the River Yeo, where William de Cantilupe established a borough, probably around the time that he obtained a fair (1228) and Tuesday market (1231). By 1272 there were 74½ burgesses and in 1353 a Guildhall ('Zuldhous'): this last still surviving at the north end of the village green, the former market-place, as does the former courthouse further to the west. No church was ever built here, probably because of Barwick's subservience to Yeovil. In 1633 the portreeve was still processing on the fair day 'guarded with four or half a dozen copper maces . . . though sometimes he be a man of verie meane estate'. The expansion of Yeovil may have been responsible for Stoford's decline although a second fair was added in 1671 by Thomas Symes and both continued to be held until World War One. Today the centre of Stoford makes a harmonious picture with its white-windowed cottages and Royal Oak Inn.

★★ *Follies and centre of Stoford village.*

BATCOMBE (F) This most attractive village, 'Bata's valley', lies north-east from Bruton and straggles along the valley formed by a tributary of the River Alham. Its modern appearance belies the successful woollen industry which flourished here until the 18th century. In 940 the manor was given by King Edmund to his kinsman Ealdorman Aelfheah (died 970/1), whose family bestowed it on Glastonbury Abbey. The last Saxon abbot of Glastonbury,

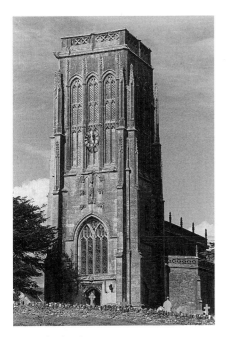

Batcombe church

Aethelnoth (1053-78), gave a substantial part of the manor to his mother Aelfilla which thereafter was lost to the abbey and became the separate estate of Westcombe in the west of the parish. Following the dissolution of Glastonbury the main manor was granted to James Bisse, whose family were prominent clothiers and also acquired the Batcombe manors of Westcombe and Spargrove ('Spertegrave', 1166: 'the grove where basket withies were cut'). The church of St Mary stands on a rise above the valley with wonderful views from the churchyard. It has a superbly ornamental 87 ft west tower, to the building of which bequests were made in 1539 and 1543. This richness is continued inside with a panelled tower arch and fan vault. The remainder is Perpendicular, the south porch added by James Bisse in 1629, and there are a number of memorials to his family, including a brass to Dr Philip Bisse, rector here 1564-1613, whose bequest of 2,000 books founded the library at Wadham College, Oxford. The church includes a second font brought from Spargrove where there was a chapel of St Lawrence by 1191, when the rector of Batcombe was trying to recover it, until 1564. At Spargrove a moated site survives but the 16th century manor-house was largely rebuilt in the later 19th century. The manor was held by the Sanzaver family by the early 13th century and the house here was later occupied by the Bisses. The latter were largely responsible for the Puritanical complexion at Batcombe in the 17th century, given added

impetus by the rector, Richard Alleine, which led in 1642 to an abortive raid on Bruton, as recorded in a well-known verse in that town's parish register:

'All praise and thanks to God still give
For our deliverance Matthias Eve (23
    February).
By his great power we put to flight
Our foes, the raging Batcombites.'
★★★ *Village, church and landscape.*

BATHEALTON (H) Lying hidden in the high wooded hills and valleys west of Wellington and south of Wiveliscombe, its name ('Badeheltone' in 1086) perhaps meaning 'Bada's remote (or possibly 'old') settlement'. After the Norman Conquest it was granted to William de Mohun of Dunster but in the 13th century was divided into three parts between the daughters of Reynold of Bathealton. One of these parts was long held by the Sydenhams, another successively by the Pouletts and the Pophams, but all passed in the 17th century to the Webber family, originally of Kittisford, who later took up residence at Bathealton Court. This substantial house, set back from the road north of the village, was rebuilt c.1766 by John Webber (died 1775) and acquired by the Moysey family in 1845. The church of St Bartholomew was completely rebuilt in 1854 but its chancel contains earlier monuments to the Webber family, while the Moyseys are commemorated by tablets below the west tower. Two miles west of the village, high above the River Tone, is an eliptical prehistoric enclosure, possibly a fort, known as the Castles.
★★ *Setting*

BAWDRIP (E) Turning off the A 39 at the west end of the Polden Hills from an uninspiring hamlet down a grubby lane towards the village, the visitor may well have second thoughts – but persevere ! Suddenly appears a delightfully-picturesque grouping of cottages, farm and school around the church. Its name seems to derive from a trap, possibly 'badger trap' ('Bagetrepe' in 1086). St Michael's church has largely escaped vandalising restoration and retains the 13th century air that its builders intended. In the same century the church was granted to Athelney Abbey by Roger of Bawdrip, although the abbey later lost possession. Cruciform in shape, it has a central crossing tower carried on open arches. There is a delightful profusion of carved heads, including four on the canopy over the effigy of Sir Simon de Bradney (died 1375), MP for

Somerset, who endowed a chantry in St Mary's chapel: probably in the north transept where his effigy lies. There are massive squints from both transepts, a tiny madonna and child set in the north wall of the chancel and a Heath-Robinson stairway which seems to hang above the west tower arch. A slate memorial behind the altar commemorates Edward Lovell, a 17th century rector, and his daughter Eleanor, stated to have died in 1681 soon after her marriage. This led to Bawdrip erroneously appropriating the folk tale of a bride entombed in an old chest on her wedding day as recounted in the Victorian song, *The Mistletoe Bough*. A gloomy vestry on the south side of the nave formerly housed the family pew of the Greenhills, lords of the manor. Their former home, Knowle Hall, an 1830s creation of Richard Carver, later became a hotel and since 1976 has been occupied by the British Institute for Brain-Damaged Children. Bradney, Crook and Peasey probably represent the sites of late Saxon settlement above the flood plain.

The parish was the birthplace in 1598 of John Atherton, who rose to become the Irish bishop of Waterford and Lismore, before being hanged for sodomy at Dublin in 1640. Rock salt was accidentally discovered here and subsequently exploited when a bore hole was sunk over 2,000 ft during an abortive search for coal in 1913.
★★ *Village centre, church and setting.*

BECKINGTON (B) This 'settlement of Becca's people' is a substantial former cloth-producing village to the north-east of Frome. Despite its early industrial success it never acquired borough status, although there was a market cross here until its demolition in 1775. It was also the birthplace of Thomas Bekynton (c.1390-1465), one of the most prominent bishops

Carved stone head, Bawdrip church

of Bath and Wells and secretary to Henry VI. The principal manor, granted to Robert Arundel after the Norman Conquest, had passed by the mid 12th century to the Erlegh family, who established a park by 1248 and obtained a fair here in 1318. The estate was bought by local clothier, Thomas Webb (died 1585), who in 1581 also acquired Beckington Priory manor, named from its ownership before 1278 by Maiden Bradley Priory (Wilts) and held after the dissolution by Dr Agostino, Henry VIII's Venetian physician, centred on Prior's Court Farm at the eastern end of the village. The main estate here was purchased c.1650 by John Ashe of Freshford (died 1659), reputedly 'the greatest clothier in England', after which it was inherited by his Methuen relations.

The church of St George (sometimes mistakenly attributed to St Gregory) stands at the upper and south-eastern limit of the village and possesses 'the most ambitious Norman tower of any Somerset parish church' (Pevsner). The chancel is 14th century (aggressively restored by the Victorians), the clerestoreyed nave, aisles and porches are all Perpendicular and Compton's aisle, to the east of the south aisle and formerly dedicated to the Blessed Virgin Mary. The last, entered by a fine Jacobean screen, was evidently built under the will of clothier John Compton (died 1484) and he and his wife Edith are commemorated by brasses in the floor. The rest of the church is also full of interesting memorials. In the north aisle is a tablet and bust (in Roman dress) to the poet Samuel Daniel (died 1619), who ended his days in the small hamlet of Rudge at the eastern edge of the parish. In the chancel are the effigies of an unidentified Erlegh lady of c.1370 and, under a superbly ornate canopy, those of Sir John de Erlegh and his wife Margaret de Bryan of 1380. In the chancel floor beneath a carpet are brasses to John St Maur (died 1485) and his wife Elizabeth Choke (died 1503), he being the most likely builder of Seymour's Court, the five-bay manor-house on the north-eastern outskirts of the village. In the south aisle a further brass commemorates Thomas Webb, 'clotheman' (died 1585), surmounted by his merchant's mark. Nearby is an elaborate plaster achievement of the royal arms of Elizabeth I (there is another on canvas of 1702 under the tower) and memorials to the Edgell family of Standerwick Court, including Rear Admiral Henry Edgell (died 1816). The church is notorious for its churchwardens having refused a royal order to remove the

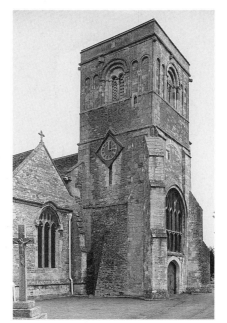

Beckington church

altar from the body of the chancel to the east end in 1635. The wardens were excommunicated by Bishop Piers, imprisoned and had to do penance at Beckington, Bath and Frome.

Beckington was a place that attracted notable visitors. Charles II and Queen Catherine rode through in 1663, Samuel Pepys stopped to feed his horses in 1668, the Duke of Monmouth and his army marched through on their way to oblivion at Sedgemoor in 1685, and George III and Queen Charlotte passed this way to Longleat in 1785. This was also the scene of an incredible eight-hour gun battle in 1766 between starving rioters and the proprietor of the flour mills, which left one dead and many wounded.

Standerwick is a village south-east down the A36 to Warminster but running at rightangles to it. It was a Domesday manor held later by the Hungerfords of Farleigh, of whom Walter, Lord Hungerford (died 1449), built a causeway across 'Stanwyk-mersshe' to improve travel through the parish. In the 18th century it was bought by the Edgells who lived at Standerwick Court, a sizeable plain mansion standing alone to the north-west of the village. The rectory, long held by Cirencester Abbey, was united with that of Beckington in the later 17th century although Standerwick church had evidently been demolished before 1454. Frome market in 1990 moved out of town to a new extensive site at the former Moors Farm here.

★★★ *Beckington church and village.*

Three-toed carving, Beer Crowcombe church

BEER CROCOMBE (J) On the Fivehead River, a tributary of the River Isle, the parish takes the first element of its name from the Saxon for 'pasture' or possibly 'grove'. The manor was granted to Godfrey de Craucombe (of Crowcombe) in 1227 and by the 14th century had adopted his surname as a suffix. The church of St James lies isolated from the small village at the end of a narrow verdant lane with extensive views from the churchyard. The nave dates from the 13th century and the west tower from the 14th: the tower arch supported by hunched three-toed grotesques. Restoration in the 19th century swept it clear of memorials, although a window on the south side of the sanctuary is dedicated to Col J.R.M. Chard (died 1897), the hero of Rorke's Drift (*see* **Hatch Beauchamp**).

★ *Church, village, setting.*

BERKLEY (F) A happy retreat immediately east of the expanding town of Frome, its name ('Berchelei', 1086, pronounced 'Burkley' *not* 'Barkley') meaning 'birch wood'. The estate here, held in 1086 by Robert under the great Roger Arundel, passed in the mid 15th century to the Newborough family from Dorset. Their heiress married John Prowse of Compton Bishop in 1670, and this couple's son, John, who died aged 34 in 1710, married Abigail (died 1763), daughter of George Hooper, bishop of Bath and Wells. The bishop spent much time in his latter years at Berkley and died here in 1727. Abigail erected the present Berkley House in 1731-2, its five-bay front designed by Nathaniel Ireson of Wincanton. It was probably her son, Thomas Prowse, amateur architect and MP for Somerset 1740-67, who conceived the new church of St Mary, immediately beside the Prowse home, built 1748-50. The church is approached up an attractive short lane, which dissolves into a lime-tree lined avenue and succeeded an older building. Michael McGarvie has persuasively argued that this can be identified with the 14th century chapel of Pikewell. For Pevsner the present building is 'the best Georgian church in any Somerset village' (although there are precious few of them). St Mary's is basically square, crowned by a central octagonal dome-like structure, decorated with ornamental rococo plasterwork and supported on four pillars. The former manorial chapel at the head of the south aisle includes a lengthy genealogical inscription to the Newboroughs. The manor itself passed in 1834 to the Mordaunt baronets, descendants of the Prowses, until the estate was split up and sold in 1890 and 1919. West of the church is the hamlet of Berkley Marsh, originating as the manor of Egforton but later known as Fairoak. It had its own chapel by the mid 12th century which was united with Berkley in 1460. An elaborate Skimmington ride to ridicule the cuckolded William Swarfe was recorded at Berkley in 1611.

★★★ Church.

BERROW (A) Sea, sand and, in particular, sand dunes bespeak this north-west Somerset coastal resort – and perhaps name it, for Berrow ('Berges' in 1196) is probably derived from the Saxon *beorgas*, meaning 'mounds'. It was jocularly christened Berrow-super-Rabbit-burrows by Joseph Leech c.1850. Its gently-sloping sands extend north from Burnham and continue to the headland of Brean Down, settlement being largely confined to both sides of the coast road. The place seems to have been included within the great estate of Brent granted by King Ine of the West Saxons to Glastonbury Abbey in 693, although the monks clearly lost the manor later. A new grant specifically of Berrow was made in 973 by King Edgar to his thegn Wulmer, and presumably the manor passed to the abbey soon after. It was apparently seized by King Harold II but restored to Glastonbury by William the Conqueror, and thereafter was retained until the dissolution of 1539. It was later held by a succession of non-resident lords and was bought by the Stanley baronets in 1740. Warding off

Berrow Sands from Brean Down

the advances of the sea was always a priority here. Ralph de Lucy granted 'the Newewalle' in Berrow to the abbey c.1310, Abbot Adam of Sodbury (1323-34) built 'a stonework at Rokusmille' ['Rokespulle' was a watercourse flowing into the sea at Berrow c.1310] to shut out the sea-waves', and tenants in 1515 had to maintain 'Shyprokys Wall'. The church of the Virgin Mary stands amid the sand dunes at the northern end of the golf course (*see* **Burnham**) at a right-angle bend in the coast road. Formerly held by the abbey, it was settled on the archdeacon of Wells in 1328 and a vicarage was ordained. The present building is basically 13th century with Perpendicular additions, including the top of the west tower. There is a 13th century quatrefoil font, a Jacobean pulpit dated 1621, a slender reader's desk of 1631 and a western gallery of 1637. The fine 15th century crosshead, depicting the Crucifixion and the Virgin Mary, missing from the cross itself outside, was discovered in the churchyard in 1926 and is preserved in the sanctuary. Outside, heavily weathered, are the 13th century effigies of a knight and his lady. In 1515 there was a Church house and 'Our-ladyhouse' (probably a former priest's house) at the southern end of the cemetery. Viscount Cave (1856-1928), Home Secretary 1916-19, is buried here and Withy Cottage was the holiday home of the playwright Ben Travers (1886-1980).

★★ Coastal scenery and church.

BICKENHALL (H) A scattered parish south-east from Taunton, whose name means 'Bica's hall' or 'hill'. The manor was held under Robert, Count of Mortain, in 1086, passed to the Portmans of nearby Orchard Portman following their marriage to the heiress of the Orchard family in the 15th century. In the late 16th century the Portmans built a mansion at Playstreet in the parish, home to Rachel Portman (died 1631), spinster sister of the first baronet. The development of Portman property in London resulted in the naming of Bickenhall Street in the capital. The Rev Fitzhardinge Berkeley Portman (died 1893) destroyed the house at Playstreet and the small medieval church of St Paul, building a new Victorian church on the Playstreet site in 1849. This redundant church has recently been converted into Neroche Parish Hall.

BICKNOLLER (D) A picturesque village of thatched 16th and 17th century cottages on the western slopes of the Quantock Hills, whose name ('Bykenalre' in 1291) means 'Bica's alder tree'. The regularity of its street plan suggests a planted settlement which can be identified with the 11th century manor of Newton. Joined with the other Domesday estate of Woolston, the united lordship was held by the chapter of Wells Cathedral from 1430 until 1857: its manor-house the late 16th century house of Wayvile (formerly 'Wayfield'). Thorncombe, an ancient freehold mentioned in 1221, is today represented by

A benchend, Bicknoller church

Thorncombe House, a fine 5-bay mansion built in 1744 by the Sweeting family with a 19th century facade. Remains of a much earlier settlement survive on Bicknoller Hill. Trendle Ring is a circular prehistoric bank and ditch 100 yds in diameter.

The church of St George has a pillar piscina with cable moulding of the 12th century in the chancel and the south wall of the nave is probably of the same period. The chancel was rebuilt and the west tower, which Pevsner believed was modelled on that of Stogumber, added in the 15th century: with the porch, north aisle and north chapel dating from the early 16th. There is excellent stone carving, both inside and out, with a fine series of Quantock benchends of c.1530 (added to in 1932), and a rood screen, not much earlier, believed to have been moved from Huish Champflower in 1726. The benchends may well have been executed by the celebrated carver, Simon Warman of Bicknoller, living married in the parish by c.1525 and who was buried here in 1585. A small plate on one pew records the Bicknoller holidays of Archbishop Temple, 1933-44. Two epitaphs cry out to be quoted. One on the outside of the south porch runs bitterly:

'O who would trust the world
   or prize what's in it,
That gives and takes and chops
   and changes ev'ry minit.'
The second, weather-worn, faces the east window from the churchyard, commemorating the family of Bartholomew Safford, Commonwealth minister 1643, 1646-62:
'Here lie three Saffords out of view
   Mabel, Mary, Bartholomew.
Bartholomew Safford's flesh and bone
   His wife, His sister and His son.
Mabel became for worms a bait
   December 9th in forty-eight.
Mary was fitted for the bier
   On March 4th that same year.
Death on Bartholomew did fixe
   On March the 2nd fifty-six.
Wife, Sister, Brother, Father dear,
   Christ's minister and parson here.'

Halsway Manor (pronounced 'Halsey'), a Domesday estate forming a detached part of Stogumber parish until 1883, lies to the east of the A 358 and south-east from Bicknoller village. Used as a residential centre for folkdancing and folksong since 1965, the property was owned from the 12th century by the Halsway family, passing by marriage to the Stradlings c.1300. Forget the story that it was a hunting lodge of Cardinal Beaufort, although he was father-in-law of Sir Edward Stradling (died 1453) and may have visited the place. It was sold in 1637 to the Cades of Wilton (near Taunton), who retained it until 1787. Parts of the medieval house, which had its own chapel in 1415, may survive in the present building: largely rebuilt and extended in the Tudor style by solicitor Charles Rowcliffe from 1875.

★★★ *Village, church, landscape.*

Halsway Manor, Bicknoller

BIDDISHAM (A) This small village, 'Biddi's meadow', midway between Axbridge and East Brent, lines a lane running north from the A 38, to which more recent settlement along the main road has been added. If a spurious charter of 1065 can be believed, its Celtic name was Tarnock, mentioned in Saxon charters of 693 and c.950 as a boundary of the great Brent estate (*see* **Badgworth**). The manor was a Saxon possession of Wells Cathedral and was assigned by Bishop Robert (1136-66) for repairs to the cathedral building and to provide its ornaments. The vicarage was similarly devoted by the 14th century to the office of schoolmaster of the cathedral. The church of St John the Baptist has a west tower which long ago lurched to the west and has since been given a modern vertical upper stage. The building seems to be Perpendicular, there is a square Norman font decorated underneath with scallops and a Jacobean pulpit. It was recorded in 1332 that tenants of the manor were given an annual Christmas feast of meat and cheese, washed down with 45 gallons of ale.

★ *Village and setting.*

BINEGAR (F) A Mendip village with much modern development which lies north of Shepton Mallet and west of the A37. Its name ('Begenhangra' in a dubious charter of 1065) probably means 'the slope where beans are grown'. It evidently formed part of the endowment of Wells Cathedral from Saxon times and in the 12th century was bestowed by Bishop Robert on the dean of Wells to endow a prebend which was known as Whitchurch. This evidently refers to a hamlet of that name to the east of Ston Easton village.

The church of the Holy Trinity has a Perpendicular west tower with a vernacular carved emblem of the Trinity on its western parapet, but the rest was rebuilt in 1858. Calamine ore for the production of zinc was mined at Merchants Hill briefly in the late 18th century, although the place was always best known for its limestone quarries and lime-burning, and many of the 19th century houses here were built to accommodate the quarrymen. To Binegar station (closed 1966) on the Somerset and Dorset line were brought by traction engine the products of Oakhill brewery, until a private branch line thence was opened in 1904. Binegar fair, formerly claimed to have been moved from Wells at a time of plague (as was also claimed for Priddy fair) in the 17th century, was in existence by 1367, and was in private hands when sold in 1592, at that time being described as Binegar *and Whitnell* (in Emborough) fair. It was held next to the church by the 18th century and lasted for most of Whitsun week. A house on Binegar Green was referred to as 'the Fair Place' in 1764. It became mainly a horse fair in the 19th century and continued until 1955.

Gurney Slade is a grey-stone settlement along the A 37, today continuously built up with Binegar, although partly lying in Ashwick parish. The Upper Mill there was rented from 1831 by George Steeds, edge-tool maker from Stoke Lane, and became Steeds' Iron Works, closing in 1934.

BISHOPS HULL (H)

BISHOPS HULL (H) A parish which once extended right into the centre of Taunton, including Taunton Castle and Castle Green, and may represent a very early settlement. As Hulle ('hill') it formed one of the five 'hundreds' into which Taunton Deane manor was divided, the 'bishops' being those of Winchester, lord of that manor. There has been considerable modern development in the present century as Taunton has expanded, but the old village has preserved its attractive character thanks to the building of its Victorian bypass, Wellington New Road (A 38), in 1838. The Manor House (which it never was), formerly known as the Great House, is a fine H-shaped Elizabethan mansion on the hill slope below the church. Built in 1586 by George Farewell (died 1609), its porch bears the date and the arms of his father, Simon (died 1568), probably rescued from an earlier house, and was held by the Farewells until 1720. It is now occupied as a nursing home.

The church of SS Peter and Paul at the top of the hill was granted to the monks of Taunton Priory (whose church had the same dedication) during the later 12th century, who from 1308 were obliged to provide a priest here. They must have paid for the 13th century tower base and its 14th century octagonal top, although the rebuilding of the chancel and north chapel c.1522-40 proved to be their swansong here. Desperate to house a larger congregation, the parishioners wrecked the nave by a major rebuilding of 1826-7 which extended the body of the church to the north and added a gallery. A fine series of 16th century benchends, some attributed to Simon Warman of Bicknoller, include an elaborate Resurrection tableau, a night watchman with club and lamp, and papal head with crossed keys. There are fine monuments to the Farewells, particularly in the chancel to the builder of the Manor House (1609). Outside against the south wall is a tombstone to Dr William Crotch, first President of the Royal Academy of Music, who died in 1847 while on a visit to his father, headmaster of Taunton grammar school. The United Reformed Church dates from 1718, although housing a congregation founded by the former vicar of Bishops Hull, Nathaniel Charlton, ejected from his living in 1662 after the Restoration.

The parish has many substantial houses, including Upcot Hall (c.1730) and Netherclay House (late 18th century). Barr House (17th century, later enlarged) was built by the Hine family and was later the home of Col Sir Charles Webb Dance (died 1844), veteran of Waterloo. This was also an area of mills. On the northern boundary with Staplegrove, on the site of the former Backbridge mills, Isaac Hawkins created a silk-throwing factory in 1802 (his son John Isaac invented the upright piano): in silk production until the 1860s. It christened Silk Mills Road which since 1979 has cut the modern village in two. On the Tone, beside an old narrow bridge at the foot of the hill, Bridge House represents a mill operated in the 18th century by the Tytherleigh family who named the nearby Tytherleigh House. This is my favourite corner of Bishops Hull from which there are fine walks along the River Tone. Upstream, Longaller Mill is under welcome restoration. On a modern estate here St Margaret's Somerset Hospice has housed a caring community since 1987.

At **Rumwell**, an attractive hamlet on the A38 towards Wellington, is an 18th century inn, two large 19th century villas and Grants, a late medieval farmhouse remodelled by Henry Bindon in the early 17th century. Also on the A 38 a steakhouse preserves the name of Stone Gallows: with Ilchester, one of the two principal execution sites in the county, in use by c.1575 until 1810 and chiefly remembered for the notorious day on 15 April 1801 when nine men were hanged together for theft.

★★ *Village, church for its memorials, walking by the Tone.*

BISHOPS LYDEARD (D)

BISHOPS LYDEARD (D) Below the south-western limit of the Quantocks extends this large and attractive village: a popular home for Taunton commuters. It is a place which has expanded rapidly since the Second World War with modern estates on its outskirts and a welcome bypass, completed in 1967, but which retains its mature heart, largely constructed from the local red sandstone. The second syllable of Lydeard ('Lidegeard' in 854) is from the Celtic garth – 'ridge', but the first syllable is not clear: possibly from led – 'grey'. The prefix 'bishops' derives from the grant of the manor by King Edward the Elder to Bishop Asser of Sherborne, transferred to the see of Wells on its foundation in 909. The estate was retained by the bishops until the mid 16th century, when they were separated from their lands by the Duke of Northumberland. In 1626 it was bought by the Stawells of Cothelstone and in 1722 by the Lethbridges of Sandhill Park. Above the village centre rises one of the finest of Somerset's 15th century church towers, looking at its best from the Minehead road when floodlit at night. The church of St Mary in Church Street is furnished with a suprisingly complete rood screen and a superb series of 16th century Quantock benches, featuring a sailing ship, windmill and stag. In the south aisle is a fine brass to Nicholas (died 1585) and Eleanor (died 1594) Grobham of Eastcombe bearing a cherub blowing bubbles. Their eldest son, Sir Richard Grobham, settled in Wiltshire but built the attractive almshouses opposite the church in 1616, later extended. In the south porch is an inscription to vicar John Geale (died 1733): buried there so that 'his friends could finally walk over him'. In the church can also be seen the original royal charter of 1291 by which Edward I granted to the bishop a Monday market and two six-day fairs. The market was held until 1878, latterly on Bell Green beside the Bell Inn. The village has four pubs, the oldest being the Lethbridge Arms which, as the Gore Inn, was a major social venue in the Taunton area during the 18th century. Its gabled fives wall is still a prominent landmark.

To the north of the village is Cedar Falls, a noted health retreat endorsed by *Which* magazine. Once known as Watts House, it was formerly occupied by the Winter family and, earlier this century, by the Boles baronets. Nearby at the northern approach to the village stands Lydeard House, built for attorney John Coles c.1750. To the west of the Minehead road lies Lynchfield (formerly Lynch) House, occupied in the later 18th century by Thomas Charter, the region's first estate agent. Further west rises Sandhill Park, a substantial mansion built as Hill House by John Periam (described as 'lately erected' in 1738, although usually attributed to 1720) and inherited by the Lethbridges in 1767. Between 1789 and his death in 1815 John (later Sir John) Lethbridge conducted a persistent legal vendetta with the Winter family of nearby Watts House, alleging poaching, slander, trespass, assault, perjury and even a threatened duel. Sandhill was sold in 1913 and, from 1919 until recently, served as a hospital. A second institution, Tone Vale Mental Hospital, was built on the grand Victorian scale at Cotford in the extreme west of the parish in 1897. (*See also* **West Somerset Railway**)

★★ *Village, church.*

BLACKFORD (F) The 'black ford', midway between Wincanton and Sparkford, crossed a stream which now feeds the lake of Compton Castle (*see* **Compton Pauncefoot,** and for Baron Blackford, who took his title from this place). King Edgar (959-75) gave the estate here to Glastonbury Abbey, but it had passed to Turstin FitzRolf before 1086. The manor was given up to the bishop under an agreement concluded in 1275 and was retained by Bath and Wells until its enforced sale to the Duke of Somerset in 1548. Latterly the rump of the estate here was bought in 1826 by John Hubert Hunt of Compton Pauncefoot. The church of St Michael retains a Norman south doorway and font, short Perpendicular west tower and chancel arch, but has been over-enthusiastically restored. There are monuments to the Gifford family (1819-1921) and Lord Blackford. East Hall Farm dates from the 17th century.

BLUE ANCHOR (D), *see* **OLD CLEEVE**

BOSSINGTON (C), *see* **SELWORTHY**

Gatehouse, Heatherton Park, Bradford-on-Tone

BRADFORD-ON-TONE (H) A comfortable and attractive village perched on a ridge above the River Tone, formerly crossed at the foot of the hill by the 'broad ford' which named it. Today the stream is spanned by a 15th century two-arch bridge, restored in 1698 and whenever a local lorry takes a bite out of it. The village, complete with shop and White Horse Inn but closed-and-converted school, retains much of its rural character with thatched cottages, the best of which is the late medieval Risdons, and 18th to 20th century replacements and infilling. The estate formed part of the 'outfaring' of the bishop of Winchester's substantial manor of Taunton Deane from Saxon times. Later it was divided into two manors between the heiresses of Sir Henry Percehay (died 1380). One, held by the FrAunceis family of Combe Florey and then the Burridges of Stoke St Mary, was centred on Bradford Court, behind the church, rebuilt in the mid 19th century and sold in 1903 to Bishop Wilkinson. The second manor was held by the Warres of Hestercombe, whose descendant owned it until 1904. A fair was held here in September 1753 instead of the usual revel.

In the centre of the village the tree-girt church of St Giles dates from c.1300, including a three-bay arcade. A chantry chapel was founded here in 1387 by the lord of one manor, Sir John de Meriet (died 1391), and it is believed to be his effigy in the south wall, although the present south chapel is 15th century and most of the windows are of that date. The three-stage west tower was added in the early 16th century but the church was reroofed 1858-9 and restored in 1867. The early 18th century pulpit is believed to have come from St Mary's in Taunton. Monuments include those to the Easton family of

land surveyors and engineers, prominent in 19th century Taunton.

Hele (Saxon *healh* – 'a corner'), a hamlet to the north-east, was held separately in 1086 but later merged with Bradford. Hele Manor and Hele Mill House both date from the 16th century. The men of Heatherton owed homage to the lord of Bradford c.1250 and Heatherton Park was built c.1750 for Sir Thomas Gunston, descended from a Taunton merchant family. The house, now subdivided, is set back to the north of the A38 beyond a late 18th century arched gatehouse, was held by the Adair family 1808-89 and from 1920 was occupied by St Katherine's private school for girls, a western chapel being added in 1927. Also on the A38 at Three Bridges is **Sheppy's Cider** (lists) where Richard Sheppy, a very individual cider maker, plies his family's trade. The end product can be inspected, tasted and purchased, and there is a museum of cidermaking and rural life.

★★★ *Village and setting, Sheppy's Cider,* ★★ *church.*

BRATTON SEYMOUR (F) Between Castle Cary and Wincanton, this small village takes its name ('Broctune', 1086), 'settlement on a brook', from its position on a tributary of the River Brue. The tesselated pavement of a Roman villa was uncovered on Cattle Hill in 1966, the occupation of which was dated from associated coins to 222-388 AD. The estate was held in 1086 by Walter of Douai, lord also of Castle Cary and Wincanton, and under him by Gerard, his steward. Gerard of Bratton, probably a descendant of the Domesday tenant, gave lands here to Bruton Priory in the late 12th century. Subsequently the manor reverted to its overlords, descending in turn to the Lovels, Seymours (from 1351, whose name was added to that of the parish) and lords Zouche. A second manor developed in the north and east of the parish known as Bratton Lynes from Cecily de la Lynde (died 1365). In the 17th century half the manor was held by the Byfleets who suffered as recusants (Roman Catholics) and were heavily fined during the Commonwealth. A rambling mansion, Bratton House, was built on top of Bratton Hill in 1868 by Charles Penruddocke. It commands magnificent views in all directions and has a kitchen modelled on that of the abbot at Glastonbury Abbey. The Hall School was evacuated hence from Weybridge during World War Two and stayed. Nearby is the church of Holy Trinity which may have been located up here because of a former pagan site, marked by a burial mound excavated away in the 19th century. The building has a Perpendicular west tower and a Norman zig-zag south doorway but was largely rebuilt in 1830. A T-junction south of the village on the A 371 is known as Jack White's Gibbet, a name which commemorates the brutal murder of Robert Sutton by his drinking companion in 1730. The culprit was publicly hanged there in chains as an object lesson to passers-by.

★★ *Views from the hill.*

BREAN (A) A coastal parish in the extreme north-west of the county whose name, derived from a Celtic root *briga* meaning 'a high place', evidently refers to the promontory of Brean Down which here juts out into the Bristol Channel and may once have been an island. Its shape has been compared to the back of a whale and rises steeply from the sea to a height of 321 ft. Pottery evidence indicates a fort at

the eastern end of the Down of about the 5th century BC but abandoned by c.300 BC. There are Bronze Age round barrows and two prehistoric field systems. Subsequently a Romano-British temple was established c.340 AD. This was succeeded at the very end of the 4th century by what may have been an extremely early rectangular Christian chapel or hermitage and 7th century burials were found further down the slope. The parish church at Brean bears the rare dedication to the Irish St Bridget, died c.525 AD, which itself suggests a Celtic foundation. Theories linking the name of the hill (*briga*) with the possible worship of the pagan goddess Brigantia and then with the name of the saint may be stretching credulity rather too far. A charter of 693 (corrected from 663 and now believed to have a genuine basis) by which Ine, King of the West Saxons, granted an estate called Brent to Glastonbury Abbey seems to include Brean within its bounds, but there is no later reference to the abbey's possession of this manor, which was held by Merlesuain in 1066 and granted after the Conquest, like Burnham and Huntspill, to Walter of Douai. Thereafter it descended with Burnham until the 16th century but was later divided, the principal estate being acquired in the late 18th century by the Wyndhams of Salisbury.

Today Brean is devoted to the pursuit of holiday pleasure with a plethora of seemingly-impermanent holiday homes, bungalows, caravan sites, strung out on each side of the coast road, and the Brean Leisure Park with swimming pool, golf course and fairground-type entertainments. Pontin's first holiday camp was opened here in 1947. At the northern end of the road is the unlikely location of an extensive

tropical bird garden (fee:lists). Mercury Communications brought their transatlantic cable ashore here in 1988. Formerly the place was sparsely populated with only eight houses and 40 inhabitants in 1791 and much of it liable to flooding from the sea or the River Axe. Efforts to reclaim tidal flats around the Axe estuary took place in the 12th and 13th centuries and again in the period 1600-40. In the great flood of 1607 seven of the nine houses in Brean were swept away and 26 people drowned. Apart from the rich pasture land here, there was also a profitable rabbit warren by 1361. John Cannon in his diary described a family raid on the warren in 1704 while the warrener was away from home, and Warren Road and Farm preserve its memory. Caerphilly cheese was incongruously produced here in the 18th century for sale in Wales. The sea wall, behind which the coast road runs, was probably built during the first decade of the 19th century. A grander project for a harbour on the north side of Brean Down began in 1864 with the construction of a pier, and plans for a branch railway line were produced in 1867. The pier was never finished and, despite the expenditure of £365,000, the works were completely swept away in a storm of 1872.

Nearby on the Down itself one of four forts to defend the Bristol Channel was built in 1867 and seven muzzle-loaders were installed. The fort was abandoned after one of its magazines blew up in July 1900, killing an unhinged naked gunner who was believed to have deliberately fired his carbine into the magazine. It served as a cafe 1905-39 but was refortified during the Second World War. The Miscellaneous Weapons Development Department, based

Brean Down

from 1941 on Birnbeck Pier at Weston-super-Mare, used the headland to test and develop secret weapons such as the Hedgehog anti-submarine device, the 'Expendable Noise-maker', and a nautical version of Barnes Wallis's bouncing bomb employed by the Dambusters. Marconi also used the promontory in 1896 for his early wireless transmission experiments, successfully sending signals to Steep and Flat Holm and eventually across the Bristol Channel to Penarth.

The headland is now owned by the National Trust, with bird sanctuary and nature reserve, and is freely accessible to walkers, with a paying carpark at the end of the coast road north from Burnham. Its flora and fauna, particularly its bird life, is extensive and varied.

The small church of St Bridget stands on the east side of the coast road. Pevsner considered that it might be 13th century, but no early features survive to date it, the southern porch tower having been restored in 1729 and given a saddleback roof, and the chancel rebuilt in 1883. There is a pulpit inscribed with the date 1620 and a Perpendicular font.

★★★★ *Brean Down for its archaeological interest (although little is now visible), walking, views and natural history.*

BRENDON HILL (D) A former iron-mining village on the summit of the Brendons ('the brown hills') which named it, lying at the east end of the B 3224 near its junction with the B 3190. Iron had been taken from the hills possibly since Roman times but systematic extraction began in 1839 when Sir Thomas Lethbridge opened Lothbrook mine south of Luxborough, followed by workings nearby at Gupworthy and then, further east, from 1852 at Raleigh's Cross.

Methodist chapel, Brendon Hill

To carry ore from the mines to Watchet Harbour, the West Somerset Mineral Railway was built between 1856 and 1861, featuring a steep (1 in 4) incline from Comberow up which trucks were drawn by wires wound around massive iron drums. By 1863 two terraces of cottages and other houses had been built, there was a school, a corrugated-iron mission church and Beulah chapel, opened by the Bible Christians in 1861. There were shops, a reading room (1865), a fife and drum band, choir, cricket team and a temperance refreshment house. The population, which included a high proportion of Cornish miners, reached its height in the mid 1870s at about 250. There was no inn and alcohol-induced fights between the miners were limited to Raleigh's Cross Inn to the east. The mines finally closed in 1883 and the village rapidly became a ghost town. The mineral railway, carrying passengers rather than

Somerset Monument, Brent Knoll church

iron ore, continued until 1898, although reopened 1907-10 (as were the mines) by the short-lived Somerset Mineral Syndicate. The ruins of many of the buildings can still be seen from the road, the overgrown incline traversed on foot and the isolated Beulah chapel, reopened in 1910, continues in use.

★★★ *Landscape,* ★★ *industrial archaeology.*

BRENT KNOLL (A) This village, formerly known as South Brent, lies to the north-east of Burnham and today bears the same name as the adjacent steep-sided conical hill (456 ft), the most prominent Somerset landmark on the M 5. 'Brent' was originally the name of the hill, from the Celtic *briga*, 'a high place'. The knoll, capped in the 14th century by a windmill, can be scaled best from the road across the north-eastern flank of the hill between Brent Knoll and

High tide at Town Bridge, Bridgwater

East Brent villages and the views across the Levels and the Bristol Channel are spectacular. The knoll is crowned with a roughly-oval Iron Age fort of some 4 acres in the care of the National Trust. Although the interior of the camp has been heavily quarried for the lias stone of which the hill is formed, evidence of burials, Roman occupation up to the 4th century and a possible temple has been found. It is possible that the summit was refortified in the early medieval period (the west and and south sides have been artificially terraced) as Richard Cotele was stated to hold the castle here in the 13th century. Colourful legends claim that the hill was created when the Devil was excavating Cheddar Gorge and a spadeful of rock fell short of the Bristol Channel. Another story refers to the knoll as *Mons Ranarum*, the Mount of Frogs, where Ider, son of Nuth, a companion of King Arthur, died after slaying three giants who lived here (although a rival version claims the incident occurred in North Wales): inspiring Arthur to give the hill and the land around it to Glastonbury Abbey. Brent, later Brentmarsh, may even have been a Romano-British estate, including not only Brent Knoll and East Brent, but also Berrow, Brean and Lympsham, and there was a Roman villa at Lakehouse Farm to the east of the knoll. It was, however, King Ine of the West Saxons and not Arthur who gave the land to Glastonbury, probably in 693, and the abbey retained it until its dissolution in 1539.

The village, which lies largely along a single road encircling the lower slopes of the hill, has a predominantly 20th century feel to it with occasional older farmhouses. Up the hill at the end of a short lane stands the church of St Michael, appropriated to Glastonbury Abbey in 1267, but lost in the struggle between abbot and bishop, and assigned to the archdeacons of Wells. A small estate here called Huish was assigned to Wells Cathedral in 1159 to endow the prebend of Huish and Brent. Of the present church, the south doorway and the ornamented pillar piscina in the north aisle are Norman, the south porch and south transept early 14th century, and the remainder Perpendicular. The fine set of benchends include a celebrated trio which depicts a mitred fox who is put into the stocks and finally hanged by geese. This is usually interpreted as a propaganda attack on the abbot of Glastonbury although it might represent Richard Fox, bishop of Bath and Wells 1492-94, who bought land here in 1519. The church also contains one of my favourite monuments, a magnificently flamboyant design with the threequarter-length effigy of John Somerset (died 1663) and those of his two wives, one in an incredible wide-brimmed hat. At the foot are two panels, one showing his family kneeling and the other depicting Somerset rising from his tomb at the Resurrection. In 1645 during the Civil War the village here was terrorised by Col John Tynte's royalist regiment of horse and 'tribute' was demanded from the villagers. John Somerset and his friend, Thomas Gilling (com

memorated on a stone in the churchyard), although both of royalist sympathies, led a spontaneous Good Friday attack on the plundering troopers, and were later both imprisoned at Bristol. The Victorian Manor House stands proudly on the hillside to the north-east of the church, designed by John Norton 1862-64. John Wesley preached four times in the parish, 1779-82.

★★★★ *Walks on (and views from) the knoll,* ★★★ *church for its benchends and monuments.*

BRIDGWATER (E) A sizeable town, former borough and port at the head of the Parrett estuary. It is a somewhat rough-and-ready, cheap-and-cheerful place: a busy popular shopping centre which is today known mainly for its magnificent carnival and its major fair. The river here became the boundary between the Saxons to the east and the Britons to the west, following the victory of King Cenwalh of the West Saxons at Penselwood in 658. Later, in 845, the men of Somerset (the earliest reference to the name) and Dorset defeated a Danish army and 'made a great slaughter' at the mouth of the river. The parish seems to have been a substantial Saxon agricultural settlement, which probably grew up at the west end of an early bridge across the river Parrett that named it ('Brugie' in 1086). The placename seems unlikely to have been derived from the Old Norse *bryggja*, 'jetty or quay', as recently claimed, since this usage appears to have been limited to the north of England. The notorious missing 'e'

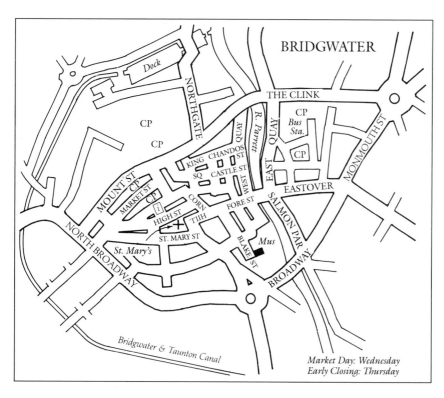

BRIDGWATER

Market Day: Wednesday
Early Closing: Thursday

1900. Behind the statue stand the dome and pillars of the Market House of c.1827, fronting the covered market hall: formerly used as the former Market House (1791) and Corn Exchange (1875). From here, High Street ran west with an elongated island of shambles and shops known as 'Cockenrewe' ('cock row'), demolished in the early 19th century, which explains the present generous width of the street. On the north side of the street Royal Clarence House has been converted from the Royal Clarence Hotel (1825-1984) and the modern covered Angel Place Shopping Centre was built in 1986 to the west of Angel Crescent. Further west, the Town Hall, designed by Richard Carver in 1823 (to which a large hall was added behind in 1865), replaced a medieval guildhall in Fore Street. Today it is also used as offices by Sedgemoor District Council and the Bridgwater Charter Trustees. High Street continues west to meet Penel Orlieu (formerly Pynel and Orlove streets, both derived from medieval personal names), the site of Pig (earlier St Andrew's) Cross and the former West Gate at the junction with North Street.

East from the Cornhill runs Fore Street, now pedestrianized, to cross the River Parrett by the Town Bridge of 1883. This succeeded an elegant Coalbrookdale iron bridge put up in 1798 and the three-arched medieval stone bridge, a little downstream, originally attributed to William Briwere but rebuilt c.1390-1400 by Sir John Trivet. In 1989 a replica of a cross formerly at Penel Orlieu was erected at the east end of Fore Street. The town's North Gate stood at the present junction of Angel Crescent and Northgate, and the South Gate towards the south end of St Mary Street. Across the bridge, East (or St John's) Gate was located at the junction of Eastover with Broadway. The south-eastern sector of the old town was known by the 14th century as Damyet, evidently referring to a mill dam on the Durleigh brook: a name that survives in that of Dampiet Street. Here, in Blake Street, stands the presumed birthplace of Robert Blake, converted in 1926 into the **Admiral Blake Museum** (lists). There are displays illustrating the varied history of the town and the career of Blake himself, including a diorama of his famous victory at Santa Cruz.

On the south-western side of the market-place rises the substantial **church of St Mary**, given by Walter of Douai to Bath Priory c.1100, passing by 1219 to the hospital of St John the Baptist (below) and, after its dissolution, to the Crown

from the middle of its name has been omitted only since the last century: surviving in the name of its American counterpart in Massachusetts. After the Norman Conquest the manor was granted, with many others beside and to the east of the Parrett, to Walter of Douai (died c.1107), from whom it became known as Bridgwater – 'Walter's bridge'. In 1199 Walter's great-grandson, Fulk Pagnell, granted the place to William Briwere (died 1226), a Devonian magnate, and it was William who founded the town's fortunes.

In 1200 a charter was obtained from King John (who visited here four times 1204-10, as did Henry III in 1250) which created a free borough and established a weekly market and an eight-day June fair. Briwere also established a deer park (from woodland west of the town) and began to build a substantial castle, the latter bounded on the east by the river and quayside, on the south by Fore Street, west by Castle Moat and north by Northgate. There was a turreted castle keep, a chapel dedicated to St Mark and a hall known as Mortimer's hall by the 1390s. Briwere's great-granddaughter had married Roger de Mortimer (died 1282), from whom the castle descended through the Mortimer earls of March to merge with the Crown in 1495. A main gate gave direct access to the market-place but the castle was neglected, fell into decay during the 16th century and

was finally destroyed after the Restoration of Charles II. A large house replaced the former keep in the late 17th century and the site was bought in 1721 by James Brydges, Duke of Chandos, who from c.1730 laid out the parallel Chandos and Castle streets: with the adjacent King Square (begun 1807 but never completed, occupying the site of the keep), the most attractive area of the present town. In Castle Street England's first Arts Centre (with its own small theatre) was opened in 1946. The fine house of the Duke's likely architect, Benjamin Holloway, the Lions of c.1730, stands nearby on West Quay. Also on the quay is all that survives of the castle today: a stretch of wall behind the houses there and the water gate, tucked away down a passage beside the Town House Hotel. The borough was incorporated with a mayor in 1468 and so continued until 1974, although the mayoralty survived the dissolution of the borough.

The medieval town was centred on a market-place known as 'Cornchepyng' and later as the Cornhill, probably extending further south than at present. Here by 1367 stood the High Cross, rebuilt 1567-8 as a covered hexagonal cross supported on columns. Its more recent successor is the fine resited statue of Robert Blake (1598-1657), Oliver Cromwell's General at Sea and Bridgwater's most famous son, sculpted by F.W. Pomeroy and set up in

Statue of Admiral Blake, Bridgwater

in the person of the Lord Chancellor. The present lofty building dates from the 14th century, work on the western tower in 1366-7 continuing in 1385, when its superb spire may have been added: a landmark for miles around. Rebuilding continued, moving eastward, until the mid 15th century. Sadly the church suffered a major restoration (1849-53) at the hands of architect W.H. Brakspear, which swept away the rood screen of 1415-20 (partly remodelled as side screens), replaced much of the internal woodwork and renewed or restored much of the roofs and tracery. Fortunately the fine Perpendicular pulpit survives as does a fine 17th century painting of mourning over the dead Christ, from a Spanish ship taken as a prize and given in 1780 by Bridgwater MP Anne Poulett (a man, but named for his godmother Queen Anne). There are two 14th century defaced civilian effigies and an elaborate wall monument depicting the figure of Francis Kingsmill (died 1620) with his kneeling sons. There was a chantry of the Blessed Virgin Mary in the chancel by 1260. There followed altars or chantries dedicated to St James, All Saints, St Catherine, Holy Trinity, St Anne, Holy Cross, St George, St Erasmus and St Saviour: those surviving swept away in 1548. At the south-eastern corner of the churchyard was the medieval St Mary's Cross. The area around the church is particularly attractive, including the 16th century Old Vicarage Restaurant and the

Tudor Cafe of c.1600. A hospital of St John the Baptist was founded by William Briwere just south of East Gate at Eastover shortly before 1213. In 1286 the master and brethren were allowed to cut a channel through a bend in the Parrett to clean out the hospital privies and the house was also used for a time from 1298 to provide accommodation for 13 poor schoolboys. In 1381, at the same time as the Peasants' Revolt in London, a mob broke into the hospital and forced the master to surrender documents, before ransacking the houses of two local lawyers, beheading two other unfortunates (one abducted from Ilchester gaol) and spiking their heads on Bridgwater bridge. The hospital was dissolved in 1539 and no trace of it or its church survives. The Grey Friars had a friary in the town, traditionally founded by the second William Briwere (died 1233) but first mentioned in 1246. It lay in the south-west of the borough beside Friarn Street, which it named, and had a master and seven friars when it was dissolved in 1538. A further chapel of St Saviour was evidently built in the 1530s outside the South Gate by a local merchant and survived at least until 1703. The expansion of Bridgwater led to the building of Holy Trinity Church in Taunton Road in 1840, demolished 1958, and St John the Baptist in Eastover, designed by John Brown of Norwich in 1846.

Bridgwater had a long nonconformist tradition. In 1683 the militia tore down a circular meeting house and burned its

furniture in a huge bonfire on the Cornhill. When toleration came in 1689, the Presbyterians built **Christ Church** in Dampiet Street with a shell-hood doorway, its facade remodelled in 1788 and its congregation became Unitarian in 1815. The poet Coleridge preached here in 1797. There were congregations of Baptists by 1653, Quakers by 1670 (visited by William Penn in 1694) and Methodists by 1753 (George Whitefield was abused here in 1739 and John Wesley visited on a number of occasions 1746-69).

From 1200 the port effectively displaced Combwich as the principal trading centre in the area. Wine was imported from Bordeaux and grain, beans, hides and cloth exported, particularly to Wales and Ireland, the place becoming a separate port from Bristol in 1402. In the late 15th century fish began to come in and, during the 16th century, mill and grindstones from the Forest of Dean. From the 17th century coal was brought from South Wales, the port acting as the main centre from which goods were distributed elsewhere in the county, particularly upstream to Taunton and Langport. Cloth manufacture, dying and spinning in the borough became increasingly important, producing broadcloth known as 'bridgwaters' with a fulling mill at the castle by the early 15th century. Later industries in the 17th and 18th centuries included brickmaking, glassmaking and from 1827 the production of Bath brick. The last product was made from

The tidal bore on the River Parrett, Bridgwater

the river slime here, named from its resemblance to Bath stone and used for domestic scouring purposes. During the 19th century several shipbuilding yards were opened but the principal industry was ornamental brick and tile making, using local marl deposits and continuing to flourish until its final decline in the 1960s. At the north end of Northgate the base of the Chandos glass kiln (c.1725) recalls the short-lived manufacture here. Across the river a restored Beehive kiln similarly commemorates the much more successful brick and tile manufacture.

Early quays were limited to the banks of the Parrett above and below the bridge and goods travelled up to Taunton and Langport by the Parrett and Tone navigations. Water traffic to Taunton from 1827 was by means of the Bridgwater and Taunton canal via Huntworth. In 1841 a dock was opened on the north side of the town and the canal extended to meet it. The area was linked with the rail network in 1871 by the construction of the Telescopic (or Black) Bridge, which could be withdrawn to the east bank to allow ships to pass upriver. The bridge survives although it is now fixed. The dock was finally closed in 1971 and has since been attractively developed as a marina with warehousing (1841) converted to apartments and new blocks put up to form Admiral's Quay. Claimed to be the oldest working steam vessel in the world, a dredger of c.1843 named *Bertha* that formerly operated here, is now

preserved at Exeter Maritime Museum. The canal, last used commercially in 1907, is now the subject of an ambitious restoration project. Its former viability was hit by the arrival of the railway from Bristol in 1841, extended to Taunton a year later.

On the national scene, Bridgwater returned two MPs by 1295 until the borough was disenfranchised in 1869, following a lengthy enquiry into corruption and bribery at elections. During the Civil War the town's sympathies were strongly for Parliament, but the place was held from 1643 by the Crown in the person of Col Edmund Wyndham. Prince Rupert was here in April 1645 and those fleeing from the Battle of Langport withdrew to the town. Much of the town was destroyed by fire when Sir Thomas Fairfax's New Model Army (including Oliver Cromwell) eventually stormed the town from Eastover on 21 July 1645, taking 2,000 prisoners. During the Duke of Monmouth's rebellion of 1685 the rebels arrived here from Taunton and the duke was proclaimed king by the corporation, he being quartered at the castle. The Duke's army returned for two days on their retreat from Norton St Philip, before marching out to defeat at Sedgemoor. Only 17 men of the town were known to have participated in the rebellion (suggesting that the presence of others was covered up), of whom three were executed, nine transported and five pardoned. Of the eight or nine hanged, drawn and quartered

here (probably on the Cornhill), none were from Bridgwater. James II visited the town in 1686 but thereafter there was a tradition of monarchical avoidance until Elizabeth II came in 1987.

Two major annual events distinguish the town. An eight-day **St Matthew's Fair**, held around St Matthew's Day (21 September) was mentioned in 1249 and was held on St Matthew's Field, beyond the West Gate by 1404. There it has continued ever since, increasingly becoming a pleasure fair during the 19th century although today held on the last Wednesday in September and the three following days, with stalls set out along West Street. The first day is now devoted to the sale of sheep and Quantock hill ponies but the principal attraction is the major fun fair. Even more celebrated is **Bridgwater Carnival**, formerly held on the 5th November but now on the Thursday nearest to it. Local Guy Fawkes celebrations here are recorded from 1854, featuring a bonfire on the Cornhill (stopped in 1924 because it melted the tarmac) and the 'squibbing'. The latter attraction is the simultaneous ignition of large squibs fixed to the end of staves known as coshes. Processions were mentioned from 1857 but only formally organised in 1881. The occasion was then no different from those of the 'bonfire boys' in other Somerset towns but progressively the Bridgwater carnivals became more elaborate. The present floats (or 'carts', as they are locally known) can be 100 ft long and the

ABOVE *The Bridgwater and Taunton canal near North Newton.* BELOW *Almshouses, Broadway*

procession stretches for over two miles: hailed as the biggest in Europe. The carnival concerts, started in 1883 to raise funds for the carnival clubs, fill the Town Hall every night for two weeks early in October. Thereafter many of the carts tour the November carnivals held in other local towns: North Petherton, Burnham-on-Sea, Shepton Mallet, Wells, Glastonbury and Weston-super-Mare.

Of the town's suburbs, **Hamp** (formerly 'Hamme' – 'meadow') was mentioned in 794 and given in 1009 by King Ethelred the Unready to Athelney Abbey, whose monks retained it until 1539. To the east, **Sydenham** ('Sideham' in 1086, 'wide meadow') was formerly a detached part of Wembdon and held by Walter of Sydenham by the mid 13th century. Walter's family held an interest in the estate until at least 1665 and from him all the many Somerset Sydenhams were descended. The 16th century former manor-house, survives incongruously isolated at the heart of Courtauld's factory complex, itself originally established as British Cellophane in 1937-8. It also names the Sydenham Community School and Sports Centre in Parkway. Other manors settled by the 11th century include Haygrove, Bower (North, South, East and West), Horsey and Dunwear.

★★★★ *Carnival and St Matthew's Fair,* ★★ *town centre (particularly West Quay, Castle Street, King Square), St Mary's church, Admiral Blake museum.*

BRIDGWATER AND TAUNTON CANAL (E/H) A canal opened in 1827 from Firepool Lock on the Tone at Taunton to the River Parrett at Huntworth in the teeth of opposition from the Conservators of the Tone, who controlled navigation on that river. It was extended in 1841 to the west of Bridgwater to join the new docks there at Newtown Lock although its economic importance ended almost immediately with the arrival of the railway. Indeed, the Great Western Railway bought up the canal in 1866, although commercial traffic continued at an ever-decreasing level until 1907. A protracted restoration project, which involved the rebuilding of

several bridges, was finally completed in 1994. There are four intermediate locks (Higher and Lower Maunsel, Kings and Standards), parking and picnic areas and summer boat trips. Pleasant towpath walks extend throughout the 14½ miles and cycling, canoeing and angling permits are available.

★★★ *Towpath walking, boating, and the locks for industrial archaeologists.*

BROADWAY (J) Strung out along a single street, this village lies to the west of Ilminster, including towards its eastern end the seven-cell range of almshouses, founded only after litigation

45

over Alexander Every's will of 1588. Its name is supposed to derive from the 'broad way' which formerly led to the medieval Neroche Forest (*see* **Staple Fitzpaine**). In 1306 Henry de Lorty obtained a Tuesday market and a nine-day fair here. Later the lordship passed to the Portman family. The church of St Aldhelm (who was missionary to East Somerset, died 709) and St Eadburga stands north-east of the village, local tradition ascribing its isolation to an outbreak of plague, The chancel and transept date from c.1300 while the rest is 15th century, including a finely carved font. An 1891 memorial set up in the south transept commemorates Humphrey Pinney, early emigrant to America in 1630, who though born in Hardington Mandeville was living in Broadway when he emigrated in 1635: probably persuaded by the Rev Joseph Hull, curate here from 1633, who sailed with him. The 16th century pulpit, bearing the five wounds of Christ, was only stripped of concealing plaster in 1900. The shaft of a fine cross survives in the churchyard, bearing two figures. In the centre of the village lies the former Congregational chapel of 1739, converted into a dwelling house.

★ *Church and village.*

BROMPTON RALPH (D) A small hillside village around two greens at the eastern end of the Brendon Hills to the north of Wiveliscombe, its name ('Burnetone', 1086) meaning 'settlement on the Brendons'. The estate here was given to Glastonbury Abbey by Queen Frithogyth c.729-40, passed to Brictric by 1066 and after the Conquest to William de Mohun of Dunster. The Mohun tenant in 1166 was William son of Durand, whose son Ralph gave his name to the place. Thereafter by 1212 the property was divided between Ralph's three daughters, becoming the manors of Brompton Ralph, Brompton Fulford (held by the Fulfords c.1490-1620) and Brompton Jacob (owned by the Jacob family in the late 15th and early 16th centuries). The main manor was held by the lords Portman from 1861 until c.1920. The church of the Blessed Virgin Mary dates largely from a rebuilding in 1738, with some reinstalled medieval features. A north aisle was added in 1847 and the whole thoroughly restored in 1880-1. The 16th century font bears a carving of the green man, the communion rail is dated 1677 and there is a reconstructed rood screen. The living was held by three members of the Camplin family, 1689-1781, and almost continuously by the Sweet Escotts 1781-

1895. Iron ore was mined at Yeanon in the north-west of the parish 1872-77. Nearby, Elworthy Barrows represent an incomplete Iron-Age hillfort.

★★ *Setting.*

BROMPTON REGIS (C) Lying at the southern limit of the county and of the Exmoor National Park, this sizeable parish is set amidst breathtaking scenery. It is a landscape occupied by scattered farms, some of which may represent former hamlets in the early Middle Ages or even before. Like Brompton Ralph it takes the first part of its name from its position on the Brendon Hills. Before the Conquest it was held by Gytha, mother of King Harold II who died at Hastings: hence 'Gytha's Tea Rooms' in the centre of the village. The estate was then inevitably seized by William the Conqueror, which explains the suffix 'Regis' – 'of the king', the place often being alternatively known as Kingsbrompton. By the later 12th century the manor had been granted to William de Say, who founded Barlynch ('barley hill') Priory, a small house of Augustinian canons, in the west of the parish beside the River Exe. Most of this monastery's lands lay in Devon although from 1478 the priory had two fairs at Bury in the south of this parish beside the River Haddeo. It was always a poor house, with never more than nine monks and occasionally (1492) as few as three. It fell to Henry VIII and today only a few fragments of stonework survive, incorporated in Barlynch Farm. The locals claimed that when the priory's great bell was taken down the Exe to Exeter its first sonorous note turned all the Devonshire cream in the city sour ! The manor passed in the 13th century to the Besil family who had a motte and bailey castle at Bury and secured a Tuesday market and two four-day fairs at Brompton. Latterly the manor was held by the earls of Carnarvon.

The church of St Mary the Virgin, with a fine airy interior, stands in the centre of the village and is probably Saxon in origin (a priest holding one hide of land being mentioned here in 1086). It has a 13th century west tower and a south transept of c.1380, the nave and north aisle being late Perpendicular. On the north wall of the chancel is an informative brass to Thomas Dyke (died 1639) and his family, including a touching epitaph to his granddaughter. The whole was brutally restored in 1853 and 1885. There is a Jacobean pulpit and reading and clerk's desks. The vicarage was in the gift of Barlynch Priory by the 13th century and exercised from 1623 by

Emmanuel College, Cambridge. Near the village Pulham's Mill has been converted into a shop for the owners' handmade timber furniture and china.

The headwaters of the River Haddeo were dammed in 1974 and four years later Wimbleball Reservoir (or **Wimbleball Lake Water Park**, as it is now dubbed) was finished and full. For those fond of statistics, it holds 4,500 million gallons and covers 374 acres. Access is well signed and there are sailing and rowing clubs, trout fishing, a nature trail and reserve, picnic and play areas, a refreshment and gift shop, carparks and scenic walks.

★★★ *Village, scenery and reservoir.*

BROOMFIELD (D) The highest village on the Quantock Hills: its name, 'the broom-covered field', being self-evident. The estate was owned after the Norman Conquest by William de Mohun of Dunster but was long held with Crowcombe manor by the de Crowcombe and Biccombe families. In 1634 their descendants sold it to Andrew Crosse and William Towill. Towill's share later passed to the Tyntes of Halswell House in Goathurst, while the Crosses became squires of Broomfield at their mansion of **Fyne Court**. For some two and a half centuries the Crosses dominated parish life, although only one of them, the last Andrew Crosse (1784-1855), is remembered today. He became a pioneer electrician and friend of Faraday, conducting storm lightning into his laboratory. It was asserted that, when he passed electricity through stones, insects of an unrecorded genus crawled out of the cracks and that Crosse had thus created life. A London lecture attended by Mary Shelley is considered to have given her the inspiration to write *Frankenstein*. Fyne Court mansion was destroyed by fire in September 1894. The rump of the estate, including several outbuildings, was left to the National Trust by John Adams (died 1967), and since 1974 the Somerset Wildlife Trust has leased the central 26 acres around the house's former site as its headquarters. There they have established an excellent interpretation centre, illustrating the natural history of the Quantocks, a Trust shop and nature trails through the surrounding woodland (lists). Crosse's laboratory is now an airy lecture hall and also houses social events and periodic exhibitions.

The church of All Saints in attractive tree-girt surroundings has an early 14th century chancel and a north aisle of the early 16th. It boasts a splendid set of Quantock

ABOVE *Broomfield.* BELOW *Monument to Aubrey Herbert, Brushford church*

benchends. The carver is identified on one as 'Simon Werman' – clearly the Simon Warman of Bicknoller who was carving at Trull in 1560. Under the tower is the decapitated brass of Richard Silverton, chaplain for 23 years until his death in 1443, who 'sumptuously repaired and magnificently decorated' the church. It is the only Somerset brass depicting a priest in his mass vestments and was discovered under floorboards in 1940. A table spanned by a copper strip at the rear of the church came from Crosse's laboratory and the scientist himself lies in the churchyard beneath a memorial recording that 'he was humble towards God and kind to his fellow creature'.

★★★ *Fyne Court, nature trail, etc., general setting,* ★★ *village, church.*

BRUSHFORD (C) A village to the south of Dulverton near the confluence of the Rivers Barle and Exe, whose name ('Brigeford' in 1086) means 'the ford by the bridge'. It lies on either side of a road running west from the B 3222 which is initially built-up with modern houses and bungalows. Here is the Carnarvon Arms Hotel, built in 1873 by the Earl of Carnarvon near the former Dulverton Station and visited by the poet Tennyson in 1891. The older and more picturesque part of the village will be found further west near the church of St Nicholas. The building is largely 15th century Perpendicular, including a restored rood screen and 16th century windows in the nave. There is a square Norman font, the south porch is dated 1725 (housing a late medieval chest and the parish stocks) and the west tower was rebuilt in 1887. What

sets Brushford church apart is the north chapel, designed in 1926 by Sir Edwin Lutyens as a shrine to the memory of Aubrey Herbert (1880-1923), 2nd son of the 4th Earl of Carnarvon, of Pixton Park (*see* **Dulverton**), on whom John Buchan based the hero of *Greenmantle*. Soldier, diplomat and Somerset MP, he lies here in effigy like a medieval knight, his sword framed above his head, coats of arms on the canopy and five late medieval benches beyond him. Until 1066 the manor here belonged to the Devon thegn Ordulf and rendered 24 sheep a year to Dulverton, but ultimately, like so many Exmoor properties, was acquired by the Aclands. Of the farmhouses, Beer dates from the 15th century, Allshire from c.1600, whilst West Nightcott was originally built as a 16th century longhouse with accommodation for livestock at its east end. Northwest from the village stands Combe House, a Tudor property obtained by Edward Sydenham when he married the heiress of William of Combe in 1482 and occupied by his descendants, lords of Dulverton manor, until its sale in 1874. The house should not be confused with Combe Sydenham Hall near Monksilver, formerly occupied by another branch of the family.

Exebridge is a picturesque hamlet with several thatched farmhouses and cottages at the east end of the parish, divided by the county boundary and the River Exe, here spanned by an 18th century bridge.

★★ *Church.*

BRUTON (F) An exceptionally attractive and interesting small town in east Somerset, 'the settlement on the River Brue', which, because of the 19th century decline in its industry and its tucked-away location, has largely escaped the architectural excesses and commercialism of the 20th century. Add to this a delightful sense of scale, idiosyncratic street names (Quaperlake, Plox and Cuckolds Row) and an excellent accumulation of buildings, and you have my favourite town in the east of the county. It is cut in two by the Brue ('Briuu' in a dubious charter of 681, from Welsh *bryw* – 'vigorous. brisk') which flows through from the north-east and is spanned by the picturesque 15th century Packhorse Bridge. The place long had a flourishing cloth industry, with several fulling mills (eg. Gant's Mill, named after John de Ghent, by 1290) powered by the Brue, succeeded from the late 18th century by silk production. Under an ancient custom,

IN ALTARE TOTA NOCTE USQUE AD MANE.

47

recorded in 1757, the tithingmen of Bruton hundred met annually at sunrise on 3 May at a gate near Pinkwood, where they recorded their attendance by inserting their rods of office in ten rings attached to a horned stick known as 'the Doating staff'.

Bruton lay within the forest of Selwood and is credited by the Domesday Book with more woodland (estimated at 9,000 acres) than any other place in Somerset. It formed a royal estate of the West Saxon kings and two churches were founded here in the late 7th century: St Mary's by King Ine and St Peter's by St Aldhelm, abbot of Malmesbury from 675. It was claimed that Aldhelm brought a carved marble altar stone back from Rome which Ine installed in St Mary's. There was later a Saxon mint here and, by the Norman Conquest a royal borough, the Domesday book recording 17 burgesses (of whom 11 were entered under Pitcombe and 1 under Castle Cary). It seems likely that this nascent town was located across the Brue north of the present church, centred on a possible market place occupying the island site at the junction of Patwell and Quaperlake streets. Soon after, the manor was granted to William de Mohun and in 1142 was used by his grandson, William, Earl of Somerset, as the initial endowment for the substantial Augustinian priory which he founded to the south of the town. To this gift was added that of the market and hundred of Bruton from the hands of Alexander de Cantilupe, and the town began four centuries of priory domination.

The first monks were evidently brought over from Normandy by the Earl and extensive lands there, including Moion from which the Mohuns originated, were also settled on the priory. It is not clear whether the present parish church of St Mary served both town and priory or if the monks had their own church based on Aldhelm's church of St Peter nearby. Certainly Sir William de Montacute requested burial in the church of SS Peter and Paul in 1319, although this is an isolated reference. I am inclined to think that there were two separate churches. In 1458 Prior John Henton established a chantry at the altar of St Aldhelm in the conventual church and also mentioned the chapel of St Laurence there, neither of which survived until 1548, suggesting that they may have been swept away at the dissolution. There were severe problems with the activities of the canons under priors John Schoyle (1418-29), who was removed from office, and Richard of Glastonbury (1429-48). A new code of behaviour (1452) imposed by

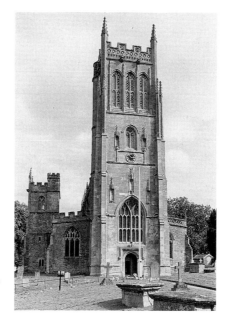

Bruton church

the bishop indicates that the canons had been gambling with dice, hunting, sharing each other's beds and entertaining women, 'especially Margaret Stawel', evidently a 'scarlet woman' of the town. Prior William Gilbert (1494-1532), according to Leland, virtually rebuilt the abbey and his visit to Rome led to the priory being transformed into an abbey in 1511. This triumph was short-lived and dissolution followed in 1539. The Bruton possessions of the abbey, with its site and buildings, were leased and then granted in 1541 to Sir Maurice Berkeley, who converted the abbey into a large square mansion where the family entertained Charles I in 1621 and again, during the Civil War, in 1644. Sir John Berkeley was rewarded for his loyalty, becoming Baron Berkeley of Stratton while in exile with Charles II in 1658. Berekeley Square, Berkeley, Bruton and Stratton streets in the West End of London were developed on lands acquired by him near Piccadilly after the Restoration. The great hall of the abbey mansion was destroyed by fire in 1763 but the building continued to be occupied by the Berkeleys until the death of the 5th and last baron in 1773. The estate here was sold in 1777 to the banking Hoares of Stourhead (Wilts) who demolished the buildings in 1786. The abbey stables survived until 1821 when they were pulled down to build the vicarage (now rectory, dated 1822) against the buttressed precinct wall in Plox and Silver Street, and this wall is all that survives of the former priory and abbey. All, that is, apart from the 15th or 16th

century roofless dovecot or Pigeon Tower. One of the first properties owned by the National Trust, it stands on a hill to the south of the town (but within the outer precinct of the abbey), although 18th century illustrations show chimneys, suggesting that it was originally occupied by people rather than doves. The last abbot, John Elye (1533-39), provided an arched market cross supported on five pillars for the town, demolished c.1790.

The Doulting-stone **Church of St Mary** stands at the northern limit of the former monastic precinct and near the junction of Silver Street and Station Road. It seems likely to occupy the site of the 7th century church built by Ine, possibly became a Saxon minster and later possessed dependent chapels at Pitcombe, Redlynch, Wyke, Witham and (South) Brewham, although these relationships may not predate the foundation of the priory. The church looks at its most noble from Silver Street on a moonlit night. The oldest surviving part of the building is the early 14th century vaulted crypt, evidently intended for the burial of members of the Mohun family and their successors. Above ground, the north aisle and north porch tower were put up in the late 14th century, followed by the nave in the early 15th. Later in the latter century the south aisle was added, then the excellent 102 ft west tower and, in the early 16th century, the nave was heightened, a wide-windowed clerestory inserted and the elaborate roofs set over the nave and both aisles. Finally in 1743 Sir Charles Berkeley built a new ornate rococco chancel, designed without an east window by Nathaniel Ireson of Wincanton, which retains its altar rails and stalls and is elegantly decorated in gold and pastel blue. In the chancel lie the effigies of Sir Maurice Berkeley (died 1581) and those of his two wives: also a bronze bust of William Godolphin, brother of poet Sydney, who died at Bruton Abbey in 1636, aged only 25. The north aisle, considered by some to have served as the parish church until the dissolution (while the abbey canons occupied the nave and chancel), housed a chapel of St Katherine and holds memorials to the staff of the King's School. At the west end of the church, where the tower screen is dated 1620, are the framed remains of a 15th century cope and cased copies of Bishop Jewell's *Apology* (1609) and the *Paraphrases* of Erasmus, both once required reading. A window at the west end of the south aisle recalls the link with the pretty box-pewed Bruton Church at Williamsburg, Virginia, USA, which was named for the 17th century emigrant, Thomas Ludwell.

Although Bruton was a Saxon borough and had a market by the 12th century (and probably long before), it never developed an independence from its lords or was granted a corporation and was administered only by its manorial officers. Later two annual fairs were granted to the abbey in 1533. High Street, to the north of and parallel to the river, was evidently laid out as a planned medieval burgage development. It includes a pleasing variety of shops and galleries, the Congregational Chapel of 1803, the 15th century half-timbered Priory House (the former abbey court house) and **Sexey's Hospital.** The last with its own chapel, hall and almshouses arranged round a quadrangle, was founded in 1638 under the will of Hugh Sexey (died 1619), a local man who accumulated a fortune as auditor to Elizabeth I. Accumulated surplus funds from the endowment were used to found a girls' school in 1877 and a boys' school in 1892. The much older **King's School** was endowed in 1519 by the bishop of London, Richard FitzJames, his nephew Sir John FitzJames and John Edmunds. Dependent for its site (in Plox) on the abbey, it fell with that house in 1539, the master receiving a pension and occupancy of the schoolhouse, which he turned into a malthouse. Only after appeals from the Bruton folk to Edward VI was the school refounded in 1550 and today, with buildings added in the 19th and 20th centuries on either side of Plox, continues to flourish, incorporating in Old School a 16th century core. The whole town is full

of intriguing corners and attractive buildings: the Georgian assembly rooms behind the Blue Ball Hotel (formerly the Unicorn), the Old Bull Inn, Patwell Pump, weavers' cottages on St Catherine's Hill, and two toll houses. (*See also* **Redlynch, Wyke Champflower**)

★★★★ *Town generally,* ★★★ *church.*

BRYMPTON D'EVERCY (J) This 'settlement where broom grows' has no village as such, but is marked by a group of Hamstone buildings which are special in their scale and juxtaposition, not merely to Somerset but to the nation. The estate lies to the west of Yeovil, was held in 1086 by Herbert under Roger de Courcelles and was sold in 1220 by Thomas of Chilthorne to Thomas D'Evercy. Although the D'Evercys gave their name to the parish, their tenure lasted little more than a century, the heiress of Sir Peter D'Evercy (died 1325) carrying it to the Glamorgans, from whom it descended successively to the Wynfords, Stourtons and, in 1434, to the Sydenhams. The latter's first manor-house is now thought to be the 15th century Chantry, Priest or Dower House to the east of the church, although this was superceded by the early 16th century west front of the present house. To this was added in the 17th century the magnificent ten-bay south front with its terrace and wonderful outlook across an extensive lawn to the lake: a view probably appreciated by the Duke of Monmouth when he was entertained here on his 1680 progress through the west. Financial problems linked with Philip Sydenham's drinking and high living meant creditor,

Thomas Penny, Receiver General for the county: the same year that the small clock tower was built on the north side of the courtyard. Bought in 1731 by Francis Fane of Bristol, the property descended from his brother, the 8th Earl of Westmorland, to the Clive-Ponsonby-Fanes. The house was occupied as a private school 1959-74 but thereafter was opened to the public by Charles and Judy Clive-Ponsonby-Fane, who courageously restored and refurnished it, making many friends and admirers in the process, until the recession sadly forced its sale in 1992. The interior boasts the longest straight staircase in England and several original overmantels.

The exquisite little church of St Andrew stands close to the house and its churchyard affords views of the house (now closed to the public). It has the same attractively top-heavy bellcot as at Ashington and Chilthorne Domer and dates mainly from the 15th century. The building contains a veritable feast of monuments to successive lords of the manor and their ladies, dating from a later 13th century D'Evercy effigy. There is a wealth of heraldry, a stone rood screen, Jacobean pulpit and 15th century font.

Houndstone, on the western outskirts of Yeovil and formerly in Odcombe, was a Domesday manor tenanted by Ansger Brito under the count of Mortain, and held by the Sydenhams with Brympton 1567-1703. It was probably in this area that the medieval hundred court of Houndsborough met. A major military camp, occupied by the Americans from 1942, was sited here.

★★★★ *Church and house.*

Sexey's Hospital, Bruton

Brympton D'Evercy

Archaeology

Somerset is extremely rich in archaeological remains although, by the very nature of the evidence, much is most readily explored in museums. A cave above Westbury-sub-Mendip has produced worked flints which may date back to 500,000 BC, which would make them the earliest evidence of man in Britain. Human remains from Palaeolithic to Roman times have been found in the Mendip caves at Cheddar Gorge, Ebbor Gorge and Wookey Hole, and can be seen at Cheddar and Wells museums. Neolithic and Bronze Age barrows are visible in considerable numbers throughout Exmoor and along the Mendip Hills. There is a Bronze Age stone circle on Porlock Common and two standing stones (Dear Leap Stones) near Ebbor Gorge.

The county is particularly rich in Iron Age hillforts and enclosures. To this period also belong the celebrated Glastonbury and Meare Lake Villages but, apart from slight bumps on the ground, little is visible and the significance of the sites is best appreciated from the excellent exhibition in the Tribunal Museum at Glastonbury. The long bank of Ponter's Ball earthwork east of Glastonbury may also belong to the Iron Age. At the Peat Moors Visitors Centre (Meare) there are two reconstructed Iron Age round houses and a stretch of Levels timber trackway, while the County Museum (Taunton) has an original section of trackway.

There is little visible to mark the presence of the Romans in Somerset apart from an amphitheatre at Charterhouse-on-Mendip, where subsequent mining operations have obliterated much of the nearby Roman lead-mining settlement. There is of course the line of the Foss Way, much of it followed by the A 303, but the only major town, Ilchester (Lindinis), has nothing to show apart from finds in its one-room museum. The best mosaic, from Low Ham villa, is in the County Museum at Taunton and lead ingots from Charterhouse are in Wells Museum. There is even less evidence to mark the passing of the Saxons. Blocks of concrete mark the positions of post holes of the West Saxon royal palace halls at Kings of Wessex Community School, Cheddar, the Caractacus Stone stands under its shelter on Winsford Hill and there is a further stone at Culbone with an inscribed cross in a circle. (*For Saxon ecclesiastical survivals see* **Churches**)

Substantial remains of medieval castles can be visited at Dunster, Farleigh Hungerford, Nunney, Stogursey and Taunton. Mounds, earthworks and hill tops marking Norman castle sites will be found at Castle Neroche (Staple Fitzpaine), Penselwood, Castle Cary, Downend (Puriton), Nether and Over Stowey, Fenny Castle (Wookey) and Montacute, and the water gate and part of the curtain wall survives of Bridgwater Castle.

Monasteries are just as well represented. At Glastonbury there are the extensive ruins of the church, the superb Abbot's Kitchen and an excellent new museum. Cleeve Abbey (Old Cleeve) has the most complete associated buildings and gatehouse, Muchelney Abbey preserves its Abbot's Lodgings and the footings of the early and later churches and the church of Stavordale Priory (Charlton Musgrove) has been converted to a private house (not open to the public). Stogursey Priory church is now the parish church, as is the Priory church at Dunster, where the monastic dovecot with its revolving ladder can be entered, although the Prior's

Caratacus stone, Winsford

Stone circle, Porlock common

Lodging is in private occupation. At Montacute there is the Priory Gatehouse, now a private house, and its dovecot. Of Taunton Priory, only one side of a gatehouse converted to a barn survives, occupied by a cricket museum, and of Bruton Abbey a length of precinct wall. Earthworks and fishponds can be seen on the site of Witham Priory (Witham Friary) and the present parish church probably represents the lay brothers' chapel, near which is a rectangular dovecot.

★★★★ Brean Down, Brent Knoll, Cheddar Caves, Dunster Castle, Farleigh Castle, Glastonbury Abbey, Cleeve Abbey (Old Cleeve), Cadbury Castle (South Cadbury), Somerset County Museum (Taunton), Wookey Hole Caves.
★★★ King John's Hunting Lodge museum (Axbridge), Chard Museum, Tribunal museum (Glastonbury), Ham Hill, Peat Moors Visitors Centre (Meare), Muchelney Abbey, Norton hillfort (Norton Fitzwarren), Nunney Castle, Stogursey Castle.
★★ Admiral Blake Museum (Bridgwater), Castle Cary Museum, Stavordale Priory (Charlton Musgrove), Cheddar Gorge Museum, Frome Museum, South Somerset Museum (Yeovil).

ABOVE *Ashen Hill Barrows, Priddy*
BELOW *Reconstructions of an Iron Age timber trackway and homestead, The Peat Moors Visitors Centre, Meare*

BUCKLAND DINHAM (B) A hilltop village on the A 362 north-west of Frome, its name meaning 'land granted by charter', possibly referring to a surviving grant by King Edred to his kinsman Aelfhere in 951. Within a century of the Conquest it had passed to a Norman, Oliver of Dinan (in Brittany), whose family name became 'Dinham' with the passage of time and was added to that of the manor to distinguish it from other Bucklands in the county. In 1239 Geoffrey de Dinham was granted a Tuesday market and three-day fair here, confirmed in 1393. The market lapsed but the fair continued until 1875. The Dinhams continued as lords until the death of Sir John Dinham in 1501, after which the manor was divided between his sisters. One half became the property of the Bampfyldes of Hardington, the other of the Hodges and later of the Stracheys of Sutton Court. In the late 19th century the Duckworths of Orchardleigh purchased property here and claimed the lordship. The church of St Michael and the tithes of hay were given to Wells Cathedral by Oliver of Dinan c.1175 to found a prebend there. I found the key to the church at nearby Court Farm, which probably represents the former manor-house. There are two Norman windows and two Norman doorways which date from the period when the prebend was established. The rest is 13th and 14th century, including a pair of worn half figures in relief set in the floor of the north chapel, identified as Sir John de Dinham (died 1332) and his wife Margaret (died 1361, *not* Joan de Brian, as often stated). A good Perpendicular west tower was added later, but the church has been over-restored inside. Near the church is the little village lock-up. Frome hundred court met by a 'big tree' on Buckland Down at a place known as Modbury.
★★ *Church.*

BUCKLAND ST MARY (H) This verdant parish lies towards the eastern end of the Blackdown Hills, its name signifying 'land granted by charter' with the addition of its church's dedication. Westcombland, one of the three tithings here, was originally held with Martock manor, evidently to provide a regular supply of timber and charcoal. The village centre is charming: flint-walled cottages and an attractive old school (thankfully still open) grouped around the substantial Victorian church of St Mary. The Rev John Edwin Lance (rector 1830-85), griefstricken over the death in childbirth of his young wife, Madalina Louisa, demolished the former

ABOVE *Memorial to Madalina Lance, Buckland St Mary church.*
RIGHT *Sea front, Burnham-on-Sea*

'neat structure' here in 1839. In its place between 1853 and 1863 he raised what Pevsner called 'a noble incongruity' to her memory, saving nothing from the old church. It is a lavish and ornate building, designed by Benjamin Ferrey, and clearly no expense was spared. On the north side of the sanctuary is an uninscribed memorial by James Forsyth to Lance's wife, showing her with her child bursting out of the tomb to resurrection. Lance also built a nine-bedroom rectory, the school and provided a drinking fountain opposite the lych-gate in 1876. Lance's daughter, Clara, later paid for a chapel of ease at the nearby hamlet of Birchwood in 1887. A stone on the road from Combe St Nicholas used to mark the site of the rape and murder of 13-year-old Betty Trump while on her way home to Buckland from Chard in 1823. A local labourer, William Flood, was acquitted of the crime. The parish features in *Larksleeve* (1985) and other recent best-selling novels by Patricia Wendorf.
★★ *Church, village and setting.*

BURNHAM-ON-SEA (E) The smaller of Somerset's two main seaside resorts, this 'settlement on a stream' (it became 'on-sea' only in 1917) to the north of the Brue and Parrett estuaries is perhaps best described as bright, cheap and cheerful. It has a seemingly endless stretch of sand and streets of friendly very individual shops behind the Esplanade. The birth of the resort was due initially to the local curate, the Rev David Davies, who in 1801 built the first lighthouse here, succeeding a candle placed in a window by a fisherman's wife to guide her husband home. The cleric's lighthouse was bought from him in 1829 for £13,681 by Trinity House and in 1832 the present 120 ft High Light was put up together with its picturesque partner, the Low Light, standing on the beach supported by stilts. From 1830 Davies

evidently used his windfall to build the Bath House (now Steart House) and several adjoining villas near the church, dubbed Daviesville, sinking two wells to exploit the supposed spa water he had discovered. The smell of this water was uncharitably described as 'very offensive, resembling that of a cesspool mixed with an odour not unlike that of horseradish'. The first esplanade had been built by 1836 and the arrival of the railway from Bristol in 1844 (followed by the Somerset Central Railway from Glastonbury in 1858) set the seal on Burnham's future. George Reed, who lived at the Manor House (later occupied by the UDC offices) built the National School, the Reed's Arms (now Queen's) Hotel and finally, in 1857, the 900 ft pier. The Royal Clarence Hotel is believed to date from the end of the 18th century. The present esplanade was laid out in 1911 and extended south in 1931 to the mouth of the River Brue, where the sailing club is sited. Walks beside the river, best at high tide when the estuary mud is covered, look across to the nature reserve and beyond to Hinkley Point Nuclear Power Station. Following severe flooding of 400 properties in 1981, Wessex Water built the present seawall 1983-88 with a curve designed to throw back the waves. To the north of the town the coastline, formerly a rabbit warren, has been occupied since 1890 by the magnificently-sited Burnham and Berrow Golf Club.

Burnham was for centuries a small village huddled behind a rudimentary seawall, for the inspection of which the Dean and

ABOVE *Burnham-on-Sea.* BELOW *Elver fisherman and Burrow Mump, Burrowbridge*

Chapter of Wells built a boat in 1681. Burnham was first mentioned in the will of King Alfred (died 899) but the manor had passed out of royal hands before the Norman Conquest, after which it was granted to the powerful Walter of Douai. Thence it descended through a succession of families, but was eventually split up and sold to the tenants by the Bampfylde baronets of Hestercombe in 1760 and 1792. The galleried church of St Andrew has a south transept which dates from a reconstruction completed in 1315. The west tower evidently developed its pronounced list soon after it was built in the late 14th century. The rest of the building is Perpendicular except for the north aisle which replaced a north transept in 1838. There is a Jacobean pulpit, fetchingly painted in light green and gold to match the roof, and one of Thomas Bayley's Bridgwater candelabra dated

1773. Around the church are distributed fragments of carving from the altarpiece produced in 1686 by Grinling Gibbons and Arnold Quellin for Whitehall Palace chapel. It was moved in 1696 to Hampton Court, in 1706 to Westminster Abbey, and brought to Burnham c.1820 by the vicar, Dr Walker King, then also bishop of Rochester. There were pre-Reformation altars to the Virgin Mary and St Nicholas. The patronage was given by John Tregoz to Gloucester Abbey in 1280, by the abbot to the bishop of Bath and Wells in 1286 and appropriated to the dean and chapter in 1306, a vicarage being ordained three years later.

Highbridge was a town formerly separate from Burnham, with which it is now continuously built up and which developed after the railway reached the place from Bristol. It is named after a major

bridge across the River Brue, mentioned in 1324. There were two fairs here by the 18th century, at which time Richard Locke (1737-1806), a celebrated agriculturalist and local historian, lived at Highbridge House. In 1772 Locke founded a religious debating group, the Burnham Society, which at one time had a library and Sunday school, and some 500 members. The church of St John the Evangelist was built at Highbridge in 1858-9 to the designs of John Norton by Mrs Luttrell of Badgworth Court, and enlarged in 1882.

★★★ *Burnham beach and the church, for its Whitehall carvings.*

BURROWBRIDGE (E) A modern parish (1840) formed around the Levels landmark of Burrow Mump, a natural conical hill topped by the chapel of St Michael, mentioned in 1231-2 as St Michael of 'la Burghe' and in 1480 as 'Myghellborough'. The village here was formerly known simply as Burrow ('hill'), its present name dating only from the early 19th century. It would be surprising if King Alfred had not used the Mump as a lookout or defensive post in 878 when he was nearby at Athelney, but there is no contemporary evidence for it. A recently-discovered Alfredian charter, possibly forged, may preserve the 9th century name of the Mump: 'Reodbeorh' – 'reed hill'. Modern excavation of the summit revealed wall footings dated to the 12th century but it is

unclear whether these represent the earliest chapel, a fortification or something else. St Michael's was certainly in use until 1548, when it was described as a free chapel belonging to Lyng, and the building seems to have been intact in 1633. The chapel may well have been damaged during the Civil War when 120 royalist troops made a vain stand on the hill after the Battle of Langport in 1645. A public subscription to rebuild St Michael's in 1793 failed to raise sufficient funds: hence the present un-finished chapel. The hill was given by Maj. A.G. Barrett as a monument to those Somerset men and women who had died in the Second World War and is now in the care of the National Trust (carpark). Until the M5 arrived, the bridge at Burrowbridge was the only crossing of the River Parrett between Bridgwater and Langport. Built in 1826, it was a toll bridge until 1945 (the tolls auctioned by sand-glass) and is believed to be the longest single-span masonry road bridge (68 ft) in the county. Below the hill, the Victorian church of St Michael is an undistinguished work by Richard Carver in 1836. Nearby, the King Alfred Inn was recorded as the Anchor in 1708, later as the Bell and took its present sign c.1806 when it was refronted. Optimistically shown off is the very table on which it used to be claimed that King Alfred displayed his burnt cakes!

★★★ *The climb up the Mump (more leisurely than Glastonbury Tor !).*

BURTLE (E) An isolated village on the Levels between Wedmore and the Polden Hills which evidently originated as a remote hermitage on a site called 'Sprauel-lissmede', endowed by William son of Godfrey of Edington, lord of Edington manor, in 1199. It was later referred to as St Stephen's chapel, by 1312 as a house of Augustinian canons under a prior, in 1335 as a collegiate church and finally as the Priory of Burtle Moor. Its patronage was granted to Glastonbury Abbey in 1285 and it continued as such until dissolved in 1536. Today it comprises Edington (or West) Burtle, where there was formerly a station and Catcott (or East) Burtle. In 1839 Anne Ruscombe Field, a wealthy spinster, financed and endowed the church of SS Philip and James at Edington Burtle, designed by Richard Carver.

BUTLEIGH (E) A sizeable but rewarding lias village, 'Budeca's clearing', south-east from Street and sited a little above the River Brue. There has been much modern development but it does not detract from the rustic streets and the essentially peaceful atmosphere. Here also is Butleigh Hospital, built to the south of the village by Sir George Bowles in 1882. The manor was granted in 801 by Egbert, king of the West Saxons, to his servant Eadgils, by whom it was given to Glastonbury Abbey, being retained by the monks until 1539. Reynald's Way in the parish preserves the name (and presumably the meeting place) of the Domesday hundred of Ringwoldes-wey. After the dissolution the estate was granted to the Duke of Somer-set and, eventually passed in 1738 to James Grenville (died 1783), a younger son of Countess Temple and in turn father of James, created in 1797 Baron Glastonbury of Butleigh (died 1825). The latter left it to his cousin, the Very Rev George Neville, dean of Windsor and master of Magdalene College, Cambridge. He took the surname Grenville and in 1845 replaced the existing manor-house with a massive Victorian pile, Butleigh Court, designed by J.C. Buckler, at the north end of the village. The dean's son, Ralph, was MP for East and Mid Somerset, and the latter's engineer son Robert (died 1936) invented a precursor of the motorcar, the Grenville Steam Carriage, in 1875 and was honoured by having a railway engine named after his home, the *Butleigh Court*. Robert's heir sold the estate in 1947 and the Court became a virtual ruin. It has been recently and happily restored, and divided up into apartments.

North-west from the village is the secondary hamlet of **Butleigh Wootton**, centred on Wootton House, built in 1722 by James Periam. In 1792 his grandaughter Elizabeth married Capt Alexander Hood, who sailed with Captain Cook but Hood was killed in action, and the captain's descendants have held Wootton House ever since. The Hoods, formerly of Dorset, had come to Butleigh in the person of the captain's great-uncle, the Rev Samuel Hood, rector here from 1723. The rector's two sons, Samuel (1724-1816) and Alexander (1726-1814), both became famous admirals and were ennobled as Viscount Hood and Viscount Bridport respectively.

The church of St Leonard has an early 14th century nave, chancel and central tower, to which were added north and south transepts in 1851, and a north aisle, full of late monuments to the Neville and Grenville families, in 1859. The thorough Victorian restoration included the installa-tion of modern misericords in the chancel. The north transept has an incredibly ornate heraldic window and three kneeling figures, taken from a lost monument to Thomas Symcocks (died 1619). The south tran-sept is a shrine to the Periams and the naval Hoods with elaborate memorials, one with a lengthy epitaph by Robert Southey, and two hatchments. Don't miss the table tomb in the churchyard which recounts the circumstances of the naval action in which Capt Alexander Hood died. His lengthy funeral procession *en route* to But-leigh brought Taunton to a standstill. A mile-long avenue of cedar trees leads to a slender Tuscan column to the memory of Viscount Hood on Windmill Hill, south-west from Butleigh Wootton. A second obelisk was set up in Copley Wood to the memory of Charles Colston, 1st Baron Roundway (died 1925).

★★★ *Village and setting.*

Butleigh Court, Butleigh

CADBURY CASTLE (F), see **SOUTH CADBURY**

CANNINGTON (D) A substantial village on the A39 north-east of Bridgwater to the east of the Quantock Hills, from which it took its name ('Cantucton' – 'settlement by the Quantocks'). By-passed since 1994, the area around the parish church is particularly attractive with Georgian houses, a pack-horse bridge and an inn, the Friendly Spirit, known until 1966 as the Blue Anchor. Traces of Mesolithic occupation have been found in the area, there is a substantial Iron Age hillfort, referred to as Cynuit Castle (so-called only from the 19th century to fit unfounded links with Hubba the Dane), on Cannington Hill to the north-west and, nearby, associated with a Romano-British settlement, a substantial pagan and Christian cemetery was excavated from 1962. Although much destroyed by stone quarrying, it has been estimated to have once contained over 5,000 graves, several grouped around the body of a young person, possibly a noble or religious figure, whose bones were reinterred in the church.

Cannington manor was left by King Alfred in his will to his son, Edward the Elder, and evidently continued in the hands of successive monarchs until granted to the Curci family of Stogursey soon after the Norman Conquest. Robert de Curci founded a priory of Benedictine nuns here c.1138, which served also as a refuge and guest house for ladies of prominent Somerset families. Such regular infusions of worldliness may have inspired an enquiry of 1351 which revealed that two nuns had

enjoyed liaisons with chaplains in the nave of the priory church, a third had produced a child and that the prioress had accepted bribes. The priory was dissolved in 1536 and its site and lands were granted to Sir Edward Rogers, whose family converted the buildings into the Court House, now Cannington Court, immediately north of the church. His descendant, Henry Rogers (died 1672 without heirs), gave £600 to found an almshouse, accommodated in the former churchhouse of c.1500, which survives in the centre of the village, restored in 1972. Following Henry Rogers' death the manor was granted to Thomas, Baron Clifford, Lord High Treasurer, who is alleged to have strangled himself in 1673. The family were Roman Catholics and by 1776 had built a lofty octagonal Catholic chapel on the site of the former cloisters, rebuilt in 1830, which survives as the impressive Clifford Hall. The house was occupied by Benedictine nuns 1807-35, 1863-67, but from 1919 was leased to Somerset County Council for the Agricultural and Horticultural College which occupies it and so much of Cannington today. **Cannington College Gardens** (fee:lists) include 7 walled gardens, 10 glasshouses (with 8 national plant collections) and magnificent views towards the Quantocks.

The parish church of St Mary is built of the Quantock red sandstone. It has a tall and slender 14th century tower, a prominent local landmark, but when the body of the church was largely rebuilt with two aisles in the later 15th century it was on a different alignment, tilted towards the south-east. The north chapel has 18th century wrought-iron gates with the

Clifford arms, there is a restored rood screen and 15th century brasses to the Dodesham family of Gurney Street. Trinity Chapel in the south aisle was the burial place of the owners of Brymore, a substantial house west of the village dating mainly from the 18th century with a south porch of c.1500. The estate was owned from the 13th century by the Pym family, who included the celebrated Parliamentarian and Puritan, John Pym (1584-1643). He was unofficial leader of the House of Commons at the outbreak of the Civil War, one of the five members whom Charles I tried vainly to arrest in 1642 and was buried (temporarily) in Westminster Abbey. There are memorials in the chapel to descendants of the Pyms, the Pleydell-Bouverie family, who in 1828 sold Brymore, which in 1951 became part of the Agricultural College. The churchyard here was the scene of a grave robbery in 1830, the culprit William Jones being caught in the act of dispatching the corpse in a hamper by stagecoach from Bridgwater to London.

There are two other substantial houses in the parish, each formerly with its own chapel. **Gurney Street**, south-east of the village, was held by the Gournay family, probably from the 13th century. A rambling house around a courtyard, it retains the vestiges of its medieval hall but was substantially extended in the 16th century, remodelled in the 17th, and has recently been restored by the Landmark Trust. It was the scene of a tragedy in 1539 when Thomas Michell murdered his wife and her sister, and then killed himself. **Blackmoor**, south-west of the village, is a remarkably unspoilt survival with chapel and kitchen wings and was probably built by London lawyer, Thomas Tremayll (died 1508), and his son John.

★★★★ *Cannington College Gardens,*
★★★ *village and church.*

CARHAMPTON (C/D) This large parish and compact village, the 'settlement by the rocks', lies mainly along the meandering A 39, praying for a bypass. It was formerly the meeting-place of a hundred which included its westerly neighbour, Dunster, and the port of Minehead. To the west, a hill is crowned by a circular Iron-Age fort known as Bat's Castle or Caesar's Camp. It has twin ramparts and entrances to the east and west. Tradition links Carhampton with the Welsh St Carantoc who may have founded a 6th century religious settlement here before he went on to evangelize Cornwall and Brittany. Colourful legends claim that he floated across the Bristol

Cannington village and church

Channel on a stone altar and tamed a dragon that was threatening the area, for which he was rewarded with a grant of land here by King Arthur. The Anglo-Saxon Chronicle records that King Egbert of the West Saxons was defeated here by an army of Danes from 35 ships in 836 (other versions of the Chronicle assign the annal to his son Ethelwulf in 843). Car-hampton was left by King Alfred (died 899) to his son and successor, Edward the Elder, and later it passed to the religious community at Cheddar and then back to the Crown, becoming part of the royal demesne in Somerset. Soon after 1066 William the Conqueror gave the manor to William de Mohun, whose descendants sold it with Dunster to the Luttrells: lords here ever since. Its local pre-eminence in Saxon times is reflected by customary payments of 12 sheep a year from the manors of Oare and Allerford (in Selworthy). There were other Domesday manors within the parish: Broadwood (also held by the Mohuns), Aller and possibly Eastbury. Lower Marsh Farm in the north-west of the parish dates from the 15th century. Marshwood, north-east from the village near Blue Anchor and dating probably from the 16th century, served as the demesne farm of the manor and had its own small deer park by 1240 until 1755. Dunster's medieval and later deer parks mainly lay within the western boundary of the parish.

The church of St John the Baptist was held with half a hide of land in Saxon times, being given after Hastings to the Conqueror's chaplain, Peter, bishop of Chester. After his death it was granted to William de Mohun, who bestowed Carhampton's tithes and a fishery here on Dunster Priory. The church itself was given in the late 12th century to Bath Priory by Simon Bozun, becoming a prebend of Wells Cathedral and a 'peculiar' of the dean and chapter there. All these early grants refer to the *churches* of Carhampton and one mentions the two individual parsons, Osbern and Robert, who held them. These references suggest that St Carantoc's church was a separate one and that it and St John's were both in use in the Middle Ages. Indeed, Leland noted in 1542 a chapel dedicated to Carantoc, which he states was formerly the parish church. In 1994 excavation revealed the cemetery possibly associated with Carantoc's church (12th to 16th centuries) 300 yds east of St John's. The present church in the village centre is Perpendicular, thoroughly restored 1862-3 and the west tower rebuilt in 1870. The

ABOVE *Market Hall, Castle Cary*
LEFT *Lock-up, Castle Cary*

superb 15th century rood screen, similar to those at Dunster and Minehead, has been repainted in colour in the medieval manner. There is an early 3-lock register chest and an 18th century pulpit. Monuments include those to the Trevelyan family, related to the baronets of Nettlecombe, and a large brass with florid inscription to Richard Escott of Escott Farm (now in Withycombe), died 1755, and his son. Opposite the church, at the 17th century Butcher's Arms the traditional ceremony of wassailing the apple orchards on Old Twelfth Night (16 January) is still performed.

★★ *Setting and church (for its screen).*

CASTLE CARY (F) A combination of picturesque narrow streets, friendly local shops and old inns make this one of the most attractive small towns in east Somerset: perhaps known best for its Round House lock-up, built in 1779. The town has no great houses but is a pleasing collection of 18th and 19th century stone buildings, so ensure that you saunter round the centre, replete with two bookshops, side by side, for bibliophiles like myself, and up High, Upper High and North streets. South of the junction of Fore and Woodcock streets, a somewhat sanitized Horse Pond borders the road with a War Memorial which seems to float in the middle. Since 1906 Castle Cary has also been a railway station, sited to the north of the town, on the main London line. King John came here briefly in 1207, as did Charles II, fleeing after the Battle of Worcester in 1651: hidden by Edward

Kirton, steward of the Duke of Somerset, probably at the old manor-house.

Originally this place was known simply as Cary, from the River Cary which has its source at Park Pond on the south side of the town. Granted after the Conquest to Walter de Douai, it was the largest of his many Somerset estates, and the first castle here may possibly have been his work. By 1138 there was a castle held by Richard Lovel which was besieged and taken by King Stephen, who rained 'showers of missiles and fire' on it. Henry de Tracy was defeated here by William of Gloucester in 1153 but no subsequent reference to the castle has been traced. Excavations south-east of the town in 1890 revealed the foundations of a Doulting-stone 78ft-square keep, the outer bailey probably lining Fore Street, and a manor-house was later built on the present site of Manor Farm, some remains of which could still be seen in 1791. The Lovels made Castle Cary the seat of their honor or barony, from whom it descended by marriage in 1351 to the lords St Maur (Seymour) and in 1409 to the lords Zouche, later passing to the lords Willoughby de Broke and dukes of Somerset. The manor was bought in the 1780s by the Hoares of Stourhead (Wilts).

Castle Cary never became a borough but the Lovels had a market here by 1352, and in 1468 a charter granted a Thursday market (changed to Tuesdays by c.1740) and two fairs, later increased to four. A market house was built here in 1616, replaced in 1855 by the present arched Market Hall (the arches possibly surviving from 1616), designed by

F.C. Penrose, which commands the central market-place. This now houses an appealing little museum (lists), which features a gallery of agricultural bygones and a small reference library. The town was a local centre for cloth production ('Cary cloth' was mentioned c.1362) until the 18th century. Thereafter factories for sailcloth and the weaving of horse-hair seating were established by the Donne (1818), Mathews (1828) and Boyd (1851) families: the horse-hair industry becoming the town's staple into the present century. Clark's Avalon Leatherboard Co. moved here in 1956. There is an abundance of surviving buildings to delight the industrial archaeologist, and Florida House, built by John Stephens Donne in 1888, is an incredible monument to the pride of a Victorian millowner. I also recommend a pint and/or a meal at the George Hotel, opposite the Market Hall.

The large lofty Perpendicular church of All Saints stands at the southern approach to the town, its striking spire visible from a distance. In its present form it is the result of a wholesale titivation by Benjamin Ferrey, completed in 1855. The church was given by Henry Lovel to Bath Priory in the later 12th century. It has a pulpit supported on a slender stem and reached by a glorified stepladder. A monument below the tower records the drowning of William Clarke in 1812, intended to show that disasters come in threes, as his uncle (1764) and father (1778) were both drowned in the Thames. Here ministered (although living at neighbouring Ansford) the Rev Samuel Woodforde (died 1771), father of the Rev James Woodforde (1740-1803), who assisted his father as curate and whose famous diary records 18th century life in the town. In 1782 the Angel Inn hosted a grand cockfighting match between the gentleman of Wales and those of Somerset. A current magazine with an old title, *The Visitor*, formerly *The Castle Cary Visitor*, affords an entertaining modern chronicle of the area, spiced with wit and gossip.
★★★ *Village*, ★★ *Museum*.

CATCOTT (E) A charming Polden village whose name suggests that it developed around a cottage (or possibly 'a shelter for sheep') settled by a Saxon called Cada. To the stranger it has a rather confusing pattern of intersecting lanes on the northern hill slope. At Cross Elm stands a column bearing the figure of a First World War soldier: one of the county's most imaginative war memorials. Catcott had to fight to retain its church of St Peter in King William Road. Formerly one of the Polden

chapels held under Moorlinch, it was mistakenly adjudged in 1548 to have been a chantry chapel and thus liable to closure and sale by Edward VI's Commissioners. It was bought by William Coke, who already held the tithes. He armed himself to keep out the parishioners and in 1552 completely demolished it. The villagers refused to pay their tithes and embarked on a succession of court cases that led to Coke being forced to rebuild the chapel, 1556-7. Today the church has a most attractive and well-kept interior. The village's two-seater stocks are set in the porch and the pews are fitted with little stools which pull out into the aisle to provide additional seating. Sexist quotations from Titus on the nave walls urge 'that the aged men be sober, grave, temperate, sound in faith, in charity, in patience, young men likewise exhort to be sober minded'. On the opposite wall a similar text, supported by two naked females and a cartoon face, requires 'the aged women likewise that they be in behaviour as becometh holiness, not false accusers, teachers of good things, that they may teach the young women to be sober, to be chaste, keepers at home, to love their husbands'.

At Catcott Heath is an important botanical reserve. (*See also* **Burtle**)
★★ *Church*.

CHAFFCOMBE (J) This delightfully wooded parish, 'Ceaffa's valley', presumably commemorating the first Saxon settler, stretches across the western slopes of the Windwhistle ridge north-east of Chard. Unusually, the manor can be traced without a break from the Norman

Text on nave wall, Catcott church

Conquest. After the Battle of Hastings four separate estates were combined and granted to the bishop of Coutances, under whom it was held by Ralph le Sor or 'the red'. It was eventually acquired by Oliver Avenel (died c.1226) and then equally divided between his two daughters, their twin estates becoming the manors of Chaffcombe Buller and Chaffcombe Poulett, reunited by John Poulett of Hinton St George in 1613. The Pouletts sold out to Holliday Hartley of Chaffcombe House in 1913 and the property was dispersed ten years later. The manor-house of Chaffcombe Poulett does not survive but probably occupied a moated site discernable beside the church. Chaffcombe Buller's manor-house, part of a substantial 15th century building, lies south of the village and is now known as Court Farm. A park was created here in 1267. The church of St Michael and All Angels at the eastern edge

Chaffcombe

ABOVE *Avishays park and house, Chaffcombe*
RIGHT *Ashton Windmill, Chapel Allerton*

of the village was almost entirely rebuilt in 1858 to the designs of J.M. Allen.

Towards the south of the parish, just north of the main Chard to Crewkerne road (A 30), a scatter of mainly 19th century houses represents the hamlet of Lidmarsh ('Libbemersa' in 1170). Avishays is a substantial brick-built 17th century mansion in the centre of the parish, given a new facade by James Marwood in 1745, probably when the extensive park was created around it. It was first recorded in 1384 as 'Aveneleseigh' and clearly took its name from Chaffcombe's lord, Oliver Avenel. At the parish's southern limit, Kingston Well Farm, known in the 16th century as 'Hynckstones Well', was evidently the home of William de Hecstanes in the 13th century and later belonged to Forde Abbey in Devon.

★ *Setting.*

CHANTRY (F) A former industrial village, based on the older hamlet of Little Elm, west of Frome, which was founded by James Fussell (1774-1845) of the family of edge-tool makers from Mells. Here he built c.1825 his solid uncompromising mansion, the Chantry, believed to take its name from the fact that it stood on land with which a chantry at Whatley church had been endowed. In the park below the house there are still the grottoes and an ice house which helped to mark the fact that James had 'arrived'. The ornamental lake below the house provided water power for the Fussell mills and around the house were built cottages that housed workers at the Chantry and Railford works in the valley, until these closed at the end of the 19th century. Beside the house James Fussell planned the Gothic church of Holy Trinity (consecrated 1846) with crocketed spirelet, designed by (the future Sir) George Gilbert

Scott, complete with external angels grasping the edge-tools and other products produced by the Fussells. James's nephew, the Rev J.G.C. Fussell (1813-83), inherited the Chantry, became its first vicar and founded in 1857 a pioneer comprehensive school here, including under one roof 'an infant school, a national school, an industrial school and a boarding school for girls'. It was pioneering in another sense because the girls were taught to play cricket in their 'bloomers'.

CHAPEL ALLERTON (A) 'Aelfweard's settlement' ('Alwarditone') is an extensive agricultural parish north-west from Wedmore, with a highly eccentric road system designed to confuse the stranger, around which farms and cottages are scattered. 'Chapel' has been prefixed to it only from 1708, to distinguish it from the adjoining hamlet of Stone Allerton. The manor was bought in 1492 by John Gunthorpe, dean of Wells, passing after his death in 1498 to the dean and chapter. The parish church, regarded as a free chapel until the early 16th century, has no known dedication. It apparently dates from the late 13th century but was remodelled in 1638 and almost rebuilt in 1858, when the north aisle was added. It has both old and new fonts, the former with a Jacobean cover. At the last restoration a 15th century embroidered cope was found and handed over to the County Museum. In the churchyard is one of the largest and oldest yews in the county. Immediately west of the church is

the former manor-house, where the manor court was held in 1650, although the present building was rebuilt in 1772 by the lessee, Robert Tudway. By the roadside between house and church lies the last remnant of the Bempstone ('Bimastane') hundred stone which was once sited in Hundredstone Field near **Ashton Windmill**. This mill (fee:lists), east of the village and sometimes identified with a mill mentioned in 1317, was rebuilt in 1549 and again in the later 18th century, grinding until 1927. A fruitless search for lead was licensed here in 1708. Stone Allerton and Ashton (formerly 'Arston') were evidently Saxon manors added to Chapel Allerton at around the time of the Domesday Book.

★ *Village, mill.*

CHARD (J) 'Welcome to Chard, Birthplace of Powered Flight' read the signs at every approach to this attractive town on the southern border of the county. For it was here that John Stringfellow (1799-1883) in June 1848 first flew a heavier-than-air steam-powered aircraft with a 10 ft wing-span down the length of a former lace mill. Stringfellow went on in 1868 to demonstrate his models at the Crystal Palace in London, although inevitably manned powered flight was to prove impossible until the invention of the petrol engine.

Chard has many other claims on the interested visitor, who should perhaps start by visiting the town's excellent **museum** (fee:lists) founded in 1970 at Godworthy House in High Street. There are areas devoted to other Chard worthies: James Gillingham (c.1840-1924), shoemaker and pioneer developer of artificial limbs, and Margaret Bondfield (1873-1953), daughter of a local lace-worker, who in 1929 became Britain's first woman cabinet minister and Privy Councillor. The complex features extensive displays illustrating the town's industries, agriculture and social life.

It used to be thought that Chard's name ('Cerdren' in a dubious charter of 1065, 'Cerdre' in 1086) was derived from a Saxon named Cerdic, which led many local institutions and businesses to take that name. In fact it comes from the Saxon word *ceart*, interpreted as 'a rough common, overgrown with gorse, bracken or broom', with the possible addition of *renn* – a house built in such a place. Before the Norman Conquest it was among the lands held by the bishop of Wells, presumably by royal grant, since lost, made at some time after the bishopric was founded in 909. The Domesday Book describes a large but

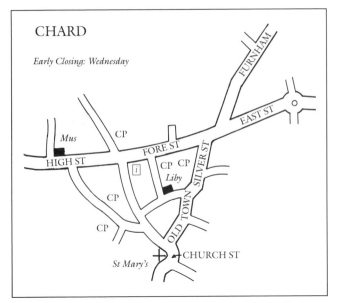

CHARD

Early Closing: Wednesday

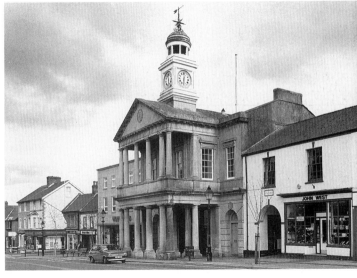

ABOVE *Guildhall, Chard.* BELOW *Turnpike Cottage, Chard*

typically agrarian settlement in 1086, probably centred on the parish church in the area still known as Old Town. In 1235 Bishop Jocelin founded a borough here to the north of the original village, laying out 52 one-acre plots on either side of a new wide thoroughfare (High and Fore streets), these plots to be leased for 12 pence a year to those willing to build on them, who would thereby become burgesses. By 1271 there was a Monday market and a fair, altered in 1292 to a Thursday market and two three-day fairs, all of which the new street was designed to accommodate. The borough was governed by a council headed by a portreeve and two bailiffs. For the bishops Chard, like Wellington, was a success story, even sending MPs to Westminster between 1313 and 1328. Cloth joined agriculture as the town's staple with a fulling mill here by 1394, and eventually a textile export trade developed with France. Even a disastrous fire on 22 June 1577, destroying buildings and goods valued at £9,000, only temporarily slowed down an expanding economy. The town even played host to the Assizes until 1667, with hangings taking place at Snowdon Hill, to the west of the town. Chard suffered from the typical West Country decline in its cloth industry from the later 18th century. The manufacture of machine-made plain lace was introduced in 1821, mopping up the surplus labour force, and throughout the 19th century fortunes were made by the owners of the principal mills in Holyrood and Perry streets, Mill Lane and at Forton. Other industries have included ironfounding, clay pipemaking and, beyond the town at Snowdon

until c.1870, stone quarrying.

During the Civil War the town was regularly visited by armies from both sides and suffered repeated plundering, particularly in 1644 when Charles I spent a week here. The Duke of Monmouth inspired some 160 men from the parish to join him in 1685, although 12 rebels were hanged, drawn and quartered at Chard after the Bloody Assizes at Taunton.

A stroll up and down the High Street and Fore Street will take in most of the town's best buildings: in High Street, the Choughs Inn, c.1600, Harvey's Hospital (almshouses founded under the will of Richard Harvey of Exeter in 1663, rebuilt 1870), Godworthy House (the museum), c.1580, Snowdon Turnpike Cottage (thatched with verandah, 1839), no.121, John Stringfellow's home. In Fore Street there are Waterloo House, c.1580, the 18th century George Hotel, the late 18th century Monmouth House (formerly the house of the grammar school headmaster), the former Grammar School (datestone 1583, but restored after a fire in 1727), and the fine Guildhall with its two-stage portico, topped with a clocktower, of 1834, when the town gained its mayoralty. The substantial church of the Virgin Mary was almost wholly rebuilt during the first half of the 15th century with a tower that seems almost too low for the rest of the building. There is a delightful monument in the north chapel to physician William Brewer (died 1618), father of 'only' eleven children, all of whom survived to maturity and are depicted with their long-suffering mother. From Chard, John Strong (c.1610-99) was an early emigrant (1635) to Massachusetts, producing 18 children, at least

148 grandchildren and descendants who include the Princess of Wales.

Hornsbury Mill (originally 'Hornsbow', referring to the bridge there) lies beside the main road to the north (A 358). The 19th century mill, succeeding earlier buildings on the site, has been converted into an hotel and restaurant, also housing a rural life museum, gift and craft shop. There is also an attractive picnic area beside the mill pond. **Tatworth** is a village on the A 358 south from Chard which has linked up with the adjoining hamlets of South Chard and Perry Street. The church of St John the Evangelist was built in Early English style to the designs of C. Pinch in 1851 and Tatworth became a parish separate from Chard in 1866. Since 1832 a meadow here has been annually auctioned while an inch of tallow candle burns, the successful bid being the last before the flame goes out.

★★★ *Town (High Street), museum, Hornsbury Mill,* ★★ *church.*

CHARLINCH (D) The Quantock settlement of 'Ceolred's hill' ('Cerdeslinc' in 1086) comprises a few houses with wonderful hillside views lining a lane leading up the hill north from the Bridgwater to Spaxton road. The church of St Mary has a Norman south doorway but was over-restored in 1886. From its pulpit in 1841 the deranged curate, the Rev H.J. Prince, began his crusade to declare himself divine, building a small meeting-house in the valley below when Bishop Law revoked his licence to preach (*see* **Spaxton**). The church was declared redundant in 1980 and at the time of my visit (in 1992) it looked untouched, overgrown and sadly neglected. Immediately west of the church is the former rectory, dating from the 17th century and now divided into two dwellings. The main manor and that of Currypool ('Curiepol' in 1086) both passed to the Earl of Egmont in the 18th century. Over a mile to the east lies Gothelney Manor, a fine manor-house with three-storey tower, dating from the later 15th century and probably built by third-generation lawyer, William Hody. The Hodys sold out to Roger Bourne in 1622, and the property later passed through the Baber and Gore families. Here was born Sir Robert Cross, one of the most prominent of Elizabeth I's naval captains, who fought against the Armada in 1588, at the burning of the Spanish fleet and at the taking of Cadiz, where he was knighted in 1596. He also foiled an assassination attempt on the queen in 1601.
★★ *Setting.*

CHARLTON ADAM (E) A rural village to the east of Somerton. There were many places in Somerset known as Charlton, 'the farmers' settlement', and this one was distinguished by the ownership of William son of Adam in the early 13th century, and William's son sold it to Bruton Priory (later Abbey) in 1258. Also known as East Charlton, it was always closely linked with its western neighbour, Charlton Mackrell, with which it was united in 1885, the two being together now known as 'the Charltons'. The Foss Way runs through the parish and traces of Roman settlement have been found at Bulland in the north-west corner. The village, largely built of the blue lias stone long quarried here, grew up around a rectangle enclosed by four lanes and formerly known as the Penning or Square. On the west side of this the church of SS Peter and Paul, formerly dedicated to St Peter alone, had been granted to Bruton Priory before 1166. For this reason the substantial Elizabethan rectory house, immediately north-east of the church and in lay hands since the Dissolution, is misleadingly known as 'the Abbey'. The present church dates from the 13th century although largely remodelled in Perpendicular style: the south chapel or Strangways aisle added in the 16th century. The right to burial in this chapel belonged to the lords of a manor centred on Manor Farm (on a detached part of the parish in Charlton Mackrell village) bought by Thomas Strangways c.1640. His descendant, lawyer Giles Strangways (died 1777), was clandestinely married to his mother's

maid and his children were born and brought up under the name of Littleton in London. The cost of establishing his identity forced the heir, Thomas Littleton Strangways, to sell up in 1796. The estate passed to the Dickinsons of Kingweston in 1805 but was dispersed in 1930. The fourth bell in the church tower, cast in 1714, bears the vernacular inscription:

'I am not now as wonce I was,
Sq[uire]. Straingwing was the caus'.
★ *Village.*

CHARLTON HORETHORNE (K) A sizeable parish to the south-west of Wincanton: its village sited at the junction of five roads. Originally known simply as Charlton ('the farmer's settlement'), it was called Charlton Kanvile by 1225. The addition of Horethorne ('Hareturna', 1084 – 'grey thornbush') marks it as the former meeting place of the hundred court of Horethorne, evidently to the south-west of the village. The hundred stone, not in its original position, now stands in front of Seven Wells Down farmhouse. In the west of the parish Bronze Age barrows at Sigwell yielded a corpse in a bark coffin and there are signs of a deserted medieval village at Whitcombe. In 1086 the lord, Robert son of Gerold, paid an annual rent of 100 cheeses (the earliest record of cheese-making in the county) and 10 'bacons'. Gerard de Camville held the manor by 1140 when he gave part of the tithes to Bermondsey Abbey, Surrey, and the church here was soon after granted by the family to Kenilworth Priory. In 1226

BELOW *The 'Abbey', Charlton Adam*
RIGHT *Charlton Horethorne manor house*

Lytes Cary, Charlton Mackrell

the Camville inheritance passed by marriage to Sir William Longespee, whose son William was granted a Monday market and three-day fair at Charlton in 1252. These had presumably lapsed by 1294 when the latter's son-in-law, Hugh de Lacy, Earl of Lincoln, received a charter for a Tuesday market and a two-day fair here. John of Cornwall was pardoned in 1353 for assaulting men at Charlton fair, but neither market nor fair survived to modern times. Latterly the manor was bought in 1791 by the Pagets, earls of Uxbridge and marquesses of Anglesea, in 1859 by the Wingfield Digbys, and in 1927 by the Parsons family. The centre of the village is graced with a small green, an impressive 17th century manor-house behind low walls with central ornamental gate piers, the Kings Arms, the 17th century Monks Place and Vine Cottage, dated 1634. South of the manor-house, the church of SS Peter and Paul (formerly St Peter alone) has an elaborate Perpendicular west tower. The south aisle is possibly 12th century, the chancel and north arcade 14th: all heavily restored in 1863. At a church ale here in 1607 one parishioner was heard to 'whoop and hallooe' after taking a powder 'to provoke drunkenness' and was drunk for 'three days together'. The kennels of the Blackmoor Vale Hunt were built here by George Wingfield Digby in 1858, amalgamating with the Sparkford Vale Harriers in 1971. The Huckworthy Basset Hounds, kennelled at the north end of the village, were registered in 1969. There was an airfield at Sigwells 1942-47.

★★ *Village centre.*

CHARLTON MACKRELL (E) This Charlton, another 'farmers' settlement', east from Somerton, was identified sometimes as West Charlton, but more often by the name of a Norman lord who has never been traced although a Herbert Makerel occurs at nearby Somerton in 1243. The Foss Way runs through the parish, Roman villa sites have been found in the north-west of the parish at the edge of Windmill Hill and to the north-west of Lytes Cary, and quarrying has revealed Roman burials. The main village around the church and former manor-house (on the site of Rookery Farm) contracted during the 19th century. Below the church, Charlton Mackrell Court, a large three-storeyed house, represents the medieval parsonage, built c.1520 and refronted in Gothic style by the Rev Richard Ford in 1792. To the north a secondary settlement developed in the 17th century where in 1726 Thomas Lyte built the substantial seven-bay Charlton House. The church of St Mary the Virgin is almost entirely the product of restorations of 1792-4 and c.1847. The circular font is early 13th century, and the Tudor benchends include the Percy arms, alluding to the ownership of half the manor by the earls of Northumberland in the 15th and 16th centuries. The south transeptal aisle housed a chantry chapel founded in 1342 by Ralph Horsey, lord of the other half of the manor. The north aisle formerly belonged to the Lyte family and once held the shapeless Purbeck marble tomb in the churchyard, representing the 13th century William le Lyte and his wife.

Much of the parish was bought up by William Dickinson of Kingweston in the first decade of the 19th century and finally sold off by the family in 1922 and 1930. There were several manors in the area which took their names from the River Cary. Cooks Cary, formerly Tuckers Cary, was named after Thomas Cooke, its owner from 1720, and Cary Fitzpaine, on the other side of the Foss Way, was briefly held by the FitzPayns in the 13th century. Chief among these Cary manors was **Lytes Cary** (fee:lists), one of those smaller ancient houses which exerts a particular appeal because it is people-sized: the kind of home which I feel I could live in. It was held in 1286 by the above William le Lyte ('the little man') and within 50 years had adopted its present name. The first house on the site was probably built by Peter le Lyte shortly before 1343, when he licensed the chapel which still stands there. No chantry priest occurs after 1433 but the building was restored in 1631, additions including a tablet which illustrates a medieval stained-glass window depicting the Lytes' earliest known ancestors, William and Agnes le Lyte, formerly in Charlton Mackrell church but since destroyed. It was John Lyte or his son Thomas who began the present house in the mid 15th century with its splendidly-roofed great hall, and another John who in 1533 added the solar wing at right-angles to it. The courtyard is completed by an 18th century farmhouse and a 20th century range. The older buildings are a riot of heraldry. The Lyte swans are everywhere: testimony to an evident pride in their family and their home, which debts sadly forced them to sell in 1755. Later also held by the Dickinsons, the house was left by Sir Walter Jenner to the National Trust in 1948. The grounds with their fine topiary are as congenial as the house and recall Henry Lyte (died 1607), translator and editor of a Dutch herbal (Henry taught the author, Robert Dodoens, to speak English), in which he incorporated references to 'the Cary Bridge Pear' and 'the Somerton Pear, an excellent pear, ripe before Kingsdon's feast'. In 1610 his son Thomas (died 1638), restorer of the chapel, was an amateur genealogist who presented James I with an elaborate but fictitious pedigree, deriving the king from Brutus of Troy, supposed to have invaded Britain c.1000 BC! In return his monarch presented him with the famous golden Lyte jewel, set with diamonds and containing James's miniature by Nicholas Hilliard: since 1898 in the British Museum as part of the Waddesdon

Bequest. Thomas's portrait of 1611 in the County Museum at Taunton depicts him proudly sporting the jewel around his neck. A later descendant was Sir Henry Maxwell-Lyte, Keeper of the Public Records and author and editor of many books on Somerset's history.

★★★★ *Lytes Cary*, ★★★ *its gardens*, ★ *Charlton Mackrell village.*

CHARLTON MUSGROVE (F) This 'farmer's settlement' to the north-east of Wincanton was held by the Mucegros family during the 13th century, whose name was added to that of the parish, from whom it passed by marriage to the lords Ferrers. In 1234 Robert de Mucegros had royal licence to create a park here, enclosed with hedge and ditch, adjoining Selwood royal forest, and to carry venison to his court at Charlton. He was also granted a charter of free warren here in 1239. The Perpendicular church of St Stephen stands in Rectory Lane, isolated from most other houses apart from the manor farm and Charlton Musgrove House, built by Thomas Bastard soon after his purchase of the farm in 1805. The living was held continuously by members of the Leir family from 1617 until 1914, who rebuilt the rectory in 1825, and their memorials up to 1976 are clustered in the chancel. Nearby is a monument to Thomas Penny (died 1730), 'a merry and chearful Companion of a free and easy Deportment . . . even amidst the incessant Tortures of the Stone, always Calm and Resign'd'. The largest settlement in the parish is at Barrow (now described as the village of Charlton Musgrove) with the small delightful Romanesque chapel of St John, put up in 1878 to the memory of the Rev Lewis Davies (died 1876) by his Leir wife.

Towards the end of a short lane north-east of Barrow stands the Augustinian priory of **Stavordale** ('valley with a stony ford' or, possibly, 'stake valley'), probably founded by a member of the Lovel family of Castle Cary in the late 12th or early 13th century. The priory church, all that remains above ground, was rebuilt under the will of John Stourton (died 1439) and consecrated in 1443. A north chapel of Jesus was added by John, Lord Zouche (died 1526), who had lost most of his lands after the Battle of Bosworth, retired to the priory and was buried there. The small priory, always poor, was united with Taunton priory in 1533 and dissolved with it in 1539. The church became the home of the Zouches until 1571. More recently the building was rescued by Frederick Sage in

1905 and converted into an attractive home (not open to the public but visible from the lane) with the addition of a north wing. Recent excavations have revealed the plan of a southern bell tower mentioned in 1374, fishponds and other details. ★★ *Priory.*

CHARTERHOUSE-ON-MENDIP (A) A wild and often bleak tract of land on top of the Mendips, extra-parochial until 1858, although often stated to be a liberty of itself or part of the liberty of Witham Friary. It takes its name from the fact that it was one of the 13th century estates of the Carthusian priory of Witham (*see* **Witham Friary**) and where, shortly before 1250, the monks had established an outlying cell. Here from Roman times, and even before, was the centre of the Mendip leadmining industry. Evidence of lead ingots shows that the workings were in progress as early as 49 AD and continued until the mid 4th century. A major Roman settlement developed here in the Blackmoor valley, complete with amphitheatre, square fort and permanent garrison. The same lead pigs suggest that the town may have been known as *Vebriacum* and, although most building remains were destroyed by later mining, brooches, engraved gems, coins and implements have been found in some quantities. The area now forms the Blackmoor Nature Reserve, owned by Somerset County Council, complete with car park. Mining activity continued during the Middle Ages. Witham monks were licensed to mine in 1283, the leadminers

receiving a hogshead of wine a year from 1387, and activity continued into the 19th century when the Mendip Mining Co were operating 1865-85.

Manor Farm, dating from the early 17th century and built by the May family, could occupy the site of the former Carthusian cell, although this may possibly have been situated at Haydon Grange to the south-east. Hidun (evidently meaning 'the hill where hay was gathered') was presumably the Saxon name for Charterhouse, and the manor bought and occupied by the May family after the dissolution until 1799 was known as Charterhouse Hydon. There was no place of worship here until 1908 when the small isolated church of St Hugh (former prior at Witham) was built, resembling a village hall with timber bellcot. ★★ *Scenery.*

CHEDDAR (A) A large sprawling village which lies at the foot of the Mendips at the end of Cheddar Gorge, a deep rugged cleft running back into the hillside. Its name ('Ceodre' c.880), is derived from the Saxon *ceodr, 'a pouch'*, referring either to the ravine itself or to the famous caves there. To most people, however, its name only means one thing – cheese. The delicacy was certainly in production in Somerset by 1086 (*see* **Charlton Horethorne**), and probably long before. Certainly by 1586, according to William Camden, Cheddar was 'famous for the excellent and prodigious great cheeses made there, some of which require more than a man's strength to set them on the table'. Early cheese-making here operated

Stavordale Priory, Charlton Musgrove

on a communal basis, referred to as the Cheddar Club in 1666. The milk from all the parish cows was literally pooled every day to produce a single cheese, such cheeses being returned in turn to the owners of cows in a sequence reflecting the number of beasts held by each. Large-scale manufacture in Cheddar itself was killed off by World War II and today cheese is made here principally for sale to the tourist. A second boost to the local economy was market-gardening and in particular straw-berry-growing, established in the 1870s. This continues to flourish and its wares are retailed from stalls along the A371.

Cheddar Gorge, whose cliffs rise over 400 ft above the road, was cut out of the Mendip limestone by the River Yeo which eventually sank underground and now has its source in a cave in the hillside. The river formerly drove 7 mills in the parish, of which 4 were fulling cloth in 1301 and 3 later produced paper. It was the caverns in the Gorge which brought visitors here by the 12th century, when Henry of Hun-tingdon wrote of 'Chederhole ... a cavity below the earth where, although many have entered and there traversed great spaces of land and streams, yet could they never come to the end'. That cave has never been rediscovered but in 1837 miller George Cox accidentally broke into what is now **Cox's Cave** (fee: lists) and introduced Victorian trippers to the wonders of stalac-tites and stalagmites. From 1890 Cox's nephew, Richard Cox Gough, a former sea captain, dug his way into the more exten-sive **Gough's Cave** (fee: lists), higher up the Gorge and where there is an excellent museum illustrating the history and the pre-history of the Gorge. Evidence of almost continuous human occupation from the Old Stone Age has been found in and around the caves. Similar remains have been located in other caverns here: Flint Jack's Cave, Great Oone's Hole, Soldier's Hole and Sun Hole Cave. Other attractions include an **Adventure Caving Centre** (fee:lists) for those who want to penetrate further into Gough's Cave, and a **Rural Village** (fee: lists), demonstrating country crafts, including pottery, coopering and cheese-making. The lower length of the Gorge is crammed with gift shops and eating places (mainly of the 'chips-with-everything' variety), while for those who appreciate simpler pleasures there are ex-cellent walks up the Gorge and above it (via the 274 steps of Jacob's Ladder). A prospect tower near the top of the ladder commands superb views over the Levels and the Cheddar Reservoir (1,300m gals),

ABOVE *A reconstruction of the royal palace at Cheddar (Drawing by Alan Sorrell)*

BELOW *The Cross, Cheddar*

completed in 1937. On the stony ledges is the only known habitat in Britain of the Cheddar Pink (*Dianthus gratianopolitanus*) which flowers in spring.

Below the Gorge in the village there is evidence of Roman settlement, perhaps a villa, near the church in the grounds of the Vicarage, and there is a possibility that a Roman port called *Ischalis* was sited nearby: maybe at Hythe on the Yeo, which served as Cheddar's medieval quay. Cheddar really came into its own under the Saxons. Excavations by Philip Rahtz, 1960-2, in the grounds of the later Kings of Wessex Community School, revealed a 'palace' of the West Saxon kings with a succession of halls dating from the 9th to 13th centuries. The post holes of the East and West halls are marked out with concrete blocks in the school grounds and the ruins of the former royal chapel of St Columbanus stand nearby. This would suggest that the royal presence here dated from the time of Alfred and that it was on this site that he entertained Guthrum the Dane after the latter's baptismal ceremonies at Aller and Wedmore. The earliest documentary reference is in the king's will when he left Cheddar to his son, Edward the Elder, and enjoined the (probably religious) 'com-munity' here to choose him as his succes-sor. The Witangemot, the royal council, met here in 941, 956 and 968, and King

Edmund had a narrow escape c.944 while hunting across Mendip when his hounds plunged into the Gorge. Monarchs after the Conquest continued to spend time here, Henry I (1121, 1130) and Henry II (1158), and King John paid out £40 to maintain 'the king's houses at Cheddar' in 1209-11. The place ceased to be a royal manor in 1204 when John gave it to Archdeacon Hugh of Wells, who as bishop of Lincoln passed it to Bishop Jocelin. Jocelin obtained a market and fair here in 1235 and a covered hexagonal market cross still stands in the centre of the village.

The main manor continued to be held by the bishops until 1548 and it was bought in 1556 by Sir John Thynne, ancestor of the marquesses of Bath, who administered the estate from Longleat. There were other manors here, known from the families that held them: Cheddar Hanham, Cheddar Fitzwalter and Cheddar Berkeley. The former royal forest of Cheddar largely comprised the parishes of Cheddar and Axbridge and was disafforested in 1337, despite a local riot, to create a park for the bishops. In 1260 Carthusian monks were prosecuted for taking a hart with mastiffs in the forest and the rector of Shipham fled when similarly accused in 1265. During the Commonwealth the parishioners assaulted the exciseman, thrust him in the stocks and called him a 'peeping rogue'.

The large Perpendicular **church of St Andrew** with its 110 ft tower and ornamented parapets lies at the south-eastern end of the village. It was a Saxon minster which before the Conquest was held by Wells cathedral, the advowson being later exercised by the dean and chapter. In the chancel is a brass depicting Thomas Chedder (died 1443), lord of the manor of Cheddar Hanham. On the floor in front of the tomb and under a carpet is another brass to Chedder's second wife Isabel (died 1476). Chedder's father, as executor of William Husee, founded a chantry here in 1362. There were two chantries, of the Holy Trinity and Virgin Mary, when they were dissolved in 1548. The chapel of St Nectan off the south aisle, with heraldic 15th century glass, was held with the manor of Cheddar Fitzwalter, whose manor-house stood on the site of the Hall in Cliff Street. A later monument in the north aisle commemorates cave-discoverer Richard Cox Gough (1827-1902). The fine 15th century stone pulpit still bears traces of early colouring and vernacular 1803 paintings of Death and Father Time hang below the tower.

Hannah More, the philanthropist, began her work at Cheddar in 1789, when there were still some inhabitants living in damp caves in the Gorge and she was advised that religion would make the poor 'lazy and useless'. A Sunday school was opened and in 1791 the first of several mass outings in wagons to Callow Hill on Mendip was attended by 517 pupils and 4,000 spectators. **Hannah More's Cottage**, containing a small exhibition of pictures, is preserved in Lower North Street and is used for social gatherings and meetings.

★★★★ *Caves, scenery, walking,*
★★ *church, Gorge museum.*

CHEDDON FITZPAINE (D) Set in lush countryside immediately north-east from Taunton, this small village is progressively being encroached on by the county town, its name ('Cedenon' in 897) possibly meaning 'wood valley'. In Saxon times it formed part of the outfaring of Taunton Deane manor but after the Conquest was granted to the great Roger Arundel, a half share descending in 1198 to Robert Fitzpayn, whose family obtained the other half in 1224 and held the estate until 1393. The manor was bought in the 16th century by Thomas More of Taunton Priory from whom it passed by marriage to the Methuens of Corsham, Wilts. The living passed with the manor until granted to William Clifton of Barrington in the 16th century, whose family sold it to the Warres of nearby Hestercombe, several of whom served as vicars. The church of St Mary retains its 13th century tower with large gargoyles, but the rest of the building was over-restored in 1861. William Otherie was prosecuted in 1623 for urinating in his pew during the sermon.

Maidenbrook Farm was mentioned in 1086 and Nerrols was formerly known as Northwalls, possibly the home of William de Northwolde in 1280. Excavations have recently revealed flint and pottery evidence in the south-west of the parish from the late Neolithic to early Bronze ages and small Romano-British settlement sites near Maidenbrook and Nerrols. There is also evidence that the medieval woodland of the priors of Taunton, hence the name Priorswood, straddled the old boundary with Taunton. (*See also* **Hestercombe**)

★ *Village.*

CHEDZOY (E) 'Cedd's island' is a small Levels village, mentioned as early as 729 and centred on a three-way junction of lanes to the east of Bridgwater and below the Polden Hills. William Stradling found a Roman villa here, complete with hypocaust, in the early 19th century but its site has since been lost. Among the cottages and former farmhouses, Cadbury House and Myrtle Cottage date from the 17th century. The manor was held with the royal estate of North Petherton, passing with it to the Erleghs, who gave the church to Buckland Priory in Durston. By 1212 the manor had been granted to the Montacute family and Simon de Montacute obtained a Tuesday market and three-day fair here in 1314. The church of St Mary in the centre of the village has 13th century arcades flanking the nave, with a chancel added a little later (rebuilt 1884-5). Above the

doorway of the south porch is a flamboyant panel dated 1579, with three sets of initials. Two are probably those of the churchwardens and the third, RB, is usually identified unconvincingly with Richard Bere, abbot of Glastonbury 1493-1524. The benchends are 16th century but more crudely executed than those in the Quantock area. In the south transept is a monument and hatchment to the Stradling family, ancestors of the antiquary who built Chilton Priory (*see* **Chilton Polden**). In the church floor near the south door is a fine brass to Richard Sydenham (died c.1500). He is often stated to have given to Chedzoy the Church Acre in Bridgwater, the lease of which is still auctioned by candle once every 21 years: the last time in 1988. In fact the land was acquired from John Foster in 1530. Note the fine equestrian monument (1946) in the churchyard. Dr Walter Ralegh, rector here from 1620, dean of Wells from 1641 and nephew of Sir Walter, suffered cruelly during the Civil War. His rectory house was plundered, his family turned out and, after imprisonment, he was murdered in 1646. In 1685 much of the activity prior to the Battle of Sedgemoor took place in the parish, the king's forces camping here, and the then rector, Andrew Paschall, later wrote a detailed account of the campaign.

★★ *Church.*

CHEWTON MENDIP (B) A substantial parish on the Mendip Hills to the north-east of Wells, the 'settlement on the river Chew', Chew being a Celtic name meaning 'river of chickens'. The village was a noted place for the manufacture of cloth by the 14th century and formed one of the four Mendip lead minories, lead continuing to be extracted until c.1910. It was also an area of several round barrows, although many were inexpertly excavated out of existence in the 19th century. The estate here was evidently an early possession of the West Saxon kings, the seat of the hundred of Chewton and was among the properties left by King Alfred (died 901) in his will to his son, Edward the Elder. It was held at the Conquest by Edith, queen of Edward the Confessor, and thereafter was seized by William the Conqueror. A later lord, Henry FitzRoger, obtained a market and three-day fair here in 1348. The FitzRoger heiress married John Bonville of Shute (Devon) and their son, William, became Lord Bonville of Chewton in 1449 before being beheaded after the Second Battle of St Albans in 1461. His great-grandson, Henry, Marquess of

Dorset, was similarly executed in 1554, whereupon Chewton was granted by Mary Tudor to one of her courtiers, Sir Edward Waldegrave (pronounced 'Wargrave'), who evidently moved into the manor-house here. He and his wife were imprisoned as recusants (Roman Catholics) in 1562 and their successors thereafter seem to have lived mainly in Essex or Norfolk. They became baronets in 1643, barons Waldegrave of Chewton in 1686 and earls Waldegrave in 1729. The widow of the 3rd Earl (and of his illegitimate elder brother), was Frances (died 1879), daughter of John Braham (an opera singer) and a celebrated society hostess in London. She bought a house at Chewton in 1850 and proceeded to build Chewton Priory (although there was never a medieval Benedictine priory here, as sometimes stated) on the site, 'an ugly Victorian monstrosity', where she lived with her third and fourth husbands, the last being Chichester Fortescue, 1st Baron Carlingford. The earls Waldegrave have continued as lords of the manor ever since, their name recalled in the name of the inn, the Waldegrave Arms, although Chewton Priory has since been demolished. In June 1643, during the Civil War, a body of royalists led by Prince Maurice and the Earl of Carnarvon pursued a body of retreating Roundheads through the village, capturing much of their baggage train. A hot engagement followed, in which Prince Maurice was wounded, taken prisoner and then rescued, before the Roundheads fled towards Bath. South-west of the village, off the B 3134, there are excellent facilities at **Chewton Cheese Dairy** (lists) for viewing all stages in the production of Cheddar cheese (carparking, licensed restaurant, well-stocked farm shop). Farm animals, including longhorn cattle, can also be inspected and the grounds are open for strolling and picnics.

The church of St Mary Magdalene stands on an elevated site above the village. It was clearly a Saxon minster with subordinate chapels at Ston Easton, Emborough, Farrington Gurney and Paulton. The church was granted by William the Conqueror to the French abbey of Jumièges by whom a vicarage was ordained in 1242, the vicar to have 'the court and curtilage' formerly occupied by the chaplains of Chewton. After the confiscation of the property of alien priories, Henry V gave the church to Bethlehem Priory at Sheen, Surrey, which held it until its dissolution. The advowson was later held by the Kingsmill family but subsequently passed to the Waldegraves. The present building

ABOVE *Manor Farm, Chilcompton*
LEFT *Church tower, Chewton Mendip*

has an east wall to the nave, north doorway and corbel table above the south door which are all Norman. The chancel and south chancel aisle (now the Lady Chapel) are mid 13th century, the nave arcade and south aisle were added in the 14th century and finally the superb 126 ft tower, with fan vault beneath, which was still incomplete in 1541. In the Lady Chapel are effigies of Henry FitzRoger (died 1353) and his wife Elizabeth (died 1388), and monuments to the Waldegrave and Braham families. There is a Jacobean lectern and, in a separate case, a copy of the Authorised Version of the Bible (1611). A churchyard cross in the churchyard has an original but damaged head.
★★ *Church.*

CHILCOMPTON (B) This Mendip village, 'the young man's settlement in the valley', south-west from Midsomer Norton (Avon), presents two faces to the traveller. The somewhat dull and predictable 19th and 20th century development along the Bath to Wells road (B 3139) and the former course of the Somerset and Dorset Railway, and the gentle older village to the north: its road running beside an idyllic stream, punctuated with weirs and attendant ducks. Here are Shell House, Eagle

House and Gainsborough House, the last reputed to have been occupied by the painter while he was labouring on canvases in Bath. A lane from this road leads west to Manor Farm (1612), sitting happily beneath the trees, and the church of St John. This church was given to Wells Cathedral in the late 12th century by Gerbert de Perci to endow a prebend and became a peculiar of the dean of Wells. Here a thief, Robert Scissor, sought sanctuary in 1243 before he abjured the realm (left the country to go into exile). The Perpendicular west tower survives from an earlier age, but the nave and aisles were rebuilt in 1839 by Jesse Gane and the chancel in 1897 by the notorious Frederick Bligh Bond (*see* **Glastonbury**). An attractive stone hall, in keeping with the older building, was added to the north of the church and dedicated by Bishop George Carey in 1990. In the 16th century the principal estate passed to the Seward family and then to the Stockers, the latter building Manor Farm and its adjacent barn. Most of their monuments, faithfully recorded by Collinson in 1791, were ejected from the church when it was rebuilt. Latterly the manor was held by the Thynne family of Longleat, marquesses of Bath. South-west from the village at Blacker's Hill is an Iron Age promontory hillfort and in this area most of the early (17th and 18th century) coalmining operations were sited. New Rock Colliery commenced operations in 1819 and closed in 1968. (See also Downside Abbey)
★★ *Old village and area round the church and Manor Farm.*

CHILLINGTON (J) On the northern slope of Windwhistle Hill between Chard and Crewkerne lies 'Ceola's settlement', originally held under the manor of South Petherton. It passed in the mid 18th century to the Notley family, who probably built the Old Manor House soon after and finally sold up in 1942. The original settlement was at Lower Chillington where 17th and 18th century farms cluster round the small mainly 14th century church of St James, whose elevated site may represent a prehistoric burial mound. The church was held as a chapelry of South Petherton by Bruton Priory and from 1542 by the chapter of Bristol Cathedral, although its tithes (and several farms here) were later acquired by the Pouletts of Hinton St George. The larger hamlet of Higher Chillington developed in the 18th century around common land at Chillington Down. Of the farms, Chibley occurs as 'Chubbeleye' in 1305 and the buildings of Hill and Sheephouse farms date from the 17th and mid 18th centuries respectively.

★ *Setting.*

CHILTHORNE DOMER (J) A village north-west from Yeovil, along a north-south lane: an attractive mix of old and new Ham stone with modern development at its southern end. The first part of its name ('Cilterne', 1086) is a British hill-name including the element *celto* – 'high'. The parish comprised three different manors in 1086 but was later two, named from the families that owned them: Chilthorne Domer (as at Pendomer) and Chilthorne Vagg, the latter name surviving in that of Vagg Farm to the south-east of the village. The former manor-house, on the west side of the street, has an outside communal loo with six seats, dated to c.1720. The small church of St Mary was granted to Bruton Priory in 1301, 'which being situate by the public street is daily crowded with the poor and needy'. The church is mainly 14th century, with a 15th century font and western bellcot, similar to those at Brympton and Ashington. Under an arch on the north side of the sanctuary is the effigy of a knight of c.1270-80, tentatively identified as Sir William de Domer but also possibly a member of the Vagg family. Higher Oakley Farm in the north of the parish has been identified with the Domesday manor of Oakley ('Achelai').

★ *Church.*

CHILTON CANTELO (J) This small village, 'the young nobleman's settlement', lies at the end of a short cul-de-sac beside the River Yeo north from Yeovil and east of Ilchester. Held initially as part of Barwick, it was owned by William de Cantilupe by 1201 and retained by a branch of that family until the death of John de Cantilupe or Cantelo in 1350, who had a manor-house, dovecot and watermill here. The manor was acquired in the 18th century by the Goodford family from Yeovil who built Chilton Cantelo House (now occupied by a private school) here in 1834 and altered the village's road system. Dr Charles Old Goodford, a second son of the family, rose to be headmaster and provost of Eton College, which he managed to serve during his time as rector of Chilton, 1848-84. It was he who was responsible for rebuilding the church of St James in 1865, although the original Perpendicular west tower with its panelled arch survived the process. The rebuilding revealed medieval wall paintings depicting the Annunciation, death, burial and resurrection of the Virgin Mary: possibly from the same hand as those which survive at Sutton Bingham. Note the gravestone of Theophilus Brome (died 1670), who hailed from Warwickshire but had relatives living at Chilton. Collinson in 1791 claimed that Brome requested his head to be severed after death but before burial and preserved in the farmhouse, Higher Farm, opposite the church. There the so-called screaming skull has remained ever since, stored in a small cupboard. 'Horrid noises, portentive of sad displeasure', have been heard whenever attempts were made to remove or bury it.

★★ *Village.*

Chilton Priory, Chilton Polden

CHILTON POLDEN (E) A blue-lias stone village on the north side of the Polden Hill ridge. The first element of its name, unlike the two other Somerset Chiltons, means 'the settlement on the limestone hill', to which has been added the name of the hills on which it lies, Polden meaning 'the hill near Pouholt'. Pouholt (possibly Celtic for 'cattle pasture') was the name of the Polden estate given to Glastonbury Abbey by King Ethelheard of the West Saxons in 729. The church of St Edward, formerly a chapelry to nearby Moorlinch, was entirely rebuilt in 1889, although several monuments were saved from the old building.

The parish's past is dominated by an eccentric antiquarian, William Stradling, who in the 1830s built a curious folly beside the A 39 and dubbed it Chilton Priory: now a private house. Stradling used the place as a private museum to house a bizarre collection of local and classical antiquities, ranging from a dirk worn at Trafalgar, an iron hook used to hang Monmouth rebels at Bridgwater, to the bedpost of the last abbot of Glastonbury. The building itself features a church-like tower, crypt and oratory, and in it Stradling incorporated architectural fragments from about a dozen Somerset churches. Among later occupiers of the house was Mrs Katherine Maltwood, 'discoverer' of the Glastonbury Zodiac, and her husband John, who devised the oxo cube.

★★ *Setting.*

CHILTON TRINITY (D/E) A village immediately to the north of Bridgwater: 'the young nobleman's settlement' with the dedication of the parish church added. The

The Rock Inn, Waterrow (Chipstable)

church occupied part of a Domesday manor called Pignes, evidently a low-lying farm or hamlet towards the River Parrett which was later abandoned. The outwardly Perpendicular church of the Holy Trinity has an inner round arch to the south doorway which has led Brian and Moira Gittos to conclude that the lower side walls of the nave and chancel belong to the 12th century. Access to the Jacobean pulpit is via the former rood-screen stair. A touching epitaph to 39-year-old John Grabham (died 1785) has him addressing his parents and opining cheerfully:

'In Heaven, where there is no pain,
I hope to see you both again.'

A Chilton revel was held on Trinity Monday in the 17th century.

CHIPSTABLE (D) The parish drops away from the Brendons to the western bank of the River Tone, its name meaning 'cippa's post'. The manor was held by Muchelney

Abbey from the Norman Conquest until the dissolution of 1538, passing thereafter to the Bluets of Greenham in Stawley, whose descendants largely split up and sold it in the 1680s. With the exception of the west tower, the church of All Saints was rebuilt in 1869 to the designs of Benjamin Ferrey. Also in the 19th century the village of **Waterrow** developed from hamlets called East and West Skirdle in a delightful valley setting beside the Tone. The Rock Inn at Waterrow had opened by 1851 on the site of a former smithy.

★★ *Setting of Waterrow.*

CHISELBOROUGH (J) lies south-west from Ham Hill, and most of the village was built from the stone quarried there: its name meaning 'gravel hill' ('Ceoselber-gon' in 1086). After the Norman Conquest it was granted to the count of Mortain, whose tenant, Alured or Alfred 'the butler' made it the focus of his barony of Chiselborough and from whom it descended through the families of Montacute, Audeham, St Clare, Chideock, Stafford and Strangways. The last sold it to John Wadham whose heirs divided the manor between them in the 17th century. These included the Fox-Strangways earls of Ilchester, who bought out the Earl of Egremont in 1857 and eventually sold off their estate in 1914, their title recalled in Ilchester Hall, built as the village school in 1870. The model Manor Farm built by the earls to the north of the village in 1861. The church of SS Peter and Paul lies at the western edge of the village at the end of a short lane from the Cat's Head Inn (dating from late 16th century). It is dominated by

an Early English central tower, topped by a splendid Perpendicular spire. Inside, the tower was supported by four rather low Gothic arches until 1911 when stones of a Norman arch, found in the walls of the tower, were somewhat incongruously re-erected in place of the fourth arch towards the nave. The chancel is 17th century, largely partitioned off to provide a vestry and church room, and the nave was rebuilt very plainly in 1842 with large light windows. At the east end of the village was the Fair Place where an October fair was held by 1529 until 1894 and led to the Punky Night tradition (*see* **Hinton St George**). Strap Farmhouse bears the date 1576.

CHURCHSTANTON (H) Until 1896 this large Blackdown parish lay in Devon but the whim of a Local Government Board Order transferred it to Somerset, paradoxically leaving it within the diocese of Exeter. Its name, 'Cheristontone' in the 13th century, has nothing to do with its church but means 'the stony settlement where cherries grow'. The manor was held by the Tudenham family by 1282, later passing in turn to the Damarels, Bonvilles and the Duke of Suffolk. Subsequently it was bought by William Clifton of London and was thereafter held for two centuries by the Pophams. There is no village of Churchstanton and the church of SS Peter and Paul is isolated from any substantial settlement. The rendered west tower may date from c.1300, judging by the worn carvings over the west door. The rest is Perpendicular with an unusually elaborate arcade to the south aisle.

Churchstanton church

Churchinford (Churchstanton)

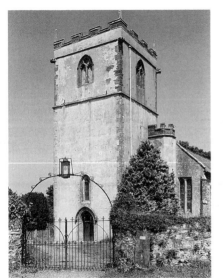

The west gallery is made up of 16th century benchends, presumably replaced in 1830 by the present box pews, and was reputedly added to accommodate silk workers from the hamlet of Stapley in the parish. Under the tower lie the three-seater stocks and a finely-carved parish bier, dated 1623. A tablet on the west wall commemorates Corp James Doble of the Coldstream Guards who 'gloriously fell' in 1854 in the Battle of Inkermann during the Crimean War, while defeating 'a vastly superior Russian force'. North-east from the church rise the aerials of Culmhead Radio Station, a major Government listening base. Nearby are **Widcombe Tropical Bird Gardens** (fee:lists): 10 acres of parkland full of azaleas and rhododendrons around a lake alive with water birds, including flamingos. There is a walled garden housing a wide variety of tropical birds, together with pets for the children, restaurant and tea gardens.

The principal village in the parish, centred on the York Inn, is **Churchinford** ('Suthchurchamford' in 1386), 'the church settlement at the ford': presumably a ford across the River Otter. A significant medieval fair was held here on St Paul's day, recalled in the name of Fairhouse Farm.

★★★ *Widcombe Bird Gardens*, ★★ *setting.*

CLATWORTHY (D) This 'homestead where burdock grows' lies on the southern side of the ridge of the Brendon Hills, north-west from Wiveliscombe. Its wooded hillsides and isolated farms are scattered around the meeting of six valleys, carrying the streams which used to form the headwaters of the River Tone. Since 1960 a lofty dam has penned back these streams to form **Clatworthy Reservoir**, holding 1,180 million gallons. There is a large carpark and viewing area commanding prospects across the water to the surrounding hills. A scenic walk encircles the lake and there are facilities for fishing and sailing.

A triangular Iron-Age enclosure known as Clatworthy Castle was sited on the wooded slopes east of the reservoir, and there are round barrows in the north of the parish. The village, comprising only a few houses, lies on the hillside south-east of the reservoir and above the Tone. By the Norman Conquest the area was divided between two manors, one probably centred on the village, the other on the former farmstead of Syndercombe, drowned when the reservoir was built and

whose name suggests early iron smelting there. Clatworthy manor was bought in 1582 by the Carew family from whom it descended with the manor of Crowcombe until largely sold off in the present century. The plain whitewashed church of St Mary Magdalene probably dates from the 12th century, as does the simple font. The farms were mostly recorded in the Middle Ages, Sedgeborough, forming an outlying grange of Forde Abbey, Dorset, by c.1300. Raleigh's Cross Inn on the northern boundary has been the site of an annual sheep and cattle fair in August or September for nearly a century. The inn is named after the remains of a medieval cross which probably marked the bounds of Nettlecombe manor.

★★★ *Reservoir and setting.*

CLEEVE ABBEY (D), *see* **OLD CLEEVE**

CLOFORD (F) A rural village south-west from Frome which straddles the Nunney brook, on which no doubt lay the 'burdock ford' which named it. The manor was held from the 16th century, by a branch of the Horners of Mells and it was the Horners who in 1633 built the tall Cloford House which stands out from the backdrop of hills and quarry when viewed from the churchyard of St Mary across the valley. The church, long held by Keynsham abbey, is sited at the end of a fine avenue of yews. It has a Perpendicular west tower but the nave was rebuilt in 1856 and the chancel in 1869. Two monuments survive to those Horners who lived here: Maurice (died 1621) and Sir George (died 1676), the latter bearing two threequarter-length effigies. South-east from the village, Postlebury Wood conceals earthworks now thought to

ABOVE *Figures on Closworth church tower* LEFT *Raleigh's Cross, Clatworthy*

be Saxon and to the west, towards East Cranmore, are the remains of Merehead Camp, a triangular Iron Age hilltop encampment with a double bank.

CLOSWORTH (J) This small exposed hill-top village, south of Yeovil, sits on the border with Dorset, its name meaning 'homestead (above) the valley' ('Clovesuurda', 1086), although the first element might be a personal name. The village comprises the church, 17th century rectory, two farms, and a few cottages, although there were 20 houses here in 1781. At Domesday the manor was granted to Robert, Count of Mortain, whose son gave it to his newly-founded priory at Montacute c.1102. After the Dissolution the estate was bought in 1560 by the Portmans of Orchard Portman who retained it into the present century. Thomas Purdue, last of a well-known dynasty of bellfounders, was casting bells in the rectory orchard 1663-97 and died here in 1710, interred under the epitaph:

'Here a bellfounder, honest and true,
Until the Resurrection lies Purdue.'

The Perpendicular church of All Saints, over-restored in 1875, has a fine west tower bearing intriguing reliefs of kneeling figures which may commemorate those who paid to build it. A 15th century missal, formerly used at the church, survives in the Bodleian Library, Oxford.

COLEFORD (F) To the west of Frome, the name of this substantial Mendip village indicates that it was coalmining which led to its foundation. Coal was worked here from medieval times and continued until the closure of the last pit at Newbury, north-east of the village, in 1927. Newbury House is a 17th century mansion, much remodelled in the 19th. It was occupied by the Moore family until in 1760 their heiress married into the Paget family (later baronets of East Cranmore). A May revel here in 1633 ended in violence. There was a chapel of the Blessed Virgin Mary at Coleford by 1488, mentioned in 1551, but probably demolished soon after. The place was part of Kilmersdon parish and its Gothic church of Holy Trinity, consecrated in 1831, became a parish church only in 1843. Much of the housing dates from the 19th and 20th centuries but there are attractive narrow winding streets below the church. At the west end of the village an acqueduct survives, built to carry the Somerset and Dorset Canal, a project abandoned c.1800.

COMBE FLOREY (D) A small village (*cwm* – 'valley') built in the warm red local sandstone to the west of the A 358 Taunton to Minehead road, near Bishops Lydeard. At the time of Domesday the manor clearly formed part of the bishop of Winchester's great estate of Taunton Deane. It was held in the early 12th century by Baldwin of Combe, who had been succeeded before 1166 by Hugh de Fleuri or Flory, whose surname was added to that of the parish. The estate descended c.1400 to the Frainceis family. Their 'auncient built mancion house' (so described,1664) was approached through a fine gatehouse, dated 1593, which survives at the eastern edge of the village. Thomas Frainceis replaced the old manor-house c.1665 (refronted 1730)

further up the hillside with the present Combe Florey House, clearly visible from the Minehead road. John Frainceis Gwyn sold the property in 1799 and, after a succession of owners, it was bought in 1956 by the celebrated novelist, Evelyn Waugh (died 1966) and is now occupied by his acerbic journalist son, Auberon Waugh. The church of SS Peter and Paul, west from the gatehouse, has a north aisle which housed at its east end from c.1313 the chantry chapel of the Virgin Mary. It features monuments to lords of the manor: the effigies of Sir John de Meriet (died 1327) and his two wives, Mary (died 1300) and Elizabeth (died 1344); brasses to Florence wife of John Frainceis (died 1485) and Nicholas Frainceis (died 1526), and (in the wall near the effigies) a heart shrine to Maud de Meriet, a Cannington nun. The rest of the building, including the west tower, is late 15th century, except for the chancel which was rebuilt c.1850. The east window commemorates the celebrated wit, the Rev Sydney Smith (rector 1828-45), who entertained many of the eminent men of his time at the rectory at the west end of the village but who died and was buried in London. There are attractive former farmhouses, again in red sandstone, on the main road and, north of the village near the railway bridge, the Farmer's Arms: a one-time cider house, immaculately rebuilt after a recent fire, complete with thatch.
★★ *Village and church.*

COMBE ST NICHOLAS (J) An extensive parish with former tithings of Clayhanger, Wadeford, Ham and Betham: its village

lying in a hollow (the 'combe' which names it) to the north-west of Chard. Bronze Age remains were excavated at Combe Beacon in 1935 and a Roman villa with mosaic floors was discovered at Wadeford in 1810. Soon after the Conquest the manor was given to the bishop of Wells and in 1234 Bishop Jocelin used it to endow the office of Cathedral provost and to generate the salaries (£6 13s 4d each) of 15 prebendaries at Wells. In consequence the name Combe features more prominently than any other on the backs of the seats in Wells Chapter House. Later the estate was transferred to the dean of Wells. The village has a 19th century feel to it, much extended in recent years but still centred on the village green and the church of St Nicholas. The church, in the absence of stained glass, has a pleasantly light and airy atmosphere. There is a fragment of a Norman doorway in the north aisle arcade but the church was reconsecrated in 1239, probably after a rebuilding. To the 13th century belongs the base of the west tower and parts of the chancel, but the rest is largely 15th century. The Bonners of Weston (formerly Waterleston) Farm are remembered by a tablet on the north wall, including Henry Bonner (died 1680) who, as a Commonwealth magistrate, married a host of couples from miles around. There is a small parish museum in the south-west corner of the church, including fossils, photographs and Combe Friendly Society staff heads.
★★ *Church.*

COMBE SYDENHAM (D), *see* **STOGUMBER**

Sir John de Meriet and his wives, Combe Florey church

Combe St Nicholas church

Compton Bishop

COMBWICH (D) A former harbour and ferry station sited by a creek on the western bank of the mouth of the river Parrett: somewhat swamped by modern development. The older area has a cheerful waterfront and its name, pronounced 'Cum-mitch', probably indicates former 'salt-works in the valley'. There was a significant Romano-British port here, the crossing to Pawlett was in use in Saxon times (with a ferry from the 13th to 19th centuries) and the place comprised two farming estates in 1086. Thereafter a successful port developed again, trading particularly with Ireland, importing a range of goods which were conveyed up the Parrett to Bridgwater and Langport in small vessels and, by 1832 until the 1930s, exporting bricks and tiles manufactured in the village. The 16th century alchemist, Thomas Charnock (*see* **Otterhampton**) had a laboratory here. Of several early inns, the Anchor, dating from c.1690, with its 18th century fives wall, and the Old Ship Inn, formerly the Passage Boat, mentioned in 1702, survive. Until the 1880s the village lay largely within Cannington parish and a chapel of St Leonard here was served from Cannington Priory by 1336 until 1549. The present aggressively-Victorian church of St Peter dates only from 1868.

★★ *Waterfront (at high tide !), old village centre.*

COMPTON BISHOP (A) This most appropriately named 'settlement in a valley' lies in a cleft in the Mendips below Crook Peak (called Ridges Tor in 1068 and used as a beacon site in the 1580s) to the west of Axbridge. It is reached by turning off the A38 through the cheerful little hamlet of

Cross: until the 1840s of considerable importance as a coach stop for changing horses on the main road between Bristol and Exeter. The New Inn and the White Hart remain of several that once operated here, now bypassed by the straightening of the main road. The estate of Compton was owned by the bishops of Winchester until 904 when it was surrendered to King Edward the Elder and subsequently settled on the 'community' at Cheddar. It is believed that King Canute gave the manor to Duduc, bishop of Wells 1033-60, who settled it on Wells Cathedral. Although the manor was repossessed by King Harold, it was restored to Wells by William the Conqueror in 1068 and was held by the bishops until forcibly surrendered to the Crown in 1548. Later it was held by the Prowse family and their heirs, the Mordaunt baronets. The church of St Andrew is beautifully situated at the northern end of the small village with magnificent views over the Levels below. It was used to endow a Cathedral prebend in the 12th century. It has a Perpendicular west tower but the rest of the building is largely 13th and 14th century, although heavily restored in 1852 and 1883. There is a fine trefoil-headed doorway to the south porch, a good south doorway, early double piscina with small aumbry cupboard. The Norman tub font has a cover dated 1617 and the stone pulpit is Perpendicular. The Prowses were remembered in an elaborate monument put up in 1751 by their descendant, Thomas Prowse of Axbridge: their former house, the 17th century Manor Farm, being sited beside the lane south from the church.

The bishops had established by 1179 a

small port called Radclive ('red cliff'), now known as Rackley, at the junction of the Rivers Yeo and Axe. There in 1189 they founded a borough with a market. This attempt to start a new town failed although there are references to the port up to 1390 and today there are only a few farms and cottages in Rackley Lane, with the possible remains of wharves. In a commanding position overlooking the M 5 is the Webbington Hotel and Leisure Club, converted and extended from Webbington House, built in 1908 by Herman Alexander Tiarks.

★★★ *Scenery.*

COMPTON DUNDON (E) A most delightfully situated parish, wonderful walking country, set in a landscape of wooded hills to the south of Street and bisected by the B 3151. Indeed it was a favourite walking haunt of Field Marshall Smuts, whose daughter had married into the Clarks of Street. Turn off west up Ham Lane to reach the oldest settlement, draped around the hill of Dundon ('valley by the hill'), from which it took its name. The hill is topped by a substantial Iron Age fort at the southern end of which is the site of an early beacon. To the east of the main road runs Compton ('the valley settlement') Street which seems to be a planned secondary settlement. At a central crossroads there are the remains of a medieval cross and it seems possible that the development might be associated with the grant of a Thursday market and a three-day fair in 1289: the fair continuing until the First World War. At the north-east end of the street is Trays Farm with a 14th century wing. From the street there are repeated

Compton Pauncefoot

views of the Hood Monument (*see* **But-leigh**). The manor may have been the 5 hides of land at 'Cumtun' given to Glastonbury abbey by Cynewulf, king of the West Saxons, in 762 and the abbey was certainly overlord here in 1086 when it was held by Roger de Courcelles with the adjoining estate of Walton. Latterly it formed part of the extensive estate of the Fox-Strangways family, earls of Ilchester. The church of St Andrew, a prebend of Wells Cathedral, possibly by gift of the Beauchamp family, stands at Dundon. It is largely Perpendicular but has an early 14th century chancel. The little pulpit, dated 1628, is enchantingly slotted over the upper rood stair opening although preachers must have to be short and agile to get up there. Don't miss the framed map of the parish at the west end by Denis Keef. In the south of the parish, Littleton was a Domesday manor and the site of at least one Roman villa of c.200 AD, to which was added a bath block with a good mosaic in the early 4th century. It was excavated by Richard Hasell (died 1819) of Littleton House, one of the earliest methodical archaeologists in Somerset, although much of the credit for his work was repeatedly stolen by Sir Richard Colt Hoare of Stourhead. Hasell also reported signs at Littleton of a Roman village or another villa, although these have never been traced.

★★★ *Scenery, walking.*

COMPTON PAUNCEFOOT (F) This 'valley settlement' is an all but perfect village with immaculately clipped hedges, south of the A 303 east of Sparkford. A prehistoric triangular enclosure, Sigwells Camp, has been almost ploughed out in the

south of the parish and flint tools have been found there. Excavations for a reservoir on Hicknoll Slait in 1966 revealed four graves with a Saxon spearhead and 7th century shield boss. The manor was held by the Pauncefoot family (the surname is a Norman nickname meaning 'round belly') from the 12th to 16th centuries. Their descendants, the Keynes family, formed a small Roman Catholic enclave here in the early 17th century, from whom sprung three prominent Jesuits. The present complexion of the parish is due to the descendants of John Hunt, who acquired the estate c.1630. To the southeast of the village John Hubert Hunt, soon before his death in 1830, built a mock Gothic house, Compton Castle, turretted and castellated, looking out over an ornamental lake. The building was occupied by Sir Alexander Hood, Bart, in 1835 and in the present century by the 1st Baron Blackford of Compton Pauncefoot (died 1947), a successful barrister, and his successors. The church of St Andrew stands at the north-western end of the village beside a three-cornered village green, the lovely Georgian rectory (featured in the TV version of Jane Austen's *Mansfield Park*) and the 18th century Manor House. The church has a Perpendicular west tower, topped with a stone spire, recently restored. In his will Sir Walter Pauncefoot (died 1485) contributed £20 towards rebuilding the church and adding a south aisle, where he founded a chantry dedicated to St Catherine (unfinished in 1523). Part of an inscription to his daughter, Anne Whiting (died 1535), and an heraldic frieze (recording Pauncefoot marriages) survive

at the east end of the aisle. There is a profusion of monuments to the Hunt family.

★★★★ *Village,* ★★ *church.*

CORFE (H) Below the Blackdown ridge and south of Taunton, this tidy well-kept village lines both sides of the road up to the hills. It has a peaceful air, apart from the noise of through traffic, and many attractive farms and cottages, such as the thatched Brook Farm at the south-east end of the village. Its means 'a cutting' and probably refers to the deep cleft cut away by the brook in the upper reaches of the parish. Corfe formerly looked towards Pitminster, of which its church was a chapelry, and like Pitminster formed a tithing within the bishop of Winchester's manor of Taunton Deane. In the mid 12th century the bishop granted to Taunton Priory an estate which straddled the Corfe and Pitminster boundary and became known as Barton Grange. After the dissolution of the priory, it was granted in 1543 to wealthy lawyer Humphrey Colles. Colles built a substantial mansion cut by the parish boundary, although his family chose to be buried at Pitminster, as did their successors, the Coventrys. On the death of Francis Coventry in 1686, the estate passed to his sister, Ultra Trajectina, wife of Sir Lacon Child. Exotic names continued at Corfe when in 1692 the couple sold out to Smart Goodenough (died 1721), from whom were descended his successors, the Earle, Newton and Spurway families. Francis Milner Newton (1720-94) was first secretary of the Royal Academy and apparently brought Gainsborough to Corfe. The former's

ABOVE *Norman font, Corfe church*
RIGHT *Cossington*

great-nephew, Francis Wheat Newton (1814-95) of Barton, was a pioneer in electrical engineering at Taunton. Most of Barton Grange was demolished in 1931 and the surviving wing is now flats.

The church of St Nicholas in the centre of the village was largely rebuilt in neo-Norman style in 1842 by Benjamin Ferrey with the addition of a tower and aisle in 1858 by C.E. Giles. There are monuments to the Newtons and the fine Norman font is preserved from the earlier building. There can be few churchyards which possess such an idyllic outlook across the valley to the woods. Of its ministers, the Rev Alexander Ainslie chaired the meeting which established Somerset County Cricket Club in 1875 and the Rev Thomas Crump was one of the prime movers in forming the Taunton and Pickeridge Golf Club in the east of the parish in 1892.

★★★ *Village and setting.*

CORTON DENHAM (K) An attractive village, appropriately named 'the settlement in a cutting' ('Corfetone', 1086), which lies between Corton Hill and Corton Ridge, south-east of Sparkford. The latter part of the name refers to the Dinant (later Dynham) family, who held the manor here by the 12th century until 1509, from whom it descended to the Arundels and then passed c.1600 to the Portmans of Orchard Portman. The church of St Andrew in the centre of the village was rebuilt 1869-70 to the designs of Charles Baker Green, Viscount Portman giving a cemetery and mortuary chapel here in 1910. North from the village is the hamlet of Whitcombe, held with Corton by the Crown in 1086, but later by the prominent Gilbert family, of whom William Gilbert was abbot of Bruton from 1495. An urn of Roman coins was dug up here in 1723.

★ *Village.*

COSSINGTON (E) Turn off the A 39 on the Polden Hills at the thatched single-storey Moon Cottage, formerly toll house to the Bridgwater Turnpike Trust, to find this tree-clad village, 'the settlement of Cusa's people'. The manor was held from Saxon times by Glastonbury Abbey and by the Brent family from 1254 until 1692. One of its trees, an elm which allegedly sheltered the Duke of Monmouth after Sedgemoor and later a preaching John Wesley, no longer stands: its stump reverently preserved in concrete. The church of St Mary dates from the 13th century but was thoroughly restored in 1900. Its treasure, now hidden beneath a blue fitted carpet, is a brass depicting the lord of the manor, John Brent, and his wife. Brent died in 1524, leaving to his cousin his 'ambling horse' called Symon. Later brasses commemorate members of the Graham family of Cossington House. Cossington Grange is a massive Victorian pile to the east of the village.

★★ *Village, setting.*

COTHELSTONE (D) One of those special places: good to look across and to look from, as well as to look at. Sited at the south-western end of the Quantocks, it clings to the hillside above Bishops Lydeard, although there is no village as such: only the old manor-house, church, farm and a few cottages. Its name means 'Cuthwulf's settlement' and the land was evidently included within the Domesday manor of Taunton. By the mid 12th century Taunton's overlord, the bishop of Winchester, had granted the manor to the de Stawell family (also known for a time as 'de Coveston' – 'of Cothelstone') and with the Stawells it remained for over six centuries. The visitor can walk from the archway up the drive towards the gatehouse of the red-sandstone manor-

house (not open to the public). A positive riot of balusters greets the eye, ornamenting every detail of the property, although their date is a puzzle. Around the side of the house to the left is a range of cottages which features a 14th century arch and may represent the medieval house. The remainder is probably of the earlier 16th century, although much was reconstructed after the Civil War and Commonwealth, and in 1855. Higher up the slope is St Agnes Well which once supplied the house with water. A fair was held in the park here in May 1758.

The church of St Thomas of Canterbury (St John the Baptist in 1499) is attractively sited behind the house; it dates mainly from the 15th century but was over-restored 1863-4. Its chief interest lies in the memorials to lords of the manor and their heraldry. Sir Matthew de Stawell (died 1379) lies in effigy with his feet on a lion, those of his wife, Eleanor, daughter of Sir Richard Merton, are supported by twin squirrels. In a corner of the south chapel are the ornate alabaster figures of Sir John Stawell (died 1603) and his second wife, Frances Dyer, having been granted an earlier divorce from his first, Mary Portman, on the grounds of her adultery. In the chancel are tablets to his son, Sir John (died 1604), and grandson, a further Sir John Stawell. The last had a truly tragic life as a result of the Civil War. Present at the first Somerset skirmish at Marshalls Elm (*see* **Street**), he fought for his king right through to the surrender of Exeter and then, wrongfully tried for treason and murder, was imprisoned in the Tower of London from 1650. The manor-house was severely damaged and was still being demolished and stripped of its lead as late as 1659, twelve men being employed daily on the destruction. Worn out, Sir John died in 1662 at his other Somerset mansion at

Low Ham (*see* **High Ham**). His elaborate funeral procession back to Cothelstone included his 23 bailiffs and 8 clergymen. His eldest son was deranged, his second had already died abroad, his third was childless and it was the fourth, Ralph, who eventually reaped the overdue reward for his father's loyalty, when he became Baron Stawell of Somerton in 1683. Lord Stawell is chiefly remembered for openly criticising the severity of the Bloody Assizes after the Battle of Sedgemoor, whereupon Judge Jeffreys ordered two rebels to be executed at Cothelstone. Ironically, one of them, former Roundhead Richard Bovet, had persecuted the Stawells during the Commonwealth but there is no contemporary evidence for hangings from the archway, as often stated. Thereafter the Stawells never lived at Cothelstone although they did not sell it until 1789. A year later it passed to the Esdaile family of London bankers, whose representatives still occupy it. Ianthe (died 1876), wife of E.J. Esdaile, was daughter of the poet Shelley and lies in the little churchyard. In 1818 on the site of the 18th century Terhill House, former home of the Slocombe family, the Esdailes built Cothelstone House, a large mansion demolished only in recent years. Its ornamental ponds survive, as does a lodge beside the lane down to Bishops Lydeard. An 18th century folly tower formerly topped Cothelstone Hill, to which there is an easy walk with magnificent views from a carpark near Buncombe.

★★★★ *Landscape, manor-house, walking,* ★★★ *church for its memorials and heraldry.*

COXLEY (E), *see* **WELLS**

CRANMORE (F), *see* **EAST CRANMORE, WEST CRANMORE**

Creech St Michael

CREECH ST MICHAEL (D) The parish ('Crice' in 1086, – 'hill') probably takes its name from the nearby Creechbarrow Hill (in West Monkton), recorded as 'Crycbeorh' in 682, although the place was recorded as 'Muchel Creech' ('great Creech') in the Middle Ages, only later adopting the church's dedication. The village has expanded considerably in recent years: homes for those who work in Taunton to the west. The manor, held in 1066 by the sister of King Harold, was seized by William the Conqueror and subsequently granted c.1100 by William, Count of Mortain, to the priory he founded at Montacute, which held it until its dissolution. The monks obtained a Tuesday market and a three-day fair here in 1269 but no evidence of their continuation has been found. Another Domesday manor lay at Adsborough east of the A38 in the extreme north of the parish, now a hamlet with three 16th century farmhouses. The River Tone runs through the parish, partnered by the Bridgwater to Taunton Canal, completed in 1827.

The church of St Michael, at the southern edge of the village was appropriated by Montacute Priory in 1336 although its vicarage was not ordained until 1362. The chancel and nave are 13th century, the west tower and north chapel slightly later, the south chapel c.1300, and the rest 15th century. A fine heraldic tomb in the north aisle marks the grave of Robert Cuff (died 1593). The Cuffs were lords of the manor, as were the Keyts, with their 18th century memorials in the sanctuary, and the Cuffs rebuilt and lived at Court Barton, dating from the 16th century and extended in the 18th, to the east of the church. The Cely family occupied the 17th century L-shaped Charlton Manor, east of the village, and

are commemorated in the south chapel with their arms in plaster on the ceiling. Initialled stones set in the churchyard wall identify landowners who maintained sections of the wall in return for common grazing. The eccentric Henry Cresswell, vicar 1813-51, indulged in cudgel fighting and playwrighting, and was suspended in 1844 for bankruptcy and violence. The parish has a long nonconformist tradition. Quakers were meeting here by 1674 and John Wesley preached four times at Charlton 1754-70. To the north of the village lies the hamlet of **Creech Heathfield**, named after common pasture enclosed in 1814, and including the 17th century Crown Inn. Creech Paper Mills, west of the village, were opened in 1875 and long dominated the economy of the parish, finally closing in 1982.

★★★ *Church.*

CREWKERNE (J) A friendly busy market town, large agricultural parish and former meeting place of a hundred on the southern boundary of the county, described in 1633 as 'reasonable large and indifferent well built'. It is a place of attractive stone houses and former industrial buildings which line streets converging on the medieval marketplace. Its name means 'the house by (or beneath) the hill', possibly referring to Bincombe Hill to the north-east. It was held by the kings of the West Saxons and first mentioned in the will of King Alfred (died 899), passing before the Conquest to Edith 'Swan's neck', mistress of King Harold II. Seized by William the Conqueror, it was granted to the Reviers, earls of Devon, descending to the Courtenays, who retained the manor with brief interruptions until the death of Edward Courtenay, Earl of Devon, in 1556. The estate was divided into quarters between his (mainly Cornish) heirs, although the Pouletts of Hinton St George became the most influential family here until their lands were largely sold off in 1810-11. The earls of Devon seem to have had a castle here at Croft in the north-west of the parish, mentioned in the early 13th century.

There was a Saxon mint here in the early 11th century, a market (later held on Saturdays) by 1086 and a fair from the 1270s, the last still taking over the centre of the town early in September each year. Despite this urban tradition, no borough was ever formally established and the place was governed by manorial and parish officers, *ad hoc* meetings of the townsmen and by the trustees of the grammar school, until a Board of Health was set up in 1854 and an Urban District Council in 1894. Although there was cloth manufacture here in the Middle Ages, the town relied principally on the trade generated at its market and income from travellers passing through on the main road between London and Exeter: travellers who included Catherine of Aragon in 1501, Parliamentary and royalist soldiery during the Civil War, and William of Orange on his way to assume the throne in 1688. They were served by a number of inns, the George, on the south side of the market-place being recorded by 1541. Thomas Hutchins, Crewkerne's postmaster in the 1620s, organized the first profitable postal system between London and Plymouth. At least 44 parishioners were implicated in the Monmouth Rebellion of 1685 and ten rebels were executed here. During the 18th century the production of webbing, sailcloth and hair-seating expanded and the first of several factories was opened in 1789 at Viney Street on the south side of the town. Others followed, the largest at Tail Mill in the north of the parish, acquired by sailcloth maker, Richard Hayward of West Chinnock, c.1825, and operated by his family until 1929. Shirt-making factories were added in Abbey Street (1875) and North Street (1880), and the industry also continued into the present century.

The Ham-stone church of St Bartholomew stands to the west of the market-place and in origin was a Saxon minster, probably founded by a king of the West Saxons, with dependent chapels at Wayford, Misterton, Eastham (in Crewkerne parish) and Seaborough (moved to Dorset in 1895). William the Conqueror gave the church to St Stephen's Abbey, Caen, but it had returned to the lords of the manor by the early 13th century. Soon after, the rectory (uniquely for Somerset) was divided into three portions, headed by a rector, deacon and subdeacon, an arrangement which continued until after the Reformation. Later it was served by curates until it became a vicarage in 1868. The present grand building is almost wholly Perpendicular, although part of a late 13th century arch is set in the south transept's east wall and the arches supporting the central tower may be early 15th century. The two turrets above the west front could be the work of William Smyth, c.1475-90, and the general richness of the work may reflect the wealth of the royal chaplains who served the rectories in the late 15th and early 16th century. The north transept was associated with the

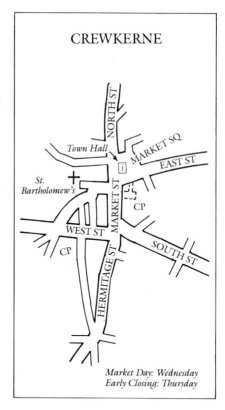

CREWKERNE

Town Hall

St. Bartholomew's

NORTH ST

MARKET SQ

EAST ST

MARKET ST

CP

WEST ST

CP

HERMITAGE ST

SOUTH ST

Market Day: Wednesday
Early Closing: Thursday

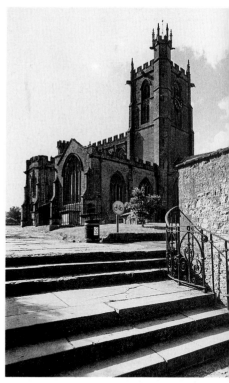

Crewkerne church

Merifield family of Woolminstone, lords of Hewish manor 1557-1752, who from 1608 lived at Merifield House in East Street. There are no fewer than seven memorial brasses: the oldest to Thomas Golde (died 1525) of Seaborough. Another commemorates Henry Trat (died 1679), headmaster of the grammar school, with a fulsome Latin tribute from his former pupil, Samuel Hill, vicar of Meare. In the south porch is an informative monument to Rear-Admiral Joseph Symes (died 1856), chronicling his colourful naval career from Trafalgar onwards. There was an anchoress (female hermit) called Odolina immured here in the late 12th century and her successors occupied a cell at the west end of the church until at least 1523. There was also a nearby hermitage by 1402 (when it was occupied by a monk from Forde Abbey, Dorset), evidently dedicated to St Edmund. A chantry of Our Lady was founded in the churchyard in 1309 by Agnes de Monceaux, then life tenant of the manor. The parish developed a strong puritan tradition in the 1580s, which led a number of families to emigrate to New England in the 1630s: the most notable being the Rev John Warham, Joseph and George Hull, William Phelps, William Gaylard and John Bartoll. To the north of the church stands the Church Hall, built in 1636 to house the former

grammar school (founded by John Combe in 1499), succeeded by Wadham Comprehensive School in 1972. Among those educated there was Nelson's captain, Sir Thomas Hardy. The Abbey, a large house put up north-west of the church by John Hussey in 1846, succeeded the surviving rectory house. The Old Almshouses in West Street were founded by 1631 with money left in the will of Matthew Chubb. They stand almost opposite the New Almshouses, established under the will of Mary Davis, dated 1707. There is a small local museum (fee:lists) in Church Street. Ralph Reader (1903-82), supremo of the Boy Scout Gang Shows, was born in the town.

To the east of the town, Eastham ('east homestead' – now **Higher Easthams**) became a separate manor from Crewkerne at the time of the Norman Conquest, held from 1803 by the Hoskyns family of North Perrott. The farmhouse, 'new built' in 1694, was used as a smallpox inoculation centre 1768-9. There was a chapel here in 1223, served by its own rectors, although the building was in ruins by 1548. Rectors of Eastham continued to be appointed, however, until the 19th century. There was also a chapel of St Reyne at the eastern end of the Windwhistle ridge by the late 13th century, which had probably been demolished by the Reformation. In the south-west of the parish the estate of

ABOVE *Crewkerne*

BELOW *Cricket Court, Cricket Malherbie*

Clapton ('farmstead near a hill') was settled by the late 12th century. There was a mill here by 1228, the precursor of the present Clapton Mill, built c.1875 and one of the few in the county still operating commercially. **Clapton Court** is a square classical block of the 18th and 19th centuries, but incorporating a long 17th century range. The attractive gardens (fee:lists) are open to the public, there is a cafe and an extensive range of plants, particularly fuschias and pelargoniums, are for sale. At Clapton in 1738 Richard Elswood murdered his uncle for having an affair with Elswood's wife. South of the town, **Henley Manor**, partly late-medieval but remodelled c.1700, was settled by 1222, owned by the Pouletts of Hinton St George, 1700-1911, and by ICI since 1946.

★★★ *Church, Clapton Court gardens,*
★★ *town.*

CRICKET MALHERBIE (J) A small parish of only 503 acres south-east from Ilminster and on the northern slope of the Windwhistle ridge, whose name, 'Cruchet' in 1086, means 'little hill'. Indeed in 1871 it had only 19 inhabitants. It is a beautiful treed landscape with fine views to the north. After the Norman Conquest the estate here was granted to the Count of Mortain, under whom it was held by Drogo (Drew) de Montagu or Montacute. The Montagues in turn bestowed the manor by the early 13th century on the Malherbie family, who gave their name as a suffix to the place and held it until 1280. Subsequent owners included the lords Dinham from the early 15th century

and the Pitt family from the 17th until the 20th centuries. The old manor-house, on a different site, was succeeded c.1820 by the present Cricket Court, built for Admiral Pitt reputedly to his own plans. It is a highly individual design with a heavy Tuscan porch. Recent occupiers have included the writer and historian, Count Nikolai Tolstoy. The small church of St Mary Magdalene with a slight tower and spire was rebuilt in 1855 (architect, J.M. Allen) and contains several monuments to the Pitt family.

★★ *Setting.*

CRICKET ST THOMAS (J) Below the majestic beeches of the appropriately-named Windwhistle ridge, the parish lies to the east of Chard, the parkland falling away to the Purtington Brook in the valley. The place was originally christened 'Cruche', an old Celtic word for 'hill', but later borrowed the form 'Cricket', 'little hill', from Cricket Malherbie, to which was added the dedication of its own church. Today the parish is almost wholly occupied by the extensive **Cricket St Thomas Wild-Life Park** (fee:lists), created by the Taylor family since 1967. It features a wide variety of animals and birds, both caged and free-range, including the Australian Black Swans, the park's emblem and first breeding success. There are gardens, restaurants, adventure playgrounds, a miniature railway, and the National Heavy Horse Centre, where Shires, Suffolk Punches, Percherons and Clydesdales can be admired.

From the 12th century the place was

probably best known for its chapel of St Wite (or Candida), just below the ridge, destroyed in 1740 after being struck by lightning 'and a man killed that stood by it'. The saint gave her name to White Down where a celebrated Whitsun livestock fair was held from 1361. In its day it attracted custom from far afield but eventually declined to become a sports day featuring wrestling and cudgel-playing before it ended c.1900.

The brook powered up to nine mills here, including fulling and edge-tool mills, one miller being killed when his millwheel fell on him in 1635. Fragments of the Elizabethan manor-house were probably used to build the Admiral's Seat, a summer-house of 1797 on the hillside. The present Cricket House (built 1786-1807), lying at the heart of the wild-life park but not open to the public, was designed by Sir John Soane after the estate was bought by the naval hero, Admiral Alexander Hood (later Baron Bridport), in 1775. Hood's great-nephew, the 2nd Baron, swept away the small village by the brook-side, formed a

succession of picturesque artificial lakes (now home to Patagonia Sea Lions) in the valley and in 1834 closed almost all the parish roads to public use. He also rebuilt the small flint-faced parish church of St Thomas, its predecessor on the same site having been fashionable for clandestine weddings during the earlier 18th century. It is dominated by elaborate monuments to members of the Hood family, including William, Earl Nelson (died 1835), brother of Admiral Lord Nelson and father-in-law of the second Baron Bridport. Among later owners of the estate from 1898 was F.J. Fry (died 1918), the chocolate manufacturer. The house was featured as 'Grantleigh Manor' in a popular TV series, *To the Manor Born*, starring Penelope Keith and Peter Bowles.

★★★ *Wild-life park and setting.*

CROSCOMBE (F) A lovely village which lies in the valley of the Doulting Water (River Sheppey) on the winding A 371, midway between Wells and Shepton Mallet, its name (from *corfweges cumb*) meaning 'the valley of the pass way'. To the north, partly in Dinder, is Maesbury Camp, a double-banked Iron-Age hill fort. At Croscombe there was early a flourishing cloth industry, particularly in the 16th and 17th centuries. It initially formed part of the royal West Saxon estate of Pilton when granted in 705 by King Ine to Glastonbury Abbey. Held under Glastonbury by Roger de Courcelles in 1086, it eventually descended through the Palton and Pomeroy families, and in 1562 to their descendants, the Fortescues of Filleigh in Devon. This last family held the estate until Hugh Fortescue, Baron, later Earl Clinton, split up and sold it in the mid 18th century. The former Palton manor-house of c.1400, or at least a part of it, survives to the north of the church: long used as a Baptist chapel but restored by the Landmark Trust in the 1970s. There are two

ABOVE *Cricket House, Cricket St Thomas*
RIGHT *Timber carving in (top) Croscombe church and (bottom) Crowcombe church*

other early houses, one at the east end of the village puzzlingly bears the initials of Abbot John Selwood of Glastonbury, the other south-west from the church on the main street. An early 'sit-in' by the inhabitants preserved the village cross from destruction by the waywardens in the 1870s. A Tuesday market and three-day Lady Day fair here were granted to John de Palton in 1343 and renewed by Sir William Palton in 1438.

The magnificent church of the Virgin Mary stands in Church Street to the north of the village centre. The nave with clerestory was built c.1420-40 (there is a roof boss with the arms of Palton) and the south chapel was added by Sir William Palton for his own burial, where in 1459 his executors endowed a chantry with two chaplains. There were also seven local guilds here, for the young men, maidens, webbers, fullers, hogglers (labourers), archers and wives. At local celebrations the archers were represented by the characters of Robin Hood and often Little John. The two-storey Treasury was added in the south-west corner and the clergy vestry at the north-east end c.1507-12 by John Carter of Exeter. The west tower is probably 14th century (dated from the tower arch) with a fan vault and spire added in the 15th (the spire was rebuilt after being struck by lightning in 1936). The glory of Croscombe is the church's Jacobean woodwork: a lofty pinnacled rood screen almost filling the chancel arch, with the royal and Fortescue arms, a high painted pulpit with heavy tester, dated 1616 and bearing the arms of Bishop Lake, side screens, chancel stalls, readers desks and high box pews (some early 16th century). Most of this was evidently provided by the Fortescues whose arms appear again on a panel high

LEFT *Crowcombe church.* ABOVE *Crowcombe Court*

up on the north chancel wall. The effect of being almost encapsulated by the dark wood is quite breathtaking. In the south aisle are brasses to James Bisse (died 1606) and his son William (died 1625), depicting their respective families, both wealthy clothiers. The north aisle has a lengthy inscription to the Parsons family, including Mary Parsons who died in the 'deadly cholera' epidemic here in 1838.

★★★★ *Church,* ★★ *village.*

CROWCOMBE (D) Nestling below the western slopes of the Quantock Hills, this village's name is self-evident: 'the valley of the crows'. The parish's landscape is one of scattered farms on medieval sites with delicious names such as Roebuck, Flaxpool, Quarkhill and Wharncliffe (formerly 'Wormeclyve'). The Doniford Brook which marks Crowcombe's western boundary once drove mills at Trowbridge and Leigh, where in 1803 the miller promised to bake 120 loaves a day should Napoleon invade. The manor, held by Wimond of Crowcombe in the early 12th century, has never been sold since that time, descending by marriage through the families of Biccombe, Carew, Trollope (related to the novelist, Anthony Trollope) and Trollope-Bellew, its present lords. The village is strung out along what was the former main road from Taunton to Minehead until bypassed in 1929. The original settlement was probably around the church at the southern end of the village, once known as Church Town. In 1227 Godfrey of Crowcombe established a weekly market and annual fair, planting a new borough, evidently represented by the northern part of the village beyond the Carew Arms. This economic experiment failed, although the

14th century market cross survives on a small triangle of roadside green. Godfrey also granted part of his estate to Studley Priory, Oxfordshire, which became the separate manor of Crowcombe Studley. With the grant went the appointment of rectors to the parish church of the Holy Ghost. This fine church, mainly built of Quantock red sandstone, bespeaks local wealth. The 14th century tower was once topped by an 80 ft spire until struck by a thunderbolt in 1725 and the tip of the spire can still be seen in the east of the churchyard. The rest of the church is mainly early 16th century with a fine south aisle and fan-vaulted porch. A superb set of benchends, including naked men fighting a dragon, a green man and a mermaid, bears the date 1534 and the octagonal carved font is of the same period. The pleasingly-simple screen, rails, altar and pulpit of 1729 replaced those destroyed by the thunderbolt. The north chapel of 1655, serving as a pew for the lords of the manor with its own private entrance, boasts an accumulation of 18th and 19th century Carew and Bernard hatchments sufficient to delight any lover of heraldry. An elegant wrought-iron chandelier by James Horrobin has graced the nave since 1974. The curious will appreciate monuments to seven domestic servants of the lords on the external wall of the north chapel. A 14th century churchyard cross possibly depicts a prioress of Studley, a bishop and St John the Baptist.

Across the road from the church stands the church house (lists), built in or soon after 1515, and which frequently hosts art and craft exhibitions. Most Somerset parishes once possessed such a building, used by the churchwardens to brew beer

and bake bread for annual revels known as Church Ales, which raised funds to repair the church fabric for the forthcoming year. Such jollifications were outlawed in the early 17th century and, in Crowcombe's case, the building became first a poorhouse and then a school, returning to parish use in 1908. The separate entrances to brewery and bakery are still preserved on the ground floor. At the northern end is the enclosure which formerly served as the manor pound. From the green in front of the church look up the drive to Crowcombe Court. It replaced a former manor-house sited beside the church and was built between 1724 and 1739 by Thomas Carew: an early use of brick for a major Somerset house. The original design was by Thomas Parker, a Devonshire joiner, but he was sacked and was later found to have stolen bags of silver coins found behind the panelling of the old house, eventually declared in the manor court to be Treasure Trove. The Wincanton architect, Nathaniel Ireson, was brought in to complete the work. The seven-bay three-storeyed facade features substantial Corinthian pilasters with a pediment above, although the massive scale of the house with its two stable wings and north range is not apparent from this viewpoint. Behind the house runs a (private) combe with cascades, a ruined folly and rustic bridge (dated 1776). In 1798 Dorothy Wordsworth was scathing about these attempts to improve on nature but still considered the valley 'romantic and beautiful', as indeed it is. The builder of the Court also planted the woods on the hill above the village. The main house is now operated as a nursing home. The village inn was known as the Three Lions

LEFT *Cucklington.* ABOVE *Culbone church*

from the early 17th century and later as the Carew Arms (the Carews bearing three black lions on their arms) from 1814. The southern wing became a market house when Thomas Carew tried vainly to revive the market in 1764. Another futile project was the sinking of a coal mine here in 1753. The three Monmouth rebels stated to have been executed at Stogumber in 1685 are traditionally claimed to have been hanged at Heddon Oak, a former landmark in this parish, only recently felled.

On Crowcombe's southern boundary, the hamlet of **Triscombe**, below a major Quantock quarry, is a noted venue for cream teas at Triscombe Stables. A thatched inn here, the Blue Ball, a favourite with walkers, takes its sign from the whortleberries found in profusion on the neighbouring hills.

★★★★ *Church and church house,*
★★★ *village.*

CUCKLINGTON (F) The 'settlement of Cucola's people' lies on the eastern border of the county to the east of Wincanton. The manor was held with that of Stoke Trister and passed with it to the Phelips family of Montacute. A weekly market and fair here, both of short duration, were granted to Henry de Lorty in 1304. The church of St Lawrence, at the end of a short lane, commands magnificent views to the west. Its south tower was evidently damaged in the great storm of 1703 and restored, as recorded in an inscription, when a perky little cupola was added to house the bell for the clock. The church dates from the 13th century but the roof was replaced and the building much restored 1873-80. There are monuments in St Barbara's south chapel to the Watts family of Shanks House, a substantial 17th and

18th century building to the south of the village, and to their heirs, the Daltons. To the south, Shanks House is a 17th century building, remodelled and extended in Georgian style. It was home to Viscount Weymouth in 1838 and to Sir Arthur Sutton, Bart., in 1931. The living was held by younger members of the Phelips family in the late 18th and 19th centuries and they were responsible for rebuilding the rectory in 1814. St Barbara was also the saint of a spring a little down the hill from the church, known as Babwell.

★★★ *Views.*

CUDWORTH (J) From the Roman Foss Way running across Windwhistle Hill, north-east from Chard, the parish drops steeply and then more gradually away. 'Cutha's homestead' probably stood on a moated site south of the church in the western of two hamlets. Another hamlet to the east at Higher Weare Green is thought to represent a second Domesday estate called Worth. Earthworks and abandoned house platforms illustrate the drop in population which now stands at barely a third of its level in the early 19th century. The manor was held by Alan de Furneaux c.1187 when he gave the church and some 30 acres to Wells Cathedral to found Cudworth prebend. The Speke family had the lordship by 1431 until 1791, when it was bought by the Pouletts of Hinton St George. The little church of St Michael comprises chancel, nave and north aisle. The north doorway and a low round-headed east window both date from the 12th century. Unless they have been reset, these may indicate that the north aisle is the original church. The nave and chancel were probably added in the late 13th century, with later modifications in the 14th and 15th, including the rebuilding of

the west wall. There is a large early 13th century font with dog-tooth and cable carving. The Old Prebendal House, near the church, was rebuilt c.1636, and for a short time provided lodging for the curates, although they generally lived elsewhere. The Windwhistle Inn on the Foss Way was mentioned in 1782 and may represent an earlier (1769) Black Horse Inn.

★★ *Church and setting.*

CULBONE (C) An Exmoor coastal parish west from Porlock, set in a sylvan landscape with wonderful clifftop walks, steep rocky clefts and sea views. Its old name was Kitnor, meaning 'the hill slope of the kites', but subsequently adopted its present title, considered to be derived from the church's early dedication to St Coulban or St Columbanus. I cannot accept the more recent opinion that it comes from a supposed Celtic *Kil Beun* – 'the church of St Bueno'. The manor passed in 1513 to the Sedborough family and then to their cousins, the Frys, whose heiress brought it to John, Lord King. His brother was ancestor of the earls of Lovelace who in the 19th century created the romantic wooded coastline of Culbone. The church, of uncertain dedication, could well be pre-Conquest in origin, possibly founded as the remote cell of a holy man. With a total length of 35 ft, a nave 12 ft 4 in wide, chancel 10 ft wide, and the pre-Reformation pews seating about 40 shoulder-to-shoulder, it has been hailed as the smallest complete parish church in England and no convincing counter-claims have come forward. The picturesque spirelet, jokingly supposed to have come from the top of Porlock's spire, was set up in the early 19th century. The porch is 13th century, the nave windows and roof were added c.1500 and the chancel re-roofed and east wall

rebuilt in a general restoration of 1888. There is a small screen of c.1400 and a Norman font. Not far from the church lay the farmhouse where under the influence of opium Coleridge penned *Kubla Khan* in 1797. The site where the intrusive 'person from Porlock' broke in upon the poet's reverie is usually identified with Ash Farm but is now thought to have been the long-demolished Withycombe Farm. A Dark Age stone inscribed with a cross in a circle stands at the end of a signed footpath from a carpark just off the A 39, opposite the Culbone Inn. Nearby to the north-east a curved stone row of some 20 stones (of which the inscribed stone may once have been one) leads through thick undergrowth to a bowl barrow.

★★★ *Scenery and walking,* ★★ *church.*

CURLAND (H) To the south-east of Taunton, the name of this small parish ('Curiland' in 1252) means 'land belonging to Curry'. The manor was long held with that of Staple Fitzpaine and, although a priest was appointed here in 1263 by the de Briwes family of Staple, the church was adjudged to be a chapelry of Curry Mallet in 1327, which may perhaps explain the parish's name. The present church of All Saints was rebuilt in 1856 to the designs of Benjamin Ferrey but closed in 1970.

CURRY MALLET (J) A scattered village on the north-western side of the Fivehead river, bearing a Celtic stream name and that of its Norman lords, and composed of three hamlets: Higher, Lower and Silver streets. The last appears to be modern and the first two, the manor-house in one and the church in the other, may well represent the two Domesday estates granted to the Courcelles family. The Mallets, one of the few families which can be proved to have

fought for the Conqueror at the Battle of Hastings, had acquired the manor by the early 12th century and it became the seat of their barony. After the death of William Mallet c.1216, it was inherited by his son-in-law Hugh Pointz, whose descendant Nicholas sold it in 1356 to the childless Sir Matthew Gournay. Gournay's widow carried it to her second husband, John, Lord Tiptoft (died 1443), after which the estate passed to the king and became, as it has remained ever since, part of the Duchy of Cornwall.

The manor-house, beside a possible former green at Higher Street, has been claimed as the home of the influential Pyne family of Curry Mallet, although in the early 17th century it was vacant, having been formerly occupied by John Poulett. It comprises a cruck-roofed hall of c.1500 and a small irregular house of c.1600, with original twisted chimneys, linked by a later wing, but much remodelled and extended c.1939 by Clough Williams-Ellis. The church of St James stands at the south-eastern end of Lower Street. It is mainly Perpendicular although the three-bay north aisle arcade dates from the 14th century. The elaborate upper part of the tower screen is 17th century, depicting the Crucifixion and the Nativity, with the Pyne coat of arms (not Mallet as in Pevsner). On top of a plain tomb in the north aisle, supposed to accommodate an early Mallet with a crippled leg, is an incongruously-placed medieval effigy. The later memorials are a delight. In the south chapel John Pyne (died 1609) and his wife kneel facing each other on a monument put up on the eve of the Civil War, as instructed by their son, Hugh Pyne of Cathanger (*see* **Fivehead**). In the chancel the half-length figure of rector Ralph Mighill (died 1633) seems to be still preaching and in the north aisle a praying

ABOVE *Curry Mallet manor house*
ABOVE LEFT *Ralph Mighill, Curry Mallet church*

wife and her two babies can be identified (from her coat of arms) as members of the Walsh family, builders of Cathanger. Humbler but just as poignant monuments are nearby in the form of craftsmen's tools fixed to the wall. At the back of the church is the wheeled parish bier (1903) and an old-style plough, used annually on Plough Sunday (Epiphany). In the churchyard a table tomb commemorates John Wimbridge, purveyor to the army in the Peninsular War, who died in 1809 aged 40 from 'the fatigue he suffered in his march through Spain' under Sir John Moore.

★★★ *Church, particularly for its fittings and monuments.*

CURRY RIVEL (EJ) This large village, set in a sizeable parish to the south-west of Langport, lies along and around the road from Taunton (A 378). Its name is a Celtic stream name of uncertain meaning, with the addition of the name of its Norman lords. Evidence of Roman settlement has been found near the village and at Stanchester to the north-east. Before and after the Conquest it was held by the Crown, possibly because it controlled the western side of the strategic crossing of the River Parrett at Langport. There may have been a Saxon fort on Herds Hill above that crossing to mirror the one at Langport Hill. Certainly until 1066 Curry Rivel received ancient dues of sheep, lambs and, in one case, iron from six other manors. By the mid 12th century it had been given to Hugh de Gundeville but this was superceded in 1190 by a new grant to Richard Revel, whose name it still bears. Richard's granddaughter carried it to the Lorty

LEFT *Burton Pynsent monument, Curry Rivel*   ABOVE *Curry Rivel church and village green*

family, the reversion being sold to the earl of Salisbury in 1331. There followed a succession of non-resident lords who, through the Beauforts, returned the manor to the Crown. Lady Margaret Beaufort, mother of Henry VII, visited the manor with her third husband, Henry Stafford, in 1467.

Thereafter the role of resident squire was supplied by the owners of **Burton Pynsent**, an estate on the western approach to the village. Held by the Jennings family in the 17th century, Burton was taken by marriage to Sir William Pynsent (died 1765), an eccentric baronet suspected of incest with his daughter, who left his estate to William Pitt the elder, whose politics he apparently admired. Pitt, later earl of Chatham (died 1778), made Burton his second home and in 1767 set up a lofty column, designed by Capability Brown, to the memory of his benefactor and added a brick extension to the house. After the death of Hester, Pitt's widow, in 1803 the estate was bought by John Pinney of Somerton who demolished the older part of the house, leaving only Pitt's extension which survives today. Heale House, north-west of the village, was built c.1620 by Samuel Powell and was long the home of the Alfords, who gave it a Georgian facade c.1725. Midelney Place, behind an impressive gateway at the north-eastern end of the village, was built by E.B. Cely Trevilian in 1870 with an inheritance from his mother, a wealthy Irish heiress. Herds Hill House, put up near Langport in the late 18th century and now a retirement home, was the last home of celebrated economist Walter Bagehot, who died there in 1877, as did his widow in 1921.

The most evocative area of Curry Rivel village lies up the slope to the north-west of the centre. Attractive thatched cottages are grouped around a village green which may once have stretched as far as the main road. Also beside the green stands the church of St Andrew, mainly Perpendicular, lofty and richly carved. Note the fine vaulted ceilings of the tower and porch. The oldest part is the 13th century north chapel which includes no fewer than six tomb recesses in its north wall. These now house a life-size knight with the Lorty arms on his shield and three smaller civilian effigies, two male and one female: all of c.1280 and presumably commemorating other Lorty individuals. In the floor are slate slabs to members of the Trevilian, Jennings and Powell families. Between the chapel and the chancel stands a major tomb bearing the booted effigies of Marmaduke Jennings (died 1625) and his son Robert (died 1630). Others of the family are depicted and named on the sides of the tomb, including babes who died in infancy. In the south window of the sanctuary are eight panels engraved by Lawrence Whistler in 1987. Above the south door are hatchments of Charles II and Hester, Countess of Chatham (buried with her husband in Westminster Abbey), and a touching memorial put up by the Countess in 1800 to one of her servants. The west tower was rebuilt 1860-1 as a copy of its predecessor, the cost including 98 pints of cider: fuel for the workmen. (*See also* **Hambridge**. *For Langport Westover see* **Langport**)

★★★ *Church, setting.*

CUTCOMBE (C) A large Exmoor parish to the south-west of Dunster, whose inhabitants formerly lived a hard, harsh existence. 'Cuda's valley', granted after the Conquest to William de Mohun of Dunster, was subsequently divided into two principal estates, known from their owners as Cutcombe Mohun and Cutcombe Ralegh. mIn 1443 Simon Ralegh's widow gave Cutcombe Ralegh to found a chantry chapel in her home church of Nettlecombe, but both manors later passed into the hands of the Pyms of Brymore in Cannington and to their descendants, the Hales and Pleydell-Bouverie families. In such an extensive area there were other early estates: Stowey ('Estaweit' in 1086), Wheddon ('Watesden' in 1201), Hawkington, Oaktrow and Kersham ('Cristeham' in 1234). Of these, Oaktrow has a late 15th century farmhouse, extended later but maybe an open-hall house. Codsend, on the upper reaches of the River Quarme, may recall the same Saxon settler who named the parish, but others like to think it represents 'God's end': a last point of civilization before venturing north-westwards onto the bleakness of the moor. For here is Dunkery Beacon, at 1,707 ft the highest point on Exmoor, where early remains of stone hearths mark the former sites of beacons used in an elaborate signalling system designed to warn of invasion. This is marvellous walking country with extensive views out over the Bristol Channel and the surrounding bleak landscape, punctuated with cairns, burial barrows and lush afforested valleys. The church of St John, whose churchyard looks out over the Brendon Hills to the south-east, was held by Bruton Priory. An adjacent green was used for playing bowls in 1633. The present building was restored in 1862 when the south aisle, south chapel and porch were added. It has a 13th century west tower and a north aisle added not much later. The Pleydell-Bouveries are lavishly commemorated: one, Henry Hales, described uncompromisingly as 'squire of this parish' in 1926. The Rev John Myers King was vicar here for 55 years until his death in 1887. His blind daughter Alice was a writer of romantic novels and a recorder of the folklore of this isolated region. Cutcombe Sheep Fair in early autumn is one of the great economic and social events on the Exmoor calendar. To the south-east **Wheddon Cross** is a modern hamlet which has mushroomed around what has been described as 'surely well up in the list for the worst cross-roads in England'. The inn sign of 'the Rest and be Thankful' must have been a welcome sight for many a thirsty traveller.

★★★ *Scenery and wallking.*

DILLINGTON (J), *see* ILMINSTER

DINDER (E) This lovely little village to the east of Wells is set in the valley below and north of the A 371, its name appropriately meaning 'the house in the valley'. The estate formed part of the early, possibly original, endowment of the bishopric of Wells, but by the 12th century had been granted away to William FitzJohn whose descendants were known as 'of Harptree' or 'Fleming'. By 1327 the manor was held by Richard de Rodney and retained by his family until sold in the mid 17th century to Richard Hickes. The Hickes heiress brought it to her husband, George Somerville (died 1776), whose son, Rev William Somerville (died 1803), built the present Dinder House, a substantial Georgian block of 1801-3. On the death of William's widow in 1830, the estate passed to his nephew, James Somerville Fownes, who took the surname of Somerville, saving the name from extinction at Dinder, a service the Fownes family had previously performed for the Luttrells of Dunster. The Somervilles continued here until the death of Admiral of the Fleet, Sir James Somerville (1882-1949). The village lies on the River Sheppey, picturesquely lined by the main street. One private house still bears the sign of the former Dragon and Wheel inn (derived from the Somerville crest, although that featured a wyvern). The Perpendicular church of St Michael is tucked behind Dinder House, although a Norman dragon-head carving, set above a south chancel window, evidently survives from a much earlier building. Initially a chapelry of Wells, although the advowson was illegally usurped by William FitzJohn, it became a prebend of Wells Cathedral in 1268 and subsequently a peculiar of the dean of Wells. The chancel was rebuilt in 1872, there is an ornate pulpit of 1621, an abundance of Somerville memorials (several high up under the tower) and an 1899 brass to John Johnes (died 1605), whose son Richard was an early emigrant to the American Massachusetts Bay Colony in 1635. Former rectors included Dr Richard Jenkyns, 1825-45, master of Balliol College, Oxford, and dean of Wells, who in 1827 built the small rectory, where he spent his academic vacations, and Francis West, 1962-71, bishop of Taunton.

★★ *Village.*

DINNINGTON (J) The 'settlement of Dynne's people' is sited between Crewkerne and Ilminster, to the north of Hinton Park, and was crossed by the Roman Foss Way. The manor was held in 1086 by Siward the falconer, passing in the 15th century to the Pouletts of Hinton St George. The most influential local family, however, were the Brices who occupied the manor-house, near the church on the site of Pondhays Farm, from 1571 to 1771 and suffered for siding with the royalists during the Civil War. The small church of St Nicholas dates from the 14th and 15th centuries but was radically restored in 1863. Initially a chapelry to Seavington St Michael, it was held with the living of Hinton St George from 1771.

DITCHEAT (F) A large parish to the north-west of Castle Cary which is bounded by the River Brue and the Foss Way, the name meaning 'dyke gate'. The dyke is thought to be a bank which marks the northern boundary and was a former trackway from the Foss to the Roman temple on Lamyatt Beacon. A Roman villa site was discovered c.1820 on the north bank of the Brue, occupied c.250-350 AD. The manor was granted in 842 by King Ethelwulf to Eanwulf, ealdorman of Wessex, and Eanwulf had passed it to Glastonbury Abbey by 855. The abbey obtained a Thursday market and a fair here in 1332 although neither survived into recent times. After the dissolution the manor was sold in 1546 to Sir Ralph Hopton whose great-nephew, Lord Hopton, died in 1652 leaving his four sisters as heirs. Edmond Dawe bought the estate c.1669 and his family lived here into the present century at the Manor House, a long two-storeyed 17th century house north of the church. The fine church of St Mary Magdalene dates from c.1300 (chancel and lower stages of the crossing tower) but was remodelled by the dean of Wells, John Gunthorpe (died 1498), rector here 1466-98. He added a clerestory to the chancel (his arms and those of Bishop Stillington and John Selwood, abbot of Glastonbury adorn the parapet), and built the body of the church with its arcades, western embattled front and south porch.

St Christopher in Ditcheat church

On the north wall is a massive painting of St Christopher, discovered under plaster in 1931 but unfortunately largely repainted. There is an attractive Jacobean pulpit and reading desk to match, an early 13th century effigy of a priest, the top of a churchyard cross sitting sadly in the south transept piscina, and a fine timber achievement of the arms of 'that worthy gentleman', Ralph Hopton, of 1610. The Leir family were rectors continuously here from 1699 to 1917. Gunthorpe was also responsible for the rectory house (lately called the Abbey, now the Priory), the oldest parts of which date from c.1475, although extended in the 19th century. William Kingston (1765-1831) was born here without arms or shoulders but managed to lift heavy weights with his teeth, perform most tasks using his feet and father 12 children by two wives. In 1584 at Ditcheat the unfortunate Margaret Cooper was claimed in a popular pamphlet to have been bewitched and tormented by the phantom of a headless bear which rolled her round her house like a football.

Alhampton, 'settlement on the Aln' stream, now the Alham, a hamlet to the south of the village, was held in 1086 by Ralph Tortesmains under Glastonbury. It generally passed with the manor but was later acquired by the Leir rectors. There is a vineyard at **Wraxall**, a hamlet west of the village and cut by the Foss Way.

★★ *Church and village.*

Arthur and Alfred

For all the wealth of words expended to link King Arthur with Somerset, there is no historical evidence whatsoever. Although the hillfort of Cadbury Castle was indeed refortified in the Dark Ages, it can never have been Camelot: a place which was an invention of the mid 12th century writer, Chretian de Troyes, and identified with Winchester by Sir Thomas Malory c.1470. It was Leland writing in 1542 who first asserted that Cadbury was Arthur's mythical capital. Popular imagination took up Arthur's presence in the West only after the monks of Glastonbury claimed to have found the twin burial of Arthur and Guinevere c.1191: an exhumation clearly designed to popularise their abbey after its destruction by fire in 1184.

Their alleged discovery inspired the development of a rich medieval folklore which included such tales as Guinevere's being spirited away to Glastonbury Tor by Melwas, King of the Summer Land, and only released after appeals by St Gildas, or the attack by Ider son of Nuth, one of Arthur's companions, on three giants who lived at Brent Knoll – 'the Mount of Frogs'. The only historical records with any pretence to antiquity are two Welsh annals which link Arthur with the battles of Mount Badon and Camlann, and a list of twelve battles enumerated by the chronicler Nennius some three centuries after they were supposed to have occurred. None of the early records refers to Arthur as a king (Nennius calls him *dux bellorum* – 'leader of battles') and none of the battle sites can be confidently identified with locations in Somerset, although some writers assign Mount Badon to Bath.

There is no such doubt of the presence of King Alfred in the county. Born at Wantage (Berks) in 849, he was the fourth son of his father, Ethelwulf, king of the West Saxons 839-58. It seems unlikely that Alfred was ever expected to become king, but he succeeded to the throne on the death of his third brother Ethelred in 871. His life had already been committed to resisting the continual raids of the Vikings and the early years of his reign were filled with a succession of bloody engagements, culminating in a surprise Christmas attack on Alfred at Chippenham. Forced into headlong retreat, the king sought refuge in 878 with a few followers on the Isle of Athelney (*see* **Lyng**), where an earlier royal West Saxon, St Aethelwin, probably had a hermitage. There he built himself a fortress and, if the stories are to be believed, took shelter with the wife of a swineherd and suffered her lashing tongue when he let her cakes burn. Another tale told how Alfred fed a disguised St Cuthbert, who in gratitude appeared to him in a vision, advising him how to defeat the Danes, while a third described his visit to the Viking camp as a minstrel to learn his enemy's secrets.

In May 878 he rode out from Athelney and, meeting up with the men of Somerset, Wiltshire and some from Hampshire at Egbert's Stone, he defeated the Danish king, Guthrum, at Edington (Wilts), pursuing his foes to the gates of Chippenham. He took hostages from them and their promises to leave his kingdom and to convert to Christianity. Three weeks later Guthrum and 30 of his leading warriors were baptized at Aller, conducted thence to Wedmore and, possibly, to the royal palace at Cheddar. Celebrations were followed by the withdrawal of the Danes to Cirencester and finally to East Anglia, where they settled.

In gratitude for his own and England's deliverance,

Cross from Arthur's 'grave', Glastonbury Abbey

King Alfred

Alfred founded an abbey at Athelney and nearby built a second fort at Lyng. This was one in a network of forts which he established throughout southern England to protect it from invasion, the record of which was compiled in the reign of his son and known as the Burghal Hidage. By this document each fort was assigned a number of hides of land which corresponded to the number of men required to patrol the defensive wall on the basis of four men to each 5½ yds of wall. Of the Somerset forts, Watchet needed 513 men, Axbridge 400, Lyng 100, Langport 600 and Bath 1,000. Of his estates in Somerset, Alfred (died 899) bequeathed in his will to his son Edward, Carhampton, Kilton, Burnham, Wedmore, Chewton and Cannington, asking the 'community' at Cheddar to choose Edward as his successor, while to his son Ethelweard were given lands at Yeovil and Crewkerne.

Centuries later, in 1693, a gold jewel enclosing an enamelled figure, probably representing Christ, and seen through a piece of rock crystal, was found at Petherton Park in North Petherton, only four miles from Athelney. It was inscribed in the Mercian dialect 'AELFRED MEC HEHT GEWYRCAN' – 'Alfred ordered me to be made'. Originally fixed to the end of a thin rod, it was probably made either as an *aestel* (book mark or pointer) or as a symbol of office. Given soon after its discovery to the Ashmolean Museum in Oxford, the

Alfred Jewel is there still: probably the most personal and tangible possession of a Saxon monarch to have come down to us.

DODINGTON (D) This small but intriguing parish lies on the north-eastern slopes of the Quantock Hills, abutting east on Nether Stowey. Indeed this place was also called Stowey ('Stawe') in 1086 but soon after took the name Dodington, 'the settlement of Dodo's people', from Dodo, its Domesday tenant. The Dodingtons of Dodington descend from the 12th century Adam de Cunteville, whose son William adopted the name of his manor. Their most notorious descendant was Cavalier Sir Francis Dodington, infamous during the Civil War for hanging those who surrendered to him and for shooting dead a defenceless priest near Taunton. The manor passed in 1720 to the prominent politician and entertaining diarist, George Bubb, who adopted the name of Dodington and died childless as Baron Melcombe in 1761. Since 1837 it has been part of the Acland, later Acland-Hood, estate. The former family home, Dodington Hall, is a substantial late-medieval open-hall house, extended in 1581 and altered in the 18th century. It adjoins Dodington House, the former rectory, and the small church of All Saints, probably dating from the 12th century. The chancel was rebuilt in the 15th century and the nave remodelled in the 16th. Finally, the south chapel was added as the family pew in 1610. They were fulling cloth here by 1518 and mining copper by 1712. Miners came from Cornwall and Derbyshire to work the seam and activity continued until 1821. Since 1883 the parish has included the oval Iron-Age hillfort of **Dowsborough** ('Dolesbery' in the 17th century), high up on the Quantocks and formerly a detached part of Stringston. The placename Walford's Gibbet identifies Dodington Green where in 1789 charcoal burner John Walford was hanged in chains for the murder of his wife. Before the murder they had been drinking at the Castle of Comfort, an inn mentioned by 1713 which became a coffee tavern in the 1880s, later a guest house and is now a private dwelling. Dodington Rit was a hilarious local revel formerly held on the Sunday before Midsummer to find the first whortleberry.

★★ *Village.*

DONYATT (J) The village, mentioned as early as 725 as 'Duunyete' ('Dunna's gate'), lies along a double bend in the road south from Horton Cross to Chard. Comprising three estates in Saxon times, it had become one by 1086. In the 14th century it was held by the Montagues who built a castle or fortified manor-house and created a park

here, probably in the area of Park Farm to the east of the village. Latterly the manor was held by the Combe family of Earnshill. Donyatt was known from medieval times until the present century for the production of earthenware manufactured from the local clay, particularly at the hamlet of Crock Street (named from the industry) to the south-west of the village (examples exhibited in the County Museum, Taunton Castle). Excavations here in 1970 produced six tons of waste pottery sherds. The 15th century Ham-stone church of St Mary, 'designed with some ambition' according to Pevsner, stands in the centre of the village. Beside it are the six-cell almshouses founded under the will of John Dunster of London (died 1625). On the southern outskirts of the village lies the 17th century Thatcher's Pond, a popular eating-place, formerly Pond Farm.

★★ *Village.*

DOULTING (F) A Mendip village delightfully situated in the valley of the River Sheppey immediately east of Shepton Mallet. Doulting is a Celtic river name (referring to the Sheppey) which might mean 'dirty stream'. It has long been famous for the light-brown limestone quarried near Chelynch to the north of the village, whence came most of the freestone for Wells Cathedral, Glastonbury Abbey, and many local parish churches. In 1381 Doulting's vicar granted an acre here to the Dean and Chapter of Wells for further stone to build the cathedral. Indeed it is the stone lorries, repeatedly ploughing a dusty furrow along the A 361, who disturb the peace of the place. Here St Aldhelm, the apostle of East Somerset, built a small wooden church and in that church he died on 25 May 709. His body was carried back to Malmesbury Abbey for burial, the route marked by stone Saxon crosses erected by Bishop Ecgwine of Worcester to mark wherever the body had rested, known as 'biscepstane' – 'bishop's stones'. At the consecration of the first stone church on the site, which included the stone on which the saint was sitting when he died, a blind woman was alleged to have recovered her sight. Indeed, the early church was probably a Saxon minster with dependent chapels at Stoke St Michael and East and West Cranmore. The present cruciform church, inevitably and appropriately dedicated to St Aldhelm, stands below the road towards the west end of the village, with a holy well dedicated to the same saint beyond it in the grounds of the 18th century vicarage. The manor here had been

ABOVE *Dodington Hall*
BELOW *The barn, Manor Farm, Doulting*

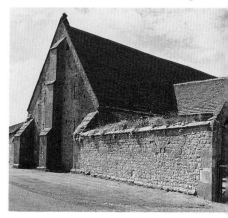

granted to Glastonbury Abbey by Ine, King of the West Saxons 688-726, and in 1266 the church was appropriated to the abbey also. From a distance the church is impressive with a tower of c.1240, surmounted by a lofty 15th century spire, and a nave which may be as early as the 12th century and transepts of the 15th. Inside, however, everything was terribly over-restored in 1869. After the abbey's dissolution in 1539 the manor was granted to the Horners of Mells, later passing to the Pagets of East Cranmore, whose memorials will be found in the south transept. To the south-east of the chancel arch is a small brass to Mary Tucker who died in childbirth in 1656, with a sad but touching verse. At the central crossroads of the village is the Abbey Barn Inn, to the south of which is Manor Farm with its fine medieval barn. The barn is unusual in having two porched entrances on each side. Most authorities date it to the 15th century but recent opinion favours a date as early as the appropriation of 1266. Southwest from the village rises Whitstone Hill on the summit of which survives the Hundred stone, marking the former meeting place of Whitestone hundred court. Beyond this, on the A371 lies the hamlet of **Prestleigh**, a separate manor by the mid 13th century. There in 1637 the five-year-old seventh son of William Gilbert alias Yeaton, 'and noe daughter borne between', was ordered by Charles I's Privy Council to be investigated for being a 'stroker': one who healed by touching the sick. Adjoining Prestleigh is the showground of the Royal Bath and West Show (*see* **Evercreech**).

★★ *Village, its setting and its church.*

DOWLISH WAKE (J) The little Dowlish Brook flows through the centre of this picture-book Ham-stone village and gives it its Celtic name (*du-glais* – 'black stream'). Often formerly called East Dowlish, its present suffix comes from the family of Ralph Wake, lord of the manor in the late 12th century, ancestor in turn of the Kaynes and Speke families, and the Spekes still hold the lordship by descent from their ancestor eight centuries ago. The village lies principally along the main street running south from the area of the church and forking towards its southern end. At the parish's northern limit, near Kingstone village, stands Wake Hill House, built by the Rev Hugh Speke c.1830 when he found the former rectory of c.1500 to be 'a poor mean house'. The latter survives at the end of a lane west of the village. From Wake Hill the lane curves past the 19th century Parke House, named for Jane Parke and her sister who from 1811 sheltered Edmund Baker, who brought the obscure sect of Joanna Southcott to the village. It flourished here until c.1850. Beside the church but behind lofty hedges stands the Manor House of c.1500. Speke Hall, which now serves as the village hall, was built by the churchyard in 1840 to house the village school, closed in 1949. Near the ford over the Dowlish Brook, itself

adjacent to an attractive footbridge, is the Dower House of 1674, leased to women of the Speke family in the 18th century. **Perry's Cider Mill** (lists), to the west of the village centre, has a smoke-blackened cruck roof, a small rural-life museum and welcomes visitors to sample and purchase its cider. In 1851 no less than one third of the inhabitants of the parish were surnamed Perry. East of the village, Mill Farm represents the former manor mill. The mill building is dated 1710 and bears the initials of the miller, Edward Symonds, whose family continued to work the mill until at least 1803. Towards the south end of the village stands the New Inn, recorded as the Horseshoe in 1769, providing welcoming refreshment and excellent food.

The church of St Andrew has an early 13th century chancel and a central three-stage crossing tower. The nave and north aisle were largely rebuilt in an over-zealous restoration of 1860-1, although the 14th century south porch survived. The north chapel is attributed in the inscription on his brass to George Speke (died 1528). Other monuments include the effigies of Isobel Wake (died 1359), who brought the manor to her husband, John Kaynes, and of her great-grandson, another John Kaynes (died 1420), and his wife, whose daughter carried Dowlish to the Spekes. The same chapel houses the monument to James Hanning Speke (died 1864), discoverer of the source of the Nile and a Victorian 'hero'. He was killed in a shooting accident and to his funeral came fellow explorer Dr David Livingstone. The Norman font in the chapel is believed to come from the former

church of **West Dowlish** (demolished by 1575), its site now marked only by its tree-lined graveyard to the west of the village, where occasional open-air services are held. Dowlish Wake was served as rector by the Rev Benjamin Speke who in 1868 caused a national sensation when he disappeared in London, distraught at his family's refusal to allow him to marry his first cousin. Thought at first to have been murdered, he was discovered at Padstow seven weeks later disguised as a bullock drover. He later married his cousin but, following her premature death in 1881, he tragically drowned himself at Wake Hill House the following day.

★★★★ *Village,* ★★★ *church.*

DOWNHEAD (F) A remote Mendip parish at 'the top of the down' ('Dunehevede' in 1196) and midway between Shepton Mallet and Frome, with disused basalt quarries to the west of the village. The manor was given to Glastonbury Abbey by King Ethelwulf (839-58) but by 1066 was held under the abbey by Erneis. This Saxon tenant retained the place after the Conquest and was probably ancestor of Ernisius of Downhead, who had a park here in the early 13th century and whose son Nicholas raised his drawbridge against the sheriff's officers in 1243. From 1303 it was generally owned by absentee lords. The estate was held from the earlier 18th century by the Portmans of Orchard Portman, of whom Henry, 1st Viscount Portman, paid for the restoration of the church in 1882. The church of All Saints, formerly a chapelry to Doulting and sited

Dower house, Dowlish Wake

Speke Monument, Dowlish Wake

Downside Abbey

DRAYCOTT (A) A village on the A 371 south-east from Cheddar, its name meaning 'cottage on a steep hill', which became a separate parish only in 1862. It is best known for its cultivation of strawberries and for the quarrying of a local golden stone, 'Draycott marble', which takes a polished finish. The church of St Peter was built in 1861 to the designs of C.E. Giles. Southwest from the village the 'island' of **Nyland** rises from the Levels, formerly known as Andersey ('Aedred's island') and later as Nyland *cum* Batcombe, an extra-parochial area until 1933 but part of the hundred of Glaston Twelve Hides. It was given to Glastonbury abbey c.670 by Cenwalh, king of the West Saxons, although later grants here by King Edgar (959-75) to Aelfswith and by her to the abbey are also recorded. Batcombe was mentioned as a small property here in 1189. The 'island' was praised in the 14th century by John of Glastonbury for its 'agreeable location' and he recorded a chapel of St Andrew here: possibly the remnant of a small Saxon monastic community.

DRAYTON (J) This small secluded village lies immediately south-east of Curry Rivel, its common name having a complicated meaning: 'the settlement near a slope for dragging loads' or 'where sledges or drays were used'. The manor was held by Muchelney Abbey before the Norman Conquest and retained by its monks until 1538. Most of the buildings in the village date from the 17th century or later, although Duck Cottage is a medieval hall house. The church of St Catherine in the middle of the village is largely 15th century with an unusually large gilded weathercock on the tower. The north aisle, its west window of c.1350, is devoted to memorials of the Trevilians: their heraldry asserting an unproven claim to be descended from the Trevelyans of Nettlecombe. In the churchyard is a fine 15th century cross, restored in the 17th century and topped with a ball finial.

Within the parish the monks also held the manor of Midelney (pronounced 'Midny' – 'the middle island'), isolated on the Levels to the south of the village. There in the late 16th century the Trevilian family built **Midelney Manor** (fee:lists), an attractive if plain Elizabethan house, traditionally put up to be occupied separately by two brothers, Ralph and Thomas. On the death of John Trevilian in 1747, the manor was inherited by his daughter and her husband, William Cely, and their descendants,

beside Manor Farm, has a Perpendicular west tower with prominent gargoyles and there is a Norman font, but the nave, chancel and porch were rebuilt in 1751. The view from the churchyard across rolling fields is marred only by the industrial workings in the valley below, graced by a little Gothic school room at its gates. Northwest of the church is Tadhill ('toad hill'), a medieval settlement formerly held under Whitnell manor in Emborough.

DOWNSIDE ABBEY (B) In 1814 a group of Benedictine monks and their pupils left Acton Burnell in Shropshire and travelled by coach, canal barge, and finally on foot to the 21-acre estate of Mount Pleasant, formerly Downside House of c.1700, in Chilcompton parish, but immediately west of the village of Stratton-on-the-Fosse. Here they re-established the Community of St Gregory the Great, founded at Douai in Flanders in 1605 by English and Welsh monks in exile to educate the sons of English Catholic families: now a well-known Catholic Public School. Persecution during the French Revolution, which led to the sacking of their monastery, persuaded them to come to England in 1794. On arrival at Downside they occupied what became known as the Old House (now encapsulated in the abbey complex) and from 1820 progressively added wings, ranges and quadrangles, including the Old

Chapel in 1823 and eventually the abbey church or basilica, the only part regularly open to visitors. To the west the rising grounds have been most attractively terraced and landscaped. The basilica of St Gregory is, without question, the most magnificent 19th or 20th century building in Somerset. The north transept was consecrated in 1882 and the superb 166 ft south tower, a landmark for miles around, was finally completed in 1938. Like a medieval cathedral, which it much resembles, it was the product of a succession of architects. The original plan, drawn up in 1872, was by Archibald Dunn and Edward Hanson and this was followed in respect of the transepts, crossing and most of the side chapels. The chancel and sanctuary of 1901-5 were by Thomas Garner, and the nave (1925) and tower by Sir Giles Gilbert Scott. The interior features a wealth of fine furnishing and artwork from the medieval to the modern, with memorials to, and relics of, many prominent English Catholics and members of the Community. The most striking is the shrine of St Oliver Plunkett, Archbishop of Armagh, martyred at Tyburn in 1681 and preserved for 250 years at Lamspring in Hanover. Visitors should turn west off the A 367 through Stratton-on-the-Fosse near the War Memorial. There is limited parking in the vicinity of the Abbey bookshop and bindery.

★★★★ *Downside Abbey Church.*

the Cely Trevilians, have held it ever since. There is a long succession of family portraits from the late 17th century and the place has a friendly lived-in feel to it. Behind the house are attractive walled gardens and a rare 18th century falconer's mews in brick.

★★★ *Midelney Manor*, ★★ *village, church.*

DULVERTON (C) A delightful small Exmoor town and extensive parish lying up the slope east of the River Barle: here spanned by the medieval Barle Bridge. This may have been preceded by a shallow crossing which named the place, 'the settlement by the hidden ford' (from Saxon *diegel* – 'concealed'). It is unspoilt, largely uncommercialised and with several attractive small shops, eating places and inns, although the majority of the buildings appear to date only from the 19th century. The place lay within the royal forest of Exmoor, the 13th century forest courts mentioning woodwards serving woods called Hawkwell, Tolchet (now Cawkett) and Dulverton here. It has also been a major centre for hunting since at least 1365, when Sir Robert Corun was prosecuted for killing a royal stag here while out hunting foxes, and it was from here in 1855 that Mordaunt Fenwick Bisset, tenant of Pixton Park, refounded the fortunes of the Devon and Somerset Staghounds.

Early settlement is represented by Iron Age hillforts: the triangular Mounsey Castle (probably named for the medieval Monceaux family) and the oval Oldberry Castle. With Exmoor Dulverton probably formed part of the estate of the West Saxon kings and was held by Harold II, killed at the Battle of Hastings. Indeed it was regarded as a hundred with its own hundred court until eventually allotted to the hundred of Williton and Freemanors. Seized by the Conqueror, the manor was granted by Henry I to the Turberville family, through whom it descended to Hawisia (died 1330), wife in turn of Thomas de Pyne, William of Luxborough and Nicholas de Bonville. William obtained

ABOVE LEFT *Midelney Manor, Drayton.* ABOVE *Dulverton.* BELOW *Exmoor House, Dulverton*

a grant of a market and fair here in 1306 and Nicholas gave his share of the manor to Taunton Priory in 1340. The church here had been granted to the monks by Richard de Turberville in the 12th century and they received the remainder of the manor from William Montagu, Earl of Salisbury, in 1337. The prior of Taunton obtained two further fairs here in 1488 and the priory continued to hold the estate until its dissolution. In 1538 they appointed John Cars as their bailiff here, granting him 10 cartloads of fuel and a robe in the prior's livery. A new grant of a Saturday market and two fairs was made in 1556 (when the place was called a borough, although 'in great ruin and decay') and a year later the manor was given to William and Elizabeth Babington, passing in 1568 to John Sydenham of Combe (in Brushford). The manor was largely dispersed in 1818, but the Sydenhams continued as lords until they sold out to the Earl of Carnarvon in 1858.

Although Dulverton's status as a

borough is dubious, the place probably developed an urban complexion in the 14th century with a dependence on the woollen industry. It is thought that the town began around a large market place below and in front of the church, which was gradually encroached on by narrow crowded streets. There was later a row of butchers' shambles (mentioned in 1539) in Fore Street, a butter cross and a brick market house, believed to date from 1760. The last was converted into the Town Hall in 1866 and given its picturesque external double stairs in 1927. Hostelries include the Lamb Hotel (formerly the Ram) in Bridge Street and the Lion Hotel (formerly the Red Lion) in Bank Square. Below the town a mill leat running south from the Barle at Weir Head, drove the Paper Mill in Lady Street, Town Mills, the Laundry in Chapel Street (originally a woollen mill, by 1830 producing crepe and later lace) and Lower Mill (grinding grain until the 1930s). There is also evidence for leadmining in the area in the 14th and 17th centuries, but

Dunster Castle

the ore was always less productive than its Mendip counterpart. Beside the Barle upstream from the bridge stands **Exmoor House**, built rather reluctantly in 1855 as the district's Union Workhouse (all others in the county were constructed in 1837). Subsequently used as Rural District Council offices, it now houses the Exmoor National Park Authority, with an information centre for the area, and adjoins the main visitors' carpark for the town. The Guildhall Heritage and Arts Centre was opened in 1994, including a permanent exhibition on Dulverton's history during the last century with a recreation of Granny Baker's cottage.

The parish church of All Saints stands at the upper end of Fore Street and was held by Taunton Priory from the 12th century until 1539 and thereafter by the Dean and chapter of Wells Cathedral. It has a plain 13th century west tower but the rest was almost totally rebuilt 1853-5 to the designs of Edward Ashworth of Exeter (also responsible for Exmoor House, above). There are monuments to the Sydenhams of Combe, including a brass to Humphrey (died 1710), and the medical Collyns family. Of the latter, Charles Palk Collyns (1793-1864) was a noted huntsman, had a pack of staghounds here 1837-41 and was author of the *Chase of the Wild Red Deer*. Windows commemorate Sir George Williams (1821-1905), founder of the YMCA, born at Ashway in the north-east of the parish, Gilbert Wills of the Bristol tobacco family (son of Sir Frederick Wills (1838-1909) of Northmoor House), created Baron Dulverton in 1929, and George Hall Peppin

(1800-72). Peppin and his family emigrated to Australia in 1850 and were responsible for breeding the Peppin Merino sheep from which most of the Australian flocks descend today. The last tombstone on the right before entering the church marks the grave of Thomas Chilcott (died 1873). This formerly bore the epitaph: 'He was neglected by his doctor / Treated cruel by his nurse / His brother robbed his widow / Which makes it still the worse'. The brother, a Tiverton coachman, took the widow to the Bishop's Consistory Court but only after a spell in Taunton Gaol did she agree to have the offending verse removed: the space now occupied by an entry recording her own death in 1881. The Congregational chapel in Milhams Lane was put up in 1831.

There were six other Saxon estates in the parish: two at Broford and one at Hollam to the north, one at Ashway to the northwest, one at Pixton ('Potesdone' in 1086) and a sixth at Hawkwell. The Sydenhams obtained Pixton by wedding the heiress of John of Pixton in 1322, but it was Elizabeth Dyke who brought it in marriage to the hunting Aclands in 1745, and Elizabeth Acland to the 2nd Earl of Carnarvon in 1796. Pixton Park, an 18th century mansion extended in Victorian times, stands in parkland to the south-east of the town. The Carnarvon earls used it as a hunting retreat from their principal home, Highclere Castle (Hants.), until it was given in 1901 to Aubrey Herbert (1880-1923), younger son of the 4th Earl. Aubrey served as Tory MP for South Somerset from 1911, and as a soldier and diplomat, developing a close relationship with the

peoples of Turkey and Albania. Claimed as the original for the hero of John Buchan's novel, *Greenmantle*, his son Auberon (1922-74) had as close a kinship with Poland, while his daughter married novelist Evelyn Waugh (hence the christening of Evelyn's journalist son, Auberon).

★★★★ *Setting,* ★★★ *town.*

DUNSTER (C) Often regarded as the gateway to Exmoor from the east, Dunster's popularity has often proved a bane to its residents, as the proliferation of gift shops and (excellent) tea-rooms have exiled many more conventional shops to nearby Minehead. To enjoy the place to the full, choose a day early or late in the holiday season if possible, when the High Street and Castle are not thronged with humanity. If you park your car at the northern end of the village, drop into the adjacent Visitors' Centre which will introduce you to both Dunster itself and Exmoor in general.

The view of the place from the A 39 is magical: the many-turreted castle dominating the settlement below it. The steep-sided hill which rises above the present castle gives the parish its name, meaning 'Dunn's Torr' and probably alluding to a Saxon lord. There may have been a Saxon or an even earlier fortification on such a superb defensive site but it was its first Norman owner, horse-loving sheriff, William de Mohun (he kept 58 brood mares at Cutcombe and Brewham), who by 1086 had built **Dunster Castle** (fee:lists) on the hill, which became the seat of his honor or barony. In 1138 the castle was held by his heir, also William, for the Empress Matilda

Dunster Yarn Market

in her civil war with King Stephen but taken by Henry de Tracy. Matilda made William an earl, ostensibly of Somerset, but Stephen failed to confirm the title and it died with its first holder. In 1265, during the baronial wars, the castle's warden, Adam Burdon, defeated Sir William de Berkeley and a band of Welshmen who had landed at Minehead intent on ravaging the area. Sir John de Mohun, last of the line and a medieval playboy, fought at Poitiers and Crecy but loaded his lands with debt. Shortly before his death, leaving three daughters, he was persuaded out of his estate by his wife Lady Joan, who in 1375 sold Dunster, Kilton, Minehead and Carhampton to Lady Elizabeth Luttrell subject to Joan's own life interest. Lady Joan lived on until 1404, when the Luttrells finally took possession, becoming one of the leading families in the county and fighting for the Lancastrians in the Wars of the Roses.

Nothing remains of the Norman castle on top of the Tor, now occupied by an octagonal summer house of 1727. Parts of the curtain wall and the lower stages of the Mohun's 13th century gateway (still with its medieval door) can be traced, the latter succeeded by a substantial gatehouse put up by Sir Hugh Luttrell, 1420-22, beneath which the modern visitor enters. The living-quarters of the castle are the result of two major remodellings, the first from 1617 by architect William Arnold for George Luttrell (1560-1629), who created a Jacobean country house with superb views across the sea to Wales. During the Civil War George's son, Thomas Luttrell (died 1644), held his home for Parliament but

was forced to surrender it to the Crown in 1643. In June 1645 it sheltered the future Charles II for two weeks before falling to a siege by Robert Blake in April 1646. Garrisoned by the Roundheads, the building was disabled as a castle in 1650 but provided a prison for the notorious Puritan pamphleteer, William Prynne. Arriving branded on his cheeks and with both ears cut off, he filled his hours by compiling a catalogue of the Luttrell archives which is still in use today. To Col Francis Luttrell (died 1690) is due the magnificent carved staircase, featuring a hunt in full cry, and the dining room with its exquisite plaster ceiling, dated 1681.

The second and most striking alterations were due to Anthony Salvin, 1867-72, for George Fownes Luttrell (the Luttrells had died out in the senior male line in the 18th century, but their heiress married Henry Fownes, who agreed to adopt the name of his in-laws). Salvin was responsible for the fairytale external appearance of the castle and much internal work. An old kitchen became the ornate billiard room, the hall was enlarged and a delightfully cosy Victorian library was created. The present Sir Walter Fownes Luttrell, now Lord Lieutenant of the county, who lives at East Quantoxhead, made over the castle to the National Trust in 1976. A fine collection of family portaits of the Luttrells and related families from the 16th century onwards fills the building and the painted leather hangings, including a decorous Cleopatra complete with asp, should not be missed. There is an exhibition of family archives, changed periodically, in the castle itself and an excellent display illustrating

the development of the site housed in the Justice Room over the Gatehouse. The 17th century stables, whose original fittings survive, has become the Trust shop. If visiting, allow sufficient time to explore the beautiful walks through the immaculately-maintained hillside gardens and also **Dunster Mill** (fee:lists) at the southern foot of the Tor.

There were mills here by 1086, the present one occupying by 1620 the combined sites of the former Newmill and Nethermill. It continued to grind until 1962 and was rescued by Arthur and Laura Capps in 1979, restored and in 1980 reopened to the public, complete with tea room and mill shop. It provides a rare opportunity to tour a working mill. Nearby are 18th century decorative bridges, arches and cataracts. There are other rewarding walks in the area, including the ascent of Conygar Hill ('rabbit warren') to a prominent folly tower, built in 1775 with a nearby artificial ruined gatehouse. Another walk from the carpark in Park Street crosses the old Gallox Bridge, a picturesque packhorse bridge, to Gallox Hill (the name is probably a corruption of 'gallows' and indicates an early execution site) with a prehistoric oval enclosure. Three of Monmouth's rebels were executed in the parish in 1685 (most likely in the market-place), one of whom, Henry Luckwill, was a carpenter here, and at least twelve Dunster men joined the duke's rising.

Dunster is often described as the archetypal English village. It is not. It was long a successful small town and trading centre. The Mohuns had established a borough here by 1197, laying out a wide market-place along the present High Street where a market was held by 1222 (on Fridays in 1633): an arrangement formalised with the burgesses by Reginald de Mohun in 1253 in return for a tun of wine. A fair was recorded in 1355 (two by 1621), continuing into the 18th century. Shambles are mentioned by the 15th century (demolished in 1825) and the picturesque covered Yarn Market was set up at the north end of High Street c.1590 and repaired in 1647 after the Civil War siege. Dunster was also a medieval port although the progressive silting up of the Avill estuary led to its abandonment after the 17th century in favour of Minehead, another Luttrell estate. Cloth was made here by the 13th century, there was a fulling mill in 1259 and four by 1430, and a particular type of kersey or broadcloth became known as 'Dunsters'. The manufacture continued until the 18th century, when it went into progressive decline. What is traditionally identified as the medieval Butter Cross was evidently removed from the centre and now stands beside the road to Alcombe. Writing in 1791 Collinson recorded that where there had been 400 houses there were then only 190. Paradoxically it was this very decline which led to Dunster's survival.

At the north end of High Street stands the **Luttrell Arms Hotel**, dating from c.1500, and claimed to have been the town house of the abbots of Cleeve. Remodelled from three houses by George Luttrell in the 1620s, it had become the Ship Inn by 1651 and was substantially reconstructed in its present form and under its present name in 1751. Further down the Hugh Street there is a **doll museum**, based on Mrs Hardwick's collection. Round the corner in the narrow Church Street rises the jettied three-storey (so-called) Nunnery, dating from the 14th century, with an untypical slate-hung facade. It was the property of Cleeve Abbey from 1346, known as the High House in 1620 and was later used as a malthouse. Further on, off West Street, lies a **model village** to captivate the younger tourist.

To the west and above the centre of the settlement stands the red sandstone **Church of St George**, possibly forming the original focus of Dunster before the borough was established. William de Mohun bestowed the church, an estate at Alcombe and two fisheries on Bath Priory c.1090, so that the monks could build (probably rebuild) it. The Bath monks not only built a new church but soon after, and certainly by 1177, established a small Benedictine priory here, constituting St George's as the priory church. There are slight remains of the Norman church in a column of the west doorway and in the crossing piers, the chancel is a 19th century reconstruction of a 13th century original, but the rest is a Perpendicular rebuilding which began c.1420. In that year William Pynsoun left money to build a new bell tower and work on a rood loft. In 1443 John Marys, a Stogursey mason, contracted to construct the top two stages of the crossing tower, complete with 'gargylles' and 'pynacles'. Later work (which continued until c.1550) was probably influenced by an agreement of 1498 which allotted the east end of the church to the monks and the remainder to the vicar and his parishioners. The superb rood screen, which spans the nave and both aisles, was probably put up as a result of

this agreement. The north aisle was rebuilt from 1504, when Thomas Upcot gave 10 tons of iron 'coming in a ship of John Cokkys' towards the cost, and there is fine wide wagon roof to the nave. The octagonal font of c.1530 is carved with the Five Wounds of Christ and the Instruments of the Passion. The church is rich in monuments, from the tomb slab of Adam of Cheddar, prior 1337-c.1355 (discovered behind a fireplace in the town), in the south transept to the many memorials of the castle's owners, mainly at the east end. The earliest of the latter is a worn effigy identified as Christian Segrave, wife of the fourth John de Mohun (c.1325). On the north side of the choir is the alabaster figure of Sir Hugh Luttrell (died 1428), the first of his family to occupy the castle, with his wife, Catherine Beaumont (died 1435). An alabaster floor slab has the outline figure of Lady Elizabeth Luttrell (died 1493). The most elaborate tomb is to Thomas Luttrell (died 1571), bearing his effigy and those of his wife, Margaret Hadley, George Luttrell (kneeling, died 1629), and wife Joan Stewkley, put up by George in 1613. Elsewhere there is a brass dated 1487 depicting John Wyther, a baker, and his wife Agnes. The church contains much heraldry including a fine painting of the royal arms (1660) and a number of Luttrell hatchments. There are three medieval chests, two of which are each fitted with five locks. The medieval church contained chapels of St Lawrence and St Leonard and an altar of the Holy Cross (mentioned 1276). Dunster Priory was always a small establishment (a prior and four monks in the 14th century) and played second fiddle to its mother house at Bath, with which it was surrendered in 1539. The priory buildings lay to the north of the church, of which the prior's lodging, restored circular dovecot (with revolving ladder) and 16th century barn survive, together with two archways across Priory Green. Much of the priory site has been converted to attractive and very peaceful public walled gardens, which provide a welcome contrast to the thronged High Street. In Conduit Lane under a 16th century well house is St Leonard's Well which provided the main water supply to the priory.

★★★★ *Dunster Castle (with its gardens) and village generally, and their setting,* ★★★ *church, mill, Luttrell Arms Hotel.*

DURLEIGH (D) Although immediately west of Bridgwater, its name means 'wood frequented by deer'. It features an attrac-

tive reservoir, created in 1938 to supply Bridgwater. Across the water can be viewed West Bower (from *bur* – 'cottage'; 'west' to distinguish it from North, South and East Bower in Bridgwater): the twin-turreted 15th century gatehouse of a formerly larger manor-house. There was an oratory here in 1339 and a chapel of St John the Baptist in 1462. Although the manor was owned by the Seymours from 1489 until 1552, there is no basis for the claim that Jane Seymour, Queen of Henry VIII, was born here. Acquired by the Halswells of Goathurst in 1553, it passed with Halswell House (*see* **Goathurst**) to the Tynte family. I can still recall the rare medieval circular dovecote of thatch and cob, complete with 745 nest holes and standing below the gatehouse, which neglect sadly destroyed in 1967. The small parish church of unknown dedication probably dates from the 12th century: the chancel rebuilt in the 13th and the nave windows replaced in the 14th, when the tower gained its saddleback roof. The rectory estate was held by St John's Hospital, Bridgwater, until the Reformation. Rexworthy Farm is 19th century but represents a Saxon site within a moated area.

DURSTON (D/E) This small village, 'Deor's settlement', lines the Taunton to Glastonbury road (A 361) north-east of Taunton. Roger Arundel held it after the Conquest but later it passed to William de Erlegh who in 1166 founded an Augustinian monastery here. Soon after, the monks were outlawed for murdering their steward and Henry II granted the house and its lands c.1186 to the Order of St John of Jerusalem. They were then used to establish a preceptory for the Knights of St John (closed in 1500) and to found the only priory in England for the nuns of that order, known as Buckland Priory or Minchin Buckland (*mynecen* – 'nun'). The priory, housing some 50 nuns, was partly destroyed by fire in 1234 and rebuilt with oak from Newton forest in North Petherton. It was finally dissolved in 1539 but no trace of the former buildings remains, the site at Lower Durston being cleared when Buckland Farm was built for Thomas Gray c.1810. The church of St John the Baptist (St Nicholas in 1540s) beside the main road at Higher Durston, was served from the preceptory as a free chapel, a burial ground authorised only in 1541. Apart from the west tower, it was completely rebuilt in 1852-3 to the designs of C.H. Knowles, although the altar table, dated 1635, was

LEFT *Lodge Farm, Durston.*   ABOVE *East Brent from Brent Knoll*

apparently saved from the older build-ing. Lodge Farm, an open-hall house immediately north of the church, dates from the 15th century and represents the manor-house retained by the Erleghs, who created a park to the north c.1223. One of Somerset's earliest known windmills was built by the Erleghs in 1324-5 to the south of Lower Durston.

EAST BRENT (A) An attractive village at the north-eastern foot of Brent Knoll hill, whose name refers to the hill, from the Celtic *briga*, 'a high place'. It is familiar to most from the rest area on the M 5, which is as near as most travellers through the parish get these days. The manor formed part of the great Saxon estate of Brent given by Ine, king of the West Saxons, to Glastonbury Abbey in 693 and held by the monks until 1539. Subsequently the manor was granted to the Duke of Somer-set, passing later to the Whitmores and eventually to the Pophams. Abbot John Selwood (1456-93) built a mansion here, possibly in the vicinity of Chapel Farm, with chapel, hall, guest chambers and a 'sumptuous porch': all sadly demolished in 1708. The two defaced 14th century priests' effigies at the church may have come from there, if Collinson is to be believed, and two stone figures from the same source are preserved at Porch House in Wedmore. The Perpendicular church of St Mary passed from Glastonbury to the bishops of Bath and Wells after the Refor-mation. It lies at the west end of the village down a short lane and has a west tower crowned by 'one of the most elegant spires in Somerset' (Pevsner), formerly whitewashed to act as a sea mark. There is an elaborate plaster nave ceiling of 1637 and a good set of 15th century benchends featuring the emblems of the evangelists, a pelican (for the arms of Bishop Richard Fox?) and the initials of Abbot Selwood,

but East Brent's real treasure is a rare 15th century eagle lectern. The pulpit is dated 1634 and the west gallery, evidently con-structed from the former rood screen, 1637. There is 15th century stained glass in the north aisle although heavily restored in 1852 and the chancel was rebuilt 1840-45. The church was served as vicar 1845-96 by Archdeacon George Anthony Denison, a colourful Anglican bigot who almost single-handedly tried to prevent the spread of non-sectarian education in the diocese and was once tried for heresy. He was also responsible for establishing in 1857 the elaborate Harvest Home celebrations which still continue with splendid gusto here annually. A board at the entrance to the churchyard displays a map of Brent Knoll hill and paths to the top. **Edingworth** (possibly 'enclosure near the ewe pasture') is a hamlet and former Domesday manor north-east from the main village. A second hamlet, **Rooks-bridge**, can be associated with Rooksmill, Rookshill and Rookspill, where there was a fishery in 1515, and at the same date a newly-built windmill was mentioned on 'the Down'.

★★★ *Setting,* ★★ *village and church.*

EAST CHINNOCK (J) Cut by the A 30 midway between Crewkerne and Yeovil, its name possibly derived from the Old English *cinu*, 'a ravine', or paradoxically *cinn*, 'a chin-shaped hill', with the addi-tion of '-ock' meaning 'little', as in 'hil-lock'. It was formerly known for the grow-ing of flax and the production of sailcloth and tiles. With Middle and West Chin-nock it seems to have formed a single Saxon estate which c.950 was held at her death by a Saxon lady, Wynflaed, under Shaftesbury Abbey, but by 1066 it had been divided into its three elements, of which East Chinnock was the largest. The Conqueror granted it to Robert, Count of

Mortain, whose son William conveyed it to his new foundation of Montacute Priory c.1100. The monks retained it until the dis-solution of the priory in 1539: indeed the last prior, Robert Shirborne, was retired to a house in East Chinnock on a pension of £80 a year. The manor was bought in 1561 by Henry Portman, son of the Lord Chief Justice, and remained in his family (note the Portman Arms inn in the village) until the estate was split up and sold by the then Viscount Portman in 1924. Before the A 30 was turnpiked in the 18th century, the main road took a less direct course to the north.

Isolated at the east end of the village is the church of the Blessed Virgin Mary. It has a 13th century font and south porch, but the rest is largely Perpendicular, although the nave was widened in the 19th century when a flat ceiling was installed. The distinctive feature of the building is its modern stained glass. An 18-year-old Luftwaffe rear-gunner, Gunther Anton, shot down over Southampton in 1944 was sent to a POW camp at Houndstone, Yeovil, and lived and worked on an East Chinnock farm 1945-48. After his return to Germany he built up a stained glass busi-ness and, in gratitude for his treatment and the survival of himself and his parents, he made a unique series of gifts to the church. Between 1962 and 1988 he crafted and installed almost all the windows in the nave and chancel and a screen of glass bricks in the tower arch, dying just six months after their dedication by Bishop George Carey in May 1989.

There are several good 17th and 18th century properties in the village and Weston House is medieval in origin. The Portmans added to the housing stock in the 19th century and there has been modern development to the west and near the church. Further west near Barrows Farm is a salt spring from which salt was distilled by the late 18th century.

EAST COKER (J) A small Ham-stone jewel of a village, south-west from Yeovil, with a cared-for feel to it and many attractive houses. It is named after the stream, Coker Water, which passes through it, from the Celtic *kukra* meaning 'crooked'. A Roman villa with mosaics was found here in 1753, occupied c.140-370, and the place long formed a single estate with West Coker, owned in 1066 by Gytha, mother of King Harold who died at Hastings. Seized by the Crown after the Conquest, a grant by William Rufus to St Stephen's abbey, Caen, never took effect and the manor was probably bestowed by Henry I on Richard de Redvers. Richard's son gave it to the de Mandevilles but, on Robert de Mandevilles's outlawry for felony in 1306, it reverted to his overlords, the Courtenays, descendants of the de Redvers family, who kept it until 1591. The manor was bought in 1616 by the Ven William Helyar, archdeacon of Barnstaple, whose heiress in the present century carried it to the Walker-Heneage family. The arms of the Helyars, a cross flory between four mullets (spur rowels), still ornament the porch of Coker Court (as they do the innsign of the village pub), a fine house up the tree-lined slope beside the church. It has a 15th century hall with Jacobean stone screen and 17th, 18th and 20th century additions.

The adjacent church of St Michael was granted with the rectory by Sir Philip Courtenay to found a chantry chapel in Exeter Cathedral, and the dean and chapter of Exeter still hold the advowson. Recent work has suggested that the nave and west wall are Saxon in origin. The building has a 13th century south arcade and 15th century north one. The chancel was rebuilt in 1711 and a transeptal north tower in 1791, replacing an earlier crossing tower. There are fine panelled arches into the transepts, which may represent the two former chantry chapels: that of the Virgin Mary founded before 1265 by Geoffrey de Mandeville and of the Holy Cross in 1344 by Hugh de Courtenay. An unidentified female effigy of c.1290-1300 lies in the north aisle and another of c.1340 near the lectern. There are late monuments to William Dampier (1651-1715), buccaneer, explorer and hydrographer, and first Englishman to set foot in Australia, born at Hymerford House (Tudor hall and two-storeyed porch) in North Coker. At the west end of the north aisle is a monument to the American poet, Thomas Stearns Eliot, whose ashes were buried here in 1965 under lines from his poem on East

ABOVE *Almshouses, East Coker*
BELOW *Allhallows School, East Cranmore*

Coker. He had traced his ancestry to Andrew Eliot, baptized here in 1627, who had emigrated to America in 1660, but the poet made only one visit here in 1937. The almshouses which point the way to church and court were founded by Archdeacon Helyar in 1640. The school-boys here held an annual Easter cock-fighting match in 1615. North of North Coker is Naish Priory, one range of a Perpendicular mansion dating from c.1400.

An attempt to found a borough called Murifield in the south of the parish was made by the de Mandevilles before 1275. In 1321 20 tenants held small burgage plots there but the place never had the success of nearby Stoford borough (*see* **Barwick**), no market or fair appears to have been granted and it was soon abandoned.

★★★ *Village and church.*

EAST CRANMORE (F) This former parish (united with West Cranmore to form the new parish of Cranmore in 1933) is set in parkland just south of the A 361 to the east of Shepton Mallet, its name meaning 'crane's marsh' or 'lake'. The manor here was retained by the Crown in 1084 but by 1249 was held by Hugh Whiting, who had a park here by 1269 and from whom it was known as Cranmore Whiting. Subsequently the manor and, indeed, the manor-house, was divided in two between coheiresses, the estate of the Bradford and Jones families being carried by Mary Moore to her husband, Dr Richard Paget. He inherited Cranmore Hall in 1791 and

the Pagets continued there until 1945, creating the park around the house and remodelling the building in stages from 1849. Between 1863 and 1865 John Moore Paget built what he called East Mendip Tower, now generally known as Cranmore Tower, on a hill to the north, complete with a cottage for the tower keeper. The most prominent member of the family was Sir Richard Paget (1832-1908), MP successively for East Somerset, Mid Somerset and Wells, and first Chairman of Somerset County Council, created a baronet in 1886. Cranmore Hall became the new home for Allhallows School, a Roman Catholic preparatory boarding school from Devon in 1946. The Pagets also demolished the medieval church of St James, formerly a chapelry to Doulting, and 1845-6 built its delicate successor, designed by Thomas Henry Wyatt, since deconsecrated and ingeniously converted into an unconventional private house. To the north-east Foster Yeoman operate a major limestone quarry, Torr Works, begun in 1932 as Merehead Quarry.

★★ *Setting.*

EAST HUNTSPILL (E), *see* **HUNTSPILL**

EAST LAMBROOK (J) A small village between South Petherton and Kingsbury Episcopi which takes its name from the small stream, 'the land (or boundary) brook', a tributary of the River Parrett. Indeed the brook formed the southern boundary of Kingsbury Episcopi in Saxon times, and the bishops of Bath and Wells and, from the mid 15th century, the dean and chapter of Wells continued to dominate the parish. It is *East* Lambrook to distinguish the village from the hamlets of West and Mid Lambrook, also within the parish. The chapel of St James, held under Kingsbury but by its own ministers, is a simple building of c.1190 with fine chancel arch and western bellcot. An attractive external stone stair gives access to the 18th century gallery supported on iron pillars. At Mid Lambrook is an early nonconformist chapel, founded in 1687, the present structure dating from 1729, and a fine late medieval farmhouse.

What draws visitors to the place today is the garden of **East Lambrook Manor** (fee: lists), a lovely house (not open to the public) dating from the 15th century, although it was never a manor-house. It was acquired by Margery Fish (1892-1969) and her husband Walter in 1937 and around it they created a garden (or rather series of gardens), and a philosophy of cottage-style cultivation which Margery popularised through her eight books. The owners since 1985, Mr and Mrs Andrew Norton, have restored the garden, rescued plants from extinction and operate a garden shop in the old malthouse. We have a very successful East Lambrook rose climbing through the branches of our old apple tree.

★★★*garden,* ★★ *Village, church.*

EAST LYDFORD (E) Northeast from Ilchester and just east of the Roman Foss Way (A 37), its name means 'the ford across the torrent', evidently referring to the River Brue, which forms the northern boundary of the parish. Down beside the Brue stood the medieval church of St Peter until replaced in 1866 by the church of St Mary the Virgin , designed by Benjamin Ferrey and built by the rector, the Rev J.J.

Moss in memory of his late wife. Its spire still forms a landmark, but the church itself has now been closed and sold. Thomas Horsey, rector 1657-90, was a great persecutor of local Quakers, even seizing a coffin from a passing Quaker funeral procession for non-payment of tithes and burying it in his dunghill in 1661. The hamlet of Cross Keys, which takes its name from the inn there, first mentioned in 1759, grew up around the crossroads formed by the Foss Way and the Langport, Somerton and Castle Cary turnpike road (B 3153). Rubbery Farm to the south takes its name from Rowborough, one of three open arable fields, recorded from the late 14th century.

EAST LYNG (E), *see* **LYNG**

EAST PENNARD (E/F) A secluded well-tended grey-stone village in a cleft below King's Hill but which takes its name from the old name for the ridge, derived from the British *penn-ardd*, 'high hill'. The estate here was granted by King Edred to Aelfgyth, a nun of Wilton (Wilts), and she transferred it to Glastonbury Abbey, which retained it until the dissolution of 1539. The manor was granted in 1549 to William Paulet, later marquess of Winchester, eventually passing in 1797 to his descendants, the Napiers of Tintinhull, lords into the present century. Pennard House with its own park is a Jacobean manor-house to the north of the village, which Gerard Napier remodelled in 1815. The church of All Saints was a Saxon minster by the 10th century. The present building is almost entirely 15th century, including a plain west tower and a 12th century font with vibrant beasts at its four corners. There is a finely-detailed 18th century pulpit and excellent additional furnishings, largely made up from earlier panels. There is a profusion of memorials to the Martin and Napier families, including one to Edward Berkeley Napier, reciting his illustrious descent from the royal houses of England and Denmark, before recording his prosaic death from gout in 1799. There was a chantry chapel at Stone in this parish until 1548.

★★ *Church and setting.*

EAST QUANTOXHEAD (D) Once called Great Quantoxhead, and with justice, this beautiful coastal parish forms a triangle running from its low cliffs on the shore up to a point at Black Ball Hill on the Quantock Hills, as its name implies. Many Bronze-Age burials, mostly on the high

ground, testify to prehistoric settlement. The parish is crossed from east to west by the A 39 from Bridgwater to Minehead but the picturesque village, several of its cottages attractively thatched, lies along a lane running north from the main road. A duckpond beside the lane raised a head of water to provide motive power for the mill until the 1920s. The millhouse was rebuilt in 1729 after a fire but probably occupies the site of the Domesday mill. Beyond the pond stretch the gardens of the Court House (not open to the public), sited on a gentle rise beside the parish church. The manor, centred on the Court House, was granted after the Norman Conquest to Ralph Pagnell and has never been sold since that time: a continuity unique in Somerset. Ralph's granddaughter, Frethesant, married Geoffrey Luttrell and their son Andrew inherited from a cousin. Although the Luttrells bought the reversion of Dunster Castle in 1376, the Court House here was occupied by junior members of the family and as a dower house until the mid 17th century. After over two centuries in the hands of tenant farmers, the Luttrells moved back in 1888. At the time of writing it is the home of Col Sir Walter Fownes Luttrell, Lord Lieutenant for the county, over 900 years since his ancester acquired it. There are remains, including a single tower, of the semi-fortified medieval manor-house but the property was largely rebuilt and extended in the early 17th century. Its magnificent position can best be appreciated from the footpath which runs north from the village beside the mill leat to the sea. I recommend the walker to continue eastwards along the coast and then turn inland again to Kilve and a well-earned pint at the Hood Arms.

The delightfully simple parish church of St Mary, unbrutalized by the Victorians, dates from the early 14th century. Its early rood screen survives, although without its loft, the benchends were added in the early 16th century, like so many in the Quantock area, and the pulpit bears the date 1633. A chest tomb on the north side of the chancel commemorates Hugh Luttrell (died 1522) and his son Andrew (died 1538), whose retainers were involved in a fracas with his stepmother over his inheritance to the estate. The Victorian east window recalls the remarkably long service as rector of Alexander Fownes Luttrell, a total of 70 years from 1818 to 1888.

Sarah Biffin was born in the parish without arms or legs in 1784 but became a celebrated mouth painter: discovered by the Earl of Morton and patronized by many members of the royal family. At nearby Kilton in 1824 she married Stephen Wright, who serenaded her in verse:

'Sweet Biffin, though admired your
  charms,
Your lover sighs not for your arms,
  He took a nobler part;
And while your happiness he plann'd.
Aware you could not give your hand,
  Aspired but to your heart.'

The Kilton register displays her firm signature on the marriage entry. She wore her wedding ring on a gold chain around her neck, survived her husband and, after her sight deteriorated, died in poverty at Liverpool in 1850.

★★★★ *Village and setting,* ★★★ *church.*

EAST SOMERSET RAILWAY (F), *see* WEST CRANMORE

EBBOR GORGE (E) A wooded unspoilt limestone cleft in the Mendip Hills to the north-west of Wookey Hole, which was given to the National Trust by Mrs G.W. Hodgkinson in memory of Sir Winston Churchill in 1967, and administered by the Nature Conservancy Council. Evidence of settlement by Neolithic man, c.3000 BC, has been found in caves here. There is a carpark at the foot of the valley with a display centre to interpret the geology, flora and fauna; waymarked nature trails.

★★★ *Scenery and walking.*

EDINGTON (E) To the north of the Polden Hills at the edge of the Levels, Edington is claimed by some (against Wiltshire's Edington) as the site of the Battle of Ethandune at which Alfred finally defeated the Danes in 878. Proximity to Wedmore and Aller, both associated with the campaign, would favour the Somerset village but it is rejected on placename evidence. The Polden village occurs in 1086 as 'Eduuintone', meaning 'Edwin's settlement', whereas the Wiltshire parish is recorded as 'Ethandune' ('waste of uncultivated hill') in a document of c.880. A presumed Roman villa site and coin moulds were found here in the 18th century. At the entrance to the village from the north is a former holy well, heavily restored in memory of Margaret Luttrell in 1937. In 1791 Collinson described its water as smelling 'like the foul barrel of a gun'. The parish church of St George, once a chapelry to Moorlinch, was wholly rebuilt in 1879 by Down and Son but includes a superb Norman font saved from its predecessor. (*See also* **Burtle**)

★ *Village.*

ABOVE *Elworthy*
BELOW *Willett Tower, Elworthy*
BOTTOM *Norman font, Edington church*

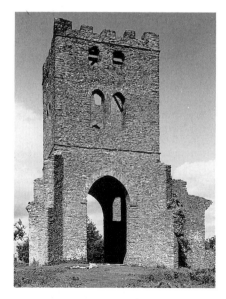

ELWORTHY (D) This parish was made up of three Domesday settlements, Elworthy ('Ella or Elli's homestead'), Willett and Coleford, and a fourth, Plash ('a shallow pool'), mentioned in 1238. All these, and other estates, came in 1811 to the wife of a future general, Daniel F. Blommart, and it was for him that c.1816 Richard Carver designed Willett House, a substantial five-bay Georgian mansion to the east of the village. Elworthy village, below the Brendons, lines the B 3188, from 1806 the turnpike road from Wiveliscombe to Watchet. The local turnpike house survives as Elworthy Cross House and a former road which skirted the village was consequently dubbed Save Penny Lane. The church of St Martin, redundant since 1979, has a 13th century nave and west tower, a late 15th century north porch and nave roof, while the chancel was rebuilt in 1846. The 17th century font is carved from Watchet alabaster. The patronage of the church was held by the Knights Hospitaller from 1233 until their extinction in 1540. John Selleck, a staunch royalist, was ousted as rector in 1645 and personally aided the escape of the future Charles II. Willett Tower, a prominent folly on Willett Hill, had been built by 1782: evidently intended merely to ornament the hunting landscape, and the surrounding woodland provides excellent walking.

★★ *Village and setting.*

EMBOROUGH (B) An isolated sparsely-populated Mendip parish north-east from Wells, whose name means 'smooth hill'. There is no village as such, only the occasional farm and small groups of

ABOVE *Emborough church and farm.*   BELOW *Enmore Castle*

houses. A lake known formerly as Lachemere Pool by 1524, when it was leased with its fishery by John Butler to the monks of Hinton Charterhouse, but now as **Emborough Pond**, is popular with anglers and ornithologists and the vale in which it lies was planted out and walks formed by the Hippisley family. The lake was also popular for winter skating with the boys from Downside Abbey. This was an area of limestone quarries, worked from 1901 onwards, the stone carried across Emborough Pond by aerial ropeways, although these have now closed. The manor was bought by John Hippisley in 1570, as had been Whitnell, a second manor in the parish now represented by Whitnell Farm, south-west from the church, in 1559. The Hippisleys effectively combined the two estates and dominated the parish until the present century, living either here in the buttressed manor-house beside the church or at their former home in Ston Easton.

The plain rendered church of the Blessed Virgin Mary has a fine outlook to the north across the Mendip plateau. It was a chapelry under Chewton Mendip: a relationship reflected by an order to the abbot of Jumieges in 1316 to reroof Emborough chapel and bell tower. In 1548 the parishioners decided it would be politic to surrender to the king the lead from the roof and tile it instead. The present pinnacled central tower is Perpendicular but the rest had new windows inserted in the 18th century and Pevsner believes this to be a virtual rebuilding. Certainly it has an unusual moulded plaster ceiling and frieze, but the whole building, now redundant, is suffering sadly from damp and neglect. There is a wealth of monuments to the Hippisleys dating from the late 17th century and, high up in the nave, an impressive profile relief portrait of Robert Bath.

Old Down is a hamlet on the Bath to Wells road (B 3139) to the east of Emborough (although in the parish of Stoneaston). It is noted for the Old Down Inn,

which was recorded as the Red Lion by 1710. It was a major posting house in the 1760s, a receiving house from 1798 and was rebuilt after a fire of 1855.

★★ *Setting, Emborough Pond.*

ENMORE (D) Between the Quantock Hills and Bridgwater, the parish's name means 'duck marsh'. From c.1100 it was long the property of the Malet family: Sir Baldwin Malet obtaining a 1401 grant of a Monday market and three-day fair here. The Malets retained it until their heiress Elizabeth (died 1682) carried the manor to her husband, the dissolute John Wilmot, Earl of Rochester. The remnants of the Malet estate were later bought by John Perceval, 2nd Earl of Egmont (died 1770), who between 1751 and 1755 set about building a ludicrous four-square baronial castle to the north of the church. Designed to feed his obsession with medieval feudalism, it came complete with a dry moat, patent drawbridge and concealed access to a basement floor where the servants were hidden away. Around this incredible pile he created an extensive park with magnificent prospects over Bridgwater Bay, diverting roads and pushing Enmore village out of sight. The work continued at the hands of the 3rd Earl, who showed off his park to Coleridge

in 1807, but the mounting costs of the operation eventually forced his successor to sell up in 1834. The castle was bought by Nicholas Broadmead of Milverton, who demolished three-quarters of it, placing domestic roofs over the remaining west wing. All this, including the wonderful view to the sea, can be seen from the north side of the churchyard. In 1795 Dr Jasper Porter, disinherited by his father in favour of his sister, left money to be used to make labelled effigies of both of them. Every 5th November these were to be processed through the village to the beat of the drum by the poor men of Enmore, before being burned on a bonfire by the church. Sadly there is no evidence that the bequest was ever carried out.

The church of St Michael has a Norman south doorway of c.1185 that was built when the Malets were still new to Enmore, as a memorial in the north aisle to their 22 generations in the parish testifies. Apart from the north aisle of 1873 and a much-restored 13th century chancel, the building is 15th century, including an ornate west tower with modern (1979) figure of St Michael in the south side niche. There is a good Jacobean pulpit, early two-lock register chest, memorials to the Broadmeads on the north wall of the nave and to successive owners of Barford Park, on the

ABOVE *Barford Park, Enmore.*

RIGHT *Evercreech church*

south wall. In the chancel is a monument to John Poole, rector here for 61 years until his death in 1857, aged 87. It was Poole who pioneered National Schools with the foundation of a free school at Enmore in 1810, which the great and the good came to inspect. Rebuilt in 1848 and extended in 1888, it now houses Enmore County Primary School in the main village street. Poole's rectory, built at Lexworthy c.1803 to replace one swept away by the Egmonts, is now a private residence, Poole House. Castle House, on the south side, was built as an inn by the Egmonts in the late 18th century, its functions now usurped by the Enmore Inn and the Tynte Arms, both opened c.1850.

North-west of the village towards Spaxton lies an exquisite country house, **Barford Park** (fee:lists), built c.1710 for the Jeanes family, which happily escaped Egmont notice. The building received a third storey and flanking wings at the hands of a Jeanes nephew, Andrew Guy (died 1798), in 1775 (date on weather vane). Guy's daughter married John Evered and their grandson, Capt John Guy Courtenay Everard, a Crimean War veteran, died three days after his 100th birthday in 1931, attributing his longevity to drinking water from a spring in the grounds. The recent and welcome restoration of the property is due to Mr and Mrs Michael Stancomb, owners since 1958. Walled and wooded gardens with views towards Bridgwater Bay complete an idyllic picture. There were three Domesday estates at Lexworthy in the east of the parish on which there were then four mills paying rent in iron.

★★★★ *Barford Park,* ★★★ *its gardens, Enmore's setting,* ★★ *church and village.*

EVERCREECH (F) A substantial grey lias-stone village midway between Shepton Mallet and Bruton, whose size reflects the fact that it was formerly the site of Evercreech Junction on the old Somerset and Dorset Railway and of a second station, Evercreech New, closed in 1966. The presence of St Ivel's major milk factory, a tile-making and an engineering works ensured the continuing importance of the place to the economy of the area. Other industries here over the years included a silk factory, rope making and mineral water production. The parish's name is likely to be derived from two Celtic elements meaning 'yew-tree hill' ('Evrecriz' in 1086). Small Down Camp, an Iron Age fort enclosing 11 barrows, crowns a hill to the north-east. The manor formed part of the endowment of Wells Cathedral, possibly from the foundation of the diocese in the 10th century, and the bishops had a country seat here, with its own chapel, and a park to the south-west of the village, marked by Evercreech Park Farm. In August 1348, from what must have seemed the relative safety of his palace here, Bishop Ralph issued prayers as the Black Death struck his diocese. This was among the estates which the bishop was forced to surrender to the duke of Somerset in 1548 and the manor seems to have been split up and sold off in the 17th century. The former bishop's residence (demolished by John Clerk, bishop 1523-41) was succeeded in 1613 by a substantial mansion put up by Sir Ralph (later Lord) Hopton, but since the 19th century the principal house here has been the plain Georgian Evercreech House, home of the Sherston family in the late 19th and early 20th centuries. The village focuses on

what anywhere else would have been the market-place, with a range of almshouses (1825-27) and a fine stepped village cross.

The church of St Peter was held by the bishops until Jocelin gave it in 1231 to the hospital of St John the Baptist, Wells. It is a fine Perpendicular building with a glorious 110 ft west tower (probably post 1475), the only later addition being the 1843 south aisle and inserted galleries. Inside there is an elaborately-panelled tower arch, a clerestorey which does not compromise the cosiness of the building, an excellent roof, whose modern red and blue painting (freshly reproducing the medieval colouring) gives a delightfully jolly effect, and monuments to the Cozens, Rodbard and Sherston families. On the outside of the south aisle are animal gargoyles of 1842 which local tradition claims represent the vicar, a publican and two local women, with whom the sculptor disagreed while lodging in the village.

North-west from the village, near the hamlet of Prestleigh, the headquarters and extensive showground of the **Royal Bath and West Show** have been sited since 1965. The society was founded in 1777 to encourage and record advances in agriculture and commerce. Chesterblade (possibly 'fort on a ledge', referring to Small Down Camp), a hamlet to the north-east, formed part of the bishop's lands by 1065 and had its own chapel by 1213 (Pevsner considers its inner doorway to be late 12th century), largely rebuilt in 1888. Roman remains found in the vicinity may suggest a former villa site here, to which the place name could also refer. The name of Stoney Stratton, a further hamlet to the east of Evercreech, means 'stony settlement on a Roman road' and may also reflect a former Roman presence.

★★★ *Evercreech church.*

EXFORD (C) This moorland parish is delightfully centred on a former 'ford over the River Exe', but long spanned by a bridge, in the heart of Exmoor. Road Castle and Staddon Hill Camp are prehistoric hillside enclosures or forts to the east of the village. Domesday Book (1086) records no fewer than eight settlements in the parish, five called Exford and others at Almsworthy ('Edmund's homestead'), Stone and Downscombe. Most seem to have been isolated farms and two were described as formerly waste. Later two estates developed: one given by the Mohuns of Dunster to Neath Abbey, co. Glamorgan, based on the manors of Exfordham and 'Cubihiete' (now Chibbet, south-west of the village), which consequently was known as Monkham, and the other centred on Almsworthy to the east of the village. In due course, like so many other Exmoor estates, Exford largely passed to the Acland family. The Aclands were closely involved with the hunting fraternity and in 1876 Montague Bisset built new kennels here for the Devon and Somerset Staghounds, joined from c.1900 by the pack of the Quarme Harriers at Edgcott. The church of St Salvyn, a Celtic dedication (although long attributed to St Mary Magdalene), stands isolated up the hill to the east of the village. The west tower is 15th century, bequests indicate that the south aisle was being put up 1532-42, but the nave, chancel and porch date mainly from 1867. A fine rood screen from the former church at West Quantoxhead was installed in 1929 and the choir stalls came from Queen's College, Cambridge. The patronage was held in the Middle Ages by Peterhouse, Cambridge. Next to the churchyard gate is the tombstone of 24-year-old Amos Cann, caught in a blizzard of March 1891 while walking home from Porlock and not found for three weeks. The annual Exford Horse Show in August is a popular event in the Exmoor calendar.

★★★ *Village, walking.*

EXMOOR (C) There are at least three different Exmoors: the ancient royal forest, the parish created in 1856, and the National Park: all three occupying differing portions of the north-western sector of the county. The **Royal Forest of Exmoor** was never wooded, as its name implies, but was an untamed, largely uninhabited waste which possibly from Saxon times was reserved (although rarely used) by the kings of England for their hunting. The forest lay entirely within Somerset, comprising in the 13th century the later parishes of Exmoor, Oare, Withypool and Hawkridge, and parts of Winsford, Exford, Porlock and Culbone. In 1301 all this was disafforested except for Exmoor and Oare, and later even Oare was excluded. The forest was administered through the forest or Swainmote court (meeting at Lanacre Bridge or Hawkridge churchyard) by a warden or forester appointed by the Crown, who also had responsibility for the other royal forests in the county. With the forestership went the manors of Hawkridge and Withypool, and in those parishes lived the 52 free suitors who had rights of pasture, fishing and cutting turf over the moor. At the time of the Norman Conquest three Saxon foresters, Dodo, Godric and Almar, shared the responsibility, but by 1086 the office had been granted to a single forester, Robert de Odburville, later descending between 1204 and 1337 from William de Wrotham through the families of Plessy and Pecche. Among subsequent holders of the office were the Mortimers, earls of March (1359-1424), under whom the poet Geoffrey Chaucer and his son Thomas exercised the post. From 1508 the forest was leased out by the Crown, being held by the Pollards of Kings Nympton (by 1537-54, 1598-1653), who regularly hunted here. The lease was assigned in 1653 to James Boevey (died 1696), who built the first house on the moor at Simonsbath, and was later held by the Walpoles, earls of Orford, and from 1767 by Sir Thomas Acland. The Aclands laid the foundations of what became the Devon and Somerset Staghounds, although enjoying a continuous existence only from 1855, thanks to Mordaunt Fenwick Bisset, tenant of Pixton Park in Dulverton. The royal forest came to an end with an Act of 1815 for its disafforestation and enclosure.

The share of the Crown was bought by John Knight, proprietor of Wolverley and Cookley ironworks (Worcs.), who later purchased the Acland interest. Knight built a wall 29 miles long, completed in 1824,

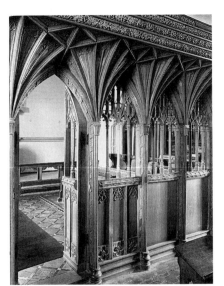

LEFT *Rood screen, Exford church.* BELOW *Exford*

North over the Horner Valley, Exmoor

around his new estate, repaired the old roads and made new ones, constructed farms and founded a village at Simonsbath around Boevey's old house. Not all his projects came to fruition. The 7 acres of Pinkworthy (pronounced, and formerly spelt, 'Pinkery') Pond were created c.1830 by damming the upper waters of the River Barle to feed a canal, optimistically designed to power a railway carrying iron ore from Simonsbath to Porlock Weir. John Knight retired to Rome in 1841, where he died in 1850, his work, particularly farm building, hedging and ditching, being continued by his son Sir Frederic (died 1897). Early attempts at arable farming were progressively abandoned in favour of pasture and stock-raising. The present complexion of Exmoor is almost entirely due to these two Worcestershire industrialists, who literally ploughed their family substance into the West Somerset soil. Their estates were sold to the earls Fortescue from Devon: as enthusiastic hunt supporters as the Aclands had been before them. The continuation of stag-hunting on Exmoor has been the professed aim of the Badgworthy Land Company which since the 1920s has been acquiring land on the moor and hunting rights over an even wider area.

The **parish of Exmoor**, which coincided with the area of the former royal forest, was formed in 1857. Apart from Simonsbath and isolated farms built by the Knights, it is still a wild and beautiful landscape of smooth hillsides, deep valleys and moorland streams. Here and there are Bronze Age round barrows and there is a single Iron Age hillfort known as Cow Castle. It is also an area rich in wildlife,

notably the Red deer and the Exmoor pony, the latter all descending from an early 19th century herd of 20 at Ashway Farm in Dulverton. (*See also* **Simonsbath**)

Exmoor National Park was established in 1954, extending from Combe Martin (Devon) in the west to Elworthy and Monksilver in the east, approximately two-thirds of which lies in Somerset, including not only Exmoor itself but also the Brendon Hills. Since 1974 the Park Authority has been based at Exmoor House in Dulverton, having taken over the offices of the former Dulverton Rural District Council, built as the Union Workhouse. Somerset villages and parishes within the Park will be found throughout the Gazetteer.

In 1958 the intention of the Forestry Commission to commence large-scale conifer planting in the area known as the Chains led to the formation of the Exmoor Society, which has continued ever since as a conservation watchdog and as a forum for those who know and love the moor. The Exmoor Press issues an annual publication, the *Exmoor Review*, with articles and comment, and has also published a succession of 'microstudies' or monographs on aspects of the history, geography and wildlife of Exmoor. Other organisations committed to the moor include the Exmoor Natural History Society and the Exmoor Pony Society.

★★★★ *Moor generally for walking, riding and driving.*

EXTON (C) A hillside village, 'the settlement on the Exe', which straggles down the slope above the Exe valley north from Dulverton. In the Middle Ages the manor

passed with the forestership of Exmoor, although later owned by the Rolles and then the Siderfins of Croydon, who sold it in 1700 to pay their debts. It is a landscape of highland farms, of which Widlake and Red Door farmhouses date from the 16th century. Further up the valley lie the farms of North and South Quarm, represented in 1086 by the Domesday manor of 'Coarme' which later split into three estates that went by a bewildering array of names. The first was called Quarm Picot, Quarm Begger or Quarm Kitnor, the second Quarm Sibyl and the third Quarm Monceaux. The church of St Peter lies at the end of a short lane leading north from the village on an elevated site above the vale. The nave has Norman herringbone masonry, the plain castellated west tower is probably 13th century and the north aisle Perpendicular. There is a monument to the 58 years of the Rev F.K. Warren as rector (died 1922) and a superb highly-painted 18th century panel to members of the Pearse family, featuring skulls and crossbones. A secondary village, **Bridgetown**, developed along the Exe beside the A 396 to take advantage of the passing traffic heading to and from Dulverton. It includes the local hostelry, the Badgers Holt, formerly known as the Rock Inn, and a magically-sited cricket field just across the river, founded in 1924 by Roy Nesfield, who was also responsible for the thatched pavilion.

★★ *Exton village.*

FARLEIGH HUNGERFORD (B) This small rural parish, the 'fern-covered clearing', occupies the extreme north-eastern corner of the county in the valley of the River Frome. A Roman villa, abandoned by the mid 4th century, was discovered half a mile to the north in 1822. Land here was granted by King Ethelred to Leofwine his huntsman in 987. From the late 11th century until 1347 the estate was held by the Montforts from whom the place was known as Farleigh Montfort. The manor was bought in 1369 by Sir Thomas Hungerford (died 1397) of Heytesbury (Wilts), MP alternately for Wiltshire and Somerset, and Speaker of the House of Commons. A protegee of Lord Burghersh and later of John of Gaunt, the king's uncle, Sir Thomas decided to move to Farleigh and build a castle here. He may well have swept away the early medieval village of Farleigh to accommodate his new works. These were well advanced, if not complete, by 1383 when he received retrospective licence to fortify his property. Sir Thomas's son, Sir Walter Hungerford (1378-1449), was also MP for both counties, Speaker, and Treasurer of England, being created Baron Hungerford in 1426. Robert, the 2nd Baron, was executed in 1464 during the Wars of the Roses (as was his eldest son in 1469), and Farleigh was granted to the Duke of Gloucester (later Richard III). Richard's sister-in-law, Isabella, wife of George, Duke of Clarence (traditionally drowned in a butt of Malmsey) gave birth at the castle to a daughter, Margaret, on 14 August 1473. The manor was given in 1483 to the Duke of Norfolk, killed at the Battle of Bosworth (1485). Thereafter Farleigh was restored to Robert's younger son, Sir Walter Hungerford (died 1516), whose only son Sir Edward (died 1522), married secondly Agnes, widow of John Cotell. She was hanged at Tyburn in 1523 for having five years before persuaded two Wiltshire men to strangle her first husband and burn his body in a furnace at Farleigh Castle. Sir Edward's son, Walter, was created Baron Hungerford of Heytesbury in 1536. He was married three times, his third wife claiming that he had locked her up in one of the castle towers for three or four years on a starvation diet and procured his chaplain to poison her. Walter himself was executed with Thomas Cromwell in 1540 for treason and sodomy with his own daughter. In the next generation, Sir Walter Hungerford (died 1596) was a great sportsman and to him is attributed the two-storey falconry at Lodge Farm, to the north of the castle, which bears the Hungerford's sickle crest. In 1568 he sued his wife for divorce, alleging adultery with William Darrell ('Wild Darrell'), and spent three years in the Fleet prison for refusing to support her or pay her legal costs.

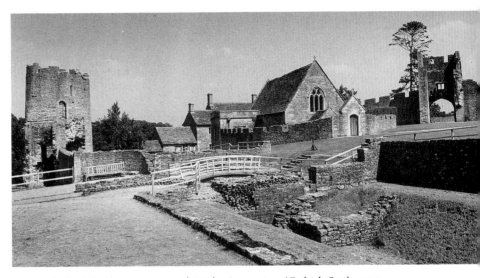

ABOVE *Farleigh Castle.* BELOW *Buck Brothers' engraving of Farleigh Castle, 1733*

During the Civil War the castle was seized from John Hungerford, who held it for the king, by his Parliamentarian half-brother, Sir Edward Hungerford (died 1648): succeeded by a third half-brother, royalist Anthony (died 1657). Anthony's younger son was a secret agent for the king but the heir, Sir Edward Hungerford was for Parliament and nursed hopes of marrying one of Cromwell's daughters although, after the Restoration, he is believed to have received Charles II at the castle. Nicknamed 'the Spendthrift, he wasted the family fortune and in 1686 was forced to sell Farleigh to Sir Henry Bayntun. It was held by the Houlton family of Trowbridge 1730-1891, and thereafter briefly by Lord Donington, whose wife was hereditary Baroness Hungerford, and then by Earl Cairns. Since 1915 it has been in the charge of English Heritage and its predecessors.

Farleigh Castle (fee:lists) is basically of two periods. Sir Thomas Hungerford's castle of c.1370-83 formed a rectangle, with a round tower at each corner and a gatehouse in the middle of its southern wall. Within this enclosure was a kitchen, possible bakehouse, first floor great hall and solar, with a courtyard and garden. It is grievous to look at the Buck brothers' engraving of 1733 and see how complete this area then was. Apart from the south-east and south-west towers and parts of the curtain wall, this northern part of the castle was demolished for building stone during the 18th century and only the foundations survive. To this Walter, Lord Hungerford, added an outer bailey c.1420-30 with a barbican in front of the inner bailey and gates to the east and west. This action enclosed the mid 14th century parish church of St Leonard, a simple rectangular structure which Sir Thomas had rebuilt to replace its 12th century predecessor, shown by recent excavations (1973-76) to have lain a little to the north of the present building. Later, c.1380-90, Sir Thomas added the chapel of St Anne to the north of the sanctuary, and this became the Hungerford chapel. Walter, Lord Hungerford, converted the church into the castle chapel and built a new parish church beyond and to the south of the castle for the parishioners (*below*). There were two chantry chapels here, one founded in 1412 in memory of Sir Thomas Hungerford by the will of his widow and the other, dedicated to the Blessed Virgin Mary, by his son Walter in 1426. There is a wealth of monuments to the family. In St Anne's chapel are the effigies of Sir Thomas Hungerford (1398) and his wife Joan (1412), and Sir Edward Hungerford (1648) and his wife Margaret (1672), and also the tombs of Sir Walter Hungerford (1596) and his son Edward (1585), and of Sir Edward Hungerford (1607) and his first wife Jane. A brass here commemorates Margaret (1613) wife of Thomas Shaa (Shaw), daughter to Walter, Lord Hungerford. In the floor of the nave is a 15th century tomb slab to one of the chantry chaplains. There are the faded remains of wall paintings towards the east end of the chapel. The 12th century font was brought here from the parish church in 1834 but is thought to have come from the earliest church on the castle site. Outside on the north side of the chapel steps lead down to the crypt underneath the Hungerford chapel. Through an iron grille can be seen the lead coffins of six adults and two children, four of which have the face of the deceased moulded on them. To the east of the chapel stands the chantry priest's house built in 1430 and extended to the north in the 17th century. It now serves as an extremely informative museum with items found during excavations and early illustrations of the castle.

The parish church of St Leonard, with wonderful views to the west, was built by Walter, Lord Hungerford, and consecrated in 1443. It is fairly typical Perpendicular work, although the chancel was Gothicized c.1830-40. Most of the monuments commemorate 19th century Houltons who occupied Farleigh House (turreted mansion set in its own park, remodelled c.1810 and c.1906, now occupied by Ravenscroft School). There is a stained-glass portrait of Sir Thomas Hungerford, builder of the castle, in a nave window.

★★★★ *Castle for its size, architecture and intriguing blood-bespattered history.*

FAULKLAND (B), *see* HEMINGTON

FIDDINGTON (D)
The 'settlement of Fita's people' lies north of the A 39 west of Cannington. The manor, granted to Roger Arundel after the Norman Conquest, was held by the Mallack family of Devon c.1647-1772, after which it was split up and sold. Illegal fairs were held here in 1242, clothmaking and tanning provided employment from the 17th century and a revel was recorded in 1675. The church of St Martin has a Perpendicular west tower and medieval south walls, but much of the rest

Fitzhead, Tithe Barn and church

was rebuilt in 1860, although the 16th century benchends and Jacobean pulpit survive, and the whole was restored in 1977. The only known Somerset example in a parish church of a Sheila-na-gig, a female erotic carving probably dating from the 12th century, appears on the outer south-east corner of the nave. Locals were fined for playing fives against the church walls on a Sunday in 1623. The separate settlement of Bonson (formerly 'Bothemeston'), north-east of the main village, was settled by the 12th century and formed a separate manor.

★★ *Village, setting.*

FITZHEAD (D)
An attractive farming village to the east of Wiveliscombe, with whose manor it was held by the bishops of Wells from Saxon times. Its name, 'Fifida' in 1178, indicates its original extent of five hides, about 600 acres: evidently modified to Fitzhead to distinguish it from Fivehead. Fitzhead Court, with armorial plaster ceiling, was built by Maj Robert Cannon (died 1685), a royalist veteran of the Civil War, succeeded by his nephew Cannon Southey (died 1768) and the latter's great-nephew Col John Southey Somerville (died 1795). Somerville's son, 14th Baron Somerville, was President of the Board of Agriculture, introduced merino sheep from Spain and devised improved ploughs. He lived in the house until 1813 and four years later laid the foundation stone of the Wellington Monument. Richard Beadon, son of Bishop Beadon, moved into the Court and bought the entire Wiveliscombe and Fitzhead estate from his father in 1827, selling out to Lord Ashburton in 1840. The Court was occupied by Ashburton's agent, John Edward Knollys (died 1892) but the estate was split up and sold in 1894. Although the Court has been sub-

divided, its buttressed wall remains a striking feature of the village.

The church of St James the Great (St Mary Magdalene in 1791) was a chapelry of Wiveliscombe until 1755 and the living is still in the gift of the vicar there. The 15th century west tower is all that is left of the medieval building. The nave and chancel were rebuilt in 1849, a vestry added in 1863 and the north aisle in 1887. There remain the superb late 15th century rood screen with its unusually wide central opening (possibly made when the screen was formerly at the west end) and 13 delicious grotesque stone heads, presumably saved from the old church, mounted on the front of the tower gallery. In the churchyard is the 14th century restored cross and the old Tithe Barn, converted into a parish room in 1910. There is also a memorial stone to William Rockwell (1591-1640), an early emigrant to America on the *Mary and John* in 1630.

★★ *Village.*

FIVEHEAD (J)
Just south of the Taunton to Langport road (A 378), this village has a name derived from its original Saxon land measurement of 'five hides'. The village's older houses are clustered in the area of the church with considerable modern expansion around all its approaches. The so-called Langford Manor in Lower Swell seems 16th century: altered internally in 1905. To the west of the village, at the end of a drive south from the main road, stands a second Domesday manor called Cathanger ('the slope of wild cats'). Given to Muchelney Abbey after the Norman Conquest, the present house was built in 1559 (datestone) by lawyer, John Walsh (died 1572), Chief Justice of the Common Pleas, whose daughter married Sir Edward Seymour, son of the attainted and executed

Duke of Somerset. Their grandson sold the house c.1615 to Hugh Pyne of Curry Mallet (died 1628), whose daughter Christabel was wetnurse to the future Charles II and wife of Sir Edmund Wyndham, royalist governor of Bridgwater in the Civil War. In 1645 Christabel herself fired a musket from the Bridgwater's defences at Oliver Cromwell and killed a man standing beside him. The Wyndham descendants retained the property until 1927. In 1785 John Wesley preached at the house although commenting that, 'having a stupid people to deal with, I spoke exceeding plain'. The building was much extended in the 18th century but retains its 16th century gatehouse and John Walsh's first floor hall, misleadingly known as the Justice room. There is no basis in the stories that Judge Jeffreys held court here or that an underground passage links the house with Curry Mallet manor-house.

Fivehead's church of St Martin has a round Norman font with cable moulding and saltire crosses around the top. The chancel is late 13th century and the rest is mainly 15th century. There are several monuments to the owners of Cathanger, including a fine reset brass to Jane Seymour (died 1565), with a cast of the reverse exhibited beside it, and a floor slab to Edmond Elyott (died 1725), page to the future James II.

★★ *Village and church.*

FOXCOTE (B) A small isolated hillside village south-east from Radstock (Avon), named for a 'fox cottage' and commanding extensive views across the valley of the Wellow Brook to Shoscombe. The estate here, apparently formerly called Weston, was granted by King Athelstan (924-39) to Ealdorman Athelstan. When the latter was received into Glastonbury Abbey as a monk he transferred it to that monastery, which had lost it before 1066. The manor was generally owned by absentee lords until the Orange family moved here in the early 17th century, passing by 1697 to Robert Smith, whose descendant sold out to Sir John Smythe of Ashton Court in 1786. It was eventually sold to the Beauchamp baronets who lived at Peasedown St John. The austere church of St James was completely rebuilt in 1721 with a Tuscan south porch and a narrow west tower. It contains monuments to the Orange and Smith families. A coal pit was sunk here from 1853, eventually reaching a depth of 1,416 ft and linked to Writhlington c.1867 by a tramway. The mine was closed in 1931 and the pithead buildings were demolished in the

1950s. (*For* **'the fair maids of Foxcote'** *see* **Norton St Philip**)

★ *Setting.*

FROME (F) A large stone-built town which dominates the far east of the county and has a long industrial history. It was also a sizeable parish and the focus for the Saxon hundred of Frome (although the hundred court met in Buckland Dinham). The place is ringed by delightful villages for which it serves as an excellent touring centre, although today it has strong economic links with Trowbridge in neighbouring Wiltshire. Its name (pronounced 'Froom') is that of the river which flows to the north of the old town and is derived from the Celtic *fram*, which can mean 'fair, fine or brisk'. The parish's name was often given as Frome Selwood, the addition referring to the great royal forest which once covered this area and extended into Wiltshire and Dorset. A Neolithic barrow, excavated away in 1965, stood on the opposite side of the river at North Hill and contained 15 burials – all lacking skulls, which are thought to have been removed for ritual purposes. There are other barrows in the area and a possible former ring of sarsen stones and a Romano-British burial, both also on North Hill.

The town had its origin in a Saxon monastery dedicated to St John, founded c.685 by St Aldhelm, then abbot at Malmesbury (Wilts), presumably on the hillside site of the present church of St John the Baptist. Its existence is confirmed and privileges were granted by an undated Papal bull (688-701) issued to Aldhelm (who died at Doulting in 709) and, at least initially, it was evidently a daughter house to Malmesbury. Aldhelm became the first bishop of Sherborne in 705, a diocese known locally as Selwoodshire. The position of the church and the settlement which grew up around it was probably determined by a natural spring in the churchyard, whose water still flows down Cheap Street. The settlement may well have become a royal Saxon *burh*, King Athelstan held a witangemot (royal council) here in 934, attended by the archbishops of Canterbury and York, and King Edred died at Frome on 23 November 955 (although buried at Winchester). These two incidents suggest that there could have been a royal residence here. The place was held by the Crown before and after the Norman Conquest and is credited in 1086 with a market, four mills and with the payment of the 'third penny'. Saxon coins with the letters 'FRO' are now generally

thought *not* to have been minted here, nor does the Domesday Book record any burgesses, which might suggest that by the 11th century the settlement was in decline. Indeed, it was never to gain borough status in the centuries that followed (although there was a vain attempt under William III) and the place ceased to be a royal estate in the early 12th century when Henry I granted it to Roger de Courcelles (dead by 1135).

The main manor descended to Roger's granddaughter and thereafter through the families of FitzBernard (1215-38), Branch (1238-1361), Wynslade (1361-1405), Leversedge (c.1405-1706) and Seaman (1706-51), after which it was sold to the Earl of Cork and Orrery of nearby Marston Bigot. The manor was known either as Frome Branch, after its medieval lords, or Frome Vallis, from the placename Vallis ('Faleise' in 1318) north-west from the town where its manor-house, now demolished, was formerly sited and where Wandrille de Courcelles had a private chapel by the later 12th century. Of its lords, William Branch in 1270 obtained a grant of a three-day fair (represented since 1871 by Frome Cheese Show) and a Saturday market, and probably entertained Edward I on a visit in 1276. Two further fairs were granted in 1492. Edmund Leversedge (died 1496), a younger son, was struck down by a mysterious illness in 1465 and had a notorious vision in which he journeyed through Hell and was addressed by an angel.

Frome was a cloth town by the early 14th century (and probably earlier) with at least five fulling mills in 1392. Indeed the place became the most important woollen production centre in the entire region, eventually growing its own woad for dyeing. Clothmaking led in the 17th and 18th centuries to substantial areas of housing being built to accommodate the industry's workers, the Trinity district on the north-west side of the town. Although much of this has been demolished in recent years, what remains is now protected: the earliest and largest such development in the county. Contemporary estimates of the numbers employed in the 18th century wool trade were inflated but Frome seems to have been nearly twice the size of Taunton at that time. From the end of the 18th century, as in most Somerset towns, the industry declined and, although Wallbridge Mills did not close until 1965, other trades mopped up the surplus labour. Prominent were ironfounders Edward Cockey and Sons Ltd,

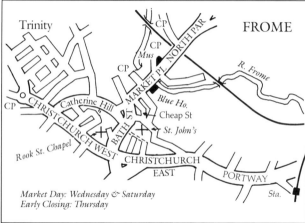

who had started casting bells c.1685 (three dated 1724 and 1746 are still in St John's), and (from c.1848) J.W. Singer, the latter producing many national monuments, notably the statue of Boadicea and her chariot on London's Embankment. The major printing firm of Butler and Tanner, located since 1908 at Adderwell near the railway, was founded off Bath Street in 1845 by W.T. Butler and local chemist William Langford, later taking Joseph Tanner into partnership. The town has a wealth of former mills and other buildings to delight the industrial archaeologist. The market was held in the Market Place and up Bath Street until 1875 when the tolls were bought from Lord Cork and the Frome Market Company opened a new market beside the river Frome on the north side of the town. In 1990 the market moved out to an extensive new site north-east of the town at Standerwick in Beckington.

The early plan of the town centre was clearly determined by the contours of the area, developing first around the church and then stretching north and north-west to the Market Place and, from c.1660, extending further west. In the Market Place are the George Hotel and Crown Inn, both with good Georgian frontages, and the former covered market hall of 1819, with assembly rooms above, now occupied by the National Westminster Bank. Near the bridge stands **the Blue House**, one of my favourite buildings anywhere in the county, even though purists criticise the mix of architectural styles. It originated as almshouses for 12 paupers founded by William Leversedge soon after 1465, rebuilt c.1620 and re-endowed by William Stafford for 14 women in 1652. The present structure was put up 1720-28 in classical pattern-book style, the central block, crowned with a cupola and clock, to accommodate the new Blue

School (opened by 1723, closed in 1921), with side wings to house almswomen. The statues on the facade represent an almswoman and schoolboy (identified in accounts as Nancy Guy and Billy Ball), while the two figures of servant girls on either side of the entrance came from an almshouse at Keyford, opened in 1803 and regrettably demolished in 1956. Across the bridge of 1667 (which still has buildings on it) in North Parade stands the Frome Scientific and Literary Institute (1869), whose premises now house **Frome Museum** (fee:lists). There are good local collections and the reconstructed interior of an old chemist's shop. Gentle Street and Cheap Street are both picturesque pedestrian ways with attractive small shops and eating places, but the whole centre has an abundance of good stone buildings and intriguing alleyways.

The **Church of St John the Baptist**, probably representing the site of Aldhelm's monastery, had evidently ceased to have a monastic status by the Norman Conquest. At that time it was one of several churches (including Milborne Port) held by Regenbald, dean of Cirencester and chancellor under Edward the Confessor and William the Conqueror. Later the church and its considerable Frome estate (about a sixth of the parish) were granted by Henry I to Cirencester Abbey on its foundation in 1133 and retained by the abbots until their dissolution in 1536. Thereafter the advowson and the church estate were granted to the future Duke of Somerset and passed by him to his secretary, Sir John Thynne, the builder of nearby Longleat House (Wilts), whose family progressively extended their estate here. The church remained with the Thynnes, created viscounts Weymouth and marquesses of Bath, until 1939. The present substantial building, west of a forecourt screen designed by Sir Jeffry Wyatville in 1814 (while working at Longleat), includes two Saxon sculpted stones in the tower and hints of a 12th century rebuilding, possibly financed by Wandrille de Courcelles, and a further cruciform reconstruction c.1300. There were three chantry chapels, the earliest being that of the Virgin Mary, endowed in 1340, and housed in the Lady Chapel on the north side of the church. St John's chantry, probably south of the sanctuary and later called St Andrew's, was founded in 1378 by Sir John Delamere of Nunney, its lands passing after 1548 to the Thynnes. St Nicholas's chantry, housed in the baptistry to the west of the Lady Chapel, was founded by John Cable in 1408, contains

Bishop Ken's tomb, Frome church

heraldic glass referring to his families alliances and is treated as a shrine by his American Cabell descendants. The present High Church Victorian structure dates from a virtual (and controversial) rebuilding between 1852 and 1866 by the Rev W.J.E. Bennett, a leading member of the Oxford Movement. Most medieval details which survive have been so reworked or repositioned as to deprive them of significance. Fortunately several of the earlier memorials survive. In the Lady Chapel are those to the Boyle earls of Cork and Orrery and their family as lords of the main manor, although almost all the Leversedge monuments were swept away and a 17th century wrought-iron chapel screen has ended up in the Victoria and Albert museum. The clergy vestry (usually locked) was originally added by Anthony Methwyn, vicar 1606-40, and contains a fine memorial depicting the figures of himself and his wife. St Andrew's chapel has been converted into a shrine to the memory of the saintly Thomas Ken, bishop of Bath and Wells 1684-89. He was deprived of his see when he refused to swear allegiance to William and Mary, having taken the same oath to James II, and lived in retirement at Longleat until his death in 1711. Poignantly he had asked to be buried in the nearest churchyard within his former diocese and at sunrise his coffin was interred immediately east of the church. There he lies beneath a low canopy and I urge on the visitor the short pilgrimage to see it. Intriguingly, the right to nominate sextons at St John's has been exercised by the lords of Orchardleigh manor since at least 1590.

A free chapel of St Catherine was founded in the 13th century, probably by the Branch family, although its former site is uncertain. It named the present Catherine Hill, had its own fair and market (held in Cross Street until 1875 and recently revived as a medieval fair in August) and its rich endowments became the manor of St Catherine. This estate was acquired by the Champneys family of Orchardleigh and sold in 1660 to clothier John Sheppard, after whose family Sheppard's Barton was named. In the 19th century an expanding population required the building of Christ Church, designed by G.A. Underwood in 1818 but enlarged by Manners and Gill from Bath 1849-51, and Holy Trinity, by H.E. Goodridge, also of Bath, 1837-8. The town has also long had a nonconformist tradition, the glory of which is **Rook Lane Congregational Chapel**, dated 1707. In plan this is a simple rectangular building (the side pavilions and gates were added in the 19th century) but with a grand classical (almost domestic) facade. After many years of neglect, a vital restoration is nearing completion. Here was buried Elizabeth Rowe (1674-1737), occupier of Rook Lane House and in her day a poetess of international repute. John Wesley preached in the town regularly from 1752, considering Frome 'a dry, barren, uncomfortable place'. The first Wesleyan chapel was completed in 1779, despite the treasurer absconding with the funds, and rebuilt 1810-12 at the meeting of Christchurch and Bath streets.

The cloth workers gave the town a Puritan flavour in the 17th century and, although the Civil War largely passed

Frome by, the forces of the Duke of Monmouth inspired at least 88 parishioners to join them in 1685. The rebel army retreated here for two days after the skirmish at Norton St Philip, the Duke traditionally staying at the gabled Monmouth Chambers in Cork Street while many of his troops deserted. The rest left for Shepton Mallet and, after the Bloody Assizes, twelve rebels were hanged, drawn and quartered here.

On the north side of the town beside Bath Road are sited Frome College, the Merlin Theatre and the Youth and Sports Centres. At the south end of the town Keyford was a separate estate by 1066, later divided between the manors of Great and Little Keyford. From the 14th century until 1585 it was held by the Twynyho family, of whom Ankarette Twynyho was kidnapped from Keyford by the Duke of Clarence in 1477. He trumped up a charge of poisoning his duchess, to whom she had been lady-in-waiting, carried her off to Warwick and there had her hanged. Southeast from the town lay the former tithings and manors of **East** and **West Woodlands**, long within Selwood and largely bought up for hunting by the Thynnes in 1611. Christmas was celebrated at East and West Woodlands in 1657 with 'drinking, playing cards and fiddling all day in disguised habits'. Indeed, the area long had an unsavoury reputation, was known as the haunt of outlaws, and an attack by local soldiery was mounted in 1693 against a gang of coiners (producing what were known locally as 'Woodland groats'). Lord Weymouth, in an attempt to tame the area, built East Woodlands church with its spired tower in 1712. In the extreme south of the parish, formerly deep in Selwood Forest and on a site now marked by St Algar's Farm beside the B 3092, the brethren of St Mary of Langley were settled by the mid 12th century. By 1235 this community moved across the border into Wiltshire to establish Longleat Priory. A chapel continued on the site with which the name of St Algar (bishop of Crediton 942-53) was linked by 1361, possibly used as a hermitage or leper hospital, and where Leland states the saint was buried.

★★★ *Centre of town and its buildings, particularly Cheap and Gentle streets, Rook Lane Chapel and the Trinity area,*
★★ *St John's Church, museum.*

FYNE COURT (D), *see* BROOMFIELD

GAULDEN MANOR (D), *see* TOLLAND

GLASTONBURY (E) This small former market-town stands on the edge of the Somerset Levels, and people have come to it over the centuries with widely differing hopes and expectations. Today it has a slightly down-at-heel look which is emphasized by the travel-worn 'New Age' pilgrims for whom the place has an irresistible attraction. The meaning of the town's name ('Glaestinga byrig' in 688) has been the subject of much debate. Dr Turner's favours 'the town of the people of the place of oak-trees' (*glastann*, Cornish for 'oak-trees'), while Philip Rahtz prefers 'the fort of Glast's people'. There is no reliable contemporary evidence for the names Ineswytrin (Welsh – 'island of glass or woad') or Avalon ever having been applied to Glastonbury at an early date. To the north-west of the town Arthur Bulleid discovered and excavated (1892-1907) a substantial (so-called) **Lake Village** of some 90 circular huts on a platform of felled timber, defended by a palisade. Evidence of occupation from c.300 BC to 100 AD included utensils, implements and pottery, but also, because of the water-logged ground, organic remains such as woven wicker-work, wooden bowls, ladles, ladders and boats. East of Glastonbury and evidently intended to defend the island of Glastonbury and/or the Tor is a long bank and eastern ditch, now divided by the A 361, known as **Ponter's Ball** (a corruption of 'Porter's Ball': land held in the 13th century by Walter, hereditary porter of Glastonbury Abbey, and not of *Pontis Vallum*, as inscribed on a nearby commemorative stone; 'ball' probably from *balgh* – 'smooth or rounded'). Excavation has failed to establish its date: Iron Age or Dark Age.

South-east of the town rises **Glastonbury Tor**, topped by the isolated tower of St Michael's chapel: the most celebrated landmark in the county. Philip Rahtz's excavations, 1964-66, on the summit and shoulder of the Tor revealed evidence of timber buildings, animal bones and metal-working from the 6th century, succeeded by cells cut into the natural rock and a rectangular wooden building, perhaps a church, of mid to late Saxon date. A possible cross-base and part of the wheel-head of a Saxon cross were found on the summit, overlaid by the medieval chapel of St Michael, of which only the 14th century tower survives (succeeding an earlier chapel destroyed by an earthquake on 11 September 1275). It seems possible that these excavations could represent evidence for the origin of Christian Glastonbury in

the form of a hermit or monastic settlement which may eventually have outgrown the top of the Tor and moved down to occupy the later site of the abbey. Also uncovered by Rahtz was the grave of John Rawle (elsewhere 'Rales') who, according to John Cannon's diary, requested burial up here in 1741 because his ancestors had been servants at the abbey and he mistakenly wished to be interred among them. Robert Thompson was also married on top of the hill in February 1754. Those wishing to scale the Tor, a steep climb but with wonderful views out over the Levels, should leave the town on the A 361 and turn up Wellhouse Lane, before striking out up the hill. Theories that interpret the scarping of the Tor slopes as a massive earthen maze rather than lynchet terracing for medieval cultivation have failed to convince me.

The ruins of **Glastonbury Abbey** (fee:lists), the foundation of which preceded the town and lie at its heart, are entered under an arch from Magdalene Street. There is a new visitors' centre with shop and an excellent museum of archaeological finds, architectural fragments and a large model representing the complete abbey just before its dissolution. Archaeological evidence takes the site back only to the 7th century, a boundary ditch, and, apart from a questionable charter of 601 issued by an unnamed British king to an Abbot Worgret, the sequence of land grants from West Saxon and Mercian kings begins in 670. Several of these charters were executed by Centwine, king of the West Saxons 676-85, who was buried at the abbey. To the east of an 'old church', the *vetusta ecclesia*, of timber and wattles, King Ine (688-726) built a stone church of SS Peter and Paul c.720. Despite many royal grants, Viking raids in the later 9th and early 10th centuries brought monastic life at Glastonbury, as elsewhere, to a virtual standstill at a time when the place was attracting Irish acolytes and becoming more of a finishing school for the sons of the wealthy. One of these pupils was the future St Dunstan (abbot 940-56), probably born nearby at Baltonsborough, who was appointed abbot by the king after Edmund I had a seemingly miraculous escape from death while hunting above Cheddar Gorge. Dunstan extended Ine's church, solicited generous land grants from King Edmund and his successors, before going on to become archbishop of Canterbury, to crown Edgar at Bath in 973 and achieve eventual canonization. Three Saxon kings, Edmund I (946), Edgar (975) and Edmund II

Ironside (1016), were buried here, five of St Dunstan's six successors as archbishop came from Glastonbury and by the Norman Conquest the monastery was the wealthiest house in England and owned one eighth of Somerset. Of the last two Saxon abbots, one died insane and the other was a profligate taken back to Normandy by William the Conqueror as a hostage in 1067. The first Norman abbot, Thurstan, disagreed with his Saxon monks who c.1083 barricaded themselves in the abbey church and sought refuge round the high altar. Norman soldiers burst in and, firing arrows from 'the upper storey', killed three monks and wounded eighteen others. A new cloister and larger church were built in the earlier 12th century, and construction continued under Abbot Henry of Blois (1126-71), simultaneously bishop of Winchester, prior of Montacute and papal legate, as well as being half-brother of King Stephen. Then disaster struck on 25 May 1184 when the abbey buildings, including the 'old church', its relics, vestments and library were almost completely destroyed by fire.

With the personal backing of Henry II, the rebuilding of the abbey followed in the form in which its ruins survive today, using stone from the abbey's quarries at Doulting. Efforts to attract pilgrims and money to pay for the work began with the alleged exhumation of St Dunstan in 1188, identified from the letters S and D on his coffin. Despite the fact that Dunstan's body rested intact in his Canterbury shrine, the monks ludicrously claimed to have rescued his body in 1012 when Canterbury was under attack by Vikings, and persisted in their assertion into the 16th century. A second attempt to draw in the pilgrims came c.1191 when, after a major dig behind screens in the abbey graveyard, the monks claimed to have unearthed the remains of 'King' Arthur and his 'second' wife, Guinevere, and for the first time identified Glastonbury with the Celtic netherworld of Avalon. The Avalon link was necessary in order to agree with the description of Arthur's end given in the over-imaginative account by the early 12th century popular historian, Geoffrey of Monmouth. A further addition to the manufactured legends of Glastonbury came in the mid 13th century, when it was asserted that the abbey had been founded soon after the Crucifixion by St Joseph of Arimathea: possibly in response to Westminster Abbey's equally ridiculous claim to have been established by St Peter. Robert de Boron, a Burgundian poet, added the Holy

Glastonbury Abbey

Grail to the St Joseph story at about the same time. No reference to the famous Holy Thorn (*Crataegus praecox*), blossoming at Christmas, has been found before 1520 and it was asserted to have sprung from St Joseph's staff only in 1716: an anecdote formerly attributed to St Benignus in a medieval life of that saint. The original thorn was destroyed in 1649 when, according to John Taylor, 'the soldiers being over zealous did cut it down in pure devotion: but a vintner dwelling in the town did save a great slip or branch of it' and 'set it in his garden'. Several such cuttings survived and since 1929 sprigs of the flowering thorn have been sent annually at Christmas to the monarch. The monks doctored the early 12th century history of the abbey by William of Malmesbury, adding the basic elements of the Arthur and St Joseph stories. The resulting concocted saga was a runaway success and for centuries very few ever questioned this revised account of Glastonbury's early years. Stories grew of saints who may have lived or visited here (Gildas, Indracht, Kea, Rumon, Bridget) and those who almost certainly didn't (Phagan, Deruvian, Columba, Patrick, Benignus, David). Tales of visits by Christ and the Virgin Mary date back little more than a century.

Sadly, the monks' efforts to reconstruct their buildings and their history coincided

with a period during which the bishops were casting jealous eyes on Glastonbury. In 1199 Savaric, bishop of Bath, backed by armed soldiery, burst into the monastery and forced the monks to enthrone him as abbot, even torturing those monks (one to death) who refused to acknowledge him. Another raid ended with five monks immured in Wells prison, and one abbot elect was suspected of having been poisoned in Rome by the bishop's agents. It was not until 1219 that an uneasy truce was achieved and the king was declared to be the abbey's patron, but only at the cost of several manors which the abbey had to surrender to the bishop. At Easter 1278 Edward I and Queen Eleanor came in state as patrons to the abbey to witness the reinterment of 'Arthur' and 'Guinevere' in a black marble mausoleum in front of the high altar. There was a further royal visit in 1331 by Edward III and his queen.

Later abbots were occupied in the accumulation of an extensive library, an impressive collection of saints' relics and the completion of the conventual buildings. In tandem with this there was an ambitious programme of drainage on the abbey's Levels estates and the construction of churches, manor-houses and barns on their country manors. Near Glastonbury the abbots had three parks, Norwood, Wirrall and Sharpham, which together eventually accommodated over a thousand deer. All this came to an end in 1539 with the dissolution of the abbey and the enforced surrender of its property. Abbot Richard Whiting, 'a very weak man and a sickly', was dragged off the Tower of London, where he was cross-examined by Thomas Cromwell himself, before being returned to Somerset for trial and conviction in the Bishop's Palace at Wells on a charge of 'robbery'. On 15 November Whiting was drawn on a hurdle from the abbey to the summit of the Torr where, with the abbey treasurer, John Thorne, and a third monk, Roger Wilfred, he was hanged. Whiting's body was brutally hacked into quarters and dispatched to Wells, Bath, Ilchester and Bridgwater for public display and his head was spiked on the abbey gateway. This was supposed to have fulfilled an old prophesy: 'when a whiteing on ye Torr is caught, then shall ye Abbey comme to nawght'.

Apart from the main gateway and porter's house, dating from c.1500 with 17th century alterations, the present remains of the abbey above ground are largely restricted to the church built after the great fire and the Abbot's Kitchen. The Norman Lady Chapel is the earliest and most complete part of the church still standing, dedicated in 1186, on the site occupied by the 'old church' before the fire. Later c.1500 a crypt was formed beneath it, of which most of the vaulting has collapsed, on which the cult of St Joseph of Arimathea centred. Unfortunately the excavation of the crypt destroyed all possible archaeological evidence of the 'old church'. The Lady Chapel was linked to the rest of the building by the early 14th century Galilee. The main church dates from the early 13th century, with twin western towers and a massive crossing tower (of which two of the four supporting piers survive), so there are some basic similarities to Wells Cathedral. The east end of the choir was reached in the 14th century and the fan-vaulted Edgar Chapel added onto the east end in the early 16th century, to house the tombs of the Saxon kings. This final extension made Glastonbury the longest church in England. To the south of the church have been excavated the Cloisters, Chapter House, Dormitory, Refectory, Monks' Kitchen, Rere-Dorter, part of the Almonry and the Abbot's House. The most complete of the monastic buildings, however, is the Abbot's Kitchen, probably early 15th century and hailed by Pevsner as 'one of the best-preserved medieval kitchens in Europe'. It has four large corner fireplaces and is crowned by

an octagonal lantern. There is also the detached chapel of St Patrick with some original stained glass. It was built in 1512 by Abbot Richard Bere to serve the women's almshouses he had founded which (having been rebuilt in the 19th century) were demolished in the 1960s. The men's almshouses survive in Magdalene Street; a 13th century barrel-roofed chapel, which formed the chancel of a medieval hall hospital. This was founded by Abbot Michael of Amesbury in 1251, having been moved from the north side of St John's church, and within the walls of the hospital a range of 16th century cottages was built. There were formerly two rows, but the southern one was criminally demolished in 1958. The abbey buildings fared no better and were used as a quarry for building stone and to repair local roads. In the early 18th century the site was held by Thomas Prew, 'a rank Presbyterian', who used gunpowder to blow up the ruins and it was at this time that the Abbot's Lodging was flattened. The destruction continued towards the end of that century at the hands of John Down, a brickmaker, who also used explosives to break up the stonework. Only the Abbots Kitchen survived: used variously as a Quaker meeting house, a stable and a barn. With the growth of interest in matters antiquarian, the abbey was treated more sympathetically by its 19th century owners, the Porch, Reeves and Austin families, and passed into the hands of the Church of England in 1907. A protracted programme of excavation began (sadly, still awaiting full publication), initially at the hands of Frederick Bligh Bond (1864-1945), great-great nephew of Capt

The Abbot's Kitchen, Glastonbury Abbey.

Bligh of HMS *Bounty*, who used seances and automatic writing to guide his investigations.

Buildings associated with the abbey which survive elsewhere in the town include the **George and Pilgrims Hotel** (formerly the George Inn) in High Street, rebuilt by Abbot John Selwood (1456-93) with a superb stone facade, bearing the arms of the abbey and of Edward IV. No visit to Glastonbury is complete without a drink or meal in the panelled lounge bar at the front of the building. Nearby is another 15th century survival, the so-called **Tribunal** (fee:lists), with a similar but early 16th century frontage, which is likely to be a former merchant's house rather than the abbot's court house. In 1735 it was described as Magdalen Moore's house, 'an ancient wine tavern'. Today it houses an excellent local museum including an extensive collection of finds from Glastonbury Lake Village (with an oak log canoe) and a miscellaneous collection of early items from the town and the abbey.

On the south-east side of the town in Bere Lane stands the magnificent seven-bay **Abbey Barn**, with twin porches and the emblems of the four evangelists on its gable ends. The elaborate base-cruck roof has been dated by dendochronology to the period after 1343-61, and documentary sources suggest the period 1375-89. The barn served the abbey's home farm, although the present farm buildings were put up in the late 19th century. The barn was given to Somerset County Council by Mrs Francis Mapstone, the adjacent farm was bought by the council in 1974 and the complex opened as **Somerset Rural Life Museum** (fee:lists) in 1978. Exhibits cover

The Tribunal, Glastonbury

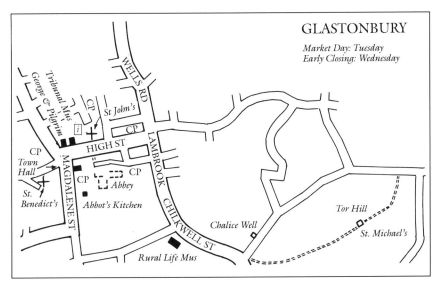

ABOVE RIGHT *Inside Somerset Rural Life Museum.* BELOW *The Market Place, Glastonbury*

the agricultural, social and domestic life of the county in the 19th and early 20th centuries, including peat digging, willow growing and cider making, and an imaginative reconstruction of the life of a Butleigh farm labourer, John Hodges (1828-91). It is deservedly the most popular museum in Somerset, with an extensive programme of special events, demonstrations and activities.

Further south-east in Chilkwell Street is **Chalice Well** (fee:lists), a chalybeate spring and formerly the principal water supply for both the abbey and the town, producing 25,000 gals a day. It was known by 1210 as the Chalk Well ('Chalcwelle'), a name surviving in that of Chilkwell Street, and gained wider notoriety in 1750 with the seemingly miraculous cure of an asthmatic, Matthew Chancellor, following a dream

in which an angel advised him to take the water on seven successive Sundays. Almost overnight Glastonbury became a spa town and up to 10,000 maimed and afflicted individuals flooded into the town, mainly from Bath and Bristol, but also from as far afield as Cornwall and Hampshire. The problem was that the gentry were insufficiently tempted, despite Anne Galloway building a pump house in Magdalene Street in 1752 (which survives as a private house next to the almshouses) and the opening of assembly rooms. The craze proved to be short-lived, a smallpox epidemic in 1753 finally killed off the spa, and an attempt to revive it in 1794 was a flop. The story that St Joseph of Arimathea hid the Holy Grail in the vicinity of the well is no older than the 19th century and was evidently inspired by the name of the

hill to the north, recorded as 'Chalewe' c.1250 and 'Chalowes' in 1515: presumably thought to be a corruption of the name Chalice. An excavation in 1961 revealed a buried well house, probably built in the early 13th century when the water was first culverted to the abbey site, and finds of flints and sherds suggesting the continuous use of the well from the Middle Stone Age. The site, bought from the Roman Catholics by Alice Buckton in 1912, is administered by the Chalice Well Trust and laid out as gardens. Visitors, some of whom still believe in the curative powers of the water, included HRH the Prince of Wales in 1990.

The town of Glastonbury presumably started as a collection of dwellings around the abbey gate to house those serving the monks. This was followed by a planted town based initially on High Street (known as 'the great street' until the early 14th century) with a market place at its western end. The settlement subsequently expanded from the market place along Northload, St Benedict and Magdalene streets. It also served an increasing number of pilgrims who converged on Glastonbury which, like most other Somerset towns, had a flourishing cloth industry. There was a Tuesday market from an early date, a September fair held at the foot of the Tor by 1243, a four-day fair around the feast of St Dunstan (19 May) granted in 1283 and two other fairs also held in the Middle Ages. Surprisingly, however, no borough seems ever to have been founded and a writ of 1319 to invite the return of two MPs went unanswered. Successive abbots clearly felt that it was against the abbey's interests to allow any autonomy to the town at their gates, although a leading role in the running of the town was played by the churchwardens of St John's. Following the dissolution of the abbey Glastonbury inevitably declined, although a band of 13 Flemish clothworkers were introduced in 1549, followed by 70 others in 1551: an experiment which proved shortlived. The town suffered during the Civil War from repeated plundering: one royalist soldier billeted here in 1643 found in the house only a mouldy cheese which was fed to his greyhounds. Nearly 30 locals joined the Monmouth Rebellion in 1685, the rebels camping out in two churches or in the abbey ruins, where great fires were lit to dry them out. After the Battle of Sedgemoor six prisoners were hanged, without trial from the White Hart innsign: their corpses stripped naked by the Wiltshire Militia. Five further rebels, sentenced at the Bloody Assizes, were hanged drawn and quartered, probably in the Market Place. It was not until 1705 that a charter established the mayoralty and corporation which survive today. Unfortunately, by the early 18th century the market had also declined because it clashed with Somerton's Tuesday market, and of the four fairs then held, three were purely for pleasure with 'pedlars, ginger bread sellers and toys', although the fourth, Tor Fair, was noted for 'the vast number of colts' sold there. The market place had a covered market cross, dated 1604, which was demolished in 1803 and the present Gothic pinnacle was put up in 1846. The **Town Hall** in Magdalene Street was built in 1814 to which a large hall was added at the rear in 1930. The entrance hall has an excellent exhibition of civic regalia with old maps and illustrations of the town, while in the council chamber upstairs are displayed portraits of past mayors. In the 19th century the town became known for the manufacture of stockings and gloves, Cyrus Clark of Street began to make rugs here in 1825, and tanning, sheepskins and leatherboard subsequently bulked large in the economy. A canal was opened in 1833 to transport coal, timber and tiles from Bridgwater and the railway (closed since 1966) replaced it in 1854. In recent years increasing numbers have been drawn hither not only by the place's religious associations but also by Glastonbury's alleged mysticism. Down an alleyway south of the High Street, the Assembly Rooms were the venue for Glastonbury Festival operatic performances by Rutland Boughton, 1914-26. These featured mainly Boughton's own works, which had a distinct Arthurian flavour, were regularly attended by George

Bernard Shaw and earned the active support of Sir Edward Elgar, Sir Thomas Beecham, Thomas Hardy and Laurence Housman. The actress Gwen Ffrangcon Davies began her career at these festivals. Modern pilgrims to Glastonbury seek the wayward ley line, earth magnetism or Katherine Maltwood's Zodiac figures, which she rashly claimed were excavated in the landscape around Glastonbury c.2700 BC.

On the north side of High Street, set back from the road, lies the **parish Church of St John the Baptist**, dominated by the abbey from the 12th century, its vicars appointed by the abbey's sacrist from 1203, from 1539 by the Crown and from the 17th century by the bishop. It had dependent chapels of St Benedict (Benignus) in Glastonbury and at West Pennard. The present building was constructed during the course of the 15th century, possibly following the collapse of a former central tower. The fine west tower is second only in height (134 ft) to St Mary's, Taunton, among Somerset parish churches. It was mentioned in 1486 and traditionally built by Abbot John Selwood in 1475, although its crown was reconstructed in 1822. It has a fan vault and a panelled tower arch. The south porch was added in 1428 and the upper storey in 1484. Altars of the Blessed Virgin Mary, St George and St Nicholas were consecrated in 1418. To the north and south of the chancel are marble-topped altar tombs to Richard Atwelle (died 1476), a wealthy clothier, and his widow, Joan (died 1485), formerly bearing brasses. Both were generous benefactors to church and parish and Joan left a pipe of wine to the abbey and a cartload of fuel to each alms-person in the town. In the south transept is a fine table tomb bearing the alabaster effigy of John Cammell (died 1487), thought to have been an official at the abbey. It is ornamented with the figures of camels, referring to his surname. There are fragments of 15th century stained glass in the sanctuary and the Glastonbury legends are depicted in a modern window of 1936. Furnishings include a fine heraldic chest with the arms of Courtenay, St George and Montagu, bought in 1421, and embroidered pall and gremial (apron), attributed to the executed Abbot Whiting. Between 1800 and 1804 French prisoners-of-war were locked up in the church overnight on four occasions. The smaller **Church of St Benedict**, in the street of that name, is believed to have been founded in 1091 following the translation of the relics of St Benignus (Beonna, see **Meare**) to Glastonbury by boat, these

having rested on the site before being moved to the abbey for reburial. The present chancel evidently dates from the late 14th century, but much of the rest, including the west tower, was rebuilt by Abbot Bere c.1520 and his initials appears on the north porch and his rebus on one of the fine roof corbels. The southern arcade and south aisle date only from 1886.

Beckery, to the west of Glastonbury, was an estate granted to the abbey by King Cenwalh in 670, its name probably meaning 'bee-keeper's island'. Excavation in 1967-8 revealed evidence of a mid Saxon monastic settlement and 63 burials, followed by at least two successive chapels dedicated to St Bridget (or in one source, St Mary Magdalene) and a priest's house, which may have continued in use until the dissolution of the abbey. From the 12th century legends developed linking the site with an actual sojourn here by the 6th century St Bridget and in the 14th century of a vision seen here by King Arthur. Nearby, on the boundary between Glastonbury and Street, the A 39 crosses the River Brue by Pomparles Bridge (originally Pons Perilis – 'dangerous bridge') from which legend claims King Arthur threw Excalibur. (**For Sharpham** see **Walton**, **for Nyland** see **Draycott**).

★★★★ *Glastonbury Abbey, for its associations; George and Pilgrims Hotel; Somerset Rural Life Museum, Glastonbury Tor, for its associations and magnificent views,*

★★★ *St John's Church; Tribunal museum,*

★ *St Benedict's Church.*

GOATHURST (D) A compact village by 'the goat hill' which lies below the Quantocks south-west from Bridgwater. Even in Saxon times there were two manors here: Goathurst itself and Halswell ('hazel spring'). Goathurst, held in 1166 by the Goathurst family, passed in the 15th century to the Paulets, a family related to the marquesses of Winchester who adopted a different spelling of their surname from that of the Pouletts of Hinton St George, although of common descent. Halswell, south-west from Goathurst village, was by 1280 also held by a family that took their name from their holding and so continued until c.1645 when Jane Halswell married John Tynte of Chelvey, the manor being settled on their son, Halswell Tynte, created a baronet in 1673. Sir Charles Kemys Tynte bought up the largest share of Goathurst manor from one of the Paulet heirs in 1753. Assiduous research led to the revival of the Wharton barony in favour of Charles Theodore Halswell Kemys-Tynte

ABOVE *Halswell House and the Temple Folly.*

RIGHT *Romulus and Remus, Green Ore*

(as time went by the names got longer) in 1916. The Kemys-Tynte home, Halswell House, which had a private chapel in 1318, was evidently rebuilt by Sir Nicholas Halswell in 1536, accommodated royalist troops during the Civil War and to the present south range was added the extensive building to the north in 1689 by Sir Halswell Tynte. For Pevsner it was 'the most important house of its date in the county', possibly designed by London architect, William Taylor. Although later altered and extended, and restored after a major fire in 1923, the substantial three-storeyed block, with small inner courtyard, stands in elysian parkland at the end of a long private drive from the centre of the village. Within the grounds Sir Charles Kemys Tynte placed a number of 18th century romantic follies, including a stepped pyramid 'in honour of a pure nymph', a monument to a horse that died winning a wager, a rotunda with ice house beneath, a temple (sadly overgrown) and an ornamental bridge. The house was sold in 1950 and subsequently subdivided, but courageous efforts to restore both house and grounds are under way.

The red sandstone church of St Edward, King and Martyr, lies in the centre of the village with a west tower to which William Paulet bequeathed money in 1424. The rest of the building is mainly 15th century and a veritable shrine to the memory of the lords of Goathurst and Halswell, with no fewer than eight heraldic hatchments below the tower. Against the north wall of the nave are impressive monuments to the Rev Sir John Tynte (died 1742), topped by a realistic bust by Rysbrack, and his brother, Sir Charles Kemys Tynte (died 1785) by Nollekens, neither of whom managed to produce issue. The south transept, furnished as the Tynte pew with a ceiling of c.1830, is surrounded by 41 coats of arms: to the east those of the Paulets and the west those of the Tyntes, with a Halswell helm, sword, gauntlets and crest exhibited in a frame. A dispute over the

transept's ownership led in 1559 to the grant of land to the Halswells for the north chapel, hidden behind a red curtain. Here is a superb memorial with effigies to Sir Nicholas Halswell (died 1633), his wife Bridget (died 1627) and their six sons and three daughters (all identified by plates around the top of the monument). Their daughter Bridget remarked in her will 'What would I not give that the bones of my faithful and dear Nicky were brought over and buried with me', her beloved brother having died in Holland. The same chapel includes a touching 1835 monument to a Tynte child by Raffaele Monti. The font is 15th century, the pulpit c.1630 with later tester. In the churchyard is a 1765 tomb bearing a Corinthian column. To the east of the church is the former Goathurst manor-house, now two dwellings: the Dower House and Church Close. Built by the Paulets in the 17th century, it became the parsonage house in 1811. West of the village is the hamlet of Andersfield which gave its name to the local hundred and includes a farmhouse possibly dating from the 15th century.

★★★★ *Church for its monuments,*
★★ *village and setting.*

GODNEY (E), *see* MEARE

GREAT ELM (B/F) A small hillside Mendip parish above the Mells river, northwest from Frome. Its name, outwardly straightforward and taken from the elm tree, occurs as 'Telma' in 1086 and as 'Teames' in 1236, evidently a contraction of *aet elm*, 'at the elm tree'. It is *Great* Elm to distinguish it from *Little* Elm, since developed as the village of Chantry. Southwest from the village across the river lies Tedbury Camp, an earthwork where a pot of Roman coins was dug up in 1691. The manor was held for the first two centuries from Domesday by the Giffards, but latterly owned by the Hodges family and then the Stracheys. The grey-stone village is centred on a small green, bordered by

the manor farm (datestone 1675), the Tudor rectory and the church of St Mary Magdalene. The church has a Norman nave and chancel with an added 13th century west tower, crowned by a solid saddleback roof. Inside it is happily unspoilt by Victorian restorers with a good plaster ceiling and 17th century woodwork. In the valley below were once woollen mills and one of the several edge-tool works operated in the 19th century by the Fussells of Mells. Since 1987 in the three-acre grounds of Bridge House has been held the annual **Great Elm Music Festival** under the presidency of Dame Joan Sutherland, founded and run by Maureen Lehane Wishart in memory of her late husband, Peter Wishart (died 1984).

★★★ *Village, church, setting.*

GREENHAM (H), *see* STAWLEY

GREEN ORE (A/E) This tiny Mendip village is sited at a crossroads on the Bath road (A 39) between Wells and Chewton Mendip. The present name is a corruption of 'Greneworth' ('green homestead') and has nothing to do with the former lead-mining here. The Carthusian monks of Hinton priory had a cell or grange on this spot where they were grazing 1,200 sheep

in the 15th century. At Hill Grove, a ruined onetime sanatorium, beside the Bath road south-west from the village, stands a sculpture mounted on pillars of Romulus and Remus being suckled by the she-wolf. It was put up by an Italian POW in gratitude for his treatment locally and who, after World War II settled at Chewton Mendip.

GREINTON (E)

A village which lines the winding Taunton to Glastonbury road (A361) at the south-eastern edge of the Polden Hills and, like so many other manors in the area, was a possession of Glastonbury Abbey by 1086. The name probably means 'Graega's settlement' and the first element may also survive in Greylake, mentioned in 1292, a location on the main road to the south-west of the village, now marked by a hotel and restaurant. The church of St Michael and All Angels is a mixture of styles from the 12th to 15th centuries. It has some fine benchends, one dated 1621, and four massive gargoyles guard its tower. The parish seems to have included a small Quaker ghetto in the later 17th century: popular because the local rector did not persecute them, as elsewhere. Among these Greinton Quakers were the Clarks, who in 1750 moved to Street where they established their shoemaking empire.

★★ *Village.*

HADSPEN (F), *see* PITCOMBE

HALSE (D)

The parish lies west of the Taunton to Minehead road (A 358) opposite Bishops Lydeard, enjoying excellent prospects of the Quantock Hills. Its name derives from the Saxon *heals*, meaning 'a neck of land'. Robert Arundel, whose family had been given the manor after the Norman Conquest, granted it together with the church to the Hospitallers of St John in 1152. The Hospitallers obtained a short-lived Monday market in 1290 and administered the manor through Buckland Priory in Durston until that monastery was dissolved in 1540. Halse House, a hospital from 1952, is a largely 18th century house of seven bays and two storeys. The village houses front onto the street, once centred on the former Halse Cross, and the tenants of four 'block houses' there were jointly responsible for the maintenance of the manor stocks. The mainly Perpendicular church of St James may stand on a pagan site. There is a well-restored rood screen, 12th century font and fine 16th century Florentine glass in the east window.

★★ *Village, setting.*

HAMBRIDGE (J)

Strung out along the Ilminster to Curry Rivel road (B 3168), its name evidently refers to the bridge that carries the road across the River Isle to the north-east of the village. It is a modern parish, created only in 1844, with the church of St James, complete with squat west tower, designed in 1842 by Benjamin Ferrey. As Pevsner cuttingly observed, 'the best thing about the church is the two splendid cedar trees by its side'. Here in the grounds of the vicarage, now a nursing home, Cecil Sharp began his folk-song collecting crusade in September 1903, by taking down *The Seeds of Love* from the lips of John England. A substantial but attractive 19th century building stands near the bridge over the Isle, marking the site of the former Hambridge brewery. To the north of the village, set well back from the road in its own park, lies Earnshill House, built of brick in 1725 by John Strachan for wealthy Bristol merchant, Henry Combe, and still occupied by the family. Earnshill ('hill by the River Earn') was formerly a parish in its own right, although ordered in 1353 to be served from Curry Rivel following depopulation caused by the Black Death. Earnshill church had been demolished by the 16th century but sinecure rectors were long appointed to serve it. In 1873 on the tennis courts of Earnshill House was played the first recorded game of lawn tennis (then called 'Sphairistike') by its inventor, Maj Walter Clopton Wingfield, a cousin of the Combe family. Further down the B 3168 the hamlet of Westport developed around the end of Westport Canal, opened in 1840 to link with Langport via the River Isle.

HAM HILL (J)

A country park administered by the local authority which commands marvellous views over the surrounding countryside and provides at its northern end the most prominent site for a war memorial in the county. There are four car parks, funished with information boards, a picnic area and a 19th century pub, the Prince of Wales.

Originally known as Hamdon, probably 'the hill among the water-meadows', it has been the source since Roman times for the golden Ham limestone from which most of the buildings in the immediate area were built and which was used further afield in the county for door and window frames and other architectural dressings. This explains the pits, holes and generally corrugated nature of the elevated plateau. There have been many Neolithic and Bronze Age finds and it was also one of the largest Iron Age hill forts in Europe, the entire L-shaped circuit of the hill being enclosed by banks and ditches. Founded probably by the Durotriges in the 1st century BC, it was captured by the Romans soon after their invasion in 43 AD and increasingly ceased to be strategically significant. Gerard in 1633 stated that 'the masons here have a pretty kind of commonwealth; they have their courtes in which all trespasses against each other are judicially tried; and the quarreys themselves seeme rather little parishes than quarryes, soe many buildings have they under the vast workes to shelter themselves in wet weather, and their wrought stones in winter'. There is still a working quarry at the south-east end of the hill. The summit was also the open-air meeting place

LEFT *Hambridge Brewery.* BELOW *Halse*

ABOVE *Ham Hill*

BELOW *Hardington Mandeville*

of the sheriff's 'tourns' or courts for the hundreds of Crewkerne, Houndsborough, Coker, South Petherton and Martock. Also here from 1872 George Mitchell of Montacute promoted great annual open-air political meetings in support of Joseph Arch's movement for an agricultural labourers' union. By c.1100 a 13-day fair was held in these lofty surroundings, owned by Montacute Priory, which continued into recent times with a fair-house near the inn. There was even a chapel of the Holy Cross up here in 1535.

★★★ *Scenery, walking and hillfort.*

HARDINGTON (B) A small farming community set in low-lying lush countryside north-west of Frome, 'the settlement of Heardred's people', sometimes called Hardington Bampfylde to distinguish it from Hardington Mandeville and united with Hemington since 1933. Some identify the place with 'Heortigtun', left in King Alfred's will to his son Edward, although this is more likely to have been Hartland in North Devon, held by Queen Edith in 1066. The manor was held from the early 14th century by the Torny and Pederton families until Agnes de Pederton married John Bampfylde c.1430. John's grandson, another John Bampfylde (died 1528), was the first of the family to live here and may have built the castellated manor-house, the ruins of which (following a fire) were still visible in 1802 and developed a park and rabbit warren. The estate continued in the Bampfylde family until sold by Lord Poltimore in 1859. The

church of St Mary stands uncomfortably hemmed in by the modern outbuildings of Manor and Park farms. The living was held by 1317 by Keynsham Abbey until its dissolution, but acquired by the Bampfyldes in the late 16th century. A Norman chancel arch of c.1150 survives from an earlier building, the tiny west tower and nave dates from the late 14th century, and the chancel was rebuilt in the early 17th century and again in 1859 (apart from the north wall). There is a Norman font, remains of wall paintings on the north nave wall, and a Georgian two-decker pulpit and Bampfylde pew. In the chancel is a superbly ornate monument to Col Warwick Bampfylde (died 1694), which also refers to his brother and sister whose memorials were destroyed in the Great Fire of London. Other tablets commemorate Sir Charles Warwick Bampfylde, Bart, who died in 1823 after being shot in London by the disgruntled husband of one of his servants, and Sir Charles's illegitimate son, the Rev C.F.B. Bampfylde (rector 1814-55), known as 'the Devil of Dunkerton', one of his other parishes. The church, long neglected, was declared redundant in 1971, has since been treated with great affection and was again under repair when I visited in 1993.

★★ *Church and countryside.*

HARDINGTON MANDEVILLE (J) This 'settlement of Heardred's people' lies south-west from Yeovil on the border with Dorset and was held before the Norman Conquest by Gunhilda, sister of King

Harold. Following her brother's overthrow she became a nun and died at Bruges, while Hardington was seized by William the Conqueror. Within a century the manor was granted to the Mandeville family, lords until the early 14th century, who gave their name to the place, and was latterly held by the Portmans. The Ham stone village lies mainly along a single lane, at the north end of which stands the church of St Mary the Virgin on a magnificent elevated site, facing across the valley of the Chinnock Brook to Coker Hill. The building retains its Perpendicular west tower, Norman font and Jacobean pulpit but the rest was largely rebuilt 1863-4. Here was baptised in 1605 Humphrey Pinney who emigrated to America in 1630 and left American descendants. To the east, down in the valley, is the later settlement of Hardington Moor and to the south the isolated farming hamlet of Hardington Marsh.

★ *Views and setting.*

HASELBURY PLUCKNETT (J) A parish

to the north-east of Crewkerne whose name means 'a hazel grove', with the addition of the surname of its medieval owners. The older part of the Ham stone village lines the A 3066, having subsequently expanded along a lane to the west. It was one of the few manors which was retained by its Saxon owner, Brismar, after the Norman Conquest and was occasionally described as a barony. A later lord, Richard of Haselbury, rebelled against King John and was hanged at Sherborne, while another, William Marshal, forfeited the manor for siding with Simon de Montfort against Henry III. The estate was granted to a Breton, Alan de Plugenet, in 1270, who obtained a grant for a Monday market here and whose widow expressed a wish to be interred at Sherborne Abbey. Her son, another Alan, buried her elsewhere and when the bishop remonstrated with him by letter to Haselbury in 1315, Plugenet forced the messenger, the unfortunate Rural Dean, to eat the parchment together with the bishop's wax seal ! In more recent times the manor was held by the Portmans of Orchard Portman.

What set Haselbury apart was the arrival in 1125 of St Wulfric, a hermit and former priest immured in a cell on the north side of the chancel of the parish church of St Michael. He wore chainmail, took cold baths and fasted regularly. He developed a widespread reputation for prophecy, second sight and healing, and his cell was personally visited by Henry I, whose death he predicted, King Stephen and the latter's queen. Even St Bernard of Clairvaux was believed to have solicited his prayers. Wulfric died in 1154 and his body was sought by the monks of Montacute, who had supported him. His remains, however, were squirrelled away by the local priest, buried in his cell and later moved into the east end of the north aisle of the church, which became known as St Wulfric's aisle. Impressive miracles were reported and the place became a popular destination for pilgrims. Wulfric's shrine was mentioned in 1531 and his cell was still standing in 1633. The present chapel, on the north side of the chancel, is Early English but there is no trace of the shrine. The rest of the building is Perpendicular

and the nave, thrown into the aisles in 1920 when the arcades were removed, is now featureless. Richard Draper in his will of 1531 refers to altars or images of the Virgin Mary, St Michael and St Erasmus, and asked that his knell should be rung every day for a year after his death. The church was given to Wells Cathedral in 1174-5 by the lord of Haselbury, William son of William, to found a prebend there.

★ *Village.*

HATCH BEAUCHAMP (J) A peaceful

village since its recent bypassing by the main Taunton/Ilminster road, it lines a single winding street. Difficult to see it today as 'a gateway' (*haecc*) to the royal forest of Neroche (*see* **Staple Fitzpaine**). Difficult also to visualise it as the seat of the medieval barony held by the powerful Beauchamp (pronounced 'Beecham') family. After the Norman Conquest the holdings of three Saxons were united and given to the Count of Mortain, under whom Hatch was held by Robert FitzIvo. Robert Beauchamp, probably related to FitzIvo, owned the manor by 1092 and his successors, lords Beauchamp of Hatch, occupied it until 1361, fortifying their mansion here in 1333. Thereafter it descended to the Seymours, Edward Seymour, brother-in-law to Henry VIII, being created Viscount Beauchamp of Hatch, and eventually by marriage to the Bruces, earls of Aylesbury and Elgin.

By 1633 the manor-house, even then called **Hatch Court** (fee:lists), lay in ruins near the church. In the early 18th century the property was bought by the Collins family of clothiers from Ilminster and in

1755 John Collins (died 1792) built 'a fine square Bath stone mansion in the Palladian style'. It stands north of the village, probably on or near the site of its predecessor, and was designed by a talented amateur architect, Thomas Prowse of Axbridge, MP for Somerset. The towers of the south front are linked by a five-arch arcade with balustrade above and the whole sits in an elegant park, stocked with fallow deer. To this curving wings were added between 1785 and 1829. Later occupiers of Hatch Court have included two MPs for Taunton, Henry Powell Collins (died 1854) and Brig Andrew Hamilton Gault (died 1958). The house features a light and airy entrance hall with cantilevered staircases, beautifully proportioned and furnished rooms and an excellent collection of family portraits and other paintings, including several by Sir Alfred Munnings. There is a small museum crammed with memorabilia of Princess Patricia's Canadian Light Infantry, a regiment raised and equipped by Hamilton Gault in 1914 at his own expense. The house is now occupied by the great-niece of the Hamilton Gaults and her husband, Dr Robin and Mrs Odgers. Don't miss the magnificent kitchen garden.

Behind Hatch Court stands the church of St John the Baptist with a carpark at the head of the Court drive. The church is almost uniformly Perpendicular except that the north chapel, south aisle, chancel arch and vestry were added in the 19th century. The south doorway is dated 1530 and the superb series of benchends are of a similar date. A three-light memorial window in the chancel commemorates Col John Rouse Merriot Chard, VC (died here 1897), the hero of the 1879 Battle of Rorke's Drift in

Hatch Court, Hatch Beauchamp

the Zulu War (played by Stanley Baker in the film *Zulu*). His brother, the Rev Charles Edward Chard was rector here 1885-1910 and both are buried in the churchyard. A wreath sent personally by Queen Victoria was long preserved beneath Col Chard's window. Other tablets recall the Uttermare family of Lodge Farm, lords of the manor from 1722, and the Raban family of Beauchamp Lodge.

A second mansion, Hatch Park was built by 1825 to the west of the village by H.P. Collins: later passing to his descendants, the Gore-Langtons. Destroyed by fire in 1940, a smaller house was later built on the site, but an attractive lodge survives, ringed by trees, towards the south end of the village.

★★★ *Village, Hatch Court and its gardens.*

HAWKRIDGE (C) This small village, named for the 'hawk ridge' above it, clings to the hillside above a tributary of the River Barle, and has a special place in the life and history of Exmoor. One of the two annual Swainmote courts which regulated the moor was held in Hawkridge churchyard and 15 of the 52 free suitors of Exmoor held farms or tenements in the parish. Today the annual highspot is the Hawkridge Revel, held on August Bank Holiday at Zeal Farm. The manor here was held in the Middle Ages by successive Foresters of Exmoor, ultimately passing into the hands of the Acland family. In the village the church of St Giles has a Norman south doorway and font, 14th century chancel and tower. The parson here was convicted in 1270 of harbouring deer poachers from Devon. There is a 13th century coffin lid which bears a Norman-French inscription to 'William . . .' attributed to the Forester and lord of the manor, William de Plessy (died 1274). There is a monument to a later hero of the moor, Ernest Bawden, huntsman to the Devon and Somerset Staghounds 1917-37.

North-east from the village **Tarr Steps**, one of the finest clapper bridges in England, spans the river Barle. The name has probably been transferred from nearby Tarr (i.e. tor) Farm. Damaged at the time of the Lynmouth flood disaster of 1952 and since, the bridge has been immaculately restored. There is good carparking, mandatory cream teas at Tarr Farm, loos, excellent picnicking and idyllic walks beside the Barle to Withypool. At Ashway Farm to the south-east was born Sir George Williams (1821-1905), founder of the YMCA.

★★★ *Tarr Steps and setting.*

Tarr Steps, Hawkridge

HEATHFIELD (D) This 'open land where heather grows' lies just north of the main road (B 3227) from Taunton to Milverton. It owed dues to the bishop of Winchester's manor of Taunton Deane from Saxon times and was given to William de Mohun after the Conquest. By 1166 the estate had passed to Talbot of Heathfield, whose successors took Talbot as their surname and the manor became known as Heathfield Talbot: later dubbed Heathfield Durborough after the family who were lords from the mid 14th century. By 1517 it had descended to the Hadleys and in 1558 to the Luttrells. The manor-house is now Manor Farm, dating from c.1600 but enlarged and refronted when the Luttrells sold it in 1803. The nearby church of St John the Baptist was granted in the late 12th century to the Hospital of St John of Jerusalem by Geoffrey Talbot. The west tower dates from the following century but the rest of the building was ruthlessly remodelled by Rector Spurway in 1869. An unusual 16th century wall monument depicts a kneeling man and woman facing each other, surmounted by two smaller figures in leg calipers. It has been associated with Arthur Hadley (died 1558) and his thrice-married sister Margaret (died 1607) but never satisfactorily identified. Later monuments commemorate the clerical Cornishes and Spurways who are credited with establishing the traditions of Taunton Cider (*see* **Norton Fitzwarren**) at their home, Heathfield Rectory, rebuilt c.1860.

HEMINGTON (B) A sizeable parish but small village to the north-west of Frome, 'the settlement of Hemmi's (or Hemma's) people'. By 1227 there was a park here, when the king gave deer from Selwood forest to Sir Robert de Courtenay. The manor was retained by the Courtenays and their relations, the Conways, until it was sold in 1544 to the Bampfyldes of Hardington. It was long remembered how the dissolute Sir Charles Bampfylde (died 1823) felled nearly all the timber on his manor to pay his debts. The Bampfylde estate was sold in 1859 and the lordship was subsequently acquired by the lords Hylton of nearby Ammerdown in Kilmersdon. The church of St Mary in the middle of the village has a Norman chancel arch, a south aisle and doorway of c.1230 and a clerestoreyed nave with Decorated windows of c.1340. The Perpendicular west tower is a scaled-down version of those at Mells and Leigh on Mendip, and the south porch is a somewhat uneasy Romanesque addition of 1856. There is a Norman scalloped font and monuments to the families of Hill (rectors almost continuously, 1678-1814), Vigor, Bampfylde and Cradock.

Another estate, now represented by Highchurch Farm, north-east of the village, was bought from the Courtenays by the Hungerfords of Farleigh c.1400, and from them by Samuel Vigor (died 1711). The Vigors were also linked from the 13th century with **Faulkland** ('land of the people'), now the largest settlement in the parish: a village which straggles along the

A 366 but is centred on an attractive green. John de Courtenay obtained a short-lived Wednesday market and three-day fair at Faulkland in 1263. Here, until demolished by Lord Hylton in 1969, stood Turner's Tower, a 185 ft column built c.1885 by James Turner to outdo the memorial pillar at Ammerdown. Hemington was the scene of a brutal murder in 1740 when Elizabeth Branch and her daughter beat their servant girl, Jane Buttersworth, to death, and were convicted and hanged at Ilchester.

★ *Church.*

HENSTRIDGE (K) A large village in the extreme south-east of the county, 'the ridge where stallions are kept' (compare this with the meaning of nearby Horsington), which lines the A 357 south of its traffic-lighted junction with the A 30. At the nearby Virginia Ash Inn it has been claimed dubiously, at least since 1836, that Sir Walter Raleigh, while smoking tobacco, was doused by a servant who thought he was on fire. Admittedly Sir Walter lived not far away, at Sherborne Castle, but there are other places which claim the story. The main estate, held by King Harold, killed at Hastings, then passed to the Conqueror and by the 12th century had been granted to the Camville family. A second manor was given by Hugh Lupus, Earl of Chester, to the abbey of St Sever in France. This estate is identified with Yenston (formerly Endeston), a hamlet to the north-west of the village, which later formed part of the endowment of St Katherine's chantry at Ilminster. The church of St Nicholas (formerly dedicated to St Michael 1516, 1526) lies in the centre of the village just off the main street. It was given by Richard de Camville to Wells Cathedral between 1175 and 1179 to form a prebend there, to which was added in 1292 by Henry de Lacy, Earl of Lincoln, a chapel at Whitchurch, a small hamlet immediately north of the village. The present church was largely rebuilt in 1873, the west tower in 1900, with the exception of the Perpendicular north aisle of the Blessed Virgin Mary. This incorporates the tomb, completed in 1463, of William Carent (died 1478) and his wife, Margaret Stourton, with their defaced effigies. Carent lived at Toomer, an estate now represented by Toomer Farm, southwest of the village, which came to him through his mother, Alice Toomer, and his family lived there until 1675. In the same aisle is a fine canopied tomb which may have housed a later William Carent (died 1516), who requested burial there.

★ *Village, church.*

The Orangery, Hestercombe House

HESTERCOMBE (D) Formerly a detached part of Kingston St Mary where its lords were buried, its name was first mentioned in 854 as 'Hegsteldescumb', probably meaning 'the bachelor's' or 'warrior's valley'. The estate was one of three held in the early 12th century by the Flory or Fleury family under the bishop of Winchester's manor of Taunton Deane, passing like Combe Florey to the Meriets, of whom Sir John de Meriet established a chapel here in 1316. This had a feast of heraldic stained glass (some apparently removed to Kingston church) until demolished in 1766. On the death of another Sir John Meriet in 1391-2, the estate descended to his son-in-law, John la Warre, in whose family Hestercombe continued for nearly five centuries. The family treasured the two-handed sword of King John of France, captured with its bearer at the Battle of Poitiers in 1356: only recently returned temporarily by a descendant for exhibition at Kingston St Mary church. Sir Francis Warre (died 1718) served as MP for both Taunton and Bridgwater, secured a baronetcy in 1672 and was involved in the ransom of the Maids of Taunton after the Monmouth Rebellion in 1685. His grandson, Copplestone Warre Bampfylde (died 1791), was a noted amateur artist and architect and two of his folly temples survive in Hestercombe's grounds. The last of the line here was Bampfylde's great-niece, Elizabeth Maria Warre. She lived in solitary spinsterhood here until her death in 1872, when over £12,000 in

notes and coin was found in the house.

The mansion and estate were bought by the 1st Viscount Portman who, in trying to economise on architects, virtually destroyed the old Tudor house. He ended up with a Victorian mock-Italian villa, enjoying a relatively imposing approach from the west up a long drive but with a jumbled featureless south front overlooking Taunton below. Even this vandalism can be forgiven in gratitude for the world-famous gardens commissioned in 1903 by the 2nd Viscount's eldest son, E.W.B. Portman (died 1911), from Sir Edwin Lutyens and Gertrude Jekyll. Below the south front of the house they created on different levels a large parterre, terraces, pergolas, water channels and a large orangery, which now features an exhibition on the history of the garden. Portman's widow died in 1951, the premises were leased to (and in 1975 bought by) Somerset County Council and now accommodate the headquarters of the County Fire Brigade. Work on replanting and restoring the gardens to their former glory commenced in 1973.

★★★★ *Gardens.*

HIGHBRIDGE (E), see **BURNHAM-ON-SEA**

HIGH HAM (E) A large rural parish lying north of Langport, whose name, originally Hamme ('meadow'), had added 'high' by the early 14th century to distinguish it from Low or Nether Ham (*see below*). The place occupies the end of a promontory of high ground with wonderful views out over King's Sedgemoor and occasional lush leafy valleys. A Roman villa one mile south of the village with two mosaics was dug up in 1861, one of several in the area west of Somerton.

Another was excavated in 1946 to the south-east of Low Ham, occupied from c.200 AD until the later 4th century, including a bath block which featured a further mosaic (now exhibited in the County Museum at Taunton Castle). This last celebrated pavement depicts four scenes of the passion of Dido and Aeneus from Virgil's *Aeneid*. Two grants of land here were made by King Edgar to Glastonbury Abbey in 965 and 973, and the abbey retained the manor until the dissolution of 1539. Thereafter it was granted by Elizabeth I to John, Lord Grey, passing in the early 17th century to the Rolles of Shapwick.

The church of St Andrew stands at the edge of a charming village green, the view fringed with tall trees, or, as German rector Adrian Schaell (1570–99) put it in his reminiscences, 'through the holesomeness of pure ayre and pleasant prospect on every side, it doth merveylously delight the comers thereunto'. The west tower is early 14th century in its lower stages but Perpendicular above. Schaell recorded that the aisled nave, with its battlements, large gargoyles and fine roof, was rebuilt in a single year (1476–77) by Abbot John Selwood and certain prominent laymen: the chancel and panelled chancel arch added at a similar period by rector John Dyer (died 1499), as mentioned on an inscribed brass. There is a substantial and detailed rood screen, an unusual (possibly Jacobean) lectern, a pulpit dated 1632 and some 15th century stained glass in the chancel. Among 16th century rectors recalled by Schaell were John Helpes, a former Glastonbury monk who died from gorging himself on brawn, and John Kenell (1560–70), who spent £400 on 'a most notorious harlot', married 'a rustique, rude and foolish woman' and died in poverty at London, aged over 90.

Stembridge Windmill (fee:lists) with its thatched cap stands alone to the south-east of the village. Owned by the National Trust, it was built c.1820, was worked until 1910, and is the only survivor of several windmills put up to catch the wind sweeping across the Levels.

In a valley south-east from High Ham lies the hamlet of **Low** (or Nether) **Ham**, formerly a medieval royal forest, where an estate was occupied by the king's forester

in Somerset. From the Odburvilles, who held that office by 1086, it passed to William de Wrotham in 1198, and in 1243 William Clome was found killed 'in the forest of Netherham'. In 1588 the main manor was bought by Sir Edward Hext, who seems to have built a new mansion on Hext Hill to the south of Low Ham church, with elaborate gardens. Hext's daughter carried the estate to the Stawells of Cothelstone and John, 2nd Lord Stawell (died 1692), demolished the first mansion and is said to have spent over £100,000 on a second house, 400 ft by 100 ft, just east of Low Ham church, which was never completed. The manor was sold to Lady Edith Phelips of Montacute c.1720, whose son-in-law, Carew Hervey Mildmay, moved the last remnant of the great house, its substantial gateway, to Hazelgrove House (*see* **Queen Camel**). Only extensive banks and terraces south and east of the church mark the sites of both buildings and their grounds. The church of Low Ham, of unknown dedication, stands isolated in the middle of a field. It was recorded as a chapelry to the parish church by the 13th century, although John de Burci failed to secure episcopal consent for a chantry there in 1316. Later it served largely as a private manorial chapel. The present early Gothic building, with a Perpendicular west tower and anachronistic rood screen, was started by Sir Edward Hext in 1620 and completed by his grandson, Col George Stawell, in 1669. The principal monuments commemorate Sir Edward Hext (died 1625), his wife Dionysia (died 1633), with their recumbent effigies, and Ralph, 1st Lord Stawell (died 1689).

The hamlet of Henley, mentioned in 973 and where there was a wood in 1282, lies at the edge of the Levels north of the main village. There was a chapel of St John the Baptist at Beer, a hamlet on the boundary with Aller until the Reformation. In this chapel a service was held on that saint's day by the parson of Pitney for those engaged in the annual wrestling matches on Sedgemoor.

★★★ *Scenery and setting.* ★★ *Parish church, Low Ham church.*

HILLFARRENCE (H) Set in the level country west of Taunton, the hill from which the place is named is presumably the slight rise to the east of the village. To this was added the name of the Ferun family, owners of the manor by 1182. From the Feruns the estate passed to the Verney family, descending eventually by marriage

to the Palmers and Aclands of Fairfield. **Allerford** ('ford by the alder trees'), today a small hamlet to the north-east, was formerly a separate manor but was united with Hillfarrence in the early 14th century when William Verney married Denise de Allerford. The Victory Inn at Allerford was built in 1835 to take advantage of passing trade on the Grand Western Canal, opened that same year. Many visitors to Hillfarrence get no further than the Anchor Inn, a popular watering (and eating) place. If they persevere they reach a peaceful village green furnished with attractive cottages, a stream and the church of the Holy Cross. The church has a fine western tower with pierced parapet bearing initials identified as those of John Peryn of Wellington, who in 1509 left money to the building of towers at West Buckland and Langford Budville. The south chapel descended with the manor until 1857, when the whole church suffered the usual heavy-handed restoration. A good set of 16th century benchends survived the treatment but are more uniform and formal than the Quantock series. The modern painting of the sanctuary ceiling with gold stars on a blue background is particularly effective. Methodism here took such a hold in 1750 that the minister was 'almost afraid of going to church to perform divine service'. Cudgel-playing was popular in the parish, a match which ended in brawling being recorded in 1650.

★★ *Village and scenery.*

HINTON ST GEORGE (J) To the north-west of Crewkerne but away from all main roads, this 'settlement on the high land' is one of the most attractive and unspoilt villages in the county. The manor, held by the Denebaud family by the early 13th century, passed by marriage to William Poulett in 1429. William's descendants increasingly dominated not only Hinton but the surrounding area, acquiring a barony in 1627 and an earldom in 1706. Their number included Sir Amias (died 1588), gaoler of Mary, Queen of Scots, who had the courage to refuse Elizabeth I's order to murder his prisoner, and John, the 1st Earl (died 1743), who served as 1st Lord of the Treasury and Lord Steward of the Household to Queen Anne. To the west of the village the Pouletts developed a substantial park from the 16th century with a major mansion, Hinton House, diverting the village street to the north to increase its seclusion. The present building dates from a rebuild which began in the late 15th century, was extended with a

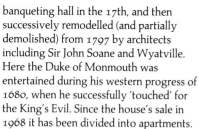

banqueting hall in the 17th, and then successively remodelled (and partially demolished) from 1797 by architects including Sir John Soane and Wyatville. Here the Duke of Monmouth was entertained during his western progress of 1680, when he successfully 'touched' for the King's Evil. Since the house's sale in 1968 it has been divided into apartments.

The church of St George at the west end of the village was granted c.1220 by Robert de Barnevill to St Bartholomew's Hospital, London. It is a fine Perpendicular building, the west tower under construction in 1487, and the rest a mix of 15th and 16th centuries. The 13th century font was recarved in the mid 15th with the Poulett arms of three swords in pile. The interior is crammed with fine memorials to the lords of the manor, particularly the Poulett pew (now closed to access) into which James Wyatt converted the north transept c.1814. Below the pew is a large knight's effigy, often identified as that of Sir John Denebaud but more likely to be his son-in-law, Sir William Poulett (died 1488). There are also excellent effigies of Sir Amias Poulett (died 1537), often alleged to have committed the future Cardinal Wolsey to the stocks, and his second wife Laura, Sir Hugh Poulett (died 1572), governor of the Isle of Jersey, and his first wife Philippa, Sir Amias Poulett (died 1588), gaoler of the Scottish queen (removed here in 1728 when St Martin-in-the Fields church, London, was rebuilt), and Sir Anthony Poulett (died 1600) and his wife Catherine. There is also an incredibly elaborate sarcophagus to John, Lord Poulett (died 1649), which Pevsner assigns to the early 18th century, and brasses to John Chudderle (c.1475) and his wife Alice, and to Adam Martin (died 1597), depicting also his wife and 11

children. One rector, Edmund Peacham, was accused of maligning James I and Bishop Montagu, tortured in the Tower of London, convicted of high treason and died in prison at Taunton Castle in 1616.

A stroll down the main village street passes the late medieval stepped village cross and a succession of attractive Hamstone houses dating from the 17th or early 18th century. One property, the Priory (a name possibly derived from its former ownership by Monkton Farleigh Priory, which had a small estate here 1227-1536), dates from the 16th century with a 14th century chapel at its east end. The Poulett Arms, complete with Fives wall behind, was known as the Hare and Hounds before 1824. Thoroughfares include Teapot Lane and Gas Lane, the latter recalling the local manufacture of gas here by 1883. In Back Lane stand almshouses built in 1872 by Lady Augusta Poulett to replace earlier ones near the church.

Two fairs here were chartered in 1632, of which that on St George's day continued until c.1947. In 1849 the future 6th Earl Poulett (died 1899) married a pilot's daughter he had met at Dublin Races, only to find out that she was already pregnant by an army captain. They immediately separated and the child, once born, led a chequered career as a singer, clown and organ grinder. He placarded his barrel organ as 'Viscount Hinton', visited the village in the 1870s and, on the death of his 'father', duly claimed the earldom. His claim was rejected and he died a pauper in Holborn Workhouse in 1909. At Gainsfords near the church Henry Fowler, compiler of the *Concise* and *Pocket Oxford Dictionaries* and *Fowler's Modern English Usage*, lived and worked in relative isolation from 1925 until his death in 1933. Punky Night, a local October custom in

the parish involving the carrying of lighted hollowed-out mangolds, allegedly commemorates the search by local women for their husbands returning late from Chiselborough fair.

★★★★ *Village and church (for its memorials).*

HOLCOMBE (F) A former Mendip coalmining village south from Midsomer Norton (Avon), whose name means 'hollow or deep valley'. It lines a road running south from Radstock (with attractive views to the south from the main village), roughly parallel to, and east of, the Foss Way. Northeast of the village on Charmborough Hill are the remains of a former chambered long barrow, Giant's Grave, marked by three large stones and largely and inexpertly excavated out of existence in 1909. Several previously disturbed burials were unearthed, together with Roman coins of c.260-330 AD, and traces of a Roman villa have been found in the parish. Half the manor was acquired with the advowson of the church by Keynsham Abbey from William de Holcombe in 1243 and retained until the dissolution. The early village presumably stood in the vicinity of Holcombe Old Church, dedicated to St Andrew, which lies to the north beyond Moore's Farm (leased to William Moore in 1674) at the end of an unfenced lane through a wheat field, set in beautiful countryside. Although the Black Death is traditionally blamed for the desertion of the site, it is more likely that the economic attractions of the main road inspired the move.

The small church is Perpendicular with an attractively-unrestored white-painted interior, furnished with box pews, west gallery and two-decker Jacobean pulpit. Particular interest centres on the reset Norman south doorway which incorporates an earlier inscribed stone set upside down in one of its capitals. Watkin believed in 1969 that in the incomplete inscription he could decipher the name 'Wrotrard', whom he identified with Hrothweard, Archbishop of York, who attended a Council at Exeter in 928: considering that he may have consecrated an earlier church here in that year. More recent work by Sally Douglas has thrown grave doubts on this. She considers that if it is Celtic it is likely to be part of a memorial: if Anglo-Saxon, to be dedicatory, but that there is too little text even to decide in which language it was written. To the north of the tower are the graves of John Edward and Hannah Scott (and their children), parents of the polar explorer, Capt Robert Falcon Scott (1868-1912), whose memorial also commemorates their son, 'who in returning from the South Pole with his Companions was translated by a Glorious Death'. In more recent years a senior citizens' development at Holcombe, Scott's Close, was opened by Sir Peter Scott. There was a major brewery in the village, opened in 1800, of which Capt Scott's father was the last manager, living in the late Georgian Manor House (the old manor was demolished in 1880). The new, rather dull, church of St Andrew was built in the village in 1884-5. The south end of the village is marked by the Duke of Cumberland Inn, opposite which is a bridge designed to span the Somerset and Dorset Canal: an ambitious project that was never finished. Coalmining began here at an early date, the only deep shaft being Edford Colliery (1862-1915). The last workings at Blackpool Wood, started by striking miners in 1921, closed in 1923.

★★ *Holcombe Old Church and its setting.*

HOLFORD (D) The village is particularly popular as a destination or departure point for Quantock walkers in the shape of the Plough Inn, recorded in 1859 and sited on the main road (A 39). Its name means simply 'the ford in the hollow'. Well-trodden walks run through the village up to the hills, through the leafy Holford and Hodders combes and past Combe House Hotel, developed from c.1840 by James Hayman as a major tannery complex. The hotel still retains a giant iron water-wheel of 1893, but the tannery closed in 1900. Industry came early to Holford. Cloth was produced here by the 16th century, there were two fulling mills in 1664, one with a dye house, and copper was mined from the late 18th century. The small church of St

Alfoxton Park, Holford

Mary the Virgin was dedicated to St John by 1175, when the living was given to Stogursey Priory by the lord of the manor, Robert son of Alfred. Between 1440 and 1978 rectors were presented by Eton College. The lower courses of the diminutive saddle-back tower may date from the 12th century, but most of the church was rebuilt in the 1840s. In the churchyard is buried Frederic Norton (died 1946), composer of the celebrated musical *Chu Chin Chow* (1916).

Alfoxton Park is a hotel with superb views to the sea which until 1886 occupied a detached part of Stringston. The estate was first recorded in 1086 as 'Alfagestone' ('Aelfheah's settlement') and was for centuries the property and residence of the St Albyn family, who obtained it in marriage with a Popham heiress in the 15th century and built the present Georgian mansion c.1710. For all that, the house is best remembered for the one year (1797-8) when it was tenanted for a rent of £23 by the poets William and Dorothy Wordsworth and regularly visited by their friend, Samuel Taylor Coleridge, from nearby Nether Stowey. All three sought inspiration from their magnificent surroundings, but their habit of wandering around a coastal area with notebooks while England was at war with France led to an hilarious spy scare in which a government agent was sent down to investigate. The nearby so-called dog pound was not intended for stray dogs, as often stated, but was the local manor pound for all stray animals. It bears the St Albyn crest of a seated wolf: evidently mistaken for a dog.

★★★★ *Scenery and walking.*

HOLTON (F) A compact village southwest from Wincanton whose name may mean 'settlement in a remote valley'. In 1086 it was occupied together with the

hamlet of Lattiford ('Lodereforda' – 'the beggar's ford') by Albric under Humphrey the chamberlain. In the 16th century it was held by Francis Hastings who by a will of c.1596 tried to discourage the holding of church ales there. The church of St Nicholas dates from the 14th century, has a Norman tub font and a north aisle added in 1888. Richard Tynes, rector 1581-83, a 16th century asset-stripper, raised money by selling the slates off the rectory roof and then having it thatched. One of his successors, Joseph Sorrell, found himself a reluctant national celebrity in 1906 when the entire parish boycotted his services.

HORNBLOTTON (E/F) This rural parish, north-west of Castle Cary, just off the Foss Way, has a colourful name: 'the horn-blower's settlement' – perhaps because the original Saxon lord may have received it for heading the king's hunt. The estate here was given by Ethelbald, king of the West Saxons 855-60, to his ealdorman Eanwulf, who transferred it to Glastonbury Abbey. The principal settlement today is Hornblotton Green, an appealing scatter of lias-stone houses. To the north stands the isolated and striking church of St Peter, at the end of a country lane beyond a farm gate, completed in 1874 to the designs of Sir T.G. Jackson by wealthy rector, Preb Godfrey Thring (died 1903), who had found the old church 'past restoration'. In the tower Thring placed an electric striking clock, the first of its kind when installed in 1883, the batteries and pendulum being housed in the substantial rectory (designed by J.L. Penrose and built for Thring by his father in 1867), now the Manor House, 130 yards away. This novelty inspired the rector of Binegar to write:

'Hail! to the workman who with
wondrous power

Has placed a Clock Electric in the tower,
Teaching the boors of Hornblotton to
    know
How, like a stream, the silent hours flow.'
In 1984 the clock mechanism was
removed to the Science Museum in
London for restoration and exhibition. In
the churchyard stands the overgrown base
of the old church tower, to the south of its
successor.

★★ *Church, for lovers of Victorian
architecture.*

HORSINGTON (K) The village is tucked
away off the A 357 immediately north-
west of Templecombe, its name meaning
'the settlement of the horse-keepers'. The
manor was owned by the Catholic Gawens
from the mid 16th century, who suffered
for their adherence to the old faith and
forfeited the estate for treason in 1653. The
manor ultimately passed in 1748 to Matthew Spencer, who built the five-bay three-
storey Manor House in the 1750s. His
son sold it in 1797 to Samuel Bailward,
whose family still occupy the property.
Horsington House, now a hotel, is an even
larger mansion, built next to the church by
William Manning Dodington in the early
19th century and held by his family until
1922. The church of St John the Baptist
stands at the end of a short lane leading
south from the shaft and steps of the
village cross. The church has a 15th
century west tower but otherwise was
completely rebuilt 1885-7 and is rather
dark and forbidding. There is a 15th
century font with angels' heads and monuments to the Gifford, Spencer, Dodington
and Wickham families, several saved from
the old church. The Wickhams were rectors
here from 1686 until 1897, occupying the
former rectory, now the Grange, dating
mainly from the 18th century with additions of 1856. Within the parish lies South
Cheriton, a separate Domesday manor but
usually held with that of Horsington. This
village also lines a lane running east from
the main road, the junction marked by the
former toll house which until recently still
displayed the tolls enforced in 1824. There
was a free chapel at South Cheriton by
1314, closed in 1548. As though in recom-
pense there are Unitarian, United Reformed
and Methodist chapels. West of the main
road is the delightfully named hamlet of
Wilkin Throop ('Wilkenthorp' in 1297;
thorp – 'farm'), Wilkin probably being the
name of a former owner, added to distinguish the place from Combe Throop,
south-east from Horsington.

★★ *Village and buildings.*

The lectern, Huish Champflower church

HUISH CHAMPFLOWER (D) This
parish stretches across the southern face of
the Brendon Hills, taking its name from
hiwisc, Saxon for 'homestead': its suffix
marking its ownership by the family of
Thomas de Champflower, lord of its manor
by 1166. Later held by the Devon
Courtenays from 1397 until the execution
of the Marquess of Exeter in 1539, it was
bought by the Trevelyans of Nettlecombe
in 1780. The place has an attractive
landscape of scattered highland farms,
although the many abandoned quarries
testify to a former harvest of stone and
slate. A house called Washbattle beside the
River Tone represents the mill which
ground Huish's corn by 1086 until World
War I. The small village of pink and white
cottages stretches along the hill slope and
includes the church of St Peter with its 15th
century rendered tower. The east window
of the north chancel chapel includes glass
claimed to be the remains of a Jesse
window from Barlynch Priory, near
Dulverton. Victorian wings complete a rare
15th century eagle lectern.

★★ *Village, setting.*

HUISH EPISCOPI (E) A former village
immediately east of Langport, and with
which it is now continuously built up. Its
name means 'household' (Saxon – *hiwisc*)
with the addition of *episcopi*, 'of the bishop',
referring to the ownership of the manor.
Much of the land is low-lying, the rivers
Yeo and Parrett meeting to the south-west
of the village, and there was substantial
quarrying of the local lias stone, particularly at Pibsbury in the east of the parish.
North of the village, strung out along an
east to west lane is the hamlet of Wearne
('alder stream'), to the south of which

Huish Episcopi church tower

Romano-British remains, including burials,
coins and *tesserae*, of the 3rd and 4th
centuries, have been periodically found.
The estate was owned by the bishops of
Bath and Wells from Saxon times until
most of it was sold off to the tenants in
1859-60. There was a park here from 1257
and a vain attempt was made to establish a
borough called Southwick or Froglane
to the west of the River Parrett south-
west from Langport, where there were 31
burgage tenements mentioned in 1458 and
1566. The church of the Blessed Virgin
Mary stands in the centre of the village
and was probably an episcopal foundation.
It had been assigned to the archdeacons of
Wells by 1199 and a vicarage was probably
ordained c.1232. There is a fine 12th century Ham stone south doorway, apparently
reddened by a major fire, possibly c.1232
when the church was rededicated and a
vicarage was ordained. The nave, chancel,
north transept and south porch are 14th
century, a superb 99 ft west tower was
added in the 15th century, featuring on a
9p postage stamp in 1972, and the south
aisle in the early 16th century. There is a
Perpendicular font, a pulpit dated 1625
and stained glass (1899) by Burne Jones
and William Morris in the east window of
the south aisle. A monument in the nave to
the Rev Thomas Keat (died 1750), rector
of Ashington and Kingweston, describes
him as 'A Gentleman of a humane
Deportment, Great Candour and strict
Integrity'.

★★ *Church.*

HUNTSPILL (E) This extensive Levels parish, 'Hun's creek', stretches from the east bank of the Parrett estuary as a landscape of scattered hamlets and farmsteads, the principal village lying mainly along and to the west of the A 38. It had its own fair by the late 18th century, discontinued before 1875. This became a wealthy area of rich pastures as the land was progressively reclaimed and sea walls built. As early as 1225 a lawsuit concerned seven dykes and the diversion of a watercourse. The process was completed with the cutting of the Huntspill River from 1940, designed not only to drain the Levels but also to supply the new (and then very secret) munitions factory at Puriton with over 3m. gallons of water a day. An estate here was granted to Glastonbury Abbey by Ethelmund with the consent of Offa, King of Mercia 757-96, but had been lost by the abbey before the Norman Conquest. The principal estate was a free manor (later forming, with Puriton, its own hundred), given before 1086 to Walter of Douai, descending in turn to the Pagnell, Cogan, FitzWaryn and Bourchier families: the last becoming earls of Bath. There were other manors here: Alston Maris (now the hamlet of Alstone, north of the village, 'Alsistune' in 1086, called 'Maris' from its ownership by the De Marisco or Marsh family), Huntspill Maris, Huntspill Delahay and Huntspill Verney. The Perpendicular church of St Peter (formerly All Saints) stands at the western end of the village, has a west tower of c.1400 and a Jacobean pulpit that came from Stogursey. Its former pulpit was destroyed in a major fire in 1878, after which the church was rebuilt. The patronage passed with the main manor until bought by John Tripp of Shipham, who presented his son to the rectory in 1708 and then sold the advowson to Balliol College, Oxford.

Signed off the A38 just to the east of the M5 lies **New Road Farm** (fee:lists), where visitors can share in most aspects of life on a Somerset Levels farm, with ferrets, goats and bees. Less predictable attractions include hand-reared badgers and foxes, a nocturnal house (to observe night creatures), a County Council Visitor Centre and an 'I Spy' farm trail. The village of **East Huntspill** lies beyond the motorway and became a separate parish in 1845. The church of All Saints was built 1839-40 in Norman style to the designs of G.P. Manners. To the north of the village the hamlet of **Bason Bridge** ('Basingebridge' in 1593) marks a crossing of the river Brue, formerly known for its major milk factory.

★★★ *New Road Farm.*

Ilchester

ILCHESTER (J) A small recently-bypassed town (and former borough) or large village midway between Somerton and Yeovil which was the principal Roman settlement in the present county and, from 1166 almost until the mid 19th century, was Somerset's county town. There is little visible evidence of this former greatness today, most of the surviving lias-stone buildings dating from the 18th and 19th centuries. A visit to the small **museum** (fee:lists) in High Street will give an appreciation of the place's heritage. Ilchester's Saxon name means 'Roman fort on the river Isle' ('Yle' in 693, a British river name, variously considered to mean 'a spring', 'to hurry' or 'to drink': now the river Yeo), but the place had an earlier name. A document of the early 8th century records a Roman town in this area called 'Lindinis' (possibly meaning 'a marshy place') and two building stones found at Hadrian's Wall dated to 369 AD are inscribed to 'a town of the Durotriges (called) Lendiniae'. The Durotriges were a native British tribe who had their capital at Dorchester and it has been suggested that Ilchester was the focus of their north-western territory. Immediately south of Ilchester is a roughly-oval late Iron-Age enclosure of some 35 acres which may have formed the site of this earlier British settlement.

At this point the Roman Foss Way from Bath crossed the navigable river Yeo, at first by a ford, later by a bridge, and the native village was replaced c.60 AD by a fort of about 17 acres immediately south of the crossing, the Durotriges having been defeated by Vespasian. There followed an urban banked enclosure of some 25 acres c.200 AD, possibly with stone gateways,

beyond which suburbs extended along the several routes which converged on the town. Stone buildings on a grid street plan progressively replaced timber ones but archaeology as yet has revealed no inscriptions or public buildings. Scattered road-side cemeteries have been excavated south of the town but a major 4th century cemetery lies just north of the Yeo in Northover, estimated to have contained 1,500 burials. After the late 5th century the town seems to have been gradually abandoned and little is known of its fortunes until 973 when a mint was established here: This mint was briefly removed to Cadbury Castle in the time of Ethelred II but returned and continued to produce coins until c.1250.

The Saxons evidently established a major *burh* here, held by the kings of the West Saxons, who became the kings of England. By the time of the Norman Conquest it had 108 burgesses with a market worth £11 a year, making it (after Bath) the most important town in Somerset. It was also sufficiently well-defended in 1087-8 to repulse the rebel Robert Mowbray, who had already burned Bath. In 1166 the county gaol was built here, effectively making Ilchester the county town of Somerset. The burgesses, having formed themselves into a guild, obtained a charter in 1183-4, reissued in 1204, making its market, later held on Wednesdays, free of toll, and placing the rule of the town under two bailiffs. Its 13th century bailiff's staff head, with the figures of an angel and three kings, is exhibited at the County Museum. From the mid 13th century the town declined, the mint closed, the county gaol and courts moved to Somerton in the 1280s, the number of churches decreased and the place ceased to return MPs in 1361. In an attempt to reverse the decline, the shire courts were moved back to Ilchester in 1366 and the county gaol returned in 1371, sited on Ilchester Bridge by 1542. From 1477 the burgesses administered the generously-endowed almshouses founded in 1426 by Robert Veel. A corporation was established by charter of 1556, on whose members the Crown settled the manor, and the right to elect two MPs was regranted in 1621 at the request of Sir Robert Phelips of Montacute. The corporation sold the manor to Tory borough-monger Sir William Manners in 1810, who had already bought the patronage in 1802 for £53,000. The playwright Sheridan was elected in 1807. Manners demolished some 100 of the 160 houses here c.1812, rendering a large number of the inhabitants homeless. These were housed in a workhouse rented from Manners but, as lodgers, were deprived of their votes. A Liberal (Whig) borough-monger, Lord Darlington, built two large tenement blocks at Ilchester Mead outside the town to house the dispossessed voters and his candidates were triumphantly returned at the 1818 election. In an incredible political demonstration, the rector persuaded the parents of 28 children to baptise them with the surnames of the new Whig MPs (Merest and Coffin!). The Reform Act of 1832 inevitably disenfranchised this corrupt borough.

A new gaol across the river in Northover was built in 1599 (joined by a house of correction soon after 1607) but the building was too small to house the many persecuted Quakers imprisoned there in the later 17th century, many having to be accommodated elsewhere in the town. The gaol was extended in 1789 and 1808-21, although the brutality of the gaoler, William Bridle, was exposed by his most famous charge, 'Orator' Henry Hunt, imprisoned here after the Peterloo 'massacre' of 1819, and Bridle was fired. A plot of ground beside the A30 immediately south of the town was the main execution site for the the county. It was probably there that 12 Monmouth rebels ended their days in 1685 and that Mary Norwood was burned for poisoning her husband in 1765. From 1811 unfortunates were hanged over the gaol entrance but in 1843 the prison was closed: succeeded by Wilton Gaol at Taunton. The Wednesday market ceased shortly before 1833, its location marked by a Tuscan pinnacle set up in 1795, although one of its

three fairs continued until c.1880. The corporation was finally dissolved in 1889, succeeded by the Ilchester Town Trust, whose responsibilities include the maintenance of the Town Hall in the market-place. This plain building dates from c.1700 but was remodelled 1812-16.

The town was unique in Somerset in having as many as six parish churches within its walls by the 13th century, reflecting its early importance. These were progressively abandoned as the place declined. Two of them, St Olave's (its dedication suggesting a Scandinavian presence, as at Exeter) and St Peter's, were not recorded after 1300, St Michael's, built over the South Gate, became a chantry chapel c.1500 and was closed in 1548, while St John the Baptist and St Mary Minor were united with St Mary Major and both demolished before the end of the 16th century. In addition there was a chapel of St Leonard on Ilchester Bridge by 1476 which was probably founded to serve the prisoners at the gaol. A leper hospital was mentioned in 1212, its site not yet traced, and the hospital of Whitehall, founded before 1220 beside the North Gate by William the Dane (which may explain the Scandinavian connection above), had become a priory of nuns by 1281, but declined to become the free chapel of the Holy Trinity by 1463: closed by 1600. The Black Friars had a friary by 1263 just outside the West Gate beside the Foss Way, last mentioned in 1536. The only parish church to survive is that of St Mary Major, near the centre of the town. The patronage was held by Muchelney Abbey until 1239, by the bishop of Bath and Wells until 1852 and since by the bishop of London. The present building has a chancel, nave and substantial west tower (octagonal at the top), all dating from the early to mid 13th century. The south aisle was added 1879-80, when the pillars of an early 13th century arcade (one of which was re-erected in the churchyard) were found embedded in the south wall, indicating a former south aisle. A Perpendicular north chapel with a fine panelled arch was added c.1500. There is a Jacobean pulpit and medieval memorial cross fragments are set in the wall of the west porch. A 1914 memorial brass commemorates the birth here c.1214 of the notable philosopher, Roger Bacon (died 1292), credited with the invention of gunpowder, camera obscura and optical lenses. He also foretold the ocean liner, submarine and aeroplane.

Immediately south of Ilchester lies the former parish of **Sock Dennis**. 'Sock' is

thought to mean 'a marshy place', while 'Dennis' is derived from the family of William the Dane, which held the manor here in the 13th century. The church, of unknown dedication, was a daughter foundation of Yeovil and sheltered altars of the Virgin Mary and St John the Baptist. It had been demolished by 1575, although surprisingly rectors continued to be appointed until 1883, when the parish was finally divided between Ilchester and Tintinhull. (*See also* **Northover**).

★★ *Town (possibly even* ★★★ *for its history and associations).*

ILMINSTER (J) A small town in south Somerset, 'the minster church on the River Isle' (now Yeo). The place seems likely to have formed the original endowment of Muchelney Abbey granted by King Ine of the West Saxons, possibly by a charter of 693 which conveyed land mainly between (and east of) the river Isle and the 'public way' (probably the Foss Way) or by a later deed of 725. Ilminster was Muchelney's most valuable possession and had to be recovered by the abbey under a charter of Ethelred the Unready in 995. By the time of Domesday it had three mills and a market, and in 1280 a two-day fair that was already old and which continued into the present century. A disastrous fire is claimed to have devastated the town in 1491 (recorded only by Collinson in 1791) and a better authenticated one in 1661, which destroyed nearly 30 houses around the market place. As was the case with most west-country towns, Ilminster's economy depended on cloth manufacture which continued here into the 19th century and was particularly buoyant in the 17th century, the town being the fourth largest in Somerset in 1670. Despite this, Ilminster never became a borough and continued to be administered by its churchwardens and by the officers of the manor on behalf of its lords. After the dissolution of Muchelney Abbey the manor was held by the Seymours, dukes of Somerset, until 1684 and, following two purchases in 1700 and 1724, by the Speke family and their successors at Dillington (*see below*). A through route was developed along West Street, Strawberry Bank and the Butts, now High Street, which took traffic away from the market place. More recently a controversial bypass to the north, opened in 1988, has restored a peace to Ilminster which it has not enjoyed for centuries. The attractive market square features an open market house on pillars, described as 'newly built' in 1813, although the range of timber tiled shambles that once accompanied it is long gone. The George Hotel accommodated the future Queen Victoria in 1819 *en route* to Sidmouth in Devon, where her parents used to stay. The town was the birthplace of John Edward Taylor (1791-1844), founder and first editor of the *(Manchester) Guardian* in 1821. In Brewery Lane the recently-opened and intimate Warehouse Theatre has begun to attract more varied entertainment to the town.

In Silver Street rises the majestic 90 ft crossing tower (c.1500) of **St Mary's minster church**. Probably founded by King Ine at about the time that he created Muchelney Abbey, Bishop Savaric persuaded a later abbot to assign the church to Wells Cathedral to create a prebend in 1201 and it was probably at this period that the parish became a royal 'peculiar', answerable only to the monarch. The present lofty cruciform church with its clerestory is uniformly Perpendicular although the nave was largely rebuilt in 1825. The airy north transept was probably built to house the tomb and brass of Sir William Wadham (died 1452) of Merryfield in Ilton (beside Joan, his mother) and later those of Nicholas Wadham (died 1609) and his wife Dorothy (died 1618), 'foundresse of Wadham Colledge in Oxforde' in 1610. The transept also housed the Wadham chantry chapel of St Katherine, swept away in 1548. The sumptuous panelled crossing has an impressive fan vault. In the south transept, beneath a crested helm, is the monument of Humphrey Walrond (died 1580) of Sea (1 mile south) and another to Col Arthur V.H. Vaughan-Lee (1862-1933) of Dillington, lord of the manor and donor of the elaborate painted reredos in the chancel. There are four fine chandeliers of 1762 by Thomas Bayley of Bridgwater.

North of the church is a group of buildings which gives the area something of the feel of a small cathedral close. These are mainly associated with the former Grammar School, whose existence was documented in a letter of 1440. This was endowed by Humphrey Walrond and Henry Greenfield in 1549, when the 15th century Cross House became the head-master's house and the adjacent building, evidently rebuilt in 1586 from the date on its sundial, housed the school itself. From 1879 it was occupied by the Girls' Grammar School, while new premises for boys were built in Wharf Lane: both closed in 1971. On his progress through the West in 1680, the Duke of Monmouth twice passed through the town, attending Divine Service at St Mary's. He returned in

1685, marching north from Lyme to Taunton with his rebel army, and encamped near the town at Winterhay. Charles Speke shook the duke's hand in the market place, an action which cost him his life after Jeffreys' Bloody Assizes, although it was his brother John who had fought at Sedgemoor. At least 57 Ilminster men joined the rebellion although of the 12 later hanged, drawn and quartered in Ilminster market place, only Charles Speke came from the town.

Horton ('settlement on muddy land'), mentioned in 1202 and (with Church Town, Winterhay and Hilcombe) one of the early tithings into which Ilminster was divided, is a hamlet to the west of the town with several attractive houses.

Dillington House, leased by Somerset County Council since 1950 as an adult residential college, with a theatre in its imposing stable block (1875), stands in an extensive park to the north of Ilminster. The 'settlement of Dylli's people' was separated from Ilminster manor c.1100 when the abbot of Muchelney granted it to Harding son of Eadnoth. The main estate was bought in 1599 by George Speke from Dowlish Wake. George's descendants served as MPs and sheriffs for the county, and in the earlier 18th century created Dillington park, upgraded and extended a Tudor farmhouse, and moved here from neighbouring Whitelackington. Anne, daughter of a later George Speke, carried the property to her husband, Frederick, Lord North (1732-92), Prime Minister and later Earl of Guilford, unfairly credited with losing our American colonies. The estate was sold in 1795 to John Hanning (died

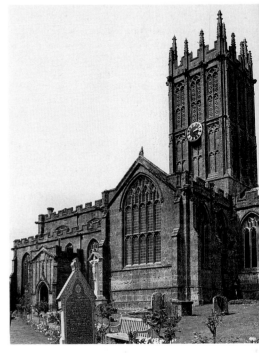

TOP *The Market House, Ilminster*
ABOVE *Ilminster church*
BELOW *The Grammar School, Ilminster*

1803) of Barrington Court, he or his son William (died 1825) added a south wing, and the next generation remodelled the house to the designs of James Pennethorne as it is today: 'Gothic in spirit, Barrington with a touch of Regency', as Robert Dunning has described it. The Hannings, who became Lees and later Vaughan-Lees for reasons of inheritance, left an heiress who in 1933 carried it to the Camerons, now living at nearby Whitelackington.

★★★ *Church, houses to the north of it and Market Square, Dillington House.*

ILTON (J) This 'settlement on the River Isle' was one of the possessions of Athelney Abbey from Saxon times until its dissolution. The village is attractively grouped around a green, flanked by the church, the Wyndham Arms and Merryfield House, built as a large vicarage in the late 19th century. There has been considerable modern development to the north of the village. South of the village at Cads Green stands a nine-cell range of almshouses founded in 1634 by John Whetstone, whom Gerard stigmatized as 'an old userer' and tradition claimed started life as an Ilton foundling discovered in a bundle of whetstones! In fact he ended his days in Dorset and made the bequest because his mother was born at Ilton. East of the village a square moated site is all that remains to mark the site of the medieval Merryfield (13th century 'Muryfeld' – 'pleasant field'), held by John of Ilminster in the 13th century. Bought probably by Sir John Wadham in the late 14th century, it continued as that family's seat until the deaths of Nicholas (1609) and Dorothy (1618) Wadham, founders of Wadham College, Oxford, both buried at Ilminster. Inherited by John Wyndham, he demolished it and with the materials is said to have built Woodhouse Farm, dated 1634, at the north end of the village. Almshouses for eight south-west of the village at Pound Corner were founded by Nicholas Wadham in 1606. The church of St Peter was given to endow a prebend in Wells Cathedral by the abbot of Athelney in the 13th century. The church dates mainly from the 14th century, with a rendered tower standing unusually on the south side, possibly on a 12th century base and topped until the earlier 19th century with a wooden spirelet. The whole was much restored and rebuilt in 1860. A female effigy of c.1475 may represent an early Wadham and a brass of 1508 depicts an earlier Nicholas Wadham in a shroud. Ashford House, dated 1703, was a

Isle Abbotts church

Domesday manor and Rapps occurs as 'les Apses' (13th century, meaning 'aspens'). In the north of the parish Merryfield aerodrome served as a bomber base 1942-44. It was reopened as HMS *Heron II*, RNAS Merryfield, and is now used principally for training helicopter pilots.

★★ *Village centre.*

ISLE ABBOTTS (J) Lying north of Ilminster, it takes its name, like that town, from the river Isle. The second part of its name derives from its ownership by Muchelney Abbey from Saxon times until the dissolution of the abbey in 1538, after which it also passed to the Earl of Hertford. The village has a regular lay-out, suggesting a planned settlement at an early period, and several houses ranging in date from the late Middle Ages to the 18th century. Bromes House (floor slab to Philip Brome, 1640, in church) has a medieval core with porch dated 1627. The church of St Mary the Virgin at the eastern end of the village is a magnificent building into which the Muchelney monks ploughed considerable resources. The four-stage 15th century west tower is rich in Ham-stone ornament, with Somerset tracery in its bell openings and, surprisingly, most of the slightly wooden-looking statues still in their niches. The fan-vaulted south porch gives access to a lofty interior almost as impressive as the tower. The chancel of c.1300 includes elaborate sedilia and piscina, and a large sarcophagus to the left of the altar. The 15th century rood screen can only be a remnant of the original or has been

introduced from elsewhere and the early benchends are relatively plain. The square Norman font bears a carving identified as a dragon, now upside down on the north side, suggesting that the bowl was inverted and the other three faces then carved.

★★★ *Church,* ★★ *village.*

ISLE BREWERS (J) Stretching east from the River Isle (*see above*) which named it, the latter part of its name comes from the Briwere family, lords here in the early 13th century. The church of All Saints originally stood near the Domesday mill towards the river and formed the earliest endowment of William Briwere's Hospital of St John the Baptist at Bridgwater in 1219. It was replaced in 1861 by a Victorian church at the opposite end of the village, designed by C.E. Giles and paid for by its eccentric vicar (1845-62), Dr Joseph Wolff. Born the son of a German Jewish rabbi, Wolff converted to Catholicism, taught Hebrew to the future Pope Pius IX and became self-appointed missionary to the Middle East. Kidnapped and sold into slavery, he walked 600 miles naked before escaping. Later in America he preached to Congress, converted to and was ordained into the Anglican church and married the daughter of the Earl of Orford. In this parish in 1681 were born Siamese twins named Aquila and Priscilla, a birth commemorated by a Donyatt plate on exhibition in the County Museum. They were exhibited at fairs by their father's landlord, even after their deaths when the latter had them stuffed. To the south and south-west of the village, on the east bank of the Isle, lay the Domesday manors of South Bradon, later held by the Wyndhams, and Goose Bradon (named from its Norman lords, the Gouvis family). South Bradon was a sinecure rectory into the present century although there had been no church there within living memory. Its parish was divided between Isle Brewers and Puckington in 1885.

KEINTON MANDEVILLE (E) The modern lias-stone village lines the B 3153, the former Langport, Somerton and Castle Cary turnpike road, although this is all 19th and 20th century development. The church lies at the end of a lane running south from the main road and this lane seems to represent the area of the Saxon and medieval village, Keinton meaning 'the king's settlement'. It was long known for its quarries, the principal source of blue lias building stone for the surrounding area. The manor was held under that of Barton St David before the Conquest and the place-name derives its suffix from William de Mandeville, lord here in the early 13th century. An estate here soon after formed part of the endowment of St John's Hospital, Wells. The church of St Mary Magdalene has an Early English chancel, a nave believed to have been rebuilt in 1800, as was the west tower (replacing an octagonal one), and a north aisle added in 1841. There is a Norman font, Jacobean pulpit and a very vernacular royal hatchment dated 1719. The famous actor, Sir Henry Irving (1838-1905), was born here as John Henry Brodribb, the son of a shopkeeper, in a cottage identified by a plaque, but left the village when aged only four.

KILMERSDON (B) A large Mendip parish and former hundred north-west of Frome, 'Cynemaer's hill' ('Kunemersdon' in 951), held by the Suleny family from the early 12th century, which included Domesday manors at Luckington and Walton within its bounds. The main manor passed through the lords of many families, of whom the last Lord Botreaux was born at Walton manor-house in 1390. It was bought by a Bristol merchant, Gabriel Goodman (died 1679) and descended to the Twyford family who in 1686 built Charlton House (now demolished). One half of the manor was obtained by a Hampshire gentleman, Thomas Samuel Jolliffe (died 1824), through his marriage to Ann Twyford in 1778, and the other half by purchase in 1787. Jolliffe built a new

Church and Jolliffe Arms, Kilmersdon

mansion, **Ammerdown House**, 1789-91, in the east of the parish, extended in 1859 and 1877, and surrounded it with an extensive park. The gardens were redesigned by Lutyens from 1901 and include an orangery of 1793 and a 150 ft slender column designed by Joseph Jopling in the form of the Eddystone lighthouse, topped by a glass dome, built 1852-3 in memory of the builder of the house, with inscriptions in English, Latin and French. The Jolliffes were regularly MPs, became baronets in 1821, barons Hylton in 1866 and the present Lord Hylton still lives at Ammerdown. Since 1973 the stable block has been operated as a residential Christian study centre and retreat, developing a national reputation for care, concern and education in idyllic surroundings.

The earliest documentary evidence for Somerset coalmining is from Kilmersdon in 1305 and the parish was long one of the major centres of the industry in this county. Individual pits often had colourful names, such as Ruth's Arse, opened in 1690, and the Hylton archives include what is claimed to be the oldest coalmining plan in existence, dated 1695. The last pit here was closed in 1973.

The attractive village today gives little hint of its former industrial activity. It has a small square as its focus, featuring the inevitable Jolliffe Arms Inn, the village lock-up (converted to a bus shelter) and a wealth of good Georgian houses. There was a church here at the Norman Conquest which may have been a Saxon minster and later had dependent chapels at Ashwick,

Coleford and Luckington. It was bestowed in 1166 by William de Erlegh on Buckland Priory at Durston, which he had founded. The present church of SS Peter and Paul has some Norman windows, a south door-way and an external frieze, but in its present form is 15th century Perpendicular with a fine lofty west tower and an excellent stone screen to the north chapel. An unusual iron grille by Singers of Frome (1878) divides nave from chancel and the east window is attributed to Burne-Jones. Also in the village are the Old School House, founded by the Rev Henry Shute in 1707, the so-called Kilmersdon Manor House with a datestone of 1674. Local claims, on no very certain grounds, assert that the nursery rhyme 'Jack and Jill' (first recorded c.1765 but possibly dating from the earlier 17th century) originated from the fall here of a husband and wife who ended up near a cottage called Tumbler's Bottom! (*See also* **Coleford**).

★★ *Village and church.*

KILTON (D) This small coastal parish to the north-east of the Quantock Hills occurs as 'Cylfantun' in the will of King Alfred, who left it to his son and successor, Edward the Elder, its name possibly meaning 'the settlement by the hill'. Since the Conquest it has been held with few interruptions by the Mohun and Luttrell families of Dunster Castle. An estate to the south-east called Heathfield was centred on the present Plud Farm, formerly known as the Constable's House and probably held by the Constable of Nether Stowey Castle during his term of office. The farm has been held with Fairfield in Stogursey since 1731. Kilton village, once surrounded by open arable fields, has apparently shrunk in size, leaving its church and village green relatively isolsted at its eastern limit. The church of St Nicholas, dating from the 14th century, was virtually rebuilt by John Norton 1861-64, but the octagonal medieval font was retained.

★★ *Setting.*

KILVE (D) A picturesque parish lying on the coast at the northern end of the Quantock Hills. Its name ('Clive' in 1086) probably means simply 'cliff', as does Old Cleeve to the west. The traveller on the A 39 passes through the principal village, formerly a hamlet called Putsham, mentioned in 1406. It includes a popular inn opened as the Chough and Anchor in 1820 but renamed the Hood Arms by 1832, although the Hoods, prominent land-owners in the area, never held a substantial estate in the parish. To the south of the road stands **Kilve Court**, a three-storeyed mansion built shortly before 1786 by Henry Sweeting. Since 1961 it has been used as a residential education centre by the County Council.

From the roadside settlement a lane runs north towards the coast, lined by the older buildings in the parish. The church of St Mary is a simple building dating from the 14th century, comprising chancel, nave (both rebuilt in the 15th century), early 17th century west tower and 19th century north vestry. Beyond the church lies the partly-ruined building known as the Priory. Originally serving as Kilve's manor-house, the premises became a college for five priests, founded by Simon de Furneaux in

1329, but had evidently reverted to a farm by 1411. The ruined portion, dating from the late 13th century, included a solar with first-floor chapel. Further north, beyond the carpark, the walker can reach Kilve Beach, site of a creek for the landing of small boats in the 16th century. *En route* to the sea is a short brick tower, last reminder of a failed experiment to extract oil from the coastal shale here in the 1920s. In the south of the parish, high up on the Quantock slope, lies Pardlestone, an early medieval settlement: now a popular riding centre for exploring the hills.

★★★ *Scenery and coastal walking,*
★ *church.*

KINGSBURY EPISCOPI (J) A large and ancient estate on the Levels, north-west of Martock. Its name, 'the king's manor' with the later addition 'of the bishop', and the fact that it belonged to the bishop of Wells both before and after 1066, suggests that it was granted by one of the West Saxon kings to endow the bishopric. As the scattered bishop's lands were collectively known as the Hundred of Kingsbury (later divided into East and West), it may well have formed part of the original endow-ment when the Cathedral was established in 909. The present focus of the village is on a central green with its octagonal Ham stone lock-up, topped with a ball finial, surrounded by cottages and farmhouses mainly of the 17th and 18th centuries. The Wyndham Arms preserves the name of later lords of the manor, the Wyndhams of Orchard Wyndham. At the eastern limit of the village, beyond a short lane lined by a terrace of cottages, the church of St Martin lies almost on the banks of the River Parrett: the danger of flooding possibly

inhibiting settlement around it. The 99ft Ham stone Perpendicular west tower is one of the county's finest, with figures surviving in several of the niches. Inside, the double panelled tower arch is magnifi-cent, although the rest of the church is rather plain in comparison. The nave is 14th century and the Perpendicular chancel superbly lit: the two divided by a surviving rood screen. One of the two chapels must be that of Our Lady where Alice Clayton requested burial in 1501. South-west from the village, Burrow Hill, topped by an iso-lated tree, rises conically above the Levels. At its foot, cider and, since 1987, Somerset Royal cider brandy are produced at Burrow Hill Farm and can be purchased there. Julian Temperley's Somerset Cider Brandy, the county's answer to Calvados, has found favour with the experts and I personally can heartily recommend it.

★★ *Church,* ★ *Village.*

KINGSDON (E) This charming unspoilt Ham-stone village lies south-east of Somerton. Remains of two Roman villas were found in the early 19th century but there are no visible remains. The village's name, meaning 'king's hill', is derived from Kingsdon Hill in the north-west of the parish and reflects the fact that the manor formed part of the royal estate of Somerton at the time of the Norman Conquest, although granted away to the Gouvis family by 1194. In 1528 the manor was bought by Thomas Arundell of Wardour, Wilts, and continued in his family (inter-rupted only by a single year following his execution in 1552) until sold by Henry, Lord Arundell, to Aaron Moody in 1801. The medieval manor-house stood north of the church but burned down in the 16th

The lock-up, Kingsbury Episcopi

Kingsdon

century. With no resident lord, it was not replaced until shortly before 1833 when Kingsdon House, a substantial lias mansion, was built by C.A. Moody to the south of the village. There the Moodys lived and, from 1864, their successors the Neals, until the house was sold to Bristol Corporation in 1952 to become Kingsdon Manor School.

The roughly triangular village was formerly surrounded by three open arable fields, the remnants of which were finally enclosed in 1810. There are many picturesque farmhouses and cottages in the village dating from the early 17th century. Humbler dwellings have often been converted to garages and outbuildings, illustrating the halving of the population since 1831. The church of All Saints dates from the 12th century and the chancel was rebuilt in the 14th century and apparently extended in the 15th. The north transeptal chapel formed the base of a 14th century tower, replaced by the present west tower one hundred years later. There is a 12th century font, Jacobean pulpit and late medieval benchends reset in the north chapel screen. The late 13th century Hamstone effigy of a knight in the north chapel may represent Brian de Gouvis, once lord of the manor. A small brass inscription on the north wall of the chancel commemorates a former rector, John Dotin (died 1561), described not only as a medical man but also an astrologer. One of his successors, Peter Hansell, was rector for 62 years from 1835 until his death aged 91 in 1897. This impressive term was, interrupted by seven years in retreat in France from 1844 after his suspension for immoral behaviour with a lady of the parish.

★★★ *Village*, ★★ *church*.

KINGSTONE (J)

A small village south-east from Ilminster, occupying a prominent ridge-top site. This 'king's settlement' ceased to justify its name as early as 940 when King Edmund gave the manor to St Dunstan as abbot of Glastonbury. The abbey lost it to the Count of Mortain after the Norman Conquest and it was later held by the Arundell family (1461-1663) and the Pouletts of Hinton St George (1663-1941). From 1280 the manor was known as Allowensay ('Alwyne's enclosure'), the name of an increasingly substantial hamlet in the east of the parish, where there was an early park to the north and a medieval chapel. A third settlement to the south-east at Ludney was mentioned in 1293. The church of St John the Evangelist and All

Saints was given in 1382 to the Vicars Choral of Wells Cathedral by the lord of the manor, Sir John Chidiock. The chancel and porch date from the 14th century: the nave, with elegant Perpendicular windows, and the central tower, a prominent local landmark, from the 15th.

★ *Setting*.

KINGSTON ST MARY (D)

A hillside parish at the southern end of the Quantocks which must have derived its name, 'the king's settlement', from having once belonged to the kings of the West Saxons before being ceded to the bishops of Winchester as part of their great manor of Taunton Deane. Indeed, one of the five 'hundreds' into which that manor was divided was named Nailesbourne ('Naegl's stream') after a small hamlet in the south of the parish. The addition of the church's dedication to the parish name dates only from the 20th century. The attractive village lies along the winding road north from Taunton up to Buncombe on the hills. The Grange, now an old people's home towards the south end of the village, is a towered house of c.1860 by Sir George Gilbert Scott, where future Prime Minister Anthony Eden used to spend his boyhood holidays with the widow of his father's cousin, Mrs Cecile Eden. Elsewhere in the village, Bobbetts has a medieval two-bay central core, remodelled in the 16th century, and Westhay, St Mary's Cottage and Quantock Cottage are all of 16th century origin. The so-called Manor House, formerly known as Lodes, dates from the mid 16th century with a porch of 1702.

The church of St Mary, just north of the village centre, was held by Taunton Priory until the dissolution and thereafter by the dean and chapter of Bristol. It has a superb pinnacled west tower of c.1490 with Somerset tracery: for Pevsner 'one of the most memorable of a district rich in towers'. The south porch of c.1520 has a fine fan vault and, inside, the nave, north and south aisles with their arcades date from the 13th century. The chancel was rebuilt in the 16th century and the excellent series of benchends, dated 1522, include two rosaries, a weaver's shuttle, and a yoke and oxen. There is a veritable feast of monuments. At the west end of the south aisle are memorials to former owners of Tetton House (north of the parish, rebuilt c.1790, enlarged 1924-6), brasses to the Dykes, their heirs the Aclands, and the Herberts, relatives of the earls of Carnarvon. One recalls Edward Herbert, grandson of the 2nd Earl, who was in 1870

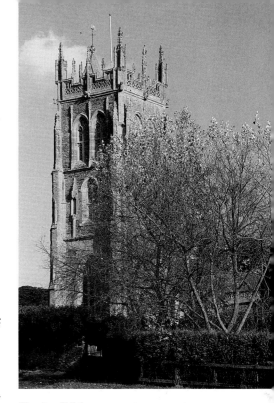

Kingston St Mary

kidnapped and murdered by Greek brigands after ten days, 'during which the huge ransom demanded was in vain offered'. At the east end of the south aisle is a massive 14th century table tomb of Purbeck marble with heraldry identifying the Warre family of Hestercombe. Other tablets and slabs commemorate later Warres and Bampfyldes of Hestercombe and armorial glass in the adjacent window was reputedly brought from Hestercombe chapel, demolished in 1766. In the north aisle are monuments to the military Chapman family of Tainfield House, an Italian-style villa built from 1808 in parkland to the east of the road south to Taunton by Lt Gen Richard Chapman (died 1812) and named after his estate of Tain in British Guiana. In 1853 it passed by marriage to William Edward Surtees (died 1889), a prominent benefactor to the parish and to Taunton. His will attested to his 'greatest objection to expensive funerals which I regard as both wasteful and ridiculous'.

The outlying areas of this parish are unusually rich in 16th and 17th century farmhouses. In 1843 two sisters named Sealey were acquitted of poisoning their father and strangling their mother at Pickney in the west of the parish, but popular sentiment forced them to emigrate for their own safety. A popular sweet cider apple, the Kingston Black, takes its name from this place. (See also **Hestercombe**).

★★★ *Church, particularly for its memorials,* ★★ *village and setting.*

The Monmouth Rebellion

In 1685 a vain attempt was made to topple the unpopular Roman Catholic monarch, James II, by a makeshift army composed principally of urban cloth-workers from Somerset, Dorset and East Devon. It was led by the illegitimate son of Charles II, James, Duke of Monmouth, a Protestant hero who had made a highly successful progress through the south-west five years before. During the 300th anniversary commemorations of 1985 the rising was misguidedly rechristened 'the Pitchfork Rebellion', giving the erroneous impression that the rebels were mainly agricultural labourers.

Landing at Lyme Regis (Dorset) from exile in Holland with 82 followers on 11 June 1685, the Duke gained some 1,500 recruits before marching north through Axminster for Taunton. Tragically Monmouth's 'passport' into Taunton, exiled goldsmith Thomas Dare, was killed at Lyme in an argument over a horse with the Duke's commander of cavalry. Marching into Somerset, the growing army passed through Chard and camped at Ilminster, before proceeding to Taunton by way of Hatch Green and Stoke St Mary. A skirmish near Ashill left four rebels dead. The Duke was greeted ecstatically at Taunton on 18 June where the next day he was presented with 27 banners by the 'Maids', pupils of a dame school, and on 20 June was proclaimed king at the High Cross. After three nights at Capt John Hucker's house (opposite the present County Hotel), Monmouth and his troops rode on to Bridgwater where the Duke put up at the castle and was again proclaimed king. Thence the rebels continued to Glastonbury, soaked to the skin, where they were dried out by great fires in the Abbey grounds, moving on to Shepton Mallet. Intending to take Bristol, the motley army made its way north to Pensford and then Keynsham, where they were attacked by royalist cavalry. The threat of a greater army at hand to oppose him led him to turn aside and, after a futile attempt to persuade Bath to surrender, withdraw to Norton St Philip. There the Duke was accommodated at the present Manor Farm but on 27 June was attacked by a royalist force, which the rebels drove off with losses on both sides. Monmouth decided to withdraw, first to Frome and then, on promise of further recruits, to Shepton Mallet. The looting of royalist wagons took the rebels to Wells, where much damage was done to the Cathedral, and finally, after a short stay at Pedwell (near Ashcott), to Bridgwater to meet a force of 'Clubmen' (once promised to comprise 10,000) of only 160.

Meanwhile a royalist army under Viscount Feversham, which had been trailing Monmouth at a respectful distance, moved from Glastonbury via Somerton to Westonzoyland. There they encamped in and around

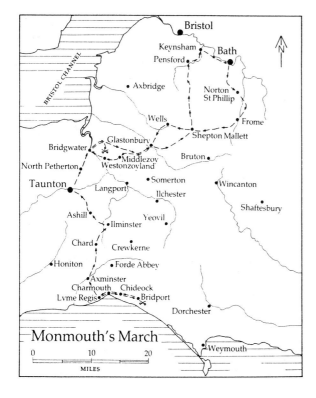

Monmouth's March

the village, with the Wiltshire militia at Middlezoy and some others at Othery. The Duke had planned to march to Axbridge and then, avoiding Bristol, to Gloucester but observing his enemy through a telescope from the tower of St Mary's, Bridgwater, he and his officers decided on a surprise night attack. The royalist army numbered 700 cavalry and 1,900 infantry while Monmouth seems to have had about 4,000 men. Although the rebels moved silently out of the town, their approach in the early hours of 6 July was betrayed by a warning shot fired probably by a royalist sentry. Prevented from assaulting Feversham's forces directly by the Bussex rhine, the rebels blazed away at the royalists and the royalists blazed back. Superior military training and cannon, several brought up by the coach horses of Bishop Mews of Winchester (formerly bishop of Bath and Wells), eventually paid off. The rebel line broke and fled back towards Bridgwater: pursued and slaughtered 'in the corne and hedges and ditches'.

The Westonzoyland churchwarden reckoned that 300 rebels were killed in the battle, 22 hanged and 500 prisoners crammed into his church, of whom five died there of their wounds. Many of the slain were buried in a mass grave and a mound raised over it. Further summary executions took place at Glastonbury (6), Wells (5) and Taunton (19). The luckless Monmouth fled and found refuge with Edward Strode at Downside near Shepton Mallet. He was finally captured at Horton (Dorset) and met his death bravely at the Tower on 15 July.

The constables of each hundred were ordered to report the names of all those who had been absent from their homes at the time of the rebellion and their lists formed the basis for prosecutions at the so-called Bloody Assizes: presided over by Judge George Jeffreys. These assizes were held in August and September at Winchester, Salisbury, Dorchester, Exeter, Taunton, Wells and Bristol – *and nowhere else*, despite alleged kangaroo courts elsewhere in Somerset recounted in popular literature. Most of the rebels were tried at Dorchester (320), Taunton (514) and Wells (518), and others were accused of seditious words or 'aiding and assisting' the rising. Some 330 were hanged, drawn and quartered, mainly in the centres of market towns throughout Somerset and Dorset, their boiled and salted quarters being displayed even more widely in those counties. Most of the remainder were transported to the West Indies to be sold into servitude. The Protestant cause, for which the rebels had fought and died, triumphed only three years later when James II fled and another invader from Holland, William III, assumed the throne.

LEFT *James, Duke of Monmouth*
TOP RIGHT *The Sedgemoor Memorial, Westonzoyland*
RIGHT *Judge Jeffreys*

KINGWESTON (E) This village's name, 'Chinwardestune' in 1086, means 'Cyneweard's settlement'. It lies north-east from Somerton, just north of the B 3153: a few farmhouses and cottages along a short lane which skirts the park of Kingweston House, leased since 1946 to Millfield School (*see* **Street**), and leads only to the house and church. Evidence of Romano-British settlement has been found in the parish, particularly in Copley Wood. After the Norman Conquest the manor was given to Eustance, Count of Boulogne, who settled it on his wife. Their descendant, Mary, Countess of Boulogne, gave the estate to Bermondsey Abbey in Surrey in 1114, which retained it until the Dissolution. Thereafter, following several generations in the hands of the Smyth family of Long Ashton, it was bought in 1740 by Caleb Dickinson (died 1783), of a family of Quaker merchants from Bristol who made a fortune from West Indies sugar plantations and slave trading and used it to build up an extensive estate around Kingweston. Caleb's son, William (died 1806), a local MP, rebuilt the somewhat severe Georgian house in the 1780s and established the present road system in the parish, avoiding the park. The Dickinsons continued here as an influential family in the county into the present century. The family's monuments fill the church of All Saints, still with its Norman font but rebuilt in 1855 with an octagonal spire by Francis Henry Dickinson (died 1890) to the designs of C.E. Giles. Kingweston House and its pleasure grounds are visible from the churchyard. An annual September revel was recorded here in 1653, when two blacksmiths beat up a soldier for refusing to drink the queen's health.

★ *Setting.*

KITTISFORD (H) Lying west of Welling-ton in lush countryside cut by the River Tone and deep high-hedged lanes, the place-name means 'Cyddi's ford'. Following the Norman Conquest the estate was granted to Roger Arundel, whose tenant William was probably ancestor of the De Kittisford family, of whom another William was murdered by three men in 1258. By 1268 it had passed to Simon of Greenham (in Stawley) and in the early 14th century, with Greenham, to the Bluets. Walter Bluet (died 1481) left the manor to his younger son Richard, who had to take his elder brother to arbitration to secure his inheritance.

Between 1485 and 1488, on a picturesque

Kingweston House

site beside the Tone in the east of the parish, Richard Bluet (died 1523) built the house he called the Court Place, now know as **Cothay Manor** ('Cotthehee', early 13th century – 'cottage in an enclosure'). To Pevsner it was 'one of the most perfect smaller English manor-houses of the late 15th century': not large but looking warm and comfortable. A contemporary gatehouse, heavily restored, bears the Bluet arms and overlooks an ornamental lake created from the former Grand Western Canal. The house itself remarkably preserves its original structure and features, including a fine hall with screened gallery, solar and parlour. On the first floor, some of the earliest surviving wall paintings in an English house portray both religious and secular themes. The Bluets continued there until John Bluet ran heavily into debt and ceded the house to his brother-in-law Richard Weekes, who moved into Cothay in 1603 and sold it two years later to William Every (died 1652), builder of the panelled dining-room west of the hall. Later Everys and their successors lived elsewhere. Cothay, which is not open to the public, became a tenanted farmhouse and its rescue and restoration were mainly due to Lt Col Reginal Cooper, 1925-37.

The church of St Nicholas, with rendered west tower and unusual timber arcade, was probably rebuilt soon after Cothay and includes small but fine brasses to the house's builder and his wife Alice. The pulpit is dated 1610 and a north chapel was added in 1659 under a bequest by Roger Wood of Overtown in the parish. Eight members of the Sweet Escott family and their ancestors were rectors here

continuously 1715-1851. Kittisford House appears to have been set up as the 17th century rectory. Kittisford Barton, dating like Cothay from the late 15th century, represents the original manor-house and was briefly occupied by the Bluets after they lost Cothay. Newhouse and Beardsley farms were erected in the late 16th and early 17th centuries respectively.

★★ *Scenery.*

KNOWLE ST GILES (J) A small parish of scattered farmsteads to the north-east of Chard. There is no obvious sign of 'the hillock' which christened it and there is no village as such. Manor Farm represents the separate Domesday manor of Illeigh ('meadow on the Isle') and there were formerly several fulling mills nearby on the River Isle, with another, Bere Mills, to the north. Woodhouse Farm, rebuilt after a fire in 1806, was probably established on cleared land c.1200. The chapel of St Giles formed part of Cudworth prebend from the late 12th century until it was totally rebuilt in 1840, but has been closed. Between 1760 and 1917 its ministers were almost all headmasters of Crewkerne, Ilminster or Chard grammar schools.

★ *Setting.*

LAMYATT (F) North-west of Bruton, the name of this small farming village probably means 'swinging gate'. Excavations on the summit of Lamyatt Beacon have revealed a significant Romano-British temple of c.300-400 AD and produced statuettes including those of Mercury, Mars, Minerva and Hercules. Some 16 associated east-west burials of the 6th to 8th centuries may indicate a very early Christian settlement there. The manor here passed into the hands of Glastonbury Abbey in Saxon times, possibly with the Ditcheat estate in the 9th century, but after the Norman Conquest was granted to Nigel the physician. By the beginning of the 13th century it was held by Robert de Columbers, whose descendants gave way to a branch of the Rodneys, by whom the manor was split up and sold in the early 17th century. The church of SS Mary and John at the north-eastern end of the village has a 13th century west tower, a Perpendicular nave and chancel and a Norman tub font with cable moulding. The living was quitclaimed by Robert de Columbers to Godstow nunnery, Oxfordshire, in 1220 and the nuns retained it until the dissolution of their house.

LANGFORD BUDVILLE (H)

The village lies west of the main road (B 3187) from Wellington to Milverton and is named from 'the long ford', presumably across the River Tone. It was not mentioned in the Domesday Book and was possibly included under the royal manor of Milverton, of which its church was a chapelry. The manor was held in 1212 by Richard de Budeville (possibly from Boutteville in Normandy) and adopted his surname to distinguish it from Langford in Burrington. It was still held by his family in the 15th century but later passed to the Clarkes and then the Sanfords of Nynehead. Langford Court is a late medieval open-hall house, successively extended in the 17th, 18th and 19th centuries. The church of St Peter dominates the village and enjoys magnificent views of the surrounding hills. In 1509 John Peryn of Wellington left 3s 4d towards the cost of the new tower and a general rebuilding of the fabric may have taken place at about that time or shortly before. The north aisle was added in 1866. Much has been made of a needle and thread carved on the most easterly pier of the south arcade, but its significance remains unclear. In the south chapel are 17th and 18th century armorial monuments to the Bacons of Harpford, a farmhouse south of the village dating from the 16th century. Other tablets commemorate the owners of Wellisford in the south-west of the parish, a Domesday estate now centred on an 18th century brick manor-house, and Bindon House, on the northern boundary with Milverton. The Langford Revel used to include the ritual of 'clipping' the church, when the parishioners joined hands to dance around the building, uttering a great shout to chase the Devil away for the

forthcoming year. This same revel got out of hand in 1650 when there was much drinking, 'fiddling and dancing', and Wellington cudgel-players on the green beat up the tithingman who tried to disperse them.
★★ *Setting.*

LANGPORT (E)

A small, slightly scruffy, but endearing little town to the west of Somerton whose name means 'long market-place', presumably referring to the Bow Street causeway across the valley of the River Parrett. This causeway may be man-made, possibly Roman, designed to link villa sites to the east and west of the crossing. Some think that the Arthurian battle of Llongborth may have taken place here although the place-name evidence is unconvincing. There was a mint here from c.930 until the 11th century and the place formed one of the Saxon forts mentioned in the early 10th century Burghal Hidage. It was a Saxon royal borough at the time of Domesday when it had 39 burgesses (the Exeter Domesday gives 29). The parish occupied a mere 171 acres and its geography suggests that it was carved out of Huish Episcopi by the kings of the West Saxons before Huish was granted to the bishop. The place, often known as Langport Eastover to distinguish it from Langport Westover (*see below*) in Curry Rivel, sent two MPs to Westminster, 1305-7, and its council was headed by bailiffs in 1280 and a portreeve by 1369. Royal charters were granted in 1563, which confirmed a Saturday market and established three fairs, and 1616, which added a fourth fair. The corporation was dissolved in 1886, to be followed by the Langport Town Trust of 1888: itself taken over by the parish council in 1966. The manor had been granted away by the Crown before 1156, when it was held by Hugh de Gundeville, and descended with Curry Rivel until the 16th century, so that both ends of the Parrett crossing were controlled by a single lord. The estate was held by Henry Fitzroy, Duke of Richmond

RIGHT *The Hanging Chapel, Langport*
BELOW *Stone carving, Langford Budville church*

(Henry VIII's illegitimate son), 1525-36, and in 1584 was leased to (and in 1604 was sold to) Hugh Sexey of Bruton who used it to endow his hospital there. Lessees under the hospital included the Berkeleys of Bruton (1634-1773), the Hoares of Stourhead (1777-1808), and Langport corporation from 1809.

The town was a significant trading centre from Saxon times, relying on river traffic up the Parrett from Bridgwater, and property was held here by the abbeys of Glastonbury and Athelney and by Taunton Priory. There was an important cloth industry here by the 15th century, when woad was imported through Southampton, but in 1548 it was described as 'sore in decaye'. Fortunes revived with the trading company founded in the 18th century by George Stuckey and Thomas Bagehot, with wharves on the Parrett by the Great Bow Bridge. By 1866 the firm owned 14 East Indiamen and 19 barges and later developed into the Somerset Trading Company. The company spawned Stuckey's Bank, a joint stock company from 1826, headed by Vincent Stuckey (died 1845) of Hill House, which absorbed 13 other banks, mainly in Somerset, before being itself taken over in 1909. At that time Stuckey's had a banknote circulation second only to the Bank of England. Water-borne trade decreased with the arrival of the railway in 1853, carried across the Levels north of the town by a prominent viaduct. Langport East and

and lady of the manor, who adopted the portcullis as her badge and certainly visited the town in 1467. Much of the remainder was evidently financed by John Heyron (died 1501), whose arms were in 1633 'on almost all the pillars' and who certainly founded a chantry of the Blessed Virgin Mary, probably in the south chapel where he was buried. The marble slab from his tomb now serves as a table-top in the vestry. The east window features the figures of ten saints in 15th century glass, including bottom left St Joseph of Arimathea, holding the two cruets in which legend claimed that he brought Christ's blood and sweat to England, long before the Holy Grail was grafted onto the St Joseph myth. The church is full of undistinguished but informative monuments to the townsfolk. The former Hill House, now a Christian centre which was occupied as St Gildas Convent from 1903, is sited opposite the church and a small enclosed green marks the site of the medieval market-place. In the 16th century there was a thatched market-house there with 12 thatched shambles and a pillory. The hilltop only began to develop its present residential complexion in the 18th century when the market moved down the hill after a new town hall was built.

From the foot of the hill Cheapside and then Bow Street run south-west to cross the Little and Great Bow bridges, leaving the town across the River Parrett. To the south of the street, Back River may formerly have given access to wharves where cargoes brought up from Bridgwater were unloaded. In Cheapside the Langport Arms, formerly the Swan or the White Swan, is a large friendly inn dating from the late 16th century. The Town Hall of 1732, on the north side of the street, succeeded a 16th century hall. It is supported on pillars with a pyramid roof, the market being held on the ground floor. Bow Street was evidently settled from c.1200 onwards and the general area below the hill, including North Street, was known in the 14th century as 'Beneathcliff' or 'Beneathwall'. Many of the house frontages there were rebuilt further back with corporation subsidies between 1844 and 1879, although drivers today still find the street narrow to negotiate. The houses lean visibly back from the street as though subsiding into the silt of the Levels.

In the Civil War the town was garrisoned for the king in 1643 and the hill fortified. In 1645 the royalists were defeated at the Battle of Langport (which actually took place in Long Sutton and High Ham) and in

TOP *Great Bow Bridge and the River Parrett, Langport.* ABOVE *Bow Street, Langport*

West stations were closed in 1964.

The original settlement occupied the summit of Langport Hill, defended by surviving embankments to the north and south-west, by the natural slope to the west and the **Hanging Chapel** to the east. This picturesque chapel stands above an arch across the road and the present building probably dates from the 15th century. It housed a chantry of the Blessed Virgin Mary by 1344 until 1548 and was apparently used for illegal Catholic masses in Edward VI's reign. Referred to as the 'Hawninge' Chapel in 1575, it served successively as the town hall (1596-1600), Langport Grammar School (1706-c.1790), a militia arms store (1809-16), a Sunday school (1818-27), a museum (1834-75) and to house the local Freemasons' Lodge (1891 to date).

On top of the hill stands the **church of All Saints**, which served as a chapel to Huish Episcopi until it became a parish church in 1882, and from the churchyard there are wonderful views across the Levels. The grave of the world-famous economist, Walter Bagehot (1826-77), Langport's most celebrated son, lies in the south-east corner. A 12th century stone lintel with lamb and cross in a circle, two angels and two saints, has been reset over the south doorway. The north aisle wall is mainly 14th century but the rest of the church, including the west tower was almost entirely rebuilt in the late 15th and early 16th century. The tower bears a portcullis device, later adopted as the seal of Langport corporation, which has led some to ascribe its building to Lady Margaret Beaufort, mother of Henry VII their flight through the town towards Bridgwater the cavaliers fired houses in Bow Street to hamper pursuit. Three Monmouth rebels were executed here in 1685, although there is no evidence that they were suspended from the Hanging Chapel, as often stated. The Black (or 'girt') dog of Langport occurs in a wassail song recorded in 1895 and its imagined outline in the landscape was allegedly traced in Katherine Maltwood's Glastonbury Zodiac. She located its tail most appropriately at Wagg in Huish Episcopi!

A borough had been established in the manor of **Langport Westover** by c.1230, when a burgage there was held by Athelney Abbey. It lay immediately west of the Great Bow Bridge beside the road into Langport from Taunton and included the single large arable Portfield to the north, all in Curry Rivel parish. In 1304 Henry de Lorty obtained a short-lived Sunday market and a 10-day fair: the latter held at least until the 15th century. There was a leper hospital of St Mary Magdalene here by 1311, which became an almshouse after the Reformation. In 1647 the nine 'poore distressed peopell' housed there complained that they had not received their alms money for three years. Numbers there were limited to ten in 1675. The former site of a windmill here was mentioned in 1806.

★★ *Town, particularly the area of the hill, and church.*

LAVERTON (B) A small village set in lush countryside to the north of Frome, whose name is of uncertain origin: possibly 'the settlement frequented by larks'. Alestan held it in 1066 but, after being held by a succession of families, the estate was acquired by the duchy of Cornwall in 1443 with which it has continued ever since. The church of St Mary has a Norman north doorway and two Norman windows, but otherwise is largely Perpendicular. There is a funny little west tower, heavily buttressed, with saddleback roof and, in the nave, a rather grand 18th century memorial to the Yerbury family. Among its rectors was the Rev William Keate, father of the famous flogging headmaster of Eton, John Keate (1773-1852). Manor Farm, north of the church, has a ribbed plaster ceiling dated 1627 and was visited in 1909 by the future George V (as Duke of Cornwall) and Queen Mary to inspect the making of Cheddar cheese.

★ *Setting.*

LEIGHLAND (D), *see* **OLD CLEEVE**

Leigh-on-Mendip church

LEIGH-ON-MENDIP (F) This Mendip quarrying village, its name (pronounced 'lye') probably meaning 'grove' or 'glade', is located roughly midway between Shepton Mallet and Frome, strung out along a single street. The estate formed part of the manor and liberty of Mells and, as such, was held by Glastonbury Abbey from Saxon times and, after the dissolution, by the Horner family. The church of St Giles was similarly a chapelry of Mells and served by chaplains and curates until it became a separate living in 1860. The Perpendicular building has an outstandingly-ornate west tower (91 ft), of similar pattern to that at Mells but later (c.1475-90). The church's warm and friendly interior has an attractive set of contemporary pews, a Norman scalloped font and monuments to the Hartgill, Moore, Johnson and Gilbert families. In 1857 one of the parishioners, having taken exception to the curate's remarks on drunkenness, fired a gun charged with a bladder of bull's blood at the unfortunate cleric while he was preaching from the pulpit. The minister was hurled back against a pillar, covered in blood, and the culprit was later sentenced to two years in prison. Although mainly a farming village, there were formerly two businesses producing spade and rake handles. One was operated by Thomas Ashman who built the Methodist chapels here and elsewhere on the eastern Mendips.

★★ *Church.*

Effigies inside Limington church

LILSTOCK (D) A small coastal parish, 'the farm of Lylla's people', to the west of Bridgwater Bay, now linked with neighbouring Stringston and including a second Domesday manor inland at Honibere. The Acland family of Fairfield , Stogursey, established a small harbour here in the early 19th century, mainly to import Welsh coal for their estate, but removed after the First World War. The church of St Andrew was demolished in 1881, with the exception of the 14th century chancel, rebuilt as a mortuary chapel and declared redundant in 1980. Its 12th century font was then removed to Stogursey.

★★ *Setting.*

LIMINGTON (J) This 'settlement on a stream' (from *lymn*, a Celtic word for stream/river) is sited immediately east from Ilchester. The estate here was held by Glastonbury Abbey before the Norman Conquest but passed by exchange to the Courcelles family soon after 1066. Later it split into three parts, a fourth property in the parish being the Domesday manor of Draycott ('cottage on a slope') on the road east to Mudford. The north-south line of the village seems to have replaced an earlier settlement to the west along Duck Lane. Limington House, north-east of the church, was built in the early 19th century by a barrister, George Thomas Williams, incorporating some remains of the old manor-house, inherited by his wife. The church of St Mary is set back from the road through the village and dates from the 13th century. Its chief glory is the northern chantry chapel with its fine groined roof. It was founded in 1329 by Sir Richard de Gyverney, who secured that third of the manor formerly held by Gregory de Wylington, uncle of his second wife, Gunnora. The effigy against the north wall, lying picturesquely on its side, is identified as Sir Richard and the lady below him with Gunnora, the heiress. The other couple may be Henry Power (died c.1362) and his wife Matilda, although their identities are far from certain. Two recesses flanking the chancel arch housed the altars of St James and St Lawrence and stalls in the chancel bear the arms of Bonville and Harrington, former lords of the manor. Intriguing grotesques support the tower arch. The rectory here was one of the first preferments (1500-09) of Thomas Wolsey, future Cardinal and chief minister of Henry VIII, and it was while here that he is supposed to have been committed to the stocks (*see* **Lopen**). Opposite the church is the charming little former school, dated 1834.

★★ *Church*, ★ *Village*.

LITTON (A/B) An attractive unspoilt village to the north of Chewton Mendip which takes its name, meaning 'settlement on the torrent', from its position on the upper reaches of the River Chew: here little more than a stream. Bishop Giso bought the manor from an Alfred (not the king, as optimistically claimed in the church guidebook) shortly after 1060 and it was settled by 1157 on the dean and subsequently used to endow a prebend in the cathedral. Thanks to the plentiful supply of water there were three mills here by 1086, traces of one being still visible at Sherborne, north-west of the village. In 1853 Bristol Waterworks dammed the Chew above the village to create two picturesque little reservoirs. The friendly Perpendicular church of St Mary is hidden down a back lane and has roses trained around the porch. There is a good Jacobean pulpit and lectern, and memorials to the Trevelyan and Salvidge families. Thomas Trevelyan was licensed to mine for lead and coal here in 1673: fortunately for the village with a noted lack of success. The west tower can be dated from the arms of Archdeacon Thomas Palton and Preb Richard Harewell to the years 1395-1416.

★★ *Village*.

LONG LOAD (J) A parish carved out of the north of Martock parish in 1895, taking

Long Sutton

its name from the Saxon word *lad* – 'watercourse'. The village is strung out along the road running north to Long Sutton, which crosses the River Yeo by the late-medieval Load Bridge. There were wharves for riverborne traffic there by 1448. The manor was held from the 12th century by the Knights Templar and then the Hospitallers of St John, passing to Winchester College in 1551. Christ Church, designed in Early-English style in 1856 by C.E. Giles, stands to the west of the village street at its junction with Load Lane. It succeeded on the same site the medieval chapel of the Virgin Mary, rebuilt c.1796, from which the Jacobean pulpit survives.

LONG SUTTON (EJ) A delightful village grouped around a central green (probably where its fair was held from 1267), built largely of the local lias stone which was formerly quarried here. Its name ('long southern settlement') presumably relates to its position south of Somerton, while its site was determined by the junction of early routes from Somerton to Martock and from Ilchester to Langport. The manor was given by King Alfred to his abbey at Athelney in the 9th century and was held by the abbey until its dissolution in 1539. This estate, centred on the E-shaped Manor Farm, dating probably from the 16th century and lying south of the churchyard, was bought in 1600 by Sir John Spencer, then Lord Mayor of London. It descended through the earls of Northampton to the dukes of Devonshire, who dispersed it in 1919. Lesser manors were Sutton Hosey, owned by the Huse family by 1249 and based on the 16th century Manor House Farm, and Bornes or Sutton St Cleers, held by the Bourne family in the 16th and 17th centuries and linked with the medieval Court House: both these properties lying at the north end of the village.

Beside the green stand the substantial

Devonshire Arms Hotel, built c.1870 to replace a former inn called the Blue Ball and then the Bull's Head, and Holy Trinity Church, a rich rebuilding completed in 1493. The church contains a fine rood screen and a superb timber pulpit of c.1455 bearing initials idetified as those of Abbot John Petherton of Athelney and vicar William Singleton. The church was given to form a prebend of Wells Cathedral early in the 13th century. There were also pre-Reformation chapels in the parish at Upton and Knole, the latter a manor held by the earls of Ilchester until sold off in 1913. The parish was a centre of Quaker worship from 1662 and an early meeting-house, built in 1717, survives at the north end of the village. George Palmer (1818-97), founder of the Huntley and Palmer biscuit firm and uncle of the 1st Baron Palmer, was born in the parish.

★★★ *Village*, ★★ *church*.

LOPEN (J) The village of 'Lufa's pen or fold' is cut by the road north from Crewkerne to Lopen Head (A 356). The three Domesday manors were bought by the Pouletts of Hinton St George in the 1560s, one, today represented by Lopen Farm, having been held from the early 13th century by the Knights Templar and then the Knights Hospitaller. The small church of All Saints to the east of the main road dates from the 14th and 15th centuries but was much restored and extended in the 19th. As Lopen chapel it was granted to Bruton Priory c.1209, becoming dependant on South Petherton church, and passed to the chapter of Bristol Cathedral, obtaining burial rights in 1574. Three years later the curate was said to be from Jersey, 'not having the perfect English tongue'. The parish was noted from the 18th century for flax growing and for the production of linen, sailcloth and twine until the end of the second World War. A noted fair was held here by 1201 and continued as the Lopen Play until the end of the 19th century, probably in Church Street, where the base of a medieval cross survives near Cross Tree. The future cardinal, Thomas Wolsey, while a youthful rector at Limington, was apparently committed to the stocks by Sir Amias Poulett and local tradition ascribes the event to Lopen fair.

LOTTISHAM (E), *see* WEST BRADLEY

LOVINGTON (F) 'Lufa's settlement', west of Castle Cary and between the rivers Brue and Cary, is a small lias-stone village grouped around the church, relatively isolated from pockets of development on the main road to Somerton and along the road to the south. Charity Farm was acquired in 1743 by the Wells Archdeaconry charity for widows and children of deceased clergy and has an 18th century mural painting, as does Church Farm with its two-storeyed summer house opposite the church. In the north of the parish by the Brue, Lovington Mill forms an attractive Georgian group of buildings and probably stands on or near the Domesday mill which was held with the manor by Serlo de Burci in 1086. In the 12th century the lofty church of St Thomas a Becket was given to Wells Cathedral by a later lord, Robert of Cary, and thereafter was held by the dean and chapter. The present building has a 13th century west tower, old benchends in the nave and, in the sanctuary, an ornate aumbry (cupboard for communion vessels) with its small wooden door.

LUCCOMBE (C) An enchanting Exmoor village south of the Minehead to Porlock road which always reminds me of a beautifully-maintained garden. Apart from a slow saunter through its lanes it has little obvious to offer: no stately home to visit and no pub, only an endearing leafy wooded perfection. Its name probably means 'Lufa's valley', although the alternative 'valley where courting was done', from the Old English *lufu*, has its attractions. The principal estate, the manor of East Luccombe, was held by Ralph de Limesi in 1086, passing by the 13th century to the Luccombe family, by marriage to the St Johns and from 1473 for three centuries to the Arundells (lords Arundell from 1664) of Trerice, Cornwall. The second manor, of West Luccombe, was held by another family called Luccombe with a manorhouse at Horner and, from 1316, an adjoining chapel of St Peter, neither of

ABOVE *Luccombe.* BELOW *Packhorse bridge, Horner (Luccombe)*

which survive. Both manors eventually passed to the Acland family, as did Wychanger, a property south-east of the village, dating from c.1600 but mentioned in 1383 and now divided into two.

The church of St Mary the Virgin is large and impressive for such a relatively small village. The chancel is Early English of c.1300, the west tower and nave of c.1450, with a south aisle separated by a slender arcade added c.1530. In front of the chancel steps (under a rug) is a fine portrait brass of William Harrison (died 1615) who lived at Wychanger. On the north wall is a slate tablet to a long-suffering former rector, Dr Henry Byam. On the outbreak of the Civil War, having been an outspoken

supporter of Charles I, he was turned out of his rectory house and imprisoned. All his five sons served in the Cavalier army, two being killed. Escaping from prison, he joined Prince Charles at Oxford, fleeing with his future king to Scilly, Jersey and to France. In an attempt to join him, his wife and daughter were drowned in the Bristol Channel. At the Restoration of 1660 Byam returned to Luccombe and died as rector in 1669 aged 89.

Horner is an idyllic hamlet north-west of the village where in 1606 there was an iron mill and later a fulling mill. The present Horner Mill is mid 19th century although long disused. There is a medieval packhorse bridge, a row of 17th century

cottages and Horner Tea Garden. South-west from Luccombe village lies Cloutsham Farm, a 17th century building enlarged in 1869. It was mentioned as early as 1243 and has long been a point of departure for the hunting fraternity. Earthworks at Sweetworthy probably represent an 11th century settlement, deserted at an early date.

★★★ *Luccombe and Horner villages and settings.*

LUFTON (J) 'Luca's settlement' to the west of Yeovil has always been a small place with a tiny population. Even at Domesday (1086) it had only three serfs and three smallholders. There is no village, only Manor Farm (now workshops for Lufton Manor College) and the small church of SS Peter and Paul both at the end of a short lane. The church was rebuilt 1865-6 by Benjamin Ferrey but the Norman font, piscina and monuments to the Clark, Hooper and Batten families were saved from the old building. Lufton Manor, a substantial brick mansion, was built in extensive grounds in 1900 by Herbert Phelips Batten (died 1918), and is now occupied by Lufton Manor College. In 1945 a Roman corridor-type villa with mosaics and an octagonal plunge-bath block, occupied c.250-370 AD, was discovered in the north of the parish.

LULLINGTON (B/F) This magical village, 'the settlement of Lulla's people', lies to the north of Frome and provides a harmonious grouping of church and cottages that in Somerset is only rivalled by Selworthy. Before the Norman Conquest the estate here belonged to King Harold, killed at Hastings. The rectory and both halves of the manor were progressively prised from their later owners by the monks of Longleat Priory, Wilts, and after the dissolution were eventually acquired by

their successors at Longleat, the Thynne family, later marquesses of Bath. The manor was sold by Lord Bath in 1820 and bought with the Orchardleigh estate by William Duckworth in 1855. Lullington village was then described as 'ruinous' and 'not worth having', but Duckworth employed George Devey to assemble a model village with new cottages, farms, rectory and school. Thus the picture postcard he created is largely 19th century, as at Selworthy. At its centre, the ornate Norman church of All Saints is anything but fake, dating from the late 11th century. Outside there is an elaborate north doorway, somewhat weathered by the elements, featuring two beasts apparently consuming the Tree of Life, surmounted by a figure of Christ in Majesty. Inside is a

superb western crossing arch with beasts and an incredibly detailed font with an inscription which translates as 'In this holy font sins perish and are washed away'. The church was restored by William Duckworth in 1862, whose family monuments are clustered in the south chapel.

★★★★ *Church and village.*

LUXBOROUGH (C) A large and remote Brendon parish whose name, 'Loloches-berie' in 1086, means 'Lulluc's hill'. Settlement and ownership were complex. The north-west formed the manor of Luxborough Picot, named after Picot of Luxborough, who held it in the late 12th century, part later being acquired by Cleeve Abbey who had a grange here in 1329. The north-east made up the manor of Luxborough Everard, named for the Everard family, owners 1280-1558. The south-west quarter comprised the manor of Luxborough Eve, named from Ives of Luxborough in the mid 13th century, whose descendants through many different families held it until the death of the gloriously-named Nutcombe Nutcombe in 1809. The south-east sector became the manors of Langham Tort, owned by Geoffrey le Tort in 1280, and Langham and Pool, held by Hugh de la Pole in the same year, after whom the hamlet of Pooltown was presumably named.

Kingsbridge is a pleasing hamlet grouped around its bridge and the 18th century Royal Oak Inn. Nearby is Chargot House, built in 1826 by the Lethbridge baronets of Sandhill Park (in Bishops Lydeard), who began to mine iron ore in the south of the parish in the 1840s. Chargot became the seat of the Malet baronets in 1926.

The third and oldest hamlet is **Churchtown** in which stands the church of St Mary with a marvellous outlook over

TOP *The Royal Oak Inn, Kingsbridge (Luxborough).* ABOVE *The Manor House, Lympsham*

the encircling hills. The church was granted to Bruton Priory in the mid 12th century by Robert of Luxborough, as lord of Luxborough Picot (the priory having been founded by his overlord, William de Mohun). The chancel seems to date from the 13th century, the tower from the 14th. The rest is Perpendicular, including the font, although in 1861 the nave was largely rebuilt, the north aisle added and the tower topped off with its saddleback gable. The only monument, surprisingly, is to a 'naturally original and quaint' Methodist preacher, Sammy Coles, the tablet having been moved here when the local chapel was closed in 1982.

★★★ *Landscape.*

LYDEARD ST LAWRENCE (D) A small working village north-west from Taunton, for whose name see Bishops Lydeard. From Saxon times the estate here was owned by the bishops of Winchester with their great manor of Taunton Deane, although granted 1081-6 to Wlward by William the Conqueror. Subsequently it was held with or under Combe Florey and indeed the Domesday estate of Pylegh ('Lega' in 1086), a hamlet south from the village beyond the B 3224 where there was a

chapel until 1548, was long known as Leigh Florey. Latterly the main manor was acquired in the 18th century by the Hancock family. The church of St Lawrence towards the south end of the village was granted to Taunton Priory by Simon de Flory in the later 12th century. The patronage was held by the Portman family for nearly two centuries from 1660. The present church has a light and lofty interior, entirely Perpendicular except for the 14th century Decorated chancel with its sedilia and ogee-arched piscina. There is a rood screen of c.1500 minus its loft, an elaborate Jacobean pulpit and a good series of early 16th century benchends. On the north side of the chancel is a monument to Dr John Goodwin, rector 1614-29, succeeded by his son, also John, who suffered after the Civil War and was ejected from the living. John Venn (1586-1650), whose family held Pyleigh, was a noted Roundhead Colonel during the Civil War, governor of Windsor Castle, a commissioner at the trial of and a signatory to the death warrant of Charles I. Local tradition claims that the Lydeard font in which he was baptised was consequently inverted after the Restoration. Venn's cousin, another John Venn (1647-87), also from Lydeard, became master of

Balliol College and Vice-Chancellor of Oxford University.

Westowe, a hamlet north-west from the village, was represented by two small estates before the Norman Conquest and largely passed to Taunton Priory in a succession of piecemeal grants in the 12th and 13th centuries. At the time of Domesday it was held by William under Roger de Courcelles together with a small estate called Holford, now known from its later owners as Rich's Holford, to distinguish it from the adjoining Treble's Holford in Combe Florey.

★ *Church.*

LYMPSHAM (A) An extensive parish to the north of Brent Knoll whose name may derive from a personal name or from *lind pyll*, 'settlement by the lime-tree pool'. It passed into the hands of the monks of Glastonbury as part of the great Saxon estate of Brent, probably by gift of King Ine in 693, remaining with them until the dissolution of 1539. Thereafter it was granted to the Duke of Somerset in 1547, passing later to the Pophams. In 1809 the Rev Joseph Adam Stephenson became rector, as did two later members of his family, and his Yorkshire-descended family dominated the place for just over a century. Joseph Adam put up the delightfully-pinnacled Gothic Manor House c.1820, and his son, the Rev Joseph Henry Stephenson (rector 1844-1901), was responsible for building some 17 houses in and around the village, the school, parish stables and, in 1875, the ornate Manor Hall. The church of St Christopher, mentioned in 1191, is largely 15th century but was converted into an incredible personal shrine by the Stephensons, who plastered black-letter texts everywhere, even on the medieval font: cramming the building with their own memorials and 19th century furnishings. Figures in the east window of 1863 depict Joseph Henry and members of his family. A visitor in 1847 criticised the rector for preaching for an hour and a half but praised the hearty singing of the congregation. On the northern boundary of the parish, beside the road to Weston-super-Mare, stands Hobbs Boat Inn, once the ferry station which by 1234 until the 19th century served a high-tide horse ferry across the river Axe. The inn sign is derived from Thomas Hobbs, Glastonbury Abbey's ferryman of 1516, and not, as claimed by local folklore, from an ill-fated Viking raid by Hubba the Dane in 878.

★★ *Victorian atmosphere of church and village.*

LYNG (E) This parish includes the twin villages of East and West Lyng which grew up along the ridge followed by the Taunton to Glastonbury road (A 361). Its name comes from the Saxon word *hlenc* meaning 'hill'. To the east and associated with Lyng lies the **Isle of Athelney** ('the island of the princes' or athelings), two low hills where in 878 King Alfred constructed a fort and established his base of operations against the Danes. Here also, according to a late 10th century life of St Neot, while musing on his parlous situation, he inadvertently allowed some cakes to burn. Such a near-contemporary source suggests the cake story could well be true. A second fortress was set up at East Lyng, linked to Athelney by a causeway which probably followed the line of Baltmoor Wall, built c.1154 and today is traced by a lane which branches off the main road at the eastern end of the village. Lyng's defences are thought to have comprised a substantial bank and ditch at right-angles to the road, at the edge of the churchyard and above the present garage, which protected the promontory against attack from the west, and are recorded in the 10th century Burghal Hidage: Edward the Elder's masterplan for defending the south of England. Thence Alfred launched the successful campaign which culminated in his victory at the Battle of Edington, Wilts.

At **Athelney** c.888 Alfred founded an abbey (possibly on the site of an earlier hermitage occupied in the 7th century by St Aethelwin, son of King Cynegils of the West Saxons), evidently in gratitude for his own and England's deliverance. Its early years were marred by the attempt of two French brethren to kill their abbot and carry his body to the door of a notorious local whore for discovery. The abbot, although wounded, survived the attack and his assailants were tortured and put to death. Possibly destroyed in later Danish raids, the monastery may have been refounded c.960. In the 14th century the abbey was plagued with having to support royal pensioners, its church was ruinous in 1321, and in 1349 at least two abbots are believed to have died in the Black Death. In 1498 the then abbot was fined for aiding the rebels led by Perkin Warbeck and in 1536 the abbey was in debt to the tune of some £870. Three years later it was surrendered and dissolved. The foundations of the church were dug up in 1674 by labourers of Capt John Hucker (later a prominent Monmouth rebel), who also squirrelled-away a gold spur, but no remains are now visible above ground. A

Benchend, East Lyng church

monument, visible from the road, was set up on the abbey site by John Slade in 1801. Resistivity tests in 1993 revealed that it stands exactly over the former crossing of the 200 ft-long church with cloisters and other buildings down the slope to the south. At the east end of the church, a small rectangular building on a slightly different alignment might represent Alfred's original 9th century abbey church.

In the village of East Lyng the church of St Bartholomew, delightfully quiet inside apart from the ponderous tick of the tower clock, has Decorated 14th century windows to the nave and chancel: the rest is Perpendicular. There is a superb set of 16th and 17th century benchends (one dated 1614), featuring a woodcutter, Green Men, a pelican, wrestlers and a monkey riding backwards on a beast (Skimmington riding ? – *see* **Montacute House**). Beneath

the tower are two large 18th century paintings of Moses and Aaron, there is a Norman tub font and an early threelock register chest. The church secured burial rights from Athelney Abbey only in 1403 and the earliest Somerset evidence for annual church ales to maintain the church fabric occurs in an agreement of 1444 between the inhabitants of East and West Lyng and 'Burgh St Michael' (*see* **Burrowbridge**). Parking on the main street, let alone crossing it, is not easy and I am inclined to suggest the carpark of the 17th century Rose and Crown and a visit to that excellent establishment. A shortlived Monday market was established here in 1267 and, from 1349, a succession of fairs were held here until the Second World War. West Lyng seems to be the former manor of 'Relengen', granted to the abbey by King Athelstan in 937. Outwood is a hamlet north of the main road in the west of the parish which expanded after the Bridgwater to Taunton Canal was completed in 1827. Beside the main road between East Lyng and Burrowbridge is an excellent basket emporium: the product made from the local withies or willows.

★★★ *For its associations with King Alfred and its Levels setting,* ★★ *church.*

LYTES CARY (E), *see* CHARLTON MACKRELL

MAPERTON (F) The 'maple settlement' (pronounced 'Mayperton') sits on a leafy hillside to the south-west of Wincanton. As well as the main manor with its two mills in Domesday, there were two further estates at Clapton ('the hillock settlement'). There are earthworks and house platforms to the east of the village, suggesting that the place was formerly of greater extent. It was one of several manors in the area in which Maperton's lord, Francis Hastings (died 1610) of North Cadbury, tried to prevent churchales being held. In 1699 a gang arrived from Charlton Horethorne and beat up several Mapertonians while trying to steal their maypole: possibly sited at Dancing Cross, where there was formerly an inn called the Three Swans. Maperton House in the centre of the village is a substantial seven-bay classical building, which Pevsner dates to c.1805, extensively restored in 1874, approached through ornamental entrance piers, topped by eagles with over-large talons. The church of SS Peter and Paul is reached by a steep footpath east of the house. It has a Perpendicular west tower, but the rest was

ABOVE *Mark from the Levels.*
RIGHT *Marston House, Marston Bigot*

rebuilt in 1869 to the designs of Henry Hall. A piece of 12th century interlaced carving and a Norman piscina, discovered in the reconstruction, are incorporated in the new building. In 1505 the rector, Thomas Sawell, bequeathed 6s 8d to every couple in the parish and 3s 4d to every widow or widower. The church was a favourite venue for clandestine marriages in the first half of the 18th century.

MARK (E) A village on the Levels, with several attractive 18th and 19th century houses, which is sited west of Wedmore and to which it was for centuries subservient. Its name ('Mercern' in a dubious charter of 1065) means 'boundary house' and it lies at the junction of two man-made causeways running west to Highbridge and east to Blackford and Wedmore, to the repair of which a local cleric left money in 1425. The estate here was given by Edith, queen of Edward the Confessor, to the bishop of Wells, and with Wedmore was used to endow the deanery of Wells Cathedral by 1157. Successive deans continued as lords until its forced surrender to the Crown in 1547. There were two annual fairs held here in the late 18th and early 19th century. The chapel of Mark, mentioned in 1176, had a rector until 1242 when it was joined to the prebend of Wedmore. Thereafter, although a vicar was appointed in 1338, it was generally served by chaplains or curates. The present church of the Holy Cross (there is no documentary evidence for a claimed dedication to St Mark) stands uneasily opposite a garage towards the east end of the village. The large lions which guard the porch were the gift of a late 19th century minister. The south aisle probably dates from a rededication of 1268 but the rest is uniformly Perpendicular. There was a chantry of the Virgin Mary here by 1425 until 1548. An

early register chest still has two of its old padlocks attached and there is a good brass chandelier of 1758.

MARSHALLS ELM (E), *see* **STREET**

MARSTON BIGOT (F) The 'settlement by the marsh' bounds the town of Frome to the south and south-west, the site of the marsh now occupied by an ornamental lake. There are the remains of a round barrow at Smithwicks and the footings of Roman buildings were found in 1823 at Cheesehill (formerly 'Chessil') towards the north of the parish. The manor, initially held under that of Wanstrow, had been acquired before 1195 by the Bigod or Bigot family who held it until c.1310. It was then forfeited to the Crown by Richard Bigot for fortifying his manor-house (near the present church and Church Lodge) without licence, and again after Charles, Lord Stourton, was hanged with a silken noose in Salisbury market-place for the murder of his steward at nearby Kilmington. Following several leases, it was held by James Orange (1596-1601) and by John Symes (1601-19), the latter being credited with the building of the original Marston House (the central section of the present building) on a new site on the side of East Hill. Thereafter, the estate passed to Sir John Hippisley in 1619 and in 1641 to Richard Boyle, 1st Earl of Cork, the descendants of

whose third son, earls of Orrery from 1660 and Cork and Orrery from 1753, retained it until 1905. It was for Charles, 4th Earl of Orrery (1674-1731), that the 'Orrery', a clockwork device produced in 1716 which imitated the movement of the planets, was named in gratitude for his patronage. At first the Boyles spent little time at Marston, but the frequency of their visits increased in the 18th century. Marston House was substantially modernised 1750-52 to the designs of the 5th Earl's son and the east and west wings added by the 7th Earl in 1776. A loggia was built along the south front c.1820 and a major remodelling by the 9th Earl took place between 1856 and 1872, a new entrance and great hall being provided on the north side and the west wing largely rebuilt to accommodate an elaborate ballroom. Following the death of the 9th Earl in 1904, Marston was sold, allegedly because of the 11th Earl's gambling debts, and passed to the Bonham-Christies. Requisition during World War II and later division into flats placed the survival of the house in jeopardy. Its salvation and restoration as the headquarters of the Foster Yeoman quarrying company since 1984 was due to the commitment and devotion of John (died 1987) and Angela Yeoman. A distant view of the house beyond its extensive park can be obtained from the lane running east from Truddoxhill.

The old church of St Leonard, originally in front of the present east wing of Marston House, was demolished in 1786 and its successor, a simple Gothic barn, built and consecrated near Church Lodge in 1789. To this the 8th Earl added a west tower with five bells in 1809 and his youngest son, the Rev Hon Richard Cavendish Townshend Boyle, rector 1836-75, built the Romanesque chancel and 'violently Normanized' the rest. In the east window were placed six panels of 16th century Flemish and Rhenish painted glass, one graphically depicting St Bernard rejecting an innkeeper's wife from his bed. Later the Rev Boyle added a High Victorian north chapel and this, and indeed the rest of the church, is a feast of 19th and 20th century memorials to the Boyles. There are superb views from the churchyard across the park to the distant wooded Wiltshire hills. (*See also* **Nunney** *for* **Trudoxhill**, *and* **Witham Friary** *for* **Gare Hill**).

★★★ *Setting,* ★★ *church for its position and its memorials.*

MARSTON MAGNA (J/K) This 'larger settlement by a marsh', sometimes called Broad or Great Marston, is sited on a double bend in the A 359, north-east from Yeovil, on a tributary of the Hornsey brook which runs picturesquely through the village. It was so called to distinguish it from Little Marston Farm (west from the village) or Marston Parva. Held as nine separate estates before the Norman Conquest, a November fair was granted in 1248 but does not occur later. By the early 18th century the manor was owned by Sir John St Barbe and descended with Ashington to the Sydenhams. The site of the medieval manor-house survives as a moat and associated fish ponds south of the village. A property known as the Manor House near the church bears the date 1613.

The lovely church of St Mary the Virgin was held by Polsloe Priory, near Exeter, from the 12th century until the Dissolution but in 1736 the rectory estate was given by the executors of Sir John St Barbe to the vicar and his successors (who thus effectively became 'rectors'). The oldest part of the present building is the Norman chancel (see the tell-tale herring-bone masonry on the outside of the north wall and one small window), and the Norman scalloped font. The east window is 13th century, the chancel arch 14th and the nave, south porch, north chapel and west tower all Perpendicular, as is the attractive

ABOVE *Gothic cottage, Marston Magna.*

BELOW *Martock market place*

screen to the chapel just inside the north door. The north chapel is evidently the Lady Chapel, mentioned in several 16th century wills. In the gallery over the screen are the workings of a former tower clock of 1710 and there is a neat Georgian pulpit with sounding board. The nearby Rectory was surprisingly occupied by King Lewanika, King of Barotseland, and his entourage at the time of Edward VII's Coronation. Opposite the church is a delightful Gothic cottage and the former school.

★★ *Village and church.*

MARTOCK (J) A sprawling parish, one of the largest in the county, lying at the southern edge of the Levels, originally bordered to the north and west by the rivers Yeo and Parrett respectively and to the south-east by the Roman Foss Way. Its name probably means 'holy place by the lake'. It has long been an industrial place at variance with its rural setting, noted for

a cloth manufacture that flourished particularly in the 18th century. In 1633 Thomas Gerard remarked on its being ruled by its farmers, 'wealthy and substantial men though none of the best bred, which is the cause their neighbours slander them with the title of clowns; but they care not much for that, knowing they have money in their purses to make them gentlemen when they are fit for that degree'.

Apart from Martock village itself, the parish includes a number of other attractive Ham-stone villages: Bower Hinton, Hurst, Coat, Stapleton, Long Load, Milton Falconbridge, Witcombe and Ash. Each of these once had its own open arable field system and boasts a remarkable number of 17th and 18th century houses. Of these settlements the most substantial are strung out along both sides of a meandering street running north through Bower Hinton and Hurst (linked before 1327 by a tithing called Newton) to Martock. The principal manor of Martock was held before the

Conquest by Edith, queen of Edward the Confessor. Seized by the Conqueror in 1066, it was granted soon after to Eustace, Count of Boulogne, from whom it descended to the Fiennes family. Among later lords were the illegitimate son of Henry VIII, Henry Fitzroy, Duke of Richmond (died 1536), and from 1603 William, Lord Morley and Monteagle, recipient of the letter which revealed the Gunpowder Plot and led to the arrest of Guy Fawkes. All that remains of the manor-house is a small building with a 1659 datestone, which until recently stood within a large moated site to the west of the church. Up to 15 further manors were created by grants from the main manor in the generations following the Norman Conquest. Of these, Stapleton was held in the 14th century by the St Clares in return for holding a towel at the royal court three times a year and at the coronation. John de Say's 14th century estate was later divided into the manors of Martock Sayes and Says Bonville.

At the heart of the parish stands the church of All Saints, probably a Saxon minster of royal foundation, with attractive gateways to the churchyard dated 1625 and 1627. The present building dates from the mid 13th century, but its chancel, twin side chapels, nave, north and south aisles, south porch and west tower are largely 15th century. It is a lavishly appointed church with high clerestory, panelled tower and chancel arches and a superbly detailed angel roof with 768 panels, dated 1513. A female effigy of c.1315 in the south aisle probably represents a member of the Fiennes family. Note the memorial to vicar Thomas Bowyer (died 1763), the first to propose public hospitals in England. A buttress on the north side of the church has footholds cut in it to aid the recovery of lost balls from the roof when the game of Fives was played against the wall there in the 18th century.

The church was generously endowed: its estate, held in 1156 by the French abbey of Mont St Michel and from 1226 divided between that abbey and successive treasurers of Wells Cathedral, comprising the twin manors of Martock Rectory and Martock Priory. Across the road from the church, and visible from it, stands the oldest inhabited house in Somerset (apart from the Bishop's Palace at Wells), known in recent times as the **Treasurer's House** (fee:lists), owned by the National Trust, but open only by appointment. Serving as the manor-house of Martock Rectory manor, its great hall was described as 'new' in

1293-4, the cross wing may be a little older, with a virtually-detached kitchen of c.1500 to the west. In 1297, when the Treasurer of Wells, John de Langton, was also Edward I's Chancellor, he left the Great Seal of England at his 'court of Martock' while absent on the king's business.

On the corner of Pound Lane, near the church stands the former Grammar School, converted from an existing court house in 1661 by William Strode of Barrington, then lord of Martock manor. Strode required that the boys should only speak Latin to each other, out of school as well as in. Here c.1720 Daniel Defoe was amused by the broad accent of the pupils. The school closed in 1862 and has been a private house since 1975. Above the entrance is inscribed the name of God in Greek, Latin and Hebrew and the ironic injunction 'Martock, neglect not thy opportunities'. Further up the lane is the graveyard of the former Pound Lane Presbyterian Chapel, licensed in 1701 and demolished in 1913, where George Whitefield preached. Martock had a long nonconformist tradition dating from 1657 when a Quaker meeting at Ash, attended by nearly 800, was broken up by 'a great company of rude people with long staves and pikes'.

East from the church the Market House of c.1753, supported on pillars, forms an attractive group with the market cross or Pinnacle and the surrounding houses, although the Pinnacle is a replica of the original, demolished by a lorry. Martock had a Tuesday market from 1247 (held on Wednesdays in 1756) and an annual fair by 1302. The name of the nearby White Hart occurs from 1736 and the Lyric Opera Company performed in its assembly rooms in 1864. The George Inn is even older: mentioned in 1631.

There were two mills here in 1086. One of these on the Parrett in the south-west of the parish, known successively as Walter's Mill and Cary's Mill from its 13th and 18th century owners, was converted to grind snuff in the early 19th century and later extended to become **the Parrett Works**, an isolated but impressive industrial complex producing machinery and later canvas and twine. Although now used mainly for warehousing, its tall square chimney remains a major local landmark.

(*See also* **Ash, Long Load**).

★★★ *Martock church, villages of Martock, Bower Hinton, Hurst and Coat for their houses, Treasurer's House,* ★★ *setting.*

MAUNSEL HOUSE (D/E), *see* **ST MICHAELCHURCH**

MEARE (E) A former island and extensive parish on the Levels to the west of Glastonbury, where it was stated in 1540 that the air 'is not very holsome, savyng to suche as have contynued long therein'. The name, in its present shortened form, means simply 'lake', but it was formerly known as 'Fearningamere' or 'Ferramere', probably meaning 'the lake of dwellers in a place where bracken grows', although the Fearningas could possibly have taken their title from a personal name. The place-name referred not only to the island but also to Meare Pool, a large lake north of the village which in 1540 was 5 miles around and a mile and a half across with 'pykes, tenches, roches and yeles', but had been totally drained by the mid 18th century. The remains of two Iron-Age (so-called) **Lake villages**, Meare East and West, were discovered in 1895 at the south-western edge of the pool. Protracted excavation (1909-56) revealed evidence of occupation, including nearly 200 hearths, from the 3rd century BC to the 2nd century AD, now thought to represent a regular but seasonal market or fair, abandoned each winter as the floodwater rose. In 670 King Cenwalh of the West Saxons gave the island of Meare and two other small islands, Westhay ('western island') and Godney ('Goda's island'), to Glastonbury abbey, which retained it until its dissolution. At Meare a holy man, Beonna, was buried and 9th century Irish monks at Glastonbury mistakenly identified him with St Benignus (Benen), a follower of St Patrick, hailing him as a 6th century abbot of Glastonbury, with the result that Beonna's body was translated to the abbey, with associated miracles, in 1091. Later and spurious writing credited the saint with miraculously creating Meare Pool to provide fish and with planting his staff in the ground so that it took root and flowered: a story subsequently transferred to St Joseph of Arimathea and the Holy Thorn.

The inhabitants of Meare seem originally to have relied on fishing. In 1086 there were 10 fisherman and three fisheries here, but also vineyards which in 1189 the tenants were required to maintain. To the east of the village and formerly on the edge of Meare Pool stands the 14th century **Abbot's Fish House** (lists), a unique survival in the county. The abbey fisherman evidently lived on the first floor: working, salting and storing fish on the ground floor. A survey of 1540 enumerated

ABOVE *Church and Manor House Farm, Meare.* BELOW *Door hinge, Meare church*

40 pairs of swans, 4 herons and 16 pheasants within the manor. At the eastern end of the village, set back north from the road, is the substantial L-shaped Manor House Farm, to which Abbot Michael retired in 1252. The present building was built c.1340 by Abbot Adam de Sodbury and was apparently used as an occasional retreat for the abbots, being altered and extended in the early 16th century by Abbot Richard Bere. After the dissolution the manor was granted in 1547 to the dukes of Somerset, whose descendants retained Manor House Farm until 1758.

The present **church of St Mary** stands close to the farm. It was rededicated in 1323 'in honour of the Blessed Virgin Mary, All Saints and especially St Benignus, confessor', from which time probably date the west tower and the chancel. The high clerestoryed nave and north and south aisles evidently put up during the abbacy of John Selwood (1456-93), whose monogram appears on the parapet of the south aisle. In the absence of stained glass (disposed of to an antiquary after 1791 !), the interior is extremely light and airy, and there is a Perpendicular font and (stone) pulpit. The south door bears magnificently ornate hinges, probably of the 14th century. After the Reformation the rectory estate passed into the Strode family who in 1627 used it to endow a hospital and grammar school at Shepton Mallet. Opposite the church is the 1844 school with bellcot and clock.

Godney is an isolated working hamlet north-east from Meare, which had a chapel dedicated to the Holy Trinity by the 14th century. This was rebuilt in 1839 to the designs of G.P. Manners, became a parish church in 1869 and has a chancel by E. Buckle of 1902. There are wonderfully atmospheric views across the Levels to Glastonbury Tor and the Mendip Hills. To the west of Meare is the hamlet of **Westhay**, set at the edge of the peat

moors. Here peat digging is turning the landscape into an eerie barren waste to serve the needs of the gardener. The industry has, however, been instrumental in revealing a network of the earliest dated trackways in Europe, the oldest of which, the Sweet Track of c.4000 BC discovered by Ray Sweet in 1973, runs from Westhay towards Shapwick. This led to the formation of the Somerset Levels Project (1973-89) which pursued an in-depth archaeological investigation of the area. Reconstructed sections of trackways can be seen at the **Peat Moors Visitors Centre** (fee:lists), south-west from Westhay, opened in

1982 and since much extended. Here there are also exhibits on the archaeology, natural history and peat industry of the area, and periodic metal-working and craft demonstrations. An Iron-Age-type settlement was reconstructed by County Council archaeologists in 1992, including two reed-thatched round houses. Along Westhay Moor Drove is sited Westhay Moor Nature Reserve.

★★★ *Levels landscape, Meare church, manor-house (not open to the public) Abbot's Fish House, Peat Moors Visitors Centre.*

MELLS (F) One of the most beautiful of Somerset parishes, set in lush countryside north-west of Frome in the valley cut by Mells river. Apart from the main village near the church, it is a strangely scattered settlement with a confusing network of lanes. Its name means simply 'mills', suggesting that water-powered industry was a feature of the area even before records begin. There are no fewer than four Iron-Age camps in the parish: Wadbury and Tedbury to the east of the village, both above the Mells river, Newbury to the north-east on Newbury Hill, and Kingsdown in the north-west: again indicating the early significance of the place. The estate here was granted by King Edmund to Earl Athelstan in 942 by a charter which describes its bounds, including 'Todanberghe' (Tedbury), 'Mordrancombe' (Murder Combe) and 'Schipperugge' (Shipperidge Wood). Earl Athelstan transferred Mells to Glastonbury Abbey although after the Norman Conquest Abbot Herluin had to recover it from Harding son of Eadnoth. Following the dissolution of the abbey, the free manor or liberty was purchased in 1543 by Thomas and John Horner, a family linked with Mells by 1442. A widely-held belief that links this transaction with the origin of the nursery rhyme Little Jack Horner can be traced back no further than the 19th century. It is alleged that 'Jack' Horner, as Glastonbury's steward, was required to take the abbey's deeds to London, secreted them under a pie crust and abstracted the 'plum': those relating to Mells, Leigh-on-Mendip and Nunney. There is no foundation in fact for such a story and the

character of Little Jack Horner can be traced back as far as the 14th century *Tale of a Basyn*. The Horner family served the county as MPs and sheriffs, and, with the Pophams, were the most prominent Somerset supporters of the Parliamentary cause during the Civil War. The Horners might be here still were it not for the First World War. Edward Horner, only son of the last Sir John Horner, was killed at the Battle of Cambrai in 1917 and the estate passed to his sister Katherine, wife of Raymond Asquith, the Prime Minister's son, and then to their son, the present earl of Oxford and Asquith.

The former Horner home, Mells Manor, lies secluded behind high walls immediately west of the church. It was originally built in the shape of the letter **H** in the years following the Horner purchase, evidently replacing an earlier house put up by the abbots. At the height of the Civil War, while the Horner estate was sequestered, Charles I spent a night at the manor-house on 17 July 1644. In the early 17th century the Horners developed an extensive deer park to the south-west of the village and there 1724-25 Thomas Strangways Horner commissioned a large Georgian mansion from the Wincanton architect, Nathaniel Ireson. Thereafter the Horners abandoned the old manor-house and even demolished its north wing from 1763 to provide stone for extending Mells Park house. The park was enlarged, planted, and ornamented with lodges, walks, bridges, a temple and 'duckery'. Reasons of domestic economy led the Horners to restore and refurbish the remaining south wing of Mells Manor,

whence they returned in 1900 and where their descendants continue to live. Mells Park was let to tenants and in 1917 was gutted by fire. A more modest house was built on the site in 1922 by Reginald McKenna (Chancellor of the Exchequer 1915-16, buried in Mells churchyard) to the designs of Sir Edwin Lutyens, incorporating some features from the older house, although not sold by the Horners until 1939. Since 1977 Mells Park has been held by the ARC quarry company.

The parish's rural appearance belies the former industrial economy of the place. There were fulling mills here from medieval times, one at Melcombe described as 'old' by 1234 and another there as 'newly built' in 1425-26. One wealthy clothier, Thomas Strete, bequeathed a woad vat in his will of 1528 and Leland described Mells as 'a praty townelet of clothing'. Later there was brewing here, and in 1744 James Fussell (died 1775) of Stoke St Michael, edge-tool maker, leased ground here to build mills. In 1803 his son, also James (died 1832), offered to supply the government with up to 2,000 pikes a week without charge from his Mells Iron Factory to oppose Napoleon. Concessions were wrung from the Horners in 1841 by threatening to build a Fussell mansion and further works in full view of Mells Park House. The business developed an international reputation but was eventually bought out by Isaac Nash in 1884 and closed in 1894. A Mells fair, supposed to have been procured c.1342, continued until the 19th century. Today quarrying is the principal activity in the area.

There is an abundance of honey-coloured

Mells Manor and church

houses and cottages throughout the parish, but particularly in the High Street of the village, which includes the welcoming 16th century Talbot Inn (this hound was the crest of the Horner family and a pair of them surmount the gate piers to the Manor). At right-angles to the High Street runs **New Street**, a rare example of medieval town-planning, the brainchild of Abbot John Selwood of Glastonbury c.1470. This is only one quarter of the original concept which was intended to form the four arms of a cross, but was never completed. On the east side Col Horner established a boys' school in 1840 which bears a plaque to mark Victoria's Golden Jubilee in 1887.

New Street leads to the delightful Perpendicular **church of St Andrew** with its substantial and ornate 104 ft west tower. The tower, which has a fine fan vault, was in progress in 1446, when £3 was bequeathed to the work by John Sammell. There is a pinnacled two-storeyed porch, also with fan vaulting, and a polygonal vestry, the gift of a London draper (presumably with Mells connections) called Garland c.1485. In the tower a faceless clock, first recorded in 1658, has since 1720 played four tunes on the bells at 3-hourly intervals throughout the day (and night). A will of 1496 mentions the chapel of the Blessed Virgin Mary and the altars of St Katherine and St Anne. The interior was modified and restored at various times

Statue of Edward Horner in Mells Church

during the 19th century, although there is a simple Norman font with cable moulding, four saints in 15th century stained glass in the north aisle, and a chancel chandelier of 1721. At the west end of the south aisle is a monument to the edge-tool wizardry of the Fussells. The church has been enriched with the work of many celebrated modern artists. The north (Horner) chapel features a fine equestrian statue of Edward Horner (died 1917), a rare sculpture by Sir Alfred Munnings on a Lutyens plinth, panels to other Horners from 1659, and a tomb chest of 1872 bearing the arms of others formerly buried here. Under the tower is a memorial to Raymond Asquith (killed on the Somme, 1916) by Lutyens and Eric Gill, and opposite a Burne-Jones peacock above an empty tomb to Laura (died 1886), sister of Margot Asquith and wife of Cabinet Minister and England cricketer, Alfred Lyttelton. A brass in the south chapel recalls Canon J.O. Hannay (rector 1924-34, died 1950), who wrote under the pen-name George Birmingham. Outside in the churchyard, the Horners and their friends are buried to the east of the church. Graves include those of Mngr Ronald Knox (1888-1957), translator of the Vulgate Bible who lived in retirement at the Manor (Mrs Asquith converted to the Roman Catholic Church in the 1920s), the war poet Siegfried Sassoon (1886-1967), who wished to be buried near Knox, and Christopher Hollis (1902-77), MP, author and son of the bishop of Taunton. John Wesley preached here for two hours in 1785 despite the fact that a wasp stung him on the lip as he began.

Elsewhere there is a Georgian rectory, a medieval barn, an impressive war memorial by Lutyens, the 18th century Blind House or lock-up (a burglar escaped from the abbot's prison here in 1225), an almshouse built in 1708 with money from the poor rates, a primary school founded in 1830 (there was a grammar school in the village in 1524), and a wealth of humbler dwellings dating from the 17th and 18th centuries, traditionally identified as former weavers' cottages. At the south-eastern end of the village by the bridge is a triangular shelter (Lutyens again) put up in memory of Mark Horner (died 1908, aged 16) by his mother, Lady Horner. She had water piped to several sites around the village, including this shelter, each with inscriptions designed by Eric Gill.

Upper and **Lower Vobster** are small appealing hamlets in the west of the parish ('Fobbestor' in 1234, 'Fobb's tor'), probably founded to house clothworkers, as the

earliest fulling mills were in their vicinity. Subsequently the area was dominated by quarries and collieries: all now disused. Vobster became a separate parish in 1852, served by the ambitious church of St Edmund (1846), designed by Benjamin Ferrey.

★★★★ *Mells church, village and setting.*

MERRIOTT (J) A sizeable village north of Crewkerne, whose name probably means 'boundary gate'. Unsubstantiated traditions of Irish colonization, founded on the parishioners' distinctive dialect, dark complexion and hair, led to the place being nicknamed 'Little Ireland'. Nicknames also proved necessary in early 17th century Merriott because of common surnames, and curlhead, noghead and boneback occur in official records. The parish generally is awash with unusual placenames: Shitrock (now Shutteroak), Eggwood House, Sockety Farm, Boozer Pit, Waterloo Farm (c.1820) and Green Nap. A fair around Ascension Day was mentioned between 1244 and 1328.

The manor was held in 1086 by Harding son of Eadnoth, whose descendants took the name of their property and continued as lords until the death of Sir John de Meriet in 1391. The village streets form a triangle around a former open arable field called Hitchen or Landshare and there are a large number of attractive 17th and 18th century stone houses, particularly in Lower and Church streets, several of them with datestones. The richness of the soil led to the early development of market-gardening here. Indeed, the earliest recorded horticultural use in England of the word 'nursery' ('noresire') occurs at Merriott in 1369. By the 17th century tithes were payable on a range of garden produce and the Whitley family, later lords of the manor, were gardeners here from 1718. Scott's Royal Nurseries were established in the parish in 1852 when John Scott bought out the Webber family's business.

The church of All Saints has a sturdy low west tower with substantial tapering walls, possibly dating from the 13th century. The rest is mainly 15th or early 16th century, but the east end of the church was rebuilt in 1860. A carved stone in the vestry with figures identified as fighting cocks may be 12th century. Alexander Atkins, vicar here 1576-1626, was deemed 'most contentious and quarrelsome', insulting from the pulpit those who were late in paying their tithes. In 1620 at a bear- and bull-baiting revel one churchwarden was accused of serving ale in the church's chalice at the bear stake,

The Kings Head, Merriott

Milborne Port Town Hall

and a curate in 1632 was described as so drunk that 'he would have cut off some of his hand to give unto his dog'. The former tithe barn near the church was restored in 1913 for parish meetings. To the north-east of the village the buildings of the one-time Bow Mill, mentioned in 1373, form an attractive group.

★★ *Village,* ★ *church.*

MIDDLE CHINNOCK (J) This small Ham stone village, delightfully unspoilt, lies to the north-east of Crewkerne and formed part of the 10th century Saxon estate of Chinnock (*see* **East Chinnock**) and which lines a short north-to-south street, including the 17th century Rectory and Manor Farm. The manor was held in 1086 by Malger under the count of Mortain and was later possessed by the Aumale and Maltravers families, descending to the Fox-Strangways earls of Ilchester. The church of St Margaret has a Norman south doorway and font, a Perpendicular west tower and south porch, but the nave, chancel and transepts were rebuilt during the 19th century. In the south porch is the mutilated effigy (head and shoulders) of a priest of c.1300. A Roman burial was found at Higher Farm, near the church, in 1930.

★★ *Village.*

MIDDLEZOY (E) A Levels parish to the south-east of Bridgwater. By the 8th century 'Sowi' was the name of Glastonbury Abbey's major estate here, *sow* being a British river name from a root meaning 'flowing', the added 'i' deriving from the Saxon *ig* for 'island'. Thus Middlezoy can translate as 'the middle stream island'. The church of the Holy Cross stands on a small hill with fine views towards the Polden Hills: the village draped around and below it. A vicarage was ordained here in 1268 after a dispute over tithes with the rector of nearby Chedzoy. Although the church had window and doorway details from c.1300, most of the building is 15th century, including a fine three-stage west tower. There is a rood screen of c.1500 (the initial 'R' and a barleycorn to the left of the door are claimed to identify the work of Abbot Richard Bere), a few surviving 16th century benchends, and a pulpit dated 1606. Beneath the nave carpet, level with the third pew from the front, is a floor slab to Louis, Chevalier de Misiers, a French mercenery with the English army for 18 years: killed at the Battle of Sedgemoor in 1685. Under the tower is a charming 'acrostick' on Anne Ames (died 1697), wife of Thomas Willis of Thorngrove, whose home, south-west of the village, was stylishly rebuilt in the late 18th century.

★ *Village and setting.*

MIDELNEY MANOR (J) *see* **DRAYTON**

MILBORNE PORT (K) A 'stragling towne' (1633) and former parliamentary borough, it is today a large village on the south-eastern border of the county with Dorset, lying athwart the main A 30, its name being that of the 'millstream' mentioned in two 10th century charters ('Mylenburna', 933), with the addition of 'port' , meaning 'town' or 'market' rather than 'harbour'. It was a royal borough before Hastings with its own mint (c.997-1035), and in the Domesday Book had a market, 6 mills and 67 burgesses: making it the third largest town in Somerset, after Bath and Ilchester. Immediately north of the present village is a triangular area which possibly represents the focus of the royal demesne, later the manor of Kingsbury Regis. The borough was administered by the proprietors of nine burgages who nominated two capital bailiffs or stewards, and there were town and guild halls, a common bakehouse and brewhouse and a tolsey (for collecting market tolls) . To the market was added one fair in 1397 with a second by the 18th century. In the centre of the village survives the picturesque 18th century Town Hall, supported on pillars and below which trading formerly took place, and nearby the Guildhall, with what must be a reused Norman doorway. The base of the former 15th century market cross has been moved to Sansomes Hill near the church. The staple industry of Milborne was cloth weaving, with an increasing emphasis on sailcloth from the 18th century, and gloving from the mid 19th.

The borough returned MPs on five occasions between 1298 and 1307 and again, after a petition, from 1628 until 1832, when as a 'rotten' borough it was deprived of the privilege by the Reform Act. The electorate was always small, sometimes as low as 80 voters, and it was this fact which brought lawyer James Medlycott (died 1731) from Berkshire to Milborne, where he succeeded his brother Thomas as MP 1710-22. Here from 1696 he built Ven House south-east of the town, a splendid

ABOVE *Ven House, Milborne Port.* BELOW *Milton Clevedon church*

13th century female effigy, possibly the foundress of a chantry here) was rebuilt in 1842, the nave, north transept and north aisle in 1867-9, although the fine Norman south doorway was reused. The Medlycott memorials cluster in the north transept (where there are four hatchments) and north chapel and in the latter there is an exhibition of early service books, including a 'Vinegar' bible, and medieval tiles. The royal arms of 1662 hang on a board in the north aisle, with an appropriate Restoration quotation from Proverbs: 'My sonne feare thou the Lord and the King and meddle not with them that are given to change'.

Milborne Wick is a charming farming hamlet to the north of the main village, with a former mill and small gallery. Alice de Horsted (1314) and Roger de Guldene (1332-4) had an oratory chapel here. East of it the earthworks of an early fort or camp survive.

★★★★ *Church*, ★★ *Village*

MILTON CLEVEDON (F) This small village lies just off the B 3081 to the north-west of Bruton: possibly called 'the middle settlement' because it lies midway between Evercreech and Bruton. In the late 12th century it was held under the Lovels of Castle Cary by William de Clevedon, who gave the church of St James to Bruton Priory (later Abbey), which retained it until its dissolution in 1539. The church, surrounded by trees with romantic rolling countryside beyond, lies at the end of a short lane through the inevitably muddy farmyard of Manor Farm, with earthworks and house platforms in its vicinity, indicating shrinkage of settlement here. There were sheep grazing in the churchyard when I visited. Collinson recorded a Norman tower and west doorway, but the tower was rebuilt in 1790 with stone appropriately taken from Bruton Abbey. The rest of the church is Perpendicular but was largely rebuilt in 1865 when the north aisle was added. In the sanctuary is the effigy of a priest of c.1325 (possibly William de Milton, vicar 1313-22), holding a chalice, but heavily recut in the 19th century. Under the tower stands an elaborate memorial to Susannah widow of Thomas Strangways (died 1718) with a touching inscription: 'ye best of Wives, A tender and Indulgent Mother'. She was the daughter of John Ridout and brought the manor to her husband, ancestor of the Fox-Strangways earls of Ilchester. There was also a medieval chapel of St Lawrence in the east of the parish.

★ *Setting of church.*

Georgian mansion, probably completed after his death. It was enlarged 1836-7 and finally sold by the family in 1957. Ludicrous electoral contests here included that of 1774 when there were rival returning officers and the Medlycotts broke into the Town Hall to steal the borough seal and so validate their return. In 1819 the Earl of Darlington (Whig) started to build 80 houses within the borough, known as Newtown, the new tenants of which would support his interest. In retaliation the Marquess of Anglesea (Tory) built Waterloo Crescent in 1820, and then went on to construct cottages in East Street, Sansomes Hill and Upper and Lower Gunville, at a total cost of £15,689. The political race ended in 1824 when Darlington sold his properties to the Marquess. It is believed that the 1831 Census totals were deliberately inflated in a vain attempt to save the place's representation. The Medlycotts gave the borough Somerset's oldest surviving fire engine

(1733) and built the Ball Court (for playing Fives) just south of the High Street 'for the health and amusement of the town', laid out as a Garden of Remembrance in 1951.

The important church of St John the Evangelist, possibly a Saxon minster, was held before and after the Conquest by Regenbald, dean of Cirencester and a chancellor of both Edward the Confessor and William I, passing like his other property, on its foundation in 1133, to Cirencester Abbey and, following that abbey's dissolution, to Winchester College in 1551 (which transferred its estate here to the Marquess of Anglesea in 1824). The crossing beneath the tower has fine late Saxon arches and capitals to the north and south, and there are remains of Saxon windows in the north and south walls of the chancel, the existing windows having been added in the 13th and 14th centuries. It is tempting to ascribe the Saxon (and early Norman) work to Regenbald himself. The south transept (with a late

144

ABOVE *Trout Hill from Elsworthy, Exmoor*
BELOW *Selworthy*
LEFT *Looking west from Daw's Castle to Watchet*

ABOVE LEFT *Podimore church*
LEFT *The Colles Monument, Pitminster*
BELOW LEFT *Pendomer*
ABOVE *Abbey Barn, Somerset Rural Life Museum*
BELOW *Huish Episcopi church*

ABOVE *Draycott Sleights Nature Reserve, the Mendips* BELOW *Cheddar Gorge*

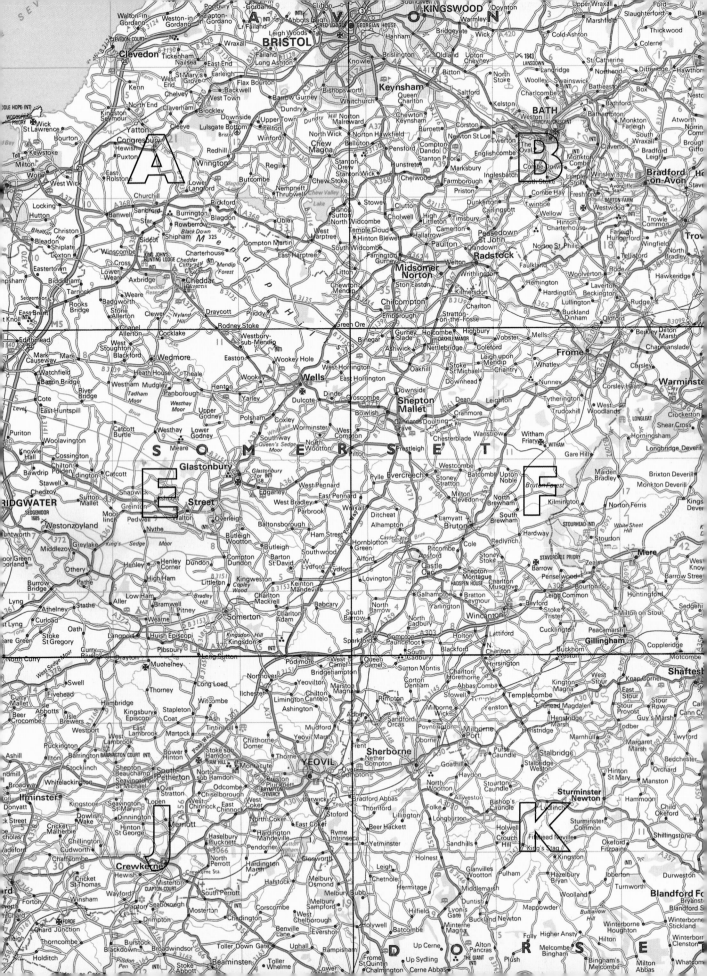

ABOVE LEFT *Dillington House*
LEFT *Hestercombe House gardens*
BELOW LEFT *Cricket St Thomas*
ABOVE *Dunster Castle*
BELOW *Lytes Cary*

LEFT *Hodders Combe, Holford*
ABOVE *Cothelstone Hill, the Quantocks*
BELOW *West Bagborough*

ABOVE *Glastonbury Tor.* BELOW *East Lyng from the Levels*

MILVERTON (D) A very appealing small town, former borough and meeting-place of its own hundred, immediately south-east from Wiveliscombe and west of Taunton. Its name means 'the settlement by the mill-ford', probably referring to the site of the Town Mills on the Hillfarrence Brook to the north of the town. A large number of Neolithic flint arrowheads and axes have been found to the west of the town and three Bronze-Age axe heads were turned up in building the welcome bypass, opened in 1975 along the line of the old railway, which runs to the north-east of the town. The place was probably a settlement established by the West Saxon kings although the earliest direct evidence is its grant shortly before the Norman Conquest by Queen Edith to Bishop Giso of Wells Cathedral, an act reversed by William the Conqueror. The manor was evidently united with the barony of Torrington (Devon), passing by 1212 to William Briwere, who in 1225 received a grant of timber from Petherton Park to build his manor-house here, but divided between the Briwere heiresses in 1233.

The somewhat shaky evidence in the Domesday Book for a pre-Conquest borough rests largely on its market and the fact that the lord of Oake had a house here. Otherwise the earliest record of a borough is mention of a burgage held by Jordan the leech in 1265. Thereafter the borough was administered under a portreeve. High Street is thought to represent the earliest settlement, the borough extending eastwards along the ridge to occupy the present gridiron of streets. These streets have a delightful sense of scale, with a succession of 18th and 19th century facades, particularly along North Street: one of the most charming Georgian thoroughfares in the county. The market, held on Saturdays in 1408, was centred on the junction of Fore, Sand and St Michaels streets, and there was also a fair by 1280. A temporary Tolsey house (for the collection of tolls) was put up for the fair in 1553: later succeeded by the Fair Cross, but the market and fair had been discontinued by 1652. A new covered Market Cross was built in 1706 and William Hulett secured a fresh grant of two fairs and a Friday market in 1708. The cross was demolished in 1851 although the base of its shaft survives in the garden of the Fort. The town's economy, like the trade of Wiveliscombe and Wellington, relied on cloth manufacture until its decline in the 18th century. Lamech Swift established a silk-throwing factory at Preston in 1819, employing up to 300 women and children in its early years.

The church of St Michael in the centre of the town was held in 1086 by Stephen, the king's chaplain. The advowson was granted by William Briwere to Bishop Jocelin in 1226, who in 1241 settled it on the archdeacon of Taunton as a prebend. The Old Parsonage to the east of the church, which Pevsner dates to the late 15th century, evidently served as the archdeacon's residence. Among those who held the archdeaconry were Stephen Gardiner (died 1555), bishop of Winchester and Chancellor of England, and Thomas Cranmer (1489-1556), archbishop of Canterbury. The present red sandstone church is mainly Perpendicular, the base of the west tower dating from c.1200, the north arcade and west doorway and window to the south aisle from the 14th century. There is a Norman font with cable decoration, a rood screen incorporating early panels with the date 1540, and a considerable series of 16th century benchends. The south aisle contains 18th and 19th century monuments to the Broadmead family of Olands and the south chapel to the Spurways (1807-1914), owners of the 17th century gabled house called the Fort, formerly known as Lancasters from its earlier owners. Until 1548 the chantry chapel of the Virgin Mary stood in the churchyard.

No fewer than 62 Milverton men are believed to have joined the Duke of Monmouth's rebel army, of whom one was executed, 17 were transported and 4 pardoned. Thomas Young (1773-1829), born

North Street, Milverton

next to the Quaker meeting-house in North Street, became professor of physics at the Royal Institution. He originated the wave theory of light, gave the word energy its scientific significance, pioneered the studies of optics and colour perception and contributed to the deciphering of Egyptian hieroglyphics.

That part of Milverton to the north of the Hillfarrence Brook formed the three Domesday estates of Preston, later the twin manors of **Preston Bowyer** and **Torrells Preston**. The former survives as an attractive hamlet along the main road east of the town, its manor settled in 1113 on the alien priory of Goldcliff, Monmouth, by the priory's founder, Robert de Chandos, and then descending with Monksilver manor. Torrells Preston was named after and held by Roger Torrell who endowed a chapel there with land which the vicar of Milverton tried to recover in 1403. There were three other Domesday estates in the parish, Manworthy, Poleshill and Leigh: all held under the Mohun's honor of Dunster. Garnival's Week to the east of the town is recorded as 'Wyke' (*wic* – 'dairy-farm'), when it was held by Henry de Gernevil. Auton Dowells, south-west from Milverton, is a converted former farmhouse which has provided a happy venue for countless wedding receptions and functions in the area. Signed off the bypass and lying to the west of the town, Frys Quaking House takes its name from the Quaker burial ground, dated 1681, lying just south of the house.

★★★ *Town, particularly North Street,*
★★ *church.*

MINEHEAD (C) This is Somerset's largest seaside resort, a former borough and port in the west of the county. Its name ('Mynheafdon' in 1046, 'Maneheve' in 1086) is that of the steep flat-topped hill to the west, now known as North Hill, on which were sited East and West Myne farms. The town's name derives from the Celtic *mynydd*, 'hill', to which was added the Saxon *dun*, also meaning 'hill'. It was this promontory which provided the natural shelter for the growing settlement and contributed to its popularity as an early watering place. Today the town is the biggest and busiest shopping centre in West Somerset. Its aspect was changed forever when Billy Butlin's extensive holiday camp, now known as **Somerwest World**, was built on the marshes to the east of the town in 1962.

From the time of the Norman Conquest the main manor was always held with that of Dunster: first by the Mohuns and then by the Luttrells. Initially it depended on agriculture, farms at Periton, Hindon, Lynch, Woodcombe, Wydon and Combeshead being mentioned by the 13th century. There was a park here by 1279, destroyed by Sir Andrew Luttrell in the early 16th century. At Myne on North Hill was a small manor, which in 1086 seems to have served as a sheep farm for Dunster. Bratton ('newly cultivated settlement'), a third Domesday manor, was centred on the present Bratton Court, a major 15th century house with chapel and gatehouse to the west of Minehead. Held under the Mohuns by the Bratton or Bracton family, it has never been sold since that time, descending through the families of Fry, and Lord King to Lord Lytton. Traditions of a link with the 13th century jurist, Henry de Bracton, have not been substantiated.

The town of Minehead developed from three distinct settlements. Upper Town on the hillside around the church was probably the earliest, Lower Town around the later market-place (now the Parade) and mills, and Bottom or Quay Town along the shoreline, and these remained separate hamlets until the 19th century. There was a Michaelmas fair by 1383-4 and a weekly market by 1424-5, the latter then held 'next to the cross opposite St Michael's church', i.e. at Upper Town. A grant of a Tuesday market and three-day fair were obtained by Lord Herbert in 1465 and a borough had been established by 1474 when a portreeve and burgesses are recorded. There was a town hall where the courts met and officers appointed, including watchers of (fish) weirs and keepers of

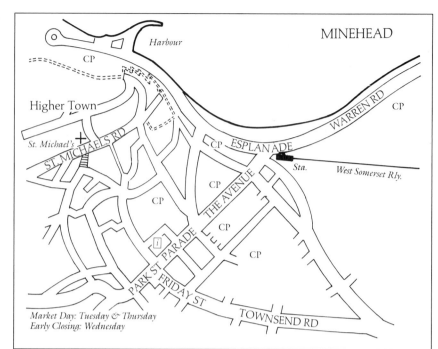

ABOVE *Minehead.* OPPOSITE *The beach at Minehead*

the waters. During the same period the Luttrells were setting up a port, evidently as Dunster's haven silted up and declined. A new jetty was built 1421-2 and trade opened up with Bristol, Wales, France and, most significantly, Ireland: importing wine and exporting fish, although the place suffered from a high-water mark which progressively receded. By the mid 16th century the port had 12 ships and 20 barks, and was bringing in beans, coal, salt, wood and iron. In 1559 a full charter of incorporation was obtained, adding a prison (the

Cockmoile), Thursday market and two fairs, but burdening the borough with the maintenance of the port (described as 'useless' in 1570), to be paid for out of the harbour dues. George Luttrell was instrumental in the borough charter being rescinded in 1607 and responsible for the building of a new harbour further west, completed in 1616. Vain attempts to regain their charter were made by the inhabitants in 1620 and 1667. The town was particularly prosperous during the 17th century and a fishing fleet left

Rood screen, Minehead church

Church Steps, Minehead

annually for the Newfoundland cod banks 1660-7. Persistent silting necessitated an extension to the harbour, encased in stone in 1714. The 18th century, however, was a saga of gradual decline which culminated in 1791 in the destruction by fire of 73 houses in Lower Town, caused by a miller's blazing pitch barrel.

Fortunately the seasonal popularity of sea-bathing, recorded here in 1794, brought growing numbers of visitors to the town's lodging houses. There were two bathing machines in 1802, and from the

1820s building began to link Upper and Lower Town. The remoteness of the place, however, made reaching it a laborious business until the building of the railway from Taunton to Watchet in 1862 reduced the time spent jolting in a coach, and the arrival at Minehead of the extended line in 1874 set the seal on the resort's success. The town gained a new town hall in 1889 (converted to the hospital in 1920), an Urban District Council in 1894, the seawall and promenade had been built by 1900 and a 700 ft pier followed in 1901 (dismantled

at the beginning of World War II). Blenheim Gardens opened in 1925, the Regal Cinema in 1934, a swimming pool was completed in 1936, and the harbour finally closed in 1947: handed over to the UDC by the Luttrells. A small local museum is planned at the restored **Townsend House** in Townsend Road.

The charter of 1559 also provided the town with two MPs, who continued to be returned until 1832, long after the charter had been rescinded. The wide electorate comprised all householders not receiving charity (including those living at Alcombe and Staunton) and generally, but not always, returned members who supported the Luttrell interest.

High on the slope of North Hill with wonderful views out over the bay, the large grey-stone **church of St Michael** was given in the later 12th century to the monks of Bruton Priory by the third William de Mohun. After the Reformation the advowson was generally held by the families of successive vicars until bought by the Luttrells in 1718. Of the present building, the 87 ft Perpendicular west tower has two well-preserved carved panels, one evidently depicting the Trinity (God holding the crucified Christ, although lacking the dove) and the other St Michael weighing souls who shelter under the skirts of the Virgin Mary. Pevsner considers the tower might be the work of John Marys of Stogursey, who completed the similar tower at Dunster from 1443. The nave and north aisle (there is no chancel arch), with

wagon roofs, contain no features earlier than the 15th century. The octagonal font with figures is also Perpendicular. A fine late 15th century rood screen spans the building, similar to those at Dunster and Carhampton, there is a superb 16th century altar table in the north chapel and a mid 17th century pulpit. Above the east window of the aisle, dated 1529, is the inscription 'We pray Jesu and Marie, Send oure neygboure safelie': evidently referring to the deliverance of seafarers. The illuminated missal of Richard Fitzjames, vicar here 1485-97 and later bishop of Rochester, Chichester and London, is exhibited at the west end. On the north wall are boards ornately painted with the ten commandments and the Creed. These were provided by Robert Quirke, who also built almshouses for 11 paupers in Market House Lane in 1630. There are several memorials to later members of his family, including two brasses. The Quirkes appropriated a 1440 brass of a woman in the chancel floor for further of their own inscriptions. Under the east bay of the arcade is the effigy of a priest of c.1410 (possibly Richard of Bruton, vicar 1401-6) beneath an ornate canopy. There are no fewer than three royal hatchments: of Charles II, 1704 and 1743. The church formerly contained the impressive statue of Queen Anne, given by Capt Sir Jacob Bancks (who in 1694 married Col Francis Luttrell's widow), moved to Wellington Square in 1894. Also in the square stands St Andrew's church, built in 1880 at the expense of Mrs Charlotte Luttrell, the vicar's wife, to the designs of G.E. Street. The small church of St Peter-on-the-Quay was converted in 1910 from a 1628 storeroom formerly known as Gibralter Cellar. The late medieval walls of Burgundy Chapel, restored 1984-5, stand in Burcombe (of which Burgundy is evidently a corruption) on the north side of North Hill. The chapel of Burcombe is mentioned in 1405 and 1420 as being served at the expense of the Luttrells.

Uniquely in Somerset, May morning is celebrated here by the antics of the Hobby Horse, although such figures were once common throughout England. One such 'horse' from St Decuman's was recorded in 1601 when it frightened children in Sampford Brett churchyard. The Minehead horse, often known as the Sailor's Horse, is first mentioned in 1830, and was augmented from c.1905 by the Town Horse. The place is also notorious for the whistling ghost of Widow Susanna Leakey (died 1634) whose spirit was alleged to appear at

Monksilver

the masthead of her son Alexander's ships when approaching the port and whistle up a wind to cast them away. These claims, recorded by Sir Walter Scott, were not mentioned in an official enquiry of 1637 into the ghost conducted by William Piers, bishop of Bath and Wells, which concluded 'there was never any such apparition at all'.

Alcombe (possibly 'alder valley') was a Domesday manor, formerly in Dunster parish, which now forms part of Minehead town on the approach from the south-east. It was given by William de Mohun c.1100 as part of the endowment of Dunster Priory and retained by its monks until 1536. Thereafter it was held by the Speke (1561-c.1720) and Escott (c.1720-1925) families. There was a pre-Reformation chapel of St Michael here and the present church of St Michael was built 1902-3 to the design of C.H. Samson, to which a chancel was added in 1937. The place became a separate parish in 1953. (*See also* **West Somerset Railway**)

★★★ *Coastal scenery,* ★★ *town, St Michael's church.*

MISTERTON (J) The parish lies immediately south-east of Crewkerne and its name, formerly 'Minsterton', illustrates its former dependence on the minster or mother church of that town and, indirectly, that Misterton formed part of Crewkerne manor. The village is strung out along the main road (A 30) running south from Crewkerne to Dorchester and a tombstone in the churchyard commemorates Mary Gear (died 1876), 'messenger and errand woman between the village and Crewkerne'. A number of fine Ham-stone

houses lie to the west of the road and around the church, the choicest being Old Court, formerly Misterton Lodge. It was held by the Spoures from 1399 (and thus called 'Sporisplace') until the late 16th century. It is remembered as the birthplace of Helen Mathers (died 1920), authoress of *Comin' thro' the Rye* and many other novels, some written at Misterton and very popular in their day. A mill called 'Paddokeslake' in 1292 is represented by Mill Farm, rebuilt in 1820. At the west end of the village in Church Lane stands the church, formerly chapel, of St Leonard, completely rebuilt in 1840 to the designs of Sampson Kempthorne. Its ministers from the mid 13th century were known, most unusually, as rector curates.

★★ *Village for its elegant Ham-stone houses.*

MONKSILVER (D) A small village lying in a valley below the Brendon Hills: a string of pink and white cottages with flower-filled gardens along a winding lane. Originally called Silver ('Sulfhere' in 897), evidently referring to the silvery stream below the village, the manor was given in 1113 by Robert de Chandos to endow his new priory at Goldcliff in Monmouthshire. Thereafter the place was commonly called Silver Monachorum ('of the monks') or Monksilver. The manor passed with the priory to Tewkesbury Abbey in 1441 and thence to the canons of Windsor in 1474. There were long-established links with the estate of Combe Sydenham in neighbouring Stogumber. Monksilver manor was leased to the Sydenhams between 1567 and 1716, and sold in 1800 to the Notleys of Combe Sydenham, who still hold the

lordship. The Notleys are also remembered on the innsign of the Notley Arms, popular port of call in the centre of the village, formerly known as the Ram Inn (1675) and the Half Moon (1785). Sadly the Notleys had no coat of arms but invented them after marrying into the armigerous Marwoods from Devon. The parish was a centre for clothmaking in the 16th and 17th centuries. The red sandstone church of All Saints has a small Norman window on the north side of the chancel, but dates mainly from the 14th century. A more elaborate south aisle and chapel were added in the 15th century, the latter probably that dedicated to St Giles by 1530. Here on 18 June 1583 the celebrated seafarer, Sir Francis Drake, married his second wife, Elizabeth Sydenham of nearby Combe Sydenham. In the churchyard rest Elizabeth Conibeer and her two daughters, victims of a mass-murderer at nearby Woodforde in 1773. The unidentified knifeman was addressed on their tombstone:

'Inhuman wretch, whoe'er thou art,
    That didst commit this horrid crime,
Repent before thou dost depart
    To meet thy awful Judge Divine.'
(*For* **Combe Sydenham** *see* **Stogumber**)
★★★ *Village and setting.*

MONTACUTE (J) This wonderful Ham stone village to the west of Yeovil houses one of Somerset's finest stately homes. The place first occurs c.680 as an estate called 'Logworesbeorh' ('Logor's hill') which was granted by Baldred, a sub-king of the West Saxons, to Glastonbury Abbey. By the 9th century it was known as 'Biscopestun' ('bishop's settlement'), possibly alluding

to Tunbeorht, abbot of Glastonbury and bishop of Winchester. who granted land here to the abbey c.875. This second name survives as a street north from the church, although the manor had adopted its present name by 1086, alluding to the *mons acutus* or 'pointed hill' which rises steeply to dominate the village from the west. It was on this hill c.1035 that a smith unearthed a black flint crucifix which Tofig, King Canute's standard-bearer, carried to Essex where it was given to a church he founded: a church which became the abbey of the Holy Cross at Waltham. The cross was an object of particular veneration by King Harold II, 'the Holy Cross' was the Saxon battle cry at Hastings and it was at Waltham that Harold was buried. Back at Montacute, Glastonbury had lost out to

Athelney Abbey before the Conquest and Athelney passed Montacute to Robert, Count of Mortain, immediately after. Mortain made it the seat of his barony by setting up a castle on the summit of the hill. Whether or not this was the calculated desecration of a spot sacred to the Saxons is unclear, but the castle was besieged in 1068 in an abortive rising against William the Conqueror.

The Mortains had established a borough here by c.1102, represented by the properties around the market-place which is still known as the Borough, although the market itself was discontinued in the 18th century. Count Robert's son William founded a Cluniac priory c.1102 on a site to the west of the present parish church, endowing it with his Montacute and other

estates. Thereafter the hilltop castle was of no strategic importance and was evidently used as a quarry for stone to build the priory, although a chapel of St Michael on the summit was in use in 1315 and was still remembered in 1633. The locals even claimed that St Joseph of Arimathea was buried on the hill and that a nail from Christ's cross had been found there. The folly tower, a prominent local landmark, was constructed on the site in 1760 and there are rewarding walks for those with energy for the climb. A three-day fair on the hill was granted in 1246 but lapsed in the 16th century. One 12th century prior was expelled for maladministration, another removed in 1285 for clipping coins and passing counterfeit money and a third accused in 1317 of supplying food and arms to the enemy when England was at war with Scotland. The monks suffered repeatedly from their links with Cluny whenever England was at war with France and finally broke free in 1407. Dissolved in 1539, the priory church of SS Peter and Paul was demolished and today all that survives of the priory is the impressive early 16th century gatehouse and an isolated square dovecot. Nearby, close to the junction of Middle Street and Bishopston, stands **the church of St Catherine**, described in the late 12th century as a chapel in the monks' graveyard. The building has a fine Norman chancel arch, the chancel, transepts and north porch remaining from a late 13th century rebuild, the nave remodelled c.1500 and a west tower added soon after. The north transept is devoted to memorials of the Phelips family who lived at Montacute by 1479 and came to dominate the whole area. Only the effigies of Thomas Phelips (died 1590) and his wife Elizabeth can be identified with certainty despite the confident later inscriptions on the bases.

The most prominent member of the family was Sir Edward Phelips (died 1614), Master of the Rolls and Speaker of the House of Commons, who bought Montacute manor in 1607. Before that acquisition, c.1590-1600, he had built **Montacute House** (fee: lists), one of the grandest houses in the county, set in extensive ornamental grounds. Its three-storeyed eastern facade is ornamented with the figures of the Nine Worthies, while its Great Hall with stone screens passage has a lively representation of a Skimmington ride, an old custom designed to ridicule henpecked or cuckolded husbands. On the first floor is an exquisite library with

A Phelips face, Montacute church

heraldic glass and on the second floor the longest long gallery in the kingdom, housing a magnificent collection of Tudor and Stuart portraits from the National Portrait Gallery. The house was extended to the west in 1786 by a later Edward Phelips, incorporating an elaborate porch from Clifton Maybank in Dorset. The house was occupied by the Phelips family into the present century and tenanted by Lord Curzon when in 1923 he awaited the summons to become Prime Minister that never came. It was acquired by the National Trust in 1931 with funds provided by Ernest Cook, grandson of Thomas Cook, founder of the travel agency.

Of two more modest properties, both standing near the entrance to Montacute House, Montacute Cottage is of c.1500, and a bay window on its southern extension, the Chantry, bears the initials of the last prior of Montacute, Robert Shirborne. Of the village's two excellent inns, the King's Arms has quenched thirsts since the later 18th century while the Phelips Arms, so named by 1835, may represent the former George Inn, recorded in 1698. Park House, formerly the vicarage, was the home of the Rev C.F. Powys, vicar 1885-1914, and there he raised his trio of literary sons, John Cowper, Theodore and Llewellyn. Llewellyn's essays paint an enchanting picture of his childhood here and of the last years of the Phelips family at Montacute House.
(*See also* **Ham Hill**)

★★★★ *Montacute House, gardens and village,* ★★★ *church, walking.*

MOORLINCH (E) A parish on the Polden Hills with sunken lanes and high banks, whose name ('Mirieling' in 971) is thought to mean 'pleasant hill' (from Saxon *myrge* and *hlinc*). It formed part of the extensive Polden estate held by Glastonbury Abbey from Saxon times until the abbey's dissolution in 1539. Thereafter it descended with Shapwick manor to the Rolle family, although latterly held by the Greenhills of Knowle Hall, Bawdrip. From 1277 a smaller estate here was accumulated by the Pyke family (of Pykesash in Martock). This led them in 1339 vainly to claim half the manor and with swords, bows and arrows to seize two stray foals which belonged to the abbey. The church of St Mary stands on an elevated site with superb views to the south over the Levels. Its rectory estate was held under that of Shapwick by Glastonbury Abbey, although Moorlinch in turn had dependent chapelries at Edington, Chilton Polden, Catcott, Stawell and Sutton Mallet. The building has a late 13th century west tower and a chancel of the late 14th with ten external consecration crosses. The rest is mainly Perpendicular, including the pulpit and a reader's desk, the latter probably assembled from pieces of a rood screen. A late 14th century female effigy is believed to represent Eleanor daughter of Hugh Beauchamp and wife of Sir Richard Pyke. Fragments of colour indicate that her elaborate headdress was yellow, her gown vermillion and that her head rested on red and green pillows with a red plinth. At Loxley Wood north-east of the village are four stones which traditionally mark the triple jump of John Swayne of Shapwick, a rebel captured after the Battle of Sedgemoor. He is supposed to have escaped from his captors when he asked, before his execution, to demonstrate his jumping prowess to his family (although the only known rebels of this name hailed from Seavington St Mary and Lyme Regis). There was a fair at Moorlinch on 20 August by 1704 (and probably some time before), discontinued in the mid 18th century. Moorlynch Vineyard (lists) was established in 1981 at Spring Farm in Spring Lane, just east of the village. There are 16 acres of vines, a pleasant restaurant, carparking, and opportunities to tour, and to taste and purchase the end product.

MUCHELNEY (J) A charming little village south of Langport, occupying a dry refuge above the floodline of the Levels and centred on the meeting of three roads, marked by a restored 15th century cross

with a former single-storey toll house of c.1830 to the north. The name of the parish, 'the great island' (as in 'many a mickle makes a muckle'), graphically describes its situation and no doubt its very isolation recommended it as the site for a monastery. At that time the estate was probably carved out of the older minster land of Martock, comprising the three islands of Muchelney, Thorney and Midelney (since transferred to Drayton).

The substance of a charter of Ine, king of the West Saxons 688-726, dated 693, once considered a forgery but now believed to be genuine, records the grant of a very substantial estate (37 hides) east of the river Isle to Abbot Froda of **Muchelney Abbey** (fee:lists), suggesting that the abbey was probably founded shortly before, possibly by Ine himself. Further grants followed, but it seems likely that, in common with other such houses, monastic life was disrupted by Danish raids and that the abbey was refounded by King Athelstan (924-39), although he is represented only by an undated forged deed. The original charter of 995 by which Ethelred the Unready confirmed the manor of Ilminster to the abbey is one of the treasures of the Somerset Record Office. In 1086 the monks had a vineyard here and two fisheries annually producing 6,000 eels, and they created a park near Thorney in 1205. Throughout the earlier 14th century Muchelney suffered from the Crown putting its aged retainers out to grass at the abbey, and in 1335 the bishop complained that the monks had provided themselves with over-ornate beds, were jogging round the countryside on horseback without permission and were not taking their meals together but in private. In 1532 one of the monks, Thomas Ine, aged 25, secured election as abbot only after paying £140 to the king's officers, a sum he obtained by illegally pledging the abbey's revenues. At the house's dissolution in 1538 he was described as 'negligent and of doubtful character' and his ten monks as 'ignorant and unlernyd'. A succession of lessees held the site from the

Crown throughout the rest of the 16th century, progressively demolishing the 247 ft abbey church for building stone, the abbey and its farm being sold in 1614 to Sir Edward Phelips of Montacute. Thereafter it was held by the Portmans of Orchard Portman (1616-1825), was taken over by the Crown in 1927, and is now administered by English Heritage. The rest of the manor had passed by 1654 from the Phelips family to the Davenants and was held by the Longs from c.1727 until split up and sold in 1921.

The abbot's lodging is a remarkably complete rebuild of the late 15th and early 16th century, with kitchen, anteroom and, on the first floor, the abbot's parlour, with its splendid overmantel (Pevsner considered it one of the finest of its date in the country), and several other chambers. The southern cloister with its upper storey survives, as does the stone-panelled north wall of the refectory. To the north of the lodgings excavations in the 1950s revealed

the location of the rest of the cloisters, the chapter house, warming house and infirmary. The footings of the abbey church were uncovered, including the foundations of the early 8th century church, with semicircular apse, incorporated in the 12th century building as a crypt. Across the road, west of the abbey church, is a 9-bay 16th century barn, while north of it the almonry survived until 1902, when it was rebuilt (the figure of a cleric was preserved above the entrance of the new building).

The **church of SS Peter and Paul** (formerly dedicated to St Peter alone) stands only 3 ft north of the site of the abbey church and is uniformly Perpendicular with a fine panelled tower arch and fan vault. The building is known principally for its painted wagon roof which features 17th century painted angels in low-cut costumes among clouds (Pevsner described them as 'lovable, very incompetent'). The sanctuary floor is composed of medieval tiles dug up from the Lady Chapel of the abbey church

ABOVE *Jacobean pews, Mudford church.* BELOW *Nether Stowey and the castle earthworks*

in 1872. There is a working barrel-organ of 1838 which accompanied the congregation's singing until 1872, although the worshippers were limited to 25 different hymn tunes and 3 double chants. A vicarage was ordained in 1308 by which the vicar was to receive his rations from the abbey cellarer: meat on Sundays and Tuesdays, fish or eggs on every other day and two gallons of ale a day.

The thatched **Priest's House** (lists), owned by the National Trust, stands across the road to the north of the church. It evidently dates from 1308, when it had a small open-roofed hall, parlour and solar at the eastern end, with a service room and guest chamber above at the western end, and a small servant's room over the screens passage. Later additions included two solar windows of c.1350, a late 15th century roof, and a floor inserted in the hall and a large fireplace in the screens passage in the mid 16th century. John Leach, grandson of the celebrated Bernard Leach of St Ives, established his own **Muchelney Pottery** here in 1965. His pottery shop is open all the year round, the workshop can be viewed by appointment and kiln firings on advertised open days.

★★★ *Village, Abbey, Priest's House, parish church.*

MUDFORD (J) A large parish north-east of Yeovil and cut by the main A 359 along which most modern development has taken place. Its name means 'muddy ford' and the sunken lane beside the parish church still bears flood-warning signs. There were no fewer than five different manors in 1086, the largest, given with the church c.1102 to Montacute Priory by its founder, William, Count of Mortain, became the manor of Mudford

Monachorum ('of the monks'), centred on the present hamlet of Up Mudford and held from 1602 by the Harbins of Newton Surmaville in Yeovil. The manor-house at Up Mudford was rebuilt after a fire in the early 17th century. A second estate, known as Mudford Terry after Theodoric or Terricus, its 12th century owner, and later as Wood Court, has been identified with a deserted site to the west of the main village. At Hinton, across the river Yeo to the north, there was a chapel in 1351 and a substantial moated manor-house, abandoned in 1440, which the 19th century locals mistakenly believed had belonged to Cardinal Wolsey. On the extreme eastern boundary with Dorset a major deserted village, Nether Adber, has been identified, held by Siward the fowler before and after Hastings, also with a chapel in 1351, and a moated manor-house: all suddenly abandoned in the mid 16th century. Settlement at West Mudford has evidently contracted, as has that at Mudford (or Old) Sock, from *soc* – 'marsh'. Stone Farm in the south

of the parish takes its name from the hundred of Stone. The actual stone where the hundred courts used to meet in the open air until the 19th century survives just north of Yeovil and the A 329.

The church of St Mary was granted by Montacute Priory to the bishop of Bath and Wells in 1239 and subsequently passed to the dean and chapter. The west tower is probably that rebuilt after its predecessor was blown down in September 1309. The present building is largely Perpendicular (the dean and chapter paying nearly £30 to rebuild the chancel, 1455-6), although the north transept was built in 1620 by John Boyse for the use of himself and his family. The Jacobean pews with shell tops were clearly carved by the same hand as those at Ashington.
★★ *Church.*

NEROCHE (H) *see* **STAPLE FITZPAINE**

NETHER STOWEY (D) A large homely village and former borough to the north-east of the Quantocks, bypassed (and partly severed) since 1968 by the A 39. Stowey means 'stone way', probably referring to the Saxon *herepath* or highway which ran through the neighbouring Over Stowey. The focus of the village is formed by the meeting of three streets, marked since Victoria's Diamond Jubilee (1897) by a small clock tower, but formerly the site of a medieval covered cross and market house. There are several good 18th century houses in St Mary Street and Castle Street, down which runs a picturesque stream, bridged at intervals and dubbed by Coleridge the 'dear gutter of Stowey'. In the area of the cross from 1304 until the 19th century were held a Tuesday market and annual fair, obtained by John de Columbers. His family were lords of the

manor by the 12th century and had established a borough here by 1225 (possibly as early as 1157-8) and an extensive park to the north. They or their predecessor, Robert de Chandos (died 1120), built a castle (possibly succeeding an earlier fort in Over Stowey) at the west end of the village at the top of Castle Street: a castle which became head of an honor or barony of 10 individual manors. Only the earthworks of the classic Norman motte survive, topped by the rectangular outline of the keep with baileys to the east and north-east. There was believed to have been a church of St Michael here although the site seems have been abandoned by 1485. Access to the castle mound, which commands superb views over Bridgwater Bay, is via a signed stile. The manor passed from the Columbers to the lords Audley in 1342, and James, Lord Audley, was extending his manor-house, Stowey Court, at the other end of the village, when he was executed for treason in 1497. Part of the courtyard walls and two gateways may date from this period, but the present substantial house appears to date from the 16th century, although reputedly damaged by fire during the Civil War. The lordship was held from 1838 by the Aclands (later Acland-Hoods) of Fairfield.

The church of St Mary stands next to Stowey Court across the A 39. Probably of Saxon origin (Winegod the priest held the estate of Budley to the east of the church in 1086), it may have been a minster, having a dependent chapel at Dodington and tithes from Otterhampton. Maud de Chandos gave the church to Wells Cathedral c.1189 and it became a 'peculiar' in the charge of the dean of Wells. The patronage, however, passed to Goldcliff Priory, co. Monmouth, founded by Maud's grandfather, Robert de Chandos, in 1113, later succeeded by Tewkesbury Abbey and in 1475 by the dean and chapter of Windsor. The present church is a rebuilding of 1849-51 (Carver and Giles of Taunton), with the exception of the medieval western tower. Two mitres on brackets in the sanctuary commemorate Henry Majendie (vicar 1790-3), later bishop of Chester and Exeter, and John Fisher (vicar 1793-6), also later bishop of Exeter. The celebrated Jesuit, Robert Parsons (1546-1610), was born in the parish, the son of a blacksmith, and educated at Stogursey and Taunton. Later, three Monmouth rebels, one from nearby Durleigh, were executed here in 1685.

Evidence for a 13th century pottery has been unearthed immediately south of the

ABOVE *Nether Stowey clock tower*
BELOW *Nettlecombe Court and church*

castle and of similar 17th century working to the north of the village. From the 16th to 18th centuries cloth manufacture seems to have been the staple of the place. Tanning brought fortune to the Poole family from the early 18th century, of whom Thomas Poole (1765-1837) lived in a fine 7-bay house in Castle Street (no.21), founded a women's friendly society c.1807 (whose annual procession and church service still continues) and built a schoolroom in 1812. He is remembered chiefly for having assembled in his house a literary circle which included Samuel Taylor Coleridge, William and Dorothy Wordsworth, Charles Lamb, Robert Southey and Sir Humphrey Davy. He was responsible for bringing Coleridge to the village, finding him a house in Lime

Street and financially supporting him here 1797-99, during which the poet produced much of his finest work. **Coleridge's Cottage** (fee:lists) has been owned by the National Trust since 1909 and its two parlours are open to visitors, featuring displays of memorabilia. The inn opposite has been renamed the Ancient Mariner to catch the passing literary trade.

★★★ *Picturesque village centre, Coleridge's cottage for its literary associations.*

NETTLECOMBE (D) This delightfully unspoilt parish, 'the valley where nettles grow', is tucked below the Brendon Hills south-west from Williton. Its original village was long ago swept away: the surrounding lush landscape, dotted with isolated farmsteads, dominated by a single estate. The manor was held before the Norman Conquest by Godwin son of King Harold, killed at the Battle of Hastings. Thereafter, seized by the Crown, it was granted c.1160 to Hugh de Ralegh, member of the Devonian family, a junior branch of which later produced the famous Sir Walter. Since that time the estate has never been sold. Ralph de Ralegh supported the barons against King John before Magna Carta and lost the manor to his younger brother. Sir John de Ralegh fought at Crecy in 1346 and Simon de Ralegh at Agincourt in 1415. Nettlecombe passed to Simon's nephew, Thomas Whalesborough, in 1440 and to Thomas's Cornish son-in-law, John Trevelyan, in 1481. The Trevelyans, showing a remarkable if confusing allegiance to the name John (there were eight of them), continued here for over five centuries. They supported Lancaster during the Wars of the Roses and the king in the Civil War, gaining a belated baronetcy for their loyalty in 1661. In 1931 Sir Walter John

Trevelyan left the estate to his daughter, whose son, John Wolseley is the present owner. Raleigh's Cross, set up by 1426, marked the boundary of the manor on the Brendons.

The manor-house, **Nettlecombe Court**, is a late-Elizabethan mansion lying at the end of a long winding drive through landscaped (c.1792) parkland in typical feudal proximity to the parish church. The adjacent village had been swept away by 1800 to improve the general aspect from the Court. The medieval house was largely encapsulated by the present building at the hands of the sixth John Trevelyan, dated 1599 on the porch. The great hall features plasterwork with elaborate pendants and an heraldic overmantel depicting the successive marriages of the Trevelyans and a hunting scene. Above the screen is an early organ, constructed in 1666 by John Loosemore, builder of the organ in Exeter Cathedral. Behind the hall fireplace in 1641 George Trevelyan (died 1653) added for his wife Margaret Strode a small block in the courtyard with a dining-room on the ground floor and elegant chamber above, both with further ornamental and heraldic plasterwork. In 1787-8 the south-west range was remodelled in the Adam style by Samuel Heal. A substantial stable block was built in 1792 to the north of the Court. Since 1967 the house has been leased to the Field Studies Council as the Leonard Wills Field Centre and become an idyllic retreat for biological, ecological and artistic courses. The house featured in the film *Tom Jones* and, although the interior is not open to the public, the polite and curious visitor may be allowed a glimpse of it if circumstances permit.

The red sandstone parish **Church of St Mary the Virgin**, dates from the 15th century. The south aisle was founded as the chantry chapel of St John the Baptist by Simon de Ralegh (died 1440) and the northern, of Our Lady and St George with interesting 16th century stained glass, under the will of Sir John Trevelyan (died 1521). In the south aisle are two effigies of early Raleghs of the late 13th and 14th centuries and a rare East Anglian-style font depicting the Seven Sacraments. The clerestory in the nave was only added in the later 19th century and a fine 20th century east window illustrates the four seasons and the Court itself. The chalice and paten of 1479 bear the date letter B and are the earliest pieces of dated church plate in England, now exhibited in the St Nicholas Church Museum at Bristol. In 1643 the rector, Robert Gay, headed a

mob which tried to destroy the Court.

The parish includes widely scattered farms and hamlets such as Woodadvent, a former manor named from its 13th century lords, the Avenants, Beggearn Huish and Lodhuish, all mentioned in Domesday (1086). Lodhuish is now represented by Huish Barton, a substantial 17th century house occupied at the time of its building by the Musgraves, a well-known family of physicians whose monogram (dated 1698) appears in a fine first-floor hall. In the hamlet of Yard stands the former parish school, designed in 1819 by Richard Carver for the Trevelyans, closed in 1980, and a mill mentioned in 1374-5 which ground grain until just before the First World War.

★★★ *Nettlecombe Court, church and countryside.*

NORTH BARROW (F) A small isolated village south-west from Castle Cary, its name means 'grove' or 'wood', from the Saxon *bearu* ('Berue' in 1086). When first settled in Saxon times it probably formed a single estate with South Barrow which was then divided by an east-west boundary into two units of 5 hides each. Held in the Domesday Book by Ralph under Walter of Douai, the lord of Bridgwater, the manor was owned from the late 17th century by the Portmans of Orchard Portman. The approach from the west to the attractive village is marred somewhat by the aggressively green corrugated-iron roof of the village hall. The church of St Nicholas retains its Perpendicular west tower, but the rest was rebuilt in 1860.

NORTH BREWHAM (F) *see* **SOUTH BREWHAM**

NORTH CADBURY (F) One of the county's most attractive villages, it formed a single estate with South Cadbury, both places taking their names from 'Cada's fort' (*see* **South Cadbury**), south-west from Castle Cary. Within a century of the Conquest the manor was held by the Newmarches (Neufmarche), descending by marriage to the Moels family c.1230, the lords Botreaux in 1337, the lords Hungerford in 1462 and the lords Hastings in 1468. The Hastings family became earls of Huntingdon in 1529 and the 3rd Earl gave Cadbury to his brother, Sir Francis Hastings, in 1586. Francis set about spending more than he could really afford in building what Gerard described in 1633 as a 'faire beautiful house' at the south end of the village, which was 'in good forwardnes' in 1592. Effectively he added a substantial seven-bay three-storey north front to an existing early 16th century west wing, now known as North Cadbury Court. In the west staircase survives the elaborate heraldic glass he inserted to proclaim his ancestry. Sadly, after the death of his first wife in 1596, he decided he could no longer bear to live here and soon after sold the Cadbury estate to his friend Matthew Ewens (died 1598), Baron of the Exchequer, thereafter living at Holwell in Dorset, the home of his second wife. Hastings (died 1610) was one of the leading Puritan spokesmen in Parliament and he bequeathed money to North Cadbury church (and three other churches on his former estates) to dissuade the parishioners from their annual church ales which lead to 'dronkennes and ryott, and the corrupting of their youthe by trayning them up in gaminge and lascvious wantonnes'. He also gave the advowson to Emmanuel College, Cambridge, which ensured the continuation of the Puritan ethic in the parish. North Cadbury Court is now occupied by the daughter of Sir Archibald Langham, who bought it in 1910.

The Court (not open to the public) is visible from its gates and from the adjacent churchyard of the superb Perpendicular church of St Michael: the approach to both down an attractive beech-lined avenue. The church's west tower was built by John Feron, rector 1390-1407, as recorded on a brass destroyed in 1567 by a falling bell. The rest of the building is described in 1423 as 'newly built' by Elizabeth, Lady Botreaux, and her grandson William, Lord Botreaux, which they provided with a lofty roof supported on angel corbels (dated 1417). In 1427 they converted the church into a collegiate church for 7 chaplains and 4 clerks, although it seems likely that it reverted to being a parish church in the early 16th century. The effigies of the foundress (died 1431) and her husband (died 1391) lie beneath the tower, where there is also a 96-line epitaph in brass by Sir Francis Hastings to his first wife and the coat of arms of the Ewens family in stone. Two Jacobean tombchests probably commemorate Sir Francis Hastings (died 1610) and the widow of Matthew Ewens (died 1611). There is a fine series of benchends, dated 1538, depicting everyday subjects such as a windmill, packhorse, and a cat devouring a mouse. On the vestry wall are two early alphabets, evidently for teaching children. On the stable wall in the churchyard are striking sculptures of the Crucifixion by John Robinson, set up in 1972.

The village is full of appealing 17th and 18th century houses with a sprinkling of thatch. The Catash Inn recalls the hundred of Catash, in which Cadbury lay, and whose court met beneath a prominent ashtree beside the road from North Cadbury to Galhampton: a tree that was stated c.1730 to have been replanted whenever the old one failed. Galhampton ('the settlement of the rent-paying peasants') occurs in 1166 and the manor-house there is dated 1723. Woolston ('Wulf's settlement'), a hamlet to the east, comprised the holdings of at least three thegns in 1066.

★★★★ Village, ★★★ church.

NORTH CHERITON (F) The 'northern

North Curry church

settlement with a church' (as distinct from South Cheriton in Horsington) is a secluded leafy village to the south-west of Wincanton, which from the Norman Conquest formed part of the distant honor or barony of Dunster, held by the Mohuns. The name of the place suggests that the church of St John the Baptist stands on a Saxon site. It has a Perpendicular west tower but was restored and enlarged in 1878 and the chancel and organ chamber built in 1886. The screen was made up of fragments of another, made 1498-1508, bought from Pilton and installed in 1883. There is a Norman tub font, a Jacobean pulpit and the former clappers of four bells with the appropriate verse (of 1898):

'Our duty done in belfry high,

Now voiceless tongues at rest we lie.'

Under the tower are the handcuffs once used by the village constable and, at the churchyard gate, the stocks, the size of both suggesting that former Cheritonian miscreants were all midgets ! Below the church is the large 19th century manor-house with a beautiful magnolia tree, in bloom at the time of my visit.

★ *Village.*

NORTH CURRY (E/J) The parish is a large one, strung out along a ridge above the Somerset Levels. The parish's name, shared with Curry Mallet, Curry Rivel and the principal estate (East Curry) in Stoke St Gregory, is apparently a Celtic stream name of uncertain meaning. The extensive manor, its very size suggesting an early origin, was held by King Harold, killed at

Hastings. Seized by William the Conqueror, it remained in royal hands until 1189 when Richard the Lion Heart gave it to the bishop of Wells. A year later the bishop settled it on the canons of Wells Cathedral and it subsequently remained with the dean and chapter. To improve their holding the new lords obtained the grant of a Wednesday market (held until 1841) and a fair from King John in 1206. Soon after, they established a borough at Newport: today only a small hamlet to the south of the main village.

North Curry village lies principally along a single street with a central area at Queen Square: named for Queen Victoria and providing a site for her memorial, irreverently dubbed 'the pepper pot'. Nearby stands the fine church of SS Peter and Paul, known locally as 'the Cathedral of the Moors', in a beautifully laid-out site overlooking the Levels, with a tree-lined avenue leading to its south porch and a 14th century cross, heavily restored in the late 19th century. The size of its Domesday estate suggests that it was originally a Saxon minster. From the outside the early octagonal central tower, probably dating from c.1300 but with later superstructure, is the principal feature. Inside the transepts are of similar date with the remainder, mainly 15th century Perpendicular. A Norman north door of c.1180 alone survives from an earlier church. In 1337 Robert Gyan, for felling the dean and chapter's timber and beating their servants, was ordered to be whipped three times round the church on three Sundays, clad only in his trousers, while carrying a candle. In the vestry a large tablet records in detail the elaborate custom of the Reeve's Christmas feast, allegedly founded to honour King John but probably even older, as a Christmas feast was mentioned here as early as 1192. A huge mince pie bearing an effigy of the king in pastry was consumed and ale was drunk by the tenants as long as two one-pound candles burned. The feast was last regularly celebrated in 1865.

Of other hamlets in the parish, Wrantage ('Wrentis' in 1196), the name possibly meaning 'stallion's pasture', formed a separate manor, as did Knapp and Newport, although all owned by Wells Cathedral. The Canal Inn, Wrantage, marks the former course of the Chard Canal. Moredon Hall was the home of John Scott Gould (died 1846), his widow Sophia (died 1871) and her family, the Barretts. The origin of their phenomenal wealth, estimated at half a million pounds in 1846, is still a mystery. Maj William Barrett (died 1914) gave nearly half the cost of restoring the parish church in 1880. Ham Mills in the west of the parish caused perennial problems to the navigation of the River Tone and led to 15th century disputes between the dean and chapter and the bishop of Winchester, as lord of Taunton Deane manor.

★★★ *Church and village.*

NORTH NEWTON (E) A modern parish formed from North Petherton in 1880, this attractive village lies to the east of the A38 beyond the M5, including at least ten farmhouses and cottages dating from the 17th century. The church of St Peter originated as the 13th century chantry chapel of Newton Placey. Apart from a medieval consecration cross on the south wall of the south aisle, there is nothing earlier than c.1635 when Sir Thomas Wroth of Petherton Park evidently rebuilt it. He was responsible for providing the fine screen, pulpit (dated 1637) and vestry door, depicting the wise and foolish virgins, probably by the same carver who worked at Thurloxton. The church was again largely rebuilt, except for the tower, in 1884. To the south, West Newton Manor also had its medieval chapel and represents the manor of Newton Comitis (of Eustace, Count of Boulogne), later known as Newton Hawys (because it was held with Castle Ewyas, co. Hereford). Although incorporating some timbers of a 14th century aisled-hall house, it was remodelled for Henry and Katherine Cheek

The vestry door, North Newton church

c.1622 (initials and date above the front door). Their granddaughter married Edward Phelips, the heir to Montacute, and the Phelips family retained it until 1810.
★ *Village.*

NORTHOVER (J) The former village immediately to the north of Ilchester ('north over' the river Yeo) and now continuously built up with it. A major 4th century Roman cemetery (evidently serving Ilchester) was discovered to the west of the village in 1982. Robert Dunning's researches suggest that the parish was the northern half of an early bridgehead settlement, of which the southern element was Ilchester, and on which a number of significant routes, including the Foss Way, converged. Before the Norman Conquest the main estate was held by Brictric under Glastonbury Abbey but by 1086 had passed to Maurice, bishop of London. Subsequently it was acquired by William Briwere who by 1219 had transferred it to the Hospital of St John the Baptist which he had founded at Bridgwater, owner until its dissolution in 1539. The manor was bought in 1566 by Thomas Raymond of Chard, descending by marriage to Col John Hody (died 1702) and similarly in 1729 to the Chichester family, whose representatives still hold the advowson. The church of St Andrew, on an elevated site towards the northern end of the village, is believed to represent a Saxon minster foundation, the mother church of Ilchester, from which the surrounding area would have been converted and which was granted to the bishop of London after the Norman Conquest. The present building, now declared redundant, has a Perpendicular west tower and Norman font, but the nave and chancel were rebuilt in 1821 and the south transept added in 1878. The 19th century Old Vicarage represents the

North Perrott

site of the former manor-house, to the south of which was a medieval ten-bay barn, burned down in 1876. The 18th century Northover Manor Hotel was the former home farm of the manor estate while the seven-bay Northover House was occupied from 1802 by the Tuson family of Ilchester solicitors. Darlington House, another 18th century building, was named for the Ilchester borough monger, Lord Darlington. (*See also* **Ilchester** for the gaol, which lay in Northover from 1599.)

NORTH PERROTT (J) A parish south-east from Crewkerne which takes its name from the River Parrett. The manor was long held with that of its neighbour, South Perrott (Dorset), early non-resident owners including the St Clare, Lorty and Daubeny families and the dukes of Somerset. The attractive village is stretched out along the A3066 although the church lies on a lane to the west, lined with Ham stone walls, which becomes one of the drives to Perrott Hill School. This private school was founded in 1946 at North Perrott Manor, the large mansion built by the Hoskyns family in 1878 in an extensive park and occupied by them until the outbreak of World War Two. It replaced an earlier house, described as 'newly built' in 1791, just after the Hoskyns's bought the estate from the Dorset Pitts. The church of St Martin is Perpendicular with a cruciform shape and central tower: its date suggested by the will of Sir John Byconyll, who in 1500 left money to buy three bells and complete the chancel and porch. The 1791 rules in verse for bellringers included the admonition

'And whosoe'er a noise does make
Or idle story tells,
Must six-pence to the ringers take
For mending of the bells.'
★ *Village.*

NORTH PETHERTON (D/E) The largest parish in the county, it takes its name from its proximity to the river Parrett ('Pedredistrem' in 725), an unexplained early river name. North Petherton village has grown up along and around the main A 38 from Taunton to Bridgwater: expanding considerably during the present century. Before and after the Norman Conquest the main manor formed part of the personal holding of the king: passing by 1157 to John de Erlegh, probably by grant of Henry I. The Erleghs, lords until 1371, had evidently founded a borough here by the mid 13th century and in 1318 obtained the grant of a Saturday market (moved to Tuesdays in 1556) and three-day fair. There was also a major park and royal forest here, probably from Saxon times, centred on the area of North Newton: indeed one of the five Newton manors recorded in 1086 was held by Anschitil the parker. Royal grants of oak trees and deer from the forest to both monasteries and private individuals were a feature of the 13th and 14th centuries. Petherton Park Farm, east of the village beyond the M5, represents the site of the foresters' headquarters. Among these foresters were the poet Geoffrey Chaucer and his son, Thomas. The present house, now divided into two dwellings, dates from the 17th century. In its vicinity was found in 1693 the celebrated Alfred Jewel (see **Arthur and Alfred**), given in 1718 to Oxford University and since kept in the Ashmolean Museum. A replica is held at the parish church and used as the insignia of the mayor of North Petherton: a post invented in 1974.

The church of St Mary stands in the centre of the village, set back from the main road beyond a stretch of featureless grass broken only by the stump of the churchyard cross. Excavations to the west of the churchyard disclosed a Saxon cemetery, the church's lands were recorded in the Domesday Book and it was probably a royal Saxon minster with dependent chapels at Chedzoy, Pawlett and St Michaelchurch. The church was given to Buckland Priory in Durston by its founder, William de Erlegh in 1166, subsequently passing to the Hospitallers of St John. Its 109 ft three-stage 15th century tower is one of Somerset's finest and a landmark for miles. The rest of the church is of similar date, including both pulpit and font but, apart from the lofty panelled tower arch, Pevsner clearly found it dull inside. Personally, I feel it has a wonderfully peaceful atmosphere. The north aisle was supposed in the 17th century to belong to

Huntworth manor and the south aisle to that of Melcombe. Much of the woodwork is modern, including a fine rood screen of 1909, but two of the benchends are dated 1596 and 1629, and there is a pleasing small gallery dated 1623 above the south door (used by the Wroths of Petherton Park) bearing an intriguing figure of Father Time. A small brass in the nave commemorates the wife (died 1652) of John Morley, vicar 1615-62, who suffered for his faith during the Commonwealth. A stone in the north chapel is inscribed to a kindred spirit, Henry Gatchell (died 1668), 'who lived a loyall subject to his King and died a true son of the Church of England'. Indeed the whole building is rich in early floor slabs. The rest of the village has few notable buildings, apart possibly from the Congregational church of 1833, remodelled in 1869, but a number of welcoming pubs.

The parish includes a number of secondary settlements. Huntworth, Melcombe, Shearston and Woolmersdon all occur as individual manors by 1066. Moorland or Northmoor Green is a village which grew up on the west bank of the Parrett and became a separate parish in 1845 with the church of SS Peter and John, designed by Benjamin Ferrey in 1844. (*See separate entries for* **North Newton** *and* **St Michaelchurch**)

★★ *Church.*

NORTH WOOTTON (E) An attractive secluded village, the 'settlement in or by a wood', south-east from Wells on the river Redlake. The 'North' was added in recent years to distinguish it from Wootton Courtney. The estate here was granted by King Edmund to Aethelnoth, his minister, in 946 and subsequently passed to Glastonbury Abbey, although there is an earlier dubious grant to the abbey by King Cynewulf of 760. Thereafter the manor was held under the abbey with Pilton. The pretty little Perpendicular church of St Peter in the centre of the village was a chapelry of Pilton, and as such formed part of the peculiar of the precentor of Wells Cathedral until it became a separate living in 1846. There is a pleasant sundial over the porch dated 1767, a Norman tub font and a slate monument to the Phippens family (1766-81). The precentor had a mill and mill leat constructed here shortly before 1269 which he then assigned to the abbey. **Wootton Vineyard** (lists) has a small roadside carpark and operates to the north-east of the village.

★ *Village.*

NORTON FITZWARREN (D) This 'northern settlement' (from Taunton) lines the winding main road from Taunton to Wiveliscombe – and suffers in consequence. A local rhyme claims that 'when Taunton was a furzy down, Norton was a market town'. This may possible refer to the extensive Bronze and Iron Age hillfort which lies above and north of the village, but could equally concern North Town, locally once called 'Nurton', to the north of Tone Bridge in Taunton itself. Crude stone tools found in the area of the fort take the occupation of the site back to 250,000 BC, but the earthwork itself dates from c.1100 BC. A substantial hoard of bronze bracelets suggests that it was a significant manufacturing and trading centre for the south-west. The enclosure was extended to the south and east during the Iron Age (c.300 BC), provided with three symmetrical 'covert ways' and continued in use until finally abandoned after c.400 AD. Archaeological and nature trails have been laid out around the earthwork starting from a carpark on the north side of the village. Unfortunately modern housing development has been allowed too close to the monument.

From Saxon times the manor owed customary dues to the bishop of Winchester's manor of Taunton Deane but was held separately before 1280 by Robert le Veel, from whom it was known as Norton Veel. Thereafter it passed in 1302 to William Paynel, descending through the families of Stapledon and Hankeford to the Bourchiers, lords FitzWarin from 1449, whose title was added to the village's name. The manor continued with the Bourchier earls of Bath until the mid 17th century.

The church of All Saints lies on the north side of the village. It has a west tower and north aisle and arcade of c.1300. The rest is 15th century Perpendicular but suffered over-enthusiastic restoration in 1851-2, the porch and chancel rebuilt and vestry added in 1866. The treasure of the building is its rood screen, bearing the name of churchwarden Ralph Harris, who died in 1509. The carved frieze is supposed to tell the story of the dragon of Norton, alleged to have risen from the putrefying bodies of those killed in a great battle at the hillfort. There are three hatchments, including one to Sir James Slade (died 1859), for whom Montys Court was built c.1840 on the road to Wiveliscombe. The south-west corner of the churchyard was reserved in the 19th century for gypsies of the Stanley family. Norton Court, beside the church, dates from c.1600 and clearly represents the former manor-house. It served during the 19th century as headquarters for Hewitt's brewery, whose former buildings survive behind the house.

The offices and factory of the **Taunton Cider Company** dominate the southern centre of the village, its buildings defined by orange rendering. Founded in 1911 by local cinema proprietor George Vickery, it was taken over by the Pallet family, became a Limited Company in 1921 and has undergone successive expansions ever since. It is now the second largest cider producer in the country and the delights of Dry Blackthorn, Brody and Diamond White have tickled many a jaded palate. A wassailing ceremony is performed here every January, for which I have acted as MC in recent years. Mulled cider is poured around the roots of trees, cider-soaked toast is placed in the branches to propitiate the robins (good spirits) and shotguns fired to scare away the evil spirits.

Norton Manor, beside the road to Minehead, was built in 1843 by Henry Roberts for Charles Noel Welman, held 1890-1904 by Wilfred George Marshall, a leader of Taunton society, and occupied in 1910 by the Queen Mother's uncle, Francis Bowes-Lyon. The military camp which surrounds it was built to house the 22nd Searchlight Militia Depot in 1939 and has been tenanted by 40 Commando since 1983.

★★★ *Norton hillfort.*

NORTON ST PHILIP (B)

A most attractive clothing village and former borough, its name meaning "the northern settlement' (probably in relation to Frome) with the addition of the parish church's dedication and long known as Philips Norton. The manor was granted after the Norman Conquest, together with that of Hinton Charterhouse (immediately to the north, which with Norton formed a separate 'liberty'), to Edward of Salisbury, sheriff of Wiltshire. Edward's grandson, Patrick (died 1168), was created Earl of Salisbury, and Patrick's granddaughter, Ela, carried both manor and title to her husband, William Longespee (died 1226), bastard brother of Richard I. In accordance with his wishes she founded a Carthusian priory at nearby Hinton in 1232, on whose monks she had already bestowed this manor, then known as Norton Comitis ('Earl's Norton' from its tenure by the earls of Salisbury) and once referred to as Norton Chartus. These monks created a formidable cloth-trading industry at Norton, obtaining a three-day fair in 1255. A second 3-day fair was transferred in 1345 to Norton from Hinton, where it had been disturbing meditations at the priory and attracting the enmity of Bath. In 1343 a Friday market, established in 1285, was supplemented or replaced by a Tuesday one, to be held 'in a vacant place on the west side of the church'. Despite this location, there is no doubt that the later market cross was situated at the hilltop road junction beside the George in the area known as the Plain. It was on a fair day here in 1401 that Thomas Neuton, the king's aulnager of wool, was set upon by 'certain evildoers', who inflicted 'a hundred mortal wounds' on him and killed several of his companions in a veritable bloodbath. After the dissolution of the priory in 1539, both Norton and Hinton eventually passed to the Hungerfords of Farleigh. One clothier who kept 'many men at work' here, William Tovy, was licensed in 1577 to extend throughout England 'the mistery of making woollen cloth, long or short, and kersies, pinned whites or plain straights, and to weave, put to rowing and weaving, and to put to sale the same'. The market here continued into the 18th century and the fairs until 1902. In 1638 the cloth fairs were held in the Fair Close, at the gates of the priory grange (now Manor Farm), in which field was a little house called Taylors' Hall, evidently where the tolls were collected. The sheep fairs were then held in a different field.

The earliest settlement was probably down in the valley in the area of the parish church of St Philip. The advowson was held by the bishop, and the living was united with that of Hinton between 1527 and 1825. The west tower, an untypical version of those at Mells and Leigh-on-Mendip. and much of the rest of the church is attributed to a substantial Norton clothier, Jeffrey Flower of the Grange (died 1644), occupied by his family from 1523. He was wealthy enough to entertain Queen Anne, consort of James I, in 1615 on her way back to Windsor from Bath. The body of the church was given a Perpendicular remodelling and an over-thorough restoration in 1847 (when the many Biblical texts were added), although Pevsner considered the south doorway to be 13th century and the south arcade early 14th. There is an unidentified effigy of a barrister of c.1460 in the south aisle and under the tower are the two heads of 'the fair maids' of Foxcote. These are reputed to have been Siamese twins, joined at the stomach, and were noted by Samuel Pepys when he visited Norton in 1668. Collinson (1791) recounted that, 'one of them dying,

George Inn, Norton St Philip

the survivor was constrained to drag about her lifeless companion, till death released her of her horrid burden'. Opposite the church is a delightfully ornate and pinnacled school of 1827.

On the hill above, to take advantage of traffic on the old Bath to Salisbury road, the monks appear to have established a planted borough with burgage plots on both sides of High Street. Certainly in 1539 there were no fewer than 27 burgage tenements, although the borough's formal structure had probably collapsed by then. Here is located the 15th century George Inn, 'one of the most remarkable medieval inns in England' (Pevsner). The only other Somerset contender would be the smaller George and Pilgrims at Glastonbury. Norton's George is a long rambling building, with a stone ground floor and two jettied timber storeys above (possibly added after a fire). Its origins are unclear. It may have started life as Hinton Priory's hospice but it was certainly not its grange, represented by Manor Farm, a late 17th century rebuild below the hill in the Barton, complete with medieval dovecot. The George was referred to under its present name by 1595, and in 1638 it was described as 'an ancient and common inn' and housed a fair loft, 'where the lynnen cloth is sould at the fare tymes'. The inn claims Pepys and the Duke of Monmouth among its guests, although no mention of the hostelry occurs in the contemporary accounts of either visit. Pepys's sojourn might equally have been at the Fleur de Lis opposite, dating from the 16th century and evidently recently converted into an inn in 1638. Monmouth was accommodated at 'the Old House': almost certainly Manor Farm, the former grange, previously visited by the queen in 1615.

The Duke of Monmouth's stay was a brief one. He retreated here from Bath with his rebel army on 26 June 1685 and the following day was engaged in a skirmish with the royal forces who advanced on the village from the north. The rebels lost some 18 men and their opponents perhaps as many as 80, but the action was inconclusive and Monmouth withdrew to Frome. No Norton men are known to have joined the Duke but 12 men, condemned at Jeffrey's Bloody Assizes at Wells, were hanged, drawn and quartered here, probably at the market-place on the hill.

★★★★ *George Inn,* ★★ *church and village.*

NORTON-SUB-HAMDON (J) This 'northern settlement below Ham Hill' is a charmingly unspoilt village of 17th and 18th century thatched cottages, built from the Ham stone whose quarrying once gave employment to many of its residents. In 1555 the tenants here were working 14 quarries, each 20 ft square. Flax was once extensively cultivated for the local manufacture of twine and sailcloth. After the Norman Conquest the manor was granted to Robert, Count of Mortain, who gave it and the church to Grestein Abbey in Normandy, whose monks administered it through Wilmington Priory in Sussex, until it was confiscated as alien property by the Crown in the 14th century. Given to the De la Pole family, the estate descended with the dukedom of Suffolk to the Seymours and in 1671 to the Earl of Aylesbury, before being broken up and sold off in 1705. The lordship was bought by the Quantock family and descended to their heirs, the Shuldhams, in the present century. The manor – or Court house – stood west of the church until its demolition c.1850, although its circular dovecot survives: now in the churchyard. The church of the Blessed Virgin Mary in the centre of the village is a lofty exquisite Perpendicular building, with an earlier 14th century south porch, although it lost its bells and most of its furnishings after a lightning strike and fire on 29 July 1894. Fragments of the original stained glass are preserved in the upper windows and the alabaster fluted font of c.1904 is a delight. A parish feast with rural sports was formerly held here in September. (*See also* **Ham Hill**)

★★ *Village, church.*

NUNNEY (F) An enchanting valley village, immediately south-west from Frome. Most visitors will probably drop down Church Street from the A 361 at Nunney Catch, passing under the inn sign of the George, which spans the road. The village's name probably means 'Nunna's island' and is unlikely to refer to the former presence of a Saxon nunnery, as was once thought. A hoard of early Roman coins in

ABOVE *Dovecote, Norton-sub-Hamdon churchyard*
RIGHT *Nunney Castle*

an earthen jug was dug up in 1869 near Westdown Farm, and a Roman villa with mosaic pavement was discovered in 1837 towards the northern boundary with Whatley, with coins of the late 3rd and early 4th century: since re-excavated with the discovery of three juvenile skeletons. An estate at Nunney was granted to Glastonbury Abbey by King Edred in the 10th century. Of the two Domesday manors, one was in the hands of Elias de Meisi by 1166, whose daughter, Grecia, carried it to her son Sir Elias de la Mare (died c.1270). His descendant, Sir John de la Mare (died 1383) had licence to crenellate his manor-house here in 1373 and so built **Nunney Castle** (lists) in the centre of the village. On an almost ludicrously ill-defended site, four lofty drum towers mark the corners of a simple four-storeyed oblong, enclosed by a moat. A surviving sketch of 1644 indicates that the centre of the castle was sheltered by a French-style high-pitched roof and that each of the towers was crowned with its own conical topknot. There was a great hall on the first floor and a chapel in the south-western tower. The builder's grandson, another Sir Elias, probably died at Agincourt in 1415 (or soon after), whereupon the castle and manor of Nunney Delamare passed to his nephew, Sir John Paulet (died 1437), continuing to his descendant, William Paulet, Marquess of Winchester (died 1572). The heirs of the last sold out in 1577 to Richard Prater, whose family were prominent Roman Catholics and occupied the castle. During the Civil War the castle was held by Richard's grandson, Col

Richard Prater (died 1651), for the king until on 19 September 1645, after a personal visit from Sir Thomas Fairfax on his march towards Bristol, the building was bombarded by three cannon and a breach made in the north-west wall. The next day Prater surrendered the garrison of 80 Irishmen together with a number of Catholic refugees. On Parliamentary orders, the castle was duly slighted by having its roof, internal walls and floors removed. Later the estate, known as the manor of Nunney Castle *alias* Nunney Glaston, passed in 1700 from the Praters to the Whitchurch family and in 1749 to their cousins, the Theobalds, from whom the Theobald Arms Inn at the south end of the village is named and who built Rockfield House in 1804. The castle was 'fitted-up' for the reception of French prisoners-of-war in 1759 but, apart from the collapse of the north-west wall in 1910, it remains much as the Roundheads left it.

A second Domesday manor was granted soon after the Conquest to the Norman abbey of St Mary de Montisburgh and held from the early 13th century by the Montforts of Farleigh Hungerford, of whom Henry de Montfort obtained a Wednesday market and three-day fair in 1260 (*not* in 1259, as regularly claimed). A claim that this market was injuring another at Frome was made in 1279. The fair continued into the late 19th century and was revived in 1959, the profits being used to re-erect the so-called market (probably churchyard) cross beside the pond in the centre of the village. This second estate, known as Nunney Mawdley from its 16th century owners, was bought in 1691 by the Whitchurches, who built and occupied the present Manor Farm to the north-west of the castle.

The **Church of All Saints** has a 13th century chancel (largely rebuilt in 1874), aisles and transepts of the 14th, with nave wagon roof (sadly ravaged by deathwatch beetle), south porch and tower of c.1500. There is a Norman font (with cover dated 1684), the fragment of a Saxon cross and the remains of a wall-painting of St George above the north arcade of the nave. The north chapel, dedicated to St Catherine, housed a chantry founded by Philip de la Mare in 1394, and the knight's effigy on the cill probably represents the founder. The other effigies in this chapel are of Sir John Paulet (died 1437), his wife Constance Ponynges (died 1422), identified from the heraldry (some now concealed behind the tomb), Richard Prater (died 1578) and his wife. The south chapel was held with the second estate and thus holds monuments to the Mawdley family and their successors, the Sambournes.

Nunney was a rural centre for cloth-making from the 13th century, Rockfield House deriving its name from the rack field, where the woollen cloth was stretched on its tenterhooks. An edge-tool manufacture was started here in 1717 by Richard Hoddinott (died 1733), who lived at what is now Nunney Court. The business was taken over from his grandson, another Richard (died 1760), by the Fussells of Mells and continued until the 1880s. Major stone quarries are worked at Holwell to the south-west of the village.

Trudoxhill ('Truttoc's hill') is an appeal-ing village in the south of the parish, centred on the White Hart Inn, with an Anglican chapel of 1899, a much older Congregational chapel, converted from a dwelling house in 1717, and plenty of modern development. An account of 1583 describes how the armour-making smiths here were all murdered in a single night by their rivals from the Forest of Dean.

★★★ *Castle, village and setting,* ★★ *church.*

NYNEHEAD (H) An attractive village immediately north of Wellington and the river Tone, whose name means 'nine hides', presumably the original size of the estate (compare Fitzhead and Fivehead, both originally meaning 'five hides'), a hide being a Saxon land unit of about 120 acres. The estate formed part of the 'outfaring' of the bishop of Winchester's manor of Taunton Deane, under which it was held

from c.900 by Wulfhere Cidding, passing by the 12th century to the Fleury or Flory family (from whom it was long known as Nynehead Florey). Thereafter it was held by the Wykes, from 1616 by the Pophams and then the Sanfords from Dulverton, the last of whom still possess it. To the west of the village stands the manor-house, Nynehead Court, a fine mansion dated 1675 but incorporating earlier features, which is now an old peoples' home. A second manor, known as Nynehead Monachorum ('of the monks'), was held by Taunton Priory and is now represented by the village of East Nynehead, reached via Nynehead Hollow: a deep cutting through the solid rock. Northwest from the main village lies Chipley Park, formerly held by the Chipley, Warre, Lottisham and Clarke families, descending by marriage to the present occupiers, the Sanford family.

The perpendicular red sandstone church of All Saints is sited in the classic position next to Nynehead Court (its formal gar-dens can be admired from the churchyard). The rectory estate was granted c.1100 to Montacute Priory but soon passed to Taunton Priory, whose monks presented vicars until the dissolution. In 1537 the vicar was allotted eight loaves and eight flagons of ale a week from the priory. Subsequently the patronage was exercised by the Crown until 1786, after which it was bought by the Sanford family. Hints of an earlier church survive in the 13th century tower arch and piscina and the south aisle was evidently built with a bequest in John Wyke's will of 1410. The interior of the church was transformed ('much pulled about' says Pevsner) by the Rev John Sanford (died 1855) and thoroughly restored in 1869, although the rood screen survived his attentions. Sanford also intro-duced fine 15th century Italian sculptures attributed to Mino da Fiesole and della Robbia. There is a substantial monument to father-of-17, Richard Wyke, of 1590, and others include the kneeling figures of Edward Clarke (died 1679) of Chipley and his wife, and a bust of John Sanford of 1835. The Sanfords, long the leaders of the community here, are generously com-memorated. In the south transept is a slate memorial to philosopher and radical John Locke (1632-1704), born at Wrington (now Avon) and a regular visitor to the Clarkes at Chipley.

★★ *Village and church*

OAKE (D/H) Lying on the Hillfarrence brook in the the valley of the River Tone, between Taunton and Milverton, its name

('Acon' in 897) testifies to the early presence of oak trees here. From Saxon times the manor formed part of the 'outfaring' of the bishop of Winchester's great manor of Taunton Deane. The modern village, including the village hall, post office, school and a positive rash of bungalows, extends along both sides of the lane running south-east to Bradford-on-Tone. An earlier village, which has since contracted, evidently lay to the west on a side lane around the church of St Bartholomew. The church is basically Perpendicular, including the impressive six-light north window with fragments of 15th century, claimed on no very certain grounds to have come from Taunton Priory. A frieze on the south porch includes initials identified as those of John Peryn of Wellington and resembles a similar frieze on Hillfarrence tower, to which Peryn contributed in 1509.

OAKHILL (F), *see* **ASHWICK**

OARE (C) Lies in the far west of the county, where Exmoor stretches into Devon, sheltering behind the coastal cliffs to the north. It is a wooded landscape with scattered farms, these being set mainly on the north side of the valley through which runs Oare Water: Oare ('Are' in 1086) being a British stream name identical to Ayr in Scotland. After the Conquest the manor was granted to Ralph de Pomeray, who had to render 12 sheep a year to the royal manor of Carhampton. For two centuries from 1315 the manor was held by the Kelly family. but later, following the death of Nicholas Cove prior to 1557, it was fragmented. Through the Spurrier family most of the estate passed to the Snows, and in the 19th century lands here were acquired by the Hallidays of Glen-thorne in Porlock. The church of St Mary, with a west tower rebuilt in the 19th century, lies in the valley and attracts visitors mainly because it was here that R.D. Blackmore set the fictional wedding of Lorna Doone to Jan Ridd and her shooting at the altar by Carver Doone. Certainly Blackmore's grandfather was rector here 1809-42 and used to ride over from his principal living, Combe Martin in Devon, to take services. There is a copy of the Blackmore memorial in Exeter Cathedral to the left of the south door. The interior is mainly 15th century but a further chancel was added in the 19th century which gives a somewhat corridor-like feel to the building. There is an intriguing piscina in the form of a man's head clasped in two

Piscina in Oare church

ABOVE *Robber's Bridge, Oare.* BELOW *Old Cleeve*

hands, possibly 15th century, which has prompted identification with the decapitated St Decuman (*see* **Watchet**). Note the crude panel painting of Moses dated 1718 and the Prince of Wales's feathers (resembling triple ram's horns), commemorating the 1868 visit by the future Edward VII. There are fine monuments to the Spurry/Spurrier, Snow and (in the sanctuary) Halliday families, particularly that to the Prince's host, Nicholas Snow (1827-1914), lord of the manor, 'an upright man, greatly skilled in woodcraft'.

Beyond Oare, a narrow winding lane leads west to **Malmsmead**, a hamlet divided by the county boundary with Devon. Here, amid beautiful Exmoor scenery on the Somerset side, the **Exmoor Natural History Society** has its **Field Centre** (lists), opposite the gate to Cloud Farm. Just across the bridge, Lorna Doone Farm offers predictable gift-shop attractions and a starting point for walks up the so-called Doone Valley. Their story belongs, however, to our sister county.

★★★ *Setting of church.*

ODCOMBE (J) A hilltop village to the west of Yeovil, whose name means 'Uda's' or 'wood valley'. Granted to the Count of Mortain after the Conquest, the church was given c.1102 by his son, William, to the latter's newly founded priory at Montacute. Under the Mortains the manor was held by Ansgar Brito and became the seat of his honor or barony of Odcombe. Latterly the manor was owned by the Phelips family of Montacute. The church of SS Peter and Paul stands on an elevated, possibly ancient, site in Higher Odcombe with commanding views. It was entirely rebuilt 1874-5, apart from the Perpendicular tower and south porch, although several of the old windows were reused. Until 1702 an old pair of shoes were hung up in the church belonging to Thomas

Coryate (1577-1617), the self-styled 'Odcombian leg-stretcher'. Son of the rector, he became unofficial court jester to Henry, Prince of Wales, before walking 2,875 miles to Venice and back in 1608, his account of the journey becoming popular under the title *Coryate's Crudities*. A second expedition took him to Jerusalem, Persia and India, but he died at Surat on his way home. He is credited with introducing the table fork to England from Italy and with popularising the umbrella here. The son of another rector, Dr Humphrey Hody (1659-1706), became Regius Professor of Greek at Oxford and founded a charity to apprentice Odcombe children. Down in the valley, Lower Odcombe was developed later but has attractive thatched cottages and an old pub, the Mason's Arms. The site of a deserted village, possibly called Barrow, was discovered in 1976 near the boundary with Lufton, yielding pottery dating from Saxon times to the 14th century.

★★ *Setting.*

OLD CLEEVE (D) This elongated parish to the west of Williton, runs south in a long strip from the coast, crossed from east to west by the main road (A 39) to Minehead. Originally Cleeve ('cliff' or

'hill'), it became known as Old Cleeve to distinguish the principal village north of the main road from the later site of Cleeve Abbey to the south. Old Cleeve is a delightful village of 18th and 19th century cottages, several thatched, all overlooked by the parish **Church of St Andrew**. Its chancel and south chapel date from the 13th century, although herringbone masonry in the north wall of the nave survives from a former Norman building. The south aisle and south porch were added c.1450 and the western tower was under construction in 1533, when John Tucker left his clothier's shears towards the cost of the work. Don't miss the unidentified effigy of c.1425 with its feet resting on a cat holding a mouse between its paws, and the porch floor with a heart laid out in cobbles, dated 1614. In the churchyard lies George Jones, the village blacksmith, who died in 1808, commemorated in a favourite epitaph for blacksmiths:

'My sledge and hammer lie reclined,
    My bellows too have lost their wind;
My fire's extinct, my forge decayed,
    An in the dust my body's laid;
My coal is burnt, my iron's gone,
    My nails are drove, my work is done.'

One of the curates here, John Tratt, was murdered in 1624 by four of his flock, who

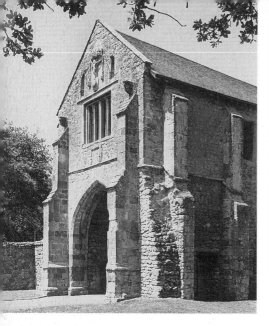

ABOVE *Blue Anchor beach (Old Cleeve)*
LEFT *The gatehouse, Cleeve Abbey*

dismembered his body, and parboiled and salted the remains to prevent them from smelling. A Wednesday market and two annual fairs were established in 1466 but did not last for long. In the village is sited **John Wood's Sheepskin Tannery**, craft shop and cafe, established in 1876, and there are regular tours of the factory in the summer months.

Washford, named from a ford recorded in the 10th century at what is now Lower Washford, is a village which today mainly lines the A39. The manor was held by the Wyndhams of Orchard Wyndham from 1542. A station on the West Somerset Railway features a museum (fee:lists) operated by the Somerset & Dorset Railway Trust with artefacts and memorabilia relating to that railway. Just east of Washford beside the A39 at Washford Cross, **Tropiquaria** (fee:lists) now occupies a former BBC Radio Station, built in 1933. Providing ideal all-weather entertainment for children, it houses a wide range of exotic birds and animals, an aquarium, adventure playground, wireless exhibition, seasonal puppet theatre, cafe and giftshop. Further west on the A39 the hamlet of **Bilbrook** ('stream in which watercress grows') was settled by 1221.

Clearly signed from Washford to the south of the A39 lies **Cleeve Abbey** (fee:lists): the most complete monastic survival in Somerset. Sited in the romantically-named Vallis Florida, 'valley of the flowers', it was founded by the lord of Old Cleeve manor, William de Roumare, 3rd Earl of Lincoln, between 1186 and 1191, and the first Cistercian monks moved in during the summer of 1198. There were 26 monks here by 1297, then increased to 28, but one receiver in the mid 14th

century was outlawed for failing to render accounts, and several abbots plunged into debt with London merchants. Major building projects were carried out in the later 15th century but, although its inmates were described as 'priests of honest life who keep great hospitality', the house was dissolved in 1537 and the remaining 15 monks pensioned off. Among these was John Hooper, who went on to become bishop of Gloucester in 1551 but was deprived of his see under Queen Mary and burned at the stake as a heretic in 1555. There is a carpark opposite the abbey and visitors enter through a two-storeyed gatehouse dating from the 13th century but remodelled in the early 16th century when a Latin inscription was added above the arch, which translates as 'gate be open, shut to no honest man'. Only the footings of the walls and pillars of the cruciform priory church survive, built c.1200-50, to which in 1232 Henry III gave oak from Newton Park to make the choir stalls. Immediately south of the church, the abbey's domestic buildings survive remarkably completely around two sides of the cloister garth. To the east the 13th century dorter range comprises the sacristy, library, chapter house, parlour and common room, with the dormitory above, although the roof has been replaced. Along the south side the refectory range was remodelled in the late 15th century to provide chambers below and a fine first-floor hall with its reader's desk and elaborate wagon-roof. A former painting of the crucifixion on the east wall has now faded away, but a late 15th century painting, featuring SS Catherine and Margaret, survives in the painted chamber to the west. The tiled pavement of the 13th

century ground-floor refectory has been excavated, projecting south from this range. The western cloister alley survives but the cellarer's range beyond it is known only from excavation. The adjoining farmhouse, created from the abbey buildings, served as the manor-house of Old Cleeve after the Dissolution. The site was bought by the Luttrells of Dunster in 1870 and to them is largely due the fine state of the abbey buildings today.

South of the abbey at the hamlet of Hungerford the monks had a grange called Stout and remains of the 14th century chapel of St Pancras survive in a cottage of that name. Other abbey granges were sited at Croydon, Leigh, Bye and Bineham. Further upstream on the Washford river, the village of **Roadwater**, formerly known as Rode, had a mill by 1243 and an inn by 1736. An Ebenezer chapel was built in 1842 (succeeded by the present Methodist chapel in 1907) and a strong temperance movement began in 1868 under the influence of the Trevelyans of Nettlecombe. The mission church and school of St Luke were opened in the 1880s. In the extreme south of Old Cleeve, the hamlet of Leighland named one of the two tithings in the parish and by 1320 had a chapel dedicated to St Giles, served by the vicar of Old Cleeve. This was replaced by the present chapel of St Giles, built 1861-2 to the design of C.E. Giles, which became a parish church in 1865. Leigh Barton, south-west from Leighland, was occupied by the Roman Catholic Poyntz family from the early 17th century until 1691. Here they sheltered a succession of Catholic priests, remains of whose chapel survive behind the present 19th century farmhouse. These priests included until c.1642 Philip Powell, brutally martyred at Tyburn in 1646.

Beside the sea extends the small resort of **Blue Anchor**, named after an inn mentioned there as long ago as 1678. Formerly known as Cleeve Bay, the settlement comprises a scatter of bungalows and beach-huts, with a leavening of small hotels and restaurants. The long sandy beach with views along the coast to Minehead is its finest asset, superb for bracing walks out of season. On the shore near Blue Anchor stood the chapel of St Mary, destroyed by a cliff collapse in 1452. It had featured a statue of the Virgin Mary which appears to have then been moved inland to a new chapel, consecrated in 1455, at what was later known as Chapel Cleeve. On the south side of this new chapel stood a guest house used by pilgrims until the dissolution of Cleeve Abbey. Around the remnants of these buildings, architect Richard Carver created a Tudor-style mansion for John Halliday, completed in 1823. Extended by the Luttrells in 1913-14, it later operated as a hotel, but is now a private house again. (*See also* **Brendon Hill**)

★★★★ *Cleeve Abbey,* ★★★ *Old Cleeve village and church, setting, Blue Anchor beach, Tropiquaria (for its entertainment value for children).*

ORCHARDLEIGH (B/F) A singularly beautiful parish and estate to the north of Frome, comprising a great wooded park of over 800 acres around a large and lovely lake. The earliest evidence of settlement at this 'glade with an orchard' (or 'with horses' is a possibility) was a chambered Neolithic long barrow on Murtry Hill in the south-west of the park, excavated out of existence from c.1803 to 1920, its site marked by two standing stones. The estate here was held by three thegns in 1066 but after the Conquest was granted to the bishop of Coutances. There was certainly woodland here in Domesday and it was mentioned again in 1243. Subsequently the estate descended through the families of Cultura and Merlaund, and c.1430 half the manor passed by marriage to Henry Champneys, who purchased the other half in 1459. It remained with the Champneys family, baronets from 1767, for four centuries and they created the lake, which now surrounds the island church, and park lodges. The old Champneys house stood beside the lake, near the church, and there Sir Thomas Mostyn-Champneys died childless in 1839. The estate was sold in 1855 by Sir Thomas's receiver in bankruptcy to

William Duckworth, a wealthy Mancunian lawyer and property speculator. Between 1856 and 1858 Duckworth erected a large chateau-like mansion on the hillside above the lake, at a cost of about £40,000. His architect was Thomas Henry Wyatt, and the old house was demolished in 1860. From the Champneys period Duckworth spared the lavish castellated gateway (pre 1816) at the east end of the park, Tudor-style lodges (c.1825) to the south, a rotunda of c.1760, and a romantic boathouse on the lake. The property continued in the Duckworth family for four generations, ending with the death of Arthur Duckworth in 1986. The following year the estate was sold and has since changed hands several times, the house having had many of its fixtures and fittings ripped out.

The small church of St Mary stands in a magical situation on a little island at the western end of the lake, linked to the shore by a footbridge. It is only accessible on foot from Lullington but it is a walk that is heartily recommended. The church comprises an unusually ornate chancel, nave and western bellcote, all of the later 13th century, with an early 19th century north chapel, and includes corbels to hold the Lenten veil, aumbry (cupboard) with original door and an early 14th century decorated font. There is an abundance of monuments to the Champneys tribe, two with wild claims that the family had held the manor since the Norman Conquest, to their successors the Duckworths, and in the churchyard several touching inscriptions to family retainers. Here also lies the poet, Sir Henry Newbolt (1862-1938), author of *Drake's Drum,* who married a granddaughter of the house builder, was a frequent visitor to Orchardleigh and based his novel, *the Old Country* (1906), here, disguising it under the name 'Gardenleigh'. Newbolt also penned the poem, *Fidele's Grassy Tomb,* which research has shown was based on the belief (probably mistaken) that a German poodle, Azor, given in 1790 to the last Champneys baronet by Frederick William II, king of Prussia, had been buried with its master in Orchardleigh church. The dog's monument, a pedestal surmounted by an urn, was moved to the churchyard in 1989.

★★★ *For the walk through the park to the church and its parkland setting.*

ORCHARD PORTMAN (H) Some two miles south-east of Taunton, sandwiched between the roads to Corfe and Staple Fitzpaine, lies the former estate of

TOP *Orchardleigh church*
ABOVE *The gateway, Orchardleigh House*

'Orceard', given by King Ethelwulf of the West Saxons to Taunton's minster church in 854. Its name may possibly supply the earliest evidence for the cultivation of the apple in Somerset but today it is better known for the playing of polo and for Taunton Racecourse, established on the former Orchard Great Field beside the Corfe road in 1927. By c.1135 the manor had passed to Elfric de Orchard: a later descendant, Christina de Orchard, carrying the estate to her husband Walter Portman: representative of a wealthy merchant family which had already represented Taunton in Parliament. Walter's great-grandson, Sir William Portman, became Lord Chief Justice in 1555, and laid the foundations of a great estate in Somerset and London (whence Portman Square). 'A large faire house, well befitting the possessions of the owners, neighboured with a parke and all other delights fitting such a place', was created in the 16th century around Orchard church. But the Portmans eventually outgrew both Orchard and Somerset and moved on: baronets from 1611, with a barony in 1837 and a viscountcy in 1873. The 'faire house' was demolished in or soon after 1843, leaving the church of St Michael relatively isolated. The church boasts a Norman north doorway and a west tower of c.1520-30, but the Portmans destroyed the medieval south aisle in 1844 and finally sold the estate to the Crown Commissioners exactly a century later.

★ *Setting.*

Industrial Archaeology

Those who are drawn to Somerset to enjoy its beautiful and varied countryside and picturesque small towns often remain unaware that it was a heavily industrialised county from the Middle Ages until the 19th century. In fact lead, silver and coal mines on the Mendip Hills were operated from Roman times and possibly before, and evidence of old lead workings can still be traced in the vicinity of Priddy and Charterhouse-on-Mendip. Although coalmining continued into recent times at the east end of the Mendips, its record on the ground has been largely obliterated with the exception of miners' housing in the nearby towns. Similarly, calamine mining for the Bristol brass industry from 1550 to 1850 at Shipham and Rowberrow, mainly surface digging, has left a legacy of uneven ground. Copper was mined briefly on the Quantocks and, in the 19th century, iron on the Brendons, where the remains of a ghost mining village and the incline down which the ore was lowered for transport to Watchet can still be explored.

Cloth manufacture was the county's principal industry by the 13th until the 18th century, continuing even later in some towns such as Frome and Wellington. Fulling mills are recorded from 1219 (Taunton) and have been noted in surprising numbers in rural parishes. With the decline of the industry some were demolished and others converted to grist mills. In the towns silk making and then lace were introduced to mop up surplus labour, and factory buildings, often converted to other uses, survive in places such as Bridgwater, Bruton, Chard, Frome, Rode, Shepton Mallet and Taunton, dating from the 18th and 19th centuries. There are substantial factory remains at Tonedale and Westford (both Wellington) and the building (and preservation) of cloth-workers' houses in the Trinity area of Frome from the 17th century is of national importance. In the south and east of the county, particularly in and around Crewkerne, the manufacture of twine, rope, webbing and sailcloth was developed from the 18th century, relying on locally-grown hemp and flax. The most impressive industrial complex, the Parrett Works at Martock, dominated by its tall chimney, was adapted for canvas and twine making. Gloving flourished at Yeovil and in the villages around it, the production of shirts and collars began at Taunton c.1870, while Castle Cary and Crewkerne featured horsehair weaving for chair seats.

Other manufactures included glassmaking at Bridgwater where the base of an early 18th century glass kiln has been excavated and preserved. The same

ABOVE *The Anglo-Bavarian Brewery, Shepton Mallet*
BELOW *Fox Factory, Tonedale, Wellington*
BELOW LEFT *Lead workings, Charterhouse-on-Mendip*

town was noted for its 19th century Bath bricks, a scouring brick made from the river slime there, and nearby at Dunball (Puriton), and also for the production of ornamental bricks and tiles. Street is a town built on the making of shoes and the Shoe Museum there graphically illustrates the industry's origins and history.

Watermills were built in almost every parish and many manor courts required their tenants to take their grain for grinding to a named manor mill ('suit of multure'). One mill, at Clapton near Crewkerne, is still working commercially and flour is also being produced at Dunster and Burcott (Wells). Dunster and Burcott are open to the public, as are two other restored mills: Orchard (Williton) and Hornsbury (Chard). Water and water power were also vital for papermaking which continues at Watchet. There were many paper mills below the Mendips and around Wells, and the production of handmade paper can still be witnessed at Wookey Hole. Other watermills were built or adapted to make edge-tools, notably the Fussells' operation in and near Mells, Chantry and Stoke St Michael. Windmills were also once common in the county (one was built at Durston as early as 1324-5) and old maps show them scattered along exposed areas like the Polden Hills. Few, however, survive and only two are accessible: Ashton, an 18th century tower mill at Chapel Allerton, and Stembridge, built c.1820 with a thatched cap at High Ham.

Somerset has been identified with cider from the earliest times, although major factory production at Norton Fitzwarren (Taunton Cider) dates only from 1911. The older farmhouse traditions are preserved and can be inspected at Sheppy's (Bradford-on-Tone) and Perry's (Dowlish Wake), and a horse-powered cider mill has been installed in Corporation Street, Taunton. Important brewery buildings still dominate Shepton Mallet, Oakhill (Ashwick), Hambridge and Wiveliscombe, but brewing continues only at the last.

Canals came comparatively late to the county. A grand design of the 1790s to link the Bristol Channel with the South Coast came to nothing and the Bridgwater and Taunton Canal was the first to open to commercial traffic in 1827. After a costly restoration of its locks and bridges it was triumphantly reopened in 1994. Other canal projects included the Glastonbury Canal (1833), the Grand Western Canal (1838, linking Taunton and Tiverton), the Westport Canal (1840, *see* Hambridge) and the Chard Canal (1842). The Westport venture survives virtually intact, but only the occasional aqueduct betrays the former course of the others. The arrival of the railways heralded the deathknell of the canals. A proposal to connect Bristol and Exeter by rail was made as early as 1825, but the main line was not completed as far as Taunton until 1842 and to Exeter in 1844. In the years that followed an elaborate network was created across the Somerset landscape by a succession of railway companies: a network that survived largely intact until the Beeching axe closed many lines in the 1960s. The spirit of the steam age lives on in the East Somerset Railway, a short stretch of line at West Cranmore, and in the 20-mile course of the West Somerset Railway between Bishops Lydeard and Minehead. Steam was also the motive power for the 19th century drainage of the Somerset Levels and can be observed in action at the Westonzoyland Pumping Station, where there is also a small museum.

Indeed, museums provide the clearest understanding of the county's industries and there are particularly good exhibitions at the Museum of South Somerset (Yeovil) and Chard Museum. Although car manufacture has never been a major activity in the county, its development can be traced at the Sparkford Motor Museum, as can the history of aviation at the Fleet Air Arm Museum at Yeovilton.

OTHERY (E) A village which lies on the Taunton to Street road (A 361), recently described as having 'a tired, traffic-trampled air'. It would be unfair, however, to judge this 'other island' only from the part seen by the through traveller. Try a stroll along North Lane to sample the other Othery with its older buildings, well-kept gardens, National School of 1827 and the parish church. Othery formed part of the Saxon estate of 'Sowi' held by Glastonbury Abbey until the dissolution of 1539, and its low-lying lands were progressively drained by the monks. In 1317 Matthew de Clevedon, lord of Aller, with a gang of 13 other men, broke down the abbey's banks in Othery and flooded 1,000 acres of crops for two years. The church of St Michael has a fine 15th century central tower supported on 14th century piers. The aisleless nave, with north and south transepts, and chancel also belong probably to the 14th century but everything was radically restored in 1846-7 and later. There are good 15th and 16th century benchends, one with initials identified as those of Abbot Richard Bere (1493-1524): also fragments of 15th century stained glass in the south transept and a framed cope of similar date, possibly foreign, illustrating the Assumption of the Virgin Mary. Outside, below the west window, note the tablet to the splendidly-named Ezekiel Athanasius Rowse (died 1822), vicar here for 46 years. At Pathe, south-west from the village, stands Pathe House, built c.1800, birthplace of the Victorian hero of Rorke's Drift, Col J.R.M. Chard, VC (see **Hatch Beauchamp**).

OTTERFORD (H) This highland parish straddles the top of the Blackdown hills to the south of Taunton. Probably from Saxon times the parish formed a tithing within the great manor of Taunton Deane, all its lands being held under the bishops of Winchester. It occurs as 'Oteriford' in a forged Taunton charter of 854 by King Ethelwulf of the West Saxons. Taking its name from a ford across the River Otter, it comprises a landscape of scattered cottages and farms. The village of Bishopswood in the south-east of the parish has grown up largely since the 19th century. The church of St Leonard stands isolated on a lane to the west of the Taunton to Honiton road across Brown Down. It was substantially restored in 1861 when the north aisle was added and, apart from the Norman font, has entirely modern furnishings. The sundial above the south porch advises that 'Our days on the Earth are as a Shadow'. In the chancel is a tablet to William Beadon

Otterhead Lakes, Otterford

(died 1864), retired physician and an influential figure in Taunton's political life. In 1841 he built Otterhead House, a large mansion whose later occupants included judge Sir John Mellor (died 1887) and Sir William Henry Goschen (1916-c.1935). The property was demolished in 1947, but the former grounds, Otterhead Lakes, acquired as a catchment area by the local water authority, still provide delightful walks and fishing. The Holman Clavel Inn was forfeited to the parish as pauper's property in the 18th century and ever since its rent has ensured that Otterford's rates, and latterly its Community Charge and Council Tax, have been the lowest in the district.

★★★ *Landscape, walking.*

OTTERHAMPTON (D) The parish follows the exposed western bank of the River Parrett as it runs into Bridgwater Bay, its name possibly meaning 'the settlement of those living in the place frequented by otters' ('Otramestone' 1086). The isolated village comprises only the former rectory and manor-house (now Otterhampton Farm) and the redundant church of All Saints. Formerly dedicated to SS Peter and Paul, the medieval building was over-restored in 1894 but retains a 16th century screen and 12th century font. Hill House, a mansion to the south-east of the village in its own small park and used since 1976 as a Christian Youth conference centre, was probably built c.1812 by John Evered, lord of the manor. Buried here in 1581 was Thomas Chanock, a noted alchemist who claimed to possess the secret of the philosopher's stone which would transform base metals into gold and who had a laboratory at Combwich.

Amid the salt marshes to the north-east of the village lies the small hamlet of **Steart** (from Saxon *steort* – 'promontory'), formerly known as Marsh and held with Stockland Bristol until 1886. A rusting notice beside the road requires visitors to obtain permission from the hayward or common-rights owner. The Bridgwater Bay Nature Reserve was established here in 1954. Cars should be left at Dowells Farm before proceeding on foot to Fenning Island, where there are hides for watching the birdlife of the estuary. Permits to visit Stert Island are obtainable from the Warden at Dowells Farm.

★★★ *Scenery and natural history of Bridgwater Bay.*

OVER STOWEY (D) A picturesque parish on the north-eastern side of the Quantock Hills which, like its neighbour, Nether Stowey, derives its name ('stone way') from the old Saxon *herepath* which passed through the place. Even earlier settlement is evidenced by cairns, barrows and an Iron Age camp in Cockercombe. The parish once supported no fewer than six fulling mills, copper was mined, 'broom squires' produced brushes and charcoal burners charcoal. Today the whole area still bears the stamp of Henry Labouchere, first and last Baron Taunton (died 1869), who in the 1830s bought up threequarters of the place, mainly from the Earl of Egmont, and from 1857 built Quantock Lodge, a Tudor-style pile designed by Henry Clutton, with a large Gothic lodge on the Nether Stowey road. Following the death of Lord Taunton's daughter Mary, wife of E.J. Stanley, MP for Bridgwater, in 1920, the estate was sold, the house being converted into a sanatorium (1925-62) and a private school in 1963.

ABOVE *Rich brother's monument, Over Stowey Church.*
RIGHT *Gothic lodge, Over Stowey*

The small village is clustered round the church of SS Peter and Paul: itself so radically restored in 1840 by Richard Carver as to be mainly of interest for its fittings. It has a fine set of 16th century Quantock benchends, a Bridgwater brass chandelier of 1775 and a series of good Victorian memorial windows to the Stanleys. In the north aisle a charming monument of 1815 to two Rich brothers bears symbols of husbandry, including a plough, harrow, rake and beehive. Christopher Rich (1647-1714), born in the parish, became London's most prominent theatrical manager. His son's staging of John Gay's celebrated *Beggar's Opera* made 'Gay rich and Rich gay'. During the Civil War a Roundhead attack from Taunton in 1645, in which 'many soldiers and commanders were slain', was opposed by the Selleck family who fortified the church tower and parsonage, summoning the villagers with the church bells.

The name of Walford's Gibbet marks the execution site of charcoal burner John Walford, who cut his wife's throat in 1789. To the north of the village a low flat mound seems to be 'the old castle precinct' mentioned in the mid 12th century, which Robert Dunning suggests could well have been the stronghold of King Harold, lord of Over Stowey, killed at Hastings, and of his Norman successors: formerly focus of a Quantock royal forest until replaced by Nether Stowey Castle. At **Plainsfield**, a manor held by the family of Admiral Robert Blake from c.1600, weavers and potters ply their trades and retail its products. The footings of a 13th century chapel of the Virgin Mary survive at **Adscombe**, probably built by the monks of Athelney Abbey who had an estate here. This was one of Coleridge's favourite haunts. Today prominent signs direct the walker to a nature trail through Forestry Commission woods.

★★★ *Nature trail and landscape generally.*
★★ *Village and church.*

PAWLETT (D/E) To the north of Bridgwater, the parish lines the east bank of the meandering River Parrett towards its mouth. The place was formerly noted for its salmon fisheries and in the 19th century for brickmaking. Its name seems to mean 'the stream with (or obstructed by) stakes'. The largely modern village, which Newman decided had 'a forlorn feeling of space and solitude', lies just off the A 38 on the south-east side of Pawlett Hill: the top of the hill once occupied by the open fields of the main manor of Pawlett Gaunts and marked from the Middle Ages by Alderigge windmill. In 1232 this estate was given by Robert de Gournay, nephew and heir of Maurice de Gaunt, to St Mark's Hospital, Bristol, whose masters obtained a fair in 1257 and kept peacocks here in the late 14th century. After the hospital's dissolution in 1539 the manor later passed to the earls of Shaftesbury and their descendants the Ponsonbys until its sale 1920-22. Another manor of Pawlett, centred on the present South Farm, was held in the 13th century by Walter of Pawlett and continued with his descendants until sold in 1548 by Sir Hugh Poulett, ancestor of the earls Poulett of Hinton St George. The heavily-rendered church of St John the Baptist has an elaborate Norman south doorway and a Perpendicular rood screen. Originally a chapelry of North Petherton, it passed to St Augustine's Abbey, Bristol, c.1140, and to St Mark's Hospital in 1251. Below the hill stretch the Pawlett Hams, rich pasture lands which were protected against flooding by the 13th century. At the west end of the Hams was the departure point from the 12th century for the ferry to Combwich, marked by 1655 until 1897 by the White House Inn. Stretcholt, a secondary hamlet, was a

Domesday manor, as was Walpole, a hamlet in the south of the parish partly destroyed when the present A 38 was diverted in 1822.

★★ *Setting and views over Bridgwater Bay.*

PENDOMER (J) One of my favourite small villages, which lies on the county boundary east of Crewkerne, at the end of lane which goes nowhere else and commands beautiful views across the surrounding countryside. Its old name, 'Penne', means either 'hill' (if Celtic) or 'enclosure' (if Saxon). From the 12th century until 1407 it was held by the Domer family (taking their name from Dummer in Hants), who added their surname to that of the manor. It was later owned by the Pouletts of Hinton St George (1630-1803) and the Helyars of Coker Court (from 1803). The immaculately-kept little church, of unknown dedication, is Perpendicular with an earlier west tower and some 15th century stained glass. In a recess in the north wall is the quite superb effigy of a knight, c.1325, identified as Sir John de Domer, elected MP for Somerset in 1306 and 1313. His coat of arms, a crescent between six billets, is still visible on his surcoat and shield, the canopy includes an angel with a small figure (bearing the knight's soul to Heaven) and the embattled cornice, supported by the figures of two peasants, still has some iron prickets to carry lighted tapers. West of the churchyard is the former manor-house.

★★★ *Village, church, setting.*

PENSELWOOD (F) A little village which lies on a wooded ridge to the north-east of Wincanton. Its name, formerly 'Penne', is Celtic for 'hill', and is generally thought to be identical with 'Peonnan' where Cenwalh, king of the West Saxons, defeated the British in 658 in a decisive battle and pursued them as far as the River Parrett. This victory marked the beginning of the Saxon conquest of Somerset. It was also probably the site of an indecisive battle between Edmund Ironside and Canute in 1016. At the northern end of the ridge, cut by the lane north from the village, is an Iron Age hillfort called Kenwalch's Castle and in the same area are the celebrated Pen Pits, once estimated at over 20,000, although now much decreased in number. They are circular holes of up to 30 ft across and 10 ft deep and were evidently excavated in the Roman or Dark Ages to quarry whetstones for querns (hand mills). Northeast of the village at Castle Orchard is a Norman motte and bailey and the earthworks of a similar construction, Ballands Castle, with two baileys, lie half a mile south-west of the church, although no documentary reference has been found for either. The estate was held in 1086 by William Geral under Roger Arundel and the two forts may be dated to around that period. On the death of Nicholas Wadham in 1609 the manor was divided between his sisters and their descendants, known locally as 'cuckoo lords' from their non-residence. The second part of the placename was added to distinguish the place from Pendomer and reflects its position at the heart of the great forest of Selwood (see **Frome**). The church of St Michael stands at the centre of the village near a small green. It is mainly Perpendicular, the nave was rebuilt in 1805 and the north aisle added in 1848. There is a fine Norman south door topped by a lintel carved with a lamb and cross, flanked by two beasts and supported by two corbel heads, sometimes optimistically identified as Alfred and Guthrum. The interior has monuments to the Biging family (1743-1917) and three roof bosses in the nave came from Stavordale Priory (see **Charlton Musgrove**).

★ *Church, setting.*

PILTON (E/F) This welcoming leafy village, south-west from Shepton Mallet, lies on and below the A 361, its houses set attractively at different levels. Its name means 'settlement on a stream' and, although the first element can also be rendered as 'creek', tales of its former importance as a port up to which Joseph of Arimathea sailed should be treated with more than caution ! The estate here was given to Glastonbury Abbey by Ine (688-726), King of the West Saxons. The substantial manor originally included Shepton Mallet, Croscombe, North Wootton and Pylle, and had two mills by 1086: a number that had increased to four by 1317. The abbots had a substantial house here together with a park which at the dissolution was three miles around and stocked with 351 deer. The manor was granted in 1551 to the Duke of Somerset and, despite his execution, was bestowed on his son, Edward, Earl of Hertford, continuing in the Seymour family until settled on their descendants, the Prynnes. Thereafter it was held by the Langtons and Gore-Langtons. The church of St John the Baptist, attractively sited amid trees in the valley, was initially held by the abbey but was lost to Wells Cathedral in the 12th

century after a complex power game between the abbot and the bishop. Subsequently the living was assigned to the Cathedral precentor (Thomas Overay, precentor 1471-92, is represented by a kneeling figure in stained glass in the chancel) and a vicarage ordained in 1342. The building retains a Norman south door, has a clerestory nave (under a fine timber roof, supported by angels) and north arcade of c.1180 and a 13th century west tower. The chancel (also with clerestory) and north aisle date from the 14th century and the east end of the latter may have been occupied by the chapel of the Virgin Mary, mentioned in 1508. Only a parclose screen remains of the full rood screen set up between 1498 and 1506, the rest having been restored away to North Cheriton. There are several monuments and small brasses to the Strode, Bethell, Hole and Clerk families, and a framed fragmentary embroidered cope of the early 16th century.

The Manor House to the south-west of the church has a Georgian five-bay facade although there are some 17th century windows at the rear. The only survivals from Glastonbury's lordship are a stone-vaulted cellar and a square dovecote. Above and south of the house is a superb 14th century Glastonbury barn over 100 ft long, with symbols of the evangelists on each of the four gables. Sadly the building was struck by lightning in 1964 and the thatch and timber roof destroyed in the resulting fire. **Pilton Manor Vineyard** (lists), established in 1966, stretches from the south-western approach to the village, recalling that the abbey had vineyards here by 1189. To a wider world Pilton means the Glastonbury pop music festival, first held in 1970 at Michael Eavis's Worthy Farm, immediately south of the village. Although restaged in 1971 as a free festival, it was again revived only in 1979 as a fund-raising exercise for CND and has brought tens of thousands to this long-suffering area almost every year since.

★★★ *Village, church, atmosphere.*

PITCOMBE (F) This sizeable parish, 'the marshy valley', lies south-west from Bruton: a town with which Pitcombe's economic fortunes were inextricably linked. In 1086, when the manor was held by Turstin son of Rolf, 11 of Bruton's 17 burgesses were entered under Pitcombe, which already had two mills. Later the manor, with the estate of Cole (formerly 'Colne', a British river name), was long held by the Lovels of Castle Cary and their

descendants, the Zouches. There was a silk factory here in 1831, with a workforce of nearly 50. The village is dominated by the viaduct which carried the Somerset and Dorset Railway until its closure in 1966. The church of St Leonard, a chapelry of Bruton from the 12th century until 1784, stands isolated to the south of the village at the end of a short lane which once led to Pitcombe House. This burned down soon after the death of its owner, Nathaniel Jekyll, in 1826 and only the picturesque lodge survives. The church has a Perpendicular west tower with panelled tower arch but the rest was rebuilt in 1858 to the designs of G.E. Street.

The estate of Hadspen in the south-west of the parish was bought in 1747 by Vickris Dickinson, a Bristol merchant (related to the family at Kingweston), who built here a 5-bay classical mansion set in its own park. The property was acquired in 1785 by Henry Hobhouse, a Bristol barrister, whose family hailed from Minehead. His descendants have lived here ever since, establishing a notable reputation for public service in the law, politics, church and local government. St Leonard's church includes monuments to the Rt Hon Henry Hobhouse (1811-62), Arthur, Baron Hobhouse (1819-1904), and the Rt Hon Henry Hobhouse (1854-1937). The eight acres of sheltered Edwardian gardens at Hadspen (fee:lists), set against a woodland backdrop are open to the public. Restored by Penelope Hobhouse in the 1970s, they were adopted in 1986 by a Canadian couple, Nori and Sandra Pope. To a traditional English garden the Popes have added their own transatlantic flair. Access is from the Castle Cary to Wincanton road (A371). Godminster ('Godmaneston', c.1210 – 'Godmann's settlement'), 16th century seat of the Cottington family, is a late medieval mansion with a 7-bay Georgian facade.

★★★ *Hadspen gardens.*

PITMINSTER (H) The parish extends south-west from Taunton to the old county boundary on the Blackdown Hills, its early Saxon name meaning 'the minster or mother church of Pippa's people', although its only known dependent chapel was at Corfe. In 938 King Athelstan, Alfred's son, gave the estate to the bishop of Winchester and thereafter it formed part of the huge manor of Taunton Deane. Subsequently one of the five major divisions of the manor, known as 'hundreds', was centred on Poundisford in the parish, where by the early 13th century the bishops had their deer park. King John is believed to have hunted there on a visit to Taunton in 1208, and in 1239, during a vacancy in the bishopric, Henry III sent his huntsman to take venison there for the royal Christmas celebrations at Winchester. Losses of horses killed in the park by wolves were also noted in 1218. The park continued until 1534 when it was sub-divided. Roger Hill, a Taunton merchant, took the northern half and built Poundis-ford Lodge, a substantial house which boasts three plaster ceilings of c.1590 and fine overmantels of the period. His son William took the southern half and from 1546 raised an even more sumptuous house, **Poundisford Park.** A tall three storeys in an H-shape (just in time for Henry VIII), it has a galleried and panelled central hall with a dining-room added to the north-east c.1692 and is set in pleasing parkland with walled gardens to the north. To the east is a range of outbuildings, including the former detached kitchen, now the Wellhouse Restaurant, and a tiled covered well in the centre of a courtyard. Later Hills served as lawyers and MPs, the splendid house eventually being sold to the Welmans in 1706, the Helyars in 1869 and the Vivian-Neals in 1928.

Pitminster village is surprisingly but delightfully located midway between the two roads running south from Taunton. The present church of SS Margaret and Andrew (formerly St Andrew alone) was built c.1300 and the octagonal tower top and leaded spire were added within the following century. Then followed the Perpendicular chancel and the twin chapels either side of the tower. It may have been a parish dispute over paying for casting the oldest bell in the tower in 1630 which prompted Richard Trott (later known as Treat) of Amberd House to emigrate to the New World c.1638. His American descendants regularly return and have commemorated their ancestor in a memorial on the north wall. The Vibarts, their successors at Amberd (Col J.M. Vibart built the present house near Staplehay in the north of the parish c.1805), are remembered in several tablets above the north door. Most impressive are the effigies of the Colles family of Barton Grange (*see* **Corfe**): Humphrey (died 1557) in the north-west chapel, on the north side of the sanctuary, his son John (died 1608) with his wife Anne Thynne of Longleat, supported by their six children, and on the south side his grandson John Colles (died 1627), his wife Elizabeth Wyndham, with their infant son at her feet and their four daughters below.

Colles monument, Pitminster church

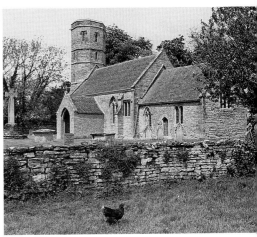

Podimore church

Two heraldic hatchments beneath the tower relate to William Hawker (died 1806) and his daughter Ann (died 1834) of Poundisford Lodge. A tablet recalls Arthur William Kinglake (1803-91) of Wilton House, Taunton, author of a celebrated travel book, *Eothen*, and the multi-volume official history of the Crimean War.

South-west of the village the delightful hamlet of **Blagdon Hill** (formerly Blagdon) lines the road up to the Blackdown Hills which named it. Here in the early 18th century the landlord of the Lamb (later the Lamb and Flag) started an annual fair on Blagdon Green on 13 August. Near Staplehay stands Canonsgrove House (c.1825), a police training centre from 1963. (For **Widcombe Wild-Life Park** *see* **Churchstanton**)

★★★ *Poundisford Park, church, setting.*

PITNEY (E) The name means 'Pytta's island' but, long before Pytta the Saxon a Bronze Age sword of c.200 BC was left on Pitney Moor and the Romans built two villas here. A fine pierced-work Saxon brooch was found here in 1898. The medieval manors of Pitney originated in grants made to Richard Revel (the Revel in Curry Rivel) from the royal manor of Somerton between 1190 and 1203. Pitney Wearne manor was granted to the Compton family in 1610 and split up and sold by their descendant, the Duke of Devonshire, in 1919. The lesser manor of Pitney Lorty was held by Henry, Lord Lorty (died 1321), and latterly by the Pyne family. In the village of thatch and blue-lias stone stands the church of St John the Baptist, probably founded as a daughter chapel to Huish Episcopi by a lord of Pitney Lorty. The church has a chancel dating from the 13th century with some well-carved roof

bosses. Here throughout the Common-wealth the Rev Cananuel Bernard (rector 1624-68) continued to marry couples from far around by the rites of the Church of England.

PODIMORE (J) A small lias stone village, north-east from Ilchester, with a scatter of thatched farmhouses and cottages and modern infilling, lining a single lane running south from the Podymore Inn. It was originally known simply as Milton, 'the middle settlement', to which was later added Podimore, 'frog moor' (*pode* – 'frog'), in order to distinguish it from other Somerset Miltons: now it is plain Podimore. Evidence of an Iron-Age and Romano-British settlement, occupied until the 4th century, has been found in two fields south-east and south-west from the village. In 966 the manor was granted by King Edgar to the monks of Glastonbury Abbey, who retained it until 1540. Thereafter it was held by the Horners of Mells. The church of St Peter in the centre of the village dates from the early 14th century with an octagonal west tower and several old table tombs to the south of the church.

PORLOCK (C) The last sizeable coastal settlement in Somerset heading westward into Devon. Surrounded by wooded hills, it is not really a village, not a town, nor a seaside resort, but a mixture of all three. Once noted more for its herring fishery and for the yarn made here to be sold at Dunster, there are still some thatched cottages near the centre. Like Dunster, it is best out of season, when its narrow streets are not jammed with traffic seem-ingly trying to pluck up courage for the ascent of Porlock Hill. A rewarding

ABOVE *Doverhay, Porlock*
RIGHT *Porlock Weir*

alternative to the hill climb is a toll road (well worth the extra cost), commanding wonderful sea views across Porlock Bay to Hurlstone Point. At the foot of the hill is the 16th century Ship Inn where Robert Southey extolled Porlock's charms in mediocre verse.

A prehistoric presence in the area is indicated by Berry Castle, a hill-slope enclosure three miles south-west from the village, and a stone circle on Porlock Common of some ten standing stones and eleven fallen ones, about 80 ft in diameter, with a nearby round barrow. From Porlock's name, meaning 'enclosure by the harbour', and from two significant landings here, it seems likely that the village was a significant settlement in Saxon times. In 914 (the year corrected from that given by the Anglo Saxon Chronicle) a Viking fleet landed at night but were successfully driven off: many of them later starving to death on the island of Steepholm in the Bristol Channel. Then in 1052 Earl Harold (the future king who died at Hastings) and his brother Leofwine put ashore here from Ireland with nine ships, defeated an army from Somerset and Devon, killed 30 thanes, and plundered the area. Thereafter Porlock did not feature as a major port: possibly explained by the silting up of the bay which forms the Marsh and which may have cut the village off from the sea. This was solved by the construction of a weir or harbour to the west at Porlock Weir, which seems to have been under way during the period 1422-27. A blockhouse was planned for Porlock in 1539 and towers armed with cannon, here and at Hurlstone, in 1586. The present harbour at Porlock Weir dates only from the 19th century and only one trading vessel was ever built there: in 1858.

The main manor was held by the Roges family from the late 12th century until

c.1332 when the heiress was pardoned (with her mother) for the murder of her husband, Robert de Mohun. In 1366 the new lord, Sir Nigel Loring, created a park here and was granted a Thursday market and two three-day fairs. Edward Rogers of Cannington bought the manor from James I in 1610, from whom it was inherited in turn by the Winters and the Blathwayts of Dyrham, Glos. The manor-house, Court Place, was rebuilt in the 19th century after a fire. The most attractive house here is the late 15th century **Doverhay** in the centre of the village (never a manor-house, as often claimed), now a Tourist Information Centre and a delightful old-style museum (lists). Within, archaeological finds jostle with gas masks, children's exercise books and antique radio sets: all with handwritten labels.

Not far away, identifiable by its truncated spire, the top of which may have been destroyed in the great storm of 1703, stands the parish church of St Dubricius (the Welsh bishop St Dyfrig, died c.550). This dedication might suggest that it was the saint himself (alleged improbably by Geoffrey of Monmouth to have crowned King Arthur) or one of his disciples who brought Christianity to the area. The low west tower is 13th century, the south arcade c.1300, with the south porch and east vestry added in the 15th century. Built into the west wall are two pieces of a Saxon cross which may hark back to the original foundation. In the south wall are two tomb recesses, one with the mutilated effigy of a cross-legged knight, identified by some as Sir Simon Roges (died 1306), lord of the manor. To the south of the chancel is a superb canopied monument bearing the alabaster effigies of a later lord, John, 4th Baron Harington (died 1418), and his wife Elizabeth Courtenay (died 1471), daughter of the Earl of Devon: both sadly

vandalised with carved initials. Under Harington's will a chantry of the Virgin Mary was founded in the south aisle in 1474, endowed with the manor of Ugborough, Devon. Its two chaplains lived in the 15th century Chantry Cottage, north-east of the churchyard. In the chancel and porch are two table tombs, probably those set up under the will of Alice Hensley of 1528 to her husband and herself. The Hensleys lived at Worthy, a substantial 16th century house at Ashley Combe, by 1424: selling out to the Stukeleys of Dunster in 1568. On the north wall of the church is a lengthy inscription to barrister baronet, Sir Charles E.H. Chadwyck-Healey (died 1919), who documented six parishes in this area in a detailed history of 1901.

West along the coast through the hamlet of West Porlock, almost entirely composed of guest houses and the occasional hotel, is **Porlock Weir**: an idyllic little harbour with a row of 17th century lime-washed cottages and the old Ship Inn. Now mainly a mooring for pleasure yachts, it was formerly the haunt of fishing boats and the last coal cargo was unloaded here c.1950. From the seashore a toll road winds up through Worthy woods: a magical landscape created by the lords King. Here at Ashley Combe, Peter, the 7th Baron, built a summer retreat in 1799. His son William, later Earl of Lovelace, married Ada, Lord Byron's only child, in 1835 and she used her fortune to extend the mansion, adding an Italianate clock tower and elaborate terraced gardens. Converted to a country club in 1950, it was later demolished. Nature has since taken over and hidden the site with trees and undergrowth, through which there is an enchanting walk to Culbone church.

★★★★ *Porlock Weir, landscape, walking,*
★★ *Porlock village, church.*

PRESTON PLUCKNETT (J) A rural parish now swallowed up by the western suburbs of Yeovil: its name, 'the priest's settlement', suggesting a Saxon religious centre. There were two early manorial estates, one known as Preston Bermondsey following its gift in 1092 by Ansgar Brito to Bermondsey Priory in Surrey, to which in 1095 his son Walter added the estate of Stone, where the hundred court of Stone (see **Mudford**) met. The priory had a cell for two monks at Preston in the early 15th century. The second manor, Preston Plucknett, was held by the Plugenet family (whose name survives here in that of a pub) from 1270, although it was occupied under them from 1380 by the Stourtons. To a 15th century John Stourton (died 1438) is ascribed the building of the stunning Abbey Farm (a recent and mistaken name), lovingly restored after war damage, with a substantial ten-bay barn, both visible from the main road. This estate was held by the Waldegrave family from the 16th century until 1725 and by the Fanes of Brympton from 1762. Opposite is the 17th century Knapp House and associated buildings. The church of St James, a former chapelry of Yeovil to the west of the manor-house, has an early 14th century chancel and transepts: the rest largely Perpendicular with a Victorian porch.

PRIDDY (A) This grey-stone village is ranged around a large green high up on the Mendip plateau: its name derived from the Celtic for 'earth'. Throughout its history it was held with and under the manor of Westbury-sub-Mendip by successive bishops of Bath and Wells and formed one of the four principal centres of leadmining and smelting on the hills until St Cuthbert's mine finally closed in 1908. North-east from the village are three Neolithic embanked circles in a line with part of a fourth further to the north, which excavation suggests (from post-hole evidence) were wood henges. East of the village on North Hill are two major groups of Bronze Age tumuli: Priddy Nine Barrows (called 'Nigheberwes' in 1296) and Ashen Hill Barrows. The church of St Lawrence was by 1164 a chapelry to Westbury (whose church has the same dedication), in which year it was given to Bruton Priory. A vicarage was ordained in 1290 but the church was generally served by curates until a a separate parish was created in 1862. The present building stands on higher ground north-east of the green and has a 13th century west tower with an inscription recording the repair of

ABOVE *The barn, Abbey Farm, Preston Plucknett.* BELOW *Priddy Fair, Priddy*

its battlements and two 'pinikls' after the great storm of 1703. There is a 14th century lancet window in the chancel which may relate to a rebuilding when the church was rededicated on 10 August (St Lawrence's day) 1352 and a bequest to the church 'work' in 1509 may date a Perpendicular contribution. The remains of the rood screen look a little sad without its loft but there is a framed 15th century altar frontal decorated with irises.

Priddy Fair, formerly held on the green on St Lawrence's day, was altered to 21 August when the calendar changed in 1752 and still continues on the nearest Wednesday. Now principally for sheep (together with a fun fair) it specialised in cloth when it was first mentioned in 1349. The king's alnager of cloth was beaten up there and his warrant and purse stolen in 1350. There is no evidence to support the claim that the fair was moved from Wells

because of the Black Death. It is popularly believed that the fair cannot continue if the picturesque stack of hurdles is not maintained on the green although there is no legal basis for this fear. East of the village, Stockhill is a Forestry Commission plantation with waymarked walks and picnic areas.

★★ *Village, setting.*

PUCKINGTON (J) The 'settlement of Puca's people' is a small but attractive village which lines each side of the Ilminster to Curry Rivel road (B 3168), including several medieval and 18th century thatched cottages. Before the Conquest it was held under Muchelney Abbey by two Saxons but after the Battle of Hastings all three lost out to Roger de Courcelles. During the Middle Ages it passed through a succession of families until, by the execution of the Duke of

171

Suffolk in 1553 for supporting his daughter, Lady Jane Grey, for the throne, it reverted to the Crown. Thereafter it was long held by the Portmans of Orchard Portman who bought it in 1557. The church of St Andrew is set back from the road: a sizeable building for such a small community, possibly explained by its short-lived status as a collegiate church of chaplains in the 14th century. The 13th century chancel includes a fine sedilia and piscina, but much of the rest was rebuilt and reroofed in the 19th century.

★★ *Village.*

PURITON (E) A leafy village, 'the settlement by the pear tree', clustered prettily at the west end of the Polden Hills. Its proximity to Bridgwater has meant much modern building around its approaches to house commuters. The landscape has changed too. A meandering loop in the nearby River Parrett (shown to have served a sizeable Roman port at the west end of the Polden ridgeway) was bypassed in 1677, the vast expanse of the Royal Ordnance Factory was established east of the village from 1939 and the motorway carved its own swathe through the parish in the 1970s.

After the Battle of Hastings the manor, held by Edward the Confessor's queen, was given by William the Conqueror to the Pope, who had blessed his English expedition: the only such papal possession in the country and one which the Pope did not hold for long. The church of St Michael and All Angels (formerly St Michael the Archangel) stands at the head of a triangular village green. Its 13th century west tower is capped by a pyramid roof but the rest of the building is mainly 15th century. Note the beams in the porch roof dated 1633, almost contemporary with a rough register chest of 1629, and the spiral stair, also in the porch, which now leads nowhere (to a former gallery ?). The north aisle is peppered with memorials to the Greenhill family of Knowle Hall in Bawdrip, lords of the manor from the late 18th century, one of whom went down with Kitchener in HMS *Hampshire* in 1916.

At the hamlet of **Downend** in the west end of the parish a borough known as Caput Montis had been planted before 1159, probably by Philip de Columbers, but was not mentioned as a borough after the mid 13th century. Apart from its grid-plan streets, no trace of the medieval town survives, although earthworks mark the site of a motte and bailey castle,

probably Norman in origin. At **Dunball** on the banks of the Parrett the river slime was formerly made into the famous Bath bricks (patented in 1827 and named from their resemblance to Bath stone) which were marketed for cleaning and scouring. Dunball also served as a major port for the Bridgwater area, known for the production of salt, lime, cement and manure.

★★ *Church and village centre.*

PYLLE (F) South-east of Pilton, this small parish's name literally means 'creek' but here probably refers to a stream and must reflect the fact that it was held in Saxon times as part of the similarly-named Pilton estate and was owned with it under Glastonbury abbey. The Domesday tenant was Serlo de Burci from whom the manor passed by 1303 to William FitzMartin and subsequently to the families of Fitzwarren, Bourchier, Berkeley and, finally, the Portmans of Orchard Portman. The present manor-house dates from 1621, the work of Sir Edward Berkeley, and was substantially remodelled and extended c.1700. It is somewhat severe and plain although the adjoining outbuildings and cottages of the latter period are delightful. The grounds feature a small ornamental lake opposite the church of St Thomas Becket, with its Perpendicular west tower. The rest was rebuilt in 1868 but there is a model of the former church under the tower, some earlier memorials and a later one of 1917 to a lieutenant in the Royal Flying Corps who died of his wounds after aerial operations over Gaza. There is also an early sculpted font and an old flute which once provided accompaniment to the singing here. The influence of Lt Col J.A. Garton, occupier of Pylle Manor 1922-69, founder of the Somerset Guild of Craftsman, led to the church's adoption by the guild, whose members have furnished and ornamented the interior. Today the main settlement in the parish is Street-on-the-Fosse, a scatter of buildings along the Foss Way (A 37) to the north-east of the church.

★ *Setting.*

QUEEN CAMEL (K) An attractive village, south-west from Sparkford, although lining the busy A 359 to Yeovil. It is blessed with pleasing houses (with an abundance of well-tended front gardens), many apparently set up after a disastrous fire of 1634 destroyed 70 properties. There were once two weekly markets and four annual fairs held here but by 1791 these had been reduced to two fairs and even they did not

last for long. Celia Fiennes praised its fine ring of bells and the brown 'nun's thread', produced here c.1690. Camel ('Cantmael', 995) seems to be derived from Camel Hill, a ridge to the north-west, the first syllable identical to that in the Quantocks: the whole meaning 'bare rim of hills'. Successive royal grants of lands in Camel were made in the 10th century by Edmund I, Edwy and Edgar but in 1066 the manor was held by Gytha (after whom the village primary school is named), mother of Harold who died at Hastings.

The manor was granted c.1202 by King John to Hubert de Burgh, later Earl of Kent, who gave the church to the monks of Cleeve Abbey. Subsequently the manor returned to the Crown and in 1275 was known as Camel Regis – King's Camel. Edward I gave it to Eleanor, his queen, and it gained its present name, Queen Camel: bestowed also on Queen Margaret in 1304. Retained by the Crown, it was finally granted away in 1558 to Sir Walter Mildmay, later Chancellor of the Exchequer and founder of Emmanuel College, Cambridge, whose family retained it until 1929.

The Mildmays, an Essex family, later lived at **Hazelgrove House**, a substantial seven-bay Tudor mansion to the north-east of the village which Carew Hervey Mildmay employed John and William Bastard of Blandford to remodel, 1730-35. A small village there, complete with village cross, shown on a map of 1573, may have been swept away in the 18th century, when an entrance gate of c.1690 from the Stawell house at Low Ham was set up near Sparkford and an extensive park created. The Mildmays sold the house in 1929 and it is now a prep school, although the old family name survives in the sign of the Mildmay Arms in the village. The spacious 14th century church of St Barnabus stands in the centre of the village where a stone marks the 1979 flood level. It has a fine panelled chancel arch, an unusual octagonal 15th century font, and a splendid rood screen and pulpit of c.1500. Chapels of SS Michael, Mary and John the Baptist occur in 15th century wills. The Mildmay memorials will be found at the east end of the south aisle, including that to Civil War cavalier, Humphrey Mildmay (died 1690). 'He sustain'd several wounds in the Warrs for his Loyalty to his Prince, King Charles the first, particularly at Newbury Fight where He served as a Major under his Uncle, the Earle of Cleavland, and was taken up among the slain'.

★★ *Village, church.*

ABOVE *Queen Camel.* BELOW *Raddington church*

RADDINGTON (D) At the southern limit of the Brendon Hills lies 'the settlement of Raeda's people', granted to Berthulf by King Alfred in 891. The former manor-house, now known as Washers Farm after a 17th century tenant, lies beside the stream at the foot of Raddington Bottom. The parish included a second Domesday estate centred on the present Chubworthy Farm, rebuilt in the 19th century, towards the eastern boundary with Chipstable. The small church of St Michael, accessible only by a stony path, lies a little north of Washers on a small eminence and is almost completely 14th century: happily over-looked by the Victorian restorer. The 13th century font survives from an earlier church and the chancel screen of c.1400 is topped by a plastered tympanum.

★★ *Church, setting.*

REDLYNCH (F) A chapelry (and parish from 1733) which lies to the south-east of Bruton and whose name ('Redlisc' in 1086) means 'reed marsh'. There was a medieval chapel here served by the monks of Bruton. In the 15th century the manor passed by marriage from the Draycots to the FitzJames family, who later lived here. Richard FitzJames (died 1542) became bishop successively of Rochester, Chichester and London, built the hall at Merton College, Oxford, and locally cofounded Bruton Grammar School. The estate and park were bought c.1670 by Sir Stephen Fox (died 1716), who built Redlynch House, and extended it in the 1740s, and his son, also Stephen (died 1776), lived here, becoming Lord Ilchester and Stavordale and Baron of Redlynch in 1747, and Earl of Ilchester in 1756. Here in

1750 he built the four-square chapel of St Peter to the designs of Nathaniel Ireson of Wincanton, its exterior looking more like a severe nonconformist chapel and replacing a medieval chapel of St Peter nearer the house. The east wing of Redlynch House was demolished in 1913 and the western portion was burned down in a suffragette demonstration in February 1914: rebuilt in 1915.

Immediately west of Redlynch is the hamlet of **Discove**, which was a Saxon manor held in 1066 by Tofig the sheriff, its name probably meaning 'Diccin's cleft' ('Digenescova' in 1086). The estate was bought by Sir Charles Berkeley in 1749 and later passed to the earls of Ilchester. Here novelist John Steinbeck found a rural retreat while working on his own version of the saga of King Arthur.

RIMPTON (K) This 'settlement on the border', north-east from Yeovil on the Dorset boundary, is a mix of thatched cottages and modern development. The estate was granted in 938 by King Athelstan to Ethaered, evidently only for his life, and in 953 to Brihtric Grim by King Eadred. Brihtric left it in his will to the Old Minster at Winchester and the bishops of Winchester held it as lords of the manor for over nine centuries until 1822, which is why the place was administered with the bishops' distant manor of Taunton Deane. Rimpton was used by the bishops as a staging post on journeys between Winchester and their principal manor of Taunton Deane, and their records provide a detailed picture of this rural manor from the early 13th century. The tenants carried the lord's corn to the markets at Ilchester, Yeovil, Castle Cary and Sherborne, bore his letters to Taunton and cultivated vines, flax, peas, beans, onions, leeks, apples and pears. In return, at Christmas the bishop provided an annual Christmas feast with meat, wheat, cheese and malt for beer. In 1498 seven wagon loads of 'bryks' were bought from Taunton: the earliest known record of their use in Somerset. Later the local blue lias stone was quarried on Rimpton Hill but mainly for road-mending rather than building. The church of St Mary is beautifully situated towards the end of Church Lane at the eastern edge of the village. It has a late 13th century chancel but the rest is Perpendicular and can be ascribed to Richard Fox, bishop of Winchester 1501-28, whose pelican badge is carved on an external parapet. The Tudor benchends were formerly at Corton Denham and the pulpit is c.1630-40. In the south chapel are monuments to the Andrews, later Genge-Andrews, family, leaders of the community in the 18th and 19th centuries. They lived at Rimpton House on the western side of the village, a building dating from the 17th century but much remodelled. The delightful Rimpton Manor, formerly Court Farm, is visible from Church Lane.

★★ *Church and its vicinity.*

ROADWATER (D) *see* **OLD CLEEVE**

RODDEN (F) A small parish, 'the roe deer valley', immediately east of Frome. The manor was bought in the 16th century by the Horners of Mells from whom it passed by marriage to the A'Court clothiers of Frome, who lived at Rodden until the 18th century and were created baronets in 1795 and barons Heytesbury in 1828. The church of Rodden of unknown dedication was made a chapelry of Boyton, Wilts, in 1289 and so continued until 1784. It was then endowed by the Rev John Methuen Rogers of Berkley, whose wife had bought the manor from the A'Courts. The present church lies in the farmyard of the former manor-house: a rebuilding of c.1640 in Perpendicular style by the then rector of Boyton, with fine views to the east. To the south-east are Grandon and Flintford farms, both mentioned in the 13th century.

★★ *Setting.*

RODE (B) This sizeable village north-east from Frome, was formerly known for its cloth manufacture and still has an industrial feel to its streets, although mellowed by time. Its name, usually spelt 'Road' until officially changed to its modern form in 1919, means 'a clearing', probably within the great forest of Selwood when it was originally settled. Held by 7 Saxon thegns before the Norman Conquest, thereafter it became a single estate which, like so many other properties in the area, passed to the St Maur (Seymour) family at the beginning of the 13th century. In 1283 Lawrence de St Maur was granted a Thursday market and a three-day fair here, the latter, often known as Rode Revel, continuing until the 19th century. Indeed, there was formerly a local couplet which ran:

'Rode Revel, Beckington Rout,

  The Devil's in Frome and cannot get out.'

The manor descended like Castle Cary from the St Maurs to the Zouches, but later was divided between coheiresses. The property known as Northfield House and later as Rode Manor at the western

Rode, stables

approach to the village was built by a Bristol merchant, Edward Andrews, who bought the estate in 1737. Subsequently held by the Pooll and Batten-Pooll families, the house was sold in 1954 and largely demolished. The grounds, however, were opened as **Tropical Bird Gardens** (fee:lists) by Donald and Betty Risdon in 1962, and provide 17 acres of ornamental trees and shrubs, a chain of lakes, and over 1,200 exotic birds of 240 different species. There is a cafeteria, pets' corner and, since 1988, a narrow gauge woodland steam railway. Nearby, at the bridge, are attractive early Georgian stables and an elaborate summer house. Rode also formerly boasted two chalybeate springs, complete with a pump room, and in 1746 Benjamin Edwards was advertising Rode mineral water in Bath.

There were several mills here in 1086, powered by the River Frome, and one called 'Scuttysmyll', evidently at Scutts Bridge, was held by a Beckington clothier in 1535. The manufacture of cloth reached its height in the 18th and early 19th centuries. A fire in the workhouses of Thomas Whittaker, clothier and dyer, threw hundreds out of work in 1764. Wheelers of Rode were even supplying fulling stocks to Yorkshire mills in 1793 and Rocabella Mill (closed c.1904) at Scutts Bridge is credited with devising the colour Royal blue for George III.

The church of St Laurence stands at the south-eastern end of the village and is mainly Perpendicular with a 14th century south doorway, although all heavily restored in 1874. Wills record a chapel of St Etheldreda in 1405 and an image of the patron saint in 1485. A copy of an intriguing painting is exhibited showing the old ceremony of 'clipping' the church, when on every Shrove Tuesday the parishioners linked hands and danced around the building, ending with a great

shout to drive away the Devil for the ensuing year. Is there a link with the name of a long barrow to the east of the church, known locally as the Devil's Bed and Bolster ? At Rode Hill on the north side of the village (formerly part of North Bradley in Wilts) the incredibly turreted Christ Church was built in 1824 to the design of H.E. Goodridge, Archdeacon Daubeney of Salisbury providing a third of the cost and most of the enthusiasm. Rode has a strong nonconformist tradition and was regularly visited by John Wesley.

Rode Hill House, later known as Langham House, was the scene of a notorious and apparently motiveless murder in 1860, when 16-year-old Constance Kent slit the throat of her 3-year-old half-brother and stuffed his body down the outside privy. The murder went unsolved until Constance confessed in 1865, her death sentence was commuted to life and she later emigrated to Australia under an assumed name, becoming matron of a nurses' hostel and dying at the age of 100 in 1944.

★★★ *Tropical Bird Gardens*, ★★ *village.*

RODNEY STOKE (A/E) An attractively-situated village midway between Cheddar and Wells below Stoke Woods (a Nature Reserve managed by the Nature Conservancy Council) on the southern slope of the Mendip Hills. Originally called simply Stoke ('place' or 'dairy farm') it adopted the names of those families which owned the manor, being known successively as Stoke Whiting, Stoke Giffard and Stoke Rodney. Remains of a Roman settlement and an urn containing coins were found on the moor below the village in 1927. By 1086 the manor was held under the bishop of Coutances by Roger Whiting ('Witen'), whose descendant, also Roger, was succeeded before 1196 by his son, Giffard Whiting. By the early 14th century the

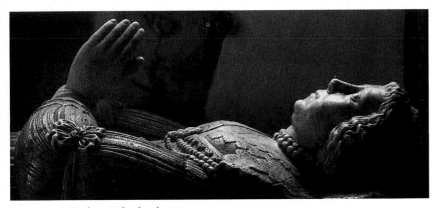

Monument in Rodney Stoke church

The Blackbrook Inn, near Ruishton

estate had passed to Sir Richard Rodney and it continued in his family until the death of Sir Edward Rodney in 1657. Sir Edward, a staunch and active royalist during the Civil War, experienced the death of his only surviving son and heir, aged 22 and unmarried, commenting in a touching memoir 'when I dye there wilbe an end of my family and the fortunes of my house'. Rodney Stoke passed to his daughter Anna, wife of Sir Thomas Brydges of Keynsham, from whom it descended to the Duke of Chandos. Member of a junior branch of the Rodney family, Admiral George Brydges Rodney, victor over the French at the Battle of the Saints, took the title Baron Rodney of Rodney Stoke in 1782, although he never lived here or owned land in the parish. North of the church there is a fine three-storey Georgian farmhouse. The only remnant of the former Rodney home is a gatehouse, which may have been an Elizabethan summer-house.

The parish church of St Leonard (St Bernard c.1200) lies down Stoke Street, facing out over the moors. It was evidently a chapelry to Westbury-sub-Mendip until 1159 but was given to Bath Priory before 1196 by Roger Whiting and transferred to the bishop in 1214. Dating mainly from the 15th century, the building contains a Jacobean screen (1625), altar (1634), conical font-cover and pulpit, with a south chapel added in 1879. The church's glory is the small north chapel, crammed with the monuments and heraldry of the Rodneys: Sir Thomas (died 1478) is depicted in his armour, Sir John (died 1526), Anne (died 1630), widow of George Rodney, the young George Rodney (died 1651), shown wrapped in his shroud and rising from his coffin, and Sir Edward (died 1657) and Lady Frances (died 1659), with their busts under a canopy.

★★★ *Village setting, church, for its memorials.*

ROWBERROW (A) This isolated settlement on top of the Mendips, well merits its name, meaning 'rough hill'. With Shipham it was until the 19th century one of the principal sources of calamine ore for the Bristol brass industry, as well as lead. The smoke from the smelting, mainly in Rowberrow Bottom, was said to have killed off all trees in the vicinity of the village. There is a squareish inclosure, possibly Roman, at the south-western end of Rowberrow Warren. By the 13th century the manor was held by St Augustine's Abbey, Bristol, passing after its dissolution to the new Bristol Cathedral. Latterly the estate was held by the Leacroft family, who are buried at the east end of the small churchyard. The church of St Michael stands to the north of the village. There is a Perpendicular west tower but the body of the church was rebuilt in 1865, incorporating a fragment of a Saxon cross discovered during the reconstruction. A burial mound south of the church yielded a dagger, cinerary urns and two burials, when opened in 1813.

RUISHTON (H) The 'settlement where rushes grow' lies near Taunton to the north-east of the A358. It is now a dormitory village for the county town and has rapidly expanded during the present century. Its tithings of Ruishton and Henlade formed part of the manor of Taunton Deane from the 9th century. The church of St George lies at the northern edge of the village close to the River Tone in Drakes Close. It was served by the canons of Taunton Priory: from 1308 with resident priests. Apart from a Norman column and capital by the south door, the building is mainly 14th-15th century with an unfinished but ornate west tower of the 16th. The octagonal richly-carved font is c.1380 and the south chapel features a host of monuments to the Proctors and their

descendants the Anderdons. In the early 19th century the latter built Henlade House, a fine mansion which, after a sensitive restoration, is now a country house hotel: the Mount Somerset. To the south of the A358 Ruishton House was built by Stuart Somerville in 1893 while to the north, set picturesquely back from the road, lies Woodlands House of c.1810, enlarged by architect Richard Carver c.1833. The Blackbrook Inn on the main road was the meeting place for the Blackbrook Corporation 1769-88, possibly a nonconformist rival to Taunton Borough, which elected its own mayor and officers but which ultimately became a drinking, dining and skittling club.

★★ *Church.*

RUNNINGTON (H) A small parish on the River Tone, almost lost in leafy lanes north-west from Wellington, whose name means either 'Runa's' or 'the councillor's settlement'. After the Conquest the estate passed into the hands of William de Mohun of Dunster, under whom it was held in 1166 by William of Elworthy. His successor, Gilbert of Elworthy, gave the church to Taunton Priory, which retained it until the dissolution. The small church of St Peter has a 15th century tower and nave, although the building was reroofed and chancel rebuilt c.1840. Runnington House, built in the early 19th century, served as the rectory until its sale in 1933.

ST AUDRIES (D) *see* **WEST QUANTOXHEAD**

ST DECUMANS (D) *see* **WATCHET** *and* **WILLITON**

ST MICHAELCHURCH (D/E) At 46 acres, once the smallest parish in the county, it is entirely surrounded by North Petherton, of which it has formed a part

ABOVE *The heart-in-hand monument, Sampford Arundel.*
BELOW *Seavington St Mary*

since 1933. In the 12th century the land of Maunsel here was given by William de Erlegh to Philip the Crossbowman, who had married William's daughter Mabel, for a token rent of two piglets. Philip's descendants took Maunsel as their surname and made their home here until 1631, building the hall of **Maunsel House** (fee:lists) c.1500. Since extended at various dates, this is now an impressive if confusing pile, attractively located near the Bridgwater to Taunton Canal. It was held by the Bacon family from Broomfield 1648-1726, and was bought in 1772 by John Slade, whose son, Gen Sir John Slade, a hero of the Peninsular War, received a baronetcy and added to the property 1827-8. The mansion is now held by the 7th baronet, Sir Benjamin Slade. Current claims that the

building is partly Saxon and that Geoffrey Chaucer 'was a frequent visitor and guest' and 'wrote part of *The Canterbury Tales* whilst staying at the house' have no basis in fact.

The church of St Michael, which named the parish and was of Saxon foundation, lies at the end of a farm track: the church-yard full of Slade tombs between the yews. The small church dates from the 15th century but was over-restored and extended in 1868 by the Slades, whose monuments also dominate the interior.
★★ *Maunsel House and setting.*

SAMPFORD ARUNDEL (H) Immediately west from Wellington, this settlement by a 'sandy ford' marks the western end of the Blackdown Hills at Sampford Point. The manor had been granted by 1086 to Roger Arundel, whose family name was added to that of the village to distinguish it from Sampford Brett. In 1225 Nicholas Arundel was pursued by his tenants here, denied sanctuary at the church and murdered: the body being placed in the manor-house, to which they then set fire, presumably to destroy the evidence. The corpse was carried off by the prior of Canonsleigh (Devon) and at least 14 of the tenants were later hanged.

The main village lies between the railway and the M5, reached through typical sunken lanes, centred on the parish church and the village school, opened in 1880. The church of the Holy Cross was given by the Arundels to Canonsleigh Priory which retained it until its dissolution.

The church has a slender 13th century west tower but the rest was rebuilt in 1867. In a recess in the north aisle a pair of sculpted hands holding a heart may mark a medieval heart burial. There is a substantial monument to Christopher Baker (died 1729), who bought the manor from Lady North of Dillington and whose grandson sold it in 1800 to Ellis Were, whose family lived at Werescote. Other monuments commemorate the Belletts of Easterlands, the Morgans and Sweets.

To the north-east of the village the Beam Bridge was an inn formerly known as the New Inn (c.1770) and the Royal Marine (1813), adopting its present name from 1832 after a nearby County bridge, rebuilt in 1754. Here was the railhead for the Bristol and Exeter Railway, 1843-4, until White Ball tunnel was cut. A newly-built windmill here was mentioned in 1798.
★★ *Setting.*

SAMPFORD BRETT (D) Just south-east of Williton, it takes its name from a 'sandy ford'. The parish includes the Domesday manor of Torweston which with Sampford manor was held by the Brett family from the 12th century until sold to the Courtenays in 1359. Indeed, Adam Brett, who procured a fair and a Monday market at Sampford in 1306, evidently intended to build a castle at Torweston in 1316, probably never completed. Their 19th century successors, the Acland-Hoods, widened the village street to provide an uninterrupted view of the church from their estate cottages. Much of the church of St George was rebuilt 1835-43, although the north transept of c.1300 and the 15th century west tower survive. The effigy of a knight in the vestry probably commemorates Sir William Brett (died c.1295) and not, as Arthur Mee and others have thought, Richard le Brett, one of the four murderers of St Thomas Becket in 1170 and a younger son of the Sampford family. It was he who broke his sword in striking the final fatal blow in Canterbury Cathedral, and his daughter, son-in-law and granddaughter all gave lands to Worspring Priory (dedicated to St Thomas) in Kewstoke to expiate Richard's part in the crime.
★★ *Village.*

SEAVINGTON ST MARY (J) A village to the east of Ilminster which, with its neighbour, Seavington St Michael, takes its name from the 'seven settlements' that originally lay within their boundaries. The manor was held by Alice Vaux c.1200 and consequently known as Seavington Vaux, passing in 1680 to the Welmans of Poundisford (Pitminster) and to the Vaughan Lees of Dillington in 1876. A windmill at Seavington, the earliest known in Somerset, was given by Robert Vaux to Montacute Priory c.1212. A second estate, known as Hurcott and Seavington Abbot, was given by King Canute to Athelney Abbey c.1030 and in 1699 also acquired by the Welmans. The church of St Mary formerly lay isolated to the north of the village, probably beside the vanished manor-house, until the present line of the A 303 was laid out in 1829. It was held as a chapelry of South Petherton church by Bruton Priory and, after 1539 by the chapter of Bristol Cathedral. The present building, redundant since 1983, dates from the 13th century, with an added porch and west tower of c.1500. There is a 12th century font and a memorial to Midshipman Arthur Hood Rowsell, who

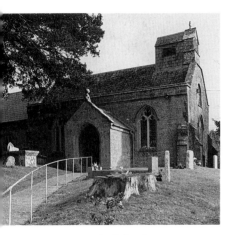

Seavington St Michael church

Thatched cottage, Selworthy

Selworthy church

died in 1824, 'a victim to his exertions', when he and his shipmates were attacked by the Ashanti on a remote African shore. Today the village is visited mainly for the Pheasant, a restaurant with an excellent reputation, converted from West Street Farm in 1971.

★ *Village and church.*

SEAVINGTON ST MICHAEL (J) This
parish was distinguished from its neighbour, Seavington St Mary (*see above*) by the addition of its church's dedication. The village is centred on the Volunteer Inn (so named by 1833), lining the A 303 east of Ilminster. Its older buildings date from the 17th century, notably Orchard Close (1689), Buckrells and Swan Thatch (the former village bakery and later post office). The manor, held by Siward the falconer in 1086, had passed by 1252 to Adam the Dane, from whom it was known as Seavington Dennis. Later owners included Glastonbury Abbey (1483-1539) and Winchester College (1551-1932). The small church of St Michael lies towards the end of a short lane at the southern edge of the village. The nave is mainly 12th century with an added chancel of the 13th. A civilian effigy of c.1290 in the chancel may represent a member of Adam the Dane's family and two 14th century corbel heads in the nave, the man with his tongue out, were formerly supports for a lost rood screen.

★★ *Village.*

SELWORTHY (C) North of the Minehead
to Porlock road (A 39) lies a favourite destination for visitors which is fortunately largely uncommercialised. The village, whose name may mean 'the homestead by the sallow copse', is not large but is a feast of thatched cottages and lush gardens.

There are large car parks beyond the village, tea rooms and an excellent National Trust shop at the edge of Selworthy Green. Those cottages around the Green were largely put up in 1828 for retired retainers by Sir Thomas Dyke Acland, who was also responsible for much of the woodland planting in the area. Selworthy forms the focus of the Holnicote (pronounced 'Honeycut') estate, over 12,000 acres, given to the National Trust in 1944 by the late Sir Richard Acland. It comprises almost all the parishes of Selworthy, Luccombe and Stoke Pero with parts of Porlock and Minehead, and encompasses marvellous walking country, particularly north of Selworthy village to the sea: crossed by the Somerset and North Devon Path. Holnicote itself, now a holiday hotel, was used as a retreat by the Aclands from their principal home at Killerton in Devon, and as a residence for junior branches of the family, although showing a distressing tendency to burn down (in 1779, 1851 and 1941). Bury Castle is a square Iron Age hillfort north-west of the village.

Selworthy itself was held before the Conquest by Edith, queen of Edward the Confessor, but after Hastings was given, together with nearby Allerford and Bossington, to Ralph de Limesi. Thereafter it descended like the manor of Luccombe until inherited by the Aclands in 1802. Bossington had been granted in Saxon times to Athelney Abbey, probably by King Alfred, and was in due course returned to the monks. It had its own 16th century chapel at Lynch, restored by the Aclands in 1885. Later lords included the Dykes from 1733 and their heirs, the Aclands, from 1745. Land at Holnicote was given by William the Conqueror to Edith, a woman whose husband was killed in his

service and was possibly one of two nuns there in 1086. Her successor in 1212 held it in return for praying for the king. Walter Barun (died 1306) had a smallholding here by the unusual service of hanging up any deer that died of the murrain on a forked piece of wood and of entertaining 'such poor decrepid persons as came to him'. In the east of the parish the manor of Blackford and Tivington was held by Montacute Priory, also passing to the Aclands in 1776. The 15th century thatched chapel of St Leonard at Tivington was restored by the Aclands in 1896: its bell believed to come from their yacht.

The whitewashed parish church of All Saints looks down over Selworthy village. It has a 14th century west tower and inside has a height emphasised by the slender four-bay arcades: all Perpendicular and magnificent. Its chief delight is the Holnicote south aisle, dated 1538 on a capital, which might suggest that it was put up by Philip Steyning of Holnicote (died 1589) a year after he inherited the manor. His brass, which records his nine sons and five daughters, is the oldest of several to the family, including one of 1634 to a child:

'This graves a cradle where an infant lyes,
Rockt fast a sleepe with deathes sad lullabyes.'

There are larger and more lavish monuments to later owners of Holnicote: Charles Steynings (died 1700), William Blackford (died 1731) and junior members of the Acland family. The aisle itself has a superbly delicate waggon roof with finely carved angels and bosses, and over the porch 'a delicious Gothic pavilion' (Pevsner), converted by the Aclands into a family pew. There is a heavily classical west gallery, dated 1750, which now houses the organ, a 16th century pulpit with sounding board and hour glass, and a balustered communion rail of c.1700. In the chancel is a brass to rector William Fleet (died 1618) bearing a very human record in verse of his ministry in 'this place of worth and fame' with its 'wholsome aire and soile'. Below the church is the converted 13th century tithe barn with one hood mould over a blocked window bearing a lamb, pig and wheatsheaf: emblems of the local produce rendered to the church.

Allerford ('alder ford'), west from Selworthy village, is a wonderfully attractive hamlet and its bridge, Packhorse Inn and cottage (with generously-proportioned chimney) form one of the most photographed views in the county. The former village school, established in 1822, now houses an appealing small **museum** (fee:lists) with antique tools, photographic exhibition, craft demonstrations and a recreated Victorian schoolroom with children's costumes for dressing up.

Bossington, the delightful 'settlement of Bosa's people', lies north-west of Allerford, centred on a green fringed with walnut and willow trees, where the Horner stream runs into the sea. The Sydenham family held the manor by 1472 until 1694 and they must have built the picturesque small chapel c.1520, near their manor-house at Lynch.

★★★★ *Selworthy village and setting,*
★★★ *Selworthy church, villages of Allerford and Bossington.*

SHAPWICK (E) A charming village of attractive low houses and the occasional grand one, mainly built of the local lias stone. Its name means 'sheep farm' and recent research suggests that Shapwick

may have formed the head of the Pouholt (Polden) estate acquired by Glastonbury Abbey in 729: an estate dependant on the grazing of livestock along the lower slopes and northwards onto the moors. This economy seems to have been replaced by one more reliant on open arable fields in strips, possibly from the 10th century. At a similar period Shapwick's village may have been laid out by the abbey on a grid-iron plan between the two arable fields and on either side of the north-south road. A painstaking examination of the parish's development, the Shapwick Project, has been proceeding since 1988.

After the dissolution of Glastonbury Abbey, the manor passed to Thomas Walton and then to the Rolle family. In 1630 Sir Henry Rolle (died 1656), Lord Chief Justice during the early years of the Commonwealth, remodelled an existing 15th century building, Shapwick House, at the north-western end of the village. Now a hotel, it was altered during the 18th century and gained a clock tower in 1865. In the grounds are an octagonal dovecote and icehouse. Shapwick Manor, to the north of the church represents the rectorial manor-house and also boasts a dovecote. The property is medieval but was remodelled for the Bull family in the early 17th century. The Bulls claimed descent from the original (Dr) John Bull, hailed by some as the composer of our National Anthem, and barrister Henry Bull, MP for Somerset, lived in the house. It descended by marriage to the Strangways family and was sold in 1944 to Lord Vesty, whose family still owns much of the parish, including the estate once attached to

Shapwick House. A windmill here blew down in 1836, injuring the miller and killing his brother.

The original church of St Andrew, probably on a Saxon site, formerly lay to the east of the present village near Beerway Farm. The new church of St Mary, petitioned for by the abbot of Glastonbury in 1329 and consecrated in 1331, stands at the centre of the village, framed by large cedars, and is a mixture of Decorated and Perpendicular with a central tower. It features stylish memorials to the Bull and Strangways families and one to William Cator of the East India Company. While *en route* to Calcutta on board the *Kent*, he 'was slain by a musket ball from a French privateer of 36 guns on 7th October 1800 in the bay of Bengal while gallantly defending the ship against the boarding of the enemy'. A twin monument commemorates Thomas Graham, nephew of George Templer (whose family bought out the Rolles), who died in the same action. The Templers are also recalled by a large hatchment on the south wall of the nave, which displays their arms. The altar rail of Australian oak was given in 1861 by Henry Bull Templer Strangways, later Premier of Australia, and the same family installed the fine, if unusual, wrought-iron screen behind the altar. The large grassy mound in the churchyard hides the Strangways family vault. Loxley Wood, south-west from the village, preserves the name of the Domesday hundred of Locheslega: later combined with Ringoldeswey (in Butleigh) to form Whitley hundred. Shapwick Heath National Nature Reserve is sited along Shapwick Road.

★★★ *Village,* ★★ *church.*

LEFT *The Packhorse bridge, Allerford*
BELOW *Shapwick*

SHEPTON BEAUCHAMP (J) This picturesque Ham-stone village north-east from Ilminster, has a Saxon name, 'sheep settlement', to which was added that of the Beachamp (pronounced 'Beecham') family who held the manor with the barony of Hatch Beauchamp from the mid 12th century until the death of John de Beauchamp in 1361. Thence it descended to the Seymours who had their manor-house to the south-west of the village, with a chapel licensed by Roger and Maud Seymour in 1408. It is recorded that Sir John Seymour lived there when sheriff of Somerset, 1515-16, possibly accompanied by his young daughter Jane, later third queen of Henry VIII. Mountfields House, a plain classical building with Tuscan porch, was built soon after 1840, just to the south of the old manor-house, which was demolished. All that remains is a small 16th century barn in which medieval window tracery, dug up in the churchyard, was inserted in 1964. There was also a much smaller estate, known in the 16th century as the manor of Shepton Poulett after its owners.

The village largely lines a single street which takes an S-shaped course through the parish. Further early expansion, inhibited by the surrounding open arable fields (mostly enclosed in 1807), was limited to Love Lane and to a hamlet called Wash Cross on the eastern boundary of the parish. In 1340 the mowing and stacking of hay was supervised by a free tenant wearing white gloves and carrying a white rod. The Tudor House, opposite the church, has a datestone of 1752 although built in the 17th century. The former New Inn, on the corner of Buttle Lane and Church Street, closed c.1960 but its Fives wall, with carved parapet and ball finial, survives behind it. In 1260 Robert de Beauchamp secured a grant of a Friday market and two fairs here, probably held at the junction of North and Church streets, a site still known as the Shambles although neither market nor fairs have been held there for some 450 years. An appealing charity was founded by Mr F. Robins in 1934 to provide sweets for the village children on their birthdays and prizes for the Shrove Tuesday egg-shackling, which still continues annually. Each child contributes a marked egg and all are shaken in a sieve, the last remaining uncracked being the winner.

The Ham-stone and lias church of St Michael, probably dates from the late 13th century and formerly had a north tower. This was replaced (or possibly supplemented) by an early 16th century richly-ornamented west tower with fine fan-vaulting and a panelled tower arch. North and south aisles were added in the 14th century and the chancel is of similar date. A fundamental restoration of 1865 included the rebuilding of the south aisle, the replacement of all roofs except that of the north aisle and the renewing of the clerestory. In 1872 the Rev Vincent S.S. Coles (died 1929) succeeded his father as rector. He was a leader of the Tractarian movement and later became librarian and principal of Pusey Hall, Oxford. He was responsible for suppressing the 'Old Shepton Play' at Easter, the celebration of Old Christmas Day and a fife and drum band. In 1874 he built a new rectory house (now Beauchamp Manor) to serve as a retreat for visiting clergy and students and introduced daily Evensong, weekly Communion, confessions and vestments. The former rectory, St Michael's, survives on the north side of North Street and dates from the 16th century. Coles's high-church practices continued under his successor as rector, Arthur Lethbridge, who in 1904 reported the presence at one of his services of 'a Protestant spy', from the Royal Commission on Disorders in the Church. ★★★ *Village,* ★★ *church.*

SHEPTON MALLET (F) An industrial town in the east of the county whose name, meaning 'sheep settlement', recalls the days up to the 18th century when wool from the backs of the Mendip flocks provided the raw material for a flourishing cloth industry. As at Yeovil, there have been too many demolitions this century in homage to the motor-car, which have left an interesting but not over-attractive town. Iron-Age pottery has been found at Shepton and the Roman Foss Way runs through Charlton to the east. Part of a significant Roman town, comprising stone buildings, walled enclosures and four small cemeteries, probably Christian, was excavated at Charlton in 1990. This settlement, occupied from the early 2nd century AD until c.400, lay beside the Foss almost midway between Camerton to the north-east and Ilchester to the south-west. In addition Roman pottery kilns were found in 1864 on the site of the Anglo-Bavarian brewery to the west of the town. Following the Saxon conquest, the whole of Shepton west of the Foss (i.e. except Charlton) was included in a grant of 702 by King Ine of the West Saxons to Glastonbury Abbey, and a 15th century tradition claimed that the Glastonbury martyr, St

Market Cross, Shepton Mallet

Indract (died c.700), and his companions were buried here. By 1086 the estate was held under the abbey by Roger de Courcelles but passed by the early 12th century to Robert Malet, whose family added their name to that of the manor and retained it until the death c.1216 of William Malet. Later it was divided between the Malet heiresses One half was long held by the lords de la Warre and the other became part of the Duchy of Cornwall. Hugh de Vivonia, William Malet's son-in-law, was granted a Thursday market (which the bishop complained would damage his market at Wells) and three-day fair in 1235, succeeded by a Monday market and fair obtained by his granddaughter, Cecily de Beauchamp, in 1318.

Although it became a town, Shepton never secured borough status and was governed by its manorial officers until the Local Board of Health was established in 1875, succeeded by its Urban District Council in 1894. Medieval settlement was centred on the Market Place with its covered Market Cross, for the building of which Walter Buckland left £20 in 1500. The central column was rebuilt in 1841 after collapsing, although the surrounding pillars and arches may date from the original building (Pevsner prefers c.1700).

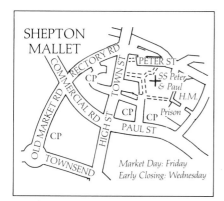

SHEPTON MALLET

Market Day: Friday
Early Closing: Wednesday

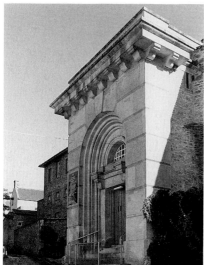

LEFT *Prison gateway, Shepton Mallet*
BELOW *The nave roof, Shepton Mallet church*

Also here ran two lines of 15th century covered market standings, the Shambles, the survivor of which was demolished in 1919, although a section was replaced on the east side of the Market Place. The area was transformed 1973-75 thanks to the generosity of Francis Showering, the works including the Amulet (a 272-seat combined theatre, cinema and hall), a new library, accommodated in the rebuilt Bunch of Grapes Inn, offices, shops and housing, and at the same time the area was paved and pedestrianised.

To the east of the Market Place, set in a slightly down-at-heel mini-cathedral close, is the majestic **Church of SS Peter and Paul** with its late 14th century west tower. An intended spire was never completed and the tower is topped with a small pyramid roof. The nave has traces of long-and-short work, suggesting that it preserves the dimensions of a simple rectangular Saxon church. The nave was pierced and arcades added in the late 12th century, when the former north and south aisles were built. The chancel followed in the early 13th century, furnished with its double piscina c.1235. The glory of the church is the nave roof with its 350 panels and 300 bosses, which Pevsner considered to be 'the most glorious of all the wagon-

roofs of England'. It was evidently put up in the early 16th century after the nave clerestory was added. There was an altar to the Virgin Mary (1520) and guilds or fraternities of the Holy Trinity and St John the Baptist (1548). The present aisles were built in 1837 and most of the chancel in 1847. Furnishings include a fine high Perpendicular stone pulpit, two unidentified effigies of knights (c.1240) at either end of the north aisle, four heraldic hatchments and a good collection of 17th and 18th century brasses, several commemorating the Barnards of Downside and the Strodes.

South of the church are the almshouses for four poor men founded by Edward Strode in 1699 and to the north the Rectory was built after 1626, also by the Strodes, to house the town's grammar school (and five shortlived almshouses for widows on the ground floor). The school had a chequered career, including the imprisonment of one headmaster in 1796, before being relocated in 1900. East from the parish church behind high grey stone walls stands **HM Shepton Mallet Prison**, claimed to be the oldest working prison in England still on its original site, first built here as a house of correction in 1625-6. It was largely rebuilt 1817-22, a chapel was added in 1849 and it suffered a severe fire in 1904. During World War Two it was occupied by the Americans as a military prison and the women's wing housed records from the Public Record Office in London, including the Domesday Book, Magna Carta and the logbook of HMS *Victory*. Other notable buildings include Sales House in Draycott Road, a forbidding Georgian group occupied as a Catholic convent 1810-30, and the Unitarian Chapel in Cowl Street, built 1696 but remodelled in 1785.

The original line of Town Street was extended to the north across the valley of the river Sheppey with the building of Waterloo Street and Bridge in 1832. Industrial development took place east and west, up and down the Sheppey valley, to harness the available water power. There are few physical remains of the former cloth industry apart from two substantial clothiers' properties at Bowlish to the west of the town: Old Bowlish House, dating from c.1650 but remodelled in Georgian style, and Bowlish House, dated 1732. Jardine's Factory (rebuilt in 1852 after a fire) in Kilver Street produced lace and, west of Bowlish at Darshill, there was a silk mill (closed 1913, demolished 1974) but the mill pond and workers' cottages remain to form an attractive group. Following the decline of the textile industry, breweries bridged the employment gap. Charlton Brewery was operated by the Berryman family from 1844 in a former woollen mill, and in the 1860s the ornate mass which became the Anglo-Bavarian Brewery rose to command the west of the town. More recently Showerings has grown to dominate the town's economy and made 'Babycham' a household word. A major crossroads to the south-east of the town has long been known as Cannard's Grave, probably from the burial there of a suicide or an executed criminal who has never been satisfactorily identified.

In the Civil War Shepton was almost solidly for the Parliamentary cause. Immediately before hostilities commenced in 1642 there was an altercation in the Market Place between the Cavalier leader, Sir Ralph Hopton, and the local Roundhead colonel, William Strode, before the royalists were forced to withdraw. In 1645 towards the end of the conflict Sir Thomas Fairfax led his New Model Army through the town to take Bristol. In the Monmouth Rebellion of 1685 the rebels were billeted at Shepton before their abortive march on Bristol and again on their return before final defeat at Sedgemoor. The Duke himself was traditionally lodged at Monmouth House, demolished in 1964, and after the battle he sought refuge with Edward Strode at Downside, just north of the town. Only eight Sheptonians are known to have joined the rebel forces, of whom six escaped and two were transported to the West Indies. Eleven others, however, were hanged, drawn and quartered in the Market Place.

★★★ *Church, particularly for its roof, industrial archaeology.*

SHEPTON MONTAGUE (F) This 'sheep settlement' to the east of Castle Cary was held in 1086 under the count of Mortain by Drew (Drogo) de Montagu and was retained by his descendants, earls of Salisbury from 1337, until their attainder in 1421, latterly passing in 1765 to the Phelips family of Montacute. With Shepton in 1086 were held the manors of Knowle and Stoney Stoke to the east, both of which were later acquired by the Fox-Strangways, earls of Ilchester. During the Civil War a Puritan clergyman was killed here by Cavaliers in 1647 and a local man was shot dead by Roundheads on his doorstep in 1649. The hillside church of St Peter was gutted by fire in 1964, which destroyed an 'extremely pretty' 18th cen-

tury gallery and 13th century font. A striking restoration, completed in 1966, did not rebuild the ruined chancel. HM the Queen contributed the royal arms above the south door to replace a 1672 hatchment that was destroyed. An inscription over the outer door, 'Port Seynt Thomas', may indicate the original dedication. Lord Rees-Mogg's ancestors, the family of Mogg *alias* Keene, hailed from Shepton and floor slabs in the nave represent some of their 17th century members. Earthworks in a field south-west from the church, may represent the site of the medieval manor-house of the Montagues.

★ *Imaginatively-restored church.*

SHIPHAM (A) A remote 'sheep farm' or 'enclosure' high up on the Mendip Hills. A site to the north of the hamlet of Star (named from an isolated inn) has revealed probable evidence of Mesolithic settlement and a Roman villa, occupied until c.355 AD. The manor was held in 1086 by Robert de Odburville under Roger de Courcelles, passing by the 13th century to the Malherbie family and in the early 14th to the Clevedons. William Malherbie in 1309 obtained a Monday market and three-day fair here. A Clevedon descendant, Lady Margaret Hungerford, sold the manor to Bishop Thomas Bekyngton to ransom her son, captured in France, and in 1478 it passed into the hands of the dean and chapter of Wells, with whom it remained. Mendip was known for its lead mines, but at Shipham the product was calamine ore to produce zinc, used in the Bristol brass industry. A licence to work the mines. grooves and pits of 'calamyntstone' on the commons here was granted in 1598. Most of the early digging was surface mining, which accounts for the uneven ground over much of the parish. By 1791 there were more than 100 mines in operation, 'many of which are in the street, in the yards, and some in the very houses'. Almost all the community were involved in the industry, Cornish miners were introduced and the place developed a widespread reputation for lawlessness. Extraction declined in the early 19th century and had ceased by 1853, although searches for new deposits continued until c.1870. Fear of contamination of the soil due to centuries of mining activity led to scares in the 1970s over the consumption of locally-grown produce.

Most of the houses in the village date from the 19th century and the church of St Leonard was rebuilt 1842-3 to the design

of James Wilson. It includes a memorial window to Hannah More (1745-1833), the zealous reformer, who established Sunday and day schools here in 1790, having found the people 'savage and depraved . . . brutal in their natures and ferocious in their manners'. There is also a monument to the Rev James Jones (died 1825), a great influence on Hannah's work and for whom she composed a verse epitaph.

SIMONSBATH (C) The most westerly village in the county, set in a remote cleft in the heart of Exmoor and a mecca for walkers. The name was first recorded by John Leland on his tour of 1542, when he referred to a wooden bridge here, although the identity of 'Simon', has never been resolved. A pack of hounds is said to have been kept here in 1598 but there was no settlement or building until the lease of the moor was bought in 1653 from Sir Hugh Pollard by James Boevey, a London merchant of Dutch descent. Within a year Boevey had built Simonsbath House ('1654' was inscribed on a beam), enclosed some 100 acres from the waste and set up a pound here. Although Boevey lived here for a time, the house was later leased as a farm, in the 18th century stallions were stabled here and the forest court began to meet, and in 1789 the building was licensed as an inn. Following the enclosure of Exmoor forest in 1815 and its purchase in 1818 by John Knight (1766-1850), he built and developed the village of Simonsbath in the local grey stone, moving into Boevey's house c.1830 and handing over in 1841 to his son Frederic, who himself lived here from 1860.

The church of St Luke was built above the village in Early English style in 1856 and became the parish church of Exmoor (which was formerly extra-parochial) a year later. It is a large barn-like building with a monument to Hugh, 5th Earl Fortescue (1888-1958), whose family succeeded the Knights as owners of the moor. In the hillside churchyard is the prominent pink marble tomb of Sir Frederic Winn Knight (1812-97), overlooking the Exmoor that he loved. Simonsbath was the scene of a murder in 1858 when William Burgess killed his little daughter Anne because he could not afford the 2s 6d a week for her lodging. The body was only found after the abandoned shaft of a nearby copper mine was drained at a cost of £350. Today there are two hotels, a pottery and craft gallery, and a visitors' carpark.

★★★ *Landscape.*

Literary Somerset

Somerset's landscape has entranced countless writers and poets over the centuries, and also inspired several of its own sons and daughters. Roger Bacon (c.1214-94), probably born at Ilchester, went on to become one of the most celebrated philosophers and scientists of the Middle Ages: inventing spectacles and prophesying the telescope, aeroplane, submarine and ocean liner. Polydore Vergil (c.1470-1555), Italian archdeacon of Wells 1508-54, was a celebrated chronicler and author of numerous treatises. Samuel Daniel (1562-1619), poet and writer of court masques, was certainly born in Somerset, some believe near Taunton, and returned in 1610 to live at Rudge, Beckington, where he was buried. One of England's first travel writers, Thomas Coryate (c.1577-1617), son of the rector of Odcombe, walked through much of Europe, publishing an account of his journey in *Coryate's Crudities* and hanging up his much-travelled shoes in Odcombe church. During a second more ambitious expedition, he died at Surat after walking to India. He is credited with popularising the umbrella and introducing the fork to England. A later travelogue of the Near East, *Eothen* (1844), was written by A.W. Kinglake (1809-91) of Wilton House, Taunton, author also of the 8-volume official history of the Crimean War.

The legends of St Joseph of Arimathea and King Arthur, associated with Glastonbury, have inspired a wealth of poetry and prose since the 13th century, including Sir Thomas Malory's *Le Morte D'Arthur*, Tennyson's *Idylls of the King*, John Cowper Powys' *A Glastonbury Romance*, and T.H. White's *Once and Future King*. J.C. Powys (1872-1963) and his literary brothers, novelists Theodore (1875-1953) and Llewellyn (1884-1939), spent much of their early years at Montacute where their father was vicar, 1885-1914.

Another novelist, Henry Fielding (1707-54), was born at Sharpham Park, near Walton, and set part of his best-known novel, *Tom Jones* (1749), in Somerset. Fielding's table is preserved in Taunton Castle and around it regularly meets the Council of the Somerset Archaeological and Natural History Society. One of literature's most celebrated diaries was kept by the Rev James Woodforde (1740-1803), while curate at Ansford and afterwards. Tom Poole, a cultured tanner, brought the poet Samuel Taylor Coleridge to Nether Stowey in 1797 and provided him with a temporary home in Lime Street, where some of his finest poetry was written. Poole was also visited regularly by Charles Lamb, Sir Humphrey Davy and William and Dorothy Wordsworth, the latter pair renting Alfoxton Park in Holford 1797-8. Hannah More (1745-1833), bluestocking playwright, novelist and philanthropist, laboured

ABOVE *William Wordsworth*
BELOW *Samuel Daniel; R.D. Blackmore*

Thomas Coryate's shoes, once in Odcombe church

amongst the poor of the Mendips, founding schools at Cheddar, Shipham and elsewhere.

The village of Combe Florey was home to the wit, letter-writer and critic, the Rev Sydney Smith (1771-1845), from 1828 until his death. Later Evelyn Waugh (1903-66) moved into Combe Florey House in 1956, writing *Unconditional Surrender* (1961) there. The parish's literary tradition continues with Evelyn's son, journalist and critic, Auberon Waugh.

One of the most famous novels set in Somerset is the Exmoor adventure story, *Lorna Doone* (1869), by Richard Doddridge Blackmore (1825-1900), which still brings tourists to revisit the wonderful wild countryside of Jan Ridd and the scene of his marriage to Lorna in Oare church. At the opposite end of the county Sir Henry Newbolt (1862-1938), author of *Drake's Drum*, married into the Duckworth family of Orchardleigh, set his novel *The Old Country* (1906) there and was buried in its island churchyard. Newbolt also used Aisholt on the Quantocks as a rural retreat. Langport was the birthplace of the great economist and constitutional writer, Walter Bagehot (1826-77), and there he is buried. He lived at Herds Hill House in nearby Curry Rivel, and his widow died there in 1921. At Trull lies Juliana Horatia Ewing (1841-85), authoress of numerous children's novels, while at Yeovil was born Walter Raymond (1852-1931), writer of popular novels and essays, most of which were set in Somerset or related to the county. Another novelist whose reputation has not survived the passage of time was Helen Mathers (1853-1920), born at Old Court in Misterton, who wrote several of her books there, including *Comin' thro' the Rye*.

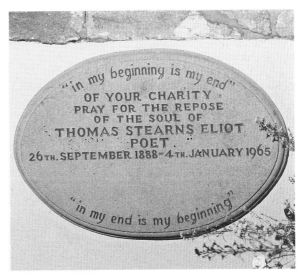

In the present century the poet Thomas Stearns Eliot (1888-1965), whose reputation has been given an unorthodox boost as unwitting librettist of the musical *Cats*, became fascinated by the origin at East Coker of his 17th century ancestor: a fascination reflected in his poem *East Coker* and the burial of his ashes there. Elizabeth Goudge (1900-84), prolific and popular novelist, was born at Wells, and Patricia Wendorf has set her recent best-selling Patteran trilogy of novels (1985-87) in her native Somerset: notably in Buckland St Mary and Taunton.

SKILGATE (C) Reached through deeply-sunken verdant lanes, the village lies west from Wellington on the Devon border, its name meaning appropriately 'boundary gate'. The estate was held in 1086 by Robert de Gatemore under the powerful Roger Arundel, together with another manor in the parish called Milton, and passed in the present century to the Ferguson-Davie baronets. The church of St John has a massive squat west tower, probably 14th century, but the rest is a plain rebuilding of 1872. Surridge Farm, west of the church, dates from the 16th century although extended a century ago.

SOCK DENNIS (J), *see* ILCHESTER

SOMERTON (E) Although never 'the ancient capital of Wessex', as has been often claimed, this large parish, former borough and small town above the river Cary was evidently the focus of an ancient tribe that gave the county its name, and the centre, particularly the market-place, the tree-lined Broad Street and Cow Square, is one of the most picturesque and satisfying urban settings in the county. It has a good restaurant and excellent new and second-hand bookshops. References to Somerton Castle in Lincolnshire have been mistaken for evidence of a castle here. Somerton literally means 'the summer settlement', the prevailing theory being that a people, Romano-British or Saxon, who lived in this vicinity, annually drove their livestock onto the Levels to graze and, as the winter floods advanced, retreated to higher ground. To the north and west of the present town the area was intensively settled in Roman times with villas,

ABOVE *Somerton market place*
BELOW *Hext's Almshouses, Somerton*
BOTTOM *The Red Lion Hotel, Somerton*

and at Catsgore there was a substantial agrarian complex which developed from c.100 AD and eventually comprised at least six farms. At Hurcot to the north-east, where alabaster was once quarried, was a further Roman farm. Passing under control of the Saxons, Somerton was taken by Ethelbald, King of Mercia, in 733 but returned to the West Saxon kings by the 9th century to become the centre of a major royal estate. The Witan or royal council met here once in 949.

Successive kings let out the manor in the Middle Ages, often to their queens, and it was finally given in 1318 to Edmund of Woodstock, second son of Edward I. Thereafter it passed through the hands of various noble and non-resident families

until bought by Sir Edward Hext of Low Ham in 1592, before being inherited by his daughter Elizabeth, wife of Sir John Stawell. The manor continued in his family (Ralph Stawell took the title Baron Stawell of Somerton in 1683) until sold to Thomas Strangways in 1700, whose grandfather had in 1638 bought the manor of Somerton St Cleers (named for the family of Robert de St Clare, owner by 1223). Thereafter both manors descended to the Fox-Strangways family, earls of Ilchester from 1756, who sold off the estate in 1874 and 1913-21. Other estates included Somerton Erleigh, held by William de Erlegh in 1176, whose family had to perform the serjeanty or service for it of carrying a towel before the king at Pentecost, and Somerton Randall, acquired by John Pretor Pinney in 1799, whose descendants still occupy its manor-house, confusingly named Somerton Erleigh, which they virtually rebuilt in 1846. Hurcot was a separate manor by 1205, its owners including Bisham Priory, Berks, 1337-56, Henry VIII's queen, Anne of Cleves, 1541-57, and latterly the Dickinsons of Kingweston.

The old town seems to have been located north-west of the parish church, the focus shifting by the late 13th century to the newly-developed market-place south of the church. The place has always been primarily an agricultural centre and a Monday market and eight-day fair were granted in 1255 and a second fair in 1320. In 1278 the shire courts were moved here from Ilchester, followed by the county gaol in 1280, remaining until they returned to Ilchester in 1366: during which brief period Somerton was effectively the county town. Old Hall in Cow Square may represent the site of the court house of this period. Although the place was a borough by the 13th century, it never achieved an incorporated mayoralty and ownership was retained by the lords of the manor. In the market-place the High Cross was mentioned in 1390, although this had presumably gone by 1615-16 when Sir Edward Hext, having set up 'a fayre shamells', was collecting subscriptions to build a covered market cross. The present covered cross is dated 1673: much restored in 1925 and 1950. The nearby Town Hall or Market House dates from the 17th century, while the Red Lion, the entrance to its yard surmounted by a large coat of arms of the earls of Ilchester, has an attractive 18th century facade. Most of the houses in the centre date from the 17th and 18th centuries, some frontages concealing medieval cores. Sir Edward Hext's almshouses in West Street for eight poor men are dated 1626, Sophia Scott Gould's homes for six women over 60 were built in 1866 at the junction of North and New streets, and the Lady Smith Memorial Hall (1901) in the market-place was named for the wife of Sir John Smith, daughter of J.F. Pinney. Montclefe Junior School derives its name from a mistaken reading of 'Seintclere' by John Collinson.

The church of St Michael and All Angels, formerly St Michael, was originally and surprisingly a daughter chapel to Queen Camel until c.1140 when the Empress Maud granted it burial rights and it passed to Muchelney Abbey. A vicarage was ordained c.1200. Owners of the advowson after the Reformation included the Seymours, later dukes of Somerset (1538-1671), the Bruces (1671-1722), and the earls of Ilchester (1762-1921). The present church is set back to the north of the market-place. To a cruciform church with crossing tower of c.1250, aisles were added and the nave rebuilt c.1350. Thereafter in the 15th century a clerestory was added to the nave and the chancel rebuilt, and c.1510 the superb nave roof. Note the carved barrel placed on the centre beam on the north side, supposed to refer to Abbot Bere of Glastonbury, although it is difficult to reconcile such an interpretation with Muchelney's tenure of the church. The benchends are of c.1500, the painted pulpit is dated 1615 and the communion table with its rotund legs 1626. The panelled chancel has the feeling of the hall of an Oxbridge college. There is an unidentified female effigy of c.1320 in the south transept and a 14th century chantry chapel of the Virgin

ABOVE *Charcroft, South Brewham*

BELOW *Alfred's Tower, South Brewham*

Mary was located at the east end of the south aisle. A chapel of St James was sited at Hurcot from c.1200 and others at Somerton Erleigh and Melbury.

★★★★ *Centre of old town and Broad Street,*
★★★ *church and setting.*

SOUTH BARROW (F) A village north of Sparkford which takes its name from a 'grove' or 'wood', to which modern development has been added at its southern end. It seems likely originally to have formed a single estate with North Barrow. In the late 12th century the manor was held by Alured de Ponsand, who gave the church to Wells. Thereafter it formed the endowment of a prebend in the Cathedral and was a 'peculiar' of the dean and chapter. The church of St Peter in the centre of the village is still reached by the avenue of fan-shaped yews which entertained Pevsner. It is basically Perpendicular but was extensively restored in 1882. There remain some early benchends, a Jacobean pulpit and a 13th century font, recarved in 1584. To the same year belongs a brass inscribed with an acrostic verse to Richard Morice. The manor has been held with that of North Barrow by the Portman family of Orchard Portman since the late 17th century.

SOUTH BREWHAM (F) The approach to the village from the south is marked at Charcroft by a picturesque timber dovecot and barn, both supported on staddle stones, beside a duck pond. This 'southern settlement on the river Brue' lies on the eastern county boundary immediately east of Bruton. In 1066 it was held, with North

Brewham, by one of Edward the Confessor's favourites, Robert son of Wimarc the Staller, but after the Conquest the manor with the church were granted to William de Mohun of Dunster, whose grandson, another William de Mohun, Earl of Somerset, gave them to his foundation of Bruton Priory. After the dissolution the manor was granted to Sir Maurice Berkeley in 1546 and subsequently passed in the 18th century, like Bruton, to banker Henry Hoare of Stourhead (Wilts). It was Hoare who in 1772 completed the 160 ft Alfred's

Cadbury Castle, South Cadbury

Tower to the south-east, just within the parish. Conceived as early as 1762 and designed by Henry Flitcroft, it was intended to mark the 'summit' where Alfred the Great 'erected his standard against the Danish Invaders' in 878 prior to the Battle of Edington (Wilts). The actual site of Alfred's rendezvous with his forces was in fact at Egbert's Stone, now believed to lie much further south at Bourton (Wilts).

The Perpendicular church of St John the Baptist stands in the centre of the village next to the former school, now the village hall. It has a three-stage south tower above an open porch from which one steps down into the church. The south aisle was added in 1826 and includes two appealing monuments to servants of the Digby and Dampier families at Colinshays. Elsewhere there are four small brasses, one with a touching verse to Edward Bennet (died 1673), Commonwealth minister at South Petherton, but ejected from his Dorset living in 1662: returning to preach at South Brewham, his birthplace, only a year before his death. Another of c.1691, to members of Bennet's family, is signed by Wincanton bellfounder, William Cockey, one of very few autographed brasses in Somerset. A third commemorates the 44-year service of Francis Lynewraye (died 1596) as steward of South Brewham manor. A sad little notice with photographs records the sale of three of the five bells to Taylors of Lough- borough in 1969. One of the surviving bells, dated 1775, ironically wishes 'suckcess to the parish'. One of two Domesday manors at Eastrip, now represented by Brewham Lodge Farm, was held by Huscarle in 1066 and 1086 and by John Huscarl in 1287: a rare instance of continuity from Saxon times. Dr Joseph Glanvill recorded a 17th century coven of witches at Brewham to which the Devil appeared in the form of a hedgehog or as 'a little man in black clothes', who left an odour of brimstone when he disappeared.

North Brewham is separated from its neighbour by the river Brue. There was never a church here but Batts Farm (Hugh Batt was its tenant in 1569) represents the former manor-house known as North Court, where the prior of Bruton had a residence in 1411 and where the hundred court of Bruton met. There were fishponds to the east of the farm by the 12th century, and until the early 19th century the tithingmen of the hundred were required to meet at a gate near the farm every 3 May at sunrise. Horseley Farm was a grange of Bruton Priory in the early 13th century.

SOUTH CADBURY (F) A small parish south-west from Sparkford, whose name, 'Cada's fort', refers to the massive hilltop fortifications known as **Cadbury Castle**, which dominate the village below and to which access can be gained by a footpath from near the church. The summit commands superb views across the surrounding countryside but it is the fortifications themselves, enclosing an area of 18 acres, which provide the main interest. These were excavated by Leslie Alcock, 1966-70, and at the time the work received national news coverage and brought thousands of visitors here. The hill was first settled by Early Neolithic man (c.3,300 BC) but the four immense banks that surround the site, with entrances from the east, north-east and south-west, were raised in the late Iron Age (c.500 BC), and circular houses, workshops and two possible temples or shrines were discovered inside the perimeter. At this time the fort was the principal defensive work in Somerset. There was a fairly continuous occupation of what amounted to a small town by the local Celtic tribe, the Durotriges, until c.70 AD, when the settlement was stormed by the Romans and the inhabitants massacred or dispersed. With an increasing threat from the Saxons, the hill was again fortified c.470 AD, a new gateway was built at the south-western corner, a timber hall of about 60ft by 30ft erected, and the fortress was occupied until the late 6th century. Was this the period at which the eponymous Cada headed the garrison ? Finally, in response to Viking raids by Thorkell the Tall in the reign of Ethelred the Unready, the mint at Ilchester was moved to the security of 'Cadanbyrig' in 1009-10, the building of a church possibly started, and a Saxon town was established. This continued only until 1019, when the moneyers moved to Bruton and Crewkerne and the settlement was abandoned. Excavations south of the church suggest that it may have been at this time that South Cadbury village was first developed. A single reference to 40 marks (£12.82) spent on 'building work at the castle of Cadbury' in 1209 may suggest a further project in King John's time, but there is no other evidence for this.

Leland, Henry VIII's itinerant antiquary, wrote in 1542 that Cadburians knew the fortress as 'Camallate' to which 'Arture much resortid'. Camelot, as King Arthur's mythical fortress, was a late addition to Arthurian literature for which Chretien de Troyes, a French writer of the mid 12th century, was responsible. Subsequently local traditions added a cavern in the hillside where Arthur and his knights lie sleeping, a causeway towards Glastonbury ridden by their ghosts, and Arthur's well (at the north-east angle of the fort) where

A303

MONKTON

A303 BRISTOL

BLACKFORD

FIELD PLACE

GRASSLAND
HORTICULTURE

(G.BUS SHEBBEAR)

A 3T
BATH
BRIS

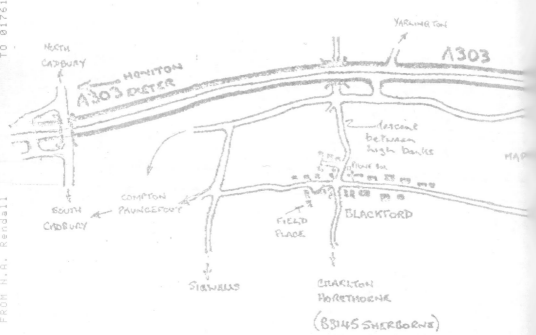

NORTH CADBURY

A303 HONITON EXETER

YARLINGTON

A303

descent between high banks

phone box

MAP

SOUTH CADBURY

COMPTON PAUNCEFOOT

FIELD PLACE

BLACKFORD

SIGWELLS

CHARLTON HORETHORNE

(B3145 SHERBORNE)

VIVIEN & NEVILLE RENDALL

FIELD PLACE

BLACKFORD

01963 440549

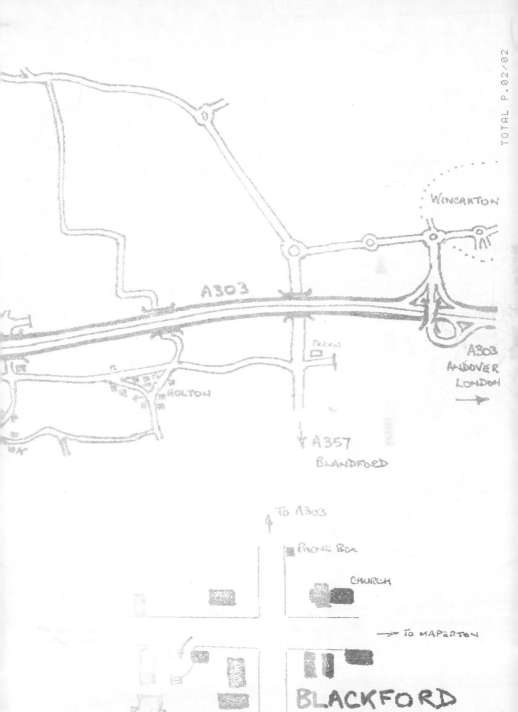

ABOVE *Barn, South Cadbury*   ABOVE RIGHT *The Blake Hall, South Petherton*   BELOW *The Ayshe monument, South Petherton church*

their hounds slake their thirsts (*see also* **Arthur and Alfred**). Another well, St Anne's or Queen Anne's well lies on the west of the hill. There is evidence for the use of one of these for superstitious purposes in 1634 when a group of local women baptized each other on a Sunday and went through certain obscene rites.

Since the Norman Conquest the manor seems always to have descended with that of North Cadbury. The village is clustered around a crossroads with the church of St Thomas a Becket on its southern arm. It has a good west tower, a south arcade of the early 14th century, a Perpendicular panelled chancel arch (although the chancel was built in 1874) and a good 15th century nave roof. The south aisle was largely rebuilt in 1853 but in a surviving splay is the 15th century painting of a bishop, popularly supposed to represent the patron saint. Opposite the church is the 18th century South Cadbury House, formerly the rectory, and nearby is Castle Farm House, dated 1687.

★★★★ *Cadbury Castle*, ★★ *Village*.

SOUTH CHERITON (K) *see* HORSINGTON

SOUTH PETHERTON (J) This 'southern settlement on the river Parrett' is an attractive large village (or small town) lying west of Yeovil. Although the centre was largely rebuilt in the 19th century, it boasts a scatter of interesting shops, such as Global Village (Third World crafts) and some selling antiques. The parish was noted for its gloving in the 19th century and local limestone quarries and the manufacture of bricks and tiles, but has always relied predominantly on agriculture. Indeed, John Willy received medals for his

account of cultivating turnips and for seed drilling, 1765-6.

Bronze-Age tools have been found nearby at Wigborough, Iron-Age and Romano-British evidence has turned up to the north-east of the village at Stoodham, and the Roman Foss Way (A 303), naming Over Stratton ('settlement on a Roman road'), runs through the south of the parish. There was a mint here before the Conquest although no borough was ever established. The manor was probably an early possession of the West Saxon kings, but there is no evidence to link the place with King Ine, as often stated. It was held by the Daubeney family by 1225 until 1541, when money troubles forced Henry Daubeney, Earl of Bridgwater, to sell to his kinsman, Thomas Arundell: continuing with the Arundells until 1792. It was the Daubeneys who built a new manor-house north of Butt Lane in the later 14th century (added to in the early 16th and mid 19th), known as 'King Ina's Palace' probably since Stukeley's writings of 1720. In 1213 a Thursday market and Midsummer fair were granted by King John to endow St James Chapel (site untraced although its name survives in St James Street in the village), the market lapsing shortly before 1870 and the fair continuing into the present century. A market house in the centre of the market-place was rebuilt in 1843. This was converted and extended in 1911 to provide a Liberal club and the Blake Hall by Robert Blake of Yeabridge in memory of his father. There are several significant houses in the parish, such as the 17th century Hayes End Manor.

On the south side of the market-place stands the church of SS Peter and Paul. A reference to Alviet the priest in 1086 suggests that there was a church here by that

date and the fact that it had several dependent chapelries means it was probably a Saxon minster in origin. The church, its lands and chapelries were given by Henry II to Bruton Priory in 1181-2, the endowment becoming known after the dissolution as the manor of Hele, held by the Ayshe family 1566-1683. The present building is a substantial cruciform rebuilding of c.1350-1450 with traces of 12th century work in the chancel. The upper octagonal central tower is Perpendicular, as are the nave, south transept and north porch (note the panel depicting Sagittarius and Leo, as at Stoke-sub-Hamdon). In the south transept (by 1305 housing the chantry of Our Lady) are the kneeling figures of Henry Compton (died 1603) of Wigborough and his wife, together with an effigy identified as Sir

Philip Daubeney (died 1294), dug up at Pitway in 1929, and a brass of Mary (died 1442), second wife of Sir Giles Daubeney (died 1446). Sir Giles's brass with that of his first wife is in the north (vestry) transept (where the chantry of St Catherine was founded in 1364) and an incredibly elaborate but rather vernacular monument to William Ayshe (died 1657) with the figures of his mother and sister, and two children, the last peering out from niches behind. A nearby brass to William Sandys (died 1679) bluntly refers to his character. 'Some will say that he was passionate/and would too quickly love and hate/ others he would too plainly tell/ his mind and that some took not well'.

Compton Durville was held by Eustace de Durville in the 12th century and is centred on a sizeable 17th century manor-house, occupied since 1962 by the Community of St Francis. **Bridge**, a hamlet settled by the late 12th century, is named for the bridge which carried the Foss Way over the Parrett. Although largely obliterated by the dual carriageway of the A 303, two associated figures, identified alternatively as the bridge's founder and his wife or two children drowned there, are preserved in the vicinity. Wigborough and Stratton occur from the 11th century, Little Lopen by 1232, Harp by 1305 and Watergore, which grew up around a road junction, from 1462. The parish was visited by troops from both sides in the Civil War, the Duke of Monmouth was feted here in 1680 and Field Marshall Lord Harding of Petherton (1896-1989) was born here.

★★ *Village, church.*

SPARKFORD (F) A village midway between Ilchester and Wincanton, bypassed since 1990 by the new course of the A 303, whose name may mean 'brushwood ford'. A Bronze Age hoard, including sickles and a chisel, was found here and is now in the County Museum. In the Middle Ages it formed part of the barony of Castle Cary, the manor being held by the Newman family in the 17th and 18th centuries, passing to the Bennetts in 1793. The church of St Mary Magdalene stands at the south-east end of the village. It has a Perpendicular west tower, south chapel and chancel, but the nave was rebuilt by the Rev Henry Bennett in 1824. The south chapel is a touching memorial to the eight local men who died in the Great War, complete with their photographs, and there is a small brass in the chancel to rector John Chyke (died 1513). The Haynes Publishing Group, which specialises in

Contemporary engraving of the 'Abode of Love', Spaxton (1851)

motorcar manuals, is based here and in 1985 John Haynes established the **Sparkford Motor Museum** (fee:lists), north of the village on the A 359 and opened appropriately by Richard Noble, holder of the land speed record. It features over 200 vehicles, spanning the history of the internal combustion engine, attractively exhibited in four large halls. I particularly liked the copies of prosecutions under the Red Flag Act. There is a display track on which the occupants are regularly exercised, a video cinema, bookshop, cafe and picnic area.

★★★ *Motor museum, recommended for vehicular addicts.*

SPAXTON (D) Between the Quantock ridge and Bridgwater a Scandinavian settler gave his name to 'Spak's tun', a sprawling parish of scattered farms. Even before the Conquest, in addition to Spaxton itself, there were separate estates at Merridge ('boundary ridge'), Pileigh, Radlet and Tuxwell. The principal manor was held by the Fichet family within a century of the Battle of Hastings, of whom Sir Thomas Fichet was clearly the terror of the region. In 1352 he was pardoned for burning down a manor-house in Wembdon, forging a will, poaching the king's deer in Petherton forest, and ordering the murder of a servant. The manor passed by marriage to the Hylles in 1396, and thereafter descended through the Cheyneys to the Waldegraves. In the 18th century, like so many other estates in the area, it was sold to the earls of Egmont. The Hylles' manor-house seems to survive as Court House Farmhouse in Splatt Lane, dating

from the 15th century. Nearby stands the 15th century church of St Margaret: heavily restored in 1895. The west tower was in building in 1434 when John Hylle left money towards the work. The effigies on the north side of the sanctuary probably represent this John (who requested burial in the chancel) and his wife Cecily. There is a three-lock 17th century almsbox and a superb series of Quantock benchends, two dated 1536 and 1561: the ownership of three pews being inscribed on them in 1728. Following the closure of Charlinch church in 1980, its altar, reredos and lectern were installed in the south aisle which thus became the Charlinch chapel. In the churchyard is a fine cross of c.1400 with its preserved head, featuring a damaged crucifixion on both faces.

At Four Forks, formerly concealed behind a high wall, stand the house and former chapel of the **Agapemone** – the Abode of Love, founded in 1846 by the Rev Henry James Prince, unfrocked curate of Charlinch, who had publicly declared himself in Weymouth Assembly Rooms to be the Son of Man and immortal. Addressed as 'Beloved' by his disciples, he gathered around him a host of besotted women, his 'soul brides', whom he fleeced of their fortunes to support his luxurious life style. In 1856 to the strains of organ music he deflowered a young virgin before the altar in the presence of a congregation which included his own wife and the girl's mother. Prince audaciously claimed that the Devil was responsible for the resulting child. The farce continued long after the 'immortal' Prince died in 1899 and even after his successor, New Messiah the Rev Hugh

Smyth Pigott, followed him in 1927: both interred beneath the front lawn. The small commune was dissolved only in 1958, the buildings were sold and a newspaper story that had run and run for over a century finally ended. In 1965 history almost seemed to repeat itself when, in the full glare of the national press, the rector of Spaxton was deprived for 'conduct unbecoming' his position.

★★★ *Church, village and landscape.*

STANDERWICK (B), *see* **BECKINGTON**

STAPLE FITZPAINE (H) This village lies in undulating countryside on the road south from Taunton up to the Blackdown Hills. Its name derives from the Old English *stapol,* meaning 'pillar' or 'post'. Some see this as referring to the sarsen stone which stands near the church. Local tradition claims that it was hurled there by the Devil and that it bleeds when pricked with a pin. This place was granted to Robert, Count of Mortain, following the Norman Conquest and was briefly known as Staple Briwes after the de Briwes family who held the manor by c.1200. Robert de Briwes obtained the grant of a Tuesday market, three-day fair and free warren (a hunting park) here in 1233. Between 1307 and 1393 the manor was owned by the Fitzpaine family, who gave their surname to it, later descending to the Percy earls of Northumberland. In 1600 it was purchased by the Portmans of nearby Orchard Portman as they expanded their estate in the area, and they continued to dominate the parish until 1944.

The church of St Peter is blessed with one of the fine Perpendicular towers for which Somerset is famous, enriched with niches and gargoyles. The rest of the church is almost a disappointment in comparison, despite a Norman south doorway and a rood screen moved from Bickenhall. The church was probably granted to Bermondsey Abbey by William de Mortain c.1140, when he became a monk there, but was bought back by Robert de Briwes in 1236. In 1318 the rector, George Roges, was fined for adultery. A later rector, Fitzhardinge Berkeley Portman, built the massive rectory (now Staple Manor) beside the church in 1840. He ruled the parish (and three others) with a rod of iron and dismissed the village schoolmistress in 1875 for being absent for three days without permission. Near the church stand fine almshouses, complete with chapel and kitchen, built in 1643 by Sir William Portman for six poor persons from Staple

and three other neighbouring parishes: each to have a blue gown lined with yellow. Today most come here to patronise the Greyhound, a popular eating and drinking house in the village which was trading under that name by the 18th century.

At the south-eastern edge of the parish, crowning a spur on the Blackdowns and on part of an excellent forest trail laid out by the Forestry Commission, lie the substantial earthworks of **Castle Neroche**. There a Norman motte-and-bailey castle was set up, probably by Robert, Count of Mortain, in response to the rising in the West against William the Conqueror in 1068. It was later abandoned, possibly in favour of Montacute (also held by Robert) or after the defeat and exile of his son William in 1106. Its name ('Nerechich' in 1236) may refer to 'a place where hunting dogs are kept', for Neroche Forest was one of five former royal forests in the county. It stretched east as far as Barrington and encompassed nearly 10,000 acres as late as 1623. The vicar of Martock was fined for netting a doe there in 1270, as was the abbot of Athelney for killing a buck with his dogs in 1365. Charles I ordered Neroche to be disafforested in 1627 but hedges and fences were thrown down by a rabble at the time of the Civil War and much remained open until finally enclosed in 1833.

★★★ *Castle Neroche, nature trail, walking,* ★★ *village, setting.*

STAPLEGROVE (D) A compact village immediately to the north-west of Taunton and with which it is almost completely built up, although preserving its own identity. Its name may mean 'the grove where posts were got', although more colourfully considered by Costen possibly to refer (on the evidence of the fieldname 'halgrove' – 'holy grove') to a phallic post worshipped in a sacred grove. The place lay from Saxon times within the bishop of Winchester's manor of Taunton Deane, giving its name not only to a tithing but also to one of the five 'hundreds' into which that manor was divided: a hundred which stretched south to the river Tone and east to include Obridge (in Taunton). The old village lies along a winding lane running east from the Taunton to Norton road. At its centre stands the church of St John the Evangelist, which by 1308 was a chapel served by priests from Taunton Priory. The chancel arch and lower stage of the south tower seem to be 13th century and the nave and chancel may be of similar date. The north aisle was added in the 14th

century, the tower completed soon after and the south aisle possibly enlarged from an existing south chapel 1619-20. An 1857 restoration added a new north arcade, extended the nave to the west, inserted new windows and removed the old pews. The wealthy Minifie family dominated the parish during the 18th century. On the south wall of the nave is a monument to James Minifie (died 1725), Taunton serge-maker, who bought Fairwater House (now part of Taunton School) in 1722. His grandson, another James Minifie, rector 1759-89, is commemorated in the south aisle. There are several tablets to the Turners of Staplegrove Manor (formerly Pinkhurst), unofficial squires in the 19th and early 20th century. Do not miss the chest tomb to the north of the church with inscriptions to Joseph Poole (died 1791), who sailed with Captain Cook, and Capt Robert Poole (died 1833), who crossed the Equator 22 times and rounded Cape Horn on no fewer than 17 occasions: quite a record for an inland parish. The Somerset Nuffield Hospital was established in 1974 around Staplegrove Elm, a house probably built to Richard Carver's designs in the 1840s. Since 1981 the parish has been home to its own vineyard and winery, producing its prize-winning Staplecombe Wines.

★★ *Village.*

STAWELL (E) This attractive village is strung out along the lane from Moorlinch to Greinton. Its name, meaning 'stony stream or well', is supposed to refer to a pond at Ford Farm which deposits lime on objects placed in it. The buildings include some fine Georgian brick houses, particularly the Manor House. The squat chapel, formerly dependent on Moorlinch church, has a very plain interior, over-restored in 1874. An arcade buried in its north wall suggests the former presence of a north aisle which was later demolished. The west tower was never completed and is topped by a low gable. An unsupported but appealing local story alleges that the tower was begun to house a ring of bells offered by the abbot of Glastonbury to whichever parish among Moorlinch and its chapelries should first solemnize three baptisms and three burials: a contest narrowly won by Moorlinch itself – hence the unfinished tower. The manor gave its name to the family of Stawell, later lords Stawell of Cothelstone and Low Ham, who owned the manor by the 13th century until 1692.

★ *Village.*

Churches

There are few counties in England which have so many superb parish churches of high quality as does Somerset: particularly in the elaborate towers put up in the Perpendicular (c.1350-1530) style. Most of the towns have sizeable churches, richly furnished, but even small parishes seem to have tried to outstrip each other in the lavishness of their buildings.

There is no standing Saxon church in the county, although the Saxon foundations of the monastic church at Muchelney and of the Cathedral at Wells are still visible (with a Saxon font inside the Cathedral), part of the shaft of a carved cross is displayed at West Camel, and other cross fragments can be seen at Porlock, Nunney and Rowberrow. There is some Saxon long-and-short work at Wilton (Taunton) and Shepton Mallet, but the most significant Saxon remains, although late, are incorporated in the imposing church of Milborne Port. The best Norman church is Lullington with its finely carved north doorway, capitals, chancel arch and exquisite font, although on a larger scale Stogursey is magnificent, despite later alterations. Witham Friary's somewhat gaunt church has an impressive simplicity, Beckington has a bold Norman tower, Stoke-sub-Hamdon an extremely satisfying interior, and there are many chancel arches and doorways of the period throughout the county. Sutton Bingham has the added bonus of extensive 13th century wall paintings.

Wells Cathedral, begun in the 1170s and consecrated 1239, is the earliest major Gothic building in England and in a class of its own in Somerset. This is not the place to exult at length on its West Front, central tower, Lady Chapel, Retrochoir and Chapter House; let alone the nearby late 13th century Bishop's Chapel (in the Palace). No one should need to be encouraged to visit Wells.

Much of the great Perpendicular rebuilding of Somerset churches was paid for from the profits of cloth manufacture, which flourished not only in the towns but also in many of the villages. The reconstruction flowered from c.1400 in the wonderful towers, the finest of any in the country, believed to have been inspired by the western towers of Wells Cathedral. The tallest and most ornate is that of Taunton St Mary (c.1488-1514), although rebuilt in the 19th century, but there are many others. Among the best are Batcombe, Bishops Lydeard, Chewton Mendip, Evercreech, Glastonbury St John, Huish Episcopi, Ilminster, Isle Abbotts, Kingsbury Episcopi, Kingston St Mary, Leigh-on-Mendip, Mells, North Petherton, Staple Fitzpaine, Taunton St James and Wells St Cuthbert.

Several timber roofs of the same period are incredibly intricate. Shepton Mallet has the best wagon roof, but the Somerset or angel roofs at Leigh-on-Mendip, Martock, Somerton and Wells St Cuthbert are a delight. Some churches reflect in their memorials the almost feudal domination of particular families, my personal favourites being Cothelstone, Crowcombe, Goathurst, Hinton St George, Montacute, Nettlecombe, Nynehead

LEFT *Saxon arch, Milborne Port church*
BELOW *Norman font, Lullington church*

and Rodney Stoke. Other buildings boast remarkably rich fittings, notably Trull (pulpit and woodwork generally) and Croscombe's complete timber interior. A number of churches, mainly in the Quantock area, have flamboyant 16th century benchends, of which the most prolific craftsman can be identified as Simon Warman of Bicknoller (fl. 1525-85): Bicknoller, Bishops Hull, Brent Knoll, Crowcombe, Hatch Beauchamp, Kingston St Mary, Lyng, Milverton, Spaxton and Stogursey.

Of later churches, the best were put up by local landlords to complement their neighbouring manor-houses: Low Ham, Babington, Berkley and Marston Bigot. The 19th century produced a considerable number of rebuilt parish churches (and many heavy-handed restorations), particularly in the towns and in the far west of the county. I favour the eccentrically-turreted Rode Hill, the octagonal church at Blackford (Wedmore), West Lydford, Hornblotton and, of course, the splendour of Downside Abbey. Nonconformist chapels in the county are distinguished largely by their austerity, with the notable exceptions of Rook Lane (Frome) and Mary Street (Taunton).
Churches

★★★★ *Brympton D'Evercy, Croscombe, Crowcombe, Downside Abbey, Goathurst, Hinton St George, Lullington, Mells, Stogursey, Stoke-sub-Hamdon, Wells Cathedral.*
★★★ *Babington, Beckington, Berkley, Bicknoller, Bradford-on-Tone, Brent Knoll, Bruton, Burnham-on-Sea, Cannington, Cothelstone, Creech St Michael, Crewkerne, Curry Mallet, Curry Rivel, Dowlish Wake, Dunster, East Coker, East Quantoxhead, Evercreech, Frome (Rook Lane Chapel), St John's Glastonbury, Great Elm, Ilminster, Isle Abbots, Kingston St Mary, Martock, Meare, Milborne Port, Montacute, Muchelney, Nettlecombe,*

North Cadbury, North Curry, Oare (setting), Old Cleeve, Pendomer, Pilton, Pitminster, Rodney Stoke, Selworthy, Shepton Mallet, Somerton, Spaxton, Stawley, Stocklinch Ottersey, Sutton Bingham, Swell, St Mary's Taunton, Mary Street Chapel (Taunton), Trull, St Decuman's Watchet, St Cuthbert's Wells, Westonzoyland, Witham Friary, St John's Yeovil.

ABOVE *Panel above tower door, Stawley church.*   BELOW *St Mary's church, Stocklinch Ottersey.*   BOTTOM *Cottage at Stocklinch*

STAWLEY (H) This 'stony glade' lies in a wooded setting above the river Tone on the county border west of Wellington. Held in 1086 by Osward and Ailward under Alured the Spaniard, the manor was long in the hands of the earls Poulett of Hinton St George. The little church of St Michael stands in magnificent countryside at the end of a winding lane which leads nowhere else and is one of my favourites. Passing a touching tombstone commemorating 'Squire Batten' (died 1991) of Kittisford Farm, the visitor enters through a 13th century door with original hinges. The interior is happily untouched by the Victorian restorer. The basic structure is evidently Norman, judging from the panels of herringbone masonry left unrendered on the outside of the north wall. The slightly off-centre chancel has an unusual 16th century square-headed east window and, just as rare, a leaded 17th century rectangular window in the north wall. The woodwork and fittings are all 18th century: box pews and pulpit with elegant canopy. The west tower has an elaborate panel above the outside doorway, inscribed to Henry Howe (not Hines, as sometimes quoted) and Agnes his wife with a date variously interpreted as 1522 or 1523. Howe probably paid for the building of the tower and in his will of 1528 asked to be buried 'within the towre and church of Stauligth'.

Appley ('apple wood') is a little hamlet south-east of the main village which was represented by two small manors at Domesday. Today it is best known for the excellent cuisine served up at the Globe Inn, converted from 17th century cottages.

Nearby on the Tone at **Tracebridge** is a former industrial site at variance with its leafy surroundings. Here by 1592 were two corn mills, converted to sawmills in the 19th century and worked until the 1950s, and two quarries. Further to the south-east Greenham, 'farm on the mill brook',

certainly had a mill by 1086 when it was held by Bretel, lord of Ashbrittle, under the Count of Mortain. Greenham Barton is a superb early 15th century L-shaped house, the work, like Cothay (in Kittisford), of the building Bluets. William de Gryndham ('of Greenham') built a chapel here in 1316 because he was too old to travel to Kittisford church. Visible through the trees from across the valley is Greenham Hall (formerly Tremlett House), a large mid 19th century Tudor-style mansion. Beside the Tone the church of St Peter, Greenham, was built in Early English form in 1860 and contains a monument to Adm Sir John Kelly (died 1936) of Greenham Hall.

★★★ *Stawley church, landscape,*
★★ *Appley village, setting of Greenham.*

STEART (D) *see* **OTTERHAMPTON**

STOCKLAND BRISTOL (D) A flat, leafy parish on the coast east of Stogursey, whose name means 'land belonging to a dairy-farm' and was held by Bristol Corporation from 1541 until 1839. It had formerly been known as Stockland Gaunts because in 1230 Maurice de Gaunt left the manor to St Mark's Hospital, Bristol, which held it until the hospital was dissolved by Henry VIII. Stockland Manor, a many-chimneyed mansion, was built c.1860 by Thomas Daniel, who had bought the estate from Bristol. Daniel also built the present church of St Mary Magdalene, 1865-66, replacing that of All Saints but preserving its 15th century font. Daniel's great-grandson began to sell off the estate in 1947.

★ *Village and its setting.*

STOCKLINCH (J) North-east from Ilminster the former twin villages of Stocklinch Magdalen and Stocklinch Ottersey have combined to form a single settlement. The name Stocklinch means 'the hill place' and the manor of Stocklinch

Ottersey was held from the late 12th century (and possibly as early as the Norman Conquest) by the king's hawker (*otricer*). Stocklinch Magdalen, its suffix taken from the church's dedication, comprises most of the surviving buildings in the two places and includes a surprising number of medieval thatched houses dating from the 14th and 15th centuries. Formerly held by the Beauchamps of Hatch, Stocklinch Magdalen manor formed from 1426 the principal endowment of Robert Veel's almshouse in Ilchester and many of these properties must have been built under the stewardship of the almshouse trustees. The church of St Mary Magdalene in the centre of the village is a small plain structure with three-bell bellcote. The west gallery has a crude picture identified as King David and there is a Norman font.

Please do not miss the church of St Mary the Virgin, Stocklinch Ottersey: as much for its position as the building itself. Go down Owl Street and turn left into Owl Lane. After a short distance, beyond the Victorian manor-house, pass through a gate on the left and make your way through a field up the slope to the church, standing in splendid but recent isolation, for in 1791 most of the houses were stated to lie around it. The church dates from the 13th century with 14th century chancel, and the south transept contains an elaborate Decorated south window. On the ledge below this window is a late 13th century female effigy, identified as the wife of William le Ostricer, probably once housed in the tomb recess in the nave. The south transept with its own piscina presumably accommodated the chantry founded in 1363 by her son, Ralph of Stocklinch. Since the 17th century it has formed a valhalla for the Jeffrey(s) lords of the manor and their heirs, the Allens. A spurious tale, suggested only by the lords' surname, told that Judge Jeffreys' coffin was secretly placed in the vault here, but no such relationship existed. The royal arms of 1664 bear an enthusiastic post-Restoration cry of euphoria: 'God save our Noble King Charles'. The church was declared redundant in 1973 but is excellently maintained.

★★★ *Village and its houses, setting of Stocklinch Ottersey church.*

STOFORD (J), *see* BARWICK

STOGUMBER (D) A most attractive village and large parish, lying between the Quantock and Brendon hills south-east from Williton. To the name Stoke ('place' or 'dairy farm') was added by 1225 the personal name 'Gunner', later 'Gomer' (the combined elements later transformed into Stogumber), although no record of an early landowner of this name has been traced. George Bernard Shaw wrote to the vicar before using the village's name for a priest in his drama *St Joan*. The parish seems always to have featured scattered farms and hamlets, and no fewer than nine separate settlements here (including Capton, Vexford, Hartrow, Combe, Coleford and Embelle) are recorded in the Domesday Book (1086). A parish held by a variety of owners continued to be its pattern. An estate eventually called Stogumber manor was held from 1286 by the Andelys family:

later owners including the Sydenhams (1396-1626) and Notleys (from 1896), both of Combe Sydenham. Hartrow was owned by the families of Lacey (c.1560-1695), Rich (1695-1727) and Escott (1771-c.1936), while the Luttrells of Dunster held Vexford and the Trevelyans of Nettlecombe owned Rowdon.

A market was held here by the Sydenham family from at least 1614 until the later 19th century, originally with two fairs, and a market hall was built c.1800 opposite the church with an assembly room over. This survived to be incorporated in the present White Horse Inn (mentioned 1748). The church of St Mary was probably founded as a Saxon minster, with a chapelry at Bicknoller, dues payable from Monksilver and properties in Clatworthy and Elworthy. There was also a substantial

church estate by 1086, later known as the manor of Stogumber Rectory and centred on Hall Farm. The advowson was given by Walter de Andelys to the bishop in 1259 and soon after passed to the dean and chapter of Wells Cathedral, who ordained a vicarage by 1291. The present red sandstone building stands in the middle of the village to the south of the former market-place. The lower stages of the tower and west end of the south aisle date from c.1300, but the rest is a rebuilding and extension of the 15th century, with octagonal font and stone pulpit of the same period. The north aisle was owned with Halsway Manor (*see* **Bicknoller**), formerly a detached part of Stogumber parish, while the south aisle was held by the Sydenham family. Here is the substantial monument to Sir George Sydenham (died 1589) between his two wives, with its delightful vernacular inscription to 'Sr. Gorge Sidnum' and the figures of three infants and their nurse at his feet. His daughter's marriage to Sir Francis Drake did not take place here, as often stated, but at neighbouring Monksilver. There is also a good armorial and portrait brass to Margery Wyndham of Kentsford (died 1586). Down the slope from the church a cottage known as Seven Crosses (they are fixed to its facade) was named by the Rev George Trevelyan (vicar 1820-71), who suffered from bouts of religious mania. Just beyond is the almshouse founded by Sir George Sydenham (died 1595) for six poor widows, converted to a single house in 1939. Three rebels from the Taunton area were hanged here in 1685 after the Monmouth Rebellion: traditionally at

ABOVE *Monument to Sir George Sydenham, Stogumber church*
BELOW *Combe Sydenham Hall, Stogumber*

Heddon Oak on the road to Crowcombe.

There is evidence for clothmaking in the parish from the mid 13th century until the 18th, with five fulling mills here for much of that time. A later industry, Stogumber Brewery, was established south of the village by George Elers shortly before 1840, and he later built Springfield Lodge for himself. Its Medicinal Pale Ale, produced with water from the nearby Harry Hill's well, earned a widespread reputation. Brewing ceased c.1910, malting c.1925 and the brewery buildings were finally demolished in 1973.

Combe Sydenham Hall (fee:lists) is a substantial house to the west of the village. The estate of Combe Allen was bought by Judge Richard Sydenham in 1367 and retained by his descendants until 1693. Later owners included the Musgrave (1693-1765) and Notley (1796-1957) families. Sir George Sydenham remodelled and extended the medieval house around 1580, this date appearing with his initials over the porch and a Latin inscription which translates as 'This door of George's is always open except to ungrateful souls'. The interior has been much altered but there is some good Elizabethan plasterwork. Also displayed is the famous stone cannonball, alleged since at least 1810 to have disrupted the marriage of Sir George's daughter Elizabeth, and supposed to have been fired across the world by Sir Francis Drake, who later married Elizabeth at Monksilver in 1583. This charming piece of folklore seems to have originated as a story relating to Drake's first wife in West Devon. Other attractions include delightful walks through the surrounding parkland, a fish farm, cafe and gift shop. The Theeds, owners since 1964, have deservedly won awards for their educational work.

Near Stogumber station on the West Somerset Railway is the **Bee World and Animal Centre** (fee:lists). There are fascinating live exhibits behind glass detailing the life cycle of the bee and its honey production, a range of rare animal breeds, country stream-side walks, shop and restaurant.

★★★ *Village, setting, Combe Sydenham,* ★★ *church, Bee World.*

STOGURSEY (D) A large coastal parish and former borough north-west from Bridgwater, whose name (originally simply 'Stoke', meaning 'place' or 'dairy farm') occurs c.1100 as 'Suntinstoch' – 'swamp in the stoke'. Following the Norman Conquest the manor was granted to

William de Falaise, whose father had fought at Hastings, and his daughter Emma carried the manor to her husband, William de Curci (died c.1114), steward of Henry I, from whose family the place became known as Stoke Curci: modified over the years to Stogursey. By 1100 William had probably built the first castle here, which became the seat of the honor or barony of Stogursey, and soon after he gave the church to Lonlay Abbey in Normandy, which had established a priory here by c.1120. The Curcis had founded a borough here by 1225, laying out an attractive wide market-place along High Street, which seems to have formed the northern edge of an open rectangular space bounded to the south by Bank Street. There was a Saturday market and a fair by 1301, and shambles in 1475. Early industry was concentrated on clothmaking (there were fulling mills at Fairfield and Durborough in the 15th century) but tanning and gloving were also recorded from the 15th century. Borough courts were held until the late 16th century and officers appointed even later. The stump of a market cross survives towards the west end of the market-place, south of which lies St Andrew's Well, mentioned in 1473. The present well-houses bear the arms of the earls of Egmont and of Sir Peregrine Fuller-Palmer-Acland, who rebuilt them in 1870. In 1869 Sir Peregrine also demolished almshouses on an island site in the market-place, founded for six poor people in the early 15th century by William Paulet of Chilton Trinity, replaced by almshouses for six women in Lime Street. A further almshouse for three men was founded in 1821. It houses the 'Ding Darling Bell', possibly from the original almshouse, which is still rung twice a day. On the village outskirts, Sir Peregrine was also responsible (as 'a thank-offering' after the recovery from illness of his daughter Isobel) for the delightful Victorian school of 1860, designed by John Norton with a host of ornate chimneys and spired bellcot. The site of the school has been identified as Tower Hill, where two Monmouth rebels were hanged drawn and quartered in 1685.

The fourth William de Curci died in 1194 and his brother-in-law and heir, William FitzGerold, acted as host to King John (from whom he seems to have won 20s at cards) here in 1210 but later fell from grace, forfeited the estate, and the destruction of the castle was ordered in 1216. FitzGerold's son-in-law, Fawkes de Breaute, 'a ferocious and sanguinary ruffian', occupied the castle which was surrendered to the Crown in 1224

and refortified in 1233. Thereafter the castle does not appear to have seen action but was maintained as a combination of manor-house and estate office until the 1530s after which it progressively decayed. Today **Stogursey Castle** comprises the ruined keep, a 12th century circular wall surrounded by a moat and formerly punctuated by drum towers: only earthworks marking the former area of the outer bailey to the east. The gatehouse was occupied in the 17th century, but replaced c.1878 by a house recently restored and converted by the Landmark Trust. A footpath from the bottom of Castle Street gives access to the east and south sides of the moat. The castle and main manor were granted to Robert FitzPayn in 1308, from whom the estate descended to the Poynings and Percy families: held by the earls of Northumberland until 1670, and from 1758 by the earls of Egmont.

The former precinct of **Stogursey Priory** stood immediately to the east of the borough. Throughout its existence the priory remained an alien house, subject to its parent abbey across the Channel, and there were squabbles with the bishop over the elections of priors and the running of the house. An enquiry of 1326 found that one spendthrift French prior had reduced the establishment to the prior himself, one monk, servants and 'useless folk'. War with France led to the confiscation of the priory by 1438 and the site with its Stogursey property was conveyed to Eton College c.1440. The college retained the premises, leased to the Bristol Merchant Venturers from 1713, demolishing the substantial prior's house c.1810 and leaving only a circular dovecot to mark the former presence of the priory. With the exception of Priory Farm, the college's estate was sold off in 1921.

Fortunately the **priory church of St Andrew** survives and is one of the ecclesiastical jewels of Somerset. The crossing tower and north and south transepts survive from a church presumably built by William de Falaise from c.1090. They have superb Norman round arches supported on elaborate capitals. There were formerly circular apses on both transepts and on a short chancel, but these were replaced c.1180 when the chancel was extended to form a choir and the chancel aisles built, with sophisticated zig-zag and dog-tooth arches. This work can presumably be linked with adaptation of the building for use by the priory. The north chancel aisle housed a chantry chapel of Our Lady until dissolved in 1548. The

The interior of Stogursey church

present floor levels are the result of excavations by the vicar in the 1940s. The Perpendicular nave, almost an anticlimax after the richness of the early work to the east, was constructed c.1500 (the fine angel roof is a reconstruction of 1865), when the chancel aisles were also rebuilt and a two-storeyed vestry added further east. The present neo-Norman east end dates from a restoration of 1864-5 by John Norton, who was also responsible for the choir stalls, low screen and the removal of the Fairfield chapel (built c.1500) from the angle between the nave and south transept. The west doorway was in place in 1836 although Pevsner doubts that it is genuine Norman work reset. The Norman tub font in the north transept has four faces and cable moulding, while another at the west end was brought from Lilstock. The highly-carved series of bench ends date to 1535-9 and the initials on one of them can be identified (from contemporary accounts) with those of Isobel and Elizabeth Symons and Robert Evered. The south chancel aisle, formerly containing an altar to the Holy Trinity, is known as the Verney aisle and contains a profusion of monuments to former owners of the Fairfield estate. There are effigies identified as those of William Verney (died 1333), holding his heart, and John Verney (died 1462), the latter bearing the Verney arms of three fern leaves. There is an excellent and massive wall memorial to Sir Thomas Wroth (died 1721) of Petherton Park and others to his Palmer relations. In the floor of the north transept is a fossil ichthyosaur, found locally and installed here in 1944. The living was served by vicars by c.1280, appointed by the prior and monks until 1352, thereafter by the Crown and since 1453 by Eton College. There was a chapel of St John the Evangelist in the churchyard in the 12th century and a mortuary chapel or Dead House spanned the stream from 1867.

Fairfield is a major house on the western boundary of the parish, held in 1166 by Goslan and carried in 1287 by Margaret Russell, probably his descendant, to the Verneys of Hillfarrence. From the Verneys the estate passed in the later 16th century by marriage to the Palmers, and in 1762 to their cousins the Aclands, later Acland-Hoods of West Quantoxhead, lords St Audries from 1911. The second Lord St Audries (died 1971) returned here from West Quantoxhead and the house is now occupied by his niece, Lady Elizabeth Gass, direct descendant of William Russell, owner in the early 13th century, and possibly of Goslan in the 12th. The present

Hinkley Point Nuclear Power Station, near Stogursey

Stoke Pero

mansion may encapsulate the building surrounded by a wall and seven towers, put up by William Verney c.1473, but in its present form is E-shaped, probably the work of Elizabeth (died 1592), wife of William Palmer, but described by Gerard as 'unfinished' in 1633. It was remodelled by Sir John Acland c.1780 and c.1815. A chapel here is recorded by 1313 until the late 16th century. There were a large number of other early estates in the parish, of which Durborough was held by Glastonbury Abbey from the late 10th century (later divided into the manors of Durborough Dodington and Durborough Verney), and those of Wyndeats ('Widiete' in 1086), Idson, Shortmansford, Shurton, Woolstone and Steyning were all recorded in the Domesday Book. At Shurton Court in 1794 Coleridge stayed on his first visit to the Quantock area in company with Robert Southey.

Stolford, recorded from 1431-2, is an isolated coastal settlement north-east from the main village, evidently occupied by fishermen who had 12 'net-stalls' and 9 fish weirs here by 1551. Here the primitive 'mud horse' or sledge is still in use to harvest shrimps, prawns, eels and skate. There was a chapel of St Michael in the hamlet by the 15th century, maintained by the earls of Egmont from 1758 but demolished by 1824. The present church of St Peter was provided in 1866 by Sir Peregrine Fuller-Palmer-Acland.

On the coast due north from Stogursey village rise the stark modern towers of **Hinkley Point Nuclear Power Station** (lists), which form a major modern landmark from the Quantocks and from all points east and west along the Somerset coast. Construction began in 1957 and the first station has produced electricity since 1965. A second station was completed in 1976 and a proposed third reactor (Hinkley 'C') has excited considerable public concern. Regular public tours are available.

★★★★ *Stogursey church,* ★★★ *Stogursey village and castle.*

STOKE PERO (C) Stoke means simply 'settlement' or 'place' (and later 'dairy farm') and even for Exmoor this is a remote area, described by James Savage in 1830 as being 'as isolated a spot as any in the whole country'. At the time of the Norman Conquest there were three small estates here: Stoke, Wilmersham ('Winemaer's farm') and Bagley. Bagley has long been abandoned but its Saxon owner, Caflo, was one of the few who retained his tiny holding after the Battle of Hastings, albeit with a Norman overlord. A fourth property in the north of the parish, Lucott, became a possession of Taunton Priory from the 12th century, accumulated mainly from small grants by the le Tort family, together with the adjoining Buckethole (formerly 'Buggedehole') in Luccombe. The same century saw the earliest evidence of the presence of the Pirou family (from Pirou in Normandy), who probably built the first church here, held the main estate until the 14th century and added their distinctive name to that of the manor. In the east of the parish the little church has no known dedication, unless it be to St Barbara, whose name appears on a 15th century bell: one of three in the 13th century gabled tower. The rest, apart from the porch and its door, was rebuilt by Sir Charles Thomas Dyke Acland in 1897, one donkey called Zulu carrying all the timbers up from Porlock. No village as such survives. In 1791 Collinson wrote of 14 houses near the church but today there is only Church Farm, dating from the 17th century. Even in so remote a place three rectors died in the Black Death of 1348-9, and in 1369 a fourth, Robert Thoryng, kidnapped the wife of Simon atte Lovecote (Lucott) at Buckethole.

★★ *Scenery.*

STOKE ST GREGORY (E) The village extends north-east along the ridge from North Curry and seems to go on for ever. Its manor, known strangely as East Curry, was throughout its history held with that of North Curry: from 1190 by the dean and chapter of Wells Cathedral. 'Stoke' means simply 'place' and the church's dedication was added to distinguish it from other Stokes. The parish boasts at least eight farmhouses dating from the 16th or 17th centuries, notably at Meare Green, Curload and in Slough Lane. Pre-eminent among these is Slough Farm, a late medieval fortified house on a moated site with a 16th century gateway. At the time of its building it seems to have belonged to a branch of the Montague family, passing by the early 17th century to the Courts of Lillesdon in North Curry.

The church of St Gregory is basically 14th century, although the upper part of the central tower with its small spire was added in the 15th century. Of the later date are the south aisle, south porch (note the statue of St Gregory) and most of the windows. The unusual font is attributed to the 14th century. There are two pleasing monuments to the Court family in the south transept, featuring a touching verse to Margaret Court who died unmarried at Bath in 1710. Egg shackling (*see* **Shepton Beauchamp**) continues at the village school on Shrove Tuesday.

Egg-shackling at Stoke St Gregory

From the centre of the village the way is signed to the **Willows and Wetlands Visitor Centre** (fee:lists) at Meare Green where the Coate family have been creating baskets from the local withies since 1819. All the processes can be viewed at close quarters, there is a basket museum, an exhibition on the natural history of the Levels and an opportunity to purchase the end product.

A final word. If you continue through Stoke St Gregory to the hamlet of Stathe and turn right, there is a rewarding drive, walk or cycle ride past the Black Smock Inn (ask about the colourful legend behind the inn-sign!) through beautiful countryside before climbing the wooded hill to Curry Rivel.

★★★ *Willows and Wetlands Centre,*
★★ *church and area round it.*

STOKE ST MARY (H) The planners have diverted the old approach south-east from Taunton through the maze of a modern housing estate. The village is made up of old farmhouses and cottages, several of them thatched, with modern additions and infilling, largely strung out along a single lane below the wooded Blackdown Hills. The manor of 'Stoc' ('place' or 'dairy farm') was granted by King Ethelwulf of the West Saxons to Taunton's minster church in 854 but soon after it passed to the bishops of Winchester to form a tithing within their great manor of Taunton Deane. The church of St Mary is a small plain building which retains its 13th century west tower and 15th century chancel. Most of the remainder dates from the 1864 restoration which added a south aisle. The church may originally have been a daughter chapel to Ruishton and from 1308 both were served by a single priest from Taunton Priory.

A word of praise for the 1960s octagonal village hall at the western end of Stoke village. The village features several substantial houses, notably Stoke Court, last home to Elizabeth Barrett Browning's favourite sister, Henrietta Surtees Cook (died 1860), who was buried nearby at Thurlbear.

★★ *Village, setting.*

STOKE ST MICHAEL (F) A pleasant Mendip quarrying village north-east of Shepton Mallet, whose name ('stoke' – 'place' or 'dairy farm') is completed by the addition of the church's dedication. The origin of its alternative and often-used name, Stoke Lane (recorded from the 14th century), is something of a mystery unless it is a corruption of the surname of John de Lison, who ceded his lands here to Glastonbury Abbey c.1253. The main manor was generally held with that of neighbouring Downhead during the Middle Ages: from the 16th century, by the Horners of Mells, who themselves came formerly from Stoke. Manor House Farm to the east of the village dates from the late 17th century. A ruined Elizabethan house north-west of the farm, often claimed on no reliable authority to have been occupied by the dukes of Buckingham, was probably an earlier manor-house. In the village itself stands the late 17th century Knatchbull Arms, named for the Knatchbulls of Babington who held the manor by the late 18th century. Nearby, the church of St Michael was a chapelry of Doulting, with a guild until 1548, whose lands funded a priest here. The present building has a Perpendicular west tower, but the rest was rebuilt in 1838. There are some earlier monuments at the west end including that to William

Cornish, who was 'Barbarously Murdered' in 1817.

Stoke was a focus for cloth manufacture at an early date, James Bisse purchasing fulling and stone mills here in 1545. These mills were probably on the river Frome to the north of the village in the valley known as Stoke Bottom, which became a major industrial centre. Henry Fussell established paper mills here c.1803, which continued to work until 1839. Here also stood Stoke House, a mansion occupied successively by the Norman, Chichester (from Northover) and Burnard families, demolished in 1928 after standing empty for several decades. The Fussells who established their edge-tool business at Mells in 1744 came formerly from Stoke, a branch of the family also operated Stoke Lane Iron Works in 1871 and the Rev William Fussell was vicar here, 1834-85. There are stone quarries to the north and south of the village, including Moonshill, producing basalt for road chippings and tarmac.

STOKE-SUB-HAMDON (J) A substantial Ham-stone village ('stoke' – 'place' or 'dairy farm') to the north of and below Ham Hill, as indicated by the latter part of its name. In fact there are two villages, East and West Stoke, both strung out along the former main road eastwards to Yeovil. The Foss Way marks the north-western parish boundary, Roman remains have been turned up at Stanchester in the north of the parish and an inscribed column at Venn Bridge. The place was a noted centre for quarrying and, from the 18th century, of gloving. Estates here passed to Glastonbury Abbey in the 10th century but after the Conquest the principal manor, held under the Count of Mortain, was granted to Robert FitzIvo. From Robert's descendants, the Beauchamps of Hatch, it was known as Stoke Beauchamp, being acquired by the Duchy of Cornwall in 1443, which still holds it. This manor was focused on West Stoke and by 1333 on a major castle or fortified manor-house of the Beauchamps (ruinous by the 15th century) on a site north-east of the village, now partly occupied by Castle Farm. By 1287 the manor-house complex included the substantial St Nicholas Chapel which in 1304 Sir John Beauchamp converted into a collegiate church (suppressed in 1549 and later demolished). The provost and priests were accommodated in extensive premises in North Street, known since 1902 misleadingly as **the Priory** and bought by the National Trust in 1946 (fee: lists).

The chancel arch, Stoke-sub-Hamdon church

Dating largely from the 15th century the property includes an open hall, first floor chapel, circular dovecot and barns, and was restored in the 1960s. West Stoke also has a number of good 17th and 18th century houses and a large Congregational Church of 1865-6. The Fleur de Lis was the former church house, probably built in 1544, and converted to an inn by the 18th century when the fine finialed fives wall was built behind it.

East Stoke was the centre of a smaller Domesday manor, sometimes known as Stockett. It may represent the earlier settlement, for the superb Norman church of St Mary the Virgin (described in the 19th century as dedicated to St Denys or St Andrew) stands here. The chancel, nave, lower tower and font survive from the 12th century, with a fine (restored) chancel arch and several windows, one of which (north-west corner of the nave) may be Saxon. In the porch above the north door is an early carved tympanum depicting the tree of life and the named zodiac signs of Sagittarius and Leo (the same signs feature at South Petherton church). The north transept, beneath the tower, includes the effigy of Thomas Strode (died 1595), a former occupier of the 'Priory', and the south transept of c.1300 the figure of a priest identified as Reginald de Monkton (died 1307), first provost of the college. (*See also* **Ham Hill**)

★★★★ *Church,* ★★ *village, setting.*

STOKE TRISTER (F) A pleasant hillside village immediately east of Wincanton and yet another Stoke ('place' or 'dairy farm'), distinguished from the others probably by the addition of a corrupt form of the name of Richard del Estre, lord in the 12th century of several manors formerly held by the count of Mortain in 1086 ('Tristrestok' in 1265). In 1314 Henry de Lorty's park here was poached of venison with 'nets and other engines', and in 1333 a Wincanton raid on the park, headed by Richard Lovel, took not only deer but also hares, rabbits, partridges and pheasant from the warren. A survey of the manor in 1547 recorded that John Chycke held a plot of land for the rent of one penny, which he was to be excused if at the tenants' Christmas feast he should 'leape over the [table]borde and lette farte'! Stoke passed with Cucklington to the Phelips family in 1765 and thereafter was held with Montacute. The manor-house dates from the earlier 15th century and was described in 1547 as 'a statly house within the parke pale, all covered with tyle which begynnethe to decaye'. The formerly-detached kitchen survives behind it. The present church of St Andrew was built in 1841 half a mile north-west from the medieval church, believed to have been destroyed by fire. **Bayford** ('Boia's ford'), a hamlet on the east side of Wincanton, was held with Stoke and included Bayford Lodge, built in 1764, later occupied until 1848 by the Messiters, a prominent Wincanton banking family, and more recently by the first and only Lord Bayford (died 1940), former Minister of Agriculture.

STOLFORD (D) *see* **STOGURSEY**

STONEASTON (B) This high Mendip village lies north-east from Chewton Mendip, with which it was long associated. Its name, at first simply 'Easton', 'the eastern settlement' (from Chewton), was prefixed with the adjective 'stoney' by the 13th century. Five Bronze Age barrows on Chewton Plain were excavated in 1941. There are claimed to have been four separate manors here in 1086, including 'Haia' (represented today by Hay Street Farm). The principal estate, later known as Easton Major, was held by the Peytevyn family in the 13th century by service of one sester of clove wine to be delivered at Christmas to the king whenever he was in England. Walter Peytevyn transferred the manor to Bruton Priory (later Abbey) in 1348 which retained it until the dissolution of 1539. The manor-house and lands were bought by John Hippisley in 1544, his descendants retaining it for the next four centuries. His son, another John (died 1570), was a successful lawyer and MP for both Bridport and Wells, and the next three generations were also trained up in the law, living sometimes at Cameley and Emborough, and following the Roundhead cause in the Civil War.

The original manor-house, now represented by Manor Farm, east of the church, was replaced by a new substantial house to the north, probably built by Preston Hippisley (died 1723) in the late 17th century. Preston's heiress married John Coxe (died 1717), MP for Milborne Port, and their son, John Hippisley Coxe (died 1769), extended and remodelled the house from 1739 to create the present Palladian mansion, **Ston Easton Park**. The project was evidently financed from his marriage to Mary Northleigh of Peamore, Devon, and their coat of arms appears over the front door. Their son, Richard Hippisley Coxe (died 1786), evidently completed the house, served as MP for Somerset 1768-84 but died single and insane. It was left to Richard's brother Henry, also MP for Somerset (1792-5), to employ Humphrey Repton in 1793 to lay out the grounds. Although Repton's 'Red Book' designs were never fully carried out, there was extensive tree-planting, the River Norr was bridged twice and a sham castle, ruined grotto and romantic walks created. Henry's widow, Elizabeth Horner (died 1843), married his distant cousin, Sir John Coxe Hippisley MP, but under Henry's will Ston Easton passed to an even more distant cousin, John Hippisley (died 1898), an early photographer, and then to John's grandson, Cdr R.J.B. Hippisley CBE (died 1956). Subsequently the house was sold to William (now Lord) Rees-Mogg, editor of *the Times*, and, following a meticulous restoration, is today run by Peter Smedley (grandson of the founder of Smedley's tinned vegetables) and his wife Christine as an elegant and distinguished country house hotel.

A second manor, Easton Minor, was centred on the present site of Clare Hall (now a nursing home) and bought by the Hippisleys from the Churchey family c.1723. There was a chapel of St Mary adjoining the manor-house by 1201 but this was evidently demolished soon after 1548 when it was decided that it 'maye welbe spared, for that Eston maior standeth within 2 furlonge and nerer the towne'. The former chapel of Easton Major, now the parish church of St Mary, lies south of

Ston Easton Park and was a chapelry of Chewton Mendip. It has a Perpendicular west tower, a (reconstructed) Norman chancel arch and a wealth of Hippisley memorials, but was radically restored by Sir Arthur Blomfield 1890-1. Here in 1594 were married Bishop John Still and Jane Horner. (*For* **Old Down** *see* **Emborough**)
★★★ *Ston Easton Park.*

STOWELL (K) A small rustic parish midway between Wincanton and Sherborne whose name means 'stony stream' or 'spring'. The most noted name linked with it was successful lawyer, John Hody (died 1441), MP, Recorder of Bristol and Lord Chief Justice from 1440. He bought Stowell manor in the 1420s and lived here, at Stowell Farm House, an L-shaped building which may date from the judge's time or soon after. The Hodys continued as lords until 1720 and the manor was bought in 1753 by the Dodingtons of Horsington. Beside the farm stands the church of St Mary Magdalene with a west tower dated 1748. The rest was rebuilt in Perpendicular style to the design of Frederick Bligh Bond in 1913. Both manor-house and church are isolated from the little village to the south-west.

STRATTON-ON-THE-FOSSE (B) A former coalmining Mendip village south-west from Radstock which lines the Roman Foss Way, its name 'Stratton', meaning 'settlement on a Roman road'. The manor here was granted to Glastonbury Abbey c.970 by Aelfthryth, queen of Edgar, but by 1263 it had passed to Beatrice de St Vigor, from whose family the place was regularly known as Stratton St Vigor. The parish church is dedicated to St Vigor, although it is not clear if this dedication was inspired by the family (who may have taken their surname from their original home, St Vigeur-le-Grand, near Bayeux, where the saint founded a monastery in the 6th century) or if the dedication christened Stratton and subsequently its lords. In 1267 Thomas de St Vigor was granted a Wednesday market (changed to Tuesday in 1282) and three-day fair here. Thomas's son sold the manor to Thomas de Gournay in 1308, whence it passed in the 15th century, like other Gournay manors, to the duchy of Cornwall which still retains it. The commons in the south of the parish may have been the earliest site of coalmining in Somerset, where there is a reference to 'the place of the ancient [coal] works' in 1477. Initial surface mining or by means of bell pits eventually gave way to

shafts. Pitcot ('Picote', 1086) was worked by 1750, Old Rock Colliery from 1786 and New Rock Colliery from 1819 until its closure in 1968. From 1545 the manor and its mines were leased by the Long family who, in the absence of resident lords, became leaders of the community, later succeeded by the Knatchbulls, both living at the early 18th century Stratton House to the north of the village. The Perpendicular church of St Vigor, looking out across fields, lies to the east of the Foss Way down a lane marked by a War Memorial in the form of a slender pinnacle. The chancel was rebuilt in 1765 and the north chapel, containing monuments to the Long and Knatchbull families, c.1780. (*See also* **Downside Abbey**, which lies immediately east of, and dominates, the village.)

STREET (E) A small town immediately south-west from Glastonbury whose economy rests on the making of shoes by a single firm: founded and developed by the Quaker family of Clark. Its Saxon name suggests a settlement on a Roman road, but its former Celtic title 'Lantokay' ('the church or sacred enclosure of Kay') would indicate that the place had a religious origin at the hands of a holy man named Kay. He can perhaps be identified with the 6th century St Kea, possibly from Glastonbury, who probably founded the church here before continuing on to Devon, Cornwall and Britanny. Tradition and the church's dedication link Street with St Gildas, a testy Celtic saint, who c.540 wrote a tract attacking the behaviour of British rulers in the face of the Saxon menace from the east. Gildas was claimed to have composed his work on Steepholm, the island in the Bristol Channel, after which it is asserted that pirate raids forced him to seek a more secure refuge here, where he built his 'chapel of happy retreat'. A charter of Haeddi, bishop of Winchester 676-703, conveyed the estate to Glastonbury Abbey, which retained it until the dissolution of 1540. The monks initially knew the place as Leigh ('a clearing'), a name which survives in three farming hamlets running in a line south from the town: Lower Leigh, Middle Leigh and Higher (or Over) Leigh, and it was included within the Domesday hundred of Ringoldsway. The adoption of the name Street could also reflect the rebuilding of the causeway linking the place with Glastonbury in the late 12th century. The abbey had a grange here by 1239 but this does not survive. It probably stood near the site of the present Grange (long known

as Street Farm) in Grange Road, dating from the early 16th century but remodelled with a colonnaded front in the early 19th. After the dissolution the Grange (whose owners were regarded as squires here) was held in turn by the Dyers (1563-1628), the Strodes of Barrington (1628-1741) and the Brownes (1755-1829). The south of the parish was occupied by the manor of Ivythorn, first mentioned c.1190, which extended into the adjacent parish of Compton Dundon and was held under the abbots by the Ivythorn family until the 15th century. The E-shaped house (of which one arm has been demolished) was possibly rebuilt in 1578 (datestone) although a stone with the monogram of Abbot John Selwood (1436-93) is incorporated in the building. The manor lands were dispersed in 1699.

Street was a village until the last century. Early industry was limited to quarrying the local blue lias stone by the 15th century, used in building both Glastonbury Abbey and Wells Cathedral. There was an annual fair and a Midsummer revel, and wool spinning and stocking knitting gave employment to the women. A major tannery was founded c.1810 at Middleleigh by Arthur Clothier, who took as his apprentice (and from 1821, partner), Cyrus Clark (1801-66), of Quaker farming parents who had moved to Higher Leigh from Greinton in 1750. In 1825 Cyrus set up his own business producing sheepskin rugs, taking his brother James (1811-1906) as an apprentice, the latter introducing the manufacture of woollen slippers called Brown Petersburgs and later boots and welted shoes. The first factory building was put up in 1829, although outwork was long a feature of the business, and thus C. & J. Clark was born. Crises in the 1840s and 1863 were weathered thanks to injections of cash by fellow Quakers and under James's son, William S. Clark (1839-1925), the concern was put on a firm financial footing, employing 1,200 workers by 1887. The Clarks ploughed much of their money back into the development of Street, notably all their profits from supplying troops in the Crimean War, later setting up a succession of public buildings and housing for their growing work force. **Crispin Hall** (1885), named for the patron saint of shoemakers and opened by orator John Bright, was built as the Street Club and Institute but now serves as a cultural centre with exhibition hall and art gallery. The old factory in the centre of the town received its clock tower (1887) and water tower (1897) to celebrate Victoria's

TOP *Clark's shoe factory, Street*
ABOVE *Street church*

TOP *Gracie Fields' clogs, the Shoe Museum*
ABOVE *Crispin Hall, Street*

Jubilees. The chimes from the clock tower are struck on four bells named after the daughters of W.S. Clark: Esther, Alice, Margaret and Hilda. Much of this factory is today occupied by **the Shoe Museum** (lists), which documents the history of the firm and also the story of shoes with original examples of footwear from Roman times onwards. Behind the factory **Clark's Factory Village** opened in 1993, featuring a succession of units operated by national names such as Laura Ashley, Dartington Crystal, Pierre Cardin and, of course, Clarks itself, all marketing goods at up to 65 per cent off normal prices. There are picnic and play areas, a cafe and access to carparking is clearly signed off the town's bypass. Opposite the factory a former cider tavern was rebuilt in 1894 as the Bear Inn temperance coffee-house, taking its name from the Strode family's crest (derived from a pun on the name Barnard, into which family the Strodes had married) and only reverting to a public house in recent years. The name of Strode is perpetuated in Strode (tertiary) College and, on the same campus, Strode Theatre.

The **church of Holy Trinity** (formerly dedicated to St Gildas) stands marooned in industrial back streets at the northern edge of the town: the price for having been sited in isolation on the Mead until the 19th century. It was believed to have been given to Glastonbury Abbey by King Ine and was regarded as one of the abbey's seven churches not subject to episcopal control. It was the mother church of Walton chapel and rectors of Street lived at Walton, paying an annual sum to the abbey's meadmaker. In the church Edward I, to avoid infringing the abbot's rights during a visit to Glastonbury, personally presided over the Somerset Assizes in 1278. The present church is early 14th century (Decorated), although the top of the tower was added in the 15th century. The north aisle was added in 1826 and the chancel reroofed in 1843. One rector, Joseph Glanvill (1672-80), wrote a best-seller on witchcraft. The Society of Friends arrived in Street in 1656, George Fox himself visited in 1663 and the stately Quaker Meeting House in Church Street is a rebuilding of 1850. **Millfield**, originally built in 1889 as a new home for W.S. Clark, became from 1935 a major independent

school with an international reputation. Founded by R.J.O. Meyer (retired 1970), it has grown progressively and occupies several other major houses in the area, including Edgarley near Glastonbury and Kingweston. East of the parish church Bowlingreen Mill was developed by the Clarks as a tanyard from the 1830s, home to the Avalon Leatherboard Company from 1878.

Marshalls Elm on the southern boundary of the parish was evidently an early execution site, probably named after a family that held Ivythorn manor during the 17th century. It is now remembered for the events of one day, 4 August 1642, when a small royalist group of 80 horse and 14 dragoons, led out of Wells by Sir John Stawell, found their progress barred by a Parliamentary force of 600 from Taunton and South Petherton, headed by John Pyne. The Cavaliers routed their more numerous opponents, who fled leaving 7 dead and a further 18 wounded who died later. These were the first deaths anywhere in the country in the Civil War which split England during the years that followed. Running west from Marshalls Elm across

ABOVE *Walton Hill, near Street*

BELOW *Wall painting, Sutton Bingham*

BELOW *Barn at Sutton Mallet*

Walton Hill is a minor road above the National Trust wooded hillside, commanding magnificent views across the Levels to the Mendip Hills.

★★★ *Shoe musem and factory village,*
★★ *town.*

STRINGSTON (D) Just north of the A 39 near Stogursey, this small village, its name meaning 'Strenge's settlement' and latterly part of the Acland-Hood estate, comprises a small group of houses round a green. There also stands the church of St Mary the Virgin, undedicated until recently, largely rebuilt in the 19th century and restored in 1912 by Sir Prior Goldney, baronet of Halse. The Prior family, ancestors of the Goldneys, were farming in the parish by the 15th century and gave their name to Priors Farm here, furnished with fine plasterwork dated 1641 and 1658. In the south transept of the church is a good series of 18th and early 19th century monuments to the St Aubyn family of Alfoxton (*see* **Holford**), formerly a detached part of the parish. The nearby hamlet of Dyche was mentioned in the Domesday Book and the eccentrically-named Gugglemoor in the 13th century. (*For* **Dowsborough hillfort** *see* **Dodington**)

★ *Village.*

SUTTON BINGHAM (J) The 'southern settlement', presumably in relation to Yeovil although it also sits on the southern boundary of the county, has been dominated since 1956 by a 142-acre reservoir holding 500 million gals. Fly fishing for trout is available and there is a sailing club. The Binghams were lords here from the 13th to 15th centuries and the manor was ultimately bought by the Helyars of Coker Court in 1814. There is no village as such and the early 17th

century manor-house and the church of All Saints stand almost alone in a short lane, overlooking the reservoir. The church is a small Norman gem with a magnificent chancel arch, simple windows and font, with cable moulding. As if this were not enough, the 1868 restoration disclosed late 13th century reddish brown wall paintings (unfortunately retraced by a 19th century hand), which almost fill the chancel, illustrating the coronation of the Virgin Mary and figures of female saints and bishops. In 1917 scenes of the death and funeral of the Virgin were discovered on the north wall of the nave, with smaller fragments elsewhere.

★★★ *Church.*

SUTTON MALLET (E) One of several Polden parishes which were once chapelries of Moorlinch, it is centred on a small but pleasant hamlet which in the 17th century was known occasionally and

delightfully as Venice Sutton or Venus Sutton. As 'the southern settlement' it gained its suffix from the ownership of the manor by the Malet family by the 12th century until the 17th. In 1720 the manor was bought by the notorious Robert Knight, cashier of the South Sea Company, whose 'bubble' burst that same year. Knight's escape to the continent with embezzled funds of the bankrupt company was engineered by his prominent friends and, although his Sutton estate was confiscated, it was later bought back by Knight's son. Apart from the west tower, the chapel, now redundant, was rebuilt in 1829 to designs of Richard Carver and preserves its original high-sided box pews, clerk's desk and pulpit. The round stone by the porch, popularly supposed to have once carried a beacon fire on top of the tower, was more likely the base of a churchyard cross.

★★ *Village and setting.*

SUTTON MONTIS (K) This 'southern settlement', probably in relation to Cadbury Castle, which lies to the north-east, was held in 1086 under the Count of Mortain by Drew de Montagu (or Montacute), whose descendants were

Swell Court

lords here until the late 15th century. Indeed the place was known as Sutton Montacute until the last century, only recently adopting its present form. The village is full of fine houses and cottages, the most notable being the Abbey House of the late 15th century and Parsonage Farm of the 17th. Both lie at the north end of the village near the church of the Holy Trinity. The Burtons and their descendants the Leaches were rectors here from 1573 until 1878. The building has a short 13th century west tower. There is a fine Norman chancel arch and in the chancel a brass to the Duports (overlooked by Connor), lords of the manor in the late 16th century. The nave was rebuilt in 1805 and an idiosyncratic porch with Tuscan pillars clapped onto the south wall.

★★ *Village,* ★ *church.*

SWELL (J) From the Langport to Taunton road (A 378) a sign 'Ancient Church' directs the visitor to a small hamlet, whose name refers to 'a swelling' in the hillside. The manor was held in medieval times with nearby Curry Rivel by the Revel and Lorty families, later passing from the Warres to the Grosvenors, ancestors of the dukes of Westminster. To reach the church of St Catherine means a short walk past the magnificent manor-house, Swell Court, dating from the 15th century. Behind the court the small church, granted to Bruton Priory by Walter de Asselegh c.1220 and formerly housing a chantry founded by Maud Revel c.1250, has a Norman south doorway but is otherwise 15th century, as are the two bells which now rest on the nave floor. The Jacobean pulpit is dated 1634 and a small brass plate in the sanctuary floor commemorates the energetic John Toose (died 1582) and his long-suffering wife, who between them produced 14 sons and 6 daughters.

★★★ *Church and its setting.*

TARR STEPS (C), *see* **HAWKRIDGE**

TATWORTH (J), *see* **CHARD**

TAUNTON (H) Somerset's county town lies at the heart of the lush, fertile valley of the river Tone, intensively farmed since Romano-British times and probably even before: its name meaning 'settlement on the Tone'. It is an attractive town at its heart although generally not a beautiful one. Most of its medieval and Tudor buildings were evidently destroyed by fire and by cannon in the Civil War sieges of 1645, there was little distinguished rebuilding and only a few architectural gems remain. Its post-war development has been patchy, although recently of much more sympathetic character. Its modern central shopping areas include the Riverside (by the Bridge), the Courtyard (off St James Street), County Walk (south of East Street), the Old Market Centre (south of the Parade), alongside the traditional attractions of Bath Place (a picturesque passage west of High Street). Indeed the town is now a major shopping centre, with the Brewhouse Theatre and Arts Centre,

cinemas, Stansell Art Gallery, Somerset County Cricket Club, two swimming pools, Blackbrook Sports Pavilion, and Youth and Community Centre. The Victorian suburbs have been vastly extended in latter decades, almost ringing the town in a sea of red brick. The arrival of the railway in 1842 and of the M5 in 1974-5 both ensured the town's economic prosperity in those eras. Taunton is celebrated for being the home of three public schools. Queen's College, named for Queen Victoria, was founded by the Wesleyans in 1843 and has occupied buildings on Trull Road since 1848. Taunton School, established by the Congregationalists in 1847, moved to its present Fairwater site on Staplegrove Road in 1870. King's College, formerly King Alfred's, was set up by Canon Woodard in 1880 in buildings of 1870 in South Road deserted by the old town grammar school. A fourth school, which occupied Fullands House (now in multiple occupation) on Shoreditch Road 1840-88, educated the future General Gordon of Khartoum and on its playing fields Somerset County Cricket Club was born in 1875.

Taunton was in origin a Saxon town at the heart of the manor of Taunton Deane, one of the largest such manors in England and divided into five 'hundreds' which surrounded the town: Hull, Nailsbourne, Staplegrove, Holway and Poundisford. Ine, king of the West Saxons, established a fortification here (although its site is uncertain) in the early 8th century, destroyed by his queen Ethelburga in 722, probably to prevent its seizure by rebels. A minster church was evidently founded soon after, traditionally by Queen Frithogyth, wife of Ine's successor. The town flourished under successive bishops of Winchester, lords of Taunton Deane by 904 (until 1822), and was a Saxon *burh* where coins were minted from the later 10th century and which had

The River Tone, Taunton

64 burgesses in 1086. A Saxon cemetery has been traced under Castle Green and Taunton Castle, probably associated with an 8th century minster church which later became St Peter's chapel in the castle. Taunton is stated to have been damaged by fire in 1111, a disaster which aeems to have stimulated a burst of civic activity. The town's first charter was granted in 1136, the bishop of Winchester started to build a castle in 1138 which led in turn to the removal of the priory (founded c.1120-25) from the castle area in 1158 to a site outside the north-east of the borough. The embanked defences around the central area of some 60 acres seem to have been laid out at around the same time, when north and east gates were mentioned, although the original course of the western boundary is uncertain.

A market was recorded by 904 and was held on the Parade, the town's central triangle, until 1929, when it moved to its present site in Priory Bridge Road. On the medieval Parade stood the Chuse (cheese ?), Rix or Ruish and High crosses, the last at the junction of High and Corporation streets until removed c.1770. St Botolph's Fair was also held on the Parade, while the site of St Thomas's Fair, granted in 1256, was evidently the present car park west of the Plaza Cinema to the north of the river. Taunton Deane manor had ten mills in 1086, of which one was almost certainly the Town mill on the site of the present Goodland Gardens. To this was added in 1218-19 the earliest recorded fulling mill in the county, both mills being powered by a leat which still runs from Frenchweir on the Tone, west of the town. This marked the beginning of cloth manufacture in the town, the bishop of Winchester contributing the raw material: 200 ewes, 200 lambs and 3 rams. Overseas trade developed through Topsham and Lyme Regis with Brittany by 1467 and with the Guinea coast of Africa by 1588. Despite reverses during the 17th century, the industry continued until its final decline during the later 18th. Silk weaving was introduced from London in the 1770s, then lacemaking and, from the 1860s, the manufacture of collars and then shirts. In the present century the production of optical instruments was begun by Avimo from 1937, British Rail's concrete works were established at Priorswood and the Admiralty Hydrographic Department was set up in the shadow of Creechbarrow Hill. Increasingly Taunton was regarded as the county town after the county court moved here from Ilchester in 1843 and Wilton

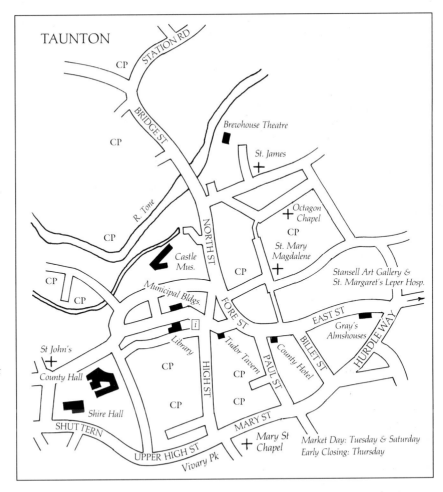

Gaol in Shuttern was enlarged to become the County Prison (closed 1884). Shire Hall, the Gothic creation of William Moffatt, was completed in 1858 and its vestibule is decorated with busts and inscriptions commemorating Somerset worthies. Finally, Somerset County Council was moved from Weston-super-Mare in 1935 to occupy Vincent Harris's County Hall: since extended in modern glass and steel.

Taunton was represented by two MPs from medieval times until 1884 (then by one until 1918), elected before 1832 by 'potwallopers': all those who had a fireplace on which to boil a pot. Among its MPs were in 1529 Thomas Cromwell, Henry VIII's minister, and Henry Labouchere (died 1869), who in 1859 resigned to become the first and only Lord Taunton. Opposition from the bishops of Winchester meant that the borough did not secure a mayor and corporation until 1627, and then only by petitioning while the bishopric was vacant. Unfortunately the town almost made a habit of forfeiting its charters: in 1660 for supporting Parliament in the Civil War

(regranted 1677), in 1792 for failing to maintain a quorum (regranted 1877) and in 1974 when it was finally swallowed up by Taunton Deane District (later Borough) Council.

On the national stage, Taunton was the scene of a skirmish between the lords Devon and Bonville during the Wars of the Roses in 1451, and Queen Margaret and her troops passed through in 1471 to defeat at the Battle of Tewkesbury. In 1497 a Cornish rebel army murdered and dismembered the provost of Penryn on the Parade and that same year Henry VII came here to cross-examine Perkin Warbeck, whose own rebellion had ended at Taunton when most of his men deserted him. During the Civil War the town was at first held for the Crown but seized in 1644 by the Roundheads and held for Parliament by Robert Blake, later Cromwell's General-at-Sea, in a protracted siege and bombardment. On the approach of Sir Thomas Fairfax's New Model Army, the royalists fired the outskirts which resulted in the destruction of much of the town before the siege was raised on 11 May 1645: an

Taunton Castle

anniversary long celebrated here. Dissension continued to fester after the Restoration of 1660 and made Taunton a natural objective for the Duke of Monmouth after his landing at Lyme Regis in 1685. The Duke himself was accommodated during his three-day stay at John Hucker's house in East Street opposite the present County Hotel, was presented with banners by local schoolgirls ('the Maids of Taunton') and proclaimed king at the High Cross on the Parade. We have the names of nearly 400 townsfolk who marched out with him (with a further 150 from adjacent parishes). After the defeat at Sedgemoor Col Percy Kirke arrived here with prisoners and two carts full of wounded and summarily hanged 19 rebels on the Parade without trial. Judge George Jeffreys later held his Bloody Assizes in the great hall of the Castle, trying 526 cases in three days, following which a further 19 prisoners were hanged, drawn and quartered in the market-place. Another 139 were ordered for execution elsewhere and most of the rest were transported to the West Indies.

The central triangle of the town and former market-place, the Parade, was occupied in the mid 18th century by no fewer than 11 inns, a medieval guildhall (with gaol under), and a market-house of c.1682 with assembly room over. All this was swept away in 1768 and the present Market House completed in 1772,

although lacking its side arcades since 1930. South of the Market House are the town's oldest surviving houses, a half-timbered range centred on the **Tudor Tavern**. The rear of this restaurant dates back to c.1350 with a facade added in 1578 by clothier Thomas Trowbridge, whose initials with those of his wife Joan appear beneath a first-floor window and whose grandson emigrated to America to found a prominent Connecticut family. One former occupier under the wealthy Portmans was Thomas Baker, a grocer and prominent supporter of the Duke of Monmouth, two of whose daughters presented banners to the Duke in 1685, giving the lie to traditions which link Judge Jeffreys with the property. East from the Parade in East Street the **County Hotel** has an impressive Georgian facade of 1784 but was first mentioned in 1528-9 as the Three Cups Inn. Further down the street, County Walk shopping precinct preserves the frontage of the former Phoenix Inn, once kept by John Gill (died 1865), better known as Manchester Jack: England's first great lion-tamer. Beyond extends a fine range of almshouses with nine diagonal chimneys, built by Robert Gray in 1635, the earliest dated use of brick in the county.

The north-western sector of the old borough was occupied from 1138 by **Taunton Castle**, which served as both court house and manor-house for the bishops of Winchester and their manor of Taunton Deane. Castle Green was the outer bailey of the Castle, its medieval east gate surviving as Castle Bow, now incorporated in the Castle Hotel of c.1820. The west gate formerly spanned the roadway beside the Winchester Arms. The Castle keep, whose footings were uncovered in the hotel garden, was ruinous by the early 17th century. The remaining buildings, enclosed by a filled moat and surrounding a courtyard, date from the 13th century but were remodelled from 1786 and in 1816 to provide courts for the Assizes and Quarter Sessions and lodgings for the judges: continuing as such until Shire Hall was completed in 1858. Since 1874 the Castle has been home to the library and offices of the Somerset Archaeological and Natural History Society, its museum taken over by the County Council in 1958 to become the **Somerset County Museum** (fee:lists), occupying the former Great Hall and adjacent galleries. The museum houses major local collections illustrating the history, archaeology and natural history of the county, including a

section of prehistoric Levels trackway, the Roman mosaic from Low Ham, and locally- produced silverware and pottery. The Castle has also accommodated the county's **Local History Library**, with extensive printed and microform holdings, since 1973 and the Somerset Light Infantry's **Military Museum** since 1974. In the courtyard, a former bay of St James's almshouses of c.1500 was re-erected in 1993. Beside the castle entrance is set a sword in a stone: last relic of a 1987 Son et Lumière which retold the Somerset legends of King Arthur. The outer bailey was also surrounded by a moat, through part of which Corporation Street was constructed in 1894, lined by the **Municipal Buildings**. The eastern part of this range was built by Bishop Richard Fox of Winchester 1522 as Taunton Free Grammar School, and its impressive great schoolroom is now the Municipal Hall, hung with portraits of local worthies. The Council Chamber above (the buildings were occupied by Taunton Borough Council from 1887) is garnished with Tauntonian memorabilia, including the staves of office of the Court Leet, which continues to meet there annually. High Street seems to have been a later addition to provide overspill for the market from the Parade. From its south end stretches **Vivary Park**, named from the 13th century *vivarium* or fishpool of Winchester's bishops and cut by a stream dug in 1332 to bring water into the town.

The park is furnished with impressive entrance gates and bandstand (both 1895), and an ornate fountain set up in 1907 as a memorial to Queen Victoria with money left over from the local celebrations of Edward VII's coronation. There are also tennis courts, a golf course, and cricket ground, all overlooked by the massive red-brick tower of Jellalabad barracks (1881), former base of the Somerset Light Infantry and named after the regiment's 19th century Afghan campaigns.

The Augustinian monks of Taunton Priory, following their 1158 grant of lands to the north-east of the borough, built their church of St Peter and Paul and seem to have laid out St James Street, Canon Street and Middle Street as a planned medieval suburb. Throughout four centuries the priory dominated the religious life of the town, the monks serving many of the churches and chapels in the area and the inhabitants of Taunton Deane manor had to be buried within the precinct. The monastery was dissolved in 1539 and most

of its buildings were swept away within a
century by the More family to build their
Priory House. All that survives is part of
the precinct wall lining Canon Street and
the Priory Barn, in origin one side of a
gateway of c.1500 and now occupied by
the **Cricket Museum** (fee:lists) of Somerset
County Cricket Club. The **Church of St
Mary Magdalene** stands at the end of
Hammet Street, a planned development
begun in 1788 by Sir Benjamin Hammet
which opened up a magnificent vista of the
four-stage 163 ft church tower. The
original tower of 1488-1514, one of the
architectural jewels of the county with
Somerset tracery in its bell openings and a
graceful pierced and pinnacled crown, was
completely rebuilt 1858-62 as a faithful
copy of its unsafe predecessor. Since 1711
it has contained a carillon of bells, playing
tunes on the hour. The five-aisled body of
the church is of similar date to the tower,
apart from the 13th century arcade
between the two north aisles, to which an
ornate south porch dated 1508 has been
added. There is a good contemporary nave
roof, painted in recent years, but most of
the fittings are 19th century. There is a
small brass to the family of Thomas More
(died 1576) of the Priory and a fine painted
effigy of Robert Gray, merchant-tailor of
London and almshouse-builder, dated 1635
(although he died and was buried in
London). From 1308 the vicars were given
responsibility for serving the churches of
Trull and Wilton and St Peter's chapel in
the Castle. There were no fewer than seven
chantry chapels and guilds of the High
Cross and Holy Sepulchre which survived
until 1548.

In St James Street the church of St James
was established to serve the priory suburb
and the growing population north of the
river, and was served directly by the
monks. It is uniformly 15th century with a
120 ft west tower that, like St Mary's, is a
rebuilding (1870-75), a superbly detailed
(but over-restored) font and a good
Jacobean pulpit dated 1633. There are
monuments to the family of Yea baronets
of Pyrland Hall (a classical house of 1758 at
the northern limit of the town, now called
King's Hall and occupied by King's College
Junior School) and the Hallidays of Yarde
House. The twin church towers form a
familiar backdrop to televised cricket
matches from the county ground. There
were medieval chapels of St Paul, outside
the castle west gate, St Leonard at Pyrland
and St Margaret 'of the sick'. The last
served St Margaret's Leper Hospital, now
in Hamilton Road towards the east end of

St Mary Magdalene church, Taunton

the town and on the former boundary
between the parishes of St Mary's and
West Monkton. Probably founded by the
monks of Taunton Priory in the early 12th
century, the present house is a rebuilding
of c.1510-15 by Richard Bere, abbot of
Glastonbury and lord of West Monkton
manor, whose monogram appears in the
front wall. Used as an almshouse for West
Monkton by 1612 until 1938, it was

occupied by the royalist forces during the
Civil War siege and latterly served as
the headquarters of the Somerset Guild
of Craftsmen and the Somerset Rural
Community Council. It has lain sadly
derelict since its thatched roof was
destroyed in two arson attacks. A growing
population led to the building of Holy
Trinity church (1842, by Richard Carver),
St John the Evangelist (1863, by Sir George

Gilbert Scott with a fine spire), St Andrew's (1881 as the railwaymen's church by J.H. Spencer, enlarged 1890), All Saints in Roman Road (1953) and St Peter's, Lyngford (1956).

The town was notorious for its Puritan complexion in the early 17th century, and from the time of the Civil War most nonconformist sects found a ready reception with the cloth factors and their workers. Paul's Meeting in Paul Street, now the United Reformed church, was founded in 1672 but sacked by the royalist mayor in 1683, when its pulpit, pews and galleries were torn out and burnt on the Parade. **Mary Street Chapel**, formerly Baptist but latterly Unitarian, preserves its fine galleried interior of 1721 with two massive Corinthian pillars, high pulpit and brass chandelier of 1728. John Wesley preached in Taunton on 26 occasions from 1743 and personally opened the Octagon chapel off Middle Street in 1776, now encapsulated in a modern housing development. The Wesleyan congregation migrated in 1811 to the Temple Methodist church, built in Upper High Street in 1808 by wealthy bookseller, James Lackington, and named after his London bookshop, the Temple of the Muses. A second Baptist church in Silver Street was put up in 1814 and given a highly-ornate Italian frontage in 1870. The Roman Catholics opened a chapel in the Crescent (an attractive terrace of houses begun by banker William Kinglake in 1807) in 1822, now the Masonic Hall, with pillared Ionic facade. In 1860 they built St George's church at the top of Billet Street to provide a smaller-scale version of the view up Hammet street to St Mary's.

Wilton, at the south-western end of the town was formerly a separate parish but has long been continuously built-up with Taunton and is notable for large and fashionable Victorian villas. The name means 'settlement by the well' and evidently centred on the Fons George, a holy well dedicated to St George. Fons George manor and its chapel were among the early endowments of Taunton Priory, although the chapel was served from 1308 by the vicar of St Mary's. The present church of St George, tucked away down a side lane from Middleway, has traces of Saxon 'long-and-short' stonework on the outer west wall of the south aisle. The rest is largely Perpendicular, although the chancel, west tower and south porch were all rebuilt in the 19th century. Sir Benjamin Hammet (died 1800), formerly MP for Taunton, lies under a large table tomb in

The Crescent, Taunton

the churchyard. Hammet lived nearby at **Wilton House**, a large mansion with a hint of Holland in its facade, now occupied as an old peoples' home. It was built in 1705 by Christopher Cooke, a wealthy clothier and sympathiser of the Duke of Monmouth, who lived in exile in Amsterdam until a free pardon lured him back. His merchant's mark appears over the entrance door although the coat of arms there are those assumed by the Kinglake family who bought out the Hammets and occupied the house until earlier this century. West from Wilton lies Galmington ('settlement of the rent-paying peasants'), a medieval hamlet largely obliterated by modern residential development. Both Sherford and Shuttern seem to take their names from the brook that links them, recorded as the Saxon 'Scitere': 'the stream in which dung is thrown'.

★★★★ *Somerset County Museum,* ★★★ *St Mary's Church (mainly for its tower), Mary Street Chapel;* ★★ *St James's Church, Municipal Hall, town generally (*★★★ *as a shopping centre), Wilton Church.*

TELLISFORD (B) A small village, partly destroyed by a major fire in 1785, to the north of Frome and on the west bank of the river Frome, which here forms the boundary with Wiltshire. Its name ('Tefleford' in 1001, 'Tablesford' in 1086) may mean 'Theabul's ford' or 'ford at a flat place'. The manor was acquired by the Hungerfords of Farleigh in the early 15th century, who used the manor-house and a fulling mill here to endow their chantry chapel in Farleigh Castle. The cloth

industry continued in the parish until 1911, the mill being reckoned as one of the largest in the Frome valley in 1821. The church of All Saints stands at the end of a long church path from the centre of the village. It has a late Norman south doorway and a font of the same period. The rest is largely Perpendicular with a pulpit dated 1608 and was heavily restored in 1854. Most of the monuments commemorate 19th century members of the Crabb family who held the mills here and lived at Crabb Hall.

TEMPLECOMBE (K) This sizeable village, originally known simply as Combe ('valley'), lies south of Wincanton, and since 1860 has been dominated by its railway station (closed 1966-83) on the main London line. It was also a station on the former Somerset and Dorset Railway ('the Slow and Dirty'), 1862-1966. The modern parish was formerly two separate estates and villages. The more northerly one was held from Saxon times by Shaftesbury Abbey and thus known as Abbascombe. The other manor was owned by Earl Leofwine, brother of Harold who died at Hastings, but after 1066 was given to William the Conqueror's half-brother, Bishop Odo of Bayeux. His descendant, Serlo FitzOdo, granted it in 1185 to the Knights Templar, who established a preceptory here and from them it became known as Templecombe. The Templars were suppressed in 1312, their estate here being granted to the Knights of St John, who converted the preceptory to their commandery, dissolved by Henry VIII in 1540. The last remains of their chapel behind the 17th century Manor Farm at the south end of the village were demolished in the 1970s, although earthworks which formerly enclosed the fishponds survive. A small Saxon cemetery with eleven burials of c.700-1000 was found in 1991 close to the northern boundary with Horsington. Lions Gate has at its core a four-bay medieval cruck house. The church of St Mary, just north of the railway, was held with Abbascombe by Shaftesbury Abbey. It is largely Perpendicular but the north aisle was added in 1834 and the chancel rebuilt in 1865. On the south wall since 1956 has hung the medieval panel painting of a head which bears an uncanny resemblance to that on the Turin Shroud. It was found above the ceiling of an outhouse in West Court off High Street in 1945 and has led to much speculation linking it with the Templars. The railway connection also made the place a popular venue for releasing racing pigeons.

THORNE (J) Evidently named for a prominent thornbush, this small but satisfying village, north-west of Yeovil, comprises 17th and 18th century Ham stone houses along a north-south street and was usually known as Thorn Coffin from the Coffin family who held the manor by 1279 until 1376. A manor here, later known as Thorne Prior, was granted to Stavordale Priory in 1441. At the northern end of the village in grounds fringed with yews stands Thorn House, a large neo-Elizabethan property built in 1882 by Sir Thomas Jackson for the lord of the manor, Judge Hooper (died 1895). The little church of St Andrew, with a western bellcot typical of this area, stands at the opposite end of the village and was probably founded by Ellis Coffin c.1300. It was restored and partly rebuilt in 1895 but retains 17th century furniture. One rector, John Hearne, was gaoled in 1608 for failing to support his bastard child.
★★ *Village.*

THORNE ST MARGARET (H) This small parish to the west of Wellington presumably takes its name from an isolated thornbush with the addition of the church's dedication. Manor Farm, at the south-western approach to the village with an enclosed forecourt, dates from the early 16th century. The porch was added in the 17th century and is faced with slates cut in the shape of playing cards. Behind is a double threshing barn with horse-engine house, dated 1830. The church of St Margaret stands on a knoll with superb views towards the Quantock Hills. It has a 15th century west tower but the rest was rebuilt in 1865, its porch flanked by stylish boot scrapers. Saved from the former building is an early tub font and a brass to John Worthe of c.1610. In 1230 the patronage of the living was given by Baldwin of Thorne to the archdeacon of Taunton and it has continued with that office ever since.
★★ *Landscape.*

THORN FALCON (H) A tiny village just off the dual carriageway from Taunton to Ilminster (A 358). To Thorn ('thornbush') was added by 1265 'Fagun', now 'Falcon': probably the Norman surname of the family of Sir Gilbert of Thorn, lords until the early 14th century, who had by that date adopted the name of their new home. It was bought from the Burridges of Lyme

Thorne

Regis by Nathaniel Butler Batten of Yeovil (died 1785), whose descendants, known as Chisholm-Batten from 1859, lived at the 16th century Court House in Thorn Lane until 1979. The church of the Holy Cross, pleasantly situated towards the top of Church Lane, dates from c.1400 and includes a good series of benchends carved in 1542. There is a plain octagonal 13th century font and monuments to the Chisholm-Battens, including a hatchment.
★ *Church and its setting.*

THURLBEAR (H) Three miles south-east from Taunton and north from the Blackdown Hills, this leafy parish has a name which seems to mean 'hill with a hollow' ('Tierleberge' in 1084). The manor was owned from the Norman Conquest by Drogo de Montague, whose descendants held it until the beheading of the Earl of Salisbury in 1400. The Montagues gave the church to Taunton Priory in the 13th century and obtained a short-lived three-day fair here in 1314. The manor was bought by Lord Chief Justice, Sir William Portman, in 1556, following another execution: that of the Duke of Suffolk. The Portmans acquired the rectory estate in 1605 and dominated the place, as they did so much of the surrounding area, until the Crown Commissioners took over in 1944. The church of St Thomas, although much restored in 1864, boasts twin Norman arcades which Pevsner dates as early as 1110. In the churchyard are buried Henrietta Surtees Cook (later Altham) of Stoke Court, favourite sister of Elizabeth Barrett Browning, and other members of her family. It was also in the churchyard on Whitsunday 1611 that Robert Harris was accused of playing at bowls and quoits and

of tempting and seducing 'certaine maides who were sent to be catechised'.
★★ *Village, setting.*

THURLOXTON (D) 'Thurlak's settlement' is a peaceful haven just off the present A 38 near North Petherton. Both manor and church were held by the monks of Taunton Priory until the dissolution, thereafter passing to the Portmans of Orchard Portman. The church of St Giles dates mainly from the 15th century with a Norman tub font and a north aisle added in 1868. A richly-carved rood screen of three arches, pulpit (dated 1634) and a font cover seem all of a piece: possibly from the same hand that carved the woodwork at North Newton church. There are 19th century monuments to the Colthurst family, manufacturers of bricks and tiles at Bridgwater, who built the Manor House beside the church c.1840.
★ *Village and church.*

TIMBERSCOMBE (C) A delightful huddle of houses and narrow streets sited between Exmoor and the Brendon Hills, just off the A 396. Taking its name from 'the wooded valley' in which it lies, the manor was divided in the late 12th century between the heiresses of the Timberscombe family, but most was acquired by the Sydenhams in the 15th. Subsequently it passed to the Hill family 1567-1647, thereafter to the Elsworthys, later known as Elsworth. It was Richard Elsworth who in 1705 paid for a new west tower to the church of St Petrock in the centre of the village. Elsworth died childless in 1714 and, among other charitable bequests, left money to found schools at Timberscombe (the building

Timberscombe

survives in the village, complete with tablet) and Cutcombe. The church is largely Perpendicular, retaining its fine rood screen and 17th century pulpit. An early 16th century mural painting of King David plucking his harp was discovered above the south door in 1955. Note the early north door with its massive lock. The church was given c.1189 to Wells Cathedral to found a prebend there by Cecily of Timberscombe and her sisters. From the village there are walks to the famous Snowdrop Valley (recommended for February) and to the deserted hamlet of Clicket. West of the village is Bickham, a Domesday manor which gave its name to the Biccombe lords of Crowcombe. The present L-shaped house, formerly occupied by the Elsworths, dates from the 17th century.

★★★ *Walking,* ★★ *village, church.*

TINTINHULL (J) The parish lies on either side of the Roman Foss Way (A 303) just south-west from Ilchester: close enough to Ham Hill for its buildings to be largely constructed of golden Ham stone. The last syllable of its name means 'hill', preceded by the British *din* – 'fort' and an uncertain second element. As was usual in Somerset, the Saxons avoided the Roman roads when siting their villages, so that Tintinhull is attractively grouped around a triangular village green to the south-east of the old Foss Way. The manor originated in two 10th century estates given to Glastonbury Abbey, which the monks exchanged for Camerton with Robert, Count of Mortain. Robert's son gave Tintinhull to endow Montacute Priory c.1102, a 13-day fair was established, and the monks retained the

manor until their dissolution in 1539. Thereafter the manor passed to the Petre family and in 1673 to their former tenants, the Nappers. The rectory estate had previously been bought by Nicholas Napper in 1559 and his family occupied its manor-house, now Tintinhull Court. They gave a 17th century look to their medieval home, which bears their coat of arms over the main door and the initials of Thomas Napper on a weathervane dated 1673. The Nappers also upgraded a 1630 farmhouse (datestone on one gable with the letter N for Napper) in the early 18th century for a younger brother, Andrew Napper, since known as **Tintinhull House**. The Nappers sold the property in 1835 and it was a learned botanist, the Rev Dr S.M.J. Price, who from 1898 laid out noted gardens which were further developed after 1933 by Mrs Ferdinand Reiss. The house has been owned by the National Trust since 1954 and the formal gardens (fee:lists) amply repay a visit. As if all this were not enough, the Nappers were also responsible for the Dower House on the north side of the green, described as 'new' in 1687. Heavily in debt, the Nappers disposed of the manor to Admiral Arbuthnot in 1792 and the estate was finally split up and sold by Viscount Arbuthnot in 1913.

The church of St Margaret dates from the early 13th century: remodelled in the 15th century. The survival of early church-wardens' accounts makes it possible to date the south porch to 1441-2, the benchends to 1511-12 (with hinged panels to provide extra aisle seats – an alternative method

Tintinhull church

to that devised at Catcott), and the top of the tower and stair-turret to 1516-17. There is a fine brass depicting the rector, John Heth (died 1464). In the churchyard is a cross by Sir Ninian Comper (c.1920) and the 'stonyng door' set up as a churchyard gateway by the prior of Montacute in 1517. The church was raided in 1642 by Roundhead troops, who contented themselves with stealing two surplices which they cut up and handed out to the poor.

★★★ *Tintinhull House gardens, church.*

TOLLAND (D) A small parish in wooded country between the Brendon and Quantock hills, whose name is believed to mean 'land on the Tone': supposing that the stream on which it lies also bore the same name as the main river. Ralph son of William gave the church here c.1180 to the Knights Hospitaller for their sisterhood at Buckland Priory in Durston and the knights presented rectors until 1539, after which the patronage was exercised by the Crown: recently in the person of the Lord Chancellor. The church of St John the Baptist, formerly St Leonard, has a short 13th century tower and north arcade. The building was radically restored in 1871 by C.E. Giles but the backs of two end pews are constructed from 15th century benchends. The west window commemorates Henry Wolcott who left Tolland for America and founded a prominent family in Connecticut, one of whom, Oliver Wolcott, signed the Declaration of Independence. The coat of arms depicted in the window, however, was illicitly appropriated from the Walcot family of Walcot in Shropshire as the Somerset Wolcotts were generally husbandmen and clothiers. Their trans-atlantic success was marked by the christening of not only a town but also a county called Tolland in Connecticut state. Tolland manor, long in the hands of the Malets of Poyntington and West Quantoxhead, was lost after Baldwin Malet mismanaged his accounts as Receiver General to the Crown in the late 17th century. It was later acquired and used by Susannah Strangways Horner to found a charity designed to increase the incomes of impoverished clergy in West of England counties. The Old Manor House, dating from the 17th century, was occupied by the Brufords 1740-1811.

A mile south-east from the church lies **Gaulden Manor** (fee:lists), originating from 13th century grants to Taunton Priory ('Gaveldene' – 'rented valley'),

Gaulden Manor, Tolland

which held it until the Dissolution of 1539. Occupied from 1525 by the Sellick family, the ownership passed through various hands until the manor was bought in 1615 by Devonian John Turberville for his son, also John. Married in 1639, this son rebuilt the house and moved in with his family in 1642. His coat of arms with those of his wife, Bridget Willoughby, are incorporated in the elaborate plasterwork of the hall, featuring religious scenes and texts. The Civil War brought Roundhead soldiers to Gaulden in 1647: such drinkers, wrote John, 'that a barrell of good beare trembles at the sight of them, and the whole house nothing but a rendesvous of tobacco and spitting'. Fortescue Turberville, the builder's grandson, finally sold up in 1699. Stories which include the 16th century Bishop Turberville of Exeter and Henry Wolcott among the house's occupants have no basis in fact, and Thomas Hardy's Turbervilles of Bere Regis in Dorset were only very distantly related to those who lived at Gaulden. Around the house the present owners have developed most attractive grounds, including bog and herb gardens.

★★ *Gaulden Manor and gardens.*

TREBOROUGH (D) This 'hill of trees' lies in a valley on the north side of the Brendon Hills, once famous for the slate which was quarried here. In 1426 Sir Hugh Luttrell bought 2,000 Treborough slates for Dunster Castle and quarrying, in the hands of the Luttrells and then the Trevelyans of Nettlecombe, continued until 1938. In 1895 'gaunt chimneys' and 'ugly pumping-houses' were features of the landscape but time has mellowed the place's surroundings and a conservation area and nature trail were opened in Treborough Woods in 1982. The village itself is a huddle of houses around the small plain church of St Peter, with a 19th century pyramid cap to its south tower. The building is mainly Perpendicular, the local slate much in evidence underfoot. In the chancel is an unusually ornate pillar piscina and, at the west end, a 1965 sculpture of a figure at prayer by Rachel Reckett.

★ *Village, nature trail.*

TRULL (H) An attractive village immediately to the south-west of Taunton. Its name, formerly 'Trendle', means 'ring' or 'circle' and may suggest a vanished prehistoric stone circle or earthwork – the original circular form of the churchyard has also been remarked on in this connection. The area formed part of the bishop of Winchester's manor of Taunton Deane from the 9th century, divided between the tithings of North and South Trendle, and commemorated in the sign of the village inn, the Winchester Arms. The church of All Saints was served by the monks of Taunton Priory until 1308, when responsibility shifted to the vicar of St Mary's, Taunton. Subsequently Trull was served by curates and did not secure its own cemetery until 1476. The west tower dates from the end of the 13th century but the rest of the building is 15th century Perpendicular. The glory of the church is its woodwork. The pulpit of c.1500 is an almost miraculous survival, bearing the undefaced figures of saints John the Evangelist, Gregory, Augustine of Hippo, Jerome and Ambrose. One of the benchends is dated 1510 although much of the work may have been carried out later, around 1560, by the Bicknoller carver, Simon Warman, as recorded above panelling at the west end of the north aisle, and his initials appear elsewhere on the benchends. A fine rood screen bears traces of original colour on its east face but lacks its original tracery.

In the churchyard is buried Juliana Horatia Ewing (died 1885), in her day a popular children's writer. Her husband, Col Alexander Ewing, composed the tune for the hymn 'Jerusalem the Golden'. Batts Park, a substantial house to the east of Trull Road (Walter Bat occurs at Trull c.1250), was demolished in 1937 and its site subsequently occupied by Sherford Army Camp, headquarters of the South Western District, but now cleared for housing. The parish provides as great a number of scattered 16th and 17th century houses as anywhere in the county: Higher Comeytrowe, Budleigh, Chilliswood, Boxen Hedge, Dipford, Higher Dipford, Greenacres, White Lodge, Trull Green, Gatchell Cottage and Spinney, Hamwood, Kings Gatchell, Reaphay and Chantry Cottage.

★★★ *Church (for its fittings), the surrounding countryside and houses.*

The pulpit, Trull church

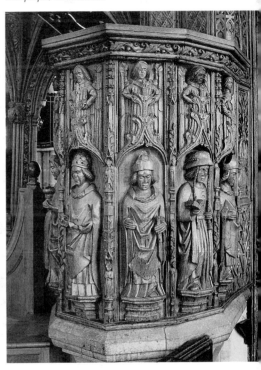

Mansions and Houses

Of major houses open to the public, the finest is Montacute: a substantial Elizabethan mansion of c.1590-1600 with contemporary plasterwork and portraits of the Phelips family who built it. An added bonus is the magnificent collection of Tudor and Stuart portraits in the Long Gallery, loaned by the National Portrait Gallery. Barrington Court is a substantial mansion built by William Clifton in the 1550s and restored internally by the Lyle family. Dunster Castle, former home of the Luttrells, is an elegant 17th century house, remodelled in the later 19th century and romantically situated within the hilltop remains of a medieval castle. Lytes Cary, home to the Lyte family by 1286 until 1755, is a delightful manor-house of the 15th and 16th centuries with a recreated Tudor garden. Poundisford Park was put up from 1546 by William Hill in the former deer park of the bishops of Winchester and is a tall three-storey building with extensive views towards the Blackdown Hills. Combe Sydenham was raised c.1580 by Sir George Sydenham, whose daughter married Sir Francis Drake. Its ongoing restoration by the Theeds has also included a small mill and there are idyllic walks through its parkland. Hatch Court, built c.1755 by John Collins with the profits of the Ilminster cloth trade, is an elegant four-square Palladian mansion in its own deer park: still replete with deer. The Jeanes family established Barford Park c.1710, with graceful side wings added in 1775 by Andrew Guy, overlooking Bridgwater Bay. Two Trevilian brothers erected Midelney Manor, a plain but inviting Elizabethan manor-house on the Levels, and the Trevilian descendants live there still. Gaulden Manor, on a site once owned by Taunton Priory, is a picturesque house dating mainly from a 1640s reconstruction by John Turberville, with fine vernacular plasterwork. Maunsel House is an impressive pile, built by the

Maunsel family from c.1500 and since extended: its lawns sloping down to the Bridgwater and Taunton Canal.

In a class of its own is the Bishop's Palace at Wells, the oldest occupied building in the county. Its central portion was the work of Bishop Jocelin in the early 13th century, with a lofty chapel and ruined great hall added soon after, and the present bishop's apartments put up in the mid 15th century. The whole is surrounded by a wall, gatehouse and moat, and a further towered

ABOVE *Gazebo at Montacute House* BELOW *Ston Easton Park*

gateway, the Bishop's Eye.

Smaller houses include the Treasurer's House at Martock, with its wonderful hall of the 1290s, and the thatched Priest's House at Muchelney, dating from 1308, both owned by the National Trust but open only by appointment. Coleridge's Cottage at Nether Stowey contains memorabilia of the poet, who occupied it 1797-99.

Other important houses to which the public has limited or unofficial access include Dillington House, the County Council's adult residential college, and Nettlecombe Court, leased by the Field Studies Council and occupied as the Leonard Wills Field Study Centre. Three fine buildings operated as hotels are Alfoxton Park near Holford, rented by William and Dorothy Wordsworth 1797-8, Ston Easton Park, former home of the Hippisley family, and the Luttrell Arms at Dunster. The best early inns in the county are the George and Pilgrim at Glastonbury and the George at Norton St Philip.

Particularly excellent buildings whose exteriors can be viewed at reasonably close quarters from adjacent churchyards include Brympton D'Evercy, Babington House, Cothelstone Manor and Whatley manor-house.

★★★★ *Barrington Court, Brympton D'Evercy, Lytes Cary (Charlton Mackrell), Cothelstone Manor, Dunster Castle, Barford Park (Enmore), George and Pilgrim (Glastonbury), Montacute House, Nettlecombe Court, George Inn (Norton St Philip), Bishop's Palace (Wells).*

★★★ *Babington House, Midelney Manor (Drayton), Luttrell Arms (Dunster), Hatch Court (Hatch Beauchamp), Treasurer's House (Martock), Priest's House (Muchelney), Coleridge's Cottage (Nether Stowey), Poundisford Park (Pitminster), Combe Sydenham (Stogumber), Ston Easton Park.*

★★ *Maunsel House (St Michaelchurch), Gaulden Manor (Tolland), Whatley Manor-house.*

TOP LEFT *Orchard Wyndham, 1839*
TOP RIGHT *Poundisford Park, 1832* BELOW *Dillington House*

UPTON (C/D) This 'upper settlement' is an isolated parish midway between Dulverton and Wiveliscombe. The original settlement evidently lay in the area of Upton Farm and the church of St James, both now on the eastern slope above Wimbleball Reservoir. Of the church held by the monks of Barlynch Priory only the 14th century west tower and the footings of nave and chancel now remain in a field of scattered tombstones. Its three old bells sit at the west end of the new parish church built in 1867 at the hamlet of Rainsbury, now known as Upton village, on the B3190. The new site was given by the Ferguson-Davie family of baronets, who are buried there and lived at Bittescombe Manor in the east of the parish. In the west stands a triangular castellated folly with hexagonal towers, formerly known as Haddon Lodge, now as Pepperpot Castle, standing beside a drive built by Lady Harriet Acland (died 1815) from her home at Pixton Park in Dulverton.

★ *Abandoned church for its atmosphere and position.*

UPTON NOBLE (F) A small village to the east of the Frome to Bruton road, 'the upper settlement', features some attractive 18th century houses and the enticing Lamb Inn. The suffix derives from the family of Sir John le Noble, who held the manor in the mid 13th century, bought by Bishop Robert Burnel in 1291. The small church of St Mary Magdalene was always a chapelry to Batcombe. The south tower is topped by a saddleback gable, there is an unusual stone crucifix in the south chapel and the building was restored in 1881.

VOBSTER (F), *see* **MELLS**

WALTON (E) A somewhat nondescript village which lines the main A39 just west of Street, blessed with two inns, the Royal Oak and the Pike and Musket. The meaning of the name is uncertain: either 'settlement in a wood or wold', or 'settlement of the Britons'. It is thought that Walton formed part of the Polden estate granted to Glastonbury Abbey by King Aethelheard of the West Saxons in 729. Certainly it was held by the abbey in 1086 when it included Compton Dundon, Ashcott and Pedwell. It formed part of the hundred of Whitley which took its name from a wood just within the eastern boundary of the parish and where the Hundred House stood beside the A39, c.1600. After the dissolution of Glastonbury in 1539 the manor was given to the

duke of Somerset, passing soon after to Sir John Thynne of Longleat (Wilts), whose descendants as marquesses of Bath held it until 1939, when it was sold off. The church of Holy Trinity was a chapelry of Street until 1886. The Perpendicular west tower has a plain slated pyramid roof, but the rest of the church was rebuilt in 1866 to the designs of John Norton. In the north-west corner of the nave is the fine effigy of a priest of c.1300. Surprisingly the rectors of Street lived at Walton in what is now the Old Rectory, to the west of the church, a substantial house of the mid 15th century. There is also the tower of a converted windmill on the Polden ridge, the Glastonbury records documenting the building of its forerunner, possibly a timber post mill, in 1342-3. Described as recently rebuilt in stone in 1742 and again in 1797, it ceased to grind c.1910.

A mile north from the village along Asney Road will bring the visitor within sight of **Sharpham Park Farm**. The estate was granted by King Edwy (955-9) to his thegn Aethelwold and probably passed to Glastonbury Abbey soon after, although a post-Conquest grant was also made by John, Count of Mortain. A mansion and chapel were built as a country retreat by Richard Bere, abbot of Glastonbury 1493-1524. It was at this house that the last abbot, Richard Whiting, faced the king's commissioners in 1539 before being dragged off to the Tower of London and finally to Glastonbury for execution. After the dissolution Sharpham was sold to the Dyers who parted with it in 1659 to the Goulds. Here in 1707 was born novelist Henry Fielding, author of *Tom Jones*, whose mother was a Gould. Davidge Gould added an additional wing in 1733, but more fundamental remodelling took place in 1799. Only the front door appears to survive of Bere's work. The place was home to Thomas Hawkins, the noted geologist and pioneer palaeontologist, 1832-45. From the road beyond the farm are superb views across the moors to Glastonbury Tor.

★★ *Setting of Sharpham.*

WAMBROOK (H/J) It was only in 1896 that this parish, west from Chard and formerly a noted producer of lime, limestone and marl, was transferred from Dorset and its manorial and ecclesiastical links were earlier always with neighbouring Chardstock, which that same year was moved from Dorset to Devon. The name of the place may mean 'crooked stream', although this is doubtful if 'Awanbruth', a

Wambrook church

9th century estate granted to Sherborne Abbey (Dorset) by King Egbert of the West Saxons, can be identified with Wambrook. The main hamlets of Higher Wambrook, Wambrook and Lower Wambrook (sometimes known as Haselcombe) lie on the side of a north-south valley. At Wortheal, an early freehold on the high ground in the west of the parish, there are substantial earthworks: possibly Iron Age. From the mid 12th century the manorial estate was owned in turn by the Olivers, the Fillols and from 1527 the Willoughbys, who sold it in 1588 to fund the building of Wollaton Hall, Notts. The name of its purchasers, the Drakes from London, survives in that of a farm at Higher Wambrook, but the manor was soon after split up and sold. The former manor-house, apparently near the church and used as a church house from 1529 until at least 1666, has long gone.

The church of St Mary the Virgin has a chancel dating from the 13th century, much altered, but the nave, porches and west tower are 15th century: all heavily restored in 1892. Wambrook was not furtunate in some of its former ministers. John Marraker, rector 1555-91, could not read or speak clearly and was accused of immorality with a female in his flock. His son, Christopher, rector 1591-1621, ran a private school but 'had no regard to the souls of his scholars'. The chalice of 1621 bears an egotistical inscription that he contributed 35s towards its cost. His successor, Gamaliel Chase, rector 1621-45, was persecuted by both sides during the Civil War and William Randall, the intruded rector 1650-62, was described as 'an idle sottish fellow'.

★★ *Setting.*

WANSTROW (F) A quiet peaceful village, its name meaning 'Waendel's tree', lying south-west from Frome on a loop off the A 359, which was the original course of the main road before Bruton Turnpike straightened it c.1810. The bishop had an estate here before the Conquest which in the 12th century was used to endow a prebend in Wells Cathedral. The manor split into two properties, one known successively as East Wanstrow and Church Wanstrow, the other as West Wanstrow, Wanstrow Rogers and Wanstrow Buller, the latter given by Hugh Sexey to endow his hospital at Bruton. This place was known for coarse earthenware made from clay dug on Wanstrow Common. The manufacture was reduced to a single pottery by 1826 where formerly there had been 11. One of the most successful was owned by John Yeoman (died 1824) who lived at the battlemented Park House, dating from the late 17th century. Nearby stands the church of St Mary, thoroughly restored in 1877. In 1866 a neighbouring clergyman commented that Wanstrow's rector, the Rev Cicero Rabbits, was cohabiting with a woman and 'is only in residence during the shooting season'. West Town is a secondary settlement of stone cottages to the west.

WASHFORD (D) *see* OLD CLEEVE

WATCHET (D) An appealing small town, port and former borough to the east of Minehead, with narrow winding streets, an attractive series of small shops, several old inns and walks along the esplanade. At the town's heart, the former Market House has housed **Watchet Museum** (fee: lists) since 1979, with displays illustrating the town's archaeology and local history. This was also the harbour from which Coleridge's ill-fated Ancient Mariner set sail, 'below the kirk, below the hill': a poem which tradition claims was begun at the Bell Inn in Market Street.

The place's name occurs as 'Waeced' in 917 and 'Wecedport' in 987, and seems to represent the Celtic for 'below the wood', although the trees above the town were felled long ago. It was clearly the most important seaport in Saxon Somerset and Viking raids here are recorded in 917, 987-8 and 997. After the first the raiders were driven off, seeking refuge on Flatholme where many of them starved to death, but following the last 'they wrought great havoc by burning and killing people'. There was also a mint here by c.980. The original site of the Saxon *burh*, first

Watchet Museum

recorded c.900 in the Burghal Hidage (the record of a network of forts to defend southern England), probably lay at Daw's Castle, an earthen bank formerly topped by a mortared wall which lies on the coast below the B 3191 to the east of the town. The present name is derived from Thomas Dawe who c.1537 rented a field called 'le castell'. The site evidently originated around the shrine of St Decuman, believed to have been a 6th century Welsh monk who, according to legend, was martyred here, carrying his severed head to a nearby holy well. There is also a gap in the coastal rocks below, which would have enabled boats to land. The site was much eroded by the sea and probably in the 11th century (when there is an hiatus in the issue of coins) a new site was settled to the east which became the present town.

The move can also be linked with a medieval feast of the translation (removal) of St Decuman, when the saint's shrine was evidently re-established on the prominent site of the present parish church to the south-west of the town. The chancel is late

Watchet Harbour

13th century but the rest of the church, with its two aisles and west tower, dates from a Perpendicular rebuilding that was evidently in progress in 1498. There are rood and side screens evidently dating from the same rebuilding, with Jacobean communion rails, altar table and pulpit. The area passed into the hands of the Wyndham family of Orchard Wyndham by purchases during the 16th and 17th century, and their monuments will be found in the north chapel with the family pew, dated 1688. There are fine portrait brasses to Sir John Wyndham (died 1574) with the wife who brought him the Orchard estate, Elizabeth Sydenham (died 1571), their son John Wyndham (died 1572) and his wife Florence Wadham (died 1596). A story has long been told that Florence 'died' soon after her marriage but revived in the family vault when the sexton tried to cut off her finger to steal her rings. A further brass depicts Sir John's second son, Edmund Wyndham (died 1616) of Kentsford. Edmund evidently rebuilt Kentsford Farm (a site on Washford river, south-west from Watchet, mentioned in the 12th century) c.1600 and it was later held by his grandson, the royalist Civil War governor of Bridgwater, Sir Edmund Wyndham (died 1683). The church was given to Wells Cathedral by Simon Brett to endow a prebend c.1190, with land formerly conveyed to it by Robert FitzUrse, and the parish formed a 'peculiar' under successive prebendaries, its estate described in the late 15th century as 'the sanctuary of St Decuman'. There was also a chapel of the Holy Cross at Watchet on the site of the present London Inn from the early 13th century until 1548, with a chantry chaplain required to pray for the

souls of members of the FitzUrse family. The same dedication was used for a chapel on the first floor of the Market House from the 1920s.

There was a market at Watchet by 1222 (continuing on Saturdays until the 1830s) and a borough had been established here before 1243, probably by the FitzUrse family. Evidence of trading developed in the same century with a quay on the north side of a large open market-place, although storms severely damaged the town in the 1450s and 1640s. Principal imports featured coal, iron and cattle from Wales, salt and wine. Alabaster from the cliffs was used to produce medieval effigies in the area's churches. There were fulling mills here by the 14th century and a cloth industry continued until the 19th. A western pier to shelter the quay was built by 1801 and extended with a breakwater and jetty 1861-2, when the eastern pier was added. With the exploitation of the Brendon Hill iron mines, the West Somerset Mineral Railway (see **Brendon Hill**) was begun in 1856 to export the iron ore to Wales, running up the valley of the Washford river from the harbour. The West Somerset Railway arrived from Taunton in 1862: extended to Minehead in 1874. The most persistent local industry was the manufacture of paper, which had begun on the Washford river to the west of the town by 1652. The mills were operated by the Wood family by 1727 until 1834, and by the Wansboroughs c.1840-1903, after which they were bought by W.H. Reed and became part of the Reed and Smith group. The harbour closed to commercial activity in 1992, although plans for its future are under consideration. It continues in use for pleasure-boating and fishing. The town was administered by Watchet Urban District Council 1902-74.

Doniford is a hamlet to the east of Watchet, named by 1196, where Old, Middle and New Stone Age flints have been found and evidence of a 4th century Romano-British settlement. William de Reigny (died 1275) had a house here, with a chapel served by the rector of Aisholt, and the Huish family held land here from 1369 until 1669 with a medieval mansion house, Doniford Farm. There was a fish weir here by 1275 and from the 16th century ore (seaweed) was collected here for drying or burning, the resulting kelp being used in the Bristol glass industry.

★★★ *Harbour, St Decuman's church,*
★★ *town, museum.*

WATERROW (D) *see* **CHIPSTABLE**

ABOVE *Wayford Manor and churchyard*

BELOW *Alabaster angel, Weare church*

WAYFORD (J) This attractive and unspoilt village, 'ford on a road', straggles along a hillside lane overlooking the Axe valley to the south of Crewkerne. The main manor estate, held by William of Wayford c.1200, passed by marriage to the Daubeney family in the early 16th century. Among their descendants, born at Wayford in 1612, was Dr Daubeney Turberville (died 1696), a famous occulist who was consulted by Samuel Pepys and Princess Anne. Wayford Manor, the Daubeney family home beside the church, was described in 1633 as 'a faire house . . . well accommodated with gardens and orchards'. It is a medieval building, remodelled by Giles Daubeney in 1602 to form an E-shape with a porch supported on Tuscan columns, and was extended c.1900 to the designs of Sir Ernest George. The house is not open to the public but the lovely gardens on the slope below the Manor, laid out by Harold Peto early this century, are occasionally opened in aid of charity. There are pleasant woodland walks off the lane beyond the village to the south. The church of St Michael is a small plain building dating from the later 13th century but much rebuilt and restored. It was formerly a daughter chapel to Crewkerne, symbolized by annually laying the key to the church's north door on the altar of Crewkerne church as late as 1833. Wayford was a popular venue for clandestine marriages 1721-53. A monument recalls the support of the church orchestra by the Bullen family, tenants of the Manor in the 19th century. Lower Bere Chapel Farm was a manor-house owned by the Portman family from 1530. Its name suggests that

there was a medieval private chapel there, although the present building dates only from the 17th century.
★★★ *Village and setting.*

WEARE (A) A parish immediately south-west from Axbridge which takes its name from a weir, possibly connected with the river Axe. The old village was formerly known as Over or Upper Weare and the main estate was granted to Walter of Douai after the Conquest, passing to the Gaunt, Gournay and Bythemore families. The church of St Gregory was given in 1257 to St Augustine's Abbey, Bristol, and after the dissolution was bestowed on the dean and chapter of Bristol. The present building is

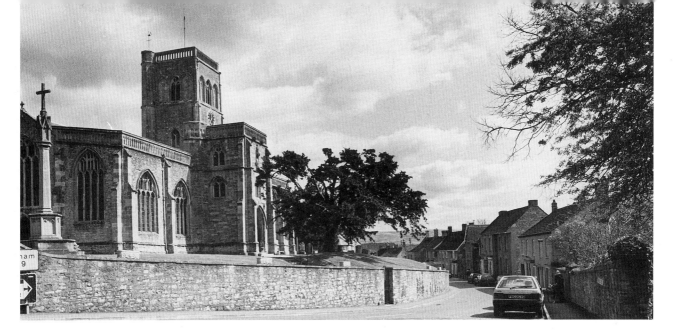

Wedmore

Perpendicular with a good west tower but was heavily restored and the north aisle added in 1846-8. There is a square Norman fluted font, a Jacobean pulpit dated 1617 with an hour glass bracket beside it. In the sanctuary is a brass depicting merchant John Bedbere of c.1500. Even a hat peg is dated 1690 and a door hinge 1755 ! Imaginative communion rails, featuring kneeling alabaster angels, were the gift in 1901 of the Luttrells of Badgworth Court.

Along the present A 38 the Gournays established a borough, possibly in opposition to the bishops' borough of Rackley (*see* **Compton Bishop**), and called it Nether (later Lower) Weare. Although in 1418 claiming privileges granted by Henry I, the process seems to have started with the grant of a Friday market and a fair to Robert de Gournay in 1241 and a borough was mentioned two years later. A new grant in 1298 to John Apadam substituted a Tuesday market and another fair, and the place even sent MPs to Westminster on three occasions, 1304-6. Burgages here were held by St Mark's Hospital, Bristol, and the building of a new mill here brought the hospital into dispute with the bishop in 1316. Thereafter the borough declined, probably because of the proximity of the much older Axbridge, although a borough court was still being held in 1603-4. Lower Weare has been home to **Ambleside Bird Gardens** (fee: lists) since 1943. There are displays of tropical birds, 'pet corner', attractive gardens and a lake, with gift shop and restaurant.

South of Weare is the hamlet of **Alston Sutton** ('Aethelnoth's settlement'), a Domesday manor held in 1286 by Walter de Sutton. There was a free chapel here which may have been Saxon in origin.Tithes were paid to the priest but it never secured a graveyard. It was 'utterly decayed' in 1548, although still with its resident chaplain, and was demolished soon after.

★★ *Ambleside Bird Gardens.*

WEDMORE (E) One of the largest parishes in the county but today a friendly closely-knit community sited in the centre of the Levels midway between Burnham and Wells. Conflicting ownerships on the moors during the Middle Ages led to unedifying squabbles between church dignitaries. The origin of its name is uncertain but seems most likely to be 'moor of shallow water' (Saxon *waed*). Recent excavations have revealed evidence of Romano-British as well as Saxon settlement. The place was a royal estate of the West Saxon kings and it was later claimed that King Centwine (676-85) had given it to St Wilfrid of York and that Wilfrid had given it to Glastonbury Abbey. The manor was clearly back in royal hands by 878 when, after the victory over the Danes at Edington and Guthrum's baptism at Aller, Alfred brought Guthrum here to conclude the Peace of Wedmore. Alfred left Wedmore to his son and heir, Edward the Elder, in 899 and it continued in royal hands until Edward the Confessor gave it to the bishop of Wells, Queen Edith adding Mudgley and Mark to the grant. The larger estate later became known picturesquely as Wedmoreland. By 1157 Bishop Robert had bestowed the manor and church on the deanery of Wells and the income was devoted to the endowment of four (later five) cathedral prebends. In 1255 a Tuesday market and three-day fair were obtained and it was probably at this time that a borough was established (described as 'new' in an undated deed c.13th century). A 14th century market cross with lantern head survives. The borough court was still appointing officials under a portreeve in 1791, and the Borough was one of the five tithings into which the parish was divided but the place never developed into a successful town. Rent was still being paid by 38 borough tenants in 1873 (one of their holdings called 'Burnt Backside') when the Court Leet was held at the George Hotel. The bishops retained a country residence at Mudgley with its own chapel, demolished by Bishop John Harewell c.1380. In 1547 Wedmore, with the other deanery estates, was surrendered to the Crown and granted to the Duke of Somerset, thereafter passing into lay hands.

The church of St Mary Magdalene stands up the slope from the centre of the village and is the rival to North Curry for the title 'Cathedral of the Moors'. It is a large cruciform building, largely Perpendicular, but with a south doorway and supporting piers and arches below the central tower of c.1200, a chancel built shortly afterwards and a south-east chapel of c.1300. There is a substantial Jacobean pulpit, above which is a vernacular painting c.1520 of St Christopher, redone more than once. In the vestry (north chapel) are two late brasses to members of the Hodges family: one to Capt Thomas Hodges who at the Siege of Antwerp, c.1583, 'with unconquerd courage wonne two Ensignes from the Enemy; where, receiving his last wound', he asked that his body be buried in Flanders but his heart returned to Wedmore for burial. The west window has a Victorian depiction of Alfred burning the cakes. Until 1548 there was a chantry chapel of the Virgin Mary here.

The centre of the village is a hive of small-scale activity with shops, restaurants and pubs. An annual revel on the Wednesday after Whitsun week occupied the people until 1830 and the popularity of cudgel-playing, a barbaric rural sport, continued even longer, John Bunn of Wedmore being declared champion in Berkshire in 1857. Porch House was the home of John Westover, a surgeon dentist in the late 17th century, who treated mental patients and, just as rarely, kept a diary. In Pilcorn Street the reforming bluestocking, Hannah More, founded one of her Sunday schools in 1799, and in Church Street John Tonkin built c.1830 a major fashion house in a grand Italianate building which is now the National Westminster Bank.

Among several secondary villages in the parish, **Blackford** to the east had a free chapel by 1176, although its present octagonal church of Holy Trinity was the work of Richard Carver in 1823 and the place only became a parish in 1844. Blackford manor, given by King Edwy (955-9) to Glastonbury Abbey, later formed one of the endowments of Hugh Sexey's hospital at Bruton, and the hospital trustees founded a secondary school here in 1899. **Theale** (meaning 'planks', referring to a wooden bridge) to the south-east also became its own parish in 1844, having commissioned Richard Carver to build Christ Church in 1820. Beyond Theale lies **Panborough** (possibly 'wayfarer's hill'), where King Edwy gave an estate to Glastonbury abbey in 956 (later the manor of Northload) which included a vineyard, mentioned again in 1086.

★★ *Wedmore village.*

WELLINGTON (H) A friendly town to the west of Taunton whose main streets house a refreshing range of small shops, drawing custom from a wide radius. The town originally lined the former main route from Taunton to Exeter, although the arrival of the railway in 1843 drew settlement north towards the river Tone and the 20th century has seen considerable residential development to the south. At the central crossroads, the former Town Hall, built in 1833, has been converted to

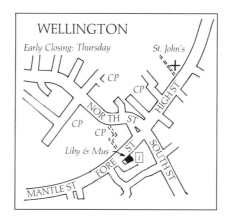

Town Hall, Wellington

an attractive shopping arcade and in Fore Street a small one-room **museum** (fee:lists) is housed in the old Squirrel Inn. In South Street is the substantial Baptist Chapel of 1833 and the independent Wellington School, founded by Benjamin Frost in 1837 but which owes its present prominence to the headmastership (1899-1938) of George Corner. In Mantle Street, Old Court may represent the original manor-house, where there was a medieval chapel of St Lawrence.

The town's complex name, originally 'Weolingtun', possibly meaning 'the settlement of the people near the [pagan] temple clearing', may suggest that the rise on which the parish church stands was an early sacred site. The place was first mentioned in an undated charter of 899 to 909, by which King Edward the Elder of the West Saxons gave the manor to Bishop Asser of Sherborne, biographer of his father, King Alfred. After the bishopric of Wells was founded in 909 the estate was

transferred to the new diocese. The bishops created a park, probably near Park Farm, in 1189 and secured the right to hunt there in 1257. Soon after, as on several of their other Somerset estates, they planted a borough here, first recorded in 1279, by laying out a new east-west street to the south of the church: sufficiently wide to accommodate the market, where a man was murdered in 1305, as well as fairs at Easter and Ascension. The shamble stalls used to line the north side of High Street until swept away c.1813. A market house on brick pillars, which also served as town hall and supported the town clock, stood in the middle of the street near the central crossroads until demolished at the end of the 18th century.

The bishops largely retained their estate until forced to sell it to the Duke of Somerset, Protector of the young Edward VI, in 1548. Forfeited on the Duke's execution, it was held by a succession of lessees from the Crown, including Queen Elizabeth's favourite, the Earl of Leicester, until sold in 1624 to Sir Francis Popham, son of Lord Chief Justice, Sir John Popham (1533-1607). Sir John, who presided over the trials of Mary, Queen of Scots, Sir Walter Raleigh and Guy Fawkes, although not lord of Wellington manor, built a grand mansion here, destroyed during the Civil War in a brief but bitter siege and excavated in 1952. It was from Wellington that Sir John sent to London the first news of the approach of the Spanish Armada, his letter endorsed frantically 'Haste, haste, I say, haste, post haste'. The Popham estate, divided into the twin manors of Wellington Borough and Wellington Landside, was sold in the mid 18th century and later bought by Parliament to present to the future Duke of Wellington in 1813.

Like most Somerset towns, Wellington produced cloth in the Middle Ages. There was a fulling mill, probably on the Tone, in 1503 and a cloth house near the marketplace by 1548. From Devon in the 1730s came a Quaker family, the Weres, to found a clothmaking business which was to dominate the town's economy for over two centuries. Tone Mills were built in 1754, the year that election riots in Taunton marked the start of the decline of that town's cloth manufacture to the east. The Weres and their descendant and successor, Thomas Fox (died 1821), went into Europe with a vengeance and, although initially spurning steam power, suggested on a personal visit by James Watt in 1782, expanded into the Culm valley (Devon) in 1797. In 1801 Thomas began to build a new woollen factory on the north side of Wellington, christened Tonedale, constructing the Basins to provide reserve supplies of water. Tonedale was rebuilt after a fire in 1821 and, adopting steam power in 1840, the firm of Fox Brothers flourished, 'discovering' the true shade of khaki at the time of the Boer War and producing 70,000 pairs of puttees a week during World War I. Quaker paternalism (as at Street) led the Foxes to provide the town with schools, a park, playing field and maternity hospital. Sadly, the recession of recent years has led to contraction and decline, and much of the Tonedale complex is now occupied by small businesses. To the west of the town at Westford, another successful textile factory was established in 1780 by the Elworthy family, closed in 1934. Two other concerns have weathered the economic storms. Bedding manufacturers Relyon developed from a factory founded in South Street by a Montacute Baptist, Joseph Price in 1858. Aerosols International originated in a chemical company started in 1910 which produced its first aerosol fly spray at Swallowfield in the late 1940s.

The **church of St John the Baptist** at the east end of the town was held with the manor by the bishops who ordained a vicarage in 1234. Typically Perpendicular, it has a slender western tower in red sandstone, a lofty airy interior.and a chancel rebuilt in 1848. In that rebuilding a defaced reredos of c.1380 was found beneath the chancel floor and is now partly exhibited in the County Museum. There is a delicate lily crucifix in stone on the mullion of the east wndow in the south aisle and the superb canopied tomb with the effigies of Sir John Popham and his wife. A second effigy in the chancel represents a 14th century priest identified as Richard David, vicar c.1310-33. Vicars have included John Cardmaker alias Taylor, burnt alive at Smithfield in 1555, John Salkeld (1613-35), personally converted from Roman Catholicism by James I, who dubbed him 'the Learned Salkeld', and William Prockter Thomas (1843-50), who divorced his wife by Act of Parliament for adultery, secured £2,000 damages from her Tiverton lover, and remarried in church to father a second family. John Wesley preached from the pulpit here in 1775. There was a long tradition of nonconformity, the Quaker presence dating back to a visit by George Fox in 1663. The Roman Catholic church of St John Fisher in Mantle Street opened in 1940 in the former Popham almshouses.

Rockwell Green is a former hamlet to the west of Wellington with which it is now almost continuously built-up. Formerly known as Rowe Green, it was often called 'Rogue Green' because of its disreputable inhabitants. Its present name was adopted c.1780 and presumably refers to the brick well at the core of the village. The church of All Saints was put up in 1888 to the designs of J. Spencer, to which a tower and spire were added in 1908.

The British military hero, Sir Arthur Wellesley, became Viscount (1809), and then Earl (1812), Marquess (1813) and Duke (1814) of Wellington: titles apparently chosen only because of the closeness of the town's name to his surname. After the duke's victory at Waterloo a subscription was launched to build on top of the Blackdowns a tall column, **the Wellington Monument**, to be crowned with a massive cast-iron statue of the Duke 'in the attitude of commanding', and three cottages at its base to be occupied by retired army veterans: an Englishman, an Irishman and a Scotsman. Work began in 1817 but funds fell short and the monument was left incomplete. It was later found that the mortar used had been soluble in water ! After the Duke's death in 1852 a further appeal was opened but failed to realise sufficient funds for the statue or cottages and the column of 170 ft was finished off with a pyramid top. The monument was made triangular in section not to resemble a Waterloo bayonet, as often stated, but so that it would only use up half as much masonry. A major restoration completed in 1892 (there have been several since) raised the height to 175 ft and the column passed into the care of the National Trust in 1934. It had originally been intended to place 24 cannon captured at Waterloo around the base of the monument but only 15 were eventually dispatched to Exeter in 1818. There was no money left to transport the guns to Wellington and eventually most were used by Exeter Corporation as bollards. Vain attempts to obtain the cannon were made in 1853 and 1890, when it was discovered that the guns were naval cannon cast in Scotland for Catherine the Great of Russia and thus could not have been captured at Waterloo. In 1911 four cannon were finally brought from Exeter and placed in front of the monument but these were removed for scrap during World War II and are believed to have been buried at Watchet. Finally in 1985 a single cannon was brought from Exeter and installed in its present position at the foot of the column. There are

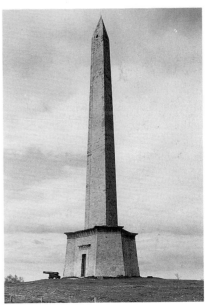

TOP *Popham memorial, Wellington church*
ABOVE *Wellington Monument*

magnificent views from the site across the vale of Taunton and an even more splendid panorama for those willing to scale the 235 steps up the interior of the monument. The key is kept at nearby Monument Farm. The intention to hold an annual fair below the pillar on the anniversary of the battle, 'the Wake of Waterloo', was dropped after the first celebration in 1819. Nonconformist reaction from the town below claimed that it would lead the poor into 'drunkenness and debauchery'. The remaining estate here of the dukes of Wellington was finally sold in 1972.

★★★ *View from the Monument,* ★★ *town and church.*

WELLS (E) It is almost impossible to be over-enthusiastic about 'England's smallest city'. Attractively sited below the Mendip Hills, Wells offers a feast of medieval and later architecture and in its central area communicates a warm and friendly atmosphere.

Wells takes its name from four natural springs, North, Central and the East Pots (the last formerly known as the Bottomless Well), which rise behind the Bishop's Palace in the bed of an L-shaped pool created c.1824 and to the west a fifth, Scotland spring: all fed by an underground stream from the Mendips and daily producing an average of 4 million gallons, often known

collectively as St Andrew's Well. Early stone-built culverts carried the water towards the cathedral and its close (with a dipping place or baptistry in the present cloisters), and the 14th century Palace moat, while in 1451 Bishop Bekynton built the well house near the springs and conveyed water to a conduit in the Market Place and down both sides of High Street. From the moat runs a mill leat which formerly drove the bishop's Inmill and Outmill. Excavation to the west of the springs revealed Neolithic flints and arrowheads, suggesting very early use of the water by man. Roman pottery was found (a possible nearby villa has been

suggested) and a Roman or later sub-Roman mausoleum of the 5th to 7th centuries, probably linked with an early church further west: in turn succeeded by a Saxon mortuary chapel. Many of the wall footings found in these excavations can be inspected in the Camery, with a plan near the entrance from the east cloister. These discoveries give the cathedral an unrivalled continuity in England as a site of religious veneration.

Ine, King of the West Saxons, is credited with founding a minster church here at about the time that St Aldhelm became first bishop of Sherborne in 705, when he was active in east Somerset. Certainly a grant of

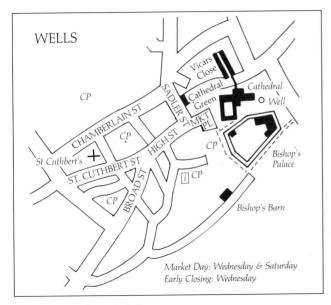

St Cuthbert's

CP

CHAMBERLAIN ST

SADLER ST

ST. CUTHBERT ST

HIGH ST

BROAD ST

CP

CP

CP

CP

i CP

Vicars Close

Cathedral Green

MKT PL

Cathedral

Well

Bishop's Palace

Bishop's Barn

Market Day: Wednesday & Saturday
Early Closing: Wednesday

OPPOSITE *Wells Cathedral*

ABOVE *The Chapter House steps, Wells Cathedral*

land by King Cynewulf in 766 was made to 'the minster by the Great Spring which they call Wells'. When the diocese of Sherborne was divided in 909, the new see was established at Wells, the minster church became **Wells Cathedral** and Aethelhelm was consecrated its first bishop.

The foundations of the Saxon cathedral run diagonally beneath the present cloisters, culminating in a rounded apse. An extension from the apse physically connected it with a chapel of St Mary on the site of the former mausoleum and mortuary chapel. This former cathedral, some 300 ft long, was on a line running from St Andrew's (or Scotland) Well, along High Street to St Cuthbert's church. Bishop Giso (1061-88) endowed St Mary's chapel and added a dormitory, refectory and cloister, possibly on the north side of the cathedral. Giso's successor, John de Villula (1088-1122), moved his see to Bath, where he began to build a new cathedral (now represented by Bath Abbey), pulled down Giso's additions so that, although a dean continued at Wells, the canons here were forced to return to lodgings in the town. However, Robert of Lewes, bishop of Bath 1136-66, rebuilt the church at Wells (consecrated in 1148), gave the place a new constitution based on that of Salisbury and restored its lands. An attempt to move the see again, to Glastonbury, failed although the abbots of Glastonbury became canons of Wells. The present church of St Andrew at Wells was begun by Bishop Reginald c.1175-79 when the bishopric was still at Bath. It was the first major English church

in the new Gothic fashion and building proceeded westwards from the choir, including the transepts and an impressive porch (giving access from the canonical houses on the north side of the Green), the new building being consecrated in 1239. By then Bishop Jocelin, born at Launcherly to the south of the town, had brought the see back here: its bishops thereafter styled as of Bath and Wells. A break in the stonework and carving just to the west of the north entrance is attributed to the period 1209-13, when the Pope placed England under an Interdict, excommunicated King John, and Bishop Jocelin was forced into exile in France. The capitals of the nave piers are superbly carved with scenes of everyday medieval life and feature a number depicting medieval toothache. Meanwhile, the intricate screen of the West Front (c.1230-50) was constructed to provide the largest gallery of 13th century sculpture in Europe (angels, apostles, saints, bishops, kings, knights, Old and New Testament tableaux), once painted in rich colours. The lowest tier was damaged by Monmouth rebels in 1685 and all have suffered from erosion, but a £2m. restoration (1975-86) culminated in an open-air eucharist on the Green when the Prince of Wales took communion. On the buttress to the left of the central door is a poignant unfinished inscription to John of Pitney, a Crewkerne chantry priest who died during the Black Death in 1348, suggesting that the sculptor also died of the plague before his work was finished. As the West Front neared completion, activity moved to the erection of the octagonal

first-floor Chapter House (over an under-croft) on the north side of the cathedral (begun c.1250, completed 1306) at the head of a most elegant and much photo-graphed stairway, lit by stained glass of c.1290. Inside, from a central pillar 36 ribs rise to shelter the labelled seats of the cathedral officers and canons beneath a sublimely graceful roof, lit by high windows. Between 1313 and 1322 the massive central tower was set up. Origi-nally much shorter, the addition of a further stage with spire led to cracking and potential collapse. This was solved by the ingenious insertion below of three scissor or strainer arches (1338-48) to support the weight, although these are often criticised for marring the original concept of the interior. The spire was destroyed by fire 1439, after which the crown was rebuilt, resulting in a 182 ft tower: the tallest in the county. During the years 1320-40 the choir with its aisles was extended eastwards (the bishop's throne and the existing wooden stalls with their 65 carved misericords – three exhibited in the retrochoir – are of this period). The great east 'Jesse' window was set up (with its 14th century glass intact, as is that in the choir aisles) and the star-vaulted Lady Chapel, at first separate, added and then linked to the choir by the beautiful many-pillared retrochoir. The final additions were the twin western towers: the southern one of c.1385-95, mainly paid for by Bishop Harewell: the northern tower following in the 1430s, built under a bequest from Bishop Bubwith (beneath which the bishops' consistory court was held). To the south of the cathedral extend

Wells Cathedral from the north transept

the vaulted cloisters: in their present form a 15th century reconstruction of the 13th century originals. The west cloister now houses the cathedral shop and restaurant with the choristers' practice room and offices above. Over the east cloister (which served as the bishop's entrance to his cathedral) is the splendidly atmospheric **Cathedral Library** (lists), built 1425-33 under the will of Bishop Bubwith and furnished in 1686, after the depredations of the Civil War and Commonwealth, with book presses, chained books and desks paid for by the cathedral treasurer, Dr Richard Busby, later a famous headmaster at Westminster. The library holds the archives of the dean and chapter, dating from 958, books owned by Erasmus and Thomas Cranmer, and there is a standing exhibition of its treasures. Above the north porch of the nave has been discovered one of the only two English Plaster-of-Paris tracing floors (the other at York Minster) on which the medieval master masons scribed their designs for mouldings and tracery.

Among the fittings, the font in the south transept is considered to be Saxon work, almost miraculously surviving from the earlier cathedral, although the saints once in its reworked arches have been removed (the painted cover is c.1635). Other early survivals are the bones of seven Saxon bishops from Siger (died 975) to Giso (died 1088), placed in the choir aisles beneath later effigies of c.1200, although recent medical examination showed the

remains to have been somewhat jumbled up, probably including the relics of other holy men. The famous clock in the north transept was made c.1390 and is second in age only to that in Salisbury Cathedral of 1386 (which merely struck the hours and probably had no dial), made by the same hands and evidently commissioned by Bishop Erghum, translated from Salisbury to Wells in 1388. The original works are now (still working) in London's Science Museum and the present mechanism was only installed in 1880. The clock face, however, is believed to be the oldest in the world, showing the hours, minutes, the days of the lunar month and the phases of the moon. The wooden quarterjack, known as Jack Blandiver, strikes the quarters with his heels and hammers the hours on a bell in front of him, while above the dial four horsemen revolve and one is felled (the same loser for six centuries !). Since c.1475 the time has been relayed to a second dial outside the transept where two standing knights strike the quarters. The substantial nave pulpit with its English text is a self-effacing memorial to Bishop William Knight (died 1547), who is buried beneath it. An excellent brass double lectern in the Lady Chapel was given in 1661 by Dean (later Bishop) Robert Creyghtone, 'upon his returne from fifteene years exile with our Soveraigne Lord Kinge Charles ye 2d'. Although there has been an organ on the pulpitum below the choir arch probably from the 14th century, the present case, surmounted by twin gilded and trumpeting angels, was put up only in 1973.

There is predictably a feast of fine monuments, particularly those bearing effigies of the bishops. William Bitton (died 1274) has one of the oldest incised slabs in the country, protected under perspex in the south choir aisle. The richness of the ornate canopy and carved heads surrounding the figure of William of March (died 1302) in the south transept may reflect the vain attempt to elevate him to sainthood in 1324. Of later episcopal tombs, I am particularly fond of those depicting bishops John Drokensford (died 1329), Thomas Bekynton (died 1465, portrayed in his vestments above his cadaver), John Still (died 1608) and Richard Kidder (died 1703, the tomb bearing a finely-carved Rubenesque matron). In the south transept is a small brass to Humphrey Willis (died 1618, aged 28), showing him kneeling penitently and illustrating the worldly pastimes he had presumably foresworn: a pack of playing cards, dice, a tennis racket and ball, and a fiddle. The cloisters are full

of memorials, many removed from the cathedral itself. They include those to Thomas Linley of Bath (died 1795) and his granddaughter, wife of the playwright Sheridan, Dr Claver Morris, surmounted by his bewigged bust, and members of the Sherston and Davis families, leaders of the Wells community in the 18th century. The fine monument to Bishop George Hooper (died 1727) in the west cloister now looks incongruously down on tourists wolfing their cream teas.

The Bishop's Palace (fee:lists), which Pevsner hailed as 'the most memorable of all bishop's palaces in England', lies immediately south of the cathedral within a five-sided turreted wall and moat. There was an earlier palace, probably in the same area, which may have accommodated King John on his four visits to Wells, 1204-8. The present building was begun by Jocelin, bishop 1206-42, probably around 1207, when he was granted land to create a park to the south-east of the city, and was continuing in 1233, when Henry III gave oak trees towards the work. Jocelin was responsible for the central part of the palace (now known as the Henderson Rooms after Edward Henderson, bishop 1960-75): a vaulted entrance hall with a superb undercroft behind it. A fine Jacobean staircase now gives access to Jocelin's first-floor solar, a long gallery and hall, the last divided into two rooms in the 19th century, when a second floor was added together with a new porch. These first-floor rooms were given an early Victorian Puginesque remodelling with ornate ribbed ceilings. They contain a fascinating collection of bishops' portraits, including those of Cardinal Wolsey (1518-23), William Laud (1626-28), who went on to become a repressive Archbishop of Canterbury, beheaded in 1644, Peter Mews (1672-85), who wore a cheek patch to cover a Civil War wound, the saintly Thomas Ken (1685-89), who objected to the cruel treatment meted out to Monmouth rebels but resigned when he refused to break his oath of allegiance to James II, and Richard Kidder (1691-1703), who kept a revealing diary and died at the palace with his wife when the great storm of 1703 brought chimney stacks crashing through their bedroom. Also exhibited are the much-copied Glastonbury Chair, made for John Thorne, Treasurer of Glastonbury Abbey, who was martyred with his abbot on Glastonbury Tor, an intricate 16th century bobbin chair (the so-called Abbot's Chair) and the coronation cope of the bishops, paid for by the ladies of the

Bishop's Palace, Wells

diocese in 1901. Since the crowning of Richard the Lionheart in 1189 the bishops here have always supported the left hand of successive sovereigns at their coronations.

To the right of the central block stands the bishop's private chapel, possibly put up by Jocelin as a two-storey building and converted to the fine Decorated chapel of St Mark and the Holy Trinity by Robert Burnell, bishop 1275-92 and Lord Chancellor of England. It has unusually large windows containing fragments of French medieval glass, of which Bishop Law (1824-45) collected 'a cartload' in post-Revolutionary France, and features an extensive collection of heraldic glass and tapestries. The arms of the bishopric depict the cross of St Andrew (for Wells Cathedral) and the keys of St Peter and sword of St Paul (for Bath Abbey). South-east of the chapel are the surviving walls of the great hall built by Bishop Burnell. This was where Edward III was entertained in 1331-2, possibly Richard II and his queen in 1382, and was the scene of the trial of Abbot Richard Whiting of Glastonbury in 1539. Its roof was destroyed for its lead after Bishop Barlow was forced to surrender the palace to the Duke of Somerset in 1550, and Bishop Law demolished the south wall of the hall 1823-5 to create a picturesque ruin. To the left of the central block, the north wing (not open to the public) was added by Thomas Bekynton, bishop 1443-66 and, although much altered at various dates, now forms the present residence and offices of the bishop. It was Ralph of

Shrewsbury, bishop 1329-63, who after years of disputes with the citizens made a fortress of the palace, surrounding it with a wall studded with bastions and incorporating a gatehouse with portcullis and drawbridge. The bridge is now permanently down but was raised as late as 1831 when Reform rioters destroyed the Bishop's Palace at Bristol. Swans on the moat, who until recently used to ring the gatehouse bell for food, have been so well fed by visitors that they have ceased to perform. If visiting the palace, make sure to walk through the grounds to see the wells themselves and the view of the cathedral pictured on the front cover of this guide. South-west from the palace stands the

Vicars' Close, Wells

substantial 15th century Bishop's Barn where royalist troops were quartered during the 'Bloody Assizes'.

In Cathedral Green the principal house is the former Deanery, a large 15th century house with its own crenellated gatehouse. It includes a fine first-floor hall built by John Gunthorpe, dean 1472-98, in which Henry VII is believed to have been entertained. **Wells Museum** (fee:lists), founded in 1893 around the Mendip collections of Herbert Balch, has been housed in the former Chancellor's House on the north side of the Green since 1932. The Tudor house was remodelled in the 18th century and again c.1850. The museum's displays still have a delightful old-style air, centred on archaeological and geological exhibits from the Mendip caves, particularly Wookey Hole (don't miss the remains of the alleged Witch of Wookey), but also illustrating the history and life of the city and its surroundings. Next to the east is the former house of the archdeacon of Wells, built by Andrew Holes, archdeacon 1450-70, but sold after the celebrated Italian chronicler and archdeacon, Polydore Vergil, criticised Henry VIII. The building was remodelled externally in 1886 and has housed the music department of the Cathedral School since 1971.

Immediately north of the Chapter House extends **Vicars' Close**, a delightful double terrace of 42 houses to accommodate the Vicars Choral (deputies for the canons at services in the cathedral), which conjures up a wonderfully intimate feeling of the Middle Ages. Work began at the hands of Bishop Ralph of Shrewsbury with the

building of a first-floor barrel-roofed common hall and store room below, kitchen and bakehouse, completed in 1348 (the entrance gateway below is evidently later). The object was evidently to keep the vicars, who had previously lodged in the city, away from the temptations of the flesh and quarrels with the citizens. Each house had a ground-floor hall with enclosed yard behind, and a single first-floor chamber reached by a rear stair, probably with latrine under: both rooms heated by fireplaces set in the front wall. Several of the units have been converted or extended, and there are now 28 dwellings, of which the facade of no. 22 has been restored to preserve its original appearance.

The date of the houses themselves is still the subject of much speculation. Some had been built by 1363 and the rest seem likely to have been completed by 1412. The fine chimney shafts were possibly heightened by Bishop Bekynton (died 1465) for they bear his canting badge (a beacon above a tun) and the arms of his three executors (note the sugar loaves for Hugh Sugar). Bekynton also linked the Vicars' hall to the cathedral by a covered bridge called the Chain Gate. At the far end of the Close the Vicars' chapel (on ground floor) with their library over had been built by 1447, but both are now used by Wells Cathedral School. The Close is still home to adult members of the cathedral choir, with some houses occupied by others working in the cathedral. East beyond the Chain Gate, Tower House (birthplace of novelist Elizabeth Goudge, 1900-84) dates from the 14th and 16th centuries and once housed the cathedral precentor, while opposite is the 15th century 'Rib', formerly home to the principal of Wells Theological College.

East from New Street runs the Liberty, a fine succession of houses now mainly occupied by Wells Cathedral School (with an almost continuous existence since the early 12th century, the oldest school in Somerset), outwardly of the 18th and 19th centuries but often concealing medieval origins. They include no.15, the Cedars, built in 1759-61 for Antiguan sugar-planter Charles Tudway by Thomas Paty of Bristol, and no.19, put up for Claver Morris, a physician who kept an entertaining diary of social life in 18th century Wells. The Cedars occupies the site of the former College of Mountroy, whose name is preserved in that of Mountery Road. This college was endowed under the will of Bishop Ralph Ergum of 1400

and built by 1430 to house the chantry and anniversary priests of the town.

West of the cathedral precinct a settlement developed, orientated on the Saxon cathedral rather than its 12th century successor. This settlement, possibly known as Tideston, was served in Saxon times by St Cuthbert's church and, subsequently, by the chapel of St Etheldreda at Southover. A market-place was established at the south-western end of High Street, now represented by a triangular island block of properties at the junction of St Cuthbert and Broad streets, and Bishop Robert of Lewes granted weekly markets and three fairs by the place's first charter c.1160. Borough status was confirmed and a fourth fair added by charters of his successor, Bishop Reginald (1166-91), while a free borough and a fifth fair were initiated under a charter of King John in 1201. It is reasonable to suppose that much of the old town between St Cuthbert's and the cathedral was laid out in burgage plots in the later 12th century.

The cathedral and palace precincts lay beyond the control of the borough, and were consequently dubbed the Liberty of St Andrew. From 1298 until 1832 the town returned two MPs to Westminster. The success of the borough was rapid and by the early 14th century Wells was the largest town in the county. It developed a successful cloth industry (as indicated by the name of Tucker Street), based on wool from the backs of Mendip sheep and by the 15th century its market had became the most successful in the area.

The market's focus moved north-east to the present Market Place (where it continues today), which was transformed by Bishop Thomas Bekynton. In 1451 he began his New Works, the terrace of buildings (now shops) lining the north-west side of the market. Access to the market was provided by twin turreted gateways: from the cathedral by the Penniless Porch (bearing Bekynton's rebus or badge on the cathedral side and named from beggars plying their trade there) and from the palace by the Bishop's Eye. Brown's Gate (named after shoemaker Richard Brown, next-door tenant in 1553), sometimes called the Dean's Eye, is a less impressive 15th century gatehouse which divides Sadler Street from the Cathedral Green.

One price of increased independence for the town was regular disputes and litigation with the bishops, particularly during the years 1340-43, when the cathedral precinct was first enclosed by a

wall to protect clerics from the citizens. Charters of incorporation were granted in 1400 and 1589, the mayoralty surviving the 1835 Municipal Reform Act and 1974 reorganization, latterly as head of the Charter Trustees. The corporation built shambles along the middle of High Street and a new town hall over them on pillars in 1571-2, and a city gaol in 1606, which partly survives at the City Arms inn. The present Town Hall was put up in 1779 (when the arched High Cross was demolished), including a spacious first-floor assembly room and, at its eastern end, the Tourist Information Centre. An open cheese market was accommodated on its ground floor until 1835 when the nearby Post Office was built as a market hall.

The Gothic fountain of 1793 replaced Bekynton's massive conduit, through which he brought water to the market from the bishop's wells. Set in the pavement in front of Bekynton's New Works is a brass commemoration of the then world-record Olympic long jump of Mary Rand, a native of Wells, in 1964. The town centre has always been plentifully supplied with inns, of which the finest of those surviving, the Swan, Star and Crown, have become hotels. From an upper window of the Crown the Quaker William Penn (after whom Pennsylvania in America was named) preached in 1695.

The Civil War brought no major conflict to Wells itself, although the place was in turn occupied by the rival armies and the future Charles II as Prince of Wales here received a petition from the independent Clubmen in 1644. Much damage was done to the Bishop's Palace, which was ransacked and sold, and to the cathedral, where on several occasions in 1642-3 the Parliamentarians smashed stained glass, defaced carvings and destroyed fittings. Bishop Peirs suffered imprisonment, as did the dean, Dr Walter Ralegh (nephew of Sir Walter), captured after the fall of Bridgwater. Confined to the Deanery under virtual house arrest, Ralegh was stabbed to death in 1646 and buried in an unmarked grave in the cathedral.

Following the restoration of 1660 Peirs was restored to his see and himself spent £5,000 on restoring the palace and his residence at Banwell. During the Monmouth Rebellion of 1685 the rebel army, retreating from Norton St Philip, arrived in the town on 1 July, but only nine Wells men are known to have joined them. They stabled their horses in the cathedral, took lead from the roof to make bullets and damaged its fittings, almost destroying the organ. After the Battle of Sedgemoor, Judge George Jeffreys held his 'Bloody Assizes' at the Market Hall in the Market Place, while 696 prisoners were housed in the City Gaol and St Cuthbert's church. Of those who were lined up in the cloisters awaiting trial, 99 were ordered for execution. One of the first, William Mangell, having pleaded not guilty, was executed immediately to discourage such temerity among those who followed him. A total of 556 were tried and it was only for want of time that the remaining 140 were bound over to the next Assizes. Eight of those condemned were hanged, drawn and quartered at Wells: probably in the Market Place rather than at the traditional execution site at Keward Green (where Susannah Davis was burned alive for poisoning her husband in 1753).

The **Church of St Cuthbert**, its dedication suggesting a Saxon origin, is too often neglected by visitors in favour of the cathedral. Although the dean and chapter long appointed its vicars, it was also the city church where the mayor and corporation came to worship, whose ministers acted as mayors' chaplains and one of whose churchwardens was nominated by the corporation. It is the largest parish church in the county and served one of the most extensive parishes. Externally, with its striking 122 ft west tower, the building appears to date from the 15th century but, inside, the arcade pillars are 13th century. When the church was rebuilt and extended to the west in Perpendicular style, and a clerestory and a fine angel roof added, these columns were heightened by some 10 ft and the capitals and arches reset on top. In the north transeptal chapel is a fine 13th century mutilated reredos, paralleled by the superb Jesse reredos of 1470 in the south transept. A former central crossing tower collapsed in 1561. There are two fine carved representations of the royal arms dated 1631 and 1660, and an ornate pulpit of 1636. Monuments include the kneeling figure of Henry Llewellyn (will dated 1604), founder of almshouses in nearby Priest Row, and a touching brass to Francis Hayes (1623). Behind the church and bordering Chamberlain Street, almshouses for 12 poor burgesses were founded in 1436 under the will of Bishop Nicholas Bubwith, to which a first floor was later added to increase the accommodation to 24. At the east end is a chapel, mentioned

in 1466 and, at the west end, the borough's former guildhall. To this Bishop John Still and his son added in 1614 six cells for 'poor and decayed' tradesmen (rebuilt 1884), Walter Bricke, woollen draper, rooms for a further four in 1638, and a final four in 1777, built by the son of Bishop Edward Willes: together known as the Old Almshouse. Nearby, Llewellyn's alms-houses in Priest Row, founded for ten women in 1630, were rebuilt in an attractive double terrace by the Victorians, incorporating Charles's Almshouse of 1828. Archibald Harper's almshouses, originally for four woolcombers, stand on the north side of Chamberlain Street.

St Thomas's church was built 1856-7 by the widow of Dean Jenkyns to serve the poorer suburb of East Wells (formerly known as 'Byestewall'). Designed with spire and apsidal chancel by S.S. Teulon in Gothic Revival 'Geometrical' style, the south aisle was added later. The church's dedication recalls the free chapel of St Thomas in the city (recorded c.1200, now the site of the Methodist Church of 1838 in Southover), thought likely to represent the earlier chapel of St Etheldreda or Audrey with a possible Saxon origin.

Wells also had its hospital or priory of St John the Baptist in Southover, its presence recalled in the names of Priory Road and St John Street. It was founded c.1212 by Archdeacon Hugh of Wells, brother of Bishop Jocelin, chantry chapels in its church were established in 1314, 1326 and 1350, and it was dissolved in 1539. Architectural fragments in a house called the Priory in St John Street are now thought not likely to represent the medieval priory, which lay to the south of the mill leat.

On the Mendip slope immediately north of the city in an idyllic situation stands **Milton Lodge**, built by Aaron Foster in 1790. Its delightful terraced gardens (fee:lists) command wonderful views across the city and cathedral, and beyond to Glastonbury Tor. They were laid out 1903-09 by Charles Tudway of the influential Wells family of landowners and MPs when he moved thence from the former family home, the Cedars, in the Liberty. The grounds have been immacu-lately restored since 1962 by David Tudway Quilter and his wife. Also open to the public is the Tudway Quilters' 7-acre arboretum, **the Combe**, on the opposite side of the Old Bristol Road.

Coxley (pronounced 'Coaxley') is a village on the Glastonbury road where the Pound Inn has been refreshing travellers at

least since the 18th century. Christ Church, designed by Richard Carver, was built by public subscription in 1839 and became a parish church in 1844.

Polsham ('Paul's meadow') is a hamlet further towards Glastonbury. North-east from Wells are the twin villages of **East and West Horrington** ('horn-like hill'). The church of St John the Evangelist, also designed by Carver and built by subscription in 1838, is now closed but became a separate parish from Wells in 1844. **Burcott** (probably 'dwelling-place') is a small hamlet to the west of the city on the B 3139 near Wookey. Opposite the attractive Burcott Inn stands the restored **Burcott Mill** (fee:lists), its 1864 water-wheel and machinery now producing flour again and incorporating a shop, cafe, and craft workshops.

Wellesley, south-east from the town, may have been the original home of the Wellesley family, later dukes of Wellington, while **Dulcote** ('cottage on the river Doulting') and **Worminster** ('Wyrm's or dragon's hill') named prebends in the cathedral by the 13th century.

★★★★ *Wells Cathedral, Bishop's Palace, Vicars' Close, centre generally,*
★★★ *St Cuthbert's Church, Wells Museum, Milton Lodge gardens,*
★★ *Burcott Mill.*

WEMBDON (D) A rural village on the north-east side of Bridgwater and rapidly being swallowed up by the expanding town. Its name probably means 'huntsman's hill', the *dun* or hill being Wembdon Hill, where Saxon burials have been found and below which the healing powers of St John's Well (later Holy Well) were being exploited by 1464, with an associated chapel in 1539.

As well as the main manor, there were several other estates including Sandford (where the manor-house incorporates a medieval open hall and a porch dated 1570) and the twin manors of Perry Fichet and Perry Furneaux, named after the families that owned them. Was it local rivalry that led Sir Thomas Fichet to burn down Simon Furneaux's house at Perry in 1352 ? It was also at Perry that Matthew Furneaux obtained an annual fair in 1296 which was held at least until the late 16th century. The church of St George in Wembdon village was granted by William Testard, lord of Wembdon manor, to St John's Hospital, Bridgwater, in 1284. The church was badly damaged by fire in March 1868 and almost wholly rebuilt.

Gardens

For a county which recorded in 1369 the earliest-known gardening use of the word 'nursery' (at Merriott), Somerset has a long horticultural history. The most prolific early gardeners were the abbots and priors, particularly those of Glastonbury and Bath, and the tradition was continued after the Reformation at the great houses. The Tudor garden of Henry Lyte, who translated and extended a celebrated herbal of 1578, has been as far as possible recreated by the National Trust at Lytes Cary. On a larger scale, work at Montacute House has produced a splendid period garden with old roses and mixed borders, set against Ham stone walls, in keeping with the former home of the Phelips family. Hadspen House has an Edwardian garden, restored by Penelope Hobhouse in the 1970s, which features a 2-acre curved-walled garden and woodland area. Milton Lodge near Wells occupies a superb site overlooking the city, with terraced gardens and a nearby 7-acre arboretum. Cannington Agricultural College has a horticultural science garden with one of the largest collections of ornamental plants in the south-west and no less than eight national plant collections, ten substantial greenhouses and seven walled gardens.

The finest Somerset garden lies in front of Hestercombe House with views across Taunton. Created for Viscount Portman from 1903 by Sir Edwin Lutyens and Gertrude Jekyll, there are raised walks, pergolas, water channels, a large parterre and an elegant orangery. Gertrude Jekyll was again engaged in 1920 to approve and amend the plans for the walled gardens established by Col Arthur Lyle at the National Trust's Barrington Court. The National Trust also hold Tintinhull House with its 2-acre compartmented garden. The latter was developed from 1898 and also influenced by Gertrude Jekyll. Dunster Castle's hillside gardens have the finest outlook of any in the county: across the Bristol Channel to Wales. Around Clapton Court near Crewkerne extend 10 acres of formal and woodland grounds, including the biggest and oldest ash tree in Britain and a plant centre specialising in the sale of fuchsias and pelargoniums. Nearby at Wayford Manor a mature hillside garden was redesigned by Harold Peto in 1902. Attractive herb and bog gardens have been established by Mr and Mrs Starkie around Gaulden Manor, and walled and woodland gardens at Barford Park command a wonderful situation overlooking Bridgwater Bay. A large restored walled kitchen garden lies behind Hatch Court, which also features an extensive park stocked with fallow deer. At East Lambrook Margery Fish's cottage-style garden has been recreated by its present owners.

Over sixty Somerset gardens are open under the National Gardens Scheme and a county booklet describing their locations and opening times is produced annually. The Somerset Gardens Trust was formed in 1991 to encourage the appreciation and conservation of the county's parks and gardens. The area is well served by many garden centres and several of the larger gardens open to the public also have plants and shrubs for sale.

★★★★ *Barrington Court, Cannington College, Dunster Castle, Hestercombe House, Montacute House.*
★★★ *Barford Park (Enmore), Clapton Court (Crewkerne), East Lambrook Manor, Hadspen House (Pitcombe), Hatch Court (Hatch Beauchamp), Lytes Cary (Charlton Mackrell), Milton Lodge (Wells), Tintinhull House.*

East Lambrook Manor

Clapton Court

ABOVE *Tintinhull*   BELOW *Hestercombe House*

WEST BAGBOROUGH (D) This attractive village clings to the southern edge of the Quantock Hills, looking down over Taunton. Its name means 'Bacga's' or possibly 'badger hill' and was known as 'west' to distinguish it from the nearby manor of East Bagborough to the south-east. The church of St Pancras lies at the end of a footpath above the village, its relative isolation attributed as usual to the desertion of the original settlement at a time of plague. It is generally 15th century and over-restored, with a north aisle added in 1839, although the 16th century benchends survive in the nave. The rest of the woodwork is modern but of high quality, by Sir Ninian Comper. Monuments and hatchments record the Popham (later Brooke-Popham) family's residence here from the early 18th century at Bagborough House, just east of the church. The fine late-Georgian house with colonnade, where Wordsworth stayed briefly in 1841, is set in parkland and can be viewed from the church path. Below the lane to Cothelstone stands a battered statue surmounting a love seat, which commands a superb view across the vale. It represents Jupiter with his dog and is the last survivor of ten classical sculptures which ornamented the grounds of Thomas Slocombe's Terhill House, demolished in 1821.

★★★ *Village and setting,* ★★ *church.*

WEST BRADLEY (E) A small scattered village south-east from Glastonbury: the 'broad clearing or wood' (the prefix 'west' is a relatively modern addition). The manor was given to Glastonbury Abbey in 746 by Ethelbald, King of Mercia, the abbey's sacrist enjoying the income in 1303, and Glastonbury retained it until the dissolution of 1539. Among its later owners was Dr Claver Morris (died 1726), the celebrated physician of Wells. The Perpendicular parish church (of unknown dedication) looks more attractive from outside than in and was long a chapelry of East Pennard, becoming a separate benefice only in 1875. From the churchyard there is an excellent view of the three-storeyed Bradley House, a square with unusual angled extensions at each corner. It was completed in 1726 by Col William Peirs with workmen from Wells and even a Dutchman to create ornamental canals, as we know from diarist John Cannon, who was sacked as the colonel's steward in that year. Further west from church and house is Court Barn, a surviving Glastonbury Abbey tithe barn, dating from the later

Court Barn, West Bradley

14th century, with the remains of a square dovecote at its eastern end. Now in the care of the National Trust, it can be viewed by calling at the nearby house. **Lottisham** ('Lott's farm') is a hamlet to the south-east granted to Glastonbury Abbey with Ditcheat c.850, but linked to West Bradley since 1879. The pretty Victorian church of St Mary was built here to the designs of Sir T.G. Jackson in 1878.

WEST BUCKLAND (H) Its name identifies 'land held by charter' – *bocland*: possibly the early 10th century charter by which Wellington and West Buckland passed to the bishop of Sherborne and in 909 to the new bishop of Wells. Thereafter West Buckland was inextricably linked in ownership with its western neighbour, the town of Wellington. The village has been considerably extended during the present century. At its western edge on a small hillock stands the church of St Mary, whose tower is a magnificent landmark from the M5, particularly at night when floodlit. The views from the churchyard towards the wooded Blackdowns are equally breathtaking. The church was served from Wellington by 1234 (and probably before) but had its own priest's house to the east of it. The chancel arch of the present building is probably 13th century, there are two two-bay 14th century arcades and a late 15th century north chapel. The west tower was in

building in 1509 when John Peryn left money towards it. The parish has a number of farmhouses built by the 17th century, of which Huntspath is late medieval and probably represents the Domesday 'Huntanapoth', and Buckland Farm is late 16th century (two plaster ceilings dated 1591) and is claimed as the birthplace of Sir George Bond, Lord Mayor of London in Armada year. The domestic jewel of West Buckland is Gerbestone Manor, sited near the M5. Dating from the late 16th century, it was extended in the 17th and restored by the late Mr and Mrs Lloyd Fox, who bought it in 1924. It probably takes its name from the 13th century Sir Gerbert of Wellington and was thereafter held by a family who adopted their name, 'Gerberdestone', from it and licensed a chapel there in 1333. Later the manor descended to the Fraunceis family of Combe Florey (who claimed the north aisle of the church in 1612), from whom it was bought in 1693 by John Elwill, whose heirs held it until 1894.

★★ *Church and its setting.*

WESTBURY-SUB-MENDIP (E) This 'western burh' or 'manor' is a long village with much recent development, stretched out along the road from Cheddar to Wells (A371) and rising up the green Mendip slope. The manor was held by the bishops of Wells before the Norman Conquest and below the village they had an extensive park by 1178, the fencing (later stone wall) of which was maintained by the bishops' tenants from a wide area beyond Westbury. The church of St Lawrence in the centre of the village was given in the 12th century to Bruton priory. Although its west tower was rebuilt in 1887, it has a Norman tower arch and north doorway, a late 13th century chancel and the remainder mainly Perpendicular. There is an elaborately-framed inscription to George Rodney (died 1586, of the Rodney Stoke family) in the south chapel, and other monuments to the Knyftons. Just up the street from the church is a substantial village cross with six steps. Westbury Friendly Society, founded 1771, is one of the few that still celebrates its annual Club day. Recent excavations have revealed two medieval farmsteads at Ramspits, abandoned in the mid 15th century. Other investigations in a quarry-face above the village revealed worked flints assigned to the Middle Pleistocene period (c.500,000 BC), claimed by some as the earliest evidence of man in Britain. An Irish terrorist attempt to steal explosives at a quarry here was foiled in 1993. Two perpetrators received Old Bailey sentences of 25 and 23 years. Immediately south-east from Westbury is the village of **Easton**, formerly part of Wells, which became a separate parish in 1844. The church of St Paul, designed by Richard Carver, was built in neo-Norman style in 1843.

★ *Village, church.*

WEST CAMEL (J) A glorious Ham-stone village with an atmosphere of spaciousness (due to the central rectangle of green in the main street), lying north-east from Yeovil and formerly called Camel Abbatis, because it was owned by Muchelney Abbey from the 10th century until 1538 (for the name

West Camel

Saxon stone in West Camel church

'Camel' *see* **Queen Camel**). Later the manor passed to the Seymours and their heirs, the Bruces. The early 14th century church of All Saints stands at the the eastern end of the village, its south tower topped with a short steeple of 1631. A fragment of a fine 10th century Saxon cross shaft, probably dating from the time when Muchelney acquired the place, is set up in the north transept. There is a fine nave roof supported by medieval ladies and a Doulting stone pulpit, both of the 15th century. The advowson passed from Muchelney Abbey to the bishops of Bath and Wells in 1239 and thereafter, as most rectors were absentee officials of bishops, the parish's ministry suffered accordingly.

Of many attractive houses here, the rectory has a medieval solar north range, although remodelled c.1600, with a south wing added in 1836. Behind the house is a substantial barn of c.1500 and circular dovecot. Of other properties in the parish, Downhead was a Domesday manor which was granted to Muchelney Abbey in 1358, Urgashay occurs as 'Orgishie' in 1618 and Slowcourt Farm was probably the home of Simon de la Slo in 1211. On Steart Hill, north of the A 303, stands an obelisk known as Parsons Steeple where in 1794 84-year-old atheist Henry Parsons was buried.

★★ *Village, church.*

WEST CHINNOCK (J) An attractive Ham-stone village north-east from Crewkerne which extends along a single street and originally was part of the 10th century estate of Chinnock, owned by Shaftesbury Abbey (*see* **East Chinnock**), which later descended with that of Middle Chinnock to the earls of Ilchester. The church of St Mary stands in the centre of the village, was always a chapelry held under the rectory of Chiselborough and was completely rebuilt in 1889-90. There are several monuments to the Hayward and Ford families, the former operating sailcloth factories in Merriott and Crewkerne. Richard Hayward (died 1852) left 5s. each to four men and four women of the parish every year on Christmas Eve. The place rejoices in a pub named The Muddled Man.

★ *Village.*

WEST COKER (J) To the south-west of Yeovil this charming Ham-stone village with narrow streets takes its name from the Coker Water ('crooked stream' from Celtic *kukro*) but is cursed by the A 30, the former main road from London to Exeter, that passes through its centre. It had a long tradition of growing hemp and flax for sailcloth manufacture, was supplying Bridport as early as 1356 and still possesses the 19th century buildings of the West of England Twine Works to the south-east of the old centre. 'Coker canvas' was highly prized by naval captains during the Napoleonic wars. A polished stone axe and a boat-shaped bronze brooch testify to early settlement, as does a former Roman villa and a bronze plate inscribed to the god Mars. Edward I stayed here briefly in 1297. Its manor descended with that of its neighbour, East Coker, until the 14th century when, together with the local hundred of Coker, it passed to a junior

ABOVE *Almshouses, West Coker*
RIGHT *East Somerset Railway, West Cranmore*

branch of the Courtenay family. The manor-house was burned down in an attack during the Wars of the Roses in 1457. Following the execution of Henry Courtenay, Marquess of Exeter, in 1539, it was held briefly by both beheaded Protectors of Edward VI, the dukes of Somerset and Northumberland. The manor-house (1591) and manor (1661) were acquired and long held by the Portmans of Orchard Portman although in the present century the much-altered and extended manor-house was home to Sir Matthew Nathan (died 1939), retired colonial diplomat, whose weighty *Annals of West Coker* were published posthumously in 1957.

The church of St Martin had its west tower rebuilt in 1765 and much of the rest in 1838-9 and 1863-4. Its benchends (dated 1633), Jacobean pulpit and 17th century monument to two Portman daughters survive. South-east of the manor-house are the almshouses founded under the will of William Ruddock (died 1718). An endowment of land was given before 1548 to ring the curfew bell 'that all travellours by the waye . . . might thereby cum into their perfect waye, or to the saide village of Westcoker'. The right to hold three fairs at Westhill was granted to Sir Philip Sydenham in 1723.
★★ *Village.*

WEST CRANMORE (F) A small village to the east of Shepton Mallet, often known simply as Cranmore since the place was united with East Cranmore in 1933, its name meaning 'crane's marsh' or 'lake'. A

Roman pavement and associated coins were found here c.1800 but the exact site has since been lost. The manor here was given by King Edwy (955-9) to his thegn Aelfheah, and by Aelfheah to Glastonbury Abbey, which retained it until the 13th century. It was then lost to the bishop as part of the price for the abbey's escaping from episcopal control. It remained with the bishopric until 1550, when it was one of the estates that the bishop was forced to surrender to the Duke of Somerset. The Strodes arrived here in the 17th century, living first at the hamlet of Dean, building the substantial Southill House c.1720 in a delightful park to the south-east of the main village, and their name survives in the sign of the Strode Arms Inn opposite the village duckpond. They were succeeded by the Chetham-Strodes (1807-96) and the Spencers (1896-1952). The Perpendicular church of St Bartholomew, formerly a chapelry to Doulting, has an ornate west tower with a figure of the patron saint on its west face, and a panelled tower arch and fan vault inside. The body of the church does not live up to the promise of the tower but is full of information-packed monuments to the Strode, Chetham-Strode and Spencer families. Beneath the tower are four heraldic hatchments, there is a brass to James Strode (1613-98) and his wife, and a tablet to Sir Edward Chetham-Strode (1774-1862), Admiral of the White.

South-west from the village is a preserved section of the **East Somerset Railway** (fee:lists), opened in 1858 and

closed to passenger traffic in 1963. The project was the brainchild of artist and conservationist, David Shepherd, and was opened by Prince Bernhardt of the Netherlands in 1975. There are regular steam-drawn trips up and down the line, a gift shop and restaurant. Northwest of the village at **Waterlip** ('water leap') Edward Strode, killed in a duel in France in 1701, built a range of almshouses in 1699, and limestone quarrying began there in the 1860s.
★★★ *East Somerset Railway for steam buffs,* ★★ *village.*

WEST HATCH (H/J) Its name indicates simply that it lies to the west of Hatch Beauchamp. As 'the land of Hatch', it was held with the royal manor of North Curry and with that manor was granted in 1189 by Richard I to the bishop. Thence it passed with North Curry to the dean and chapter of Wells Cathedral, although separate courts for the manor were always held. Meare Court Farm occurs as 'Mere' as early as 1192, and its tenant in 1314 was obliged to superintend the mowing and haymaking in Kingsmead while wearing white gloves and carrying a white rod. The countryside here is made up of winding lanes, lined with high hedges, scattered groups of cottages, and with attractive views up to wooded hills. The church of St Andrew stands at the end of a short lane in the centre of the parish. There was a chapel here by 1234, when the vicar of North Curry agreed to serve it, and it only achieved its own vicarage in 1866. The church was fundamentally restored in 1861, when the north aisle and the vestry were added and the tower rebuilt, although the basic 15th century fabric was retained. A cruel fire on 21 August 1989 destroyed the roof and severely damaged the building, but this small community rallied to restore its church: triumphantly rededicated by Bishop Jim Thompson in 1992. At Little Creech is the home of the RSPCA's domestic and wildlife animal centre, which regularly features in the national media whenever birds need de-oiling or animals have to be rescued.

★ *Setting.*

WESTHAY (E), *see* MEARE

WEST LYDFORD (E)

A picturesque village on a loop off the Foss Way, north-east from Somerton, whose name, 'ford over the torrent' (Saxon – *hlyde*), refers to its position on the River Brue. After the Conquest it passed to the FitzMartins who in 1260 obtained a Tuesday market, a three-day fair and, later, a park, presumably sited at Park Farm to the north-east. The fair, with another added in the 17th century, was held at the Fair Place until the last century. Also in the 17th century the manor was bought from the heirs of Sir Edward Hungerford by Edward Colston (died 1721), the great benefactor of Bristol, and it was his successor, Edward Francis Colston, who rebuilt the church 1844-6 in unusually attractive early Victorian style to the design of Benjamin Ferrey. Interesting early service books are exhibited at the west end of the north aisle. The building, its manicured churchyard beside the river Brue and the five-arched stone bridge with pierced parapet make an attractive combination. The church was given to Wells by Robert de Boleville in the 12th century and thereafter formed a prebend in the cathedral. A medicinal spring, whose water produced a purging effect, was noted here in 1707. West Lydford was the birthplace in 1684 of diarist John Cannon, son of Sir Edward Hungerford's bailiff. Cannon recalled his brother's juvenile frame being passed through a split ash tree in 1687 to cure a rupture, and the rector, Edward Jacob (died 1690), blind in his latter years, who 'preached by strength of memory out of the reading desk'. The elderly Jacob, catechising the young Cannon, asked the boy who made him and received the answer, 'God – but my father and mother found the stuff'.

★ *Village centre.*

WEST MONKTON (D)

An extensive parish immediately east of Taunton which once stretched into the county town as far as the bottom of East Reach. It is named for the monks of Glastonbury Abbey, to whom the manor was granted, possibly by King Centwine in 682. It was 'West' in relation to other Glastonbury estates which made up the hundred of Whitley, of which West Monkton was a detached part. After the abbey's dissolution the manor was granted to William Paulet, Marquess of Winchester, passing in 1616 to the Warres of Hestercombe and in 1872 to Viscount Portman. The old village is cosily tucked away to the west of the A38, and the church of St Augustine is equally secluded at the end of what appears to be a private drive. The tall 14th century tower is austere in comparison with the nave's wagon-roof of a century later, with its attractively carved angels. The small brass of a priest in the sanctuary has been identified as that of Henry Abyndon, rector 1436-57. In the chancel a slate inscription to physician William Kinglake (died 1660) records:

'Contentions Doubtfull
Where two Champions bee.
Thou hast conquerd death,
Now death hath conquerd thee.'

The rest of the church is rich in memorials to former gentry of the parish: the Gatchels, Musgraves, Kinglakes, Beadons, Pophams and Brickdales. The last of these lived at the Court House near the church, the remnant of which has served as the rectory since 1933. Matthew Brickdale, MP, was forced to sell up after Taunton's first bank, founded by him in 1776, went spectacularly bankrupt in 1816. Walford House, overlooking the A38, was described as 'newly erected' by the Rev John Sanford in 1745, but had to be rebuilt c.1780 by his son Henry William (died 1806) after a fire.

Bathpool is a major hamlet near Taunton which grew up around the bridge over the River Tone carrying the main road from Bridgwater. Complaints were made from 1382 that Glastonbury Abbey's corn and fulling mills here were obstructing river traffic. Trade was improved much later when the Bridgwater to Taunton Canal was completed in 1827. The Creech Castle Hotel, a prominent pile near Bathpool, was built c.1848 as Creechbarrow House by Capt George Beadon RN (died 1889). He was a junior member of the Beadons of Gotten Manor in the parish and claimed to have invented the screw propeller. Captain Beadon's Hill is a local name for the original Creechbarrow Hill, a major landmark which flanks the eastern approach to Taunton and occurs in the Monkton charter of 682 as 'the hill which is called in the British tongue Cructan, by us Crycbeorh'. Monkton Heathfield is another expanding settlement whose name recalls common pasture finally enclosed in 1812.

★★ *Village and church.*

WESTON BAMPFYLDE (F)

This 'western settlement' lies just to the south of Sparkford and is so named presumably because it is west from Cadbury Castle (*see* **South Cadbury**). The suffix reflects the ownership of the manor by the Bampfylde family by 1316 until recent times. The church of the Holy Cross stands at the end of a short lane. It has a west tower with a 13th century base and an octagonal top, and below it are exhibited three 15th century bell clappers. The font is Norman and the pulpit Jacobean. There is an intriguing monument to Grace (died 1726) wife of Nathaniel Mist of London. What family tragedy lay behind the statement that 'in Prisons and Dungeons her Resolution and Fidelity were his comfort and support'? The manor-house of the Bampfyldes, east of the church, dates from the 17th century.

WESTONZOYLAND (E)

A sturdy agricultural village on the Levels lining the winding A372 from Bridgwater to Othery, which has been considerably developed to the north in the present century. It formed part of Glastonbury Abbey's 8th century estate of Sowi, the place's name translating long-windedly as 'the western settlement in the land of the stream island'. Little remains from the time of the abbey's lordship apart from the medieval core of the Sedgemoor Inn and the splendid church of St Mary the Virgin. The church's lofty four-stage west tower is superb but the nave roof with its host of carved angels and bosses is even more impressive. All this and the rest of the church is 15th century Perpendicular, except for the chancel which has Decorated two-light windows. The south transept, which includes good heraldic glass removed from the Old Court House, bears on a buttress the initials of Richard Bere, abbot of Glastonbury 1499-1524, repeated on one of the benchends. Oldest of all is the effigy of a priest, c.1300, in the north transept. A fine rood screen was inserted in the 1930s. A memorial to 13 men of the RAF buried here recalls the Air Ministry airfield developed to the east of the village from

1925, converted to wartime use in 1939, with its officers' mess at Townsend House. Upgraded in 1943, it was occupied briefly by the Americans in 1944, continuing in use until 1946 and reactivated 1952-58.

Westonzoyland is remembered chiefly, however, for the events of 6 July 1685 when the rebel forces of the Protestant Duke of Monmouth (see **The Monmouth Rebellion**), illegitimate son of Charles II, were defeated at the Battle of Sedgemoor north-west of the village by the royal army of Catholic James II. Contemporary accounts of the battle, claimed as the last to be fought on English soil, can be seen in the church where some 500 rebels, many of them wounded and dying, were herded, and the building later had to be fumigated with frankincense, pitch and resin. Several were summarily hanged without trial, a mass grave received those killed in the fight (some wounded were allegedly buried alive) and the rest were carried off to face trial, execution or transportation. North of the village is a small granite memorial 'in memory of all who, doing the right as they gave it, fell in the Battle of Sedgemoor', put up in 1928 and including within the enclosure stone mushrooms recording later battles. The inscription is awkward, the monument far from impressive but, in its bleak situation with the Levels stretching away into the distance, the effect on me has always been intensely moving. A nearby steam-powered pumping station of 1830, the first to be built for draining the Levels at times of flood, has been restored and is open periodically for aficionados of industrial archaeology. The engine can be seen working, there is a small forge and an exhibition recounting the centuries-old struggle against the flood waters.

★★★★ *Battlefield for its associations,*
★★★ *church.*

WEST PENNARD (E) The village borders the A 361 Glastonbury to Shepton Mallet road (for its name *see* **East Pennard**) and was one of the oldest possessions of Glastonbury Abbey, traditionally granted by Baldred, king of the Mercians, in 681. It was retained by the abbey until the dissolution of 1539 and was among those manors granted to the Duke of Somerset. The church of St Nicholas was a chapelry to St John's, Glastonbury, until 1824. It stands at the end of a cul-de-sac below Pennard Hill and has an elaborate Perpendicular west tower and panelled tower arch, north and south aisles and rood screen.

On 28 June 1839 the milk of 737 cows from the area was pooled to produce a monster octagonal cheese bearing the royal arms and weighing 11 cwt. This was presented to Queen Victoria in 1840 by a deputation of local farmers, subsequently known jocularly (after the names of their farms) as the Marquess of Sticklinch, the Duke of Woodlands and Lord East-Street. Temporarily rejected by the queen as unripe, the cheese was exhibited at the Egyptian Hall in London, the farmers living a high life on the takings, until a crowd of disgruntled milk contributors came up from Somerset to display a plaster cast of the cheese and close their rivals down with an injunction. The cheese was later returned to Somerset, shown off in various towns and ultimately ended its days as pig food. The carved 'follower' or lid of the mould is preserved in the village hall. (*For* **Court Barn** *see* **West Bradley**)

WEST QUANTOXHEAD (D) Standing between the sea and the head of the Quantock Hills, as its name indicates, it is best approached from the south through the village of Weacombe (pronounced 'Weecum') so that the emparked valley leading to the sea gradually opens up in front of you. From this viewpoint, at the foot of the slope to the right, stands the parish church of St Etheldreda, from whose dedication the parish derives its alternative name of St Audries. To the left is the small picturesque village school of 1857, closed in 1962, and ahead, just visible through the trees, is the manor-house of St Audries. This entire scene is a 19th century creation – a stage set devised by its lords. The main road was built from 1828 to replace an

earlier coastal route to the north. The church, its tower crowned by a spirelet, was completed by John Norton in 1856, retaining only the simple 12th century font from its predecessor. The little village which stood here was progressively demolished in the earlier 19th century to complete the park.

The manor was held from the early 13th century by the Cauntelo family, and for 350 years until 1736 by the Malets. It was bought in 1835 by the triple-barrelled Sir Peregrine Fuller-Palmer-Acland for his daughter Isabel and her husband, Sir Alexander Acland-Hood. The medieval manor-house was almost entirely rebuilt in Victorian-Tudor style over the following 35 years: in its latter stages to designs by Norton. Even a small harbour was constructed to land coal directly from

BELOW *St Audries, West Quantoxhead.* ABOVE *The nave roof, Westonzoyland church*

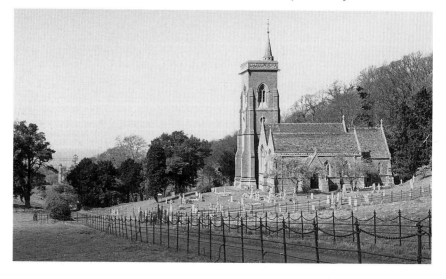

WHATLEY (F) An attractive rural parish to the west of Frome, 'the glade where wheat is grown', somewhat bruised by the major quarrying operations at the New Frome Quarry, although geography mercifully hides these from the village. A Roman villa with hypocausts and pavements was discovered in 1837 on the boundary between this parish and Nunney. Recently re-excavated, it seems to have had a relatively short existence, c.300-350 AD. The manor here was granted by King Edmund to Glastonbury Abbey in 940. Subsequent owners included the Servingtons from the early 14th until the late 16th century, the Chaffins of Dorset and latterly the Horners of Mells. David Servington obtained a three-day fair here in 1442, held at least until 1729. The church of St George, with west tower crowned by a spire, dates from the 13th century but was over-restored in 1859 and 1870. The south transept evidently represents the chantry of St Edmund, founded in 1350 by Sir Oliver de Servington, whose fine effigy it contains, or by his widow Elizabeth. Richard Church, rector 1853-71, was made Dean of St Paul's Cathedral (1871-90) by Gladstone but returned here for burial near the south chancel wall. Stroll round to the north side of the church to view the delightful manor-house complex with its medieval gatehouse and slightly cock-eyed porch. East from the church in the grounds of the Old Rectory have been established **Whatley Vineyard and Herb Garden** (lists).

★★ *Manor-house, vineyard and herb garden.*

Wales and the manor-house was provided with its own private gas-works. Sir Alexander's son, another Alexander, MP for West Somerset, was ennobled in 1911 as Lord St Audries. The 2nd Baron sold the house in 1925, retiring to Fairfield in Stogursey, and it was home to a well-known girls' school from 1934 to 1991.

Weacombe was a separate estate as long ago as Domesday and Weacombe House, visible from the road, is a fine mid 18th century building. St Audries Bay Holiday Camp, further east along the coast, has brought many thousands to the parish since the 1930s.

★★★ *Setting.*

WEST SOMERSET RAILWAY (C/D)
The longest privately-owned railway (20 miles) in the country, restored, maintained and manned by volunteers and running regular steam (and diesel) services between Bishops Lydeard and Minehead through the leafy countryside west of the Quantock Hills and along the coast. The original company was formed in 1857 (its first engineer was the celebrated Brunel), the line was opened from Taunton to Watchet in 1862, reaching Minehead in 1874. Absorbed in turn by the Great Western Railway in 1897 and British Railways in 1947, it fell a victim to Dr Beeching's axe and closed in 1971. A private (later public) company was formed to save the line only four months after its closure and partial services restarted in 1976, the complete line reopening three years later. There are stations at Bishops Lydeard, Crowcombe Heathfield, Stogumber, Williton, Doniford Beach, Watchet, Washford, Blue Anchor, Dunster and Minehead. Although hopes of running trains into Taunton have never been realised there is a connecting bus service between Taunton main-line station and Bishops Lydeard..

★★★★ *Railway for steam buffs.*

WHEATHILL (E) A delightful little hamlet, 'the hill where wheat is grown', north-east from Ilchester, marred only by its proximity to the main London railway line. It lies at the end of a lane which comprises a few lias-stone farmhouses and the redundant medieval church of St John the Baptist, recently converted into an attractive house. The manor was granted to Glastonbury Abbey by King Edgar, probably in 965, but the abbey lost it at the time of the Conquest. Later it was held from the 16th century by the Waldegraves, being sold to the Phelips family of Montacute c.1730 and descending to the Harbins of Newton Surmaville in 1803.

★ *Village*

WHEDDON CROSS (C), *see* CUTCOMBE

BELOW *Whatley manor-house.* ABOVE *West Somerset Railway, Bishops Lydeard Station*

Wildlife and Nature Reserves

Somerset's flora and fauna can most readily be appreciated over its wide open spaces, particularly across the Levels, on the shores of Bridgwater Bay and high up on the Quantock, Mendip, Blackdown and Brendon Hills and, of course, on Exmoor.

Exmoor, a National Park since 1954 and including most of the Brendons, is administered from Exmoor House, Dulverton, where there is also an information centre. At Dunster a visitors' centre includes natural history exhibits. The moor is best known for its red deer, but there are also lesser populations of roe and fallow deer and muntjac, and over 30 other species of mammal, including badger, weasel, stoat and red fox. Resident birds include robins, buzzards and dippers, and there are seasonal visits from swallows, warblers and auks in summer and fieldfare, woodcock, turnstone and brambling in winter. About a tenth of the moor is wooded, with ancient woodland in the Horner and Barle valleys, much in the National Trust's Holnicote estate. Coastal flora, under some threat from the ever-encroaching rhododendron, can best be appreciated from the Somerset and North Devon Coastal Path westwards from Minehead and there is also a 3-mile nature trail at North Hill. Another 3-mile nature trail runs from Webber's Post carpark near Cloutsham (Luccombe). The high moors have ground cover of heather, grass and sedge, and were formerly systematically plundered in summer for their harvest of whortleberries (known locally as 'worts'), as also were the Quantocks. Most of the Exmoor streams provide their own harvest of brown trout. Nettlecombe Court, set in a beautiful Brendon valley, is leased by the Field

Fyne Court, Broomfield, home of the Somerset Wildlife Trust

Studies Council and operated as the Leonard Wills Field Study Centre, offering an impressive range of courses.

The Quantock Hills, like Exmoor, have heather and bracken-covered higher slopes and wooded combes. The red deer (introduced from Exmoor c.1860), fox and badger can be regularly seen and, among its birds, kestrels, buzzards and meadow pipits. The Somerset Wildlife Trust has its offices and an interpretation centre at Fyne Court, near Broomfield, where there is also a woodland nature trail. The Trust owns or manages 64 nature reserves scattered across the face of the county, to 41 of which there is open access and to the rest there are varying degrees of access, usually by permit. The Trust publishes a detailed list of these with contact telephone numbers, and information cards are available (with detailed descriptions, locations and footpath maps) to 20 of the most interesting reserves. A forest trail from Seven Wells Bridge or Ramscombe Picnic Place, near Over Stowey, leads through Forestry Commission woods and the National Trust holds heathland at Longstone Hill (near Holford), woodland and heath at Willoughby Cleeve and Shervage Wood.

The natural habitat of the wetland pasture of the Somerset Levels has in recent years been under the twin threats of intensive agriculture and peat extraction. It is the finest breeding area for wading birds in the south-west, particularly lapwing, curlew, redshank and snipe, and is one of the few British breeding grounds of the black-tailed godwit. Mute swans nest beside the rhines and grey heron feed here regularly. Bewick swans winter here, as do plover, redwing, fieldfare and other migrant birds. From a study of the peat measures, the meadow flora has remained remarkably consistent over the centuries in undisturbed areas – with plants such as ragged robin, marsh orchid and kingcup. The rhines and waterways support water-loving plants, although machine-clearing, formerly done by hand, inhibits their growth. Otters, mainly north of the Poldens, now have to compete with mink, although badgers, foxes and roe deer are regularly found. The Levels are of national importance for their water beetles, dragonflies, butterflies, grasshoppers and crickets. Seaward from the Levels, Bridgwater Bay has since 1954 been a National Nature Reserve, covering 6,323 acres, and is the country's principal autumn moulting ground for shelduck. There is a resident warden at Stolford and hides for observing birds on Fenning Island.

The east-west limestone ridge of the Mendips is also at risk from the farmer, but ever-increasing quarrying poses an even greater threat. The picturesque clefts in the hillside provide the greatest variety of flora and fauna and it is possible to escape from the crowds in Cheddar Gorge to enjoy the place's natural charms. Much is made of the Cheddar pink, which grows only there and nowhere else, but there are other plant rarities in the area. Off the Gorge road is a

ABOVE *Red deer on Ley Hill above Porlock*

BELOW *On the Levels at Pathe near Othery*

nature trail through Black Rock Nature Reserve, another through Long Wood (good for lichens) and nearby is Velvet Bottom Reserve, recommended for its butterflies. Ebbor Gorge, another National Nature Reserve, has captivating woodland nature trails and a display centre. To the east, Asham Wood provides access to classic ancient woodland. There are some red and roe deer and plenty of foxes but fewer badgers and rabbits than formerly. Bats still occupy the caves but have fallen in numbers as caving has increased. The promontory of Brean Down, an extension of the Mendips and a further nature reserve, is owned by the National Trust and is an important staging post for migrant birds in spring and autumn.

The ridge of the Blackdown Hills, separating Somerset from Devon, is more heavily wooded than the Brendons but with similar plants and animals. A nature trail at Otterhead, near Otterford, takes in two lakes, marsh and woodland across a catchment area owned by Wessex Water. Further east, a forest trail has been laid out around Castle Neroche (above Staple Fitzpaine). The forestry there is mainly 20th century but the nature lover can ramble through mature beech woodland at Dommett Wood near Buckland St Mary.

Away from the hills there are fewer reserves, but attractive hill and lakeside walks have been laid out at Cricket St Thomas Wild-Life Park, a 4-mile moors trail has been established from Easton church to Wookey and there is bird-watching and walking at Bee World and Animal Centre, near Stogumber.

WHITELACKINGTON (J) The parish lies to the east of Ilminster, cut by the A 303, whose name records 'the settlement of Wihtlac's people'. The older village, south of the main road, is centred on the manor-house and church, while earthworks in the surrounding fields testify to the former presence of other dwellings. Medieval development favoured a line running north from the main road. The manor, granted to Roger Arundel after the Norman Conquest, supported seven swineherds in 1086, whose rent was delivered in the tangible form of 40 pigs. From the 12th to the 14th centuries the estate was held by the Montsorel family, later passing c.1430 by marriage to the Speke family, who moved here from Dowlish Wake.

The present manor-house, visible from the south side of the churchyard dates from the 16th and 17th centuries and in its grounds until blown down in 1897 stood a sweet chestnut tree 49 ft tall with a trunk over 12 ft in diameter. Beneath its branches the Duke of Monmouth, while on a progress through the South-west in 1680, was lionized by 20,000 (probably an understandable over-estimate) of the local countryfolk who broke down the park paling to get near him. He was entertained at the manor-house by George Speke on his journey down to Exeter and again on his return, which later led the authorities to search the house fruitlessly for arms but did not deter John Speke from riding out in the Duke's support in 1685. The Spekes had bought Dillington (*see* **Ilminster**) in 1599 and their descendants increasingly lived there until both Whitelackington and Dillington were sold to John Hanning of Barrington in 1795. One of the lodges and entrance gates to Dillington are sited almost opposite to the church. From Hanning descend the Camerons who still occupy Whitelackington Manor.

The church of St Mary is separated from the main road by what was probably the village green, in the middle of which is a rather isolated war memorial. The church has early 14th century transepts, the rest being a Perpendicular rebuild. The south transept includes two 14th century effigies, one of c.1350 which may represent John of Bridport, lord of the manor in 1346, and the other an unidentified knight of c.1370. In the north transept is a fine monument to Sir George Speke (identified from its heraldry), died c.1583, with helms mounted on the wall.

★★ *Group of manor-house and church.*

Whitestaunton Manor

WHITESTAUNTON (H) This leafy parish lies at the eastern end of the Blackdown Hills. Originally called just Staunton, 'stone settlement', the prefix 'white' had been added by 1333 and probably refers to former limestone quarries here. It has a landscape of steep-sided wooded hills and narrow valleys, and was settled from an early date. Stone-Age chert implements have been found, there is a prehistoric oval camp south from Howley and a barrow north of Northey. A Roman villa was discovered c.1845 in the vicinity of a holy well dedicated to St Agnes (the water reputedly good for sprains), both near the manor-house, which suggests an intriguing continuity of occupation. The village is little more than a hamlet near the manor-house and church, and the only other sizeable settlement is at Howley where the Rising Sun is recorded by 1766. The area was cultivated from scattered farms, several taking their names from their 17th century tenants: Brownsey, Browns and Parisees. The manor was held by the Staunton family (taking their name from their holding) by 1166 until at least 1370, the Bretts from the mid 15th century until 1718 and the Eltons, 1718-1923. A small manor-house of the later 15th century was encapsulated by the Bretts in a larger structure of the late 16th and early 17th century with major facades to the north and west. The Bretts continued as Roman Catholics long after the Reformation, gathering a small enclave of Catholicism around them, evidently under their protection. Between 1623 and 1630 there was even a dame school taught by a Catholic almswoman. Charles I stayed here for a night in 1644. The manor-house has been home to the Dobell family since 1947.

The chancel of the church of St Andrew may date from the 13th century and the nave and south porch from the later 14th, but the building was provided with new windows in the 15th century and has a uniformly Perpendicular feel to it. There are north and south chapels to the chancel, that on the south extended under the will of John Brett (died 1588) and housing Brett memorials. A plain west tower was put up in the 16th century and the rood screen and some benchends are of similar date. The church suffered the usual 19th century restoration which renewed the roofs. The Rev Joseph Greenfield (rector 1615-c.51) was ejected from his living during the Civil War, imprisoned at Taunton Castle and eventually died in a London gaol. The former rectory house at the east end of the village dates from the 16th century but was extended for the Rev W.T. Elton, rector 1827-74, son and brother of Elton lords of the manor.

★★ *Village, church and setting.*

WILLITON (D) A large village south from Watchet lying at the junction between the A 358 from Taunton and the A 39 from Bridgwater to Minehead, although main roads avoided Williton until new turnpike roads were established here from 1807 and 1829. Its name ('Willettun' in 904) means 'the settlement on the Willett', a stream name of uncertain (possibly Celtic) origin. The centre of the village is largely 19th century with a number of local shops and a convenient carpark, focusing on the Egremont (formerly the Wyndham) Hotel, which replaced an earlier inn, the Coach and Horses, demolished c.1830. At the other end of the village, in Long Street, Honeysuckle Cottage is a modified medieval hall-house, there is a terrace of three cottages dated 1624, and Williton Hospital was built 1838-40 as Williton Union Workhouse, designed by William Moffatt and later known as Townsend House. Formerly the meeting-place of its own hundred, with a prison in 1276, and dependent on agriculture, fairs and later markets were held here from the later 18th century. Williton Rural District Council was established in 1894 and departments of West Somerset District Council have been located here since 1974. Williton, however, only became a separate parish in 1902, until then having formed part of St Decumans. There has been a station on the West Somerset Railway at the north-east end of the village since 1862 and the *West Somerset Free Press* has had its offices here since its foundation in 1860.

At the time of the Norman Conquest the estate here formed part of the king's holding but was granted soon after 1086 to William de Falaise. Maud, probably William's granddaughter, carried the property to her husband, Richard FitzUrse, whose son Reginald lived at Williton and was the leader of the four murderers of Thomas Becket at Canterbury Cathedral in 1170 and is believed to have struck the first blow. Indeed, following the assassination, Reginald and two of the other knights, Hugh de Morville and Richard le Bret (of Sampford Brett), were together at Williton before journeying to Rome. The FitzUrse house evidently stood near the present St Peter's church. Probably to expiate his crime Reginald gave half his estate to the Knights Templar from whom it passed in 1332 to the Knights Hospitaller, being known as the manor of Williton Temple, Williton Hospital or Williton Regis ('of the king') with a manor-house near the southern side of Bridge Street. After Sir Ralph FitzUrse (died 1350), the rest of the estate was divided between his daughters, known as the manors of Williton Hadley and Williton Fulford from the families which inherited them. A further holding, obtained in 1287 from Cleeve Abbey by Thomas of Orchard, descended from 1529 through a succession

of families to Elizabeth Sydenham, wife of John Wyndham.

The manor-house of **Orchard Wyndham** (fee:lists), set in its own park to the south-west of the village, is built around a medieval hall-house, to which John Sydenham (died 1521) added a second hall, cross wings and a chapel licensed in 1499, and where the Wyndhams live to this day. During the 16th and 17th century the family bought up most of the parish to form the core of their substantial Somerset estate. They acquired a baronetcy from Oliver Cromwell in 1658 (regranted by Charles II in 1661) and Charles Wyndham (died 1763), MP for Bridgwater and Taunton, and Chancellor of the Exchequer to Queen Anne, inherited the earldom of Egremont from his uncle in 1750: a title retained by the family until 1845.

Orchard Mill (fee:lists), clearly signed from the centre of Williton, was probably first built by Sir John Wyndham shortly before 1617, although the present buildings date from the early 19th century. Following restoration of the overshot water-wheel, the premises were opened to the public in 1979. There is a small farming museum, craft shop, garden and restaurant.

The church of St Peter (of All Saints in the early 14th century), was a chapelry of St Decuman's church by 1202, maintained even after the Restoration (until 1688) by an annual revel or chapel ale at Whitsun. The present building includes some medieval walling and windows but the south aisle was added in 1810-12 and the whole radically restored and vestry and north aisle built 1856-59. West from the village stands **Bardon House**, occupied, initially under the Wyndhams, by the Leigh family from c.1590 until 1924. Here in 1834 were discovered crucial archives

(known as the Bardon Papers and later sold to the British Library) relating to the imprisonment and trial of Mary, Queen of Scots: thought possibly to have been brought here by the Throckmortons, lords of Sampford Brett manor 1763-1846, whose ancestors were conspirators with Queen Mary, or alternatively to have passed to the Leighs from Sir Christopher Hatton, Elizabeth I's Lord Chancellor, via the Scudamores. There is also the persistent legend of a white dove inside an attic at Bardon, beating against the window to presage a death in the family. Just north of Williton village an area known as Battlegore ('Bytelgore' in the 14th century) is marked by three Bronze Age barrows, almost opposite Danesfield, a Middle school in the comprehensive system since 1971.

★★★ *Orchard Wyndham,* ★★ *setting,* ★ *village.*

WILTON (H) *see* TAUNTON

WIMBLEBALL (C) *see* BROMPTON REGIS

WINCANTON (F) An attractive former market town in the south-east of the county. Its name means 'settlement on the Wincawel stream' ('Wincaleton' in 1086), the Wincawel ('the white Cale') being the Celtic name for the Bow brook, a tributary of the River Cale, mentioned in 956. It still has surprisingly busy streets despite having been bypassed in the 1970s by the new route of the A 303 to the south. There are countryside prospects from most of its main streets and, despite modern shop-fronts, there is a wealth of good 18th and 19th century buildings, some the result of rebuildings after major fires. The centre has

The Union Workhouse, Williton

ABOVE *Wincanton*

BELOW *The Greyhound Inn sign, Wincanton*

several appealing old inns including the Bear (sundial dated 1720), the White Horse (dated 1737) and the Greyhound, which boasts of a visit from the future Queen Victoria (presumably *en route* with her parents to Sidmouth). Don't miss the advertising board of Alfred Jordan, chimneysweep, in the entrance to the library. His claim to have to have been 'patronised by royalty' probably rests on having swept the chimneys at the Greyhound !

The estate was granted after the Norman Conquest to Walter of Douai and descended with the barony of Castle Cary through the St Mawr (Seymour) and Lovel families. The Lovels lived nearby at Marsh where a moated enclosure marks the site of their manor-house. They had a chapel of St Andrew there by 1278 and Sir Richard Lovel celebrated a birth in the family with a great feast at Marsh in 1344. The early village of Wincanton evidently stood on the east bank of the Cale near the church where various routes converged. Here the Lovels obtained a Monday market in 1235 and subsequently (certainly by 1345) created a borough, probably by laying out burgage plots around a market-place and along the High Street, extending up the hill to the east. No borough administration survived the Middle Ages and a charter of 1556 which established two fairs and a Wednesday market was made to 10 nominated trustees, as was a further charter of 1706. Commissioners were appointed to pave, clean and light the place in 1798, a Union Workhouse was built on a pleasant site north-west of the town in 1837 (used

as an infirmary called Town View when demolished in 1973), but it was only a Parish Council that administered the town from 1894, although Wincanton Rural District Council was seated here 1894-1974. A town clock was mentioned from 1644 and a market-house, demolished by vandals, was in 1769 replaced by a Town Hall, in turn destroyed by fire in 1877 and succeeded by the present building in the Market Place, complete with clock tower. There is a small local history museum (fee:lists), with posters and old photo-graphs, housed in a cottage in the High Street.

Like most Somerset towns early Wincanton subsisted on cloth manufacture, specializing in the early 18th century in making Spanish medley cloth and later linen, dowlas and ticking. As elsewhere, this production declined during the later 18th century, flax cultivation and linen-weaving being the last to go. The 18th century also saw quite a colony of clock-makers established. Nathaniel Ireson (1686-1769) moved here c.1726, having built Stourhead (Wilts) to Colin Campbell's designs, but became a successful architect in his own right. Among his noted buildings were Ven House at Milborne Port, Mells Park, Berkley House, Crow-combe Court, the completion of churches at Redlynch and Blandford (Dorset), adding a chancel to Wincanton church in 1748, and building Ireson House here for himself. A local bed of clay provided him with the raw material for brickmaking and for his Delft pottery (dated pieces 1737-48): now very collectable. His striking monument in

the churchyard bears a terracotta statue which he is believed to have sculpted himself. Moulton Messiter (died 1786) moved here as an attorney from Wiltshire in 1754 and, as bankers and property owners, the family became the most prominent in the 19th century town, serving as Treasurers of the county until 1879 but living for a time at Bayford Lodge in nearby Stoke Trister. The town's position on the main coach route from Exeter to London long ensured its pros-perity, as later did its station on the Somerset and Dorset Joint Railway from 1862 until closure in 1966. The present century was marked by the building of the substantial Cow and Gate (later Unigate) milk factory to the south of the town in the early 1930s.

The Duke of Monmouth found at least 18 recruits here for his rebel army in 1685 and 6 men, none of them local, were hanged, drawn and quartered: their heads traditionally displayed at the east gate of the churchyard. In 1688 Wincanton was the scene of the first clash between the forces of William, Prince of Orange (later William III), on their march from Brixham to London, and those of James II. A force of some 25 of the Prince's men, sent to obtain horses here, was attacked at the east end of the town by about 120 royalist Irish troops and 15 soldiers were killed, including both commanders. The Prince himself was later lodged briefly at Richard Churchey's house, now known as Wincanton Manor (formerly 'the Dogs') in South Street, before proceeding to London to assume (with his wife) the vacant throne. During the Napoleonic Wars (1804-12) French POWs on parole were accommodated in the town. The illegitimate child of one of them was nicknamed 'Doughfig' and a stone in the churchyard commemorates two who died here, 1806-7.

The **church of SS Peter and Paul** at the west end of the town was granted to Stavordale Priory in 1374 and thereafter was served by poorly-paid curates. One of these, John Sacheveral, was minister during the Commonwealth and forced to leave in 1662 after his parishioners had burned him in effigy when he preached against Charles II. The local clergy were also involved in the 1664 trial of three Wincanton witches (and one from Stoke Trister). The west tower is 15th century (heightened by 12 ft in 1793) but the body of the church was rebuilt 1887-9 by J.D. Sedding with an ornate north porch. Inside this porch is a mutilated medieval carving of St Eligius shoeing the detached leg of a restless horse before restoring it to the animal. The south porch may be a surviving example of Ireson's work of 1735. South Street is dominated by the twin towers of the Roman Catholic church of SS Luke and Teresa (1908), adjoining the Carmelite priory (1888-9). Methodism was slow to catch on here, John Wesley commenting (1769-70) that the inhabitants 'had just as much feeling as the benches on which they sat' and that Wincanton was 'one of the dullest places in all the county'.

South of the town at **Horwood** Richard Messiter and William Capper established a bath-house over a mineral spring c.1805. Known as Horwood Well House or Physicwell House, it enjoyed a short-lived popularity as a spa, distributing its bottled water from four London warehouses. It even had its own bank, although this stopped payment in 1810 and Messiter

went bankrupt in 1819. West from the town beside the A 371 is the Holbrook House Hotel, a fine two-storeyed Georgian mansion, extended in the 19th century
★★★ *Town centre.*

WINSFORD (C) One of the prettiest villages on Exmoor and probably one of the oldest, since no fewer than six lanes make a meandering bee-line for it and there are many prehistoric remains in the area. To the north-west there are hillforts at Road Castle (above Exford) and on Staddon Hill, while on Winsford Hill to the west are the Wambarrows and, beneath a shelter set up in 1906, one of the most celebrated of Somerset monuments: the 'Langeston' or Caratacus Stone. This long stone bears the words 'CARATACI NEPUS', 'kinsman of Caratacus': possibly set up in the 5th century to a local chieftain who boasted of his descent from the 1st century British leader. Others consider that the inscription should be read 'Caranaci nepus' and may refer to a relation of St Carantoc. The place's name must surely mean 'the ford of the Winn Brook', which may derive from the Saxon *winn* – 'meadow'. The manor was held before the Conquest by Tostig, brother of King Harold II who died at Hastings, but latterly became part of the Acland estate. The village is encircled by wooded hills, has a picturesque green and no fewer than seven little bridges which span the Winn Brook and the Exe. The thatched Royal Oak Inn, now a hotel, was originally a traditional farmhouse, dating from c.1600 but subse- quently enlarged. Several cottages in the village and farmhouses elsewhere in the parish are of similar date. A 19th century cottage bears a plaque identifying it as the birthplace of Ernest Bevin, former Foreign Secretary, in 1881. He was the illegitimate son of the widowed Diana Bevin: evidently

by Thomas Pearse, a local butcher. The church of St Mary Magdalene (formerly St Peter) was held by the monks of Barlynch Priory who appointed vicars here from 1281, as did Emmanuel College, Cambridge, from 1589. The building is approached through a ford (the one which named the village?) up a lane rightly named the Steep. The church dominates the village and inside has a pleasantly light and airy feel to it. It is mainly Perpendicular except for a 13th century chancel and a Norman south doorway, possibly reset. There is a Norman font and a fine panel of the Royal Arms dated 1609, supposed to be one of only four which survive from the reign of James I.
★★★★ *Village,* ★★ *church.*

WINSHAM (J) A sizeable parish and village, 'Wine's settlement', on the county boundary south-east from Chard. The manor evidently formed part of the estate of Wells Cathedral in Saxon times and, although granted away, probably by Harold II, was restored to Wells by William the Conqueror. It supported five canons at the Cathedral, later merged with the prebends of Combe St Nicholas, and in 1262 a Wednesday market was granted, and also a fair which continued into the 18th century. The remains of a medieval cross stand at the north end of the village street where five lanes converge on a former village green. Halfway down the street, the church of St Stephen is Norman in plan but Decorated and Perpendicular in detail, with chancel, central tower and nave. A large mid 16th century painting of the Crucifixion, which formerly filled the space above the rood screen, hangs high up on the inner north wall of the tower. In the sanctuary is a monument to Robert Henley of Leigh House (died 1639), depicted clad in his shroud and rising from the tomb.

Winsford from the south

Leigh is an E-shaped mansion built by Henry Henley c.1617, standing in parkland to the west of the village and held until 1917 by his family, who provided Taunton with its first mayor (Andrew Henley, 1627). Street (named for the Foss Way which ran through the west of the parish) and Leigh were both Domesday manors which later passed to nearby Forde Abbey in Devon. In the 19th century villagers were employed either on the Cricket St Thomas estate (Lord Bridport provided the present Jubilee Hall in 1887) to the north or at a cloth factory at the south end of the village. Some still tell of the daily tour by Johnny Rowsell's wagon to collect human urine, used in the cloth processing: regular 'savers' being rewarded with the gift of a sacking apron at Christmas! There were two mills here by 1086, possibly those later found at Whatley and Ammerham, together with tucking and blade mills in the 17th century.

★★ *Village and church.*

WITHAM FRIARY (F) This rural parish, 'Witta's homestead', south-west from Frome, was held as two estates in 1086, the larger formerly belonging to Brewham. The rectory estate was given to Bruton priory soon after its foundation in 1142 and the monks had a chapel here. Following the murder of St Thomas Becket at Canterbury in 1170, Henry II undertook in expiation to found three monasteries, of which Witham c.1178 became the first Carthusian priory in England. By a series of exchanges the king obtained Witham estates from Gilbert of Norfolk and Geoffrey of Wanstrow and the church here from the monks of Bruton, assigning all three to the Carthusians. The subsequent grudging support of Henry II meant that it was only with the appointment of the third prior, Hugh of Avalon, in 1179, that the priory literally got off the ground. Excavations in 1965-69 concluded that the priory was sited in a field to the south of Witham Hall Farm, nearly a mile north-east from the present village, and established the outline of the cloister and the possible position of the priory church on its north side. Hugh left in 1186 to become bishop of Lincoln (and later a saint) but regularly visited Witham up until his death in 1200. A royal letter of 1354 to the priory records that 'all their servants and retainers died in the last pestilence' (the Black Death). The monks had ironworkings in the parish and secured valuable leadmining areas around Charterhouse-on-Mendip which they exploited until their house was surrendered

Trumpeting angel, Witham Friary church

to Henry VIII in 1539. The Witham property was granted to Ralph Hopton in 1544, descending to Ralph, Lord Hopton, the king's general in the West during the Civil War (died 1652), the family adapting the monastic buildings for their own occupation. The future Charles II dined as Prince of Wales with Hopton at Witham in July 1644. The manor passed to the Wyndhams, descendants of Lord Hopton's eldest sister, and by 1717 Sir William Wyndham had built a Palladian mansion here, demolished in the early 19th century. The estate was sold in 1762 to Alderman William Beckford (died 1770) who commissioned Robert Adam to erect another house to the south of the monastic precinct. This was never completed and the Alderman's famous son, William, sold the property, held by successive dukes of Somerset 1812-1954, the present Duke continuing as patron of the living.

The village of Witham Friary may occupy the site of the original settlement before the foundation of the priory. Its suffix has nothing to do with 'friars' but appears to be a corruption of the French word *frerie*: identifying the home of the lay brothers. The church of St Mary, St John the Baptist and All Saints may represent the original chapel held here by Bruton priory. It is a plain severe early Norman structure with a rounded apse at the east end, high round-headed windows and a vaulted and ribbed

stone roof. Externally the restoration of 1875-6 added flying buttresses to give very necessary support and a tall three-bell bellcot, replacing a west tower of 1828. The restoration also added a western bay to the building. Over the east door are the arms of Sir Arthur Hopton and the date 1586, although thought to have been added much later, and there is a fine early 19th century organ with trumpeting angels. The font can be dated to 1459 when the building effectively became a parish church although strictly speaking Witham was a 'liberty' rather than a parish and the church was the only peculiar in private hands in the diocese. Opposite the church is a converted rectangular dovecote of the late 14th century. The Seymour Arms was built by the Duke of Somerset 1864-66, succeeding the village's former port of call, the Red Lion, recorded from 1788. A Friendly Society mentioned in 1786 continues to meet.

Gare Hill, a hamlet to the east on the county boundary, is mentioned as 'la Gahere' (possibly 'the grassy place' from Saxon *gaers* – 'grass') in 1298. It was largely settled by squatters from the later 17th century onwards. In 1857 it secured its own church of St Michael, an untypical work of William Butterfield, the creator of Keble College, Oxford. It was built following the efforts of the Rev R.C.T. Boyle of Marston Bigot and a bequest from the 8th Earl of Cork and Orrery. There are fine views from its churchyard, but it was declared redundant and closed in 1979.

★★★ *Witham church*, ★★ *Village.*

WITHIEL FLOREY (C) Lying isolated in a cleft high on the Brendon Hills, its name means 'willow' or 'withy wood'. It was a detached member of the 'outfaring' of Taunton Deane manor, having been granted in 737 by King Aethelheard to Winchester Cathedral, possibly confirmed by King Athelstan in 938 and thereafter held by the bishops of Winchester, under whom it was tenanted by the Fleury or Flory family in the 13th century. There were evidently lands excepted from the original gift, as there are genuine Saxon charters of estates here by later monarchs to their ministers in 956 and 961. The church of St Mary Magdalene is tucked away behind Castle Hill Farm. Its west tower dates from the 13th century but the rest is Perpendicular, heavily restored and externally enthusiastically rendered. The porch is dated 1693 and there is a comprehensive memorial to 18th century members of the Bryant family. A small community of 17th century Quakers worshipped here at Swansea Farm, east of the church, then held by the stout-hearted Lyddon family.

★ *Setting.*

WITHYCOMBE (D) This homely red sandstone village, with the occasional thatched survival, lies south-east of Dunster, at the bottom of 'the willow valley' which named it. In the Middle Ages there were two manors, Withycombe Wyke and Withycombe Hadley, both named from their owners and both eventually passing to the Luttrells of Dunster. The roughcast church of St Nicholas is relatively plain outside. It has a chancel of c.1300, 14th century south tower and is unusual in having escaped both Perpendicular enlargement and Victorian restoration. There is a Norman font with vertical ribs and cable moulding, but the church's finest feature is the five-bay rood screen of c.1500. In the nave are two early effigies. On a cill the figure of a woman, identified as Lucy de Meriet (died c.1315), lady of one third of the manor, lies between two beautifully-carved stone candleholders. A slightly earlier civilian figure in the south wall, almost hidden by pews, probably represents Lucy's second husband, Thomas de Timworth (died 1297), one-time Constable of Taunton Castle. Both effigies hold hearts, suggesting that only their hearts were buried here. In the chancel is a small brass to the thrice-married Joan Carne (died 1612) of Sandell. Local tradition identifies her as 'the witch of Withycombe' who murdered all her husbands and claims

Chapel of St Bartholomew, Rodhuish, Withycombe

that, after her funeral, her ghost was observed frying up bacon and eggs for the mourners! Sandell is now Sandhill Farm, east of the village, dating from the late 16th century with an enclosed forecourt.

Two lanes from the village lead south to the Domesday hamlet of **Rodhuish**, where there is the little 15th century church (formerly chapel) of St Bartholomew with a Norman font from Carhampton church. Further south, beyond Felons Oak (probably recalling an execution carried out near the site of a crime) is Croydon Hall, c.1700, now a Special School. Until 1914 it was home to Count Conrad von Hochberg, a German Anglophile forced to

return to his homeland at the outbreak of World War I. East from Rodhuish is the 17th century Escott Farm which christened the prominent landowning family of that name.

★★ *Village, church, Rodhuish hamlet, walking.*

WITHYPOOL (C) An Exmoor village at the confluence of Pennycombe Water and the river Barle, where there must once have been a 'withy pool' which named it. It is a remote spot where it used formerly to be said that there were four harvests a year — snow, frost, rain and muck ! The presence of Bronze Age man is marked by a 120 ft

River Barle, Withypool

Wiveliscombe

stone circle on Withypool Hill and there are burial mounds there and at Bright-worthy Barrows and Green Barrow on Withypool Common. With Hawkridge it was one of two estates which had a special relationship with the Royal Forest of Exmoor. The forest pound stood here and the manor was held with the Forestership of the moor, descending through the medieval families of Odburville, Wrotham and Plessy. The two annual Swainmote courts which administered the moor from the Middle Ages were held in the open air at Hawkridge churchyard and at the 15th century five-arched Lanacre or Landacre (originally 'Long Acre') Bridge which crosses the Barle upstream from the village. Here also lived 37 of the 52 free suitors of Exmoor, who were obliged to attend the courts and held delightfully-named properties such as Foxtwitchen, Garli-combe, Sweetwalls and Brightworthy. The church of St Andrew, formerly a chapelry to Hawkridge, retains its squat 17th century tower but the rest was almost wholly restored and rebuilt in 1887 and 1902. Only the fine Norman font with chevron carving survived unscathed.

★★★ *Landscape and walking.*

WIVELISCOMBE (D) A former borough, market and clothing town to the north-west of Wellington and most attractively situated below the Brendon Hills, but which wears a somewhat nondescript appearance today. Although formerly centred on the Square, through-traffic has been diverted along Croft Way

since 1980. It was an ancient possession of the bishops of Bath and Wells, who by the 13th century had a substantial and favourite palace here (with its own chapel and park) to the south of the church and Church Street. There bishops John Drokensford (1329), Ralph of Shrewsbury (1363) and Ralph Erghum (1400) appear to have died, and the second of these certainly took refuge there during the Black Death, administering his stricken diocese from Wiveliscombe. The archbishop of Canterbury celebrated his birthday there in 1331 and Bishop Knight fondly recalled the hangings in his 'great dynyng chamber' in 1547. The great kitchen survived into the 19th century but now there remains only the arched gateway, visible from the east end of the churchyard. The adjoining church fared little better than the palace. It had been granted to the Chapter of Wells by Bishop Savaric (1192-1205), given to endow a Cathedral prebend in 1214 and was stated to have been rebuilt by Bishop Ralph of Shrewsbury (1329-63). A crack which developed in the tower decided the parishioners on a wholesale rebuilding (1827-29), although the arcade pillars were so firmly seated that they had to be blown up with gunpowder. The replacement is in red sandstone by Richard Carver, whose name appears prominently on the west gallery, although the chancel was reconstructed in 1872. Carver excavated an extensive crypt which during the Second World War provided a safe haven for stained glass from Exeter and Salisbury cathedrals, the diocesan records of Bath

and Wells, Exeter, Salisbury and Lichfield, other documents from London's Guildhall, and treasures from Bristol and London churches. There is a fine monument in the south aisle to Humphrey Wyndham (died 1622), a younger son of the Orchard family, and his wife Margery (died 1628) with their effigies in alabaster. Her healing talents are over-graphically commemorated:

'His Matchles Wife, whose heaven blest
    skill and cost
Curd sundry, (Whome the Surgeon held
    for lost)
Of Dangerous wounds, dym eies, and
    festered sores,
Sent Maymed criples crutchles from her
    dore.'

North from the church stands Bournes, a 17th century house with a later porch, possibly named for John Bourne of Gothelney, a royalist who compounded for his estate at Wiveliscombe after the Civil War.

The bishops obtained a grant for a market and three-day fair here in 1285 and probably at around that date established a borough, first mentioned in 1301, although its lay-out is far from clear in the town's present street plan. There are references to 31 burgesses in the 14th and 15th centuries, headed by a portreeve, and a prison and the Rye Cross (where grain was presumably traded) were recorded in 1559. Following the Monmouth Rebellion of 1685 three rebels were executed in the town, although no local men are known to have joined the Duke. The old market-house, which once had a row of covered shambles in front of it, was replaced from 1841 by the present Town Hall financed by Lord Ashburton, then lord of the manor. From the Middle Ages the economy here depended on cloth, its carriage to Taunton and thence to London providing consider-able employment for the Taunton carriers. Felt hats called Carolinas were being produced c.1700 and a flourishing trade later developed in cheap cloth to clothe slaves in the West Indies. although their emancipation killed the business. Hancock's Brewery, founded by William Hancock (1769-1845) in 1806 and moved to Golden Hill a year later, began to dominate the town visually and economically: at one time hailed as the largest brewery in the West of England. Indeed the Hancocks, farmers from Ford, progressively became the dominant family in the area as brewers, bankers, solicitors and landowners. The brewery, with 85 'tied' houses in 1906, became Arnold and Hancock in 1927 but closed after a takeover in 1959. Part of the old building returned to brewing in 1979 and Exmoor Ale was named 'Best Bitter of the Year' in 1980.

To the west of the town lies Abbotsfield, a substantial house with large tower (all now subdivided), designed c.1872 by Owen Jones for Charles Lukey Collard. The Collards were celebrated London piano manufacturers and Abbotsfield is stated to have been visited by Richard Wagner, when from the terrace Adelina Patti sang to an audience seated below. The tenant of Oakhampton House ('Acumentun' in 1065), north-east from Wiveliscombe, was formerly obliged to attend the bishop's court with a horn slung across his shoulder and a hound on the leash, ready to assist at the bishop's hunt. The present building dates from 1734. It was formerly occupied by the Yea family, ancestors of the Yea baronets of Pyrland Hall, Taunton. There is a major disused slate quarry at Oakhampton, closed in the 1880s.

There are two early enclosures in the parish: King's Castle, an eliptical hilltop fort to the east of the town, partly quarried away, where Roman coins were found in 1711 and 1946, and Nunnington Park ('Nunnetun' in 1065), a plain square bank to the south, probably of Roman origin.

★★ *Setting*, ★ *church, town.*

WOOKEY (E)

This compact village, immediately west of Wells, is not to be confused with the tourist honeypot of Wookey Hole (*see below*), 2 miles to the north-east. The origin of the name is far from certain: perhaps from the Old English *wocig*, 'a noose or snare', maybe referring to an animal trap or to the cave itself. Current opinion favours a Celtic word *ogof* – 'cave'. The manor here clearly formed part of the larger estate of Wells, and thus part of the original endowment of the bishops from the 10th century. Bishop Jocelin (1206-42) built a moated manor-house with its own chapel, now represented by Court Farm, and this became a favourite resort for successive bishops in the 14th and 15th centuries and was where Bishop Nicholas Bubwith drew up his will and died in 1424.Its surrender to the Duke of Somerset (executed 1552) was enforced in 1549, and the estate was later held by the Dunche family of London (1553-1626), one of whom married Oliver Cromwell's aunt, and the Rolles of Shapwick (1626- 1768). The manor was split up and sold off in 1769. At Court Farm little more than a doorway, possibly

leading to the chapel, survives of Jocelin's work. The rest is 16th century, perhaps the work of the lessee from 1544, Thomas Clerke, brother of Bishop John Clerke.

The church of St Matthew stands in the centre of the village and was granted to the dean of Wells by Bishop Robert (1136-66). It was dedicated, probably after a rebuilding, by Bishop Reginald (1174-91) and assigned to the subdean of the cathedral in 1209. In 1437 the dedication day (16 September) was changed to the Sunday after 30 September to avoid clashing with the harvest. Inside it is a broad friendly building, the oldest part being the 13th century chancel. The south porch, chancel arch, west tower and south arcade date from the 14th century, and the south aisle and arcade from the 15th. The south chancel chapel is thought to have been built to house the substantial memorial to Thomas Clerke (died 1556): the altar rails are dated 1635. An original copy of the Authorised Version of the Bible (1611) is displayed in a case, as is a stuffed swift to commemorate the escape of the church when the tower was struck by lightning in 1906. Beside the church stands the early 19th century castellated Gothic extravaganza of Mellifont Abbey, standing on the site of the former rectory house and incorporating medieval and Tudor fragments, believed to have come from Court Farm. The name was apparently bestowed on it by its occupant, Lady Elizabeth Bertie, died 1781, and refers to the original abbey near Drogheda in Ireland, former seat of the earls of Drogheda and scene of a bloody siege in 1641.

To the west along the road to Wedmore lie the successive hamlets of Worth, Yarley, Henton and Bleadney. Henton had a free chapel of St Thomas,demolished in 1550. The Victorian Christchurch, designed by Benjamin Ferrey, was consecrated there in 1847. **Bleadney** was the site of a bridge over (and/or a harbour on) the River Axe, when granted to Glastonbury Abbey by the bishop of Sherborne in 712. **Fenny Castle**, 2 miles south-west of Wookey village (where the locals used to claim that King Alfred was buried !), appears to be a former Norman motte and bailey castle. William of Worcester c.1470 recorded it under that name and observed that it was then 'a ruin and had been built of stones, and traces of the offices of the house are now visible': Its presence by 1327 is suggested by the name of William 'atte Castle' at Yarley and Leland also observed the ruins in 1546. In 1825 the Rev John

Skinner excavated the footings of the curtain wall and reported that the farmer here had dug up over 20 skeletons. It is difficult to see any other builder for it than an early Norman bishop. The nearby hamlet of **Castle** has the remains of a cross and a hotel there preserves the name of Fenny Castle.

★★ *Village, church.*

WOOKEY HOLE (E)

A natural cavern in the Mendip cliffs, north-west from Wells, out of which flows the River Axe (*for the name Wookey, see above*). There are 25 chambers running back into the hillside, of which only the first three were accessible to the public until 1975, when an artificial tunnel was cut to enable visitors to view chambers seven, eight and nine. Unlike the caves at Cheddar, which had to be found by 19th century digging, the first five caverns at Wookey have always been known and have a long history of human occupation. Archaeological investigations from c.1820 produced remains dating from c.250 BC to 400 AD which can be viewed at Wells Museum. Just below the main cave, the Hyaena Den was discovered in 1852 and revealed 36 Palaeolithic tools, dating back to 35,000 BC, with bones including those of hyaenas, lions, mammoths, bears and woolly rhinoceros. Clement of Alexandria in 189 AD is thought to have referred to Wookey when likening the sound made by the wind blowing into a British cave to 'the clashing of numerous cymbals'. William of Worcester described c.1470 how those entering the cave, carrying torches made of 'shevys of reed-sedge', had to ask permission of the Porter, a stalagmite near the entrance, later called the Sentinel. He referred to the chambers as the kitchen, the 'ost' (oast for drying barley), the parlour and the 'holie-hole', and mentioned that 'the figure of a woman is there clad and holding in her girdle a spinning distaff'. This famous stalagmite was referred to as the Witch of Wookey by 1694 and led to a wealth of folklore and the possibility of animal or even human sacrifice. John Cannon, writing in the 1730s, described 'the statue of an old woman which they call the old witch of a white stone like alabaster, . . . a flitch of bacon, four together, a woman big with child, organ pipes very like those in our churches, . . . a melodious eccho, the likeness of a chimney, a stone table, a huge massy stone called the great gun which, being taken up and let fall, will make a noise as a cannon'. He also noted the discovery of a new cavern in 1736 in which was 'a boat of a handsom size'. Since that time Wookey Hole has been regularly and repeatedly visited.

Below the cave the River Axe provided motive power for fulling mills by 1425 and for the manufacture of paper by 1610. The paper mills were taken over in the mid 19th century by the Hodgkinsons from London, who virtually created the village of Wookey Hole, building the church of St Mary Magdalene in 1874 (which houses many of their memorials), the Village Club in 1883 and their own home, Glencot, c.1895. They were also responsible for exploiting the cave itself (fee:lists) which, with their mills, was sold to Madame Tussauds in 1973 who greatly expanded the operation. Today the tour includes hand-made paper-making, Lady Bangor's fairground museum and an Edwardian penny arcade. There is a restaurant, easy carparking, and the whole package provides an excellent outing for a family. (*See also* **Ebbor Gorge**)

★★★★ *Caves, mill, setting.*

WOOLAVINGTON (E) This pleasant village, 'the settlement of Hunlaf's people' ('Hunlavintone' in 1086), lies to the north-east of Bridgwater. Before the Norman Conquest there were two estates here which much later were known from the families that owned them as Woolavington Throckmorton, centred on the present Manor House, and Woolavington Pym, whose focus was the Grange. The Manor House, on the north side of the church,

probably dates from the 16th century and features an 18th century folly wall with castellated porch: possibly intended to hide the vegetable garden. The Grange, now divided, appears to be 17th century, as is the fascinating survival in its grounds: a circular thatched cockpit, 14 ft across.

I cannot resist quoting the will of one manorial lord, William Pym of Woolavington, made in 1608. He bequeathed to his wife Agnes, 'that I did a long tyme take for my wife, till of late she hath denyed me to be her husband, altho' we were married with our friends consent, her father, mother and uncle at yt, and now she sweareth she will never love me, neither will be persuaded by preachers nor any other, which hath happened within these few years, and Toby Andrews the begynner, which I did see with myne own eyes, when he did more than was fitting, and this by the means of Robert Musgrove and their abettors, I have lived a miserable life these 6 or 7 years, and now I leave the revenge to God and £10 to buy her a great horse, for I could not these many years please her with one great enough'.

The church of St Peter was granted in the early 12th century to Goldcliff Priory in Monmouthshire by its founder, Robert de Chandos, lord of the main Woolavington manor, but passed in the 15th century to the canons of Windsor, who still present the vicars. The west tower may represent the crossing tower of an earlier church of c.1300, to which the present nave and chancel were added in the 15th century.

There is a blocked Norman north door and the whole was thoroughly restored in 1880. Set in the blocked door is the so-called Hody stone, bearing the mono-gram JH. It may commemorate John Hody, who died in 1441 as Chief Justice of England and requested burial at Woolavington ('for the love that he hadde to hyt, for ther he beganne hys fyrst lernyng'), or his uncle of the same name. The 13th century north chapel probably housed a chantry founded by Gilbert of Woolavington in 1285 and served from Cleeve Abbey. The churchyard provides a final resting place for Henry Hunt, hanged at Exeter for horse-stealing in 1804.

A livestock fair was held here from 1777 until the First World War. The old White Lion Inn in the Square was home to 'the Rational Sick and Burial Society Lodge' until the temperance movement closed it in 1913, but the Prince of Wales Inn continues to minister to the thirsty.

★★ *Village*, ★ *church.*

WOOLVERTON (B) This 'settlement of Wulfhere's people', on the west bank of the river Frome, opposite Rode, features the Red Lion Inn and Woolverton House Hotel, a sizeable Victorian pile. The manor was evidently included under Rode in the Domesday Book, but for most of the Middle Ages was held by the Turney family until acquired by the Hungerfords of Farleigh in the 16th century and thereafter passed with Rode manor. The east wall of the church of St Laurence informs us that we are '212 feet above the sea'. The church, at the end of a leafy lane, is over-restored (1838-9) Perpendicular with an attractive west tower, crowned with a spirelet. There is an ornate Perpendicular font with Tudor roses. Monuments include those to the Meade family of Whatley Lodge and to the Rev Charles Glossop (died 1874, aged 92), rector here for 62 years.

WOOTTON COURTNEY (C) A valley village, 'the settlement in the wood', which lies midway between Minehead and Dunkery Beacon. It is a place of thatched cottages and pink walls which William the Conqueror took from Algar and gave to William of Falaise. The manor passed in the 13th century to John de Courtenay, whose family later became earls of Devon and gave their name to both manor and parish. Medieval domestic survivals include Fairgarden Farm, south-west from the village and dating from the late 15th century, considered to be one of the finest

Paper-making, Wookey Hole

longhouses in the county, and a little to the east a former 15th century farmhouse converted into a barn adjoining the 17th century Burrow Farm. The church of All Saints is set back above the village street and has a 13th century west tower, finished off by a saddleback roof of 1866. The remainder, including the octagonal font, is mainly 15th century but, in common with so many Somerset churches, was drastically restored in the 19th century. The screen was carved in 1921 by local hands and there is a monument to the 1st bishop of Colombo, James Chapman (died 1879), who was rector here for 15 years. The successor to the Domesday mill is now occupied by a local pottery. The Minehead Harriers have their kennels here and the village hit the headlines recently when parishioners clubbed together to buy up the village shop and forestall its closure.
★★ *Village.*

WYKE CHAMPFLOWER (F) An

idyllically-sited hamlet and former parish (*wic* – 'dairy-farm'), immediately west of Bruton. The latter part of its name reflects its ownership by the Champflower family by 1166 until the mid 13th century. The Georgian manor-house is attached to the small chapel of St Peter. There was a chapel here, 'built during time of war' by the 12th century, served by the canons of Bruton Priory until 1539 and by curates thereafter. Becoming dilapidated and allegedly used for Roman Catholic worship, it was rebuilt in 1623 by Henry Southworth (died 1625) and retains its Jacobean box pews, pulpit and panelling, a generous supply of Southworth heraldry and the builder's tomb in the chancel. The state of its structure cries out for another Southworth. The place became a parish in 1748 but was reunited with Bruton in 1971.
★★ *Setting and chapel.*

YARLINGTON (F) This small parish,

south-east from Castle Cary, has a name ('Gerlincgetuna', 1086) which probably means 'the settlement of Gerla's people'. The manor passed in the 12th century to the Montagues, later earls of Salisbury, and so continued until the attainder and execution (1541) of Margaret, Countess of Salisbury. King John was here twice in 1209, Simon de Montague in 1313 had licence to fortify his manor-house here and a year later obtained a grant of a market and fair: the fair discontinued only in 1900. The manor was settled by Henry VIII on his last wife, Katherine Parr, and it was held

by a branch of the Berkeleys of Bruton from 1592 until their descendant, Lord Carmarthen, sold it to John Rogers in 1782. Rogers built Yarlington House to the south of the village, at which a passing George III is reported to have exclaimed 'a bold man, a bold man to build a house there'. The church of St Mary, facing the Stag's Head Inn, has a Perpendicular south tower, but the chancel was rebuilt in 1822 and the rest in 1870. It features memorials of the Rogers family from 1836 to 1973. Around the church and Manor Farm are the traces of a moat, possibly the last remnants of Simon de Montague's defences of 1313. Southwest from the village, Woolston was an ancient freehold, described in the early 17th century as Great Woolston *alias* Woolston Gyon, there being Gyons living in the area in the 14th century.

YEOVIL (J) A sizeable town on the

south-east border of the county, with an important livestock market, written off by many because of the systematic way so much of its heritage has been demolished. Those who can master the road system will find pedestrianised streets, some old inns, several attractive 18th and 19th century buildings and a modern and attractive shopping complex, including the recently opened Quedam Centre (an old Yeovil street name of unclear origin although it is Latin for 'a certain'). Compensations have included a modern college, hospital and the Octagon Theatre.

A Bronze-Age golden torque (twisted collar) has been found at Hendford and evidence of a Roman settlement, including a mosaic pavement, was excavated at Westland in 1927-8. The town's name is a variant of that of the river Yeo or Ivel which flows to the east, recorded as 'Gifle' (from Celtic, 'forked river') when King Alfred (died 901) left the estate here to his younger son Aethelweard. The Domesday Book (1086) records 22 holdings added to one of the two manors which correspond to the 22 burgesses later mentioned as comprising the borough. This suggests a possible royal Saxon *burh* deprived of its liberties by the Norman Conquest, after which the manor, later known as Hendford, was granted to the Count of Eu and his tenant, Hugh Maltravers. Hugh's family and their descendants, the earls of Arundel, retained the lordship until 1561. A borough, referred to as 'the Tenement', was evidently established by a lost charter of the earlier 12th century and settled, most unusually, on the rector of Yeovil, appointed by the Maltravers family. They sold the advowson in 1415 to Henry V who gave it to the abbess and convent of Syon at Isleworth (Middx.), who thereby became lords of the town, retained the rectory and thereafter presented vicars of St John's. In addition to an existing market, the convent also received from the king in 1421 the right to hold two three-day fairs in the borough After the dissolution the lordship was held by the Horsey (1538- 1610) and Phelips (1611-1846)

The High Street, Yeovil

243

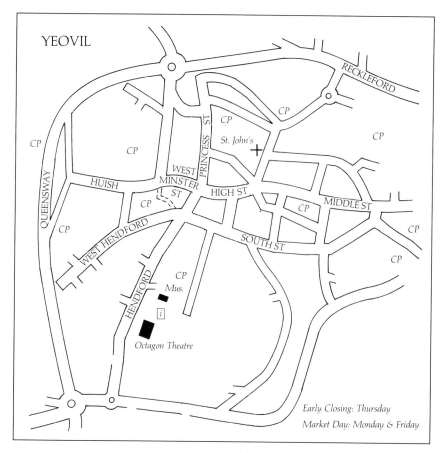

YEOVIL

QUEENSWAY
RECKLEFORD
HUISH
WEST HENDFORD
HENDFORD
PRINCESS ST
WEST MINSTER ST
HIGH ST
MIDDLE ST
SOUTH ST
St. John's
CP

Mus.
[i]
Octagon Theatre

Early Closing: Thursday
Market Day: Monday & Friday

King George Street, Yeovil

LIBRARY

PEDESTRIAN ZONE

families, and later by the Harbins of Newton Surmaville. It was a nice touch that the building opened in 1969 to house County Council and Government offices was named Maltravers House after the medieval lords of the borough and Hendford.

The borough centred on a market-place at the junction of the present High, Silver, Middle and Wine streets. Here formerly stood the medieval Market House and covered Shambles (both demolished in 1849), the Toll House and Parish (or Church) House. Yeovil's townsfolk were

probably governed by a portreeve from the beginning, although there were periodic and regular disputes over jurisdiction with the church and the lords. Town Commissioners were appointed in 1830, but the first charter of incorporation was not granted until 1854 together with a mayoralty that continued until 1974, when Yeovil borough was submerged in South Somerset District Council. Subsequent mayors have headed only the Charter Trustees.

Yeovil was a relatively small town before the 19th century with a population of some 2,800 in 1801. As in other Somerset towns, cloth manufacture was an important element in the economy until the 18th century, with particular emphasis on hemp, thread and sailcloth. Gloving and tanning were recorded from the early 14th century, reaching their height in the 19th, when the streets abounded in glove factories and annual production (1834) was estimated at over three million pairs.

This tradition continues in the tannery of Messrs Pittard at Pen Mill. Aplin and Barrett founded a cheese and butter marketing company here in 1888, which in 1901 adopted the trademark of the fictional 'St Ivel' (derived from an earlier form of the town's name). A major employer in the area, the business was taken over by Unigate in 1960 and closed in 1976.

The principal industry today is the design and production of Westland helicopters, a threat to whose continued health led two cabinet ministers to resign in 1986 and whose operations occupy an extensive area west of the town centre. It originated in James B. Petter's engines produced by 1882, and his son, Sir Ernest Petter, began in 1915 the manu- facture of air-craft for World War One on the Westland site.

Early in the Civil War a spirited engagement on Babylon Hill, to the east of the town, resulted in the Earl of Bedford's Roundheads forcing back Sir Ralph Hopton's Cavaliers to Sherborne. Only seven Yeovil men are known to have joined the Duke of Monmouth in 1685 but eight rebels, none of them known to be from the town, were hanged, drawn and quartered here. Other disasters to strike the town included major fires in 1449 and 1640 (destroying 83 houses), and a severe outbreak of plague killed 'manie hundred soules' in 1646-7.

The **church of St John the Baptist** stands in the north-western corner of the old borough to the west of Silver Street in

ABOVE *Yeovil church.* BELOW *Newton Surmaville*

a neatly-mown precinct reminiscent of a mini cathedral close and where, in the churchyard, the early rectors held their borough courts. A church evidently stood here by c.950 when Wynflaed, a Saxon lady of Chinnock, left a gift to it in her will. The present impressive building, which accommodated at least five medieval chantry chapels, dates from the later 14th century, is almost all of that period and was begun by Robert de Samborne (rector 1362-82). The design has been attributed to William Wynford, the master mason of Wells Cathedral, although much of the details were probably executed by local craftsmen.

The only older portion is the crypt of c.1300 below the chancel (where Gerard states the town's archives were stored in 1633), although a low medieval chapel to the south-west of the tower housed the town's charity (later grammar) school from its foundation in 1573 until demolished in 1854. There are corbel heads in the chancel which formerly supported the Lenten veil and an extremely rare brass lectern of c.1450, inscribed by the donor, Brother Martin Forester. A fine brass depicts lawyer Giles Penne and his wife Isabel, erected after the wife's death in 1519. The husband's death date is left blank as he moved to East Coker before his death in 1560.

There are other brasses to the Hawker and Prowse families, and several memorials to the Harbins of Newton Surmaville in the north transept. The church was the scene of a riot in 1349 when the bishop's visitation was disrupted by a violent mob (possibly terrified by the Black Death), blood was shed in the church and Bishop Ralph of Shrewsbury was besieged in the rectory until the next day. The church of Holy Trinity was put up in South Street to the designs of Benjamin Ferrey, 1843-6, to serve the new parish of Hendford.

The small **Museum of South Somerset** (lists) has been housed since 1965 in the former coach house of Hendford Manor (itself a fine 18th century mansion). It includes material from local Roman excavations, displays on the leather, glove, twine, sailcloth and aircraft industries, and exhibits of costume, firearms and painting.

Kingston was a separate Domesday manor lying to the north and north-east of the old borough, its name suggesting its former ownership by King Alfred. After the Conquest the estate was held by the Say family until 1226, after which it was divided between Gilbert de Say's

The Fleet Air Arm Museum, Yeovilton

daughters. Kingston seems originally to
have been regarded as a separate parish
and, although the chapel of All Saints there
was described in 1548 as 'utterly decayde
and fallen down longe ago', rectors
continued to be appointed to the sinecure
of 'Kingston Pitney'.

Newton Surmaville, recorded in 1208, is
an estate south-east of the town beside the
Yeo: presumably 'new' in relation to Yeovil
and deriving its suffix from its former lord,
Philip de Surmaville (died 1232). The
manor was bought in 1608 by Robert
Harbin (died 1621, aged 95) who by 1612
had built the fine Ham-stone house, still
occupied by his descendant, Mrs Sophia
Rawlins. (*See also* **Preston Plucknett**)

★★★ *St John's church,* ★★ *museum,*
★ *town* (★★★ *for shopping).*

YEOVILTON (J) The parish lies just east
of Ilchester, its name meaning 'the
settlement on the Yeo'. It was mentioned in
two 10th century grants by kings Edward
the Elder and Edwy, although its estates
were generally held by absentee lords. In
1254 William de Yeovilton was granted
the right to hold a short-lived St
Bartholomew's fair. Since 1940 the area has
been progressively dominated by the
Royal Naval Air Station, HMS *Heron*,
which has led Somerset to play a major
part in conflicts such as the Falklands War
and regularly brought serving members of
the royal family to the county. Today most
visitors come to tour the **Fleet Air Arm
Museum** (fee:lists), opened by HRH the
Duke of Edinburgh in 1964.

Since regularly extended, it now houses a
wide range of over 40 historic aircraft
from the early days of naval flying through
two World Wars to modern engagements,
including Concorde 002, and features
audio-visual displays, documents and
photographs.

The church of St Bartholomew has a
west tower that was in building in 1486,
although Norman fragments survive in
the vestry. In the east of the parish the
estate of Bridgehampton and Speckington,
probably Saxon in origin and combined
by 1315, centred on Speckington Manor,
a 19th century remodelling of a 17th
century house. The manor was held by the
Hunt family from 1618 until 1827 and
there was a medieval chapel at Speckington
in 1314.

★★★★ *Fleet Air Arm Museum.*

Glossary

Advowson. The right to present a rector or vicar to the bishop for institution to a parish.

Assizes. Courts of justice held four times a year in Somerset by the king's judges on circuit, which tended to try more serious crimes than those heard before JPs at Quarter Sessions.

Barony or **honor**. A medieval grouping of a number of lordships or manors in one ownership.

Barrow or **tumulus**. A prehistoric burial mound.

Borough. A town or potential town which had been granted a royal charter freeing it from certain tolls and usually establishing markets and fairs. A market-place and new streets were often laid out by the lord of the manor in which the site of the borough lay, along which were marked out burgage tenements, to be occupied by burgesses. These burgesses were freed from performing labour services for the lord and paid a monetary rent in lieu. The lord would hope to recoup on his investment by means of the market and fair tolls as well as the rents. Some boroughs later obtained charters of incorporation, which established a mayor (or portreeve) and corporation, and thus achieved a greater degree of independence and self-government.

Burh. A Saxon settlement, usually fortified: sometimes the precursor of a medieval borough.

Chantry. A chapel, often within a parish church, endowed before the Reformation with lands. The income from these lands supported a chantry priest who, in return, regularly said masses for the repose of the soul of the founder and sometimes other specified members of his family. Most chantries were suppressed in 1548 and their endowments sold off.

Church house. A building in most Somerset parishes usually devoted from the 15th or early 16th century in which ale was produced and bread baked. These were consumed at a 'church ale', held once a year to raise funds for the repair and maintenance of the parish church. The practice was killed off in the early 17th century and most church houses became parish workhouses or schools, or were simply sold off. The best survives at Crowcombe.

Clerestory. An upper row of church windows above the walls of the nave.

Decorated. An ornate architectural style of c.1300-50.

Demesne. Land within a manor retained in the hands of the lord, often farmed directly from the manor-house and on which his tenants had to work for a certain number of days each year, depending on the customs of the individual manor. Estates retained by the Crown were known as the royal demesne.

Domesday Book. A detailed account of manors and estates compiled in 1086 by order of William the Conqueror. It recorded their ownership, value, population, mills and markets. The Exeter Domesday (held in Exeter Cathedral Library), the original draft for the western counties, added further details such as livestock on the demesne not included in the final (Exchequer) version. Domesday often contains the earliest surviving mention of many settlements.

Fulling mill. A watermill built or converted for fulling cloth. The mill wheel tripped mallets to beat the cloth in order to compact it and raise the nap.

Hundred. An administrative subdivision of the county with its own court, originally containing a hundred hides (a Saxon land measurement of about 120 acres) of reclaimed land.

Liberty. A manor or group of manors not subject to the jurisdiction of the sheriff or any hundred court.

Manor. An estate whose owner was known as the lord of the manor and whose tenants were governed by a manor court, presided over by the lord himself or his steward. Changes of tenancy were recorded at the Court Baron, while minor offences were punished by fines at the Court Leet.

Ordination (*of a vicarage*). When a church and its glebe lands (rectory estate) were granted to a monastery or other medieval institution, a document called an ordination was often drawn up to arrange for the future appointment of vicars and their conditions of service.

Peculiar. A parish not subject to the jurisdiction of the bishop or archdeacon, holding its own church court, in which the wills of its inhabitants were proved until 1858.

Perpendicular. An architectural style (emphasizing the vertical line) of c.1350-1550.

Prebend. The manor or rectory estate of a parish church assigned to support a prebendary or canon of a cathedral chapter.

Rector. A parish priest who occupied the glebe land and received all the tithes from a parish for his support. If the church, its lands and tithes were given (or 'appropriated') to a monastery or other medieval institution, a vicar or curate had to be appointed to serve the parish. Vicars commonly received the 'small' tithes (those other than on grain) while curates were usually paid a small salary. After the dissolution of the monasteries many rectory estates were sold to private individuals, who thus became 'lay rectors': receiving the great tithes but continuing to be responsible for repairing the chancels of their parish churches.

Rhine. A local term for a drainage ditch, usually on the Somerset Levels: pronounced 'reen'.

Skimmington ride. A custom to ridicule cuckolded or henpecked husbands in which the man (in person or in effigy) was carried on a pole or tied backwards on a donkey while a crowd banged pots and pans and jeered at him. The custom continued in Somerset into the beginning of this century.

Tithing. The subdivision of a manor, the inhabitants of which were represented at the manor and hundred courts by an annually-elected tithingman. The tithing originated as a group of ten men (or boys aged 12 and over) responsible to the manor court for each other's behaviour, the regulation of this system being by 'View of Frankpledge' held at the same court. *See also manor.*

Wassailing. An old custom, once widespread and still practised at Norton Fitzwarren and Carhampton, to ensure a good harvest of apples and thus a plentiful supply of cider. Toast soaked in cider is placed in the branches of apple trees to propitiate the robins (the good spirits), cider poured over the roots and shotguns fired through the branches to frighten off the evil spirits. Traditional wassailing songs are also sung.

Acknowledgements

This book has been a three-year labour of love on the heritage of my adopted county: a county that I found, of course, that I knew only superficially. I hope that it will be a work of interest and value not only to the tourist and resident but also to the local and family historian. To that end, I trust that references to such strange 'creatures' as prebends, ordinations of vicarages, Skimmington rides, hundreds and chantry chapels will be excused and a short glossary has been included to explain certain terms which may be unfamiliar to some.

The discipline of trying to visit every town and village within the county's boundaries (the only justification for the rash inclusion of 'complete' in the guide's title) has opened my eyes to Somerset's wonderful diversity. Some places were already favourites of mine but many were totally new to me and it was a delight to discover for myself the attractions of villages such as Compton Pauncefoot, Compton Bishop, Lullington, Stawley and North Cadbury. One great sadness was the increasing number of churches whose doors I found locked against me. I can understand the reluctance of parishes to leave their treasures at the mercy of the looter (Axbridge, for instance, has to date lost a 1729 chandelier, a 1621 chest and the parish bier), but I wish that those responsible for access to churches would give some indication as to where the key can be obtained. Far too many do not and in a few cases I have had to rely on descriptions of interiors by others.

This is an historian's guide to Somerset and some may feel that there are far too many dates. In mitigation I can only say that I have tried to provide as much accurate and precise information as was possible within the limited compass available to me, and to avoid slavishly repeating what previous county guide-books have included. I have endeavoured to lay to rest a number of hoary old stories which have no foundation in fact and to incorporate the findings of recent research and excavation, although I am bound to have overlooked some papers and articles. In a work on this scale it is not possible to contemplate extensive research into original sources except in a minority of cases and I am only too well aware that I have often been at the mercy of the accuracy of a host of church and local guide-books and of their proof-readers. All things must have an end but inevitably I wish that I had had another month, another year . . .

It is not practicable to supply a detailed bibliography of the hundreds, indeed thousands, of books and articles that have been consulted, but some works must be mentioned. I have made full use of the descriptions of towns and villages already covered by the four topographical volumes of the *Victoria History of Somerset* (iii-vi), written by Robert Dunning, Mary Siraut and myself, as also of the earlier general volumes (i-ii, 1906, 1911). *The Proceedings of the Somerset Archaeological and Natural History Society, Somerset & Dorset Notes & Queries* and the publications of the Somerset Record Society have been repeatedly consulted. For the origins of place-names I have generally (but not always) relied on Eilert Ekwall's *Oxford Dictionary of English Place-Names*, while architecturally Sir Nikolaus Pevsner's two Somerset volumes of his *Buildings of England* series, although compiled over 35 years ago, are still invaluable.

I am grateful to the following for help with illustrations: Mark Sorrell for the reconstruction of the Saxon palace at Cheddar by his father, Alan Sorrell; Cambridge Aerial Survey for the photograph of Ashen Hill Barrows, Priddy; Somerset Archaeological and Natural History Society for the engravings of Orchard Wyndham and Poundisford Park; Christopher Chaplin for drawing the maps.

I must also acknowledge work published in recent decades by the following writers, to whom the people of Somerset owe a great debt of gratitude: Noel Allen, Michael Aston, Robin Atthill, T.G. Barnes, J.H. Bettey, Hilary Binding, Leslie Brooke, Ian Burrow, J.P. Carley, Linzee Colchester, Nick Corcos, Michael Costen, Robert Dunning, Heather Edwards, Ann Ellison, H.P.R. Finberg, John H. Harvey, Hazel Hudson, Peter Leach, Roger Leech, Michael McGarvie, Tom Mayberry, Stephen Morland, Frances Neale, Paul Newman, Philip Rahtz, Warwick Rodwell, Anthony Scrase, Mary Siraut, Douglas Stevens, David Underdown, MacDonald Wigfield and Michael Williams.

My labours on this present guide have been largely solitary but I am happy to acknowledge the generous help of David Bromwich and Liz Clarke of Somerset's Local History Library; the staff at Somerset's Tourist Information Centres, particularly those at Taunton; Jenny Hoyle at Taunton Deane's Economic Development and Tourism Dept; Steve Minnitt; Tom Mayberry, and my former colleagues and friends at the Somerset Record Office.

This is the second book on which I have worked in harness with my friend and photographer, Julian Comrie, and I am sure that it will not be the last. I know of no other person who has so imaginatively and capably conjured up the visual beauty of our county. Finally, my thanks to my wife Hilary who has earned her dedication of this work the hard way. In 1791 John Collinson dedicated his account of Somerset to King George III. I can only hope that Hilary appreciates the compliment as much as His Majesty did!

ROBIN BUSH

The Lists

Contents

These are not lists of everything that you can see in Somerset but mainly lists of places which have opening times or events which occur at certain times of the year, although details of other attractions have been added. Further and fuller descriptions of many of them can be found under their entries in the Gazetteer where their map reference letter is also given. Landscapes, villages and towns are not included but will be found in the Gazetteer and, if especially good, in the introductory Land of Summer and in the various double-page spread sections on specific subjects. In all cases their map reference letters are given at the start of their entries in the Gazetteer.

Unless otherwise stated the months in the Lists are complete, e.g. Mar to Sept means March 1st to September 30th. All the information was correct when this edition of the Guide went to press, but telephone numbers are given wherever possible and winter opening times should be checked, especially if you are making a long journey. Although the Lists have been carefully compiled, we have had to rely on advance information, some of which may prove to be inaccurate. Tourist Information Offices are reliable and will be happy to help where they can. They are shown on the town maps and a list of them, with telephone numbers, is given below. We apologise for any mistakes or omissions.

Price Guide: A: 10p-£1, B: £1.10-£2, C: £2.10-£3, D: £3.10-£4, E: over £4. The key gives the price of a single adult ticket, but most places give reductions for children, Old Age Pensioners and parties, some offer family tickets and in certain places combined tickets are available for more than one attraction. Not all of the places charge for admission.

Abbeys

Cleeve Abbey, Old Cleeve (English Heritage). The most complete (except for church) monastic buildings in the county (Cistercian) in rural setting south of Washford. Good Fri or 1 Apr to Oct daily 10 am-6 pm, winter Wed to Sun 10 am-4 pm (closed 24-26 Dec, 1 Jan). Price: B. (01984) 40377.

Glastonbury Abbey, Glastonbury. Place of legend and history, substantial remains of monastic church (Benedictine) and Abbot's Kitchen, excellent Visitors Centre (museum). Daily (except 25 Dec) 9.30-6.00 (9.00 June to Aug). Price: B. (01458) 832267.

Muchelney Abbey, Muchelney (English Heritage). Well-preserved remains of Abbot's Lodgings, excavated footings of rest, including 8th century abbey church (Benedictine). Apr to Sept daily, 10am- 1pm, 2-6 pm. Price: B. (01458) 250664.

Angling

Details of fisheries and angling associations in the Somerset area are included in a leaflet published annually by the Wessex Region of the National Rivers Authority. Further information and copies of fishing byelaws can be obtained from the Somerset Area Fisheries and Recreation Officer, NRA Wessex Region, Rivers House, East Quay, Bridgwater, TA6 4YS, Tel. (01278) 457333. A similar angling leaflet is issued by Wessex Water for their five reservoirs. Contact their fisheries and recreation officer (01935) 873087. Principal reservoirs: Chard, Cheddar, Clatworthy, Durleigh, Hawkridge (Aisholt), Otterhead (Otterford), Sutton Bingham, Wimbleball.

Animals, Birds and Fishes

Ambleside Bird Gardens, Weare. Tropical birds, pets corner, lakeside gardens, restaurant. Mar to Oct daily, 10 am-5 pm. Price: B. (01934) 732362.

Animal Farm Country Park & the Land of Legend, Red Road, Berrow. Large and small animals, exhibition of figures and scenes of local legends and folklore. Easter to Oct daily, 10 am-5.30 pm. (01278) 751628.

Bee World and Animal Centre, Stogumber. Life story of bees, rare breed farm animals, birdwatching, aquarium, shop, restaurant. Easter to Oct daily, 10 am-6 pm. Price: C. (01984) 56545.

Brean Tropical Bird Garden, Brean. Tropical birds (large collection of parrots), shop, restaurant. Mar to Oct daily, 9 am-dusk. Price: B. (01278) 751209.

Chewton Cheese Dairy, Chewton Mendip - farm animals (see Cider and Cheese list).

Cricket St Thomas Wild-Life Park, Cricket St Thomas. Heartily recommended for family outing. Wide range of exotic animals and birds in valley and lakeside setting, National Heavy Horse Centre, Crinkley Bottom Village and Blobby Land, adventure playground, restaurants, pub, shops. Apr to Oct daily, 10 am-6 pm, Nov to Mar 10 am-5 pm or dusk. Price: E. (01460) 30755.

Ferne Animal Sanctuary, Wambrook. Sanctuary founded by Nina, Duchess of Hamilton, now funded by a Trust. Apr to Sept, Wed, Sat, Sun 2-5 pm. No charge, donations invited. (01460) 65214.

Goat House, Bristol Road, Brent Knoll. Herd of 200 goats, shop for goat produce, meat and fleeces, cafe. No charge. Daily. (01278) 760995.

Home Farm, Blue Anchor, Minehead. Farm animals, woodland walks, picnics. Apr to Sept, Sun to Fri, 11 am-5 pm. Price: B. (01984) 40817.

Mad Hatter's Animal & Bird Garden, 1 South Street, Montacute. Also TV and Radio collection and crafts. Easter to Oct, Wed to Mon (incl. Bank Holiday Mon), 10 am-5 pm, Sun 2-5.30 pm (and 11 am-12 noon in June and July). Price: B. (01935) 823124.

Norwood Farm Rare Breeds Centre, Norton St Philip. Contact with range of rare breeds of farm stock, cafe, shop. Apr to Sept daily, 11 am-5 pm. Shop open all year round. Price: C. (01373) 834356.

Rode Bird Gardens, Rode. 17 acre gardens, lake, aviaries (over 200 species), pets corner, miniature steam railway, cafeteria. Daily (except 25 Dec), summer 10 am-6.30 pm, winter 10 am-dusk. Price: D. (01373) 830326.

Secret World, New Road Farm, Huntspill. A mixed Levels farm, over 60 breeds of animals (including badgers and foxes), nocturnal house, visitors centre, nature trails, cafe, farm shop. Mar to Oct daily, 10 am-6 pm, Nov to Mar, Sat and Sun, 10 am-5 pm. Price: D. (01278) 783250.

Thorney Moor Farm Park, Muchelney. Farm animals, rare breeds, nature trails, picnic area, refreshments. Mar to Oct, Tues to Sun, 10 am-6 pm. Price: C. (01458) 252943.

Tropiquaria, Washford Cross, Old Cleeve. Animals, birds, reptiles, spiders, puppets (summer only), adventure playground, cafe. Mar to Oct daily, 10 am-6 pm, winter weekends, school holidays, 28 Dec-3 Jan 11 am-4 pm. Price: D. (01984) 40688.

Widcombe Wildlife and Country Park (formerly Widcombe Tropical Bird Garden), Widcombe House, Culmhead, Churchstanton. 20-acre park, birds, small animals, shop, cafe. Apr to Oct daily, 10.30 am-5.30 pm. Price: C. (01823) 421268.

Annual Events

January: Wassailing at Butcher's Arms, Carhampton, and Taunton Cider, Norton Fitzwarren.

Shrove Tuesday: Egg-Shackling at Stoke St Gregory and Shepton Beauchamp.

April: Taunton Marathon, Mells Daffodil Festival.

May: Hobby Horse at Minehead and Dunster, Heavy Horse Show and Steam Rally at Cricket St Thomas, Highbridge Festival of the Arts, Westbury-sub-Mendip Friendly Society Club Day.

May/June: Royal Bath and West Show, Dunster Festival.

June: Stogumber Music Festival, Taunton Trade Fair, South Petherton Festival, Tintinhull Carnival, Glastonbury Church of England and Roman Catholic Pilgrimages, Glastonbury Festival (Pilton).

June/July: Great Elm Music Festival, Parrett Music Festival.

July: Moat Boat Race at Bishops Palace (Wells), Watchet Carnival, Minehead and Exmoor Festival, Somerton Summer Arts Festival.

July/August: Minehead Carnival.

August: Dulverton Festival, Dunster Show, Taunton Flower Show, Taunton Agricultural Show, Mid Somerset Agricultural Show (Shepton Mallet), Priddy Sheep Fair, St Catherine's Medieval Fair (Frome).

Aug/September: Porlock Carnival, Watchet Summer Fayre, Harvest Homes at Mark, Wedmore, East Brent, East Huntspill and Allerton.

September: Bridgwater Fair, Wellington Carnival, Frome Cheese Show, Frome Carnival, Axbridge Blackberry Fair.

October: Ilminster Carnival, Dulverton Carnival, Chard Carnival, Southwest Dairy Show (Shepton Mallet), Taunton Carnival and Cider Barrel Race, Castle Cary Carnival, Wincanton Carnival, Punky Night at Hinton St George Village Festival, Yeovil Carnival.

November: Bridgwater, North Petherton, Burnham and Highbridge, Shepton Mallet, Wells and Glastonbury Carnivals.

Castles

Dunster Castle, Dunster (see Houses list).

Farleigh Castle, Farleigh Hungerford (English Heritage). Impressive ruined castle of Hungerford family with chapel and tombs, small museum. Good Fri or 1 Apr to Oct daily, 10 am-6 pm, winter Wed to Sun 10 am-4 pm (closed 24-26 Dec, 1 Jan). Price: B. (01225) 754126.

Nunney Castle, Nunney. Ruined moated castle of c.1373 with four drum towers in village. Open freely without charge.

Stogursey Castle, Stogursey. 12th century ruined castle with 19th century gatehouse converted to holiday apartments. Free access to east and south sides of moat by public footpath.

Taunton Castle, Taunton (see Museums list).

Caves

Adventure Caving Centre, Cheddar. (minimum age 12 yrs). One-and-a-half-hours guided expeditions (special clothing and helmet lamp provided) into Gough's Cave beyond the public area. Daily 9.30, 11.30 am, 2 pm, 4 pm (advance booking advised). Price: E. (01934) 742343.

Cox's and Gough's Caves, Cheddar. Lofty chambers and delicate stalagmites and stalactites, museum, 'Crystal Quest' fantasy adventure. Easter to Sept daily, 10 am-5.30 pm, rest of year 10.30 am-4.30 pm (closed 24-25 Dec). Price (combined ticket): E. (01934) 742343.

Wookey Hole Cave, Wookey Hole. Spectacular limestone caves, papermill, fairground exhibition, museum, shops, restaurant. Excellent family outing. Daily (except 17-15 Dec), summer 9.30 am-5.30 pm, winter 10.30 am-4.30 pm. Price: E. (01749) 672243.

Cider and Cheese

Cheddar Rural Village, Cheddar Gorge, Cheddar. Country crafts, pottery, cheese factory, sweet-making, restaurant. May to Sept daily, 10 am-6 pm, mid Mar to Apr and Oct, 10 am-4 pm. Price: C. (01934) 742810.

Chewton Cheese Dairy, Chewton Mendip. Cheddar cheese making, farm animals (including longhorns), video, farm shop, restaurant. Daily (no cheese making Thur and Sun) 9 am-4.30 pm. Price: B. (01761) 241666.

Coombes Cider Farm and Museum, Japonica Farm, Mark. Cider museum, tasting, shop. Shop, Mon to Sat 8.30 am-6 pm, Sun 12 noon-2 pm. Museum Easter to Oct, same times. No charge. (01278) 641265.

Henry's Farmhouse Scrumpy, Tanpits Cider Farm, Bathpool, Taunton. Small cider exhibition. Mon to Sat 8.30 am-8 pm. No charge. (01823) 270663.

Perry's Cider Mill, Dowlish Wake. Shop, small rural life museum, tasting. Mon to Fri. 9 am-1 pm, 1.30-5.30 pm, Sat 9.30 am-1 pm, 1.30-4.30 pm, Sun 10 am-1 pm, Spring and Summer Bank Hols 9.30 am-1 pm, 1.30-4.30 pm. Closed winter Bank Hols. No charge. (01460) 52681.

Rosie's Cider, Rose Farm, Lattiford, Wincanton. Traditional cider, mug display, souvenirs. Mon to Fri 8.30 am-6.30 pm, Sun 12 noon-3 pm. No charge. (01963) 33680.

Sheppy's Farmhouse Cider, Three Bridges, Bradford-on-Tone. Draught and bottled cider, rural life museum, farm trails and tours, shop, refreshments. Easter to Christmas, Mon to Sat 8.30 am-6 pm (7 pm in summer), Sun 12

noon-2 pm. Winter - farm shop only. Price: B. (01823) 461233.

Somerset Cider Brandy Co & Burrow Hill Cider, Burrow Hill, Kingsbury Episcopi. Cider distillery, orchards, copper stills. Mon to Sat 9 am-5 pm. (01460) 40782.

Country Parks

Clatworthy Reservoir, Clatworthy. Walking, sailing, angling. Ranger (01984) 623549.

Combe Sydenham, Stogumber (see Houses list).

Cricket St Thomas Wild-Life Park (see Animals, Birds and Fishes list).

Fyne Court, Broomfield. Former home of Andrew Crosse, experimental electrician, headquarters of Somerset Wildlife Trust, woodland and nature trails, interpretation centre, shop. Special events and exhibitions. Daily 9 am-6 pm. No charge (car park, price: A). Shop Easter to Christmas daily 2-5 pm. Office Mon to Fri 9 am-5 pm. (01823) 451587.

Ham Hill Country Park. Iron Age hillfort and former quarry site. Excellent walking and views. Free car parking. Ranger (01935) 823617 or (01860) 876179 (mobile).

Town Tree Nature Gardens and Reserve, Stapleton, Martock. Nature trail, marshland, farm gardens. Daily 10 am to 90 mins before sunset. Price: A. (01935) 823203.

Widcombe Wildlife and Country Park (see Animals, Birds and Fishes list).

Wimbleball Lake Water Park (South West Water), Brompton Regis. Walking, sailing, rowing, angling, cafe, shop. (013987) 372.

Crafts

Burcott Mill, Burcott, Wells. Craft workshops (see Mills list).

East Lydeard Country Farm, Bishops Lydeard. Handcrafted cricket bats (Millichamp & Hall), farm trails, cafe. Workshop, Feb to Aug, Mon to Fri, 11 am-5 pm, weekends by appointment. No charge. (01823) 433881. Country Farm June to Aug daily. Farm walks (from 1.30 pm) and teas (2.30-5.30 pm). (01823) 433556/432668.

English Basket and Hurdle Centre (Nigel Hector), Curload, Stoke St Gregory. Baskets and hurdles, tour works, walk through willow beds, large showroom. Mon to Fri 9 am-5 pm, Sat and Sun 10 am-4 pm. No charge. (01823) 698418.

John Wood's Sheepskin Tannery, Old Cleeve. Tours of workshops, factory shop, cafe. Mon to Fri 9 am-5 pm, Sats and Bank Holidays 10 am-4 pm. Factory tours Easter to Oct, Mon to Fri, 10.45 am, 11.30 am, 2.15 pm, 3 pm or by arrangement. Tours, price: A. (01984) 40291.

Muchelney Pottery (John Leach), Muchelney. Woodfired stoneware, mainly kitchen pots, workshop viewing. Mon to Fri 9 am-1 pm, 2-5 pm, Sat 9 am-1 pm. (01458) 250324.

Quantock Pottery, Chapel Cottages, West Bagborough. Stoneware pottery, restaurant. Mon to Fri 9 am-5 pm, Sat and Sun 11 am-5 pm. (01823) 433057.

Somerset Levels Basket and Craft Centre Ltd, Lyng Road, Burrowbridge. Willow basketware and wicker furniture. Mon to Sat 9 am-5.30 pm and Bank Hols (not Christmas). (01823) 698688.

Willows and Wetlands Visitors Centre (P.H. Coate & Son), Stoke St Gregory. Basket-making, guided tours, basket museum, excellent wetlands exhibition. Mon to Sat 9 am-5 pm, showroom and shop only on Sat, tours only Mon to Fri 10 am-12 noon, 1-4 pm. Price: B. (01823) 490249.

There are many small craft shops and workshops, particularly potteries, throughout the county but they are too numerous to list in detail.

Gardens

Barrington Court, Barrington (National Trust). Walled gardens influenced by Gertrude Jekyll. Mar to Sept daily (except Fri) 11 am-5.30 pm. Price: D. (Court House Wed 11 am-5.30 pm. Price: E - including gardens). (01460) 241938.

Cannington Heritage Gardens and Specialist Plant Centre, Cannington Agricultural College, Cannington. Extensive walled gardens and tropical glass houses. Easter to Oct daily 2-5 pm. Price: B. (01278) 652226.

Clapton Court, Crewkerne. 10 acre formal and woodland gardens, plant centre. Mar to Oct Mon to Fri 10.30 am-5 pm, Sun (not Nov and Feb) and Easter Sat 2-5 pm. Price: C. (01460) 73220/72200.

East Lambrook Manor, East Lambrook. Restored cottage-style garden of Margery Fish, cafe, plant shop. Mar to Oct, Mon to Sat and Bank Hol weekends, 10 am-5 pm. Price: B. (01460) 240328.

Hadspen House, Pitcombe. Restored 8-acre Edwardian garden. Mar to Sept, Thur to Sun and Bank Hols 9 am-6 pm. Price: B. (01963) 50939.

Hestercombe House, nr Taunton. Immaculate Edwardian gardens, orangery, etc., designed by Sir Edwin Lutyens and Gertrude Jekyll. Wonderful setting above Vale of Taunton. Daily Mon to Fri 9 am-5 pm, Sat and Sun 2-5 pm. Price: B. (01823) 337222, ext 316.

Milton Lodge, Wells. Idyllic mature hillside terraced gardens overlooking Wells, separate 7-acre arboretum. Easter to Oct, Sun to Fri, 2-6 pm. Teas on Suns and Bank Hols. Price: B. (01749) 672168.

Tintinhull House, Tintinhull (National Trust). Formal gardens surrounding 17th century house (not open). Mar to Sept, Tues to Sun, Bank Hol Mons 2-6 pm. Price: C. (01985) 847777.

Whatley Vineyard and Herb Garden, Whatley (see Vineyards list).

(And see Houses list)

Golf Courses

Brean Golf Club, Coast Road, Brean. (0127875) 15970.

Burnham and Berrow Golf Club, St Christopher's Way, Burnham-on-Sea. (01278) 783137.

Cannington Golf Course, Cannington (9 holes). (01278) 652226.

Enmore Park Golf Club, Enmore. (0127867) 244.

Fosseway Country Club, Charlton Lane, Midsomer Norton (9 holes). (01761) 412214.

Mendip Golf Club, Gurney Slade. (01749) 840570.

Minehead and West Somerset Golf Club, The Warren, Minehead. (01643) 702057.

Oake Manor Golf Club, Oake. (01823) 461993.

Taunton and Pickeridge Golf Club, Corfe, Taunton. (0182342) 537.

Taunton Vale Golf Club, Creech Heathfield, Taunton. (01823) 412220/412880.

Vivary Park Golf Course, Vivary Park, Taunton. (01823) 333875.

Wells Golf Club, East Horrington Road, Wells. (01749) 75005.

Windwhistle Golf, Squash and Country Club, Cricket St Thomas, Chard. (01460) 30231.

(All courses have 18 holes unless otherwise stated)

Houses

Abbot's Fish House, Meare. A unique 14th century survival, built for the abbot of Glastonbury. Open at 'any reasonable time'. When locked, key available from Manor House Farm, near Meare church. No charge.

Barford Park, Enmore. Delightfully furnished 18th century house and wooded, walled and water gardens. May to Sept, Wed, Thur, and Bank Hol weekends, 2-5 pm, or by appointment. Price: C. (01278) 671269.

Barrington Court, Barrington. 16th century mansion: interior restored and re-panelled by Lyle family. Open only to those patronising Stuart Interiors, except Wed 11 am-5.30 pm, Price: E - including gardens (see also Gardens).

Bishop's Palace, Wells. Finest bishop's palace in England. Moated and dating from 13th century with portraits of bishops, gardens, wells, chapel, restaurant. Apr to Oct, Tues, Thur, Bank Hol Mons (daily in Aug) 11 am-6 pm, Sun 2-6 pm. Price: B. (01749) 678691.

Church House, Crowcombe. The finest surviving church house in the county, built c.1515. June to Sept, Mon to Fri, 2.30-4.30 pm, and at other times when art exhibitions staged there. No charge.

Coleridge Cottage, Nether Stowey (National Trust). Two rooms in home of poet S.T. Coleridge 1797-1800, small collection of memorabilia. Mar to Sept, Tues to Thur, Sun 2-5 pm and by appointment. Price: B. (01278) 732662.

Combe Sydenham Hall, Stogumber. Mansion of 1580, home of Elizabeth Sydenham, 2nd wife of Sir Francis Drake, restored cornmill, park and woodland walks, fish farm, farm shop, cafe. Mar to Oct, Sun to Fri, 10 am-5 pm. Price: D. (01984) 56284.

Dodington Hall, Dodington. Small Tudor manor-house, semi-formal garden. Certain days in June and July. Phone call advised. Donations invited. (01278) 741400.

Dunster Castle, Dunster (National Trust). Romantic castle on hilltop site, former home of Luttrell family, remodelled in 19th century, fine furnishings and portraits (steep climb on foot from village), shop. Mar to Oct, Sat to Wed, 11 am-5 pm (4 pm in Oct). Garden and park Feb to Dec daily 11 am-4 pm (5 pm Apr to Sept). Price: E. (01643) 821314.

Gaulden Manor, Tolland. 17th century manor-house, plasterwork, gardens, shop, teas. Easter Sunday and Monday, summer Bank Hols, 1st Sun in May until 1st Sun in September on Suns and Thurs, 2-5.30 pm. Price: C. (019847) 213.

Hatch Court, Hatch Beauchamp. Elegant Palladian mansion of 1755, small Canadian military museum, china room, deer park, walled kitchen garden. June to Sept, Thur and Aug Bank Hol Mon 2.30-5.30 pm. Price: C. (Separate admission to garden only, price: B) (01823) 480058.

Kentsford House, Watchet. Medieval manor-house largely rebuilt c.1600 and remodelled in late 17th century. By written appointment with occupier, Mr H. Dibble. Donations to renovation of fabric.

King John's Hunting Lodge, Axbridge (see Museums list).

Lytes Cary, Charlton Mackrell (National Trust). Delightful small medieval manor-house, chapel, formal Elizabethan garden. Mar to Oct, Mon, Wed, Sat 2-6 pm. Price: D. (01985) 847777.

Maunsel House, St Michaelchurch, North Newton. Impressive pile dating from c.1500, former home of Slade baronets, but unpredictable access. Tel (01895) 272929 during office hours for details of admission, times, charges, etc. Local no. (01278) 663413.

Midelney Manor, Drayton. 16th century manor-house built and still occupied by the Trevilian family. Booked parties and functions only. (01458) 251229.

Montacute House, Montacute (National Trust). Superb late Elizabethan mansion, National Portrait Gallery exhibition of Tudor and Stuart portraits, fine furnishings, formal gardens and park, shop, cafe. March to Oct, Wed to Mon, 12 noon-5 pm, closed Good Fri. Price: E. Garden and park, daily except Tues, 11 am-5.30 pm or dusk, price C. (01935) 823289.

Orchard Wyndham, Williton. Medieval hall-house extended in 15th century, home of Wyndham family. Tues and Wed in Aug, 2-5 pm. Guided tours only, 15 people maximum (last tour begins 4 pm). Phone call advised. Price: C. (01984) 632309.

Poundisford Park, Pitminster (now closed).

Priest's House, Muchelney (National Trust). Thatched house of c.1308, with later alterations. Easter to Sept, Sun and Mon, 2-5 pm. Price: B. (01458) 252621.

The Priory, Stoke-sub-Hamdon (National Trust). Complex of buildings to house chantry priests, dating from 14th century, admission to great hall only. Daily 10 am-6 pm or sunset. No charge. (01985) 847777.

Treasurer's House, Martock (National Trust). Oldest inhabited house in Somerset, dating from 13th century. Open (great hall and kitchen) by appointment only. Price: B. (01935) 823288.

Mills

Ashton Windmill, Chapel Allerton. 18th century windmill restored to working condition. Easter to Sept, Suns and Bank Hols 2.30-4.30 pm. No charge, donations invited. (01934) 712823/712260.

Burcott Mill, Burcott, Wells. Restored working watermill and craft workshops, shop. July to Sept, Wed to Fri, 2-5.30 pm, Sat and Sun 11 am-5.30 pm, winter Sat and Sun 2-4 pm. Price: B. (01749) 73118.

Dunster Mill, Dunster. Working mill, rural life exhibits, shop, restaurant. Apr to June, Sept to Oct Mon to Sat 11 am-5 pm, July to Aug 11 am-5 pm daily. Closed Nov to Mar. Price: B. (01643) 821759.

Hornsbury Mill, Chard. Restored 19th century mill and rural life museum, picnic area, shop, restaurant and hotel. Daily 10 am-6 pm. Price: B. (01460) 63317.

Orchard Mill, Williton. Restored 19th century watermill, farming museum, craft shop, restaurant. Mar to Oct, Dec, Wed to Sun, 10 am-5 pm, Jan, Feb, Nov, Fri to Sun, 10 am-5 pm, Bank Hols except Boxing Day 10 am-5 pm. Price: B. (01984) 32133.

Stembridge Windmill, High Ham (National Trust). Restored windmill of c.1820. Easter to Sept, Sun, Mon, Wed, 2-5 pm. Price: B. (01458) 250818.

Other Industrial Archaeology

Allermoor Pumping Station, Burrowbridge. Restored steam-powered drainage engine. For access and charges phone (01823) 412713.

Bridgwater and Taunton Canal. Contact Bridgwater and Taunton Canal Boat Co.

(01884) 253345. Cycling and fishing permits: (01873) 830328. Canoeing permits, Bridgwater YMCA, Friarn Ave, Bridgwater (01278) 422511. Boat trips during summer months from Tone Bridge, Taunton; Creech St Michael; Bridgwater YMCA. Check with Tourist Information Centres at Bridgwater or Taunton (see below) for current boat trip information.

East Somerset Railway, West Cranmore. Steam trains, museum, wildlife information centre, restaurant, play area. May to Sept, Wed to Sun, 10 am-5.30 pm, Mar to Apr, Oct to Dec, Sat and Sun, 10 am-4 pm. Also 1 Jan and Bank Hols. Price: D. (01749) 880417.

Westonzoyland Pumping Station, Westonzoyland. 19th century steam-powered engine, exhibition on history of Levels drainage. Apr to Oct, 1st Sun in month, Easter, May Day, Spring and Aug Bank Hols, Sun and Mon, 1 Jan 2-5 pm. Price: B. (01823) 412713.

West Somerset Railway, Bishops Lydeard to Minehead. At 20 miles, the longest privately owned railway in Britain. For details of timetable and steam trains contact Minehead Station, (01643) 704996.

Wookey Hole Paper Mill, Wookey Hole (see Caves list).

Museums

Admiral Blake Museum, Blake Street, Bridgwater. Local and maritime history, Robert Blake, Battle of Sedgemoor and Monmouth Rebellion, ship models. Daily, Mon to Sat 11 am-5 pm, Sun and Bank Holidays 2-5 pm (closed 25-26 Dec). No charge. (01278) 456127.

Allerford Museum, Allerford, Selworthy. Rural life, Victorian kitchen and schoolroom. April to Oct, 10.30 am-12.30 pm, 2-4.30 pm. Price: A. (01643) 862529.

Castle Cary Museum, Castle Cary. Local history collections, agricultural bygones. Apr to Oct, Mon to Sat, 10 am-12 noon, 2.30-4.30 pm. No charge. (01963) 50277.

Chard Museum, Chard. Local history and rural and urban life collections, John Stringfellow (inventor of powered flight), James Gillingham (pioneer artificial limb-maker). May to early Oct, Mon to Sat

(Suns in July and Aug) 10.30 am-4.30 pm. Price: B. (01460) 20250.

Cheddar Cave Museum, Cheddar (see Caves list).

Crewkerne Museum, Crewkerne. (temporarily closed).

Doll Museum, Dunster. Based on Mrs Hardwick's doll collection. Apr to Oct, Sun to Fri, 10.30 am-5 pm. Price: A. (01643) 821029.

Fleet Air Arm Museum, Yeovilton. Excellent family outing. Over 40 naval aircraft, Concorde 002, WWI, WWII, Korea, Falklands, audio-visual displays, adventure playground, restaurant. Daily (except 24-26 Dec) 10 am-5.30 pm (4.30 pm in winter). Price: E. (01935) 840565.

Frome and East Mendip Museum, North Parade, Frome. Local history collections, reconstructed chemist's shop. Daily Wed to Sat 10 am-4 pm. Price: A.

Glastonbury Abbey Museum, Glastonbury (see Abbeys list).

Haynes Motor Museum, Sparkford. Over 200 vintage, veteran and classic cars, motorcycles, video cinema, cafe. Daily (closed 25-26 Dec, 1 Jan) 9.30 am-5.30 pm. Price: D. (01963) 40804.

Hornsbury Mill, Chard (see Mills list).

Ilchester Museum, Ilchester. Local history collection, particularly re Roman Ilchester. Easter to Sept, Thurs and Sat, 10 am-4 pm. No charge. (01935) 841247.

King John's Hunting Lodge, The Square, Axbridge. Jettied timber-framed house of c.1500 housing local history and archaeology displays, pictures and photographs. Easter to Sept daily 2-5 pm. Price: B. (01934) 732012.

Montacute TV and Radio Museum (see Mad Hatter's Animal and Bird Garden under Animals, Birds and Fishes list).

Peat Moors Visitors' Centre, Shapwick Road, Westhay, Meare. Displays of natural history, archaeology and peat cutting, two reconstructed Iron Age round houses and prehistoric trackways, craft demonstrations, tea rooms. Daily, 12 July to 25 Oct, Sat and Sun for rest of year, 10 am-4.30 pm. Price: B. (014586) 257/389.

Porlock Museum, Doverhay, Porlock. Delightful old-style museum, local history collections. Mon to Fri 10 am-1 pm, 2-5 pm, Sat 10 am-1 pm, 2.30-4.30 pm. No charge.

Shepton Mallet Local History Museum, Shepton Mallet. Local history collections. Easter to Sept, Mon to Sat, 2-5 pm. No charge. (01749) 345258.

Shoe Museum, C. & J. Clark Ltd, Street. Shoes from Roman times to present, history of C. & J. Clark, housed in old factory, shop. Daily, Mon to Fri, 10 am-4.45 pm, Sat 10 am-6 pm, Sun 12 noon-6 pm. No charge. (01458) 43131.

Somerset and Dorset Railway Museum, Washford Station, Old Cleeve. Railway memorabilia, rolling stock, etc. Mar to Oct 10 am-5 pm (when trains are running on West Somerset Railway). Price: A. (01984) 40869/ (01308) 424630.

Somerset County Museum, Taunton Castle, Taunton, and Military Museum (Somerset Light Infantry). Extensive local history, archaeology, natural history collections housed in castle dating from 13th century. Mon to Sat 10 am-5 pm (closed Good Fri, 25-26 Dec, 1 Jan). Price: B. (01823) 255504.

Somerset Cricket Museum, Priory Barn, Priory Avenue, Taunton. Displays of cricketing memorabilia of SCCC from its foundation in 1875 in converted 'barn' (former gatehouse) of Taunton Priory, c.1500. Daily, Mon to Sat, 10 am-4 pm. Phone call to confirm Oct to Mar (open only to cricket spectators during 1st class matches). Price: A. (01823) 275893.

Somerset Rural Life Museum, Glastonbury. Excellent and extensive agricultural and rural life collections mainly of 19th and 20th centuries, 14th century abbey barn, many special events and demonstrations. Daily, Mon to Fri, 10 am-5 pm, also Sat and Sun, Easter to Oct, 2-6 pm, Nov to Easter, Sat 11 am-4 pm. Price: B. (01458) 31197.

South Somerset, Museum of, Wyndham House, Hendford, Yeovil. Archaeology, local history, industrial archaeology, shop. Tues to Sat 10 am-4 pm. No charge, donations invited. (01935) 24774.

The Tribunal, Glastonbury. Archaeological collections re Glastonbury and Meare Lake Villages. Mid Mar to mid Oct daily 10 am-1 pm, 2-6 pm. Price: B. (01458) 832949.

Watchet Market House Museum, Watchet. Local history and archaeological collections, audio-visual show. Easter, and mid May to Sept, daily 10.30 am-12.30 pm, 2.30-4.30 pm (also 7-9 pm July and Aug). Price: A. (01643) 707132.

Wellington Museum, Mantle Street, Wellington. Local history and rural life collections in former Squirrel Inn. Easter to Oct, Mon to Sat, 10 am-4 pm. No charge. (01823) 664747.

Wells Museum, Cathedral Green, Wells. Local history collection, Wookey Hole archaeology, Mendip mines. Easter to Sept, Mon to Sat, 10 am-5.30 pm, Sun 11 am-5.30 pm, Oct to Easter, Wed to Sun, 11 am-4 pm. Price: B. (01749) 673477.

Wheelwrights Working Museum & Gypsy Folklore Collection, Webbington, Loxton, Axbridge. Working wheelwright, Romany museum, gypsy caravans, old-tyme fairground, restaurant, shop. Mar to Dec, Wed to Sun. Price: C. (01934) 750841.

Willows and Wetlands Visitor Centre, Stoke St Gregory (see Crafts list).

Wincanton Museum, Wincanton. Local history collection. May to Sept, Sat 10 am-4 pm. No charge, donations invited.

Radio and TV, Local

BBC Somerset Sound (MW 1323), 14/15 Paul Street, Taunton. (01823) 252437; 1 North Lane, Yeovil (01935) 32071.

BBC Radio Bristol (FM 94.9, 95.5, 104.6; MW 1548), 3 Tyndalls Park Road, Bristol. (01272) 741111.

Orchard FM (FM 97.1 [Yeovil], 102.6 [Taunton]), Haygrove House, Shoreditch, Taunton. (01823) 338448 (commercial radio).

All three of the above carry regular 'What's On' features, local news, weather and travel information.

BBC West (Television), Whiteladies Road, Bristol. (01272) 732211.

HTV West, 43/44 High Street, Taunton. (01823) 270293 (ITV based in Bristol).

Westcountry TV, Foundry Cottage, St James Street, Taunton. (01823) 322335 (ITV based in Plymouth).

The two commercial TV stations compete for coverage of the west of the county and both include Somerset in their local news, weather, 'What's On' and documentary features.

Swimming Pools

Bridgwater, Sedgemoor Splash Leisure Pool, Mount Street. (01278) 425636.

Burnham-on-Sea, Burnham Pool, Berrow Road. (01278) 785909.

Chard, Cresta Kingfisher Pool, Holyrood Community School, Zembard Lane. (01460) 64084.

Cheddar, Cheddar Pool, Redcliffe Street. (01934) 742073.

Frome, Frome Sports Centre, Princess Anne Road. (01373) 465446.

Minehead, Somerwest World. (01643) 703331.

Minehead, Aquasplash Leisure Pool, Seaward Way. (01643) 708000.

Shepton Mallet, Outdoor (May to Aug), Shaftgate Street. (01749) 342126.

Street, Strode Swimming Pool, Strode Road. (01458) 43918.

Street, Greenbank Swimming Pool (outdoor, summer only), Wilfred Road. (01458) 42468.

Taunton, Taunton Pool, Station Road. (01823) 284108. (Also St James Street pools for private hire, clubs, etc.).

Wells, Wells Leisure Centre, Charterway, off Portway. (01749) 670055.

Yeovil, Golden Stones Pools & Leisure Centre, Brunswick Street. (01935) 74166.

Theatres

Amulet Community and Arts Centre, 7 Market Place, Shepton Mallet. Box Office (01749) 344688.

Brewhouse Theatre and Arts Centre, Coal Orchard, Taunton. Also stages regular exhibitions of contemporary art. Box Office (01823) 283244.

Bridgwater Arts Centre, 11 Castle Street, Bridgwater. Features periodic art exhibitions. (01278) 422700.

Ilminster Warehouse Theatre, Brewery Lane, Ilminster. Box Office (01460) 57086.

Merlin Theatre, Bath Road, Frome. Box Office (01373) 465949.

Octagon Theatre, Yeovil. Box Office (01935) 22884.

Strode Theatre, Church Road, Street. Box Office (01458) 42846.

Swan Theatre, Park Street, Yeovil. Run by Yeovil Dramatic Society, mainly for amateur productions. (01935) 28646.

Wells Little Theatre, Chamberlain Street, Wells. Box Office (01749) 672280.

Take Art!, an arts organization funded by SouthWest Arts and local councils, annually promotes a wide range of professional performances in villages throughout the county. See local press for advertisements. (01458) 840992.

Vineyards

Avalon Vineyard, The Drove, East Pennard. 3¼ acre organic vineyard, shop. (01749) 860393.

Bagborough Vineyard, Bagborough Lane, Pylle. 3 acre vineyard, shop. (01749) 831146.

Castle Cary Vineyard, Honeywick House, Hadspen, Castle Cary. 5 acre vineyard, shop. (01963) 50323.

Cheddar Valley Vineyards, Hillside, Axbridge. Wine tasting, shop, restaurant. Mar to Oct, Wed to Sun. (01934) 732280.

Moorlynch Vineyard, Moorlinch. 16 acre vineyard and winery, winebar, restaurant, visitor centre, farm trails, guided tours and tasting. Daily from 10 am (Sun wine sales only from 12 noon). Enquire re evening openings. Price: C. (01458) 210393.

Oatley Vineyard, Cannington. 5 acre vineyard. (01278) 671340.

Pilton Manor Vineyard, Pilton. 16 acre vineyard, winebar, shop. (01749) 890325.

Staplecombe Vineyards, Burlands Farm, Staplegrove. 4 acre vineyard, shop. April to Oct, Mon to Sat, 2-5 pm. Phone call advised at other times. (01823) 451217.

Whatley Vineyard and Herb Garden, Whatley. 4 acre vineyard and cruciform herb garden. Tours and tasting by arrangement. Apr to Sept Wed to Sat and Bank Holidays 10 am-1.00 pm, 2-6 pm, Sun 12 noon-5 pm. (01373) 836467.

Wootton Vineyard, North Wootton. 6 acre vineyard, dry white wine, cider wine and cider, inspection of winery. Mon to Sat 10 am-1 pm, 2-5 pm. No charge. (0174989) 359.

Wraxall Vineyard, Ditcheat. 6 acre vineyard, shop. (01749) 344462/860331.

Walking

With its many wide open spaces, Somerset is a perfect county for walkers. Many individual books of walks are available, particularly for Exmoor, the Quantocks and the Mendips. Most of the District Councils have published further guides, particularly South Somerset and Taunton Deane. The former has also laid out the Leland Trail, retracing the route taken by the 16th century antiquarian, John Leland, through the south-east of the county, and the Liberty Trail: the notional route south to Lyme Regis (Dorset) taken by those walking to join the Duke of Monmouth's rebellion in 1685. The West Mendip Way, laid out by local Rotary Clubs, runs some 30 miles from Wells, climbing the hills above Cheddar and continuing via Crook Peak to Uphill, near Weston-super-Mare. The Parrett Trail, following that river from its source to the sea, is being laid out by an arts organization, Take Art! A range of walking guides can generally be obtained from the Tourist Information Centres in the relevant areas.

Miscellaneous

Alfred's Tower, South Brewham. Monument of 1772 to Alfred's victory over the Danes in 878, wonderful views over Somerset and Wiltshire. End of Mar to Oct daily (not Mon or Fri) 2-5.30 pm. Price: B. (01985) 844785.

Brean Leisure Park, Brean Sands, Brean. Funfair, golf, swimming, night club, restaurant, pub, special events. Easter to Sept, Sat and Sun, May to early Sept, daily, 11 am-dusk. No admission charge. (01278) 751595.

Chalice Well, Chilkwell Street, Glastonbury. Mineral spring where some legends claim St Joseph of Arimathea hid the Holy Grail, gardens. Mar to Oct daily 10 am-6 pm, Nov to Feb daily 1-4 pm. Price: A. (01458) 831154.

Cranmore Tower, Cranmore. Folly tower, garden. Apr to Sept, Sat and Sun, 10 am-5 pm. Price: A.

Exmoor Natural History Society Field Centre. Malmsmead, Oare. NBatural History displays, games, slide show. Wed and Thur (mid May to Sept), Tues (late July to early Sept), 1.30-5pm. (01643) 703760

Hinkley Point Nuclear Power Station, Stogursey. Visitor Centre and tours. Also one-mile nature trail. No charge. (01278) 652461.

Mill on the Brue Activity Centre, Trendle Farm, Tower Hill, Bruton. Outdoor pursuits centre, day/residential, instruction and equipment provided. Feb to Dec daily. (01749) 812706.

Model Village, Dunster (now closed).

Monkeys, Tweentown, Cheddar. Children's indoor adventure play centre (up to 12 yrs), cafe. Somerset School hols and Bank Hols, daily 10.30 am-5.30 pm, Somerset Term time, Mon to Fri, 3.30-5.30, Sat and Sun 10.30 am-5.30 pm. Adults no charge. (01934) 742270/712304.

Somerset Local History Library, Taunton Castle, Castle Green, Taunton. (To move to new Central Library, Paul Street, Taunton, 1994/5.) Printed sources on Somerset history. Tues to Fri 9.30 am-1 pm, 2.-5.30 pm, Sat 9.30 am-1 pm, 2-4 pm. (01823) 288871.

Somerset Record Office, Obridge Road Taunton. Historic archives on Somerset history from 705 AD. Mon 10.30 am-4.45 pm, Tues to Thur 9 am-4.45 pm, Fri 9 am-4.15 pm, 1st and 3rd Sats each month 9.15 am-12.15 pm. Appointments advised (and required for Sats). Searchroom appointments (01823) 337600, other enquiries (01823) 278805.

Somerwest World (Butlin's), Minehead. Major holiday camp with full range of attractions, day visitors welcome. Apr to Oct daily 10 am-12 midnight. Daily price: E. (01643) 703331.

Stansell Gallery, Viney Court (off East Reach), Taunton. A recently-opened gallery featuring regular exhibitions, mainly by contemporary artists (see local press for details). Generally no charge. (01823) 325493.

Taunton Racecourse, Orchard Portman, Taunton. (01823) 337172.

Wells Cathedral Library, Wells. Exhibition of bibliographical treasures. Easter to Sept, Mon to Fri (Sats in July and Aug), 2.30-4.30 pm. Price: A. (01749) 674483.

Wincanton Racecourse, Wincanton. National Hunt racing. (01963) 32344.

Tourist Information Centres, etc.

Bridgwater TIC*, Town Hall, High Street, Bridgwater. (01278) 427652.

Burnham-on-Sea TIC, South Esplanade, Burnham-on-Sea. (01278) 787852.

Chard TIC, The Guildhall, Fore Street, Chard. (01460) 67463.

Cheddar TIC*, The Gorge, Cheddar. (01934) 744071.

Exmoor Information Centre, Exmoor House, Dulverton. (01398) 23841.

Exmoor National Park Information Centre, Dulverton Heritage Centre, The Guildhall, Dulverton. (01398) 23841.

Exmoor National Park Visitor Centre, Dunster Steep, Dunster. (01643) 821835.

Frome Information Centre, Cattle Market Car Park, Frome. (01373) 467271.

Glastonbury TIC, 1 Marchant Buildings, Northload Street, Glastonbury. (01458) 832954.

Minehead TIC, 17 Friday Street, Minehead. (01643) 702624.

Porlock Information Centre*, Doverhay, Porlock.

Porlock Tourist Association, Dept 5, Post Office, Porlock. (01643) 862296.

Shepton Mallet Information Centre, 2 Petticoat Lane, Shepton Mallet. (01749) 345258.

Somerset Visitor Centre*, Podimore Roundabout (A 303), Yeovil. (01935) 841302

Somerset Visitor Centre, Sedgemoor Services, M5 South, Axbridge. (01934) 750833.

Taunton TIC, The Library, Corporation Street, Taunton. (01823) 274785.

Watchet Tourism Office, 6 The Esplanade, Watchet.

Wellington TIC, The Museum, 28 Fore Street, Wellington. (01823) 664747.

Wells TIC, Town Hall, Market Place, Wells. (01749) 672552.

Wincanton Information Centre, The Library, 7 Carrington Way, Wincanton. (01963) 34063.

Yeovil TIC, Petters House, Petters Way, Yeovil. (01935) 71279.

Yeovilton TIC, Fleet Air Arm Museum, RNAS, Yeovilton. (01935) 841083.

(* Open only part of the year, usually summer)